THE DEFENCE OF THE FAITH

OUTREMER: STUDIES IN THE CRUSADES AND THE LATIN EAST

VOLUME 15

General Editor
Prof. Alan V. Murray, *University of Leeds*

Editorial Board
Prof. Alfred Andrea, *University of Vermont*
Dr Jessalynn Bird, *Saint Mary's College, Notre Dame*
Dr Niall Christie, *Langara College, Vancouver*
Prof. John France, *Swansea University*
Prof. Nikolas Jaspert, *University of Heidelberg*
Prof. Kurt Villads Jensen, *Stockholm University*
Prof. Peter Lock, *York St John University*
Prof. Graham Loud, *University of Leeds*
Dr Christoph Maier, *University of Zürich*
Prof. Helen Nicholson, *Cardiff University*
Dr Guy Perry, *University of Oxford*
Dr Angus Stewart, *University of St Andrews*

The Defence of the Faith

Crusading on the Frontiers of Latin Christendom in the Late Middle Ages

edited by
PAUL SRODECKI AND NORBERT KERSKEN

BREPOLS

Cover illustration: The battle of Nicopolis, 25 September 1396. Picture by Jean Colombe. Taken from Sébastien Mamerot, *Les passages faiz oultremer par les Roys de france et autres princes et seigneurs francois contre les turcqs et autres sarrazins et mores oultre marins* (s.l., 1474), Bibliothèque nationale de France, Paris, Département des Manuscrits, Fr. 5594, fol. 263v, available online at https://w.wiki/3UAC [accessed 23 November 2023], licence CC0 1.0 Universal.

© 2024, Brepols Publishers n.v., Turnhout, Belgium.

All rights reserved. No part of this publication may be reproduced, stored in a retrieval system, or transmitted, in any form or by any means, electronic, mechanical, photocopying, recording, or otherwise without the prior permission of the publisher.

D/2024/0095/8
ISBN 978-2-503-58882-7
eISBN 978-2-503-58883-4
DOI 10.1484/M.OUTREMER-EB.5.119681
ISSN 2565-8794
eISSN 2565-988X

Printed in the EU on acid-free paper.

In memoriam
Francis Michael Ipgrave
(1983–2023)

Contents

List of Illustrations   11

List of Contributors   15

List of Abbreviations   19

A Note on Names   25

Preface and Acknowledgements   27

Introduction

Crusading on the Periphery in the Later Middle Ages. Key Research Issues and Debates
Paul SRODECKI   33

Part I
Campaigning and Recruiting

Communication between Centre and Periphery in Fifteenth-Century Crusading
Norman HOUSLEY   67

Crusade Campaigning by Friars of the Observant Franciscan Establishment in the Holy Land
Marianne P. RITSEMA VAN ECK   81

Crusading and Military Orders in the Crowns of Aragon and Castile in the Late Middle Ages
Maria BONET DONATO   95

Army Inspection and Crusade. Wallachia and the Crusade Plans of Pope Leo X
Mihai-D. Grigore 113

Part II
Chivalry and Nobility

The Bohemo-Moravian Nobility and the Baltic Crusades of the Bohemian Kings Ottokar II Premislas and John of Luxemburg in the Thirteenth and Fourteenth Centuries
Dalibor Janiš 127

How to Uphold a Dying Institution. English Support for the Teutonic Order's Baltic Crusades in the Early Fifteenth Century
Benjámin Borbás 141

Lithuanian Participation in the Crusading Movement in the Long Fifteenth Century
Darius Baronas 155

Part III
From Expansion to Defence

The Crusade of Nicopolis and Its Significance for the Western Image of the Ottoman Turks around 1400
Paul Srodecki 173

Hungary and the *passagium particulare* after Nicopolis (1396–1437)
Attila Bárany 199

The Last Crusades in the Balkans from 1443–44 or the Union between Central and South-Eastern Europe against the Ottoman Invasion
Nevyan Mitev 219

Converting Heretics into Crusaders on the Fringes of Latin Christendom. Shifting Crusading Paradigms in Medieval Bosnia
Emir O. Filipović 237

Ziel oder Ausgangsort? Das Großfürstentum Litauen als verlängerter
Arm der Kreuzzugsbewegung vom Ende des 14. bis zum Beginn des
16. Jahrhunderts
Rimvydas PETRAUSKAS 253

Fighting Pagans and Relations between Poland and the Teutonic
Order after 1466
Adam SZWEDA 267

Part IV
Legitimation and Propaganda

Infideles et perfidi schismatici. Crusades and Christianisation as
Political Tools of the Polish Kings in the Fourteenth Century
Andrzej MARZEC 283

Against *Tartari, Rutheni et Litfani, hostes fidei.* The Role and
Ambivalence of the Crusading Idea in the Integration of Ruthenia
into the Polish Crown in the Second Half of the Fourteenth Century
Sven JAROS 295

Playing the Crusade Card. Rhetorical References to Outremer and
Iberian Crusades in the Conflict between the Teutonic Order and the
Crown of Poland in the Early Fifteenth Century
Paul SRODECKI 313

Zwischen Kreuzzugsrhetorik und Bündnissen. Die Ostpolitik des
Großfürsten Witold von Litauen (1392–1430)
Sergey POLEKHOV 339

Legitimising the Hussite Wars. Anti-Heretical Crusading in the
Fifteenth Century
Pavel SOUKUP 361

Index 377

List of Illustrations

Paul Srodecki

Fig. 1. The expansion of Latin Christianity, c. 1386. 35
Fig. 2. Mid-sixteenth-century depictions of two of the most famous late medieval anti-Ottoman crusades, i.e. Nicopolis (1396, left picture) and Varna (1444, right picture). 37
Fig. 3. The expansion of Latin Christianity, c. 1500. 38
Fig. 4. The title pages of the fourth volume of Joseph-François Michaud's *Histoire des croisades*, 7 vols (Paris, 1812–22), and of the first volume of Nicolae Iorga's source edition *Notes et extraits pour servir à l'histoire des croisades au XVe siècle*, 6 vols (Paris, 1899–1916), as two examples of nineteenth-century historical research on late medieval crusades. 46
Fig. 5. Territories of the military orders in Iberia towards the end of the fifteenth century. 57
Fig. 6. Voivode Neagoe Basarab V of Wallachia and his wife Milica Despina pictured on the murals of the Curtea de Argeș Monastery, Romania, sixteenth century. 58
Fig. 7. Left: contemporary seals of the Bohemian kings Ottokar II Premislas (r. 1253–78, top) and John of Luxemburg (r. 1311–46, bottom). Right: early-fifteenth-century depictions of both rulers from the *Gelnhausen Codex*. 59
Fig. 8. Seals of Vladislas Jogaila, king of Poland and grand duke of Lithuania, from 1388 and of his cousin Vytautas the Great, grand duke of Lithuania, from 1407. 60
Fig. 9. Andrew of Castagno's fresco of the condottiere Filippo Scolari alias Pippo Spano, c. 1450, Villa Carducci in Florence, Italy. 61
Fig. 10. The anti-Ottoman crusades of the Polono-Hungarian king Vladislas the Jagiellonian and John of Hunyad, 1443–44. 62
Fig. 11. An illustration of the anti-Hussite crusades from the *Jena Codex* (c. 1500), fol. 56a. 63

Maria Bonet Donato

Fig. 12. Equestrian seals of Alfonso X of Castile (top, from 1262), the founder of the Order of St Mary of Spain, and James II the Just of Aragon (bottom, from 1295), the founder of the Order of Montesa. 111

Benjámin Borbás

Tbl. 1. Non-trade-related correspondence between the Teutonic Order and
England in the 1410s. 154

Darius Baronas

Fig. 13. Seal of Duke Kęstutis of Trakai from 1379. Courtesy of Edmundas Rimša. 158
Fig. 14. An early-fifteenth-century depiction of Vladislas II Jogaila, king of Poland
and grand duke of Lithuania, as a defender of the faith from the Holy Trinity
Chapel in Lublin Castle, Poland. 163

Paul Srodecki

Fig. 15. The crusade of Nicopolis, 1396. 184
Fig. 16 The battle of Nicopolis, 25 September 1396 (top); execution of the
Christian prisoners by the Ottoman Turks (bottom) — both pictures by
Jean Colombe, 1474. 186
Fig. 17. The massacre of the Christians by the Ottomans after the battle of Nicopolis
as a revenge for the preceding Rahova by the crusaders as depicted in a late-
fifteenth-century (s. l., c. 1470) version of Jean Froissart's *Chronicles*. 192

Attila Bárany

Fig. 18. Anti-Ottoman campaigns of Sigismund of Luxemburg, 1387–1437. 205

Nevyan Mitev

Fig. 19. The Long Campaign of 1443–44. 224
Fig. 20. The crusade of Varna, 1444. 230

Andrzej Marzec

Fig. 21. Contemporary royal seals of the Polish kings Vladislas the Elbow-High
(top) and his son Casimir III the Great (bottom) as used in the late 1320s
and the second half of the 1330s respectively. 293

Sven Jaros

Tbl. 2.	Papal correspondence concerning the eastern politics of Casimir III, 1340–63.	298
Fig. 22.	The Re-Occupation of Ruthenia: Wealth and Education (painting by Jan Matejko, 1888). Muzeum Narodowe in Warsaw, Poland.	308
Fig. 23.	Crown Ruthenia within the crown of Poland (including the duchy of Masovia as a Polish fiefdom as well as temporarily dependent territories such as Chełm, Bełz and Western Podolia) and the localisation of objects in Casimir's charters concerning Crown Ruthenia (1340–70).	309
Tbl. 3.	Subjects of the Polish king Casimir the Great's charters concerning Crown Ruthenia (1340–70).	310

Paul Srodecki

Fig. 24.	*The Battle of Grunwald* (painting by Jan Matejko, 1878), Muzeum Narodowe, Warsaw, Poland.	314
Fig. 25.	(1) *The Defence of the Thorn Tree Castle in 1231* (painting by an anonymous artist, c. 1600), Stadtmuseum in Sterzing, Italy.	317
Fig. 26.	*The Prussian Homage* (painting by Marcello Bacciarelli, 1796).	336

List of Contributors

Attila Bárány is professor in medieval history at the Department of History at the Debrecen University, Hungary. His fields of research include Anglo-Hungarian and imperial relations in the Middle Ages, medieval Hungarian diplomacy, and later medieval military and crusade history. He also published on the history of medieval England.

Darius Baronas is chief research fellow at the Department of the History of the Grand Duchy of Lithuania at the Lithuanian Institute of History and part-time professor at Vilnius University. His scholarly interests focus on the medieval history of Lithuania, with a special emphasis on Christianisation, and her international and cultural relations with neighbouring countries.

Maria Bonet Donato is senior lecturer in medieval history at the Rovira i Virgili University in Tarragona, Spain. Her research is focussed on military orders, mainly related to the Hospitallers. She has also studied social and economic relationships in Catalonia.

Benjámin Borbás is a Ph.D. Candidate at the Eötvös Loránd University and research assistant at the Institute of History, Research Centre for the Humanities (both Budapest, Hungary). He is currently writing his doctoral dissertation on the importance of war booty in the thirteenth-century Holy Land. He has already published articles on customs regulating the distribution of spoils of war during the crusades, as well as on the role of falcons in service of the Teutonic Order at the turn of the fourteenth to fifteenth centuries.

Emir O. Filipović is associate professor in medieval history and head of the doctoral studies programme in history at the University of Sarajevo, Bosnia. He has authored an illustrated history of Bosnia during the Middle Ages as well as monograph studies on the Ottoman conquest of the Bosnian kingdom and the construction of dynastic identity in late medieval Bosnia. His research so far has focused on the early expansion of the Ottomans in the Balkans and the various aspects of chivalry, courtly culture and heraldry in the kingdom of Bosnia.

Mihai-D. Grigore is research fellow at the Institute of European History in Mainz, Germany. He holds a Ph.D. in historical theology with a dissertation on symbolic communication in the early medieval West-Frankish *pax Dei* councils. He also wrote another book on compared political thinking in sixteenth-century Europe.

Norman HOUSLEY is professor emeritus at the University of Leicester, United Kingdom, where he taught medieval history from 1983 to 2016. In his many publications, Housley studied the theory and practice of crusading from the mid-thirteenth century onwards. In the last years of his career, he focused on attempts to revive the crusade against the Ottoman Turks.

Dalibor JANIŠ is lecturer in medieval history at the University of Ostrava, Czechia. His main areas of interest are medieval and early modern law and judiciary, peace movement (*Landfrieden*), medieval nobility, castles and fortified manors. He is the author of several books on these topics and has also published several critical editions of historical (legal) sources.

Sven JAROS is postdoctoral researcher at the Martin Luther University in Halle (Saale), Germany. His research is focussed on premodern political and cultural entanglements in Eastern Europe. He is the author of the book *Iterationen im Grenzraum: Akteure und Felder multikonfessioneller Herrschaftsaushandlung in Kronruthenien (1340–1434)* (2021).

Andrzej MARZEC is assistant professor at the Institute of History of the Jagiellonian University of Cracow, Poland. His interests focus mainly on the social and political histories of Poland in the late Middle Ages and on the auxiliary sciences of history, in particular on diplomatics, genealogy, historical geography and epigraphy.

Nevyan MITEV holds a Ph.D. degree from the University of Veliko Tarnovo, Bulgaria. He is director of the Park Museum of Military Friendship 'Vladislav Varnenchik', branch of the National Museum of Military History, Sofia. His main research interests focus on medieval history, archaeology and numismatics.

Rimvydas PETRAUSKAS is professor of medieval history and (since 2020) rector of Vilnius University, Lithuania. His main research interests include the political and social histories of the grand duchy of Lithuania from the thirteenth to the sixteenth centuries as well as the image of the Middle Ages in modern society.

Sergey V. POLEKHOV is senior research fellow at the Institute of Social Sciences of the Russian Academy of National Economy and Public Administration. His research is focused on the socio-political and international history of the grand duchy of Lithuania and the lands of Rus (Moscow, Novgorod, Pskov), history of early modern Russia and publication of historical sources.

Marianne P. RITSEMA VAN ECK is postdoctoral research fellow at the Norwegian Institute in Rome (University of Oslo). As a historian specialised in late medieval and early modern period, she is particularly interested in expressions of religion at the intersection of visual, material and textual culture. Areas of expertise include Franciscan studies, the cult of the saints, pilgrimage and travel to the Middle East, historical cartography and Italian *sacri monti*.

Pavel SOUKUP is a researcher at the Centre for Medieval Studies, Institute of Philosophy, at the Czech Academy of Sciences in Prague. His research deals with late medieval religious history, anti-heretical polemics and crusades in Central Europe.

Paul SRODECKI is a medievalist who has been working as an assistant and visiting professor, research fellow and lecturer at the universities of Giessen, Kiel and Flensburg (all three Germany), Ostrava (Czechia), Poznań (Poland) and Sønderborg (Denmark). He has published several treatises on alterity and alienity discourses, crusading on the frontiers of Latin Christendom as well as historical deconstruction.

Adam SZWEDA is professor at the Department of Medieval History and Auxiliary Sciences of History at Nicolaus Copernicus University, Toruń, Poland. His research interests include medieval diplomacy, Polono-Teutonic relations from the thirteenth to the sixteenth centuries, and the relations of Polish kings with dependent rulers in the late Middle Ages, as well as diplomatics (especially the functioning of notary instruments).

List of Abbreviations

AAV	Archivum Apostolicum Vaticanum (until October 2019 Archivum Secretum Vaticanum; RA = Registra Lateranensia; RS = Registra supplicum; RV = Registra Vaticana), Civitas Vaticana
AB	*Annales de Bourgogne*, ed. Henri Drouot et al., 86 vols (Dijon, 1929–)
ACA	Archivo de la Corona de Aragón, Barcelona (RC = Registro de Cancillería)
ACC	*Acta concilii Constanciensis*, ed. Heinrich Finke, 4 vols (Münster i. W., 1896–1928)
Acta Anni	'A leleszi konvent országos levéltárában lévő Acta anni sorozatának oklevelei', ed. Norbert C. Tóth, 2 pts, 1 (1387–99): *A Nyíregyházi Jósa András Múzeum évkönyve* 47 (2005), 235–344; 2 (1400–10): *A Nyíregyházi Jósa András Múzeum évkönyve* 48 (2006), 323–442
Acta Clem. VI	*Acta Clementis PP. VI (1342–52) e regestis vaticanis aliisque fontibus collegit*, ed. Aloysius Tăutu, CCO 3/9 (Roma, 1960)
Acta Inn. VI	*Acta Innocentii PP. VI (1352–62) e regestis vaticanis aliisque fontibus collegit*, ed. Aloysius Tăutu, CCO 3/10 (Roma, 1961)
Acta Urb. V	*Acta Urbani PP. V (1362–70) e regestis vaticanis aliisque fontibus collegit*, ed. Aloysius Tăutu, CCO 3/11 (Roma, 1964)
AHC	*Annuarium Historiae Conciliorum*, ed. Walter Brandmüller et al., 50 vols (Padeborn, 1969–)
AHN	Archivo Histórico Nacional (OOMM = Órdenes militares), Madrid
ASPK	*Akta stanów Prus Królewskich*, ed. Karol Górski, Marian Biskup and Irena Janosz-Biskupowa, 8 vols (Toruń, 1955–93)
AT	*Acta Tomiciana: Epistolarum. Legationum. Responsorum. Actionum et rerum gestarum. Serenissimi principis Sigismundi primi regis Poloniæ magni ducis Lithuaniæ. Per Stanislaum Górski, canonicum Cracoviensem et Plocensem*, ed. Adam Tytus Działyński et al., 18 vols (Poznań, 1852–1999)
AV	*Analecta Vaticana 1202–1366*, ed. Jan Ptaśnik, MPV 3 (Kraków, 1914)
BAV	Bibliotheca Apostolica Vaticana, Vatican City
BF	*Bullarium Franciscanum*, ed. Giovanni Giacinto Sbaraglia, 11 vols in 2 sers (Roma, 1759–1990)
BGDO	*Die Berichte der Generalprokuratoren des Deutschen Ordens an der Kurie*, ed. Kurt Forstreuter and Hans Koeppen, 4 vols (Göttingen, 1960–76)
BNM	Bibljoteka Nazzjonali ta' Malta — The National Library of Malta (AOM = L-Arkivji tal-Ordni ta' San Ġwann ta' Ġerusalemm, ta' Rodi,

	u ta' Malta [The Archives of the Order of St John of Jerusalem, of Rhodes and of Malta]), Valletta
BP	*Bullarium Poloniae*, ed. Irena Sułkowska-Kuraś et al., 7 vols (Roma, 1982–2006)
CCO	Codificazione Canonica Orientale: Fonti (Fontes), 45 fascs and 15 vols in 3 srs (Roma, 1931–)
CCR	*Calendar of the Close Rolls Preserved in the Public Record Office*, 59 vols (London, 1892–1953)
CDAC	*Codex diplomaticus Arpadianus continuatus*, ed. Gusztáv Wenzel, 12 vols (Pest, 1860–70)
CDCDS	*Codex diplomaticus regni Croatiae, Dalmatiae et Slavoniae*, ed. Tade Smičiklas, Jakov Stipišić and Miljen Šamšalović, 18 vols (Zagreb, 1904–98)
CDEB	*Codex diplomaticus et epistolaris regni Bohemiae*, ed. Gustav Friedrich et al., 7 vols (Praha, 1904–)
CDECDV	*Codex diplomaticus ecclesiae cathedralis necnon dioeceseos Vilnensis*, ed. Jan Fijałek and Władysław Semkowicz, 1 vol. (Kraków, 1932–48)
CDEM	*Codex diplomaticus et epistolaris Moraviae*, ed. Anton Boczek, 15 vols (Olomouc, 1836–1903)
CDH	*Codex diplomaticvs Hungariae ecclesiasticvs ac civilis*, ed. György Fejér, 12 vols, 45 bks (Budae, 1829–66)
CDM	*Codex diplomaticus et commemorationum Masoviae generalis* [since vol. 2: *Codex diplomaticus Masoviae novus*, ed. Jan Karol Kochanowski, Irena Sułkowska-Kuraś and Stanisław Kuraś, 3 vols (Warszawa, 1919–2000)
CDMP	*Codex diplomaticus Maioris Poloniae*, ed. Ignacy Zakrzewski and Franciszek Piekosiński, 5 vols (Poznań, 1877–1990)
CDPL	*Codex diplomaticus Regni Poloniae et Magni Ducatus Lituaniae*, ed. Maciej Dogiel, 5 vols (Wilno, 1758–64)
CDPM	*Codex diplomaticus Poloniae Minoris*, ed. Franciszek Piekosiński, 4 vols (Kraków, 1876–1905)
CDPr	*Codex diplomaticus Prussicus: Urkunden-Sammlung zur ältern Geschichte Preussens aus dem Königl. Geheimen Archiv zu Königsberg nebst Regesten*, ed. Johannes Voigt, 6 vols (Königsberg, 1836–61)
CDS	*Die Chroniken der deutschen Städte vom 14. Bis in's 16. Jahrhundert*, ed. Karl von Hegel, 37 vols (Leipzig, 1862–1968)
CESDQ	*Codex epistolaris saeculi decimi quinti*, ed. August Sokołowski, Józef Szujski and Anatol Lewicki, 3 vols (Kraków, 1876–94)
CEV	*Codex epistolaris Vitoldi magni ducis Lithuaniae 1376–1430*, ed. Antoni Prochaska (Kraków, 1882)
CGOH	*Cartulaire général de l'Ordre des Hospitaliers de Saint-Jean de Jérusalem (1100–1310)*, ed. Joseph Delaville Le Roulx, 4 vols (Paris, 1894–1906)
CLR	*Calendar of the Liberate Rolls preserved in the Public Records Office, Henry III*, ed. Henry C. Maxwell Lyte, 6 vols (London, 1916–64)

CPR	Calendar of Patent Rolls: Preserved in the Public Record Office, 1232–1582, 72 vols (London, 1891–)
CRM	Cahiers de recherches médiévales (since 2010 Cahiers de recherches médiévales et humanistes), ed. Bernard Ribémont et al., 45 vols (Paris, 1996–)
Crusades	Crusades: The Journal of the Society for the Study of the Crusades and the Latin East, ed. Jonathan Phillips et al., 22 vols (London, 2002–)
DD	Diplomatarium Danicum, ed. Aksel Emanuel Christensen et al., 40 vols in 3 sers (København, 1938–)
DIR	Documente privitóre la istoria romanilor, 30 vols in 2 sers, ed. Eudoxiu Hurmuzaki and Nicolae Densuşianu (Bucureşti, 1876–1942)
DIRC	Documentos Internacionales de los Reyes Católicos, Antonio de la Torre, 6 vols (Barcelona, 1949–66)
DP	La documentación pontificia hasta Inocencio III, ed Demetrio Mansilla (Roma, 1955)
DPRHU	Documenta Pontificum Romanorum Historiam Ucrainae illustrantia (1075–1953), ed. Atanasii Velykii, 2 vols (Rome, 1953–54)
DRH	Decreta Regni Hungariae 1301–1457, ed. Franciscus Döry, Georgius Bónis and Vera Bácskai, 2 vols (Budapest, 1976–89)
DRMH	Decreta regni Medievalis Hungariae: The Laws of the Medieval Kingdom of Hungary, ed. János M. Bak et al., 4 vols (Salt Lake City, 1989–2012)
DRRR	Diplomatarium relationum reipublicae Ragusanae cum regno Hungariae, ed. József Gelcich and Lajos Thallóczy (Budapest, 1887)
DRVM	ДРВМ — Древняя Русь. Вопросы медиевистики, ed. E. L. Konyavskaya, 93 vols (2000–)
EFE	Elementa ad fontium editiones, ed. Polski Instytut Historyczny w Rzymie, 76 vols (Romae, 1960–92)
EHR	The English Historical Review, ed. Mandell Creighton et al., 138 vols (Oxford, 1886–)
GStA PK	Geheimes Staatsarchiv Preußischer Kulturbesitz (HA = Hauptabteilung, OBA = Ordensbriefarchiv, OF = Ordensfolianten), Berlin
HC	A History of the Crusades, ed. Kenneth M. Setton, 6 vols (Madison, 1955–89)
HHFD	Historiae Hungaricae Fontes Domestici, ed. Flórián Mátyás, 4 vols (Leipzig, 1881–85)
IRR	Itineraria regum et reginarum, 1382–1438, ed. Pál Engel and Norbert C. Tóth (Budapest, 2005)
JBS	Journal of Baltic Studies (until 1971 Bullettin of Baltic Studies), ed. Edgar Anderson et al., 54 vols (Uppsala, 1970–)
JGO	Jahrbücher für Geschichte Osteuropas (until 1934 Jahrbücher für Kultur und Geschichte der Slaven; NF = Neue Folge), ed. Hans Übersberger et al., 70 vols (1925–)

LIST OF ABBREVIATIONS

KH	*Kwartalnik Historyczny*, ed. Franciszek Ksawery Liske et al., 130 vols (Lwów, 1887–)
LAPM	*Listy i akta Piotra Myszkowskiego, generalnego starosty ziem ruskich króla Jana Olbrachta*, ed. Anatol Lewicki (Kraków, 1898)
LHS	*Lithuanian Historical Studies*, ed. Lithuanian Institute of History, 26 vols (Leiden, 1996–)
Lites	*Lites ac res gestae inter Polonos Ordinemque Cruciferorum*, ed. Adam Tytus Działyński et al., 7 vols in 3 sers (Posnaniae, 1855–1970)
LM	*Lietuvos Metrika: Užrašymų knyga*, ed. Egidijus Banionis et al., 53 vols (Vilnius, 1993–)
LMAVB RS	Lietuvos Mokslų akademijos Vrublevskių bibliotekos Rankraščių skyrius, Vilnius
LUB	*Liv-, Esth- und Curländisches Urkundenbuch nebst Regesten*, ed. Friedrich Georg von Bunge et al., 17 vols in 2 sers (Reval, 1853–)
MCG	*Monumenta conciliorum generalium seculi decimi quinti : Concilium Basileense*, ed. František Palacký et al., 4 vols (Wien, 1857–1935)
MGH	Monumenta Germaniae Historica
MGH DC	MGH Deutsche Chroniken und andere Geschichtsbücher des Mittelalters, 6 vols (Hannover, 1877–1909)
MGH SS	*MGH Scriptores (in folio)*, ed. Georg Heinrich Pertz et al., 39 vols (Hannover, 1826–)
MGH SRG	MGH Scriptores rerum Germanicarum in usum scholarum separatim editi, 81 vols (Hannoverae, 1841–)
MGH SRG n. s.	MGH Scriptores rerum Germanicarum, nova series, 25 vols (Berlin, 1922–)
MHSM	*Monumenta historica Slavorum Meridionalium*, ed. Vicentio Macuscev, 2 vols (Varsaviae, 1874–82)
MIÖG	*Mitteilungen des Instituts für Österreichische Geschichtsforschung*, ed. Engelbert Mühlbacher et al., 131 vols (Wien, 1880–)
MKL	*Mátyás király levelei. Külügyi osztály / Mathiae Corvini Hungariae Regis epistolae exterae 1458–90*, ed. Vilmos Fraknói, 2 vols (Budapest, 1893–95 [reprint Budapest, 2008])
MM	*Micae Mediaevales: Fiatal történészek dolgozatai a középkori Magyarországról és Európáról*, Zsófia Kádár et al., 9 vols (Budapest, 2020–)
MNL	Magyar Nemzeti Levéltár (Diplomatikai Fényképgyűjtemény = DF, Diplomatikai Levéltár = DL)
MPH	*Monumenta Poloniae historica*, ed. August Bielowski et al., 6 vols (Lwów, 1864–93)
MPH n. s.	Monumenta Poloniae historica, nova series, 16 vols (Kraków, 1946–)
MPV	*Monumenta Poloniae Vaticana*, ed. Jan Ptaśnik et al., 10 vols (Kraków, 1913–2002)
MVA	*Magyarország világi archontológiája 1301–1457*, ed. Pál Engel, 2 vols (Budapest, 1996)

MVHH	*Monumenta Vaticana historiam Regni Hungariae illustrantia*, ed. Arnold Ipolyi et al., 9 vols in 2 sers (Budapest, 1884–1909)
MVRGB	*Monumenta Vaticana res gestas Bohemicas illustrantia*, ed. Ladislav Klicman et al., 8 vols (Praha, 1903–2003)
NPL	*Новгородская первая летопись старшего и младшего изводов*, ed. Arsenii N. Nasonov (Moskva, 1950)
OT	*Oklevelek Temesvármegye és Temesvárváros történetéhez*, ed. Frigyes Pesty et al., 2 vols (Pozsony, 1896–2014)
PCsL	*A Perényi család levéltára 1222–1526*, ed. István Tringli (Budapest, 2008)
PH	*Zeszyty Naukowe Uniwersytetu Jagiellońskiego: Prace Historyczne*, Krzysztof Baczkowski et al., 149 vols (Kraków, 1955–)
PrzH	*Przegląd Historyczny*, ed Jan Karol Kochanowski et al., 114 vols (Warszawa, 1905–)
PL	*Patrologia cursus completus: Series latina*, ed. Jacques-Paul Migne, 221 vols (Lutetiæ Parisiorum, 1844–64)
PLP	*Псковские летописи*, ed. Arsenii N. Nasonov, 2 vols (Moskva, 1941–55)
PSRL	Полное собрание русских летописей [Polnoe sobranie russkikh letopisei], ed., 43 vols (St. Petersburg, 1841–)
QMAN	*Quaestiones Medii Aevi Novae*, ed. Wojciech Fałkowski (Warszawa, 1994–)
RDBM	*Regesta diplomatica nec non epistolaria Bohemiae et Moraviae*, ed. Karel Jaromír Erben, Josef Emler and Bedrich Mendel, 8 vols (Prague, 1855–2017)
RESEE	*Revue des Études Sud-Est Européennes*, ed. Victor Papacostea et al., 60 vols (București, 1963–)
RH	*Roczniki Historyczne*, ed. Kazimierz Tymieniecki et al., 88 vols (Poznań, 1925–)
RHC Occ.	*Recueil des historiens des croisades : Historiens occidentaux*, ed. L'Académie des inscriptions et belles-lettres, 5 vols (1844–95)
RHGF	*Recueil des historiens des Gaules et de la France*, ed. Martin Bouquet et al., 24 vols (Paris, 1738–1904 [the first 19 vols have been reprinted from 1869 to 1880])
RHP	*Regesta Honorii Papae III*, ed. Petrus Pressutti, 2 vols (Rome, 1888–95)
RL	*Rocznik Lituanistyczny*, ed. Urszula Augustyniak et al., 8 vols (Warszawa, 2015–)
RRH	*Regesta regni Hierosolymitani*, and *Additamentum*, ed. Reinhold Röhricht, 2 vols (Innsbruck, 1893–1904)
RS	Rerum Britannicarum Medii Aevi Scriptores (Rolls Series), 253 vols (London, 1858–1911)
RTA	*Deutsche Reichstagsakten (ÄR = Ältere Reihe, MR = Mittlere Reihe, JR = Jüngere Reihe)*, ed. Julius Weizsäcker et al., 58 vols, 102 bks (Gotha, 1867–)

SMHD	*Scriptores minores historiæ danicæ medii ævi*, ed. Martin Clarentius Gertz, 2 vols (København, 1917–20)
SOF	*Südost-Forschungen*, ed. Fritz Valjavec et al., 81 vols (München, 1936–)
SR	*Средневековая Русь*, ed. A. A. Gorsky et al., 14 vols (Moskva, 1996–)
SRH	*Scriptores rerum Hungaricarum*, ed. Imre Szentpétery, 2 vols (Budapest, 1937–38, repr. 1999)
SRP	*Scriptores rerum Prussicarum*, ed. Theodor Hirsch, Max Toeppen and Walther Hubatsch, 6 vols (Leipzig, 1861–1968)
SSDOP	*Die Staatsschriften des Deutschen Ordens in Preußen im 15. Jahrhundert, Bd. 1: Die Traktate vor dem Konstanzer Konzil (1414–18) über das Recht des Deutschen Ordens am Lande Preußen*, ed. Erich Weise (Göttingen, 1970)
SVDOP	*Die Staatsverträge des Deutschen Ordens in Preußen im 15. Jahrhundert*, ed. Erich Weise, 3 vols (Königsberg, 1939–70)
UBGH	*Urkundliche Beiträge zur Geschichte des Hussitenkrieges vom Jahre 1419 an*, ed. Franz Palacký, 2 vols (Prag, 1872–73)
VMHH	*Vetera monumenta historica Hungariam Sacram illustrantia*, ed. Augustin Theiner, 2 vols (Romae, 1859–60)
VMPL	*Vetera monumenta Poloniae et Lithuaniae gentiumque finitimarum historiam illustrantia*, ed. Augustin Theiner, 4 vols (Roma, 1860–64)
VMSM	*Vetera monumenta Slavorum Meridionalium historiam illustrantia*, ed. Augustin Theiner, 2 vols (Romae, 1863–75)
VPUB	*Das virtuelle Preußische Urkundenbuch: Regesten und Texte zur Geschichte Preußens und des Deutschen Ordens*, ed. Jürgen Sarnowsky (Hamburg, 1999–), <https://t1p.de/fexj> [accessed 18 May 2021]
VSMH	*Veterum scriptorum et monumentorum historicorum dogmatorum moralium amplissima collectio*, ed. Edmund Martene and Ursinus Durand, 9 vols (Parisiis, 1724–33 [repr. New York, 1968])
ZDM	*Zbiór dokumentów Małopolskich*, ed. Stanisław Kuraś and Irena Sułkowska-Kuraś, 8 vols (Wrocław, 1962–75)
ZfO	*Zeitschrift für Ostforschung* (since 1995 *Zeitschrift für Ostmitteleuropa-Forschung*), ed. Hermann Aubin et al., 72 vols (Marburg, 1952–)
ZH	*Zapiski Historyczne*, ed. Towarzystwo Naukowe, 88 vols (Toruń, 1908–)
ZsO	*Zsigmondkori oklevéltár*, ed. Elemér Mályusz et al., 14 vols (Budapest, 1951–2020)

A Note on Names

As general guidelines the chapters in this volume follow the *MHRA Style Guide* and the approach in *The Crusades: An Encyclopedia*. Where there are current anglicised equivalents for foreign personal names (especially with regard to monarchs ruling various realms in personal union), place-names and names of regions, we have decided to use these forms (e.g. *Alexander* for *Aleksandr/Aleksander/Aleksandras*, *Casimir* for *Kazimierz/Kazimieras*, *Cracow* for *Kraków*, *Hedwig* for *Jadwiga/Hedvig*, *Henry* for *Heinrich/Henryk/Jindřich*, *Kiev* for *Kyiv*, *Vladislas/Ladislas* for *Władysław/Vladislav/Ulászló/László*, *Louis* for *Ludwig/Lajos/Ljudevit/Ludwik* [and the quaint English form *Lewis*], *Vienna* for *Wien* etc.), but we have opted to avoid obsolete ones (e.g. *Alfonso* not *Alphons[e]*, *Frankfurt* not *Frankfort* etc.). This applies above all to individuals and toponyms belonging to the Latin West. However, especially with regard to the late Middle Ages, we have used the 'native' forms where there are first and last names handed down in the sources (e.g. *Đurađ Branković* instead of *George Branković*, *Jakub Świnka* instead of *Jacob Świnka*, *Mikołaj Lasocki* instead of *Nicholas Lasocki* etc.). This has also been done for literary figures and for any other persons who are habitually known by the foreign forms in scholarship as well as for all German ruling houses as the *Habsburgs* or the *Luxemburgs* (and not *Hapsburgs* or *Luxembourgs*), for whom the German forms were used. We also gave priority to historical place-names, i.e. those current and/or in use by the dominant local elites at the respective time (e.g. *Christburg* instead of *Dzierzgoń*, *Constantinople* instead of *Istanbul*, *Danzig* instead of *Gdańsk*, *Kholm* instead of *Chełm*, *Pressburg* instead of *Bratislava* etc.). Besides well-known historical cities such as Constantinople, in all cases where medieval names differ from modern forms the current location is provided in parentheses at the first mention in the respective chapter. In order to help readers, the various place and personal names have been cross-referenced in the index.

We have also decided to distinguish between *Rus* and *Russia*. Omitting the sometimes pedantically overused apostrophe — a transliteration of the Cyrillic soft sign — in the interest of improved readability, the former describes the loose federation of the East Slavic peoples with its centres in Kiev and Novgorod, whereas the latter denotes the early modern state, the tsardom of Russia, which developed from the grand principality of Moscow, and all its successor states (the Russian Empire, Soviet Russia and the Russian Federation). The names used in this book for the various East Slavic peoples inhabiting the Rus are *Rus* or rather *Ruthenian(s)*, the latter being derived from the contemporary Latin and being most accepted by Eastern European historians. It should be emphasised, however, that the term *Ruthenian(s)* also changes conceptually through history and is largely used from the fifteenth century onwards, and above all in the early modern period, to distinguish the East Slavic population of the Polono-Lithuanian commonwealth from the so-called Moscovite Rus and later Russia.

The debate surrounding the terms *Mongols* or *Tatars* is also a relatively longstanding one in Medieval Studies, especially among historians of East-Central and Eastern Europe, and can certainly only be resolved with great difficulty in a single publication, the focus of which is predominantly on other issues. Following the principles of the so-called *Begriffsgeschichte*, we have decided to differentiate the terms depending on what time the source written. While the term Mongol(s) is used almost exclusively for the Mongol invasions in the thirteenth century, the etymological double pair Mongol(s)/Tatar(s) is used for issues that extend into the fourteenth century. From the breakup of the Golden Horde in the fifteenth century, the term Tatar(s) is used exclusively for the successor khanates.

Preface and Acknowledgements

If a survey were to be held today to find out what is meant by a crusade, the answer which would probably be given most frequently is that it refers to the wars of the Latin Christians of the high Middle Ages in the Holy Land. The extent to which this traditional depiction is still widespread among the general public is shown by countless popular or rather pseudo-scientific publications on the subject (whether in print or as TV productions), which reduce the crusade phenomenon of the Middle Ages solely to the conflict 'between Orient and Occident, between Christianity and Islam', as postulated by the short documentary *Kreuzzüge* produced some years ago by the German public television station ZDF.[1] At the same time, the various popular-scientific publications and television productions, most of which have been compiled in a rather superficial and very fragmentary manner, serve to further disseminate and cement this simplified image. However, for medieval contemporaries, the term crusade (or better: the various Latin crusading terms such as *cruciata*, *expeditio*, *iter*, *via*, *peregrinatio*, *profectio* or *passagium*, as well as their respective national language equivalents), had a much broader range than the description of the military campaigns for the protection or rather the reconquest of Christianity's sacred sites in the Holy Land. Using the crusade as justification, the popes also legitimised numerous armed endeavours outside the Levant. With only a few exceptions, the latter campaigns only received limited attention in Western studies from the beginning of modern historiography in the nineteenth until well into the twentieth centuries. In the past two to three decades, however, new and very fruitful insights have been made into the crusading movement on the fringes of Latin Christendom.

Against this background, the international conference *Crusading and the Crusader Movement in the Peripheries of the Christian West, 1100–1500*, held in Marburg, Germany, on 5–7 October 2017, aimed to trace the manifold manifestations of the peripheral crusades in a comparative perspective spanning the entire European region and (with North Africa) even beyond. At this point we would like once again to thank all the participants who contributed to the fruitful output of the conference through their lectures, as moderators or by participating in the lively discussions. Special thanks are due to the *Herder Institute for Historical Research on East-Central Europe* in Marburg for providing the conference facilities and for the organisational support for the conference.

---

1 'Kreuzzüge', in *ZDF Kultur — God's Cloud*, 6 November 2014 <https://t1p.de/qw82> [accessed 5 May 2020].

The positive feedback, both from participants and the audience, as well as the stimulating reviews[2] and expressions of interest from those who were unable to attend the conference due to time constraints, encouraged both of us in our plans to make the respective lectures available to the wider public in the form of an anthology. The breadth of the topics, both in terms of time and space, led us to the decision to publish two volumes, which — supplemented by additional essays — are intended to shed light on the problems of the peripheral crusades. We decided on a temporal division into one volume on the high Middle Ages and one on the late Middle Ages. The present volume offers a comparative approach to the crusade movement on the fringes of Latin Christendom in the time frame from approximately 1300 to the beginning of the sixteenth century, bringing a regional focus to research on these peripheral phenomena. It covers a period widely considered as a time of change and transition. A period in which Western Christianity was on the one hand still on expansion (*vide* Lithuania and the western Rus and later the Spanish, Portuguese, French and English expansion in the Americas, Africa and South-East Asia) and on the other hand had to face two mighty opponents on its most eastern and south-eastern borders: the Ottoman Empire and Muscovy. The book features several key questions: Which military campaigns were propagated as crusades on the peripheries of the Christian West? What efforts were made to gain recognition for them as crusades and what effects did these have? What value did the crusade movement have for societies at the *fines christianitatis*? What role did the armed pilgrimages have in strengthening a pan-Western sense of togetherness and solidarity, and what role did they have in the creation of a crusader and frontier identity? The nineteen papers, ranging in scope from the southern and eastern Baltic regions to Iberia and Italy, Western and Central Europe to the Balkans, provide new insights into the ways in which crusade rhetoric was reflected in the culture and literature of countries involved in late medieval crusading.

During the completion of the present volume, we received suggestions, advice and support from numerous people from the academic community, for which we would all like to express our sincere thanks. In addition to the aforementioned Herder Institute in Marburg, we would also like to thank the Christian-Albrechts-University Foundation as well as the Fritz Thyssen Foundation for their financial support of the conference and thus, ultimately, for making this book project possible. We are also very grateful to Annelie Thom of the Christian-Albrechts-University of Kiel for her tireless and conscientious checking of the footnotes and her contribution to the compilation of the register. For his inclusion of the volume in the *Outremer* series, we would like to thank the general editor Alan Murray

---

2 See, for instance, the review of the conference published on H-Soz.Kult by Robert Friedrich (German Historical Institute Paris) on 26 February 2018: 'Tagungsbericht: Crusading and the Crusader Movement on the Peripheries of the Christian West 1100–1500, 05.10.2017–07.10.2017 Marburg', *H-Soz-Kult*, 26 February 2018, <www.hsozkult.de/conferencereport/id/tagungsberichte-7573> [accessed 5 May 2020].

(University of Leeds), who has always constructively shared with us valuable tips and critical advice. The editors would also like to thank Brepols Publishers, and in particular Chris VandenBorre and Eva Anagnostaki, for taking the final steps towards publication.

Last, we would like to pay our heartfelt gratitude and our deepest respects to our beloved colleague and friend, Francis Michael Ipgrave. Francis passed away far too early after a sudden and severe illness in November 2023. It was his thorough proofreading of the English-language contributions that made both volumes possible. This book is dedicated to him.

Paul Srodecki and Norbert Kersken, February 2024

Introduction

PAUL SRODECKI

Crusading on the Periphery in the Later Middle Ages

Key Research Issues and Debates

The late thirteenth century marked the end of the era of the Latin Christian presence in the Levante and, related to this, also the end of major crusade campaigns in the region. Nevertheless, the conflict between Christians and Muslims did continue in other forms, such as ongoing territorial disputes and religious conflicts in Iberia, Eastern and South-Eastern Europe and the Mediterranean. A main characteristic of the transition phase from high to late medieval crusading was the switch in legitimising rhetoric: the Holy Land, the site of Christ's crucifixion and resurrection, remained a focal point of most of the anti-Muslim campaigns, despite the loss of key territories like Jerusalem to Muslim forces. However, as early as with the Second Council of Lyon (1274) and certainly at the beginning of the fourteenth century, *passagia* — as one of the main medieval terms for a crusade — to the Holy Land were being divided into general (*passagium generale*) and particular (*passagium generale*) crusades. While Jerusalem and all the other Levantine holy sites of the Christians remained the main goals of the former, the latter just meant a *primum passagium* ('first passage') or a *passagium parvum* ('small passage'). These smaller crusades were understood as preliminary steps with limited objectives to achieve the final purpose, i.e. the recovery of the Holy Land.[1] In contrast to the high Middle Ages, alongside the loss of the Holy Land, and besides the Christian conquest and the Western European colonisation of the Americas, however, Latin Christian expansion came to a gradual halt at the turn

---

1 On both forms of the *passagia* in late medieval crusade thinking, see Cornel Bontea, 'The Theory of the Passagium Particulare: A Commercial Blockade of the Mediterranean in the Early Fourteenth Century?', in *A Military History of the Mediterranean Sea: Aspects of War, Diplomacy and Military Elites*, ed. Georgios Theotokis and Aysel Yildiz (Leiden, 2018), pp. 202–19; Benjamin Weber, 'Vain Hope or Insincere Justification? Jerusalem in 15th Century's Papal Letters', in *Fighting for the Faith: The Many Crusades*, ed. Kurt Villads Jensen, Carsten Selch Jensen and Janus Møller Jensen (Stockholm, 2018), pp. 395–414; Constantinos Georgiou, 'Propagating the Hospitallers' Passagium: Crusade Preaching and Liturgy in 1308–1309', in *Islands and Military Orders, c. 1291–c. 1798*, ed. Emanuel Buttigieg and Simon Philipps (Farnham, 2013), pp. 53–64; Attila Bárány, 'King Sigismund and the passagium generale (1391–96)', in *Confernita internationala Sigismund de Luxemburg, Oradea, 6–9 Decembrie, 2007*, ed. Florena Ciure and Alexandru Simon (Oradea, 2007), pp. 88–90.

The Defence of the Faith, Outremer: Studies in the Crusades and the Latin East, 15 (Turnhout: Brepols, 2024), pp. 33–64

of the late medieval and early modern periods. Alone the political, logistical and ultimately also military feasibility of a large-scale crusade to liberate Jerusalem has now receded into a purely theoretical and practically almost unenforceable far distance.

It is possible, therefore, to distinguish two diametrically opposed periods of late medieval crusading which clearly demonstrate the switch from Western expansion to religious warfare as an instrument for defensive purposes against non-Latin Christian outer-groups: firstly, in the fourteenth and early fifteenth centuries, the boundaries of the Roman Catholic church were still being extended in the eastern Baltic Sea region and in the frontier region between the Polish and Ruthenian lands. Further southwards, the Angevin kings Charles I Robert and his son Louis the Great managed to expand the Hungarian crown's sphere of influence far into the Balkans.[2] Crusades against internal enemies, such as political opponents (see the Italian crusades of 1254–1343) or heretical Hussites (1419–34), were also clearly aimed at enlarging or at least maintaining papal influence in Europe. This was also the case on the opposite periphery of the European continent, where the Iberian *Reconquista* slowly began to reach its conclusion, with the Spanish conquest of Granada in 1492 the culminating campaign.[3] The expansionist efforts of the Portuguese and Spaniards swept over to the other side of the Mediterranean Sea and even as far as to the North-Western African Atlantic coast: drawing upon the traditions of similar thirteenth-century expeditions such as the so-called African crusade of King Alfonso X of Castile in 1260, numerous campaigns were led in the name of the cross against strategically important coastal cities, with the sieges and captures of Ceuta (1415), Ksar es-Seghir (1458) and Asilah (1471) or the battles of Tangier (1437) and — even as late as the second half of the sixteenth century! — Alcácer Quibir (1578) perhaps the best known.[4]

---

2 On both kings' crusades and crusade plans, see, most recently, Attila Bárány, 'The Hungarian Angevins and the Crusade: King Charles I (1301–1342)', in *Zwischen Ostsee und Adria: Ostmitteleuropa im Mittelalter und in der Frühen Neuzeit. Politische, wirtschaftlichen, religiöse und wissenschaftliche Beziehungen*, ed. Bárány, Roman Czaja and László Pósán (Debrecen, 2023), pp. 41–80; László Pósán, 'Die Feldzüge des ungarischen Königs Ludwig I. von Anjou nach Litauen', in *Zwischen Mittelmeer und Baltikum: Festschrift für Hubert Houben zum 70. Geburtstag*, ed. Udo Arnold, Roman Czaja and Jürgen Sarnowski (Ilmtal-Weinstraße, 2023), pp. 383–404.

3 See Joseph F. O'Callaghan, *The Last Crusade in the West: Castile and the Conquest of Granada* (Philadelphia, 2014); O'Callaghan, *The Gibraltar Crusade: Castile and the Battle for the Strait* (Philadelphia, 2011).

4 For an overview, see Adam Simmons, 'The African Adoption of the Portuguese Crusade during the Fifteenth and Sixteenth Centuries', *The Historical Journal* 65 (2022), 571–90; *Croisades en Afrique: Les expeditions occidentales à destination du continent africain, XIIIe–XVIe siècle*, ed. Benjamin Weber (Toulouse, 2019); Vitor Luís Gaspar Rodrigues, 'The Portuguese Art of War in Northern Morocco during the 15th Century', *Athens Journal of History* 3 (2017), 321–36; A. R. Disney, *A History of Portugal and the Portuguese Empire: From Beginnings to 1807*, 2 vols (Cambridge, 2009–12), 2: 1–83; Luís Adão da Fonseca, Maria Cristina Pimenta and Paula Maria de Carvalho Pinto Costa, 'The Papacy and the Crusades in XVth Century Portugal', in *La Papauté et les croisades*, ed. Michel Balard (Ashgate, 2011), pp. 141–54; José Manuel Rodríguez García, 'Idea and Reality of Crusade in Alfonso's X Reign: Castile and Leon, 1252–1284', in *Autour de la premiére croisade: Actes du colloque*

CRUSADING ON THE PERIPHERY IN THE LATER MIDDLE AGES

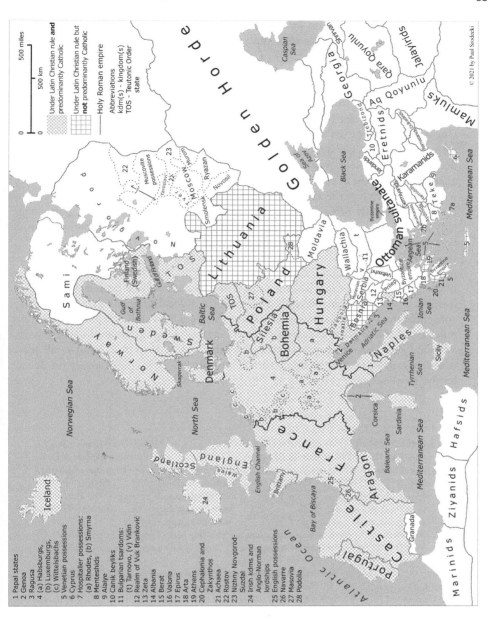

Fig. 1. The expansion of Latin Christianity, c. 1386. Map by Paul Srodecki

However, since the late fourteenth century onwards, the most prominent among anti-Muslim ventures were the various campaigns against the Ottomans, which brings us to the second type of late medieval crusading. As was already the case with the anti-Mongol expeditions of the thirteenth century,[5] these anti-Ottoman crusades largely lacked any of the expansionist characteristics of the high Middle Ages. Aside from prominent exceptions to this rule, such as the ill-fated crusades of Nicopolis (1396) and Varna (1444), which were both pictured by Christian propagandists as being in the tradition of the Levantine crusades, the majority of campaigns aimed mostly at the defence of Christian territories. Indeed, crusade ideology was now used as a welcome military and legitimising tool guarding against the expansion of the Ottoman Empire into the north-west. Thus, with the exception of the aforementioned examples, it is therefore more appropriate and historically justifiable to summarise the late medieval crusades, particularly around 1400 onwards, as an age of primarily *defensive crusades*: Europe was now under siege! This image was mirrored in numerous bulwark depictions and served as the main source of the emerging *antemurale* rhetoric, which in turn has provided one of the major pillars of Polish, Hungarian and Croatian national identities up to the present day. The fifteenth century sustainably cemented this transformation process.[6] Bringing with it a new form of local defensive crusades and, consequently, also a new form of crusaders, this paradigm shift was probably best reflected in the prominent figures of the Hungarian kings Sigismund of Luxemburg and Matthias Corvinus as well as the latter's father John of Hunyad — all of whom instrumentalised the aged crusade formula in a new guise, namely for defensive purposes against the mighty Ottoman Empire.[7]

---

de la Society for the Study of the Crusades and the Latin East (1995), ed. Michel Balard (Paris, 1996), pp. 379–90; John L. Vogt, 'Crusading and Commercial Elements in the Portuguese Capture of Ceuta (1415)', *The Muslim World* 59 (1969), 287–99; Charles-Emmanuel Dufourcq, 'Un projet castillan du XIIIe siècle : la croisade d'Afrique', *Revue d'histoire et de civilization du Maghreb* 2 (1967), 32–53.

5 See Paul Srodecki, 'Fighting the "Eastern Plague": Anti-Mongol Crusade Ventures in the Thirteenth Century', in *The Expansion of the Faith: Crusading on the Frontiers of Latin Christendom in the High Middle Ages*, ed. Srodecki and Norbert Kersken (Turnhout, 2022), pp. 303–27.

6 See Alan V. Murray, 'Conclusion: Transformations of Crusading in the Long Fifteenth Century', in *The Crusade in the Fifteenth Century: Converging and Competing Cultures*, ed. Norman J. Housley (London, 2017), pp. 206–10.

7 See János M. Bak, 'Hungary and Crusading in the Fifteenth Century', in *Crusading in the Fifteenth Century: Message and Impact*, ed. Norman J. Housley (Basingstoke, 2004), pp. 116–27; Attila Bárány, 'The Crusading Letters of Matthias Corvinus', *Christian-Muslim Relations: A Bibliographical History*, ed. David Thomas et al., 21 vols (Leiden, 2013), 5: 568–82; Andrei Pogacias, 'John Hunyadi and the Late Crusade', in *Life and Religion in the Middle Ages*, ed. Flocel Sabaté Curull (Cambridge, 2015), pp. 327–34; Ovidiu Mureşan, 'John Hunyadi— the Ideal Crusader — in Aeneas Piccolomini's Letters and Historical Writings', in *Extincta est lucerne orbis: John Hunyadi and His Time. In memoriam Zsigmond Jakó*, ed. Ana Dumitran, Lorand Máldy and Alexandru Simon (Cluj-Napoca, 2009), pp. 35–42; Dan Ioan Mureşan, 'Croisade, Union des Églises et humanisme dans le royaume de Hongrie pendant la première moitié du règne de Matthias Corvin', in *Church Union and Crusading in the Fourteenth and Fifteenth Centuries*, ed. Christian Gastgeber et al. (Cluj-Napoca, 2009), pp. 339–66;

Fig. 2. Mid-sixteenth-century depictions of two of the most famous late medieval anti-Ottoman crusades, i.e. Nicopolis (1396, left picture) and Varna (1444, right picture). Reproduced by Paul Srodecki from Hans Schiltberger, *Ein wunderbarliche, vnnd kurtzweylige, Histori, wie Schildtberger, eyner auß der stadt München, in Bayren, von den Türcken gefangen, in die Heydenschafft defüret, vnnd wider heim kommen: Item, was sich für Krieg, vnnd wunderbarlicher thatten, dieweil er inn der Heydenschafft gewesen, zugetragen, gantz kurtzweylig zu lessen* (Nürnberg, c. 1549), front cover, available online at <https://w.wiki/76vf> [accessed 20 September 2023], licence public domain; Marcin Bielski, *Kronika wszythkiego świátá, ná dźiesięciry księgi rozdźieloná, záwieriąc w sobie sześć wiekow świátá, á cżterzy Monárchie, z rozmáitych Kronik thákież Historykow wybrana, ták Greckich, táko Láciński ch* (Kraków, 1564), fol. 245r., available online at <https://w.wiki/76ve> [accessed 20 September 2023], licence public domain

In the later Middle Ages, the so-called merchant crusades can certainly be regarded as lying somewhere between offensive and defensive crusade warfare. Although they had a fundamentally offensive character, they did not serve any major expansionist goals due to their limited geographical scope (mostly concerning only strategic trading posts) and the comparatively small size of the armies involved. Rather, they were initiated to defend and secure important trade routes for the respective actors such as the maritime republics of Venice and Genoa. Through being classified as crusades by the Holy See, such ventures could attain numerous financial and legitimising benefits, not to mention a significant gain in prestige. Furthermore, this also allowed them to recruit additional combatants from all over Latin Europe. Largely organised by the Venetians and Genoese in association with local powers such as the kingdom of Cyprus or the Byzantine Empire, these merchant crusades reached their peak in the fourteenth century, with campaigns such as the various Aegean crusades (for instance Smyrna 1344,

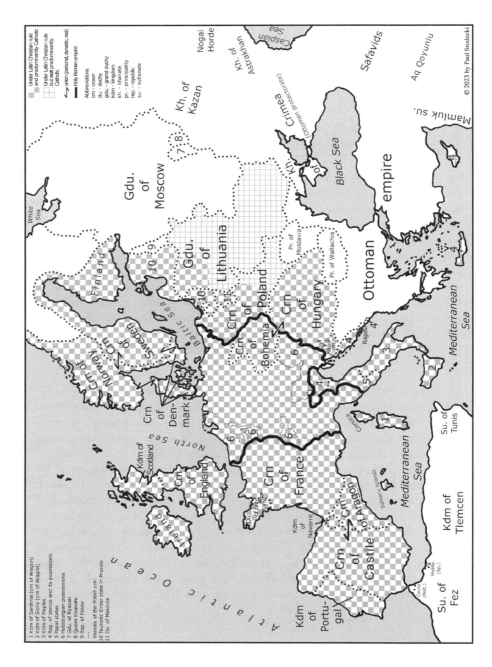

Fig. 3. The expansion of Latin Christianity, c. 1500. Map by Paul Srodecki

Lampsakos 1359, Adalia 1361 or Gallipoli 1366) or the Franco-Genoese Barbary Crusade against the Tunisian coastal city of Mahdia in 1390.[8]

A further variant of the high medieval crusades, which carried over into the late Middle Ages and the beginning of the early modern period, were the campaigns against the Orthodox schismatics of Eastern and South-Eastern Europe, conducted under the banner of the cross. For a long time — not least in the light of East-West antagonism during the Cold War —, the Great Schism was purported to have marked the beginning of a deep rift between Latin and Orthodox Christianity. In diametric opposition to this view, other researchers formulated untenable theories and misconceptions about a self-contained and unified pre-modern Europe with no religious or cultural boundaries, in which there was 'no Eastern Christianity, [...] no Latin West or Byzantine East'.[9] However, more recent balanced studies have indicated that, just as in the twelfth or thirteenth centuries, the relationship between Latin and Orthodox Christianity in the fourteenth, fifteenth or sixteenth centuries was more than ambivalent. In the border zones of Eastern Europe in particular, depending upon the current political weather conditions and caught between schism rhetoric and church union talks, the Orthodox neighbours could serve as adversaries or allies of crusading companies.[10] As was the case with anti-Ottoman crusades, Teutonic,

---

Benjamin Weber, 'La croisade impossible: Étude sur les relations entre Sixte IV et Mathias Corvin (1471–1484)', in *Byzance et ses périphéries: Hommage Alain Ducellier* (Toulouse, 2004), pp. 309–21.

8 On the merchant crusades of the fourteenth century, see Urs Brachthäuser, *Der Kreuzzug gegen Mahdiya 1390: Konstruktionen eines Ereignisses im spätmittelalterlichen Mediterraneum* (Leiden, 2017); Georg Christ, 'Kreuzzug und Seeherrschaft: Clemens V., Venedig und das Handelsembargo von 1308', in *Maritimes Mittelalter: Meere als Kommunikationsräume*, ed. Michael Borgolte and Nikolas Jaspert (Ostfildern, 2016), pp. 261–82; Mike Carr, *Merchant Crusaders in the Aegean 1291–1352* (Woodbridge, 2015); Liviu Pilat and Ovidiu Cristea, *The Ottoman Threat and Crusading on the Eastern Border of Christendom during the 15th Century* (Leiden, 2015), pp. 32–49; Kate Fleet, 'Turks, Mamluks, and Latin Merchants: Commerce, Conflict, and Cooperation in the Eastern Mediterranean', in *Byzantines, Latins, and Turks in the Eastern Mediterranean World after 1150*, ed. Jonathan P. Harris, Catherine J. Holmes and Eugenia Russell (Oxford, 2012) pp. 327–44; Léon Mirot, 'Une expédition française en Tunisie au XIVe siècle: Le siège de Mahdia, 1390', *Revue des Études Historiques* 47 (1931), 357–406.

9 As was recently stated in an article on the narrative 'roots' of Christian Europe by Mihai-D. Grigore, 'Europa — Christianitas — Europa Christiana: Zur Geschichte eines umstrittenen Narratives anhand mittelalterlicher Quellen', in *Christentum und Europa: XVI. Europäischer Kongress für Theologie (10.–13. September 2017 in Wien)*, ed. Michael Meyer-Blanck (Leipzig, 2019), pp. 457–73 (here 471).

10 Most recently on this issue, with further references: Anti Selart, 'Between Schism and Union: Rus Adversaries and Allies of the Crusaders in the Thirteenth and Fourteenth Centuries', in *The Expansion of the Faith*, pp. 251–66; Nikolaos G. Chrissis, 'Tearing Christ's Seamless Tunic? The "Eastern Schism" and Crusades against the Greeks in the Thirteenth Century', in *The Expansion of the Faith*, pp. 229–50; Mikhail Krom, 'Changing Allegiances in the Age of State Building: The Border between the Grand Duchy of Lithuania and the Grand Principality of Moscow', in *Imagined, Negotiated, Remembered: Constructing European Borders and Borderlands*, ed. Kimmo Katajala and Maria Lähteenmäki (Berlin, 2012), pp. 15–30. On efforts to unify the Catholic and Orthodox churches in the late Middle Ages, see Darius Baronas, 'King Ladislas II Jogaila of Poland, Grand

Polish, Lithuanian or Swedish military campaigns against Muscovy, especially, as the new rising great power in Eastern Europe, gradually turned from offensive to defensive at the turn of the medieval and early modern periods.[11]

***

Before introducing the articles included in this second volume on crusading on the periphery, I will provide a brief overview of the existing research history on the late medieval crusades and the key research issues and debates linked to it.

A Brief Outline of the Research History

Even if the nineteenth century saw the emergence of modern crusade research as scholars began to critically examine the historical records and narratives surrounding the various campaigns led in the name of the cross, for a long time the focus within Western countries remained on the Levantine crusades. Renowned scholars such as Friedrich Wilken, Charles Mills, Henry Stebbing, François Valentin, George Proctor, Charles Farine or Thomas Andrew Archer had very narrow conceptions and definitions of the crusades, and set them strictly within the period between Pope Urban II's call for the liberation of Jerusalem at the Council of Clermont in 1095 and the fall of Acre in 1291.[12] It is therefore

---

Duke Vytautas of Lithuania and the Roman Catholic and Greek Orthodox Church Union', in *Unions and Divisions: New Forms of Rule in Medieval and Renaissance Europe*, ed. Paul Srodecki and Norbert Kersken (London, 2023), pp. 237–47; Marie-Hélène Blanchet, 'Image de l'Union et de la croisade dans le dialogue avec un moine contre les Latins de Théodore Agallianos (1442)', in *Italy and Europe's Eastern Border (1204–1669)*, ed. Iulian Mihai Damian et al. (Wien, 2012), pp. 31–44; Katherine Walsh, 'Zwischen Mission und Dialog: Zu den Bemühungen um Aussöhnung mit den Ostkirchen im Vorfeld des Konzils von Ferrara-Florenz', in *Toleranz im Mittelalter*, ed. Alexander Patschovksy and Harald Zimmermann (Sigmaringen, 1998), pp. 297–333.

11 Tore S. Nyberg, 'The Shield of the Kalmar to the East: Sweden and the Crusade against the Russians, 1495–1497', in *Fighting for the Faith*, pp. 219–36; Anti Selart, 'Switching the Tracks: Baltic Crusades against Russia in the Fifteenth Century', in *The Crusade in the Fifteenth Century*, pp. 90–105; Janus Møller Jensen, *Denmark and the Crusades 1400–1650* (Leiden, 2007), pp. 132–48, 162–63, 170–71. See also Vladimir Shirogorov, *War on the Eve of Nations: Conflicts and Militaries in Eastern Europe, 1450–1500* (London, 2021).

12 Friedrich Wilken, *Geschichte der Kreuzzüge nach morgenländischen und abendländischen Berichten*, 7 pts [8 vols] (Leipzig, 1807–32); Charles Mills, *The History of the Crusades, for the Recovery and Repossession of the Holy Land* (London, 1820); Henry Stebbing, *History of Chivalry and the Crusades*, 2 vols (Edinburgh, 1830); François Valentin, *Abrégé de l'histoire des croisades (1095–1291)* (Paris, 1837); George Proctor, *History of the Crusades: Their Rise, Progress, and Results* (London, 1854); Charles Farine, *L'Histoire des croisades*, 4th edn (Paris, 1863); Thomas Andrew Archer, *The Story of the Crusades: The Story of the Latin Kingdom of Jerusalem* (London, 1894). For a general overview, see Paul Srodecki, 'Crusading on the Periphery in the High Middle Ages: Main Debates, New Approaches', in *The Expansion of the Faith*, pp. 29–52; Paul E. Chevedden, 'Crusade Creationism versus Pope Urban II's Conceptualization of the Crusades', *The Historian: A Journal of History* 75 (2013), 1–46; Christopher Tyerman, *The Debate on the Crusades* (Manchester, 2011); Andrew A. Latham, 'Theorizing the Crusades: Identity, Institutions, and Religious War in Medieval Latin Christendom', *International Studies Quarterly* 55 (2011), 223–43; Giles Constable,

not at all surprising that, while having been overshadowed by the high medieval Holy Land campaigns, research on late medieval crusades has always reflected the current debates and key issues of general crusade research.

In contrast to research on Outremer crusading, which was dominated from the outset by French and English but also German historians, studies on late medieval crusades were largely the domain of German-speaking scholars in the nineteenth century. This was mainly due to the political, cultural and historical dichotomy between the two most important and influential German countries, i.e. Austria and Prussia. Situated on the eastern flanks of the Holy Roman Empire, border discourses formed pillars of identity for both states from the outset. Beginning with narratives of the defensive battles against the heathen Magyars in the late ninth and early tenth centuries and up to the Mongol invasions of the thirteenth century, the centuries-long wars with the Ottoman Empire played a particularly important role in building an Austrian collective memory. In the nineteenth century, Orientalism emerged as a dominant approach, emphasising the East-West cultural antagonism and portraying the crusades as a clash of civilisations. One of the most influential scholars of the late medieval anti-Ottoman and anti-Tatar crusades was Joseph von Hammer-Purgstall, an Austrian orientalist, historian and founder of modern Ottoman studies, who wrote extensively on the Ottoman Empire as well as the Golden Horde and the khanate of Crimea, and the latter polities' conflicts with the Christian powers of Europe. Building his research upon previously little-known Ottoman sources, his works, such as *Geschichte des osmanischen Reiches* (1827–35), *Geschichte der Goldenen Horde in Kiptschak* (1840) or *Geschichte der Chane der Krim unter osmanischer Herrschaft* (1856) were instrumental in shaping the modern understanding not only of Ottoman history but also that of the late medieval anti-Ottoman crusades from non-Christian sources, as well as their significance for the history of Europe and the Middle East.[13] Also worthy of mention is the vast research output of another German historian, the Byzantinist Gustav Friedrich Hertzberg, whose works on the fall of the Byzantine Empire and the simultaneous rise of the Ottomans were essential in understanding the late medieval anti-Ottoman crusades.[14]

Subsequent German and East-Central European historians such as Alois Brauner, Gustav Kling, Ferdo Šišić, Dávid Angyal, Jan Dąbrowski, Radu Rosetti

---

'The Historiography of the Crusades', in *The Crusades from the Perspective of Byzantium and the Muslim World*, ed. Angeliki E. Laiou and Parviz Mottahedeh (Washington, D. C., 2001), pp. 1–22.

13 Joseph von Hammer-Purgstall, *Geschichte des osmanischen Reiches*, 10 vols (Wien, 1827–35); Hammer-Purgstall, *Geschichte der Goldenen Horde in Kiptschak. Das ist: Der Mongolen in Russland. Mit neun Beylagen und einer Stammtafel, nebst Verzeichnis von vierhundert Quellen* (Pest, 1840); Hammer-Purgstall, *Geschichte der Chane der Krim unter osmanischer Herrschaft: Aus türkischen Quellen zusammengetragen mit der Zugabe eines Gasels Schahingerai's* (Wien, 1856).

14 Gustav Friedrich Hertzberg, *Vom lateinischen Kreuzzugs bis zur Vollendung der osmanischen Eroberung (1204–1470)* (Gotha, 1877); Hertzberg, *Von der Vollendung der osmanischen Eroberung bis zur Erhebung der Neugriechen gegen die Pforte (1470–1821)* (Gotha, 1878); Hertzberg, *Geschichte der Byzantiner und des Osmanischen Reiches bis gegen Ende des sechszehnten Jahrhunderts* (Berlin, 1883).

or Oskar Halecki took inspiration from Hammer-Purgstall, Hertzberg and their ilk's research and published several studies on better known events such as the crusades of Nicopolis and Varna.[15] In the first half of the nineteenth century, Paul Wittek should also be mentioned in this respect. His works, such as *The Rise of the Ottoman Empire* (1938), emphasised the role of the Ottoman military and the importance of understanding the Ottoman perspective on the crusades.[16] With regard to early Ottoman history, the impact of the oeuvre of Franz Babinger cannot also not be understated. In particular, his works on the crusade of Varna, Mehmed the Conqueror and the anti-Ottoman crusade plans of the second half of the fifteenth century would prove to be groundbreaking for subsequent generations of crusade researchers.[17]

A rich tradition of research on the late medieval and early modern anti-Ottoman crusades and military campaigns can also be found in Hungary where, from the onset of modern historiography, entire generations of researchers have endeavored to illuminate the Hungaro-Ottoman conflicts from ever new perspectives.[18] However, due to the specific nature of the issue, Hungarian historians of the nineteenth and early twentieth centuries such as Mihály Horváth, Salamon Ferenc or the controversial Gyula Szekfű mostly wrote about anti-Ottoman crusades, if at all, in the larger context of their broader studies on Hungarian history. This changed in the second half of the twentieth century when scholars such as Gyula Kristó, Elemér Mályusz, Géza Dávid, Pál Fodor, János M. Bak or — from the newer generation — Tamás Pálosfalvi and Attila Bárány contributed significantly to our understanding of the Hungarian anti-Ottoman crusades, shedding light on the historical context, key events and the impact of these conflicts on both Hungary and the Ottoman Empire. Studies on fortification systems, siege warfare and military tactics at the Hungaro-Ottoman military frontier in

---

15 Alois Brauner, *Die Schlacht bei Nikopolis 1396* (Breslau, 1876); Wilhelm Pecz, 'Das Gedicht des Paraspondylos Zotikos über die Schlacht bei Varna', *Ungarische Revue* 14 (1894), 85–88; Ferdo Šišić, 'Die Schlacht bei Nicopolis (25. September 1396)', *Wissenschaftliche Mittheilungen aus Bosnien und der Hercegovina* 6 (1899), 291–327; Gustav Kling, *Die Schlacht bei Nikopolis im Jahre 1396* (Berlin, 1906); Dávid Angyal, 'Murád útja Várna felé 1444-ben', *Hadtörténelmi közlemények* 11 (1910), 252–53; Angyal, 'Die diplomatische Vorbereitung der Schlacht von Varna (1444)', *Ungarische Rundschau für historische und soziale Wissenschaften* 2 (1913), 518–21; Jan Dąbrowski, 'La Pologne et l'expédition de Varna en 1444', *Revue des études slaves* 10 (1930), 57–75; Radu Rosetti, 'Notes on the Battle of Nicopolis (1396)', *The Slavonic and East European Review* 15 (1937), 629–38; Oskar Halecki, 'La croisade de Varna', *Bulletin of the International Committee of Historical Science* 11 (1939), 485–95; Halecki *The Crusade of Varna: A Discussion of Controversial Problems* (New York, NY, 1943).
16 Paul Wittek, *The Rise of the Ottoman Empire* (London, 1938).
17 A selection of the most relevant works include: Franz Babinger, 'Von Amurath zu Amurath: Vor- und Nachspiel der Schlacht bei Varna (1444)', *Oriens* 3 (1950), 229–65; Babinger, 'Maometto II, il conquistatore, e l'Italia', *Rivista storica italiana* 63 (1951), 469–505; Babinger, 'Mehmed der Eroberer in östlicher und westlicher Beleuchtung', *SOF* 22 (1963), 281–93; Babinger, 'Pio II e l'oriente maomettano', in *Enea Silvio Piccolomini Papa Pio II. Atti del Convegno per il quinto centenario della morte e altri scritti* (Siena, 1968), pp. 1–13.
18 Oskar Halecki, 'The Last Century of the Crusades — from Smyrna to Varna (1344–1444)', *Bulletin of the Polish Institute of Arts and Sciences in America* 3 (1944/45), 300–7.

particular, as well as those on socio-political aspects of the Ottoman Empire, provided valuable insights not only into the Hungarian efforts to stop the Ottoman expansion in South-Eastern Europe but also into the organisation, administration and cultural dynamics of the Ottoman state in the occupied Balkans.[19]

Although Brandenburg, with Berlin, formed its political centre, the kingdom of Prussia traced its very name and history back to a crusader state which, by conquering pagan lands, had established one of the most famous theocracies of the entire Middle Ages, i.e. the Teutonic Order state in the south-eastern Baltic Sea region. Accordingly, and by contrast to Western European historians, those German historians who devoted themselves to the so-called *Ostforschung* ('Eastern studies'), as well as medievalists specialising in the history of the Teutonic Order, have, from the very beginning, classified the military campaigns against the Wends, Pomeranians or, above all, the Prussians, Lithuanians, Livs and schismatics of the Rus as an important part of the pan-European crusading movement.[20] From the nineteenth century onwards, whole generations of German scholars, including personalities such as Max Toeppen and the controversial Heinrich von Treitschke and Erich Maschke, or renowned medievalists such as Kurt Forstreuter, Erich Weise, Helmut Beumann, Hans Koeppen, Hans-Dietrich Kahl, Hartmut Boockmann, Udo Arnold, Bernhart Jähnig, Klaus Militzer, Werner Paravicini, Marie-Luise Favreau-Lilie, Jürgen Sarnowsky and the Swedish-German historian Sven Ekdahl dedicated their scientific output to the German *Heidenmission* in the Middle Ages and explicitly linked the *Heidenkampf* in the southern and eastern Baltic Sea region to the medieval crusading idea.[21]

---

19 See, for example, most recently: *Ottomans, Hungarians, and Habsburgs in Central Europe: The Military Confines in the Era of Ottoman Conquest*, ed. Pál Fodor and Geza David (Leiden, 2021); *The Battle for Central Europe: The Siege of Szigetvár and the Death of Süleyman the Magnificent and Nicholas Zrínyi (1566)*, ed. Pál Fodor (Leiden, 2019); Tamás Pálosfalvi, *From Nicopolis to Mohács: A History of Ottoman-Hungarian Warfare, 1389–1526* (Leiden, 2018).
20 For on overview of the Wendish and Pomeranian crusades as well as the *Preußen-, Litauer-* and *Livlandreisen* and the armed pilgrimages against the Orthodox schismatics of the Rus, see Zdzisław Pentek, 'Why Did So Few Crusaders from East-Central and Eastern Europe Participate in the Crusades to the Holy Land?', in *The Expansion of the Faith*, pp. 55–67; 'The Periphery of Europe and the Idea of Crusade: Adaptation and Evolution of Crusader Ideology in Poland under the Piast Dynasty (1100–47)', in *The Expansion of the Faith*, pp. 69–88; Norbert Kersken, 'The Crusade Idea in the Areas of the North-Western Slavs around the Time of the Second Crusade', in *The Expansion of the Faith*, pp. 113–30; Kristjan Kaljusaar, 'A North German Prince on a Pilgrimage in Arms: Political Implications of the Livonian Crusade of Albert I, Duke of Saxony', in *The Expansion of the Faith*, pp. 131–45; David Sychra, 'The Role Played by Bishop Bruno of Olomouc in the Prussian Crusades of the Bohemian King Ottokar II Premislas', in *The Expansion of the Faith*, pp. 147–63; Martin Schürrer, 'Ein folgenloser Kreuzzug? Die Herrschaftsbereiche Graf Adolfs II. von Schauenburg und des Abodritenfürsten Niklot nach dem Wendenkreuzzug von 1147', in *The Expansion of the Faith*, pp. 183–95; Oliver Auge, 'The Conquest of the Island of Rugia, 1168/1169: A Danish Crusade?', in *The Expansion of the Faith*, pp. 197–208; Selart, 'Between Schism and Union'.
21 For the respective authors' works on the Teutonic Order, see <https://t1p.de/6sh8> [accessed 29 September 2021].

The discussion of the crusade phenomenon in East-Central, Eastern, South-Eastern and North-Eastern Europe has also always been quite different to that in Western Europe. Almost without exception, in these regions, the armed pilgrimages of Latin Christians against the pagans of the southern and eastern Baltic Sea region, the Orthodox Slavs in Eastern and South-Eastern Europe or non-Catholic Christians defamed as *heretics* such as the Bogomils or Hussites, legitimised by papal crusade bulls, were defined as crusades. Above all in Poland, Lithuania and Russia there remains an unbroken interest in the Teutonic Order as well as the Baltic crusades of the thirteenth, fourteenth and early fifteenth centuries up to the present day and, in the collective memory of these countries, they are all too often representative of the idea of the crusader period as a mission propelled by fire and sword which, on the whole, is perceived as a perversion of the original missionary objective. Incidentally, this latter argumentation has a long tradition in Polish and Lithuanian research on the Baltic crusades and was already put forth at the Council of Constance (1414–18) by the Polish jurist Paweł Włodkowic (Latinised as Paulus Vladimiri), who defended his own country and all native non-Christian tribes of the southern and eastern Baltic Sea region against the Teutonic Knights and the crusading movement in general.[22] Following this idea of a perverted mission grounded in coercion, the Teutonic Order became equated in Poland in the nineteenth and early twentieth centuries — a time at which there was no independent Polish state — with the eternally hostile German nation, particularly following Bismarck's anti-Polish policies and the programmatic *Drang nach Osten* topos ('Drive to the East'). Numerous works were dedicated to the struggle with and final victory over the order in the late Middle Ages, above all to the battle of Tannenberg/Grunwald/Žalgiris in 1410, the Thirteen Years' War in 1453–66 and the so-called Prussian Homage in 1525 (Pol. *Hołd pruski*), that is the formal investment of Albert of Brandenburg-Ansbach as duke of Prussia following the dissolution and transformation of the Teutonic Order state in Prussia into a secular hereditary duchy under Polish suzerainty.[23] Jan Matejko's monumental paintings of the battle of Tannenberg and the Prussian Homage continue to enjoy a national and sacred status in Poland to the present day — with the novel

---

22 On the dispute between the Polish-Lithuanian representatives and advocates of the Teutonic Order at the Council of Constance, see Aleksandra Lenartowicz, 'Paweł Włodkowic and Andreas Laskary as the Authors of the Polish Revindication Programme against the State of the Teutonic Order in 1412–1418', in *Arguments and Counter-Arguments: The Political Thought of the 14th–15th Centuries during the Polish-Teutonic Order Trials and Disputes*, ed. Wiesław Sieradzan (Toruń, 2012), pp. 111–22; Russell, 'Paulus Vladimiri's Attack on the Just War'; Hartmut Boockmann, *Johannes Falkenberg, der Deutsche Orden und die polnische Politik: Untersuchungen zur politischen Theorie des späteren Mittelalters: Mit einem Anhang: Die Satira des Johannes Falkenberg* (Göttingen, 1975).

23 For a general overview, see Darius von Güttner-Sporzyński, 'The End of the Crusade State in Prussia: The Treaty of Kraków 1525', in *Fighting for the Faith: The Many Crusades*, ed. Kurt Villads Jensen, Carsten Selch Jensen and Janus Møller Jensen (Stockholm, 2018), pp. 331–59; Renata Knyspel-Kopeć, *Grunwald w świadomości społeczeństwa polskiego w drugiej połowie XIX i w XX wieku* (Toruń, 2014), pp. 13–62.

Krzyżacy ('Knights of the Cross') by Henryk Sienkiewicz providing a literary equivalent.[24] In light of this cultural-historical background, research on the Baltic crusades and the contrast drawn between the state of the Teutonic Order in Prussia and the Polish crown in the Middle Ages has a long history. Generations of Polish historians have dedicated their scientific output to the topic, with Gerard Labuda and Marian Biskup as well as Zenon Hubert Nowak, the founder of the series *Ordines Militares*, arguably the most formative figures in Polish research on the Teutonic Order in the last century.[25]

Research on the Baltic crusades also has a long tradition in the Baltic states and in Russia. In Lithuania, the reception of the Baltic crusades is closely linked to the prevailing conceptions in Poland while, in Latvia and Estonia, the armed pilgrimages of the Middle Ages to Livonia are also associated with the Sword Brethren as well as the expansionist efforts of the Danes.[26] In Russia, the conflicts against the Western crusaders were already stylised in medieval chronicles as a battle between Catholicism and Orthodoxy.[27]

Compared to these numerous works of German, Polish, Lithuanian or Russian historiographies on the Baltic and anti-Ottoman crusades, Western European research on late medieval crusading has largely been limited to campaigns carried out in the Eastern Mediterranean and/or those with French or English participation, such as the crusade of Nicopolis or the Smyrniote crusades (1343–51).[28]

---

24 See with further references Knyspel-Kopeć, *Grunwald*, pp. 63–230; Tadeusz Bujnicki, 'Trzy literackie wyobrażenia bitwy pod Grunwaldem (Kraszewski – Sienkiewicz – Przyborowski)', in *Conflictus magnus apud Grunwald 1410: Między historią a tradycją: Materiały z międzynarodowej konferencji naukowej 'Grunwald — Tannenberg — Žalgiris' zorganizowanej 20–24 września 2010 r. w Malborku i Krakowie*, ed. Krzysztof Ożóg and Janusz Trupinda (Malbork, 2013), pp. 321–28; Udo Arnold, 'Tannenberg/Grunwald als politisches Symbol im 19./20. Jahrhundert', in *Krajobraz grunwaldzki w dziejach polsko-krzyżackich i polsko-niemieckich na przestrzeni wieków: Wokół mitów i rzeczywistości: Tradycje kulturowe i historyczne ziem pruskich*, ed. Jan Gancewski (Olsztyn, 2009), pp. 7–18.

25 For an overview of Polish research on the Teutonic Order in the twentieth century, see Marian Biskup, 'Die polnische Geschichtsschreibung zum Deutschen Orden', in *Zwischen Konfrontation und Kompromiß: Oldenburger Symposium: 'Interethnische Beziehungen in Ostmitteleuropa als historiographisches Problem der 1930er/1940er Jahre'*, ed. Michael Garleff (München, 1995), pp. 73–94; *Der Deutschordensstaat Preußen in der polnischen Geschichtsschreibung der Gegenwart*, ed. Udo Arnold and Marian Biskup (Marburg, 1982). For the most recent Polish bibliography covering the period after 1990, see Anita Romulewicz, Anna Wysocka and Sylwia Białecka, *Bibliografia grunwaldzka za lata 1990–2010* (Olsztyn, 2010). For the various volumes of *Ordines Militares*, a journal devoted to the history of military orders, initiated by Zenon Hubert Nowak in 1981 (first volume published in 1983), see <https://t1p.de/dfh2> [accessed 29 September 2023].

26 Alvydas Nikzentaitis, 'Das Bild des Deutschen Ordens in der litauischen Geschichtsschreibung und Publizistik', in *Vergangenheit und Gegenwart der Ritterorden: Die Rezeption der Idee und die Wirklichkeit*, ed. Zenon H. Nowak and Roman Czaja (Toruń, 2001), pp. 115–31; Gert von Pistohlkors, 'Die Stellung der Deutschen in der Geschichte der Esten, Letten und Litauer', *Nordost-Archiv*, n.s. 1 (1992), 89–122.

27 On this topic, with further references, see Anti Selart, 'Between Schism and Union'.

28 On both topics, see representatively Henry L. Savage, 'Euguerrand de Coucy VII and the Campaign of Nicopolis', *Speculum* 14 (1939), 423–42; Mihály Benkő, *Csata Nikápolynál* (Móra, 1987); *Nicopolis, 1396–1996: Actes du colloque international*, ed. Jacques Paviot and Martine Chauney-

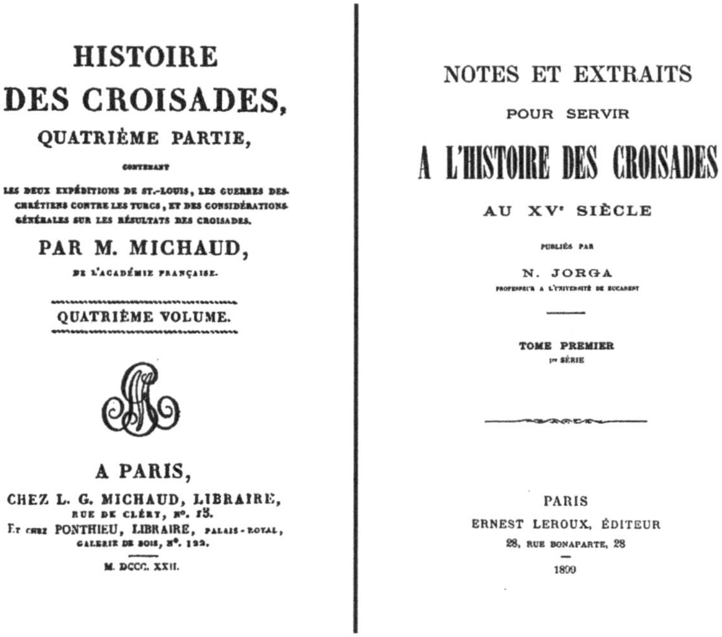
HISTOIRE
DES CROISADES,
QUATRIÈME PARTIE,
CONTENANT
LES DEUX EXPÉDITIONS DE ST.-LOUIS, LES GUERRES DES CHRÉTIENS CONTRE LES TURCS, ET DES CONSIDÉRATIONS GÉNÉRALES SUR LES RÉSULTATS DES CROISADES.
PAR M. MICHAUD,
DE L'ACADÉMIE FRANÇAISE.
QUATRIÈME VOLUME.
A PARIS,
CHEZ L. G. MICHAUD, LIBRAIRE,
RUE DE CLÉRY, N°. 13.
ET CHEZ PONTHIEU, LIBRAIRE, PALAIS-ROYAL,
GALERIE DE BOIS, N°. 122.
M. DCCC. XXII.

NOTES ET EXTRAITS
POUR SERVIR
A L'HISTOIRE DES CROISADES
AU XVe SIÈCLE
PUBLIÉS PAR
N. JORGA
PROFESSEUR A L'UNIVERSITÉ DE BUCAREST
TOME PREMIER
1re SÉRIE
PARIS
ERNEST LEROUX, ÉDITEUR
28, RUE BONAPARTE, 28
1899

Fig. 4. The title pages of the fourth volume of Joseph-François Michaud's *Histoire des croisades*, 7 vols (Paris, 1812–22), and of the first volume of Nicolae Iorga's source edition *Notes et extraits pour servir à l'histoire des croisades au XVe siècle*, 6 vols (Paris, 1899–1916), as two examples of nineteenth-century historical research on late medieval crusades. Reproduced and reworked by Paul Srodecki from <https://t1p.de/c1mpy> and <https://w.wiki/776m> [both accessed 29 September 2023], both illustrations under public domain licence

Furthermore, even if the *Preußen-* and later the *Litauerfahrten* organised by the Teutonic Order certainly became an increasingly accepted form of crusading among the European aristocracy in the thirteenth century, and reached an undeniable popularity in the fourteenth century in particular, when compared to the numerous treatises on the so-called *classical* crusades to the Levant published year after year, research on the Baltic crusades, this important phenomenon within the European aristocratic culture of the Middle Ages, remained more or less a marginal topic within Western European medieval studies until the very end of the last century.[29] It may thus come as no surprise that the absence of explicitly Western European treatises on late medieval crusading was the rule in the nineteenth and first half of the twentieth centuries, since, if they did so at all, scholars gave only incidental coverage to the issue in the framework of larger national-historical accounts.[30]

Rare exceptions in this regard were isolated studies by such renowned historians as Jules Gay, or, above all, Nicolae Iorga and Aziz Suryal Atiya. The latter two, although they were Romanian and Egyptian respectively, published extensively in English or French.[31] Joseph-François Michaud's internationally renowned *opus magnum*, *Histoire des croisades*, which was translated into numerous languages, must in a certain sense also be considered as an exception to the rule: although Michaud dedicated a considerable part of his multi-volume work to the *Croisades contre les Turcs* — which he categorised as *nouvelles Croisades*, i.e. 'new crusades' —, his considerations on late medieval crusading seem only to have had a barely perceptible impact on either crusade research or the wider popular imagination concerning the subject.[32] The works of the aforementioned Wilken, Mills,

---

Bouillot (Dijon, 1997); Veszprémy László, 'A nikápolyi hadjárat és értékelése', *Iskolakultúra* 7 (1997), 48–59; Kelly R. DeVries, 'The Battle of Nicopolis', *Medieval History Magazin* 2 (2003), 22–27; Bertrand Schnerb, '1396: Bataille de Nicopolis', in *Histoire du monde au XVe siècle*, ed. Patrick Boucheron (Paris, 2009), pp. 295–98; Cristea Ovidiu, 'La croisade de Nicopolis (1396): Controverses autour d'une bataille', in *Church Union and Crusading in the Fourteenth and Fifteenth Centuries*, ed. Christian Gastgeber et al. (Cluj-Napoca, 2009), pp. 31–56; Dražen Nemet, 'Križarski pohod i bitka kod Nikopola 1396. Godine', *Radovi: Zavod za Hrvatsku Povijest* 41 (2009), 55–113. See also László Veszprémy, 'Some Remarks on Recent Historiography of the Crusade of Nicopolis (1396)', in *The Crusades and the Military Orders: Expanding the Frontiers of Medieval Latin Christianity — In Memoriam Sir Steven Runciman (1903–2000)*, ed. Zsolt Hunyadi and József Laszlovszky (Budapest, 2001), pp. 223–30.

29 On the popularity of the *Preußen-* and *Litauerreisen* among the European nobility of the thirteenth and fourteenth centuries, see with further references Werner Paravicini, *Die Preussenreisen des europäischen Adels*, 4 vols (Sigmaringen, 1989–2023).

30 See, for instance, Pierre Antoine Noël Bruno Daru, *Histoire de la république de Venise*, 7 vols (Paris, 1819), 1: 527–33, 601–3, 623, 627, 2: 102–10, 442–54, 3: 197–202, 295, 359, 450, 4: 1, 525; pp. 494–95; Victor Duruy, *Histoire de France*, 2 vols (1862–64), 1: 429–31.

31 Jules Gay, *Le pape Clément VI et les affaires d'Orient* (Paris, 1904); Nicolae Iorga, *Philippe de Mézières 1327–1405 et la croisade au XIVe siècle* (Paris, 1896); *Notes et extraits pour servir à l'histoire des croisades au XVe siècle*, ed. Iorga, 6 vols (Paris, 1899–1916); Iorga, 'Deux ouvrages sur les croisades', *Revue historique du sud-est européen* 18 (1941), 26–30; Aziz Suryal Atiya, *The Crusade of Nicopolis* (London, 1934); Atiya, *The Crusades in the Later Middle Ages* (London, 1938); Atiya, *The Crusade* (Bloomington, 1962); Atiya, *The Crusade: Historiography and Bibliography* (Bloomington, 1962); Atiya, *Crusade, Commerce and Culture* (Bloomington, 1962).

32 Joseph-François Michaud, *Histoire des croisades*, 7 vols (Paris, 1812–22), 4: 489–608; 5: 1–161. See also the relevant parts on the late medieval crusades in the translated versions of Michaud's multi-volume work: Michaud, *Geschichte der Kreuzzüge*, trans. F. H. Ungewitter and L. G. Förster, 7 vols (Quedlinburg, 1827–32), 6: 131–352; Michaud, *Storia delle Crociate*, trans. Luigi Rossi, 9 vols (Napoli, 1831–32): 10: 164–80, 11: 5–180, 12: 5–201; Michaud, *Historia de las cruzadas*, trans. M. B. García Suelto and F. A. Pendaries, 12 vols (Madrid, 1830–32), 10: 1–310; Michaud, *The History of the Crusades*, trans. William Robson, 3 vols (Redfield, 1852), 3: 92–250.

Stebbing, Valentin, Proctor, Farine, Archer and others seem to have been more influential in this regard, since the traditionalist narrow perceptions of crusades and crusading as phenomena limited exclusively to the Outremer campaigns between the late eleventh and late thirteenth centuries have remained dominant in the collective consciousness of the West up to the present day.

However, research over the last four to five decades has contributed to the slow but steady disintegration of this traditionalist conception and periodisation of crusades and crusading. Even if the popular image of the crusades as solely religious military campaigns in the Levant does seem to persist (in part due to support from the entertainment media such as Hollywood films or even pretentiously ambitious television documentaries), a lot has changed in research since the last quarter of the twentieth century. In the context of changing discourses within Levantine crusade research, revisionist approaches gained in importance in the mid-twentieth century, while scholars began to challenge prevailing narratives and to offer alternative interpretations. Alongside the aforementioned Aziz S. Atiya, historians such as Kenneth Meyer Setton and Anthony T. Luttrell should also be mentioned in this respect. As the general editor of the six-volume work *A History of the Crusades*, Setton (as well as the authors of the respective articles) broke openly with the crusading tradition of the traditionalists by devoting the third volume solely to the crusades of the fourteenth and fifteenth centuries. In another essential work, the multi-volume *The Papacy and the Levant (1204–1571)*, Setton furthermore opened up completely new perspectives on the relationship of the crusade phenomenon to the late medieval papacy and its instrumentalisation by them.[33] Drawing upon earlier research by the Italian Ettore Rossi, Anthony T. Luttrell significantly broadened our knowledge on the Hospitallers at Rhodes and their struggle against the rising Ottoman Empire at the turn of the medieval and early modern period.[34] Outside the aforementioned German, Polish, Lithuanian, Latvian, Estonian and Russian historiographical traditions on the Baltic crusades, it was particularly the American medievalist William L. Urban whose numerous works on the Teutonic Knights and their holy warfare in the south-eastern and eastern Baltic Sea region significantly contributed to a popularisation of this topic

---

33 Kenneth M. Setton, *The Papacy and the Levant (1204–1571)*, 4 vols (Philadelphia, 1976–84).
34 To mention only the most relevant monographies: Anthony T. Luttrell, *Studies on the Hospitallers after 1306: Rhodes and the West* (Aldershot, 2007); Luttrell, *The Hospitaller State on Rhodes and Its Western Provinces, 1306–1462* (Ashgate, 1999); Luttrell, *The Hospitallers of Rhodes and Their Mediterranean World* (Aldershot, 1992); Luttrell, *Latin Greece, the Hospitallers and the Crusades, 1291–1440* (London, 1982); Luttrell, *The Hospitallers in Cyprus, Rhodes, Greece and the West 1291–1440: Collected Studies* (London, 1978); Luttrell, *Juan Fernández de Heredia, Castellan of Amposta, 1347–77, Grand Master of the Order of St. John at Rhodes, 1377–96* (Oxford, 1959). Ettore Rossi's most important works on the Hospitallers in the Mediterranean include *Storia della marina dell'Ordine di S. Giovanni di Gerusalemme di Rodi e di Malta* (Roma, 1926), and *Il dominio degli spagnoli e dei Cavalieri di Malta a Tripoli, (1530–51)* (Roma, 1942).

in the academic as well as non-academic circles of the Anglosphere.[35] Consequent research by other English-speaking scholars such as Alan V. Murray, Stephen R. Turnbull, Burnam W. Reynolds or, most recently, by upcoming young academics as Gregory Leighton followed this path.[36] All these *new* crusade historians also questioned the traditional view of crusaders as heroic figures and explored the complex motivations of the individuals involved. They highlighted economic factors, territorial ambitions, and internal power struggles within the respective European regions.

More recent research has expanded the understanding of the crusades beyond political and military events. Scholars have explored social, economic and cultural aspects, such as the impact on trade, the role of women and the impact of encounters between different religious and cultural groups. Postcolonial theory has also influenced late medieval crusade research, with its focus on power dynamics, cultural imperialism and the long-lasting effects of the Baltic or anti-Ottoman crusades on the East-West relationship. In parallel with research on the Outremer crusades, scholars have explored the influence of late medieval crusading on

---

35 See representatively only the most relevant monographies: William L. Urban, *The Last Years of the Teutonic Knights* (London, 2019); Urban, *Teutonic Knights: A Military History* (London, 2003); Urban, *Tannenberg and After* (Chicago, IL, 1999); Urban, *The Samogitian Crusade* (Chicago, IL, 1989); Urban, *The Livonian Crusade* (Washington, DC, 1981); Urban, *The Prussian Crusade* (Lanham, MD, 1980); Urban, *The Baltic Crusade* (Dekalb, IL, 1975).

36 Alan V. Murray, 'Heathens, Devils and Saracens: Crusader Concepts of the Pagan Enemy during the Baltic Crusades (Twelfth to Fifteenth Centuries)', in *Crusading on the Edge: Ideas and Practice of Crusading in Iberia and the Baltic Region, 1100–1500*, ed. Torben K. Nielsen and Iben Fonnesberg-Schmidt (Turnhout, 2016), pp. 199–224; Murray, 'The Saracens of the Baltic: Pagan and Christian Lithuanians in the Perception of English and French Crusaders to Late Medieval Prussia', *JBS* 41 (2010), 413–30; *The Clash of Cultures on the Medieval Baltic Frontier*, ed. Murray (Farnham, 2009); *Crusade and Conversion on the Baltic Frontier, 1150–1500* (Aldershot, 2001); Stephen R. Turnbull, *Tannenberg 1410: Disaster for the Teutonic Knights* (Westport, CT, 2005); Turnbull, *Crusader Castles of the Teutonic Knights. Vol. 2: The Stone Castles of Latvia and Estonia 1185–1560* (Oxford, 2004); Turnbull, *Tannenberg 1410* (Oxford, 2003); Burnam W. Reynolds, *The Prehistory of the Crusades: Missionary War and the Baltic Crusades* (London, 2016); Reynolds, 'The Prehistory of the Crusades: Toward a Developmental Taxonomy', *History Compass* 6 (2008), 884–97; Gregory Leighton, 'The Baltic Crusades (1147–1300)', in *The Routledge Handbook of East Central and Eastern Europe in the Middle Ages, 500–1300*, ed. Florin Curta (London, 2022), pp. 393–408; Leighton, 'The Teutonic Order and the Origins of Its State as an Example of a Crusading Landscape in Fourteenth-Century Prussia', in *Legacies of the Crusades: Proceedings of the Ninth Conference of the Society for the Study of the Crusades and the Latin East, Odense, 27 June – 1 July 2016*, ed. Torben K. Nielsen and Kurt Villads Jensen (Turnhout, 2021), pp. 285–304; Leighton, 'Crusading and Holy War in the Teutonic Order's Struggle for Žemaitija: Written and Visual Perspectives', *Acta Historica Universitatis Klaipedensis* 41 (2020), 25–52; Leighton, 'The Relics of St Barbara at Althaus Kulm: History, Patronages, and Insight into the Teutonic Order and the Christian Population in Prussia (Thirteenth-Fifteenth Centuries)', *ZH* 85 (2020), 5–50; Leighton, '"Reysa in laudem: Dei et virginis Marie contra paganos": The Experience of Crusading in Prussia during the Thirteenth and Fourteenth Centuries', *ZfO* 69 (2020), 1–25; Leighton, 'Military Order Castles in the Holy Land and Prussia: A Case for Cultural History', in *The Templars, the Hospitallers and the Crusades: Essays in Homage to Alan J. Forey*, ed. Helen J. Nicholson and Jochen Burgtorf (London, 2020), pp. 167–82.

colonial ventures and modern perceptions of the West. Contemporary research on the later crusades often takes a multidisciplinary approach, incorporating insights from archaeology, art history, the history of emotions and mentalities, the history of cartography and mental mapping, intellectual history and the history of ideas, literary and gender studies, studies on late medieval nation-building and those on collective identities and mnemonic culture etc., as well as more traditional fields of research such as political, economic or military histories.[37] These interdisciplinary approaches have enabled a more nuanced understanding of the late medieval and early modern crusades and their significance.

In addition to smaller essays in the form of general overviews and numerous publications in more traditional historical sub-disciplines such as political history or the auxiliary sciences of history, the number of international research projects and studies on comparative late medieval crusading history has increased in the last half century, not least within the context of the European unification process.[38] The English historian Norman J. Housley, who has published several relevant monographs, articles and edited volumes on the subject since the 1980s, has played and continues to play a prominent role in this regard.[39] Almost all

---

37 To show the vast variety of different research fields mentioned, here just a short selection of the most recent studies: Nikolas Jaspert, 'Crusades in 15th-Century Iberia and the Vexed Issue of Late Medieval Nation-Building', in *Spanien auf dem Weg zum religiösen Einheitsstaat (15. Jh.)*, ed. Klaus Herbers and Teresa Jiménez Calvente (Wolfenbüttel, 2022), pp. 33–57; *The Countryside of Hospitaller Rhodes 1306–1423: Original Texts and English Summaries*, ed. Anthony T. Luttrell and Gregory O'Malley (London, 2019); Alan V. Murray, 'Contrasting Masculinities in the Baltic Crusades: Teutonic Knights and Secular Crusaders at War and Peace in Late Medieval Prussia', in *Crusading and Masculinities*, ed. Natasha R. Hodgson, Katherine J. Lewis and Matthew M. Mesley (London, 2019), pp. 113–28; Michael Losse, 'Angriffs- und Verteidigungsmittel bei Kämpfen um Burgen und Befestigungen der Johanniter in der Ägäis 1480 bis 1522 — insbesondere bei der türkischen Belagerung von Rhodos 1480', in *Die umkämpfte Burg: Studien zur Effizienz der Wehrelemente. Kolloquium des Wissenschaftlichen Beirats der Deutschen Burgenvereinigung Göttingen 2015*, ed. Joachim Zeune (Braubach, 2018), pp. 95–113; Charles-Louis Morand Metivier, 'Narrating a Massacre: The Writing of History and Emotions as Response to the Battle of Nicopolis (1396)', in *Affective and Emotional Economies in Medieval and Early Modern Europe*, ed. Andreea Marculescu and Charles-Louis Morand Métivier (Cham, 2018), pp. 195–210; Christoph Mauntel, 'Linking Seas and Lands in Medieval Geographic Thinking during the Crusades and the Discovery of the Atlantic World', in *Entre Mers — Outre-Mer: Spaces, Modes and Agents of Indo-Mediterranean Connectivity*, ed. Nikolas Jaspert and Sebastian Kolditz (Heidelberg, 2018), pp. 107–28; Gion Wallmeyer, 'Wie der Kreuzzug marktfähig wurde: Überlegungen zur Anwendung des Marktbegriffs auf das höfische Ratgeberwesen des 13. und 14. Jahrhunderts', in *Wissen und Wirtschaft: Expertenkulturen vom 13. bis 18. Jahrhundert*, ed. Marian Füssel, Philip Knäble und Nina Elsemann (Göttingen, 2017), pp. 279–312; Elizabeth J. Moodey, *Illuminated Crusader Histories for Philip the Good of Burgundy* (Turnhout, 2012); *Documents Concerning Cyprus: From the Hospital's Rhodian Archives, 1409–59*, ed. Karl Borchardt, Anthony T. Luttrell and Ekhard Schöffler (Nicosia, 2011); *Hospitaller Women in the Middle Ages*, ed. Anthony Luttrell and Helen J. Nicholson (Aldershot, 2006).
38 See representatively *Holy War in Late Medieval and Early Modern East-Central Europe*, ed. Janusz Smołucha, John Jefferson and Andrzej Wadas (Kraków, 2017).
39 To list only the most relevant monographies as well as collective volumes and source collections edited by Housley: *The Crusade in the Fifteenth Century*; *Reconfiguring the Fifteenth-Century Crusade*,

recent studies share the same aim of breaking with the older national-historical patterns of thought which saw the final days of the crusade movement in French king Louis IX's Tunis campaign of 1270 (from a French perspective), in Edward Longshanks's Holy Land crusade of 1272 (from an English perspective) or, at least, in the fall of Acre in 1291 (from a crusader states' perspective). The Toulouse-based series *Méridiennes: Croisades tardives* may serve as an example here: originating in a cooperation between French and Czech historians, seven volumes have thus far been published — mostly written in French — shedding light on numerous aspects of the late medieval crusades.[40] Remarkably, from a popular science perspective, monographies dedicated to the search for the *last crusade* also helped post-1291 crusades to step out from under the shadow of their high medieval predecessors — at least in the consciousness of the history-interested public. A number of ventures have been labelled as *last crusades*: most prominently, Nicopolis (1396) has been described over the years as 'the last episode in the long history of the Crusade', as too — although to a lesser extent — have been Varna (1444), Granada (1492), Beirut (1520), Lepanto (1571), Alcácer Quibir (1578) or even the battle of Vienna in 1683.[41] However, the late

---

ed. Housley (London, 2017); Housley, *Crusading and the Ottoman Threat: 1453–1505* (Oxford, 2013); *Crusading in the Fifteenth Century: Message and Impact*, ed. Housley (Basingstoke, 2004); Housley, *Religious Warfare in Europe, 1400–1536* (Oxford, 2002); Housley, *Crusading and Warfare in Medieval and Renaissance Europe* (Aldershot, 2001); *Documents on the Later Crusades, 1274–1560*, ed. Housley (Basingstoke, 1996); Housley, *The Later Crusades, 1274–1580: From Lyons to Alcazar* (Oxford, 1992); Housley, *The Avignon Papacy and the Crusades: 1305–78* (Oxford, 1986); Housley, *The Italian Crusades: The Papal-Angevin Alliance and the Crusades against Christian Lay Powers, 1254–1343* (Oxford, 1982).

40 *Crusading Ideas and Fear of the Turks in Late Medieval and Early Modern Europe*, ed. Magnus Ressel (Toulouse, 2021); *Croisades en Afrique*, ed. Weber; *La guerra de Granada en su contexto internacional*, ed. Daniel Baloup and Raúl González Arévalo (Toulouse, 2017); *Partir en croisade à la fin du Moyen Âge: Financement et logistique*, ed. Daniel Baloup and Manuel Sánchez Martínez (Toulouse, 2015); *Histoires et mémoires des croisades à la fin du Moyen Âge*, ed. Martin Nejedlý and Jaroslav Svátek (Toulouse, 2015); *La noblesse et la croisade à la fin du Moyen Âge*, ed. Martin Nejedlý and Jaroslav Svátek (Toulouse, 2015); *Les projets de croisade: Géostratégie et diplomatie européenne du XIVe au XVIIe siècle*, ed. Jacques Paviot (Toulouse, 2014).

41 C. Waddy, 'The Crusade of Nicopolis: By A. S. Atiya' [review], *The Journal of the Royal Asiatic Society* (1935), 426–28; David Nicolle, *Nicopolis 1396: The Last Crusade* (Oxford, 1999). On other campaigns labelled as *last crusades*, see Snezhana Rakova, 'The Last Crusaders: Felix Petancic and the Unfulfilled Crusade of 1502', in *Au nord et au sud du Danube: Dynamiques politiques, sociales et religieuses dans le passé / North and South of the Danube: Political, Social and Religious Aspects of the Past*, ed. Rakova and Gheorghe Lazăr (Brăila, 2019), pp. 49–74; Albrecht Fuess, 'Prelude to a Stronger Involvement in the Middle East: French Attacks on Beirut in the Years 1403 and 1520', in *Al-Masāq* 17 (2005), 171–92 (here 172): '[…] the failed last crusader style attack of 1520 […]'; Christopher Duffy, *The Fortress in the Age of Vauban and Frederick the Great 1660–1789* (London, 2015), pp. 218–52; Thomas F. Madden, *Venice: A New History* (New York, NY, 2009), p. 333: 'The Battle of Lepanto […] was, in a real sense, Christendom's last Crusade'; Barnaby Rogerson, *The Last Crusaders: The Hundred-Year Battle for the Center of the World* (New York, NY, 2009); O'Callaghan, *The Last Crusade in the West*; Paul Ayris, 'Preaching the Last Crusade: Thomas Cranmer and the "Devotion" Money of 1543', *The Journal of Ecclesiastical History* 49 (1998), 683–701; Delno C. jr.

medieval and early modern *last crusades* still have to compete with the traditionalist view of what *really* was the *last crusade* which, as mentioned above, has tended to be the end of Christian rule in the Holy Land in the late thirteenth century.[42]

In recent years, new impulses in late medieval crusade research have also come from the spatial turn in the humanities, which is reflected in numerous studies on research into border areas or, for example, spatial perception and spatial concepts.[43] The emphasis has been primarily on the centre-periphery model, with a special focus on the role of East-Central and South-Eastern Europe as 'forewalls', 'ramparts' or 'bulwarks' of Latin Christianity against the Tatar successor khanates of the Mongolian Empire, Muscovy and the Ottoman Empire.[44] The interdisciplinary interweaving of historical spatial research with network analyses borrowed from the social sciences may be considered significant in this regard, since it allowed for the hypothesis that interpersonal networks, in particular, contributed to the formation of Latin Christianity's eastern peripheries as an imaginary, closely interwoven geographical frontier region. In particular, research on Renaissance humanists — accurately described in a recent study as 'mercenaries of knowledge'[45] — as influential players not only in politics in general but also

---

West, 'Christopher Columbus, Lost Biblical Sites, and the Last Crusade', *The Catholic Historical Review* 78 (1992), 519–41; William B. Munson, *The Last Crusade* (Dubuque, 1969); John Bonham Morton, 'Sobieski and the Relief of Vienna', *Blackfriars Monthly Review* 25 (1944), 243–48 (here 244).

42 Margaret Ann Hubbard, *Saint Louis and the Last Crusade* (San Francisco, CA, 2013); Wayne B. Bartlett, *The Last Crusade: The Seventh Crusade and the Final Battle for the Holy Land* (Stroud, 2007).

43 *Livland — eine Region am Ende der Welt? Forschungen zum Verhältnis zwischen Zentrum und Peripherie im späten Mittelalter / Livonia — a Region at the End of the World? Studies on the Relations between Centre and Periphery in the Later Middle Ages*, ed. Anti Selart and Matthias Thumser (Köln, 2017); Mats Roslund, 'Bringing "the Periphery" into Focus: Social Interaction between Baltic Finns and the Svear in the Viking Age and Crusade Period (c. 800 to 1200)', in *Identity Formation and Diversity in the Early Medieval Baltic and Beyond*, ed. Johan Callmer, Ingrid Gustin and Mats Roslund (Leiden, 2017), pp. 168–204; Dennis Hormuth, *Livonia est omnis divisa in partes tres: Studien zum mental mapping der livländischen Chronistik in der Frühen Neuzeit (1558–1721)* (Stuttgart, 2012).

44 Representatively, see Paul Srodecki, *Antemurale Christianitatis: Zur Genese der Bollwerksrhetorik im östlichen Mitteleuropa an der Schwelle vom Mittelalter zur Frühen Neuzeit* (Husum, 2015); Srodecki, 'Veränderungen im europäischen Wehrbau an der Schwelle vom Mittelalter zur Frühen Neuzeit im Spiegel humanistischer Bollwerksrhetorik', in *Von der Burg zur Festung: Der Wehrbau in Deutschland und Europa zwischen 1450 und 1600*, ed. Guido von Büren, Georg Ulrich Großmann and Christian Ottersbach (Petersberg, 2020), pp. 46–53; Srodecki, 'Der Ausbau der livländischen Burgen Weißenstein und Wolmar zu frühneuzeitlichen Festungsanlagen vor dem Hintergrund der Nordischen Kriege', in *Castles and Fortifications of the Reformation Period*, ed. Rainer Atzbach, Christian Ottersbach and Claus Frederik Sørensen (Bonn, 2020), pp. 71–88; Thomas Ott, '*Livonia est propugnaculum Imperii': Eine Studie zur Schilderung und Wahrnehmung des Livländischen Krieges (1558–82/83) nach den deutschen und lateinischen Flugschriften der Zeit* (München, 1996); *Antemurale Christianitatis — Crkva i društvo na području Središnje Hrvatske krajem 15. i početkom 16. Stoljeća*, ed. Tomislav Matić and Stipica Grgić (Sisak, 2021).

45 See Fabien Montcher, *Mercenaries of Knowledge: Vicente Nogueira, the Republic of Letters, and the Making of Late Renaissance Politics* (Cambridge, 2023).

in late medieval crusade rhetoric and propaganda specifically proved to be very fruitful.[46]

On the other hand, drawing upon theories from identity and alterity studies, various recent studies have also emphasised the impact of late medieval crusade rhetoric on the construction of the *other*.[47] Discourse analytical perspectives also provided new perspectives which focussed on crusade propaganda and crusading as a rhetoric tool in the later Middle Ages.[48]

Key Objectives and New Approaches in This Volume

Even if research on late medieval crusading and crusades is generally regarded as the junior sibling of the vast research on the Outremer crusades, entire libraries of Alexandrian dimensions would not be able to hold all the previous studies

---

46 Srodecki, *Antemurale Christianitatis*, pp. 151–62; Johannes Helmrath, 'Pius II. und die Türken', in *Europa und die Türken in der Renaissance*, ed. Bodo Guthmüller and Wilhelm Kühlmann (Tübingen, 2000), pp. 79–138; Dieter Mertens, 'Europa, id est patria, domus propria, sedes nostra … : Zu Funktionen und Überlieferung lateinischer Türkenreden im 15. Jahrhundert', in *Europa und die osmanische Expansion im ausgehenden Mittelalter*, ed. Franz-Reiner Erkens (Berlin, 1997), pp. 39–57; Jürgen Blusch, 'Enea Silvio Piccolomini und Giannantonio Campano: Die unterschiedlichen Darstellungsprinzipien in ihren Türkenreden', *Humanistica Lovaniensia: Journal of Neo-Latin Studies* 28 (1979), 78–138; Rigomera Eysser, 'Papst Pius II. und der Kreuzzug gegen die Türken', in *Mélanges d'histoire* 2 (1938), 1–134.

47 Paul Srodecki, 'Die Angst vor dem Osten: Europa und die religiös motivierten Identitäts-, Alteritäts- und Alienitätskonstruktionen im Mittelalter und der Frühen Neuzeit', in *Identitätsentwürfe im östlichen Europa — im Spannungsfeld von Selbst- und Fremdwahrnehmung*, ed. Hans-Jürgen Bömelburg et al. (Wiesbaden, 2018), pp. 11–34; Srodecki, 'Antemurale-Based Frontier Identities in East Central Europe and Their Ideological Roots in Medieval/Early Modern Alterity and Alienity Discourses', in *Collective Identity in the Context of Medieval Studies*, ed. Michaela Antonín Malaníková et al. (Ostrava, 2016) pp. 97–120.

48 Nancy P. Pope, 'Burgundian Crusade Propaganda in a Middle English Manuscript', *Viator* 52 (2021), 293–311; Paul Srodecki, 'Mediating Actors in the Conflict between the Teutonic Order and the Kingdom of Poland in the Early Fifteenth Century', in *Der Deutsche Orden auf dem Konstanzer Konzil: Pläne — Strategien — Erwartungen*, ed. Helmut Flachenecker (Weimar, 2020), pp. 15–34; Srodecki, 'Murus et antemurale pollens et propugnaculum tocius christianitatis: Der Traktatenstreit zwischen dem Deutschen Orden und dem Königreich Polen auf dem Konstanzer Konzil', *Schweizerische Zeitschrift für Religions- und Kulturgeschichte* 109 (2015), 47–65; Dan Ioan Mureșan, 'Bessarion's Orations against the Turks and Crusade Propaganda at the Große Christentag of Regensburg (1471)', in *Reconfiguring the Fifteenth-Century Crusade*, pp. 207–43; Stefan Erik Kristiaan Vander Elst, *The Knight, the Cross, and the Song: Crusade Propaganda and Chivalric Literature, 1100–1400* (Philadelphia, PA, 2017); Matthew J. Punyi, 'A New Crusade: Johannes Tinctor's Sec of Witches', *Constellations* 6 (2014), available online at <https://t1p.de/8gcua> [accessed 29 September 2023]; David Joseph Wrisley, 'The Loss of Constantinople and Imagining Crusade at the Fifteenth-Century Court of Burgundy', *al-Abhath* 55 (2007-8), 85–112; Nancy B. Black, 'La Belle Hélène de Constantinople and Crusade Propaganda at the Court of Philip the Good', *Fifteenth Century Studies* 26 (2001), 42–51; Oswald A. W. Dilke, 'Mapping a Crusade: Propaganda and War in 14th-Century Palestine', *History Today* 39.8 (1989), 31–35; Richard J. Walsh, 'Charles the Bold and the Crusade: Politics and Propaganda', *Journal of Medieval History* 3 (1977), 53–86.

and possible future treatises required to encompass the phenomenon in its entirety. Rather, this book is intended to present the reader with some interesting current research perspectives and thus to provide an impression of the diversity of research. We have decided to focus on the Latin Christian peripheries and the transformations which turned the crusading movement from a tool of Western expansionism (as highlighted in the first volume) into a useful military and propaganda instrument of defensive warfare. The emphasis will therefore largely be on the North-Eastern, East-Central and South-Eastern European theatres of war (with an Iberian example serving as a mirror for these regions). Through their focus on the questions outlined above, and based on examples drawn from across Europe, the contributions to this publication aim to establish a comparability between their findings which moves beyond the mere juxtaposition of individual results. The articles collected here also provide a good impression of the paradigm shift which was touched upon in the final chapter of the previous volume, i.e. that dealing with the anti-Mongol crusade ventures of the thirteenth century.

The first four chapters address issues linked to late medieval campaigning and recruiting. Norman J. Housley's article on communications between centre and periphery in fifteenth-century crusading serves as a valuable introductory sketch, outlining the issues related to communication, with its aims, methods and constraints, as 'one of the most fertile areas of discussion and research into crusading'.[49] While numerous questions have been raised and answered to varying degrees of satisfaction in recent years with regard to crusade memorialisation in late medieval and early modern writings, as have those on the interconnections between remembrance and the communication of the crusade message itself, Housley examines 'a third process of communication, one which played a crucial role in the initiation of crusade: this is the variety of ways by which frontline powers and communities in the fifteenth century attempted to persuade Christian authorities to organise and deploy crusading resources to come to their assistance'.[50] Acknowledging the interdependence between a more or less fluid centre and a periphery, which 'rarely spoke with a single voice', Housley's chapter broadens our perspective on the cross-analysis of late medieval crusade communication as a 'two-way process', based on a give-and-take, in which 'the dialogue morphed into one about expectations and guarantees' between the respective players.[51] In the face of the Ottoman threat and anti-Ottoman crusade plans in particular, the processes of communication were 'dense and fluent', since 'centre and periphery spoke the same language, both literally in their shared latinity, and in terms of the themes and rhetorical devices that each deployed'.[52] However, while in the latter

---

49 Norman Housley, 'Communication between Centre and Periphery in Fifteenth-Century Crusading', in *The Defence of the Faith: Crusading on the Frontiers of Latin Christendom in the Late Middle Ages*, ed. Paul Srodecki and Norbert Kersken (Turnhout, 2023), pp. 63–76 (here 63).
50 Housley, 'Communication', pp. 63–64.
51 Housley, 'Communication', p. 64.
52 Housley, 'Communication', p. 72.

case 'ideas and arguments were exchanged by means of circulated texts, formal orations and [...] informal liaison' and 'friendship networks based on shared interests, affiliations and education were common', things were quite the opposite with regard to union discussions with the Greeks at the councils of Constance and Basle.[53] Housley uses the contrast between the fruitful resolution of the Hussite crisis and the inability to engage in union talks with the Greeks to show what impact communication and miscommunication had on Christian unity in general, and joint crusade ventures against outer threats as the aforementioned Ottoman Turks in particular.

Even if — as mentioned above — crusade goals in the fourteenth and fifteenth centuries certainly differed from the expansive high medieval ventures in the name of the cross and had a more defensive tone, the recapture of the Holy Land and Jerusalem remained the ultimate objective, at least in crusade preaching and propaganda. Through a case study of crusade campaigning by the Franciscan establishment in the Holy Land, Marianne Ritsema van Eck explains why it is important to bring 'together various ideological, diplomatic, liturgical, textual, cartographical, and sermonical exponents [...] in order to characterise the crusading interests and efforts of the Franciscan Observants at this religious frontier'.[54] Ritsema van Eck emphasises that 'the textual culture that developed at Mount Sion was independent' from the ideas raised by such prominent thirteenth- and early-fourteenth-century Franciscan authors as Gilbert of Tournai, Fidentius of Padua, Ramon Llull and Galvano da Levanto.[55] Unlike the latter, the Franciscans in the Holy Land 'produced several compilation manuscripts with historical texts in various combinations, which expressed a clear nostalgia for the classical crusader era, but no calls for renewed crusade'.[56] However, this started to change in the second half of the fifteenth century and several treatises with explicit calls for the recovery of the Levant for Latin Christianity can be found well into the seventeenth century.

The picture is diametrically different when examining crusade preaching, campaigning and recruiting on the other side of the Mediterranean basin, where, in the course of the *Reconquista*, Christians had been on the advance on the Iberian Peninsula for centuries. In her contribution, Maria Bonet Donato takes a closer look at 'the evolution of the crusader movement in relation to the role played by the military orders in the crowns of Aragon and Castile in the late medieval period'.[57] As in the preceding two chapters, communication looms large in the interaction between the respective actors. Bonet Donato underlines how, on the

---

53 Housley, 'Communication', p. 72.
54 Marianne P. Ritsema van Eck, 'Crusade Campaigning by Friars of the Observant Franciscan Establishment in the Holy Land', in *The Defence of the Faith*, pp. 77–89 (here 78).
55 Ritsema van Eck, 'Crusade Campaigning', p. 89.
56 Ritsema van Eck, 'Crusade Campaigning', p. 89.
57 Maria Bonet Donato, 'Crusading and Military Orders in the Crowns of Aragon and Castile in the Late Middle Ages', in *The Defence of the Faith*, pp. 91–107 (here 92).

one hand, 'the crusade ideal continued to be central in the identification and services of the military orders' whilst, on the other, the latter, in turn, 'adapted to the changing geopolitical realities'.[58] This was clearly evident after the *Reconquista* slowed down in the mid-thirteenth century and 'the military alliance between the orders and the crowns of Castile and Aragon evolved in keeping with the new military and political needs'.[59] Even if Iberia became entirely Christian at the end of the fifteenth century, 'the increasing dependence on the various royal houses arising from the changing political conditions did not mean an abandonment of the high medieval crusade doctrine' by the Hispanic military orders, since 'appeals to the holy war and to the defence of the Catholic faith against its enemies remained widespread constants' in their 'quite dogmatic and [...] somehow quixotic self-perception'.[60]

The extent to which changing geopolitical situations exerted an influence on auto- and hetero-stereotypes, political alliances and diplomatic networks is demonstrated in Mihai-D. Grigore's article, in which he examines the place of Orthodox Wallachia in the crusade plans of Pope Leo X. Outlining the geographically wide-spread efforts of Prince Neagoe Basarab of Wallachia to gain support from the papacy, Venice, Hungary and Poland against the seemingly unstoppable Ottomans, Grigore departs from the classic approach by showing how interconfessional relations aimed at organising a crusade broke the 'dichotomy between a "core" and a "periphery" in the crusading phenomenology' at the threshold of the medieval and early modern periods.[61] Grigore points out that — besides the Holy See — it was the East-Central and South-Eastern European rulers of the fifteenth and sixteenth centuries who provided 'the most dynamic impulses on the path to the late crusades', rather than the Latin Christian regions situated further in to the west which were commonly regarded as the centre of the Christian West.[62] In order to join forces against the almighty threat which the Ottoman Empire undoubtedly posed, 'confessional differences were therefore replaced by common Christian beliefs which, in the crusade, saw the justified modality of combatting the infidels on all levels, religious, symbolical, military, and propagandistic'.[63]

Besides political actors, diplomats, clergymen and crusading propagandists, high medieval continuities within the late medieval crusade movement were also kept alive by chivalric culture. The four chapters in the second part of this volume examine the impact that crusade narratives and myths had on late medieval chivalry and nobility as well as on the materialisation of actual crusade ventures. Contrasting the reigns of the last Přemyslids and the early Luxemburgs, Dalibor

---

58 Bonet Donato, 'Crusading', p. 92.
59 Bonet Donato, 'Crusading', p. 92.
60 Bonet Donato, 'Crusading', p. 107.
61 Mihai-D. Grigore, 'Army Inspection and Crusade: Wallachia and the Crusade Plans of Pope Leo X', in *The Defence of the Faith*, pp. 109–19 (here 119).
62 Grigore, 'Army', p. 119.
63 Grigore, 'Army', p. 119.

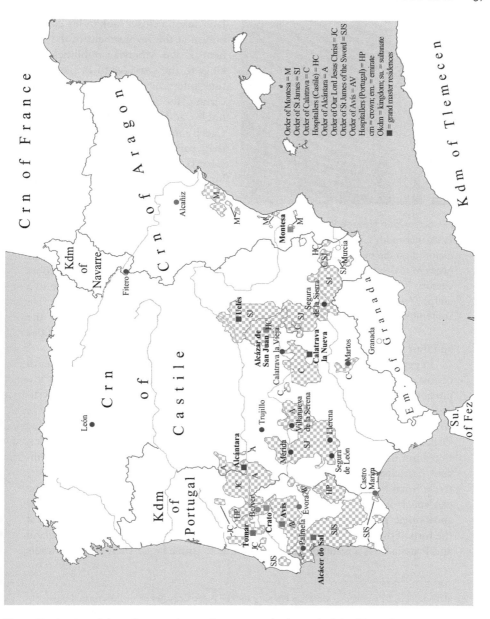

Fig. 5. Territories of the military orders in Iberia towards the end of the fifteenth century. Reproduced and reworked by Paul Srodecki from *Territorios de las órdenes militares de los reinos ibéricos hacia finales del siglo XV*, map by Tyk, available online at <https://w.wiki/6iUj> [accessed 20 September 2023], licence CC BY-SA 3.0.

Fig. 6. Voivode Neagoe Basarab V of Wallachia and his wife Milica Despina pictured on the murals of the Curtea de Argeș Monastery, Romania, sixteenth century. Reproduced by Paul Srodecki from <https://w.wiki/76rE> [accessed 20 September 2023], licence public domain

Janiš takes a closer look in his contribution at the involvement of the Bohemian and Moravian nobilities and kings in the crusades to Prussia, and thus offers new interpretations concerning the self-identification of the nobles and their relationship to the Czech monarch. Janiš emphasises that, particularly in the case of Ottokar II Premislas and John of Luxemburg, both very active participants in numerous Baltic crusades of the Teutonic Order, 'an important element [...] was the active creation of the image of an ideal king, protecting Christians and fighting pagans and enemies of the faith'.[64] Praised by various court poets, the crusade deeds of these two kings served to provide glorious role models worthy of imitation for the Bohemian and Moravian nobilities and thus strongly influenced knightly culture in the Czech lands.

In general, the Baltic crusades of the thirteenth, fourteenth and early fifteenth centuries, as shown above, served the European gentry as probably the most important arenas for the preservation and further development of high medieval crusade culture and it is hard to identify the very few regions of Latin Christianity in which local nobilities did not participate in the so-called *Reisen* of the Teutonic Order. Examining the case study of English support for the Baltic crusades, Benjámin Borbás seeks to answer the questions of 'what factors led to the significant participation of the English nobility in the Lithuanian campaigns' respectively 'what benefits England sought to gain from this support' and whether one can 'speak of a continuous and unchanging assistance' in these ventures.[65] Borbás shows that 'paradoxically, at the zenith of English participation in the *Reisen* (at the turn of the 1380s and 1390s), there was a commercial rivalry between England and Prussia'.[66] As a result of English attempts to gain a larger share of Baltic trade,

---

64 Dalibor Janiš, 'The Bohemo-Moravian Nobility and the Baltic Crusades of the Bohemian Kings Ottokar II Premislas and John of Luxemburg in the Thirteenth and Fourteenth Centuries', in *The Defence of the Faith*, pp. 123–35 (here 134–35).

65 Benjámin Borbás, 'How to Uphold a Dying Institution: English Support for the Teutonic Order's Baltic Crusades in the Early Fifteenth Century', in *The Defence of the Faith*, pp. 137–52 (here 137). On this issue, see also, most recently, Barbara Bombi, 'The Teutonic Order and England between the Fourteenth and Fifteenth Centuries: Notes on Five Documents Preserved at The National Archives', in *Zwischen Mittelmeer und Baltikum*, pp. 18–31.

66 Borbás, 'How to Uphold a Dying Institution', p. 148.

Anglo-Hanseatic relations worsened at the end of the fourteenth century, and this also led to strained relations with the Teutonic Knights who were seeking to protect their Prussian cities.

The drying up of English and Western support for the Baltic crusades of the Teutonic Order at the turn of the fourteenth and fifteenth centuries was closely related to the initiation of the Polono-Lithuanian union in 1386 and the formal conversion of the Lithuanians to Christianity. This removed the basis of legitimacy of the Teutonic Order state in Prussia in one fell swoop. Rather, the Lithuanian neophytes now developed a keen interest in Western chivalric culture and, over the course of the fifteenth century, adopted the crusade ideology for their own purposes, as presented in the following chapter by Darius Baronas.[67] He illustrates how the perceptions of the two Gediminid princes Jogaila and his cousin Vytautas in particular transformed Western depictions of the dynasty from that of savage heathens to that of most praiseworthy *athletae Christi*.

The third part of the volume is dedicated to a central specific feature of the late medieval crusades: as already described above, the Latin West went on the defensive, especially on its north-eastern, eastern and south-

Fig. 7. Left: contemporary seals of the Bohemian kings Ottokar II Premislas (r. 1253–78, top) and John of Luxemburg (r. 1311–46, bottom). Right: early-fifteenth-century depictions of both rulers from the *Gelnhausen Codex*. Reproduced by Paul Srodecki from *Die österreichisch-ungarische Monarchie in Wort und Bild*, ed. Crown Prince Rudolf of Austria and Princess Stéphanie of Belgium, 24 vols (Wien, 1886–1902), 14: 243; *Die Siegel der deutschen Kaiser und Könige von 751–1806 und 1871–1913*, ed. Otto Posse, 5 vols (Dresden, 1909–13), 1: fig. 49.1; John of Gelnhausen, *Gelnhausen Codex* (Jihlava, c. 1400–08). Available online at <https://t1p.de/l1qaq>, <https://w.wiki/6gUB>, <https://w.wiki/6gUQ> and <https://w.wiki/6gUR> [all accessed 20 September 2023], all illustrations under public domain licence.

eastern peripheries, and was increasingly pushed back by the aspiring Ottoman and Muscovite powers. An attempt to turn the tide and to regain the initiative was the crusade of Nicopolis in 1396, without exaggeration one of the last two supranational campaigns of the high medieval crusade type (the other being the Varna crusade of 1444). In the first chapter of this section, following a brief outline of

---

67 Darius Baronas, 'Lithuanian Participation in the Crusading Movement in the Long Fifteenth Century', in *The Defence of the Faith*, pp. 153–68.

Fig. 8. Seals of Vladislas Jogaila, king of Poland and grand duke of Lithuania, from 1388 and of his cousin Vytautas the Great, grand duke of Lithuania, from 1407. Reproduced by Paul Srodecki from Friedrich August Vossberg, *Siegel des Mittelalters von Polen, Lithauen, Schlesien, Pommern und Preussen: Ein Beitrag zur Förderung diplomatischer, genealogischer, numismatischer und kunstgeschichtlicher Studien über ursprünglich slavische Theile der preussischen Monarchie* (Berlin, 1854), fig. 7a; <https://w.wiki/76uq> [accessed 20 September 2023], licence public domain

this undertaking and its fourteenth-century predecessors, I will turn to a lesser-known topic, namely the importance of Nicopolis for the first formation of a somewhat more or less precise Western image of the Ottoman Turks.[68] While they had been almost indistinguishable from other Anatolian Turks or even Muslim peoples before the crusade, with their victory over the Christians at the gates of Nicopolis the Ottomans muscled their way into the public consciousness of the West. This marked at least the first expression of an increased interest in their alien culture from a Latin Christian perspective.

Following the failure of the international crusade army at Nicopolis, a radical rethink took place, especially within the crown of Hungary, which was one of the main victims of Ottoman expansion: the offensive great power policy of the Angevin kings Charles Robert and Louis the Great were successively replaced by a coordinated *passagium particulare* under King Sigismund of Luxemburg. For Attila Bárány, the latter monarch serves as an example of the fifteenth century 'modern crusader', for whom 'there was no longer any point in organising *passagia*' in the old sense, and for whom Jerusalem and its recuperation 'no longer [...] formed the goal of the struggle, but rather Christendom itself which was under assault'.[69] In fact, the defence doctrine developed under Sigismund served all his successors on the Hungarian throne as an important motivator of Hungarian foreign policy. Foreign military specialists, such as the Florentine condottiere Filippo Scolari, for instance, were hired to establish an effective defence system in the southern Hungarian border counties. Tragic exceptions, such as the offensive crusades of 1443–44 led by the young Polono-Hungarian king Vladislas the Jagiellonian and depicted by Neven Mityev in his chapter, were painful reminders for the Hungarians of the changed political situation in the

---

68 Paul Srodecki, 'The Crusade of Nicopolis and Its Significance for the Western Image of the Ottoman Turks around 1400', in *The Defence of the Faith*, pp. 171–95.
69 Attila Bárany, 'Hungary and the passagium particulare after Nicopolis (1396–1437)', in *The Defence of the Faith*, pp. 197–216 (here 216).

Balkans, in which Hungary was forced to use her limited military resources wisely in order to defeat the increasingly powerful Ottomans.[70]

Alongside the development of a dense defensive belt with several fortresses on the central Danube, the smaller principalities between Hungary and the Ottoman Empire gained in regio-strategic importance. Countries such as Bosnia, which in the thirteenth century had still served as a destination of numerous crusade calls, were now stylised as important outposts of Latin Christianity, as illustrated by Emir O. Filipović in his chapter.[71] There are also interesting parallels here with Lithuania. As mentioned above, although it had a political and military importance far greater than that of small Bosnia, Lithuania also transformed from the object of crusades to a crusading country. Nevertheless, at the turn of the medieval and early modern periods, the changing political circumstances of the Latin Christian eastern peripheries also cast their shadow on the crusade movement and crusading in this part of Europe: in his article, Rimvydas Petrauskas shows how defensive rhetoric increasingly replaced older expansionist motifs in fifteenth century crusade discourses in Lithuania.[72] Along with Poland, the Lithuanian grand duchy was promoted to the role of the gatekeeper of Latin Christianity in the east, on whose existence the security of the European hinterland against Tatar and Muscovite armies depended. The section closes with another example that clearly shows the consequences of the changed regio-political circumstances on the crusade movement and, as a result, on the self-image of the countries and nations on the peripheries of Latin Christianity. More than any other polity, it was the Teutonic Order who was forced to adapt to these new conditions, especially after it saw itself demoted to the status of a vassal of the Polish crown in 1466. In his chapter, Adam Szweda examines the fascinating question of the importance of the religious struggle for

Fig. 9. Andrew of Castagno's fresco of the condottiere Filippo Scolari alias Pippo Spano, c. 1450, Villa Carducci in Florence, Italy. Reproduced by Paul Srodecki from <https://w.wiki/6fsz> [accessed 20 September 2023], licence public domain.

---

70 See Nevyan Mitev, 'The Last Crusade in the Balkans from 1443–44 or the Union between Central and South-Eastern Europe against the Ottoman Invasion', in *The Defence of the Faith*, pp. 217–34; John Jefferson, *The Holy Wars of King Wladislas and Sultan Murad: The Ottoman-Christian Conflict from 1438–1444* (Leiden, 2012).
71 Emir O. Filipović, 'Converting Heretics into Crusaders on the Fringes of Latin Christendom: Shifting Crusading Paradigms in Medieval Bosnia', in *The Defence of the Faith*, pp. 235–50.
72 Rimvydas Petrauskas, 'Ziel oder Ausgangsort? Das Großfürstentum Litauen als verlängerter Arm der Kreuzzugsbewegung vom Ende des 14. bis zum Beginn des 16. Jahrhunderts', in *The Defence of the Faith*, pp. 251–63.

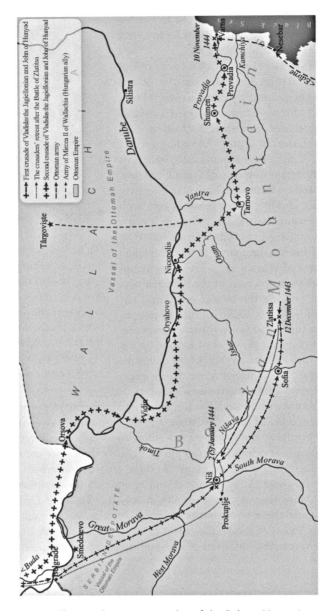

Fig. 10. The anti-Ottoman crusades of the Polono-Hungarian king Vladislas the Jagiellonian and John of Hunyad, 1443–44. Reproduced and reworked by Paul Srodecki from *Map of the Crusades of Vladislav III Varnenchik and Janos Hunyadi against the Ottoman Empire (October 1443–November 1444)*, map by Kandi, available online at <https://w.wiki/6iUN> [accessed 20 September 2023], licence CC BY-SA 4.0.

the Teutonic Knights as vassals of the Polish kings between the end of the Thirteen Years' War (1453–66) and the dissolution of the order's state in Prussia in 1525.[73]

Despite offensive crusades coming to a gradual halt in the late Middle Ages, the rhetoric of crusading once again flourished. Here too, however, the content and the programme had to be adapted to meet the rapidly changing political circumstances, as is shown very clearly in the last five chapters of the book on the basis of selected examples. Two essays trace the incorporation of Red Ruthenia into the Polish crown in the fourteenth century. Andrzej Marzec describes the instrumentalisation of the crusade motif in the fight and defence against the Lithuanian pagans and Ruthenian schismatics, as well as in the enforcement of dynastic claims in Galicia and Volhynia at the end of the Piast period.[74] Sven Jaros then goes into the propaganda legitimising the integration of the Galician and Volhynian principalities by the Poles as Crown Ruthenia.[75] Although, as shown in the previous volume, the motif of defending the faith has been present in Poland since the era of the high medieval Pomeranian, Prussian and, last but not least, Mongolian crusades,[76] it becomes clear in both chapters how defensive motifs were increasingly repeated in chancellery language but also in various historiographical as well as literary and poetic compositions and ultimately became the dominant pillars of Polish crusade rhetoric.

Fig. 11. An illustration of the anti-Hussite crusades from the *Jena Codex* (c. 1500), fol. 56a. Reproduced by Paul Srodecki from <https://w.wiki/6ft3> [accessed 20 September 2023], licence public domain.

This latter development leads seamlessly to my reflections on the importance of bulwark rhetoric for the collective self-awareness of Poles in the late Middle Ages. Of greatest importance in the final formation of this self-image was the long-standing dispute between the Polish crown and the Teutonic Order, another self-proclaimed shield of Christianity. In my chapter, I address a less noticed

---

73 Adam Szweda, 'Fighting Pagans and Relations between Poland and the Teutonic Order after 1466', in *The Defence of the Faith*, pp. 265–78.
74 Andrzej Marzec, 'Infideles et perfidii schismatici: Crusades and Christianisation as Political Tools of the Polish Kings in the Fourteenth Century', in *The Defence of the Faith*, pp. 281–91.
75 Sven Jaros, 'Against Tartari, Rutheni et Litfani, hostes fidei: The Role and Ambivalence of the Crusading Idea in the Integration of Ruthenia into the Polish Crown in the Second Half of the Fourteenth Century', in *The Defence of the Faith*, pp. 293–312.
76 See Güttner-Sporzyński, 'The Periphery of Europe'; Kersken, 'The Crusade Idea'; Srodecki, 'Fighting the "Eastern Plague"'.

phenomenon, namely the rhetorical references of the two opposing polities to the Outremer and Iberian crusades in the early fifteenth century and beyond.[77] Especially on the periphery, the bulwark argument often served as a decisive argument against critical voices from the West, according to which the countries on the periphery were insecure Christians since, depending on the political weather, they had often made pacts with non-Latins against other Western countries. In his chapter, Sergey V. Polekhov uses the example of the Lithuanian grand duke Vytautas to show what (not always unfounded) prejudices and diplomatic difficulties the Lithuanian neophytes had to contend with and what importance the crusade motif gained in grand ducal diplomacy at the turn of the fourteenth and fifteenth centuries.[78]

This section on legitimation and propaganda, and thus the volume, concludes with Pavel Soukup's chapter on the Hussite crusades. This may come as a surprise since, at first glance, the matter seemed clear from a legitimising perspective. After all, 'crusading against heretics was endorsed by the legal and theological theories developed since the twelfth century'.[79] Outlining 'briefly how the ideologues of the anti-Hussite crusade attempted to provide legitimacy', Soukup identifies 'some areas where this need arose'.[80] Indeed, there were two major issues where the respective ecclesiastical and secular players found it necessary to legitimise the anti-Hussite crusade: similar to the high medieval crusades against Orthodox Christians, heretical Cathars or Bogomils, one of the central questions was a religious and moral one, 'regarding whether it was admissible to fight physically against erring Christians'.[81] Furthermore, anti-Hussite crusades also had to deal with a diplomatic question of legitimation, i.e. whether a 'crusade as the most appropriate option for dealing with heresy' was — to paraphrase Carl von Clausewitz — a just tool in the continuation of inner-Christian policies by other means.[82]

---

77 Paul Srodecki, 'Playing the Crusade Card: Rhetorical References to Outremer and Iberian Crusades in the Conflict between the Teutonic Order and the Kingdom of Poland in the Early Fifteenth Century', in *The Defence of the Faith*, pp. 313–38.
78 Sergey V. Polekhov, 'Zwischen Kreuzzugsrhetorik und Bündnissen: Die Ostpolitik des Großfürsten Witold von Litauen (1392–1430)', in *The Defence of the Faith*, pp. 339–60.
79 Pavel Soukup, 'Legitimising the Hussite Wars: Anti-Heretical Crusading in the Fifteenth Century', in *The Defence of the Faith*, pp. 361–75 (here 361).
80 Pavel Soukup, 'Legitimising the Hussite Wars', p. 362.
81 Pavel Soukup, 'Legitimising the Hussite Wars', p. 374.
82 Pavel Soukup, 'Legitimising the Hussite Wars', p. 374.

Part I

Campaigning and Recruiting

NORMAN HOUSLEY

Communication between Centre and Periphery in Fifteenth-Century Crusading

> And at this sound the crowd gathered and was bewildered, because each one heard them speaking in the native language of each. Amazed and astonished, they asked, 'Are not all these who are speaking Galileans? And how is it that we hear, each of us, in our own native language?'
>
> Acts of the Apostles, 2:6–8

Communication — its goals, methods and constraints — has long been one of the most fertile areas of discussion and research into crusading. This applied first and foremost to the way the crusading message was conveyed to the faithful, through preaching, liturgical practices, the oral transmission of texts and, in the later fifteenth century, printed propaganda and newsletters.[1] In recent years much effort has been devoted, with very pleasing results, to the ways in which crusading became memorialised after the event.[2] In many instances recording and remembering were interlocked with the communication of the message itself, because past successes were pressed into service to rouse contemporaries to fresh action.[3] In this paper, I want to examine a third process of communication, one which played a crucial role in the initiation of crusade: this is the variety of ways by which frontline powers and communities in the fifteenth century attempted to persuade Christian authorities to organise and deploy crusading resources

---

1 For changing methods of communicating the message in the fifteenth century, see Karoline Dominika Döring, *Türkenkrieg und Medienwandel im 15. Jahrhundert* (Husum, 2013).
2 *Remembering the Crusades: Myth, Image, and Identity*, ed. Nicholas Paul and Suzanne Yeager (Baltimore, 2012); *Histoires et mémoires des croisades à la fin du Moyen Âge*, ed. Martin Nejedlý and Jaroslav Svátek (Toulouse, 2015).
3 See the classic study by E. A. R. Brown and M. W. Cothren, 'The Twelfth-Century Crusading Window of the Abbey of Saint-Denis: *praeteritorum enim recordatio futurorum est exhibitio*', *Journal of the Warburg and Courtauld Institutes* 49 (1986), 1–40.

to come to their assistance. It was of course a two-way process. If the frontier agencies were intent on accentuating the gravity of their military situation, and the ways in which their needs related to the Christian community at large, the authorities were equally intent on separating the wheat from the chaff in the body of data, assertions, promises and threats that was set before them. If resources *were* granted, the dialogue morphed into one about expectations and guarantees.

There was nothing inherently new about this, as studies of earlier crusading have amply demonstrated.[4] But the circumstances of the 1400s make it a particularly promising field of research. Contemporaries were fascinated by the arts of persuasion and convinced of the importance of reaching a wide audience. This predated humanism and printing, as Daniel Hobbins showed in his groundbreaking study of Jean Gerson. Hobbins established the significance of the tract, 'the central and even the defining genre in the works of fifteenth-century schoolmen'.[5] He also emphasised that public discourse was supremely ready for printing, 'print did not create demand, it responded to it'.[6] In no respect was this truer than of crusading, as Dan Ioan Mureşan has shown in his analysis of the relationship between the 1471 Ratisbon diet and the dissemination of Guillaume Fichet's print-run of Bessarion's *Orations against the Turks*. As Mureşan put it,

> we have to admire the entrepreneurial spirit of an editor who succeeded in publishing in record time a manuscript received in January 1471 and then in identifying across the breadth of Europe a public which would be interested in a topic of a highly specific nature.[7]

In humanistic oratory — of which Bessarion's *Orations* form one of the finest examples — the period produced a new and exciting way of setting out a case. Much attention has been paid to the precise moment when this oratory made its debut in German crusading discourse: this was 15 October 1454, when Enea Silvio Piccolomini gave his oration *Constantinopolitana clades* at the Frankfurt Reichstag.[8]

The venue for Piccolomini's oration alerts us to something else that was characteristic of the fifteenth century. The crusading 'centre' was pluralistic. The first half of the century was an age of church councils, and the material bequeathed by Constance and Basle for information exchange, and above all for the lobbying

---

4 Jonathan Phillips, *Defenders of the Holy Land: Relations between the Latin East and the West, 1119–87* (Oxford, 1996).
5 Daniel Hobbins, *Authorship and Publicity before Print: Jean Gerson and the Transformation of Late Medieval Learning* (Philadelphia, 2009), p. 143.
6 Hobbins, *Authorship and Publicity*, p. 184.
7 Dan Ioan Mureşan, 'Bessarion's *Orations against the Turks* and Crusade Propaganda at the *Große Christentag* of Regensburg (1471)', in *Reconfiguring the Fifteenth-Century Crusade*, ed. Norman Housley (London, 2017), pp. 207–43 (here 225).
8 See Johannes Helmrath, 'The German *Reichstage* and the Crusade', in *Crusading in the Fifteenth Century: Message and Impact*, ed. Norman Housley (Basingstoke, 2004), pp. 53–69, 191–203 (here 60–62). The authoritative edition is now *RTA ÄR* 5/2: 463–565.

process, is admirably rich and varied. But it was also a period when imperial diets, like the ones held at Frankfurt in 1454 and Ratisbon in 1471, played an unprecedented role in crusade discussions. The major fora for reaching and implementing decisions about military activity were situated on a north-south axis that comprised the respective polities of the Holy Roman Empire, i. e. the multiple German principalities and the Italian states. Even after Pope Eugene IV's victory over the Council of Basle (1431–49), there could be no question of the centre of authority simply returning to Rome. For sound logistical reasons, Pius II chose to convene the century's greatest crusade assembly at Mantua; and the regularity with which crusade featured on the agenda of the imperial diets showed how far crusade had come to depend on the mobilisation of imperial resources, problematic though contemporaries knew that to be.

Communication about crusading hinged on a shared set of values which in turn generated a common discourse, and in the fifteenth century this revolved around the concept of the *antemurale Christianitatis*. This has recently attracted much attention from scholars investigating crusading activity from the Baltic to the Balkans and the eastern Mediterranean. It is a pleasure in particular to salute Paul Srodecki's comprehensive analysis of what he terms 'bulwark rhetoric' and it has become possible to delineate the key features of that rhetoric.[9] Although its roots were ancient, bulwark rhetoric received a powerful impetus in the thirteenth century from the Mongol incursions into eastern Europe. In the Baltic region, the Teutonic Knights found the image of bulwark or shield a useful complement to its missionary brief, arguing that the lands they had converted and colonised constituted a rampart against the enemy.

In the fifteenth century, a number of elements converged to confirm the dominance of the new discourse. One was the response of military architects to siege artillery, exemplified by Hungary's defensive fortresses along the Danube, and Michelozzo's great curtain wall at Ragusa (mod. Dubrovnik, Croatia). For the humanists the classical resonances of bulwark rhetoric held obvious appeal and led them substantially to refurbish traditional crusading ideas as a war for the defence of European civilisation against Asiatic barbarism.[10] The seemingly implacable hostility and ambitions of the Ottomans invested the core idea of an *antemurale* with substance.[11] More importantly, it made plausible the urgent appeals of envoys for the bulwark's reinforcement. Orators from Hungary and Croatia became adept at compiling lists of recent Ottoman conquests, with the

---

9 Paul Srodecki, *Antemurale Christianitatis: Zur Genese der Bollwerksrhetorik im östlichen Mitteleuropa an der Schwelle vom Mittelalter zur frühen Neuzeit* (Husum, 2015).
10 See the studies by Nancy Bisaha, *Creating East and West: Renaissance Humanists and the Ottoman Turks* (Philadelphia, 2004), and Margaret Meserve, *Empires of Islam in Renaissance Historical Thought* (Cambridge, MA, 2008).
11 Nikolay Antov, 'Crusading in the Fifteenth Century and Its Relation to the Development of Ottoman Dynastic Legitimacy, Self-Image and the Ottoman Consolidation of Authority', in *The Crusade in the Fifteenth Century: Converging and Competing Cultures*, ed. Norman Housley (Abingdon, 2017), pp. 15–33.

aim of showing that Italy, Austria or both would be invaded if the *antemurale* was breached. There was, at least on the face of it, no tension between the defence of *patria*, religious belief, and the new learning. Nor was there any contradiction between self-interest and the charitable and meritorious deed of helping embattled fellow-believers. Indeed, it is hard to take issue with Srodecki's judgement that after *Constantinopolitana clades*, no major additions were made to an argumentation which was used well into the seventeenth century.[12]

Human traffic flowed constantly between Hungary, Croatia, Italy and the German lands for purposes of education, patronage, trade and diplomacy, and orators from the east European and Balkan *antemurale* states had little difficulty in mastering and disseminating the new discourse. Klára Pajorin has argued that a close connection existed between early Hungarian humanism and crusade, and Croatian humanism displays a similar pattern.[13] Emir O. Filipović has now discussed Bosnia's integration into the conversation.[14] Even in the far-off Danubian principalities bulwark rhetoric came to be employed by the political elite, perhaps due to the influence of the Venetians and Franciscans who were active there.[15]

What the centre could offer, and what the periphery wanted, was trained fighting men, war galleys and above all financial subsidies. The point needs stressing because the period's most successful anti-Ottoman crusade was composed almost entirely of non-professional volunteers raised by one man's charismatic preaching in circumstances of crisis. I am referring of course to the relief of Belgrade, but nobody argued for replicating that crusade: it was an inspiration, not a template, for future campaigns.[16] Much more characteristic of the period than the heady excitement of 1456 was the written exchange of views between Paul II and King Matthias nine years later. Pius II's grand plan for a crusade had mutated into a triple alliance between the curia, Venice and Hungary. Paul tried to expand its membership, but in the spring of 1465, he was rebuffed by Florence, Milan and Naples. He had to tell Matthias that the best he could offer was indulgences and prayers, plus the person of the Ottoman pretender, or *turchetto*. Matthias was unimpressed and made peace overtures to Mehmed II. Paul responded with a text which has a good deal to tell us about the way the Renaissance Papacy interpreted relations between the centre (itself) and the periphery (the king). The key point was that Matthias had not entered an ordinary military alliance:

---

12 Srodecki, *Antemurale Christianitatis*, p. 366.
13 Klára Pajorin, 'The Crusades and Early Humanism in Hungary', in *Infima Aetas Pannonica: Studies in Late Medieval Hungarian History*, ed. Péter E. Kovács and Kornél Szovák (Budapest, 2009), pp. 237–49; Norman Housley, 'Christendom's Bulwark: Croatian Identity and the Response to the Ottoman Advance, Fifteenth to Sixteenth Centuries', in *Transactions of the Royal Historical Society*, 6th ser. 24 (2014), 149–64.
14 See his essay in this volume.
15 Sergiu Iosipescu, 'The Romanian Concept of Crusade in the Fifteenth Century', in *The Crusade in the Fifteenth Century*, pp. 187–205.
16 Norman Housley, 'Giovanni da Capistrano and the Crusade of 1456', in *Crusading in the Fifteenth Century*, pp. 94–115, 215–24.

This war was indeed proclaimed and initiated not by one individual or another, but by the prince of the faith, the high pontiff, Christ's vicar, by the decree and with the advice of [the college of cardinals]. And not just one but many past popes have sanctioned the conduct of such a war when the faith urgently needed it, in defence of Christ's Gospel, calling on every orthodox prince and all of the faithful, in the name of their common faith and shared peril.[17]

From this certain things followed. In the first place, if Matthias reached a separate peace with Mehmed, he would be guilty of desertion, 'than which the founders of civil law judged nothing to be more serious'.[18] In the second place, the king would place his own soul in danger, for Pius II had declared that taking part in such a war was a matter of faith (*de necessitate salutis*). And in the third place, any peace reached with Mehmed would be null and void, because 'our holy fathers, and popes long past, abominate every agreement made with the infidels once the Church had proclaimed war against them'.[19]

Matthias duly responded with arguments that are textbook examples of the alternative view, the situation as seen from the *antemurale*. The pope should not believe everything he heard, for the king would always be the enemy of the Turks. But to fight them he needed money, and 'if your holiness really wants to stop me making peace with the enemies of the faith, he has to give me the means to keep the war going'.[20] Financial need was complemented by strategic common sense. Matthias argued that fighting against the Turks on a limited scale, through what he termed 'particular expeditions' (*particularibus expeditionibus*), was counterproductive. It was far better to assemble a strong force and use it to strike a blow at the enemy's heartlands (*viscera*). Not long afterwards he would claim that Venetian sea power was of less use to him than land-based forces, for 'we know from experience that the enemy can neither be damaged, nor damage us much, by way of the sea'.[21]

The centre was well aware of the self-interest of the periphery and resorted to a number of stratagems to neutralise or at least manage it. One was to turn the core *antemurale* argument on its head: those most at risk should be prepared to contribute most. As Pope Alexander VI advised his legate Pietro Isvalies to

---

17 MVHH 1/6: 64–65: *Hoc quidem bellum non ab uno vel altero, sed a fidei principe, summo pontifice, Christi vicario, decreto atque consulto sacri senatus ecclesie denuntiatum est et inductum; nec unus tantum, sed multi retro pontifices indixerunt, qui bellum hoc pro extrema fidei necessitate, pro tuendo Christi evangelio gerendum atque prosequendum sanxerunt, et universos principes orthodoxos, cunctosque fideles ad communem fidem, communeque periculum invitarunt.*
18 MVHH 1/6: 65: *[...] quo nihi gravius etiam legum civilium conditores existimarunt.*
19 MVHH 1/6: p. 66: *[...] enim sancti patres nostri, priscique pontifices post bellum generaliter ab ecclesia contra infideles indictum omnem conventionem cum ipsis infidelibus execrati sunt.*
20 MKL 1: 126: *In summa: si sanctitas vestra omnino ita vult, ne pacem cum fidei hostibus habeam, providae, ut bellum sustinere possim.*
21 MKL 1: 195: *Experientia docet hostem nec offendi, nec offendere satis posse per viam maris.* See also Housley, *Crusading and the Ottoman Threat*, pp. 88–91.

say to the Hungarians in 1500, 'this may look like a common war for the cause of God and the Christian religion, but the fact remains that it is the particular concern of those who are suffering the brunt of Turkish aggression'.[22] The pope was drawing an implicit distinction between frontier defence and crusade, a distinction which decades earlier Nicholas of Cusa had acknowledged by calling the former *resistentia* and the latter *passagium*.[23] A second stratagem was to strive to compile accurate data so as to control the 'fake news' reaching it from the periphery. Particularly striking was the unending search for reliable information about the enemy's ambitions, strengths and weaknesses. One example of this was the detailed study of Ottoman military techniques by the humanist Lampugnino Birago, which was almost certainly commissioned by Nicholas V.[24] Possessing such knowledge was clearly the key to evaluating King Matthias's assertions about the best times and ways to engage the Turks.

Nothing, however, was more important than despatching reliable and well-briefed legates who could carry out their own fact-finding and make judgements based on it. Legates were major conduits between the centre and the periphery. Their role was very diverse and to date it has not received enough attention, though this is changing.[25] Not least, they acted as relayers of up-to-date information. In a letter dated June 1444 at Vienna, Piccolomini, writing on behalf of Frederick III's chancellor Kaspar Schlick, asked Cardinal Giuliano Cesarini why envoys coming from Buda brought no news from Cesarini, 'because as you know we agreed that you would report Hungarian affairs to me and I would reciprocate with news from Germany'.[26] The mild rebuke is all the more interesting given that cardinal and secretary held diametrically opposing views about the crusade that Cesarini was busily promoting—contrary to Habsburg interests—and on which he would soon perish. It is an excellent example of how a friendship network could sustain even the strain imposed by the Hungarian succession crisis.

***

If the centre was fluid, the periphery rarely spoke with a single voice. Venice and Hungary would probably have been at war on several occasions in the fifteenth century but for their shared fear of the Turks, which drove them into alliance with papal encouragement. But the situation was far worse in the northeast after

---

22 *VMPL* 2, no. 297, p. 270: [...] *etsi pro dei et christiane religionis causa bellum hoc commune videatur, tamen ad eos, quos Turcus precipue invasit, et de quorum statu, ut dictum est, nunc precipue agitur*. See also Housley, *Crusading and the Ottoman Threat*, pp. 86–87.
23 Darío Cabanelas Rodríguez, *Juan de Segovia y el problema islámico* (Madrid, 1952), p. 313.
24 *Lo Strategicon adversum Turcos di Lampugnino Birago*, ed. Iulian Mihai Damian (Roma, 2017).
25 *Legati, delegati e l'impresa d'Oltremare (secoli XII–XIII)*, ed. Maria Pia Alberzoni and Pascal Montaubin (Turnhout, 2014); Antonin Kalous, 'Papal Legates and Crusading Activity in Central Europe: The Hussites and the Ottoman Turks', in *The Crusade in the Fifteenth Century*, pp. 75–89.
26 *Der Briefwechsel des Eneas Silvius Piccolomini, I Abteilung, Briefe aus der Laienzeit (1431–45), II Band: Amtliche Briefe*, ed. Rudolf Wolkan (Vienna, 1909), no. 90, pp. 151–53 (here 152): *Scitis ita inter nos esse condictum, ut et vos mihi Hungarica et ego vobis facta Teutonica renuntiem*.

the emergence of the grand-duchy of Lithuania as a substantial and ambitious Catholic power. The Teutonic Order's claim to be the region's *antemurale* state, a claim that had been intermittently challenged by the kingdom of Poland since the fourteenth century,[27] now came under severe stress and the polemics that this generated at the Council of Constance (1414–18) have justifiably attracted close attention.[28] The exchanges that occurred between 1414 and 1418 were shaped by a very different military situation from that of the post-1453 Balkans. But the issues at stake were just as momentous, including the future of the order and its lands, the right to control and convert Samogitia, and relations with the Orthodox principalities.

The most striking characteristic of information exchange at Constance was the sheer volume of written material and the diversity of both viewpoints and style of argument that it brought to bear. Substantial texts originated from both sides in the contest. *Lugubre et multum inauditum* of early 1415 was possibly written by the procurator-general of the Teutonic Order, Peter of Wormditt. It is a highly tendentious review of recent events which comes close to giving us the order's viewpoint.[29] In July 1417, Johannes Urbach, the order's best lobbyist, wrote *Licet insignis*, a robust and partisan but learned text summing up the Teutonic Knights' position.[30] But the order's contributions were overshadowed by two texts by the Cracovian canon lawyer Paweł Włodkowic, the most brilliant of the Polish envoys. His 52 *Conclusiones*, sometimes called the *Opinio Hostiensis*, and probably written in June 1416, was a sophisticated overview of the situation in the Baltic lands based on juridical premises.[31] Between November 1416 and January 1417, Włodkowic followed it up with his *Articuli contra cruciferos*, a very detailed account of the recent fighting which was just as one-sided as *Lugubre et multum inauditum* had been.[32]

There were other texts and, as Paul Srodecki shows in his paper in this collection on Andrés Dias de Escobar and his advocacy of the Teutonic Order at the Council of Constance, some came from unexpected sources, men whose personal ties with the Baltic were slender and who contributed because of conviction, persuasion or payment. Some texts, most famously Włodkowic's *Conclusiones*, argued in legal terms. This was not unique in fifteenth-century crusading — there was a similar debate about the validity of Portuguese crusading plans in Morocco

---

27 Paul W. Knoll, 'Poland as *Antemurale Christianitatis* in the Late Middle Ages', in *Catholic Historical Review* 60 (1974), 381–401.
28 For an overview, see Walter Brandmüller, *Das Konzil von Konstanz*, 2 vols (Paderborn, 1991–97), 2: 150–75. The classic study remains Hartmut Boockmann, *Johannes Falkenberg, der Deutsche Orden und die polnische Politik: Untersuchungen zur politischen Theorie des späteren Mittelalters* (Göttingen, 1975).
29 *SSDOP* 1: 65–111.
30 *SSDOP* 1: 309–80.
31 Stanislaus F. Belch, *Paulus Vladimiri and His Doctrine Concerning International Law and Politics*, 2 vols (London, 1965), 2: 845–84. Boockmann, *Johannes Falkenberg*, p. 226, n. 179, sets out the case, 'nahezu sicher', for June 1416.
32 Belch, *Paulus Vladimiri* 2: 905–88.

in 1434–36.[33] On the other hand, such juridical discussion played little or no part in the discussions about a crusade against the Turks, whose sheer belligerence made it redundant. The other dominant framework for the Baltic polemic was recent history. The counterpart at Constance to the long narratives by frontier envoys outlining Ottoman conquests and atrocities was similar narratives, if anything even longer, detailing the aggression, deceit and war crimes of the lobbyist's Christian enemies. If the immediate objective was to secure conciliar support in regard to the future of Samogitia and the 1411 peace of Thorn, there is no doubt that the order's future — and that of Baltic crusading generally — were scarcely less important considerations. The author of *Lugubre*, for example, called for the rescinding of the papal ban on indulgences for the Teutonic Knights' war, a ban imposed in response to 'importunate and false tales constantly bandied around'.[34] And in his *Articuli*, Włodkowic concluded that the Teutonic Order's past misdeeds revealed them to be guilty of a 'Prussian heresy', naked aggression, that was 'not less but rather much greater, more horrible, worse and damnable, than those of the Wycliffites and Hussites'.[35]

As such shrill rhetoric implies, the protagonists at Constance were playing for high stakes, and this generated moments of remarkable drama. The first occurred in 1416 when no fewer than sixty Samogitians made their entry to the city. They had come to plead that the Poles and Lithuanians be allowed to undertake the conversion of their people. The appearance of these eyewitnesses to the alleged misdeeds of the Teutonic Order surely made a deep impression on the Church fathers, and the debate about the conversion of Samogitia generated its own collection of texts, characterised, as Hartmut Boockmann put it, by 'a certain spontaneity' thanks to the pressurised circumstances in which they were written.[36] But the excitement caused by the appearance of dozens of people from Europe's last corner of paganism was exceeded a few months later by the *cause célèbre* of Johannes Falkenberg's heresy trial. This attempt to blacken the name of the Teutonic Knights by associating it with an eccentric text written some years earlier by one of the order's lobbyists failed, but it showed how astute the Poles had become in exploiting their opponents' weaknesses.[37]

Two years before the start of the Falkenberg crisis, Jogaila and Vytautas sent a letter to the council expressing their enthusiasm for converting their schismatic and unbelieving subjects, and lamenting Sigismund of Hungary's recent defeat at the hands of the Turks. If certain unnamed individuals had not impeded the process of conversion, not only would the Church have expanded in the

---

33 Norman Housley, *Religious Warfare in Europe, 1400–1536* (Oxford, 2002), pp. 182–88.
34 *SSDOP* 1: 106: *inportunis ac falsis sepe circumventi relacionibus*.
35 Belch, *Paulus Vladimiri* 2: 917: *[…] haeresis Prussianae — quae non minor videtur, immo multo maior, horribilior, deterior et damnabilior, quam Wicklephistarum et Hussonistarum*.
36 *CEV*, pp. 1001–38; Boockmann, *Johannes Falkenberg*, pp. 205–8, 219–25 (quote at p. 225).
37 Boockmann, *Johannes Falkenberg*, which includes an edition of the text at pp. 312–53.

north, but the two princes could have assisted its defence in the south.[38] *Mutatis mutandis*, this clever text could have come from Matthias Corvinus, and it shows how the Polish chancery, benefiting from close contacts with the university of Cracow, had absorbed the various themes of Catholic diplomatic parlance about crusade — an eclectic mixture of apologia, noble aspiration and sly denigration — which had flourished in courts further west since the 1200s. Like the diffusion of *antemurale* imagery, this and similar letters reveal a commonality of discourse between centre and periphery. Vytautas returned to the attack the following year during the Samogitian exchanges. If only his conversion had led to an alliance between his people and the order, rather than the latter's vicious hostility towards the newly-converted, what might not have been achieved![39] It was high time, Vytautas brazenly concluded, that the Teutonic Knights were packed off to fight against the Tatars and Turks.[40]

Taking their cue from such suggestions, some historians have concluded that the Teutonic Order was faltering in its ability to persuade, a process that both mirrored and aggravated its recent setbacks on the battlefield.[41] There is some truth in this generalisation. Evidence exists that compared with its adversaries at Constance, who enjoyed the services of eight doctors of law, the order was deficient in both money and expertise. Its procurators at the council had sensibly brought with them fur-lined cloaks to bribe the conciliar fathers, and in a south German winter these were much appreciated. But a constant refrain in letters to Marienburg was shortage of cash: the procurators could not themselves dress well and their credit was exhausted. This was a big problem because, lacking a cadre of experts trained and based at a university in Prussia, the order had to hire articulate defenders, and in their reports the Teutonic Knights' envoys complained that they did not have the wherewithal to pay for such help.[42]

This mattered because to some extent even a powerful message depended for its impact on its effective delivery, whether this was achieved through a *coup de théâtre* like sixty Samogitians or the humanistic *Schwung* of an oration like Piccolomini's *Constantinopolitana clades*. But it is possible to exaggerate the weakness of the Teutonic Order's position and indeed of its performance at Constance. The loss of the missionary brief in Samogitia was a severe blow both practically and symbolically, but Falkenberg was not condemned — much to the fury of the Poles — and the Knights suffered neither retrospective blame nor prospective exile. The order was not called on to explain in detail its stance that it still had work to do in the north in furthering its dual mission of conversion

---

38 *Sacrorum conciliorum nova et amplissima collectio*, ed. J. D. Mansi, 55 vols (Florence, 1759–1962), 28 : cols 221–24; Brandmüller, *Das Konzil von Konstanz* 2: 155–56, comments.
39 CEV, p. 1011.
40 CEV, p. 1017.
41 E.g. Boockmann, *Johannes Falkenberg*, p. 79, n. 115, in relation to the loss of crusade status for the *Reisen* in 1403.
42 Boockmann, *Johannes Falkenberg*, pp. 164, 235 (referencing a payment of 100 fl.).

and protection. That said, the best the Knights could anticipate was managed decline. During the cut and thrust of the Samogitian debate, when both sides had to work up their responses within a tight time scale, the *proposiciones* of the Poles and Samogitians possess a flair that is generally lacking in the order's responses; indeed, at times the latter are incoherent and splenetic.[43]

One advantage of the relatively 'open' nature of the Constance debates and the volume of material that they left is that we can occasionally perceive the response of the Church fathers to the information and arguments of the rival parties. Unsurprisingly, it was not a unified response, so it was just as well that the council had no major decision to make about the Baltic beyond resolving the Samogitian question. One gets a sense of broadly national alignments. A telling example is the French 'nation'. In the course of the debate about Falkenberg's *Satira* in 1417, we can see the legacy of crusading helping to shape their views on whether the Dominican's scandalous call for the murder of Jogaila constituted heresy. The vicar-general of the Franciscans was uneasy about condemning Falkenberg's text because there were occasions other than self-defence when the act of killing carried no sin: and a glaring one was crusade.[44] The danger involved in challenging the validity of crusading *per se* had been foreseen by Włodkowic in his 52 *Conclusiones*: with great care he had distinguished between the order's unjust wars in the north and the just conflicts waged in Palestine and Iberia.[45] But the unease of the Franciscan vicar-general points towards concern about any argument that would reflect badly on the broader crusading past, not to speak of the repercussions for much of Europe's chivalric nobility of accepting that the *Preussenreisen* had been not just a morally tainted venture, but borderline heresy.

***

The scenario we have considered so far was one in which communication between centre and periphery was dense and fluent. There was no need for the Pentecostal miracle described in chapter two of *Acts*. Ideas and arguments were exchanged by means of circulated texts, formal orations and, we must assume — since by definition it left few traces — informal liaison. Friendship networks based on shared interests, affiliations and education were common.[46] Centre and periphery spoke the same language, both literally in their shared latinity, and in terms of the themes and rhetorical devices that each deployed. To that extent the truism that the crusade was the instrument of a united Christian community held water; indeed, it explains the remarkable persistence of crusade as the proposed solution to that community's problems. But there was another side to the picture, and in

---

43 E.g. *CEV*, p. 1030. As Brandmüller comments, *Das Konzil von Konstanz* 2: 160, 'erstaunlich ist der arrogante Ton'.
44 Boockmann, *Johannes Falkenberg*, p. 272.
45 Belch, *Paulus Vladimiri* 2: 870, 878.
46 See, e.g., Erich Meuthen, 'Ein "deutscher" Freundeskreis an der römischen Kurie in der Mitte des 15. Jahrhunderts: Von Cesarini bis zu den Piccolomini', *AHC* 27/28 (1995/96), 487–542.

the last part of this essay I want to explore some of the obstacles to effective communication which arose and the problems they led to, particularly at Constance and Basle. The Council of Basle offers a particularly instructive example, in the contrast between its successful resolution of the Hussite crisis and its inability to engage in union talks with the Greeks.[47] The contrast was not entirely down to issues of communication. Hussites and Catholics alike were war-weary after a decade of fighting, and Giuliano Cesarini was able to capitalise on this to drive forward a settlement despite the huge obstacles that, time and again, threatened to derail the negotiations. Initiating talks about Church union, on the other hand, posed particular problems for the council because its fragile finances made it so difficult to bring the Greek delegation to the west. At the same time the issue proved to be a catalyst, exposing the chasm that was opening up between moderates and radicals over the council's relations with the pope. For his part, Eugene IV was able to exploit both of these difficulties and achieve the spectacular coup of union at his own Council of Ferrara/Florence (1438–45).

That said, there can be no doubt that issues of communication played a significant role in bringing Basle success with the Hussites and failure with the Greeks. The discussions that took place with the Hussites were protracted and heated — and splendidly well documented — but the two sides could follow each other's arguments, and they were able to meet at a number of different locations — not just Basle and Prague — without any great difficulty or expense.[48] Though theologically at odds, culturally and socially they were on common ground. With the Greeks, on the other hand, the reverse applied. The fathers at Basle found the Greek schism perplexing. Cesarini reported that they wanted from the start to focus on the Hussite crisis, which threatened the stability of the faith throughout central Europe, and that they regarded the schism with the east with impatience— why should the burgeoning crisis north of the Alps play second fiddle to 'this ballad [*cantilena*] about the Greeks [which] has been going on for 300 years now'?[49] They did not understand the theological controversies that lay behind the schism and there was the intractable problem of language: Cesarini had to undertake to learn Greek in preparation for the arrival of the Greek delegation.[50]

Distrust and incomprehension were reciprocated by the Greeks. The status of the council of Basle was as mysterious to them as their own view of the Church was to the conciliar fathers. By contrast, their past relations with Rome had taught them all about papal primacy. Much of the complex preliminary discussion about Basle's union programme focused on where the Greeks would agree to come. In

---

47 For what follows, see my essay 'Ending and Starting Crusades at the Council of Basel', *Crusades* 16 (2017), 115–45.
48 See the classic study by Ernest F. Jacob, 'The Bohemians at the Council of Basel, 1433', in *Prague Essays*, ed. R. W. Seton-Watson (Oxford, 1949), pp. 81–123.
49 MCG 2: 105: *et quod ista cantilena de Grecis iam tricentis annis duravit, et omni anno renovatur.* Cf. p. 111.
50 Gerald Christianson, *Cesarini: The Conciliar Cardinal. The Basel Years, 1431–38* (St. Ottilien, 1979), p. 142.

this, as in most respects, Pope Eugene held superior cards. The best that Basle could offer was Avignon, while Eugene could offer a range of Italian cities which from all points of view suited the Greeks much better. Humanist links between Italy and Constantinople were already strong in the 1430s and the arrival of the Greek delegation provided a remarkable spur to the discovery and dissemination of classical texts. Language, theology, logistics and cultural preferences all played into the hands of Rome, but underpinning them all was the basic consideration that Basle naturally looked northwards while the Eugenian curia looked towards the Mediterranean. Moreover, the revived papal monarchy was already evincing a lively curiosity about what lay beyond the periphery of the Catholic world and indeed beyond the enemies who threatened that periphery, and Benjamin Weber has recently outlined the considerable efforts made by Eugene's successors to add to its knowledge in that respect.[51]

We can appreciate why the Greeks, facing destruction, resolved to cling to the familiar in this way. Catholic rulers in a much less perilous situation also saw the advantages of working with Rome. The pope's possession of a *plenitudo potestatis* made it easier to get a decision, once the importance of the cardinals and — increasingly as the century progressed — the pope's family was brought into the picture. Experienced rulers like the doge of Venice and the kings of Hungary and Poland got to know exactly how the curia worked. By contrast, the decision-making process followed at Constance and Basle was opaque, and it changed radically between the two councils. Unlike Constance, Basle did take crusading initiatives, issuing indulgences, bestowing crosses and organising a small crusade flotilla, but the process was complicated and fraught with difficulties.[52] By contrast, once union had been proclaimed in 1439 one can see Eugene's curia moving without noticeable difficulty into the promotion of crusading activity, using the services of legates like Cesarini and the preaching skills of the Franciscan Observants.[53]

Perhaps the finest tribute to Eugene's success in re-establishing Rome's position as the premier location for future crusading initiatives is the criticism that crusading enthusiasts directed against Pope Nicholas V following the fall of Constantinople. Writing to Juan Carvajal, whom he knew to be supportive of a crusade against the Ottomans, Piccolomini listed what Nicholas had done in terms of his subsidies to Gjergj Kastrioti in Albania and the Knights of St John on Rhodes, the 40,000 ducats he had spent on shipping, and his attempt to liaise with Mehmed II's main Turkish rival, the emir of Karaman. In Piccolomini's view it was wholly insufficient. *Ex officio*, it was the pope's job to take the lead, he had the instruments to do so, and he must be more proactive. John of Capestrano

---

51 Benjamin Weber, 'Toward a Global Crusade? The Papacy and the Non-Latin World in the Fifteenth Century', in *Reconfiguring the Fifteenth-Century Crusade*, pp. 11–44.
52 Full details in Housley, 'Ending and Starting Crusades'.
53 See Benjamin Weber, *Lutter contre les Turcs: Les formes nouvelles de la croisade pontificale au XVe siècle* (Rome, 2013).

was more caustic in his complaints about Nicholas's prioritisation of his ambitious building programme at Rome: it was wrong, he declared, to put stone before Christian lives.[54]

Christendom's other main forum for crusading discussions, the imperial diets, lacked the clarity of the papal curia's procedures. Indeed, the way in which urgent crusading matters were handled at the diets can make the labyrinthine procedures followed at the council of Basle seem straightforward. Cardinal Bessarion — a Greek, but a thoroughly westernised one — had a particularly bruising experience when he attended the diets of Nuremberg and Vienna as Pius II's legate in 1460. Bessarion, who was new to Germany, had the brief of bringing about implementation of the imperial promises that had been made at Mantua. He may have been informed of the recent Turkish onslaught on the Peloponnese, which would have made him the more eager to secure rapid action. But he did not reckon with the capacity of the princely envoys at the diets for endless prevarication. What particularly annoyed Bessarion was their argument that the obligation solemnly agreed at Mantua — the provision of 42,000 troops, the backbone of the planned crusade — was not binding. For Bessarion this was intolerable. It meant that lengthy discussions conducted at no fewer than five diets plus a general congress were pointless. Bessarion did not mince words: 'The time has come to set aside words and come to deeds. Distinguished listeners: our agenda is weapons; I repeat weapons, not words. A well-organised army, not ornate and polished oratory. Strong soldiers, not verbal display'.[55] For the envoys the point of the diet was to avoid obligations on the part of their princely masters. Bessarion refused to play their game of endless deferral, and simply brought the curtain down on proceedings. Not unfairly he described the envoys as 'inconsistent and evasive people', and what followed was a polemical exchange of accusation and injured innocence.[56]

'A well-organised army, not ornate and polished oratory': for the purposes of this paper Bessarion's phrase is telling. At the Vienna *Reichstag* of September 1460, as at most of the diets, councils and congresses of the period, the oratory was indeed impressive, and the resulting activity disappointing. Envoys from Hungary became all too familiar with this, and it goes some way towards explaining the scepticism regularly voiced by Matthias Corvinus and the republic of Venice. So angry did Venice's patriciate become when nobody would assist them in recovering Negroponte (Gr. Euboea), that the doge refused even to take part in

---

54 Housley, *Crusading and the Ottoman Threat*, p. 73.
55 Ludwig Mohler, *Kardinal Bessarion als Theologe, Humanist und Staatsmann: Funde und Forschungen*, 3 vols (Paderborn, 1923–42), 3: 384–98 (here 384): *Iam tempus est, ut omissis verbis ad rem veniamus. Armis, armis, inquam, opus est, viri praestantes, non verbis; exercitu bene instructo, non compta et perpolita oratione; robore militum, non verborum magnificentia.*
56 Mohler, *Kardinal Bessarion* 3: 403: *divertentium et tergiversantium hominum*. For the whole sequence, see Housley, *Crusading and the Ottoman Threat*, pp. 79–81.

the crusading discussions triggered by the fall of Otranto a decade later.[57] But to write off the process of communication on such grounds is to miss much of its historical value. And luckily, thanks to the writings of Jürgen Miethke and Johannes Helmrath on the Church councils, and to those German scholars who in recent years have begun looking closely at the imperial diets held from the 1450s onwards, we are less likely than we once were to fall into that trap.[58]

For such assemblies had the effect of bringing together elites who were normally widely separated, and of enabling them to focus on issues which otherwise would have been obscured if not swamped by other concerns. By so doing they facilitated the rapid exchange of new ideas, data and viewpoints. In an age when the universities were producing a highly-educated and critical group of people with an insatiable appetite for information, this was bound to be significant. We have seen something of the impact this had at Constance, where as Miethke put it, the council's debate on the Baltic crusade places before us 'the full range of opportunities of the fifteenth century'.[59] But the effect was greater at Basle, which lasted longer than any previous Church council and was more proactive about crusading than Constance had been. In his seminal 1981 *Deutsches Archiv* article, Miethke wrote of the 'electrifying effect of the council [of Basle] on Europe's intellectuals', and described their incessant copying of new texts as well as their frustration when they found that key texts were not to hand.[60] The humanists gave a fresh impetus to this thirst for written material and — *mutatis mutandis* — it is probable that it became a feature of the Italian congresses — Mantua in 1459, Rome in 1490 — and of the imperial diets whose published proceedings now constitute a valuable tranche of evidence. The constant exchanges between centre and periphery in the fifteenth century will take some time to explore in full; but when they are more fully elucidated, their impact is likely to confirm that, for many contemporaries, the period's intellectual vitality embraced the promotion of a crusade.

---

57 Francesco Somaini, 'La curia romana e la crisi di Otranto', in *La conquista turca di Otranto (1480) tra storia e mito*, ed. Hubert Houben, 2 vols (Galatina, 2008), 1: 211–62 (esp. 240–41).

58 *Europa, das Reich und die Osmanen: Die Türkenreichstage von 1454/55 nach dem Fall von Konstantinopel. Johannes Helmrath zum 60. Geburtstag*, ed. Marika Bacsóka et al. (Frankfurt am Main, 2014).

59 Jürgen Miethke, 'Heiliger Heidenkrieg? Theoretische Kontroversen zwischen Deutschem Orden und dem Königreich Polen vor und auf dem Konstanzer Konzil', in *Heilige Kriege — religiöse Begründungen militärischer Gewaltanwendung: Judentum, Christentum und Islam im Vergleich*, ed. Klaus Schreiner (Munich, 2008), pp. 109–25 (here 109).

60 Jürgen Miethke, 'Die Konzilien als Forum der öffentlichen Meinung im 15. Jahrhundert', *Deutsches Archiv für Erforschung des Mittelalters* 37 (1981), 736–73 (here 763).

MARIANNE P. RITSEMA VAN ECK

Crusade Campaigning by Friars of the Observant Franciscan Establishment in the Holy Land

Several Franciscan brethren played a substantial role in late medieval crusade propagation. Well-known examples include Friar Fidentius of Padua's recovery treatise and the preaching of the Observant John of Capestrano. This paper seeks to highlight a strand of Observant Franciscan crusade campaigning which has remained more marginalised: the efforts of the Franciscan custody of Mount Sion to incite a crusade to the Holy Land from the fifteenth century onward. Even though this Franciscan establishment had its headquarters in Jerusalem, it can arguably be described as geographically peripheral when compared to the main arenas of crusading action at the time: East-Central Europe and the Iberian Peninsula. From their marginalised, yet ideologically charged, position at the *fines christianitatis*, the friars of Mount Sion called for a crusade which differed from the Spanish *Reconquista* and the anti-Ottoman campaigns. While their activities were related to — and sometimes in contact with — these more eye-catching contemporary crusading movements, the campaigning of the custody of Mount Sion emerges as distinct, both in terms of its goals and its methods. Operating first under Mamluk and then later under Ottoman rule, the friars of this custody were compelled to voice their sentiments in different, often more subtle ways.

Given these 'marginal' qualities, it is perhaps unsurprising that crusade campaigning by the Observant Franciscans of Mount Sion has received relatively little attention.[1] From its foundation in 1333, the establishment of this Franciscan custody was based on treaties and contracts with the Mamluk authorities, rather than on armed resistance, and was aimed at hosting and assisting pilgrims.[2] As

---

1 Exceptions include Valentina Covaci, 'Praying for the Liberation of the Holy Sepulchre: Franciscan Liturgy in Fifteenth Century Jerusalem', *Institutum Romanum Norvegiae Acta ad Archaeologiam et Artium Historiam Pertinentia* 31 (2019), 177–95; Marianne P. Ritsema van Eck, *The Holy Land in Observant Franciscan Texts (c. 1480–1650): Theology, Travel, and Territoriality* (Leiden, 2019), pp. 140–60, 182–200.
2 Paolo Evangelisti, 'Il 1333 e la Custodia di Terra Santa: Condizioni Politiche e Culturali alle Origini di un'Istituzione Francescana di Lunga Durata', *Frate Francesco: Rivista di Cultura Francescano* n.s. 82

a result, the existing literature is primarily focused on these friars' considerable influence on pilgrimage to the Holy Land, shaping both the practical experience *in situ* and its cultural expressions in Western Europe.[3] Nevertheless, it is worthwhile to examine how the Franciscans of Mount Sion engaged with the idea of renewed Holy Land crusade, and to explore which actions they took in order to realise this goal. Determining the ways in which this Franciscan crusading movement *ad limites* intersects with, and diverges from, the main action in Europe at the time, can help to accentuate some ideological features of the latter which are sometimes too easily overlooked. Moreover, as important cultural brokers of the Jerusalem pilgrimage for Western Europeans, the friars of Mount Sion were able to communicate their crusading zeal to wide audiences through a variety of media, even if it occasionally had to be voiced in more subtle tones.

In order to characterise the crusading interests and efforts of the Franciscan Observants at this religious frontier, this paper brings together various ideological, diplomatic, liturgical, textual, cartographical, and sermonical exponents. The combined picture will be placed in the context of, and differentiated from, the wider currents of crusading at the time, including — for example — Observant Franciscan crusade preaching and rapprochements with prominent crusade-minded monarchs and popes. In order to accommodate a full appreciation of the above, I will first offer a short sketch of the foundation of this Franciscan establishment and its main *modus operandi* from the later Middle Ages onward.

The Franciscan Establishment on Mount Sion

The first attempts to install a non-military, mendicant order in the Holy Land were undertaken by the crown of Aragon in 1319–23 and involved the Dominicans. Aragon made a second, unsuccessful attempt in 1327, this time with the Franciscan Order.[4] In 1333, Robert of Anjou (1278–1334), king of Naples, and his wife Queen Consort Sancha of Majorca (c. 1285–1345) successfully concluded negotiations with the Mamluk sultan al-Nāṣir Muḥammad (1285–1341), with the

---

(2016), 49–195 (here 49–63); Evangelisti, *Dopo Francesco, oltre il Mito: I Frati Minori fra Terra Santa ed Europa (XIII–XV Secolo)* (Roma, 2020), pp. 137–52.

3 Beatrice Saletti, *I Francescani in Terrasanta (1291–1517)* (Padova, 2016), pp. 69–200; Nicole Chareyron, *Pilgrims to Jerusalem in the Middle Ages*, trans. W. Donald Wilson (New York, 2005), pp. 82–85; Michele Campopiano, 'Islam, Jews and Eastern Christianity in Late Medieval Pilgrims' Guidebooks: Some Examples from the Franciscan Convent of Mount Sion', *Al-Masaq* 24 (2012), 75–89; Kathryn Blair Moore, *The Architecture of the Christian Holy Land: Reception from Late Antiquity through the Renaissance* (Cambridge, 2017), pp. 117–63, 211–21; Michele Campopiano, *Writing the Holy Land: The Franciscans of Mount Zion and the Construction of a Cultural Memory, 1300–1550* (Cham, 2020).

4 Kaspar Elm, 'La Custodia di Terra Santa: Franziskanisches Ordensleben in der Tradition der lateinischen Kirche Palästinas', in *Vitasfratrum: Beiträge zur Geschichte der Eremiten- und Mendikantenorden des zwölften und dreizehnten Jahrhunderts*, ed. Dieter Berg (Werl, 1994), pp. 241–62 (here 242–43).

friars minor as the main beneficiaries. As a result, the Franciscans were granted the right to officiate in the Holy Sepulchre Church in Jerusalem, the Nativity Basilica in Bethlehem, and two chapels on the Mount of Olives. They were also allowed to establish a convent on Mount Sion, the traditional location of the Last Supper, just outside of Jerusalem. From there, several daughter establishments were founded, beginning with a convent in Bethlehem ten years later, and this Franciscan custody soon assumed a pivotal role in the business of Holy Land pilgrimage, receiving and conducting all pilgrims from Western Europe.[5]

During the medieval period the Franciscan order was organised into provinces, which were subdivided into several custodies, which in turn typically contained several convents. The Franciscan province of the Holy Land (also called *oltramare* or overseas province) already existed before 1333: it was instituted at the order's chapter meeting at Porziuncola (Italy) in 1217. This province initially encompassed a large part of the Eastern Mediterranean area, where the order aspired to establish itself. In 1260, it was divided into the province of Romania (consisting of three custodies in Greece: Negroponte, Thebes, and Glarentza) and the province of the Holy Land, with the latter now narrowed down to convents on Cyprus (the custody of Nicosia) and in the Levantine crusader states (the custody of Syria). There were convents in Acre, Tripoli, Sidon, Tyre, Antioch and Jaffa, which all disappeared following the fall of Acre in 1291. For a while the Franciscan province of the Holy Land only existed on Cyprus.[6]

The foundational agreement of the custody of Mount Sion in 1333 was momentous in several senses. For the Franciscans it meant re-establishment in the Holy Land and at its sacred centre, Jerusalem: a location that combined symbolical significance with practical advantages for facilitating pilgrimage.[7] More generally, the re-introduction of the Franciscan Order was significant because it was the only (religious) organisation from Western Europe to be allowed to resettle in the Holy Land after 1291. As a result, the Franciscans became the only permanently present representatives of Roman Catholicism there for centuries to come. This was a unique prerogative which they cherished and guarded, especially

---

5 Elm, 'La Custodia', pp. 243–46; Saletti, *I Francescani*, pp. 69–130; Evangelisti, 'Il 1333', pp. 49–59; Leonhard Lemmens, *Die Franziskaner auf dem Sion (1335–1552)*, 2nd edn (Münster, 1925), pp. 37–73, 149–78.
6 Saletti, *I Francescani*, pp. 39–46; Giovanni Claudio Bottini, 'Presenza e Attività Culturale dei Francescani in Medio Oriente', in *Itinerari e Cronache Francescani di Terra Santa (1500–1800)*, ed. Marco Galateri di Genola (Milano, 2017), pp. 15–44 (here 16–18). Until 1527, the guardian of the Mount Sion custody remained answerable to the provincial minister of the Holy Land based in Nicosia. See Ritsema van Eck, *The Holy Land*, p. 4.
7 There is one single indication that there may have been a Franciscan establishment in Jerusalem prior to this in the travelogue of the Dominican Ricoldo da Monte Croce (c. 1243–1320), but further evidence is lacking, suggesting that the foundation was ephemeral. See Saletti, *I Francescani*, p. 46; Bottini, 'Presenza e Attività', p. 18; Lemmens, *Die Franziskaner*, pp. 9–14.

from the early seventeenth century onward, when the Jesuit and Capuchin orders became interested in establishing a presence in the Holy Land.[8]

Two defining aspects of the 1333 agreement are that it had its roots in a diplomatic enterprise, exhibiting great sensitivity for political contexts, and that it was a grass-roots initiative. Paolo Evangelisti convincingly draws attention to the autonomous character of the Franciscan attempt to establish in the Holy Land. Papal backing only arrived in 1342, when Clement VI issued the bulls *Gratias Agimus* and *Nuper Carissimae*, and even then, their wording did not anywhere claim any credit for the initiative for the papacy.[9] Moreover, the project depended on diplomatic, rather than military, success. This aspect of the project was adroitly managed by its Franciscan instigators, who seem to have carefully chosen their royal allies with much sensitivity to political circumstances and expediency.[10] Since the Franciscan establishment on Mount Sion was based on an unarmed, diplomatic endeavour which explicitly recognised Mamluk authority, it can arguably be characterised as a 'post-crusade project'.[11] According to Evangelisti, this 'peaceable' option was one of several ways in which the Franciscan Order engaged with Islam, while the alternatives included crusade preaching and drawing up plans for military reconquest.[12]

Without meaning to argue against these very cogent points, this essay aims to complicate the picture sketched above, by showcasing the multiple options for engaging with religious otherness in more militant ways which came into existence (and indeed diversified) at the Franciscan establishment in Jerusalem from the later fifteenth century onward.

Crusade Campaigning by Observants

The role of the Jerusalem Franciscans in papal attempts to establish contacts in the Levant with an eye to Holy Land crusading during the central decades of the fifteenth century has received a degree of attention. Franciscan friars emerge as likely candidates for such papal embassies, given the practical expediency of their existing establishments in the Holy Land.[13] Seen from this perspective, the Jerusalem friars may come across as pawns in papal schemes: convenient minions with little agency or intrinsic interest in crusade. By turning the perspective around and approaching the subject from the angle of the Holy Land Franciscans

---

8 Ritsema van Eck, *The Holy Land*, pp. 171–77.
9 Evangelisti, 'Il 1333', pp. 49–51. Cf. Evangelisti, *Dopo Francesco, oltre il Mito*, pp. 139–42.
10 Evangelisti, 'Il 1333', pp. 54–60; Evangelisti, *Dopo Francesco, oltre il Mito*, pp. 143–49.
11 Evangelisti, 'Il 1333', p. 55: 'il progetto minoritico post-crociatistico di insediamento gerosolimitano'.
12 Evangelisti, 'Il 1333', p. 62.
13 Benjamin Weber, 'Toward a Global Crusade? The Papacy and the Non-Latin World in the Fifteenth Century', in *Reconfiguring the Fifteenth-Century Crusade*, ed. Norman Housley (London, 2017), pp. 11–44 (here 21–23); Thomas Tanase, *'Jusqu'aux Limites du Monde': La Papauté et la Mission Franciscaine de l'Asie de Marco Polo à l'Amérique de Christophe Colomb* (Rome, 2013), pp. 696–728.

themselves, it becomes possible to assess whether more agency can be attributed to them, to examine their motives, and to gauge how the dual dynamic of their geographically peripheral, yet ideologically central location may have played into their crusade campaigning.

The custody's archives are of little help in this, unfortunately. Due to a hesitancy towards (and even regulations against) recordkeeping, calamities, and translocations in Jerusalem, its archives contain a mere 63 documents issued by European authorities (mostly papal bulls) and 110 issued by Mamluk authorities, for the period from the custody's foundation to 1517.[14] In order to understand crusade campaigning by the friars of Mount Sion, we have to rely on the traces that their activities have left elsewhere. The Holy Land Franciscans seem to have looked to the West in garnering support for their crusade initiatives, and — given the modest size of their establishment — they were rather successful in doing so.[15] The discussion below is primarily structured around their rapprochements with the Burgundian court, offering a chronological narrative which aims to illustrate the significance of the order's Observant branch which they became a part of, as well as these friars' private initiative vis-à-vis papal incentives.

The conversion of the custody of Mount Sion to Observant Franciscanism during the late 1430s is an important development for understanding crusade campaigning by its friars. The Observance was a reform movement within the order which promoted a return to more austere observance of (their interpretation of) Franciscan ideals, such as poverty. It quickly grew from the late fourteenth century onward and eventually culminated in a formal separation between the Conventual and Observant branches in 1517.[16] During the fifteenth century, the Franciscan Observance produced highly capable preachers, some of whom became famous while engaged in papal crusade preaching campaigns. At the same time, we should not forget that crusading formed a core part of the order's ideological backbone right from its foundation in the thirteenth century and that assuming Conventual disinterest in this topic *a priori* is unhelpful.[17]

In the case of the custody of Mount Sion, the Conventual Franciscan brethren, in place in Jerusalem prior to the 1430s, do not appear to have taken much

---

14 Narcyz Stanisław Klimas, *Storia dell'Archivio Storico della Custodia di Terra Santa* (Milano, 2013), pp. 17–23, 191–216.
15 In the 1480s, Friar Paul Walter of Guglingen reports twenty-four friars at Mount Sion, a few female tertiaries living nearby, two friars at the Holy Sepulchre and six in Bethlehem, adding up to around thirty members in the Holy Land in total. MS Neuburg an der Donau, Staatliche Bibliothek, 04/Hs. INR 10, p. 365; numbers seem to have increased towards the early sixteenth century, when Friar Nikolaus Wanckel reports around fifty friars and five female tertiaries. Nikolaus Wanckel, *Ein Kurtze Vermerckung der Heyligen Stet des Heyligen Landts: In und umb Jerusalem* (Nürnberg, 1517), [no pagination]. For more on these authors and their works, see Ritsema van Eck, *The Holy Land*, pp. 19–29, 64–66.
16 James Mixson, 'Introduction', in *A Companion to Observant Reform in the Late Middle Ages and Beyond*, ed. James D. Mixson and Bert Roest (Leiden, 2015), pp. 1–20.
17 Paolo Evangelisti's recent book offers an in-depth discussion of Franciscan crusade engagement during earlier stages of the order's history. Evangelisti, *Dopo Francesco, oltre il Mito* (Roma, 2020).

concrete action toward, or shown much interest in, calling for a crusade (or if they did, their attempts have left few traces). There is the example of Gerárd Calvet, guardian of Mount Sion, who arrived at the French court in 1393, and who appears to have renewed interest in crusade there. King Charles VI, Count John of Nevers (later better known under his cognomen 'the Fearless'), the son of Duke Philip the Bold of Burgundy, and Duke Louis of Orléans were also moved to direct considerable donations to Mount Sion.[18] However, the — exiled — patriarchs of Jerusalem (residing in Cyprus from 1291 and then as titular bishops at the Basilica di San Lorenzo fuori le Mura near Rome from 1374), the canons regular of the Holy Sepulchre, bishops of Bethlehem (now residing in the diocese of Bethléem à Clamecy in France), and previous monks of Mount Sion and the Vale of Josaphat were reluctant to cede their proprietary rights to the Franciscans, possibly tempering the friars' crusading zeal. In case of a successful Latin recovery of the Holy Land, the friars might have had to make way for Catholic prelates and monastics returning from exile, also including their rights to officiating in important churches in the Holy Land. Only in 1421 did Martin V confirm the Franciscans' rights in the Holy Land *in perpetuum*, meaning that a successful crusade would no longer threaten to cost the friars their privileges and properties, in favour of exiled religious of the former Levantine Crusader states.[19] Whether the apparent Conventual disinterest in crusading should be attributed to worries about proprietary rights, a lack of surviving sources, or perhaps to the initially 'post-crusade' character of this custody, is difficult to determine. However, the significance of the later Observant affiliation is clear.

The Jerusalem convent became Observant following an extended power struggle. Luigi da Bologna is sometimes mistakenly identified as the first Observant guardian of Mount Sion in 1430, based on a confusion with a synonymous Observant preacher. Giacomo Delfino was nominated by the pope in 1434 (instead of the Conventual friar elected by the order), but does not seem to have been able to successfully take up this post, probably due to Conventual resistance. The Observance seems to have become consolidated at Mount Sion with the guardianship of Gandolfo of Sicily in 1439. What stands out about this slightly fuzzy period of transition, is that both Pope Eugene IV and prominent members of the Observance, Albert of Sarteano and John of Capestrano, were involved in effecting this change.[20] This underlines not only papal interest in crusading in this region, but also the desire of the Observants to control this ideologically crucial establishment.[21] Apart from the obvious attraction of controlling the most

---

18 Jacques Paviot, *Les Ducs de Bourgogne, la Croisade et l'Orient* (Paris, 2003), p. 22.
19 Elm, 'La Custodia', pp. 247–48, 253–57.
20 Pierre Santoni, 'Alberto de Sarteano Observant et Humaniste, Envoyé Pontifical à Jérusalem et au Caire', *Mélanges de l'Ecole Française de Rome* 86 (1975), 165–211 (here 181–86); Lemmens, *Die Franziskaner*, pp. 94–103. See also Girolamo Golubovich, *Serie Cronologica dei Reverendissimi Superiori di Terra Santa* (Gerusalemme, 1898), pp. 22–24; Ritsema van Eck, *The Holy Land*, pp. 3–4.
21 Weber, 'Toward a Global Crusade?', pp. 21–22.

important pilgrimage sites for Roman Catholicism, Observant interest in Holy Land crusade also emerges as a likely motive for establishing in Jerusalem. This is corroborated by several letters written by the aforementioned Albert and John to Philip the Good of Burgundy (duke 1419–67), promoting this type of crusade.

As discussed by Jacques Paviot, the Valois dukes of Burgundy espoused a relatively traditional ideal of Holy Land crusade at a time when the Ottoman advance loomed large over Europe. Philip the Good exhibited a particular interest in this old-fashioned type of crusade, aiming to safeguard Christian worship in the Holy Land.[22] The friars of Mount Sion were therefore in a favourable position to attract Philip's generosity.[23] The duke's liberality really took wing in the 1430s, coinciding with the Observants' growing interest in this custody. In 1432, Philip gave 4,000 francs to the Franciscans of Mount Sion. In the summer of 1435, Pierre Clarey, a friar from Jerusalem, received 17 livres and, in March 1436, Philip gave another 9 livres to another Franciscan for pilgrimage to Jerusalem. Paviot conjectures that Pierre Clarey may have been sent by the Observant preacher Albert of Sarteano, then residing in Jerusalem, to look for financial aid.[24] It is clear that Eugene IV sent Albert there in 1435; contemporary documents do not reveal Albert's mission, but it is very likely that it was to effect the Holy Land Franciscans' transition to the Observance.[25] Apart from collecting donations, crusade was also on Albert's mind. On 6 October 1436, he sent a letter to Philip from Mount Sion, suggesting that the duke's generosity and devotion might also extend to retaking the Holy Places.[26]

From this moment on, both financial donations and crusade plans characterise the interactions between Philip the Good and the friars of Mount Sion. In 1436–37, Eugene IV sought to assemble a fleet to retake the Holy Land. When the papal envoy came to discuss this plan with Philip, the duke invited Simon of Verdeau, a friar connected to the Franciscan convent in Bethlehem, to participate in the discussions. The planned crusading fleet came to naught but, in the summer of 1437, Simon did go back to the Holy Land carrying a gift of forty-three livres for a chalice, a breviary, and a window with the duke's arms to be installed in the Franciscan church on Mount Sion.[27] Meanwhile, Albert of Sarteano left Jerusalem in 1437 but continued to search for a suitable candidate to become the new

---

22 Jacques Paviot, 'Burgundy and the Crusade', in *Crusading in the Fifteenth Century: Message and Impact*, ed. Norman Housley (Basingstroke, 2004), pp. 70–80 (here 70–71); also see Paviot, *Les Ducs*.
23 Jacques Paviot, 'La Devotion Vis-à-vis de la Terre Sainte au xve Siècle: l'Exemple de Philippe le Bon, Duc de Bourgogne (1396–1467)', in *Autour de la Première Croisade*, ed. Michel Balard (Paris, 1996), pp. 401–11; also see Paviot, *Les Ducs*.
24 Paviot, *Les Ducs*, pp. 72–80.
25 Santoni, 'Albert de Sarteano', pp. 181–86; Enrico Cerulli, 'Berdini, Alberto', *Dizionario Biografico degli Italiani* 8 (1966), 800–4; Lemmens, *Die Franziskaner*, pp. 95–102.
26 *Beati Alberti a Sarthiano Ord. Min. Reg. Observ. Operia Omnia in Ordinem Redacta*, ed. Francis Harold (Roma, 1688), no. 44, pp. 273–74; Paviot, 'Burgundy and the Crusade', p. 75; Paviot, 'La Devotion', pp. 404–5; Paviot, *Les Ducs*, p. 81.
27 Paviot, *Les Ducs*, p. 82.

Observant superior there, eventually leading to Gandolfo of Sicily's guardianship. He was installed by John of Capestrano, who travelled to Jerusalem for this purpose in 1439.[28]

Albert of Sarteano and John of Capestrano emerge as important Observant actors. Both were involved in the conversion of the Franciscan custody of Mount Sion to the Observance, both tried to direct both the generosity and the crusading zeal of Philip the Good towards the Holy Land, and both participated actively in the crusading projects of consecutive popes. In 1439, Albert was named apostolic envoy to Egypt, Ethiopia, and India by Eugene IV, and in this capacity he wrote to Philip once again, from Rhodes in December 1440, exhorting him to imitate his ancestor Godfrey of Bouillon and fight for Christendom.[29] At the behest of Eugene IV and Albert of Sarteano (now vicar general of the order), John of Capestrano paid a visit to Philip in Dijon in the autumn of 1442 and the spring of 1443 and seems to have inspired the duke to begin preparing for crusade.[30] Although John is particularly famous for his crusade preaching in the anti-Ottoman campaign in East-Central Europe in 1453–56, he did also care about the prospect of recovering the Holy Land.[31]

In March 1454, John wrote to Philip the Good from Upper Hungarian Pressburg (mod. Bratislava, Slovakia), suggesting that the duke could raise an army to recover the Holy Land, and to 'restore and recover the Holy Sepulchre of our Lord'.[32] This suggests that John saw the anti-Ottoman crusade in East-Central Europe as a prelude to a Holy Land crusade, which he hoped/expected to follow from the first campaign. In June 1455, he wrote to the newly elected and crusade-minded pope Callixtus III, describing a plan for putting together a massive army in cooperation with John of Hunyad. Once this army had reconquered Europe, John expected that it could then also retake Jerusalem within three months.[33] A year later, in August 1456, John wrote to the pope again, explaining in apparently vehement terms, that *now* was the right time to recover Jerusalem.[34] John of Capestrano's call for a campaign to the Holy Land in the midst of the Ottoman

---

28 Santoni, 'Albert de Sarteano', pp. 185–86; Johannes Hofer, *Johannes Kapistran* (Heidelberg, 1964), pp. 222–26; Lemmens, *Die Franziskaner*, pp. 100–2; Paviot, *Les Ducs*, p. 93.
29 Weber, 'Toward a Global Crusade?', pp. 21–24; *Beati Alberti Opera Omnia*, no. 45, pp. 330–31; Paviot, 'Burgundy and the Crusade', p. 75; Paviot, 'La Devotion', pp. 404–5; Paviot, *Les Ducs*, pp. 86–88.
30 Paviot, *Les Ducs*, pp. 93–94.
31 Norman Housley, *Crusading and the Ottoman Threat, 1453–1505* (Oxford, 2013), pp. 147–48; Norman Housley, 'Giovanni da Capistrano and the Crusade of 1456', in *Crusading in the Fifteenth Century*, pp. 94–115 (here 94–99).
32 G. de Beaucourt, 'Lettre de Saint Jean de Capistran au Duc de Bourgogne. 19 Mars 1454', *Annuaire-Bulletin de la Société de l'Histoire de France* 2 (1864), 160–66; Paviot, 'Burgundy and the Crusade', pp. 75–76; Paviot, *Les Ducs*, p. 135.
33 Housley, 'Giovanni da Capistrano', pp. 97–98.
34 *Acta Sanctorum Octobris*, ed. Joannes Stilting et al., 14 vols (Antwerp, 1765–1875), 10: 384: *idcirco ecce nunc tempus acceptabile, ecce nunc tempus salutis populi christiani: ecce nunc tempus implendi desiderium V. S. ut progrediamur, nedum ad recuperandam Graeciam et Europam, sed ad recuperandam Terram sanctam Hierusalem.* See Housley, 'Giovanni da Capistrano', p. 99.

crusade in East-Central Europe was not eccentric. It seems that Callixtus III was eager for the same, as Eugene VI had been two decades previously, and the aim of recovering the Holy Land remained a central tenet of the later crusades.[35] The degree to which John's personal connection to the (now Observant) Franciscan custody in Jerusalem contributed to his clearly serious and sincere efforts to push for a campaign to the Holy Land is difficult to say. We may reasonably assume, however, that it did matter, and that the Holy Land was central rather than peripheral to his vision of crusade.

Apart from well-known figures such as Albert of Sarteano and John of Capestrano, who integrated the Holy Land and its Franciscan custody in their activities for papal crusading incentives, there are additional indications that the friars of Mount Sion were interested in propagating crusade. For example, Friar Jean Marquet paid a visit to Philip the Good in Dijon in 1442 to ask the duke to assist the Holy Land Franciscans.[36] Proposing and collecting donations for the recovery of the Holy Land formed a central part of this friar's work. In 1443, Jean obtained bulls from the pope in Siena which allowed him to travel freely to propagate the recovery of the Holy Land and to collect donations for this purpose.[37] In subsequent years, Jean Marquet would repeatedly re-visit Philip, and it is reasonable to assume that a Holy Land crusade was on the agenda during these meetings, alongside financial donations to the Franciscan *custodia Terrae Sanctae*; an audience on 19 November 1447, concerned 'certain things touching on the recovery and reunion of the said Holy Land', according to the ducal administration.[38]

Thanks to Philip the Good's well-documented and well-studied interest in recovering the Holy Land, we know that several Franciscans connected to Mount Sion — including (but certainly not limited to) Albert of Sarteano, John of Capestrano and Jean Marquet — successfully encouraged the duke toward that goal. It is clear, however, that the duke of Burgundy was not the only prince who the friars tried to spur into action. For example, on 8 October 1454, the guardian of Mount Sion, Baldassare da Santa Maria, wrote a letter to Francesco Sforza of Milan (duke 1450–66), imploring the duke (and other princes along with him) to recover the Holy Land.[39] Moreover, during the later decades of the fifteenth century, Queen Isabella I of Castile (r. 1474–1504) and her husband King Ferdinand II of Aragon (r. 1479–1516), the so-called 'Catholic Monarchs', regularly received friars from the Holy Land and donated large sums to the Mount Sion custody. It is likely that their generosity was at least partly inspired by an interest in preserving the Holy

---

35 Housley, 'Giovanni da Capistrano', pp. 96–97; Weber, 'Toward a Global Crusade?', pp. 23, 25–26, 31, 33–34; Norman Housley, *The Later Crusades: From Lyons to Alcazar, 1274–1580* (Oxford, 1992), pp. 46–48.
36 Paviot, *Les Ducs*, p. 91.
37 BF 2/1, no. 682, p. 321 (31 May 1443), and no. 691, p. 324 (22 June 1443, *Iohanni de Baldironibus*); Paviot, *Les Ducs*, p. 92.
38 Paviot, *Les Ducs*, pp. 109, 111, 113–15.
39 Saletti, *I Francescani*, pp. 183–84.

Places and crusading, although we do not know for certain whether this topic was broached by these Franciscan envoys.[40]

Of the Holy Land Franciscans that the Catholic Monarchs received, Friar Mauro Hispano (guardian of Mount Sion from 1501–4) is most clearly linked to a crusade project involving several potentates on the Iberian Peninsula.[41] In 1504, Friar Mauro left the Holy Land as envoy of the Mamluk sultan Qansuh al-Ghuri (r. 1501–16), first stopping in Venice and Rome to deliver the sultan's messages during the spring and summer, before moving to the Spanish court in the early autumn of the same year. There he stayed for around eight months and was present during the turmoil that followed Queen Isabella's death on 26 November 1504. There is no documentation to prove it, but it is likely that Mauro contributed to the crusade project that his fellow Observant Franciscan, Cardinal Francisco Jiménez de Cisneros (1436–1517), began to develop in earnest following his queen's dying wish for a North African campaign.[42] In May 1505, Mauro departed for the court of Manuel I of Portugal (r. 1495–1521) to deliver the last of Qansuh Al-Ghuri's missives, to which Manuel seems to have responded with crusading zeal and a large donation for the custody of Mount Sion. After visits to the pope and Egypt, Mauro disappeared into obscurity, but Manuel I and Cisneros continued actively to develop a crusade project together from 1506, aiming to conquer North Africa and retake the Holy Land, based on the united efforts of Portugal, Spain and England.[43]

Further evidence of crusade activism by the Observant Franciscans of Mount Sion may still emerge from the archives of these and other rulers with whom they were in contact. My purpose has been to foreground the importance of this custody's transition to the Observance, and to demonstrate that its friars (and their crusade campaigning) amounted to more than just extensions of the pope in the Levant. Mount Sion's conversion to the Observance was promoted by both Albert of Sarteano and John of Capestrano, as well as by Eugene IV. Once this transition was complete there can be no underestimating the significance of the Observant Franciscan network that the custody could subsequently tap into. The (epistolary) eloquence of Observant preachers like Albert and John could now help to valorise the enduring ideological centrality of Jerusalem in crusading schemes and to direct it at powerful rulers. Given the custody's geographical peripherality, connecting to the right overseas benefactors was crucial. Moreover, the Franciscan Observance is well-known for its anti-Ottoman crusade

---

40 José Garcia Oro, 'La Cruzada del Cardenal Cisneros: De Granada a Jerusalén', in *Archivo Ibero-Americano* 51 (1991), 724–63 (here 725–40); John Edwards, 'Reconquista and Crusade in Fifteenth-Century Spain', in *Crusading in the Fifteenth Century*, pp. 163–81; Housley, *The Later Crusades*, pp. 301–6.

41 Ritsema van Eck, *The Holy Land*, pp. 158–59.

42 Garcia Oro, 'La Cruzada', pp. 740–47.

43 Charles-Martial de Witte, 'Un Projet Portugais de Reconquête de la Terre Sainte (1505–07)', *Congresso International de História dos Descobrimentos: Actas* 5 (1961), 419–99; Garcia Oro, 'La Cruzada', pp. 747–63.

preaching — ordered by the papacy — during the fifteenth century.[44] Although these preachers seem to have generally been convinced of that cause, the Holy Land crusade which could be promoted in connection to the Mount Sion custody was likely even closer to their hearts, given that the recapture of Jerusalem was a *sine qua non* in the Franciscan Joachimite Apocalyptic which many of them espoused.[45]

Observant Franciscanism thus probably boosted ideological interest in crusading at Mount Sion, as is also testified by the embassies of less well-known friars such as Jean Marquet and Mauro Hispano. In the latter's case, affiliation to the Observance meant advantageous networking opportunities through influential confrères like Cardinal Cisneros and Henrique de Coimbra, Manuel I's Observant Franciscan confessor and advisor.[46] Moreover, the same example also illustrates that the representatives of Mount Sion were astute in identifying political and ideological contexts conducive to their requests for donations and crusading. The vibrant atmosphere of apocalyptic expectation on the Iberian peninsula around 1500 offered such a potentially receptive context, where Arnold of Vilanova's prediction that 'someone from Spain would restore the wealth of Zion' was often interpreted politically — influenced by Franciscan circles — as referring to the Catholic Monarchs.[47] In addition, Cisneros's expectation (based on the prophecies of various mystics) that his crusading would ultimately make him pope in Jerusalem, surely also provided fertile soil for overtures from Mount Sion.[48] Even if these receptive circumstances were merely a happy coincidence, the Jerusalem Franciscans did make the most of them. Their sensitivity to political and ideological contexts (Burgundian, Iberian, etc.) testifies to these friars' continued diplomatic acumen, echoing the 'post-crusade' foundational negotiations in the 1330s, now aimed at mobilising a Holy Land crusade. Moreover, like the 1333 foundational treaty, crusade campaigning by the custody of Mount Sion was clearly driven by more than papal initiative. Indeed, sentiments that the Holy Land Observants expressed through various cultural media offer further testimony of their intrinsic interest in crusade.

---

44 Housley, *Crusading and the Ottoman Threat*, pp. 135–59.
45 Ritsema van Eck, *The Holy Land*, pp. 138–40.
46 De Witte, 'Un Projet Portugais', pp. 419–21.
47 Alain Milhou, *Colón y su Mentalidad Mesiánica en el Ambiente Franciscanista Español* (Valladolid, 1983), throughout, see, for example, pp. 169–87, 234–65; Roberto Rusconi, 'Introduction', in *The Book of Prophecies edited by Christopher Columbus*, ed. Rusconi (Berkeley, 1997), pp. 31–32, 316–17; Tanase, *Jusqu'aux Limites*, pp. 728–45.
48 Marcel Bataillon, *Erasme et l'Espagne* (Genève, 1991), pp. 55–75; Erika Rummel, *Jiménez de Cisneros: On the Threshold of Spain's Golden Age* (Tempe, AZ, 1999), pp. 42–45.

Cultural Expressions and Longevity

Cecilia Gaposchkin describes crusader liturgies as 'moments of sacred communication with God about the core ideals of the Christian community'.[49] It is therefore worth remarking that three thirteenth to fourteenth-century liturgical manuscripts preserved at the Franciscan library in Jerusalem contain fifteenth-century additions, including, twice, a *Missa devota ad sepulchrum recuperandum Terram Sanctam* and a militant *Ad Sanctum Sepulchrum Domini introitus*, as discussed by Valentina Covaci.[50] Liturgies for the recovery of the Holy Land were not rare during the fifteenth century (on the contrary), but indications of when, where, and by whom these liturgies were performed — the Franciscans in Jerusalem in this case — are less common. Moreover, given that innovation in this characteristically conservative medium often derives from context, it is all the more relevant that the Jerusalem friars (who imported most of their liturgical books from Europe and rarely altered or annotated these for local use) added crusader prayers to three of these.[51] This suggests that the friars aimed to perform their ideas about crusading in what they viewed as a sacred act of communication with God.[52]

Another ritual practice that testifies to the interest of the Mount Sion Franciscans in militant religiosity, is their involvement in the dubbing of knights at the Holy Sepulchre. Although the term *miles sancti sepulcri* was used during the classical crusader era, the dubbing ritual — first reported in 1336 — is less old. After a friar celebrated mass in the Holy Sepulchre, a knight (possibly a Franciscan tertiary) would perform the dubbing. This changed at the end of the fifteenth century, when the Franciscan superior of Mount Sion began to dub the knights himself.[53] The Franciscan friar Nikolaus Wanckel (in Jerusalem in 1510) describes the ceremony. Wanckel first enumerates the twelve rules or *professio* of the knighthood (the reconquest of Jerusalem is not included). After the candidate has made his pledge, he is taken from Mount Sion to the Holy Sepulchre chapel. There the guardian puts on a sword belt and spurs on his feet. The candidate then takes the sword from the guardian's sheath, kneels before the altar of the Holy Sepulchre, and is dubbed by the guardian, who hands back the sword to the new knight, who then in turn puts it back in the guardian's sheath.[54] Even if Wanckel's account of ceremony does not explicitly invoke crusading (as some

---

49 Cecilia M. Gaposchkin, *Invisible Weapons: Liturgy and the Making of Crusade Ideology* (Ithaca, 2017), p. 8.
50 Covaci, 'Praying for the Liberation', pp. 177–95; Valentina Covaci, 'Between Traditions: The Franciscans of Mount Sion and their Rituals (1330–1517)' (unpublished doctoral dissertation, University of Amsterdam, 2017), pp. 60–76.
51 Gaposchkin, *Invisible Weapons*, 8–9, 229–30; Covaci, 'Praying for the Liberation', p. 182.
52 Compare Gaposchkin, *Invisible Weapons*, pp. 8, 259.
53 Covaci, 'Between Traditions', pp. 76–83.
54 Wanckel, *Ein Kurtze Vermerckung*, 'Das zwellft Capitel von der Regel der Ritterschafft' [no pagination]. For more on Wanckel, see Ritsema van Eck, *The Holy Land*, pp. 64–66.

previous descriptions do), the bellicose image of the Franciscan superior donning spurs and a sword belt 'institutionalised' by this ceremony is telling.

The friars of Mount Sion also expressed their ideas about crusading through other media. Several Franciscan authors such as Gilbert of Tournai, Fidentius of Padua, Ramon Llull and Galvano da Levanto wrote recovery treatises prior to (re-) establishment in the Holy land.[55] The textual culture that developed at Mount Sion was independent from these treatises, however. From the late fourteenth century the convent's library produced several compilation manuscripts with historical texts in various combinations, which expressed a clear nostalgia for the classical crusader era, but no calls for renewed crusade.[56] In 1463, an anonymous friar connected to Mount Sion wrote a description of the Holy Land, the final sentence of which calls for its recovery.[57] A more elaborate call for crusade is found in a late fifteenth-century treatise on the Holy Land by the Observant Paul Walter of Guglingen, which also integrates the Franciscans of Mount Sion into the supporting historical framework that gives urgency to his call.[58] Later examples of Observant Franciscans of the Holy Land calling for crusade include Bernardino Amico, in the preface to his *Trattato* (1610 and 1619) with plates of the Holy Places, and the towering scholarly figure Francesco Quaresmio (1583–1650).[59] At Easter 1626, Quaresmio delivered a sermon in the Holy Sepulchre Church urging Philip IV of Spain to retake the Holy Land; it was printed in Milan in 1631 but apparently suppressed.[60] Quaresmio's *Terrae Sanctae Elucidatio* (1639) did become a widely distributed and influential publication; it features a map derivative of Vesconte's Holy Land map in Sanudo's famous recovery treatise, and in the preface it also contains an urgent call on Catholic princes to recover the Holy Land, which is then fleshed out further on.[61]

Enduringly then, the Observant Franciscans of the Holy Land developed their voice as crusade proponents from the 1430s, through diplomatic endeavours, rituals, texts, sermons, and maps. The duality of their location — at once geographically peripheral for the sovereigns they called on, yet central to their vision of salvation history — runs through these expressions as a common thread.

---

55 Evangelisti, *Dopo Francesco, oltre il Mito*, 27–136; Anthony Leopold, *How to Recover the Holy Land: The Crusade Proposals of the late Thirteenth and Early Fourteenth Centuries* (Aldershot, 2000), pp. 13–34.

56 Campopiano, 'Islam, Jews and Eastern Christianity', pp. 75–89; Campopiano, *Writing the Holy Land*, 127–84.

57 Ch. Kohler, 'Description de la Terre Sainte par un Franciscain Anonyme 1463', *Revue de l'Orient Latin* 12 (1911), 1–67 (here 59). Philip the Good may have been the addressee of this tract, compare Paviot, *Le Ducs*, p. 114, and Covaci, 'Praying for the Liberation', pp. 180–81.

58 This part of Guglingen's treatise was also taken over in Bernard of Breydenbach's well-known *Peregrinatio in Terram Sanctam* (1486), but the Franciscans were edited out. Ritsema van Eck, *The Holy Land*, pp. 19–28, 140–52.

59 On Amico, see Ritsema van Eck, *The Holy Land*, pp. 182–85.

60 Ritsema van Eck, *The Holy Land*, pp. 185–91; Chad Leahy and Ken Tully, *Jerusalem Afflicted: Quaresmius, Spain, and the Idea of a 17th-Century Crusade* (New York, 2019), pp. 74–86.

61 Ritsema van Eck, *The Holy Land*, pp. 191–201.

MARIA BONET DONATO

Crusading and Military Orders in the Crowns of Aragon and Castile in the Late Middle Ages[*]

The Military Orders in the New Political Scenario of the Later Middle Ages

In the military campaigns against Islam on the Hispanic front, operations headed by Castile were coordinated with others directed from Aragon and Portugal in two key periods: firstly, during the so-called Battle of the Strait (Span. *Batalla del Estrecho*), i.e. the long-lasting military conflict mostly from 1274 to 1350, between these Christian kingdoms contesting mainly the ports in the Straits of Gibraltar and, secondly, during the fifteenth century, in the Granada crusades, which culminated in the campaigns of the so-called Catholic Monarchs, i.e. the married royal couple Queen Isabella of Castile and King Ferdinand II of Aragon.[1] However, throughout, the issue of border defence continued to involve the military orders. Besides, the collapse of the crusades in the Latin East in the thirteenth century, and the abolition of the Templars in the early fourteenth century, meant the consolidation of the Hospitallers in the Eastern Mediterranean. The latter, especially those coming from the kingdom of Aragon, contributed financial and military resources to the defence of the Christian stronghold on the island of Rhodes. From the era of the Catholic Monarchs, the traditional Castilian expansionary policy around the Strait of Gibraltar merged with the expansionist fifteenth century Aragonese policy in the Mediterranean. This was encapsulated in the moment that Ferdinand the Catholic obtained the title of king of Jerusalem from Julius II.[2]

---

[*] This article was drawn up within the framework of the research project PGC 2018-098306-B-100 (Ministry of Science and Innovation of the government of Spain).
[1] For a general overview on both topics, see with further references Joseph F. O'Callaghan, *The Gibraltar Crusade: Castile and the Battle for the Strait* (Philadelphia, PA, 2011); O'Callaghan, *The Last Crusade in the West: Castile and the Conquest of Granada* (Philadelphia, PA, 2014).
[2] José Ángel Sesma Muñoz, *Fernando de Aragón: Hispaniarum rex* (Zaragoza, 1992), p. 9.

This chapter provides an overview of the evolution of the crusader movement in relation to the role played by the military orders in the crowns of Aragon and Castile in the late medieval period. Given the scope of the topic and the enormous amount of literature on the subject, I propose an interpretative synthesis, which aims to underline how the crusade ideal continued to be central in the identification and services of the military orders. These orders, in turn, adapted to the changing geopolitical realities. After the *Reconquista* slowed down in the mid-thirteenth century, the military alliance between the orders and the crowns of Castile and Aragon evolved in keeping with the new military and political needs. From the first decades of the fourteenth century, the Hispanic orders, especially those of Castile, Santiago, Calatrava and Alcántara, and later the Valencian order of Montesa, consolidated their position alongside the monarchy, while the Hospitallers defined a new alignment with the Aragonese crown. By setting these events in a larger, supra-regional pan-European context, parallels can be drawn in particular to the Teutonic Order, the third great medieval military order, and to its fifteenth-century identity crisis, as discussed in Paul Srodecki and Adam Szweda's chapters in this book.

After the Great Conquests of Al-Andalus: Politicisation and Border Defence

The end of the most expansive period of the *Reconquista* and, in some ways, the crisis in Outremer, altered the military and political coordinates on the Iberian Peninsula. This impacted upon the role played by the military orders as well as on their ties with certain monarchical institutions. There was a change in the relationship between the kings and the military organisations, who were active in the *Reconquista* and in the military consolidation of the conquered areas, and their functions were reoriented. However, despite the transformation of context, the military orders clearly remained active in the fight and defence against Islam in the crowns of Castile and Aragon.[3] Besides the vicissitudes, their actions continued to be identified with the crusade movement.

Following the great Christian conquests in Iberia, there were certain changes in the military orders which involved a greater interference on the part of the monarchies and a certain crisis concerning the crusade ideology. In the fourteenth and fifteenth centuries, these organisations became more involved in internal conflicts within kingdoms, between kingdoms and even in conflicts at an international

---

3 Philippe Josserand, *Église et pouvoir dans la Péninsule Ibérique: Les ordres militaires dans le royaume de Castille (1252–1369)* (Madrid, 2004), pp. 233–97; Anthony Luttrell, *The Hospitallers of Rhodes and Their Mediterranean World* (Aldershot, 1992); Luttrell, *The Hospitaller State on Rhodes and Its Western Provinces, 1306–1462* (Aldershot, 1999); Maria Bonet Donato, *La orden del Hospital en la Corona de Aragón: Poder y gobierno en la Castellanía de Amposta (siglos XII–XV)* (Madrid, 1994), pp. 51–80.

level, than they were in military campaigns against Muslims.[4] In some situations, the monarchs even demanded that their obligations in conflicts including battles within the kingdoms take priority over the orders' commitments to defending the Holy Land. For example, in 1290, Alfonso III the Liberal demanded that the Hospitaller commander of *Hispania* not send goods to the Latin East, since the Hospitallers had served him in his wars with the kings of France and Castile.[5] The order's obligations to the crown prevailed over their crusade mission in the eastern Mediterranean. However, in the framework of the military paradigm shift that started in the mid thirteenth century, the papacy intervened to reassert the orders' military obligations to combat Islam. King James I of Aragon (1213–76, r. 1213–76) complained to the pope that the Templars and Hospitallers did not cooperate militarily as they should, and the pope reminded them of their commitments in the fight against the enemies of the faith in letter from 18 March 1250.[6] Some of the pontifical interventions aimed to correct the specific flaws of the military orders in their duties to defending the borders. In 1319 and 1320, Pope John XXII encouraged the Order of Calatrava in its fight against the infidels and in the defence of Christianity and asked his papal legate to investigate why the orders of Santiago, Calatrava, Alcántara and the Hospital neglected the defence of the Granada border.[7]

The tendency of the military orders towards a degree of ambiguity became clear from the middle of the thirteenth and during the fourteenth centuries in Aragon and, more occasionally, in Castile.[8] However, during this period, the monarchies found certain mechanism to correct the absences of the orders. Faced with the threat of attacks from the Moroccan king in 1283, the Aragonese king Peter III established that, should breaches occur in the defence of the Valencian borders by the Hospitallers, Templars, the Knights of Santiago and other orders,

---

4 On this topic, see, to mention some significant examples, Carlos de Ayala Martínez, 'Pedro I de Castilla y las órdenes militares', *Memoria y Civilización* 22 (2019), 63–91; Pablo Sanahuja Ferrer, '¿Defensora de la fe o protectora del reino: La orden de Santa María de Montesa y la Guerra de los dos Pedros (1356–69)', in *Santa María de Montesa: La orden militar del Reino de Valencia (siglos XIV–XV)*, ed. Enric Guinot, Fernando Andrés and Juan F. Pardo (Valencia, 2019), pp. 139–53; Julia Pavón Benito and Maria Bonet Donato, 'La orden del Hospital en un mundo en cambio (finales del XV y comienzos del XVI): Proyección mediterránea y giros políticos' in *Carlos V y la Orden de Malta*, ed. Javier Alvarado and Jaime Salazar (Madrid, 2020), pp. 103–29 (here 115–20). This had been happening more clearly since the last third of the thirteenth century (Josserand, *Église et pouvoir*, pp. 234–38) and the orders were also active in civil wars, as in the time of Alfonso X the Wise. See Carlos de Ayala Martínez, 'La monarquía y las órdenes militares durante el reinado de Alfonso X', *Hispania* 51 (1991), 409–65.
5 *CGOH* 3, no. 4081, p. 555.
6 *CGOH* 2, no. 2517, p. 686. See Alan Forey, 'The Military Orders and the Spanish Reconquest in the Twelfth and Thirteenth Centuries', in Forey, *Military Orders and Crusades* (Aldershot, 1994), pp. 197–234 (here 231).
7 Carlos de Ayala Martínez, *Las órdenes militares hispánicas en la Edad Media* (Madrid, 2003), p. 599.
8 José Vicente Cabezuelo Pliego, 'Las órdenes militares y la frontera valenciana: Siglos XIII–XIV', in *Las órdenes militares: un puntal de la historia de Occidente*, ed. Margarita Torres Sevilla (Soria, 2006), pp. 73–105 (here 82).

they would have to redeem themselves through payments known as *redenciones*, which the Templars paid in 1275 and 1285.[9] The threat of the confiscation of assets emerged in order to reverse these breaches in military commitments; however, they were also the result of a greater willingness and capability for royal intervention, as Alfonso III the Liberal showed in 1287.[10] These interventionist actions crystallised in the threat of confiscating *responsiones* which the Aragonese kings deployed on those occasions when they did not comply with their obligations, such as in 1329, in order to cover the expedition to Granada and in 1330, when they did not go to the border for the crusade. The argument was that these taxes would serve to meet the expenses of the campaign.[11] However, when Peter IV the Ceremonious prohibited the sending of taxes to the convent of Rhodes in 1340, he did so for other reasons.[12] It is important to remember that the *responsiones* were contributions from the western commanderies for maintaining the order's positions in the eastern Mediterranean, and that the king therefore prioritised the peninsular crusades.

Changes in the ideological context affected the expectations and demands that fell on the orders, in particular the international ones, but also the national ones. The result was the reaffirmation of the ideology of the struggle against Islam. Some diatribes had much to do with the loss of the crusader territories and lasted through the first decades of the fourteenth century, although no movement was formed responding to the orders' demands.[13] In line with these criticisms, the Templars and Hospitallers claimed that their contributions against the Muslims were conducted under pontifical patronage, although they fundamentally referred to the Latin East in this respect. In order to do so, they copied papal bulls highlighting their role in the defence of the Holy Land and recalled epic episodes in order to fix their contributions in institutional memory from the second half of the thirteenth century onwards.[14] The existence of the two main international organisations were justified by their role in the eastern crusades, which the late medieval Hospitallers continued to be involved in. In this regard, the Hospitaller grand master and prominent intellectual, Juan Fernández de Heredia (r. 1377–

---

9 *CGOH* 3, no. 3827, p. 443; Alan J. Forey, *The Templars in the Crown of Aragon* (London, 1973), pp. 134–35; Regina Sáinz de la Maza, *La Orden de Santiago en la Corona de Aragón. La encomienda de Montalbán (1210–1327)* (Zaragoza, 1980), p. 82.
10 Forey, 'The Military Orders and the Spanish Reconquest', p. 231.
11 Manuel Sánchez Martínez, 'Las órdenes militares en la cruzada granadina', *Anuario de Estudios Medievales* 28 (1988), 31–58 (here 37).
12 Anthony Luttrell, 'The Aragonese Crown and the Knights Hospitallers of Rhodes, 1291–1350', *EHR* 76 (1961), 1–19 (here 12–13).
13 Alan Forey, 'The Military Orders in the Crusading Proposals of the Late Thirteenth and Early Fourteenth Centuries', *Traditio* 36 (1980), 317–45; *Église et pouvoir dans la Péninsule Ibérique*, pp. 37–96.
14 Maria Bonet Donato and Julia Pavón Benito, 'Cuestiones sobre la ortodoxia, la disciplina y la oposición a templarios y hospitalarios en la Corona de Aragón y Navarra (siglos XII–XIII)', in *Creences a l'època medieval: ortodoxia i heretgia*, ed. Karen Stöber (Lleida, 2018), pp. 63–99 (here 78–79).

96), left a vision of history which emphasised the order's mission in terms of imposing Christianity. Furthermore, in his *Crónica de los conqueridores* ('Chronicle of the Conquerors'), he placed the struggles in the East and the conquests against the Moors in the Iberian Peninsula on the same level.[15] With its roots in other peripheral crusades of the high Middle Ages, such as those against various pagans in the Baltic Sea region, this perception raises a lot of interesting parallels to the Teutonic Knights and their repeated equation of the *Preußen-* and *Litauerfahrten* with the Levantine crusades as ventures allegedly conducted for the same purpose of defending the faith.[16]

The military actions of the orders in the peninsular regions neighbouring Muslim regions had, in a sense, received the same consideration in terms of the defence of the Christian faith as the actions carried out in the eastern Mediterranean. In 1275, therefore, the pontiff Gregory X ordered the papal tax collectors that the Hispanic orders committed to the battle against the Muslims of Africa be exonerated from the tenth. Let us remember that his goal was to gather resources for the crusades in the Holy Land.[17] Similarly, Clement V authorised kings Ferdinand IV of Castile and James II of Aragon to collect taxes for three years in order to pay for the Granada campaign of 1309, in which the military orders participated.[18] This equation of the two crusade fronts was also translated into the spiritual privileges and benefits granted by the popes in the fight against Islam on the Iberian Peninsula, such as the indulgences granted by Nicholas IV in 1291 to those who provided help to the Order of Santiago in a bull of a clear crusade content.[19]

The Defence of Borders within a Crusading Ideology Context

The military orders had been emblematic and central organisations in the conquests led by the Hispanic monarchies in the mid twelfth and thirteenth

---

15 Alfredo Morel-Fatio, *Libro de los fechos et conquistas del Principado de Morea* (Genève, 1885), p. xxii; Maria Bonet Donato, 'Los hospitalarios hispanos. Entre la identidad transmediterránea y la pertenencia territorial', in *Tra il Tirreno e Gibilterra: Un Mediterraneo iberico?*, ed. Luciano Gallinari and Flocel Sabaté Curull (Roma, 2015), pp. 365–437 (here 379–81).
16 See the various chapters on this topic in the volume *The Expansion of the Faith: Crusading on the Frontiers of Latin Christendom in the High Middle Ages*, ed. Paul Srodecki and Norbert Kersken (Turnhout, 2022), as well as Srodecki's chapter in this volume on the ideological parallels between the Iberian *Reconquista* and the Prussian and Lithuanian crusades in the Teutonic Order's late medieval propaganda.
17 Ayala Martínez, *Las órdenes militares*, p. 444.
18 José Goñi Gaztambide, *Historia de la bula de la cruzada en España* (Vitoria, 1958), pp. 270–75.
19 Antonio Francisco Aguado de Córdoba, José López Agurleta and Antonio Alfonso Alemán Rosales, *Bullarium equestris ordinis S. Iacobi de Spatha* (Madrid, 1719), pp. 235–36, or previously, pp. 181–82 (1250). In general, the equation of fighting against Muslims in the Levant and the Iberian Peninsula proposed by the papacy can be traced back to the beginning of the twelfth century.

centuries. Moreover, the main activity of these organisations until the middle of the thirteenth century was the defence of the castle systems which controlled the conquered territories and functioned as strongholds from which to launch quick attacks against enemy positions.[20] From this period, the kings became increasingly interventionist with regard to the orders.[21] They even founded several new ones, justified by the new military requirements of defending the kingdoms' military frontiers. Alfonso X the Wise established the order of Saint Mary of Spain sometime after 1270, whose purpose was to survey and defend the maritime border of the kingdom, with strongholds near the Strait of Gibraltar; however, this order did not last long.[22] The project also included the creation of a Hispanic order under the direct authority of the sovereign, whose ambitious task was to defend the entire Spanish coastline, not only in the Andalusian border area. All this had its roots in the plans of Alfonso X the Wise for peninsular hegemony, as indicated by Carlos de Ayala Martínez.[23] After its failure, the order merged with the Order of Santiago in 1280.

The military orders were involved in the defence of the southern borders against Islam in the final decades of the thirteenth century and throughout the fourteenth century. This activity required a great effort in the investment of resources, and some knights even lost their lives.[24] This was one of the main military strategies of the crowns of Castile and Aragon, in accordance with the political and clearly instrumental aims of these institutions in the late medieval period. Moreover, this activity was intertwined with a second offensive phase beyond the established borders, which was not without its problems and failures, during the Battle of the Strait. In the Castilian sphere, the military orders were very present in the process of stabilising the border with Granada, where the orders of Calatrava and Santiago obtained fortresses, as well as in relation to the new objectives in Morocco. This second programme, which Castile would continue to pursue into the early modern period, allowed the crusade ideology

---

20 Maria Bonet Donato, 'Las órdenes militares en la expansión feudal de la corona de Aragón', *Anales de la universidad de Alicante. Historia medieval* 17 (2011), 245–402 (here 223–43). On castles and fortresses in relation to their military role, see Alan Forey, *The Military Orders: From the Twelfth to the Early Fourteenth Centuries* (London, 1992), pp. 64–67; Enrique Rodríguez Picavea, *Los monjes guerreros en los reinos hispanos en la Península Ibérica durante la Edad Media* (Madrid, 2008), pp. 153–65.

21 Manuel González Jiménez, 'Relaciones de las órdenes militares castellanas con la corona', *Historia: Instituciones. Documentos* 18 (1991), 209–22 (here 217); Josserand, *Église et pouvoir*, pp. 461–650. The Castilian orders were also subject to a secularisation in the mid-fourteenth century in relation to their service to King Peter I. See Ayala Martínez, 'Pedro I de Castilla y las órdenes militares', p. 64.

22 Juan Torres Fontes, 'La Orden de Santa María de España', *Miscelánea medieval murciana* 3 (1977), 73–118; Ramón Menéndez Pidal, 'Noticias acerca de la Orden Militar de Santa María de España instituida por Alfonso X', *Revista de Archivos, Bibliotecas y Museos* 11 (1907), 161–80; Miguel Ángel Ladero Quesada, 'Grenade', in *Prier et combattre. Dictionnaire européen des ordres militaires au Moyen Âge*, ed. Nicolé Bériou et Phillippe Josserand (París, 2009), p. 401.

23 Ayala Martínez, *Las órdenes militares*, pp. 108–12.

24 Josserand, *Église et pouvoir*, p. 29.

to be kept alive. It went beyond what it meant to attack a peninsular emirate, such as Granada, which was also a fiefdom of Castile.[25] In *Liber de fine*, written in 1305 by Ramon Llull, it is mentioned that one of the five itineraries for reaching Outremer was the North African route, which included conquering the emirate of Granada, crossing the Strait, then Ceuta, and following the North African coast until reaching Jerusalem.[26]

In the first decades of the fourteenth century, the crusade ideology was also present in the changes that affected the military orders, as seen in the crown of Aragon following the abolition of the Templars. When the Hospitallers became established in Rhodes in 1309, they reaffirmed their role as defenders of Latin Christianity in Outremer. Clement V and John XXII referred to this function and to the support of the Holy Land in many of the decrees they issued relating to the order.[27] A long process then began in which the Hospitallers were identified as the main protectors of Christendom against the Muslim threat in the eastern Mediterranean, and this impacted upon their organisation in the Hispanic world. In this context, and for this purpose, the assets of the Templars went to the Hospitallers. King James II of Aragon began a long negotiation that resulted in this transfer in Catalonia and Aragon, leaving the Hospitallers as the main military order in the lands of the crown of Aragon. However, the monarch also managed to create a new order for the kingdom of Valencia, which was subject to the order of Calatrava, and whose headquarters were established in the castle of Montesa. The monarch argued that the 'strength of the order of the Hospital would jeopardise the defence of the kingdom, since a single order would defend from a single point'.[28] Thus, it was essential to create a permanent and strong knighthood in Montesa which would occupy the castles of that region for the purpose of their defence.[29]

During the negotiations with Pope John XXII, James II presented Montesa as a fortress on the border to al-Andalus, and although this was not exactly the case, this justification did reflect the importance of the military function of defence against Islam.[30] He created a Valencian "national" order, whose task was to defend the southern border against the Andalusians and, by extension, to protect the

---

25 Ayala Martínez, *Las órdenes militares*, p. 442.
26 Ramon Llull, *Darrer llibre sobre la conquesta de Terra Santa (Liber de Fine)* (Barcelona, 2002); Benjamin Kedar, *Crusade and Mission: European Approaches towards Muslims* (Princeton, 1984), p. 196.
27 BNM, AOM 10, docs 20, 28 and 50 (from Clement V); 1126, fols 196–99; 1136, fols 130–34v and 167 (from John XXII).
28 Maria Bonet Donato, 'L'orde de l'Hospital i l'herencia del Temple a la Corona d'Aragó: Polititzaciò i internacionalitzaciò', in *Santa María de Montesa*, pp. 55–72 (here 59–61).
29 For the requests and reasons made by James II to the pontiff in 1312, see Heinrich Finke, *Papsttum und Untergang des Templerordens*, 2 vols (Münster, 1907), 2: nos 113, 118, 125, 134, 139, pp. 212–16, 223–24, 230–38, 265–68, 279–85.
30 ACA, RC, no. 336, fol. 172v. See also Luis García-Guijarro, 'Algunos aspectos sobre la extinción del Temple', in *Santa María de Montesa*, pp. 25–42 (here 32).

entire kingdom in periods of the consolidation of the new Christian political formations, which were governing a predominantly Muslim conquered population. However, the Order of Montesa was above all an institution at the service of the interests of the monarchy. Earlier, in 1202, King Peter II the Catholic had founded another military order, which would prove to be more modest, the Order of Saint George of Alfama, destined to defend the coast against Muslim pirate attacks.[31] This would end up under the guardianship of the Order of Montesa in 1401. In another vein, and as a counterpoint to the formation of orders such as Montesa or, in Portugal, the Order of Christ, thanks to the transfer of Templar properties, it is important to note that, in 1327, the papacy did not allow King Alfonso XI to create a similar new Castilian order, like those mentioned, questioning its usefulness.[32]

From the Battle of the Strait to the Granada Crusades

The so-called Battle of the Strait resulted from the position that the Marinids had managed to establish on both shores of the Strait of Gibraltar, and came after the crown of Castile had already fought to expel them from the northern shore for almost half a century. In keeping with the foreign policy of the Castilian crown, it was the Castilian military orders who were most active in the Battle of the Strait, although the Hospitallers also made some military contributions. They were involved, for example, in the battle of Río Salado (1340) and, in the Castilian army, in other expeditions against Islamic territory or sieges on strongholds.[33] In this period, the crown of Aragon looked towards the Mediterranean but continued to cooperate with the crown of Castile in its fight against Islam, as was evident in the Battle of the Strait. In this regard, the crown of Aragon remained active in the defence of the southern border, and both kingdoms fought to placate the fifth column that they had identified in the Mudéjar uprisings, counting on the military orders to do so. The collaboration between the two kingdoms had a crusade ideology at its base. Here it is worth mentioning the treaty of Alcalá de Henares of 1308, in which the two kings began to revive the *Reconquista*, agreeing on joint attacks and distributing responsibilities;[34] as well as the Madrid agreements of

---

31 Regina Sáinz de la Maza, *L'orde català de Sant Jordi d'Alfama (1201–1400)* (Lleida, 1991).
32 Philippe Josserand, *Église et pouvoir*, pp. 81, 625–26; Ayala Martínez, 'La orden de Calatrava en el contexto del nacimiento de Montesa', in *Santa María de Montesa*, pp. 43–53. In a second bull from 1331, the pope insisted on the limited utility of the orders of Montesa and Christ, AAV, RV 116, fols 84v–85r.
33 Carlos Barquero Goñi, *Los caballeros hospitalarios durante la edad media en España* (Burgos, 2003), pp. 159–60.
34 Antonio Benavides, *Memorias de Don Fernando IV de Castilla copiada de un códice existente en la Biblioteca Nacional*, 2 vols (Madrid, 1860), 2: 621–26; César González Mínguez, 'Fernando IV de Castilla (1295–1312): perfil de un reinado', *Espacio, Tiempo y Forma: Serie III. Historia medieval* 17 (2004), 223–44 (here 235–38).

1329 and 1339, which served to jointly organise the defence against the Muslims and to request the necessary aid.[35]

Carlos de Ayala Martínez has analysed and written extensively on the participation of the Castilian military orders in the Battle of the Strait and Granada Wars. In this article, we only refer to certain data that are significant for the subject of this particular study. At the end of the thirteenth century, the orders of Santiago, Alcántara and Calatrava had participated in the Castilian offensive and in the conquest of Tarifa (1292), which was followed by further punitive acts in the fertile plain of Granada at the beginning of the fourteenth century. Alfonso XI launched a new offensive and involved the orders in military developments between 1329 and the failed campaign at Gibraltar in 1333. He returned to the border again in 1339, accompanied by the masters, prior and members of the orders of Santiago, Calatrava, Alcántara and the Hospital.[36]

In the context of the aforementioned collaboration in the southern crusade, the Aragonese king Alfonso IV the Benign organised a crusade against the kingdom of Granada between 1329 and 1334, in which he demanded the presence of the orders in the crown of Aragon. The Hospitallers were not fully committed to this expedition, and some commanderies did not comply with the service requested, refusing to go to the border, abandoning it or sending only a few contingents. It is interesting to note that the king reacted by taking the *responsiones* due to the master of Rhodes[37] and trying to form an army paid with these taxes.[38] It is understandable that Alfonso the Benign considered that these resources should be devoted to the obligations against Islam in the same peninsular campaigns[39]. However, the Order of Montesa fulfilled their obligations. Its master participated in the raid of 1330, and the Order of Calatrava also attacked the kingdom of Granada in 1331, although without success. The crown of Aragon also had ambitions to complete the southern conquest, but the political-social context of the time rendered these impossible.

After a series of difficulties, Alfonso XI promoted a new crusade, which was supported by the benefits granted by Benedict XII, and which also included the strength of the military orders and the presence of their dignitaries. It had been intended as another campaign by the Christian kingdoms of the Iberian Peninsula, although it was pre-eminently Castilian, and culminated in the battle

---

35 *Colección de documentos inéditos del Archivo General de la Corona de Aragón*, ed. Prospéro de Bofarull y Mascaró and Manuel de Bofarull y de Sartorio, 41 vols (Barcelona, 1847–1910), 7: no. 5, pp. 87–96. See Manuel López Fernández, 'Algunas precisiones sobre la aplicación del Tratado de Madrid de 1339, entre Castilla y Aragón', *Espacio, Tiempo y Forma. Serie III, Historia Medieval* 21 (2008), 185–208.
36 Ayala Martínez, *Las órdenes militares*, pp. 449–62.
37 Luttrell, 'The Aragonese Crown', pp. 9–11.
38 Manuel Sánchez Martínez, 'Las órdenes militares en la cruzada granadina', *Anuario de Estudios Medievales* 28 (1988), 31–58.
39 He ordered to invest some of these *responsiones* in this crusade of Granada: ACA, RC, no. 541, fol. 185r–v.

of Salado in 1340, in which the master of Santiago was prominent.[40] Within this framework of cooperation, Peter IV the Ceremonious tried to gather military and financial resources and counted upon the border services of the military orders. These actions made it possible for him to reinforce the kingdom's defensive network in the face of the Marinid threat to the kingdom of Valencia in 1339.[41] However, he contributed very little to the Castilian attempt to lift the maritime blockade in Tarifa, while the Portuguese, represented by the Order of the Hospital and the Order of Aviz, the Order of Christ and the Order of Santiago, participated in the battle of Salado.[42] Other later developments confirm the full unity of purpose between the orders and the monarchy. One example of these is that the logistical responsibility for supplies of all kinds, as in the siege of Algeciras in 1344, which was also considered a crusade,[43] was placed in the hands of the masters of Calatrava and Alcántara;[44] another is the participation of the leaders of the orders of Santiago and Alcántara in the Siege of Gibraltar in 1349–50.

The decline of the Marinids focused the war against the Nasrid emirate of Granada. However, during the second half of the fourteenth century, Castile reached a series of peace agreements with its rulers, who was subject to the vassalage of the Castilian king. The crusade ideology was already strengthened in the fifteenth century and this, with renewed papal support and other geopolitical changes, favoured a series of military attempts that culminated in the conquest of the Nasrid kingdom (1492). Martin V again proclaimed a crusade to conquer Granada in 1430, granting indulgences to all who helped the king financially in his campaign.[45] A series of crusades in which the military orders participated followed, one after the other, until the kingdom was taken.[46] The orders had increasingly become instruments of the monarchy, i.e. an institution with greater authority. They played a role that was rather symbolic and offered the king material support. As Carlos de Ayala Martínez accurately points out, these transformations led to the monarchy absorbing the orders, which had some background in the actions of Ferdinand of Antequera who tried to control them by putting his children partly in charge of their administration.[47] The four stages of the so-called 'Granada Wars' in the fifteenth century were the capture of Antequera in 1410, the

---

40 Ayala Martínez, *Las órdenes militares*, pp. 449–62.
41 Manuel Sánchez Martínez and Sílvia Gassiot Pintori, 'La *Cort General* de Barcelona (1340) y la contribución catalana a la guerra del Estrecho', in *Les corts a Catalunya: Actes del Congrés d'Història Institucional, 28, 29 i 30 d'Abril 1988* (Barcelona, 1991), pp. 222–40 (here 224); Maria Teresa Ferrer i Mallol, *La frontera amb l'Islam al segle XIV* (Barcelona, 1988), nos 63–64, pp. 140–42.
42 Enrique Rodríguez Picavea, *Los monjes guerreros*, p. 202.
43 José Enrique López de Coca Castañer, 'El reino de Granada y las cruzadas tardías (siglo XIV)', *Baetica* 36–37 (2015), 89–117 (here 101–04).
44 Philippe Josserand, *Église et pouvoir*, p. 268.
45 José Goñi Gaztambide, *Historia de la bula*, p. 342.
46 Norman Housley, *The Later Crusades: From Lyon to Alcazar 1274–1580* (Oxford, 1992), pp. 291–304.
47 Ayala Martínez, *Las órdenes militares*, pp. 472, 474.

battle of La Higueruela in 1431, the crusade of Henry IV (1455), and the final conquest of the emirate in 1482–92.[48]

The fourth and definitive Granada War was a primary and highly coveted objective for validating the project of the Catholic Monarchs, Isabella and Ferdinand, and they made full use of the crusade momentum.[49] All the Castilian military orders participated, as did the Hospitallers and the Order of Montesa. The grand master of Santiago, Alonso de Cárdenas, played a leading role.[50] He was the highest in command of the defence of the western part of the border throughout practically the entire war, from where he also undertook important offensive actions such as the one, he led against Baza in 1489. The military orders contributed over thirty percent of the cavalry troops mobilised throughout the Granada War.[51] In addition to the military benefits, the orders also contributed with levies and charges for the victuals demanded by the crowns.

The Hospitallers and the Legacy of Outremer Defence in the Crown of Aragon

The establishment of the Order of the Hospital of Saint John in Rhodes, their renewed crusade role in the east and the Catalano-Aragonese interests in the Mediterranean provided the order with a new position in the crown of Aragon, since it was the main military order at the time. The efforts of the Hospitallers focussed on the gathering of financial resources, in the form of *responsiones* or other payments, and on the contribution of military resources to Rhodes. However, the eastern enclave served other western political and commercial interests, which strengthened the network of trans-Mediterranean relations in accordance with the expansive policies of the crown of Aragon in the Mediterranean. Before the order became established in Rhodes, James II had already intervened to maintain support for the Hospitallers in the Holy Land.[52] Nevertheless, the organisation's double dependence, on the crown and on the master of Rhodes, led to several malfunctions. This could be seen when the master of Rhodes appointed the position of prior of Catalonia or castellan of Amposta, the highest dignitary of the

---

48 Luis Suárez Fernández, 'Los trastámaras de Castilla y Aragón en el siglo XV (1407–74)', in *Historia de España*, ed. Ramón Menéndez Pidal and José María Jover Zamora, 42 vols (1935–2004), 15: 225–29; Suárez Fernández, *Las órdenes militares y la guerra de Granada* (Sevilla, 1992), pp. 6–7.
49 John Edwards, 'Reconquista and Crusade in Fifteenth-Century Spain', in *Crusading in the Fifteenth Century*, ed. Norman Housley (London, 2004), pp. 163–81.
50 Francisco de Rades y Andrada, *Crónica de las Tres Órdenes y Caballerías de Santiago, Calatrava y Alcántara* (Toledo, 1572), pp. 71–72.
51 Ayala Martínez, *Las órdenes militares*, pp. 480–85; Miguel Ángel Ladero Quesada, *Castilla y la conquista del reino de Granada* (Granada, 1988), pp. 280–81, and on other matters concerning the participation of the orders, pp. 31–33.
52 Maria Bonet Donato, 'Los hospitalarios hispanos', p. 419.

order in Aragon and some Catalan commanderies, and the king tried to impose his own candidate.[53]

Throughout the fourteenth and fifteenth centuries, Rhodes's tax demands on western priories evolved and generally increased, while resentment and breaches of them proliferated. The organisation's *raison d'etre* in the fight against Islam and the defence of Rhodes, heir to the Holy Land, continued to be in place to justify the mobilisation of human and material resources by the Hospitallers, despite all the vicissitudes. The central years of the fifteenth century and the following decades were especially difficult for Rhodes. It sought to cope with these difficulties by increasing the tax demand or by resorting to borrowing, especially from merchants, particularly in loans provided by the Catalans.[54] As an example we can take the request, in 1454, by Master Jean de Lastic to the castellan of Amposta, for a very high extraordinary tax to fund the war against the infidels. This was urgently needed to reinforce the defence of the island of Rhodes and its castles, and to provide them with supplies.[55] This request was ratified by King Alfonso V the Magnanimous, whose policies in the Mediterranean led to him helping directly in the defence of Rhodes.[56] He sent his fleet and committed large sums to this objective.[57] This clearly shows the synergies between the military and commercial interests of the crown of Aragon and those of the order.[58] The protection of Catalan and Spanish merchants was continued by his nephew King Ferdinand II.[59]

Pope Nicholas V also supported the demands of the convent in their Western commitments at the time, insisting on obligations in the fight against the Turks.[60] These exactions generated chronic indebtedness among the commanderies of the Hispanic Hospitallers. Among them, those of the crown of Aragon were the most committed to such payments, as their dignitary complained in 1470.[61] They even

---

53 Joseph Delaville Le Roulx, *Les Hospitaliers à Rhodes 1310–1421* (London, 1974), pp. 64–67; Josep Alanya i Roig, 'Procés inquisitorial contra el castellà d'Amposta Fra Pedro Roiç de Moros a la cúria pontifícia del papa Benet XIII (1414–18)', *Anuario de Estudios Medievales* 32 (2002), 199–293 (here 206–8, 210).
54 María Bonet Donato, 'Obligaciones y contribuciones de los hospitalarios hispanos al convento de Rodas', in *Financiar el reino terrenal: La contribución de la iglesia a finales de la edad media (siglos XIII–XVI)*, ed. Jordi Morelló Baget (Barcelona, 2013), pp. 169–279.
55 BNM 364, fol. 65r, and similarly fols 133 r–v and 134 r.
56 AHN, OOMM, San Juan de Jerusalén, codex 606, fols 66–67.
57 Constantin Marinescu, *La politique orientale d'Alfonse V d'Aragon, roi de Naples (1416–58)* (Barcelona, 1994), pp. 48, 50–53.
58 Mario del Treppo, *I mercanti catalani e l'espansione della Corona d'Aragona nel secolo XV* (Napoli, 1972), p. 600.
59 *DIRC* 1, no. 68, pp. 172–74; 2, nos 16–17, 104, pp. 286–87, 446–47; 3, nos 48–49, 93, pp. 90–92, 215–17.
60 BNM, Sacra Capitula Generalia 282, fol. 7: [...] *questo nostro convento possa sustentare le karigi* [...] *che sono maiori che mai fossero per la guerra deli infideli et per star sempre preveduti aço che lo Gran Turcho nostro viçino e mortal inimico ex improviso non ne faça danno.*
61 AHN, OOMM, San Juan de Jerusalén, codex 607, fols 101–2; BNM 379, fols 66–67.

paid the bills of exchange drawn in Rhodes in favour of the Catalan merchants on the Eastern Mediterranean island.[62] It should be noted that the Hospitallers from the Aragonese and Catalan priories stood out among the Hispanic conventuals, that is, the western residents of Rhodes, as the most numerous and active.[63] There were also outstanding masters from Aragon and Catalonia, such as Juan Fernández de Heredia, Anthony of Fluvià (r. 1421–37) and Pere Ramon Sacosta (r. 1461–67). All this was consistent with the mercantile, maritime and political interests of the crown of Aragon in Rhodes and in the eastern Mediterranean in the late Middle Ages.[64]

The popes supported and reinforced the late crusader missions of the Hospitallers, and provided them leadership in this task in the east, intensifying its intervention from the beginning of the fourteenth century.[65] Rome also favoured obtaining resources through the granting of indulgences by Clement VII to those who paid the alms for the works on the fortification of the Hostpitallers' Anatolian outpost Smyrna in 1391 — calls that were in particular satisfied by the Catalans and Navarrese who supported the grand master's emissaries with generous payments.[66] In addition, other Church institutions were also required, in exchange for papal indulgences, to help the Hospitallers fulfil their obligations in the east, for example the Franciscans of Pamplona and Tudela.[67] The spiritual benefits that the crusaders had obtained in previous times could now be achieved, thanks to the aforementioned alms, through the Hospitallers, who defended the last crusader enclaves.

The Fusion of Castilian and Aragonese Policies in the Era of the Catholic Monarchs

The monarchy's intervention in the military orders reached its peak in the era of the Catholic Monarchs, when the *maestrazgos* — jurisdictions under a grand master — of the orders of Santiago, Calatrava and Alcántara passed to the crown; first King Ferdinand assumed the administration, and then the crown took it on from 1523.[68] This also affected the Order of Saint John, since there was a greater

---

62 Bonet Donato, 'Obligaciones y contribuciones', pp. 308–10.
63 Pierre Bonneaud, *Els hospitalers catalans a la fi de l'edat Mitjana: L'orde de l'Hospital a Catalunya i a la Mediterrània, 1396–1472* (Lleida, 2008).
64 *Els catalans a la Mediterrània oriental a l'edat mitjana*, ed. Maria Teresa Ferrer i Mallol (Barcelona, 2003); Treppo, *I mercanti catalani*, pp. 2–92.
65 Delaville Le Roulx, *Les Hospitaliers*, pp. 25–27.
66 Carlos Barquero Goñi, *La Orden de San Juan de Jerusalén en Navarra, siglos XIV and XV* (Pamplona, 2004), p. 157. They continued to be charged in 1393, and the master appointed two treasurers for Hispania for that purpose: BNM, AOM 327, fols 93v–94r.
67 AHN, OOMM, San Juan de Jerusalén, folder 862, no 66–67 (1432).
68 Kevin Augerand, 'El camino hacia la incorporación de los maestrazgos de las órdenes militares castellanas en la Corona de Castilla 1476–1523', in *Palacios, plazas, patíbulos: la sociedad española*

interventionism in the appointment of positions in the crown of Castile. However, the same did not happen in the orders of the crown of Aragon, which continued to be named as before, although a letter of royal execution was necessary, which went beyond the mere oath of fidelity fixed in the time of James II.[69]

In relation to this order, and continuing the policies of Alfonso V the Magnanimous, we should mention the alignment of Mediterranean policies between the convent of Rhodes and Ferdinand II the Catholic and, later, his grandson Charles V. In Naples, Alfonso's only son, King Ferrante, also followed his father's path when, in 1480, he commanded ships to face the siege of the island, also foreshadowing the Catholic Monarchs' Mediterranean policies in relation to the order.[70] Therefore, there was an increased interest in aiding the resistance of the Rhodes stronghold, and the Hispanic fleet was present in the defence of the siege of Rhodes, helping the supply of the knights from peninsular domains from 1476 and, especially, from 1480.[71] In this year, the convent of Rhodes sent an appeal to their priories, insisting that the prior of Catalonia and the castellan of Amposta pay what they owed, given the extreme difficulties imposed by the siege, and also that they send knights.[72] In addition, Ferdinand II took the Hospitallers under his protection in the same year, and Queen Isabella issued a document safeguarding and providing clemency to those enrolled in the armada sent to Rhodes.[73] In keeping with this commitment to the defence of the Mediterranean, Ferdinand II consented to sending cereals from his kingdoms in 1481 and 1483, given the extreme needs on the island, as he expressed directly to the master of Rhodes.[74] Furthermore, the kings also intervened to ensure that the priories' shipments to the convent were sufficient and effective, and even arranged that certain sums collected for the peninsular crusade could be diverted to the convent of Rhodes.[75]

The full correlation between the eastern interests of the Hospital of St John and those of the Spanish monarchy corresponded well with the international policy of Ferdinand II the Catholic, who had a prominent interest in the region in Sicily. It should be remembered that a Christian league was organised against

---

moderna entre el cambio y las resistencias, ed. James S. Amelang et al. (Valencia, 2018), pp. 487–99 (here 490).

69 Barquero Goñi, *Los caballeros*, pp. 228–29.

70 Ettore Rossi, *Storia della marina: Dell'origine di S. Giovanni di Gerusalemme di Rodi e di Malta* (Roma, 1926), p. 24; Rossi, 'The Hospitallers at Rhodes, 1421–1523', in *The Fourteenth and Fifteenth Centuries*, ed. Harry W. Hazard, HC 3 (Madison, 1975), pp. 314–39 (here 325).

71 Fernando Suárez Bilbao, 'La orden de San Juan de Jerusalén en la defensa de Rodas, un bastión en el Mediterráneo', in *Actas del primer simposio histórico de la orden de San Juan en España* (Toledo, 2003), pp. 259–62.

72 BNM, AOM 387, fols 64v–65r, 126r.

73 *DIRC* 1, no. 67, pp. 107–8; Luis Suárez Fernández, *Los Reyes Católicos: El Tiempo de la Guerra de Granada* (Madrid, 1989), pp. 11–12, 26–27; Luis Suárez Fernández, *Política Internacional de Isabel la Católica* (Valladolid, 1965), p. 484.

74 Enric Bassegoda Pineda, 'Vida i obra de fra Bernat Hug de Rocabertí' (unpublished doctoral dissertation Univerity of Girona, 2009), p. 148.

75 Miguel Ángel Ladero Quesada, *La Hacienda Real de Castilla en el siglo XV* (La Laguna, 1973), p. 237.

the Turks in 1501, including Venice, Spain, Portugal, France, the papacy and the Hospitallers. The latter contributed four ships, each commanded by a leading figure from one tongue, such as the castellan of Amposta for the langue of Aragon.[76] After the conquest of Naples by Ferdinand II in 1504, Spain became the main power in the central Mediterranean, in keeping with Castilian North African policy.[77] The crown of Aragon, now in the Spanish context, recovered its Mediterranean dominion and was reoriented in accordance with Castilian traditions and interests. However, we should not forget the increasing strength of the Turks in the first decades of the sixteenth century, which practically only the Spanish Empire under Charles V could and did confront.[78] The actions carried out by the Catholic Kings constituted a political turn[79], which later crystallised in the donation by Emperor Charles V of the island of Malta to the Hospitallers, where, in a certain way, the Aragonese tradition was put at the service of the Castilian tradition. Malta's strategic position was justified by the conflict between Muslims and Christians for control of North Africa, in this case, between the Ottoman Empire and Spain. Charles V's donation sought to constitute the defence line pursued by the Castilians in Iberia in previous centuries. After the fall of Granada, Spain embarked on an expansive policy, not only in the Americas, but also beyond the Strait of Gibraltar in Africa. This led to the establishment of strongholds along the North African coast, authorised by the papacy and inspired by the old idea of reaching the Holy Land by this route.[80]

Concluding Thoughts

After the important conquests of al-Andalus, the Hispanic military orders became more dependent on the framework of royal and military policies, since they were preferred agents of the evolving crusading projects. In the final decades of the thirteenth and first decades of the fourteenth centuries, there were significant changes in the relationship between the monarchy, the papacy and the military orders. These new relationships corresponded to new situations, such as that following the abolition of the Temple. Although there were some breaches by these organisations, in general terms they met the new expectations.

Frontier military positions and obligations became increasingly relevant in the late Middle Ages, especially in the kingdom of Castile, although often in coordination with the crown of Aragon. Due to the different structure of the respective institutions in both polities and the royal policies regarding the Iberian

---

76 Giacomo Bosio, *Dell'istoria della sacra religione et illustrissima militia di San Giovanni gierosolimitano*, 3 vols (Roma, 1594–1602), 2: 441.
77 Norman Housley, *The Later Crusades*, p. 306.
78 Henry J. A. Sire, *The Knights of Malta* (New Haven, 1994), p. 60.
79 Barquero Goñi, *Los caballeros*, pp. 224–27.
80 Pavón Benito and Bonet Donato, 'La orden del Hospital en un mundo en cambio', p. 129.

Peninsula and the Mediterranean, the two crowns used the orders in different manners. In Castile, the orders were especially involved in the process of guarding a long frontier, contributing with all means, and they were object of greater interventionism. In Aragon, there was a certain ambiguity in the Hospitallers' commitment towards the *Reconquista*, as they were more involved in supporting Rhodes, especially with financial resources. Moreover, in the fifteenth century, Catalan and Aragonese commercial and political interests in the Eastern Mediterranean aligned with those of the Hospitallers.

It is important to underline that the comparisons or differentiations between the fight against Islam in neighbouring Hispanic regions, such as in the Strait of Gibraltar region in the case of Castile, and the fight in Outremer were present in the background of many of the demands and crusader discourses involving the orders. These parallels were highlighted, for example, at times such as in the middle of the offensive at Granada, when the Catholic Monarchs decided to send resources that had been collected for the peninsular crusade for the defence of Rhodes. However, some Aragonese kings had previously stopped the Hospitallers sending resources to Rhodes due to military breaches on the regional fronts against the enemies of the faith. The commitments of the Hospitallers in Outremer did not always correspond with their obligations, fundamentally with those due to the crown of Aragon. Nevertheless, in the mid-fifteenth century, these realities merged into a Mediterranean project which transcended the conquest of Granada in 1492 with the dynastic union that united the traditional Castilian policies around the Strait of Gibraltar with those of the crown of Aragon. This culminated in the order moving to Malta.

It is worth noting that there were papal actions which rewarded the military orders' support in the fight against Islam in the Iberian Peninsula with spiritual benefits, as participation in crusades had been rewarded at other times. This specificity of orders was reflected in the creation of military institutes in the service of the monarchy with specific crusade missions, as was the case with the ephemeral Order of Saint Mary of Spain and the Order of Montesa. This entanglement of interests between the military orders and the respective crowns raises interesting parallels with similar processes in the rest of Europe, as discussed in Paul Srodecki and Adam Szweda's chapters on the Teutonic Order's changing relations with the Polish crown in the fifteenth century. There are also certain similarities with regard to the ideological orientation of the respective orders. In fact, the increasing dependence on the various royal houses arising from the changing political conditions did not mean an abandonment of the high medieval crusade doctrine. Quite the opposite was the case: while simultaneously comparing their own efforts and ventures to the Levantine crusades, appeals to the holy war and to the defence of the Catholic faith against its enemies remained widespread constants in the quite dogmatic and — with regard to the intellectual changes of the renaissance zeitgeist — somehow quixotic self-perception of the military orders in Spain.[81]

Fig. 12. Equestrian seals of Alfonso X of Castile (top, from 1262), the founder of the Order of St Mary of Spain, and James II the Just of Aragon (bottom, from 1295), the founder of the Order of Montesa. Reproduced by Paul Srodecki from *Die Siegel der deutschen Kaiser und Könige von 751–1806 und 1871–1913*, ed. Otto Posse, 5 vols (Dresden, 1909–13), 1: fig. 38.1; Ferràn de Sagarra, *Sigillografía catalana: Invetari, descripció i estudi dels segells de Catalunya*, 5 vols (Barcelona, 1915-32), 1: fig. 40. Available online at https://w.wiki/8DDH and https://t1p.de/24pao [both accessed 20 November 2023], illustrations under public domain license.

---

81 On the ideological parallels between the various military orders' involvement in the Iberian *Reconquista* and the Teutonic Order's crusades in the Baltics, and on the awareness and perception of these parallels among respective contemporary players, see Paul Srodecki's chapter on the Teutonic Order in this volume.

MIHAI-D. GRIGORE

Army Inspection and Crusade

Wallachia and the Crusade Plans of Pope Leo X

At the beginning of the sixteenth century, Wallachia was not in an advantageous geopolitical position. Not only did its direct vicinity to the Ottoman Empire create a state of insecurity, but the plans of the sultans to launch a new offensive in Europe also considerably increased the risk that this Danube principality could possibly lose its autonomy and become — like Greece, Bulgaria and Serbia — an Ottoman province. The era of the so-called 'soldier-rulers' of Wallachia, as well as of Moldavia, were over; Vlad III 'the Impaler' died miserably in the 1470s, betrayed by his boyars. Stephen the Great of Moldavia, the only papal crusader of the Byzantine rite in the last decades of the fifteenth century, died in 1504, having submitted his country to Polish sovereignty and re-started payment of tribute to the Ottomans, whom he had so gloriously defied for a long time.[1]

In Wallachia, the period following the armed resistance to Ottoman expansion was one of suffering and consciousness of its own weakness. Romanian historians refer to it as the 'Romanian Baroque', an era characterised by military impotence on the one hand, but great cultural achievements and luxurious monuments on the other.[2] Wallachia's only hopes of ridding themselves of the Ottoman threat

---

1 Alexandru Simon, 'From Wallachia to Dacia: International Politics and Political Ideology in the Last Decades of the Fifteenth Century', in *Government and Law in Medieval Moldavia, Transylvania and Wallachia*, ed. Martyn Rady and Simon (Leicester, 2013), pp. 91–100 (here 91); Ștefan Ștefănescu, *Bănia în Țara Românească* (București, 1965), p. 101; Șerban Papacostea, 'La Moldavie état tributaire de l'Empire Ottoman au XVe siècle, le cadre international des rapports etablis en 1455–1456', *Revue roumaine d'histoire* 13 (1974), 445–61; Nicolae Stoicescu, *Vlad Țepeș* (București, 1976); Veniamin Ciobanu, *Țările Române și Polonia* (București, 1985), pp. 78–79; Ștefan S. Gorovei, 'Pacea moldo-otomană din 1486: Observații pe marginea unor texte', in *Ștefan cel Mare și Sfânt: Portret în istorie*, ed. Mitropolia Rădăuților (Putna, 2004), pp. 496–515; Ovidiu Cristea, 'Pacea din 1486 și relațiile lui Ștefan cel Mare cu Imperiul Otoman în ultima parte a domniei', in *Revista istorică* 15 (2004), 25–36; Eugen Denize, *Românii între Leu și Semilună. Relațiile turco-venețiene și influența lor asupra spațiului românesc sec XV-XVI* (Târgoviște, 2009), p. 127; Liviu Pilat and Ovidiu Cristea, *The Ottoman Threat and Crusading on the Eastern Border of Christendom During the 15th Century* (Leiden, 2018), p. 180.

2 Edgar Papu, *Barocul ca tip de existență*, 2 vols (București, 1977), 2: 250–51; Edgar Papu, *Din clasicii noștri. Contribuții la ideea unui protocronism românesc* (București, 1977), pp. 20–22.

vanished at Kosovo Field (1389, 1448), Nicopolis (1396) and Varna (1444).[3] Under Vlad Dracul and his son, Vlad the Impaler, there were only minor attempts to keep the almighty Ottoman Turks at bay.[4] Under the princes Radu the Great (r. 1495–1508) and Neagoe Basarab (r. 1512–21), Wallachia had a lengthy and quiet period in which to develop its economy and culture, albeit with the hard price of the tribute imposed by the Ottomans increasing from 8,000 ducats at the end of the fifteenth century to 10,000 ducats during the reign of Neagoe Basarab.[5]

However, the dreams of throwing off the Ottoman yoke never disappeared from the political actions of the Wallachian rulers at the beginning of the sixteenth century. Not only did they try to influence the civil war in the Ottoman Empire in the final years of Sultan Bayezid II's reign (1481–1512) in their favour, as shown below, they also created a broad network among the Christian European powers, with the goal of waging a powerful and well-organised crusade (although they never used this term) or such capable of throwing the Ottomans back in Asia and — why not — reconquering Constantinople, that symbol of Eastern Christianity and — third to Jerusalem and Rome — also of the Christian West.[6]

At the heart of this ambitious and very subversive policy was a most unlikely ruler: Neagoe Basarab, who ruled Wallachia from 1512 through 1521, was a scholar prince, a boyar's offspring from outside the dynastic succession of the country, who was not well viewed by the new Ottoman sultan Selim I (r. 1512–20). It was Basarab who responded immediately to the crusade plans of Pope Leo X (r. 1513–21), and who pushed the Hungarians and Poles to build a new Christian alliance in order to free the European southeast from the Ottomans.

In the following, I will begin by analysing the geopolitical situation of Wallachia at the beginning of the sixteenth century in the context of the Ottoman Civil War (1509–13). After that I will discuss Prince Neagoe Basarab and his diplomatic network, with a special focus on his legations to the Venetians and to Pope Leo X, as well as on his contacts with the Hungarian and Polish courts in the matter of crusade, before finally closing with several short theoretical conclusions.

---

3 Carl Göllner, 'Zur Problematik der Kreuzzüge und der Türkenkriege im 16. Jahrhundert', *RESEE* 13 (1975), 1–19 (here 2).
4 Sergiu Columbeanu, *Radu Valentin, Vlad Dracul (1436–42, 1443–47)* (București, 1978), pp. 71, 88; Vasile Mărculeț, *Ioan de Hunedoara și cruciada antiotomană târzie în viziunea istoriografiei bizantine din secolele XV–XVI* (București, 2004), pp. 41–42; Liviu Pilat, 'The 1487 Crusade: A Turning Point in the Moldavian-Polish Relations', *Medieval and Early Modern Studies for Central and Eastern Europe* 2 (2010), 123–36; Matei Cazacu, *Dracula* (Leiden, 2011), p. 43.
5 Tashin Gemil, *Românii și otomanii în secolele XIV–XVI* (București, 1991), p. 77. See also Mihail Guboglu, 'Le tribute payé par les principautés roumaines à la Porte jusqu'au début du XVIe siècle, d'apres les sources turques', *Revue des études islamiques* 1 (1969), 49–80 (here 62–64); Vlad Georgescu, Stelian Neagoe, *Istoria Românilor de la origini până în zilele noastre* (București, 1995), p. 67; Bogdan Murgescu, *Țările Române între Imperiul Otoman și Europa Creștină* (Iași, 2012), pp. 136–37.
6 Simon, 'From Wallachia', pp. 97–100; Mihai-D. Grigore, *Neagoe Basarab — Princeps Christianus: Christianitas-Semantik im Vergleich mit Erasmus, Luther und Machiavelli (1513–23)* (Frankfurt am Main, 2015), p. 73.

Sow the Wind and Reap the Whirlwind

The merits of the Wallachian princes Mihnea 'the Evil' (r. 1508–9) and Vlad the Young (r. 1510–12) were that they tried once more to emancipate Wallachia from Ottoman influence and to restore its independence.[7] However, their policy of force was condemned to fail in the context of the strengthening Ottoman power at the beginning of the sixteenth century. Vlad the Young, a mere boy at sixteen years of age, was able enough to find an important ally against the Ottomans, taking an oath of allegiance to the Jagiellonian king Vladislas II of Bohemia (r. 1271–1516) and of Hungary (r. 1490–1516) in 1510.[8] Moreover, he also sought to benefit from the Ottoman Civil War in Sultan Bayezid II's final years.[9]

The elderly and infirm sultan sought to determine his successor during his lifetime, identifying his eldest son, Ahmed. He was attempting to ensure a smooth transition to a new ruler, even killing his own offspring who were already intriguing to gain the throne at the expense of Ahmed: therefore, Bayezid II had two of his sons, Şehinşah and Mehmed, put to death and proclaimed Ahmed as his successor. He was too hasty in doing so, however, because he had not taken the time to persuade the Janissaries to support Ahmed. He would also have needed more money in order to bribe them, and he certainly did not take into account their stubbornness and loyalty to his other son, Selim, who at the time was governor of Trebizond (Turk. Trabzon). Selim rebelled against the decision of his father and, in 1511, with Tatar assistance, challenged the troops of the old sultan in Thrace.[10]

This was the moment for the Wallachian prince Vlad the Young to intervene and to offer military aid to Selim against his father.[11] The sources do not comment

---

7 Alexandru Lapedatu, 'Mihnea-cel-Rău și ungurii 1508–1510', *Anuarul Institutului de Istorie Națională Cluj* 1 (1921–22), 46–77; Constantin C. Giurescu and Dinu C. Giurescu, *Istoria Românilor*, 2 vols (București, 1975), 2: 223–25. See for instance the letter of Vlad the Young to the patricians of Hermannstadt (mod. Sibiu, Romania), asking them in 1511 for weapons against the Ottoman Turks. Nicolae Iorga, *Scrisori de boieri, scrisori de domni*, 2nd edn (Vălenii de Munte, 1925), no. 12, pp. 181–82.
8 Constantin Rezachevici, *Cronologia critică a domnilor din Țara Românească și Moldova* (București, 2001), p. 140; *Istoria politicii externe românești în date*, ed. Ion Calafeteanu (București, 2003), p. 39–40; George Coandă, *Istoria Târgoviștei: cronologie enciclopedică* (Târgoviște, 2005), p. 78.
9 *Der fromme Sultan Bayezid: Die Geschichte seiner Herrschaft (1481–1512) nach den altosmanischen Chroniken des Oruç und des Anonymus Hanivaldanus*, ed. Richard F. Kreutel (Graz, 1978), pp. 10–17; Hedda Reindl, *Männer um Bayezid: Eine prosopographische Studie über die Epoche Sultan Bayezids II. (1481–1512)* (Berlin, 1983), pp. 85–99; Douglas A. Howard, *Das Osmanische Reich 1300–1924* (Darmstadt, 2018), pp. 116–17.
10 Selim married a Tatar princess as a letter of Sigismund the Jagiellonian, king of Poland and grand duke of Lithuania (1507–48), informs in 1511, *DIR* 2/3, no. 27, p. 24. Selim had also strong familial bonds to the Tatars, as shown by a letter of the same Sigismund, *DIR* 2/3, no. 35, p. 30 (see also no 53, pp. 45–46).
11 Radu Popescu Vornicul, 'Istoriile Domnilor Țărâi Rumânești', in *Cronicari munteni*, ed. by Mihail Gregorian (București, 1961), pp. 225–577 (here 260–62); Kreutel, *Sultan Bayezid*, pp. 254–60; Manole Neagoe, *Neagoe Basarab* (București, 1971), pp. 47–52. The alliance of the 'Wallachians' —

on this, but it can be supposed that the young prince hoped that, in aiding Selim, he would prolong the war and thereby win time for other subjects of the Ottoman Empire to rise against their suppressors, as was the case with the numerous rebellions of the Shiite Qizilbash in the eastern provinces instigated by the Persian shah. Selim and his Wallachian and Tartar allies lost the battle in Thrace and was forced to flee to Crimea. The other pretender to the throne, Ahmed, succeeded in conquering the strategic town of Karaman and advanced on Constantinople. In the middle of such intrigues and betrayal, the old sultan Bayezid lost his head and, fearing that Ahmed would kill him in order to gain the throne, forbade him to enter the city. This gave Selim enough time to obtain the aid of the Janissaries and to force his father to declare him sultan. In this position, he executed his other two brothers, Ahmed and Korkut, together with all his nephews, so that there were no longer any rivals to the throne.

Vlad also had to pay dearly for the aid he offered Selim in 1511. In January 1512 — Selim was not sultan yet –, he was confronted with a powerful Ottoman army from Nicopolis, led by Mihailoglu Mehmed, who brought with him a new pretender to the Wallachian throne, Neagoe Basarab (born around 1482), the offspring of the Craiovescu boyar family. After the lost battle near Bucharest, Vlad the Young was beheaded.[12] Neagoe Basarab thus started his promising reign by usurping the throne of Wallachia illegitimately.[13]

Wallachian Machiavellianism

Neagoe Basarab would prove not to be the docile marionette on the northern border that the Ottomans were hoping for. On the contrary he tried — as Radu the Great had previously done[14] — to balance Ottoman influence and power by cultivating close relations with the Christian powers in the West. Neagoe Basarab acceded to the Wallachian throne at the end of January 1512. Three months later, Selim became sultan of the Ottoman Empire. He was not happy at all to see his supporter, Vlad the Young, dead and Wallachia's throne in the hands of a non-dynastic successor with issues of legitimacy.

---

meant is for sure Vlad the Young — with Selim is mentioned in a letter of Sigismund the Jagiellonian from 1512, *DIR* 2/3, no. 46, p. 40.

12 Gavriil Protul, *Viața Sfântului Nifon*, ed. Vasile Grecu (București, 1944), pp. 135–37; Anonymus Cantacuzenos, 'Istoriia Țării Românești de când au descălecat pravoslavnicii creștini', in *Cronicari munteni*, ed. by Mihail Gregorian (București, 1961), pp. 81–224 (here 98); Rezachevici, *Cronologia*, pp. 141–42.

13 Grigore, *Neagoe Basarab*, pp. 41–46.

14 Radu the Great provided the Transylvanians and the Hungarians with information about the Ottomans and their moves. He had, in return, the pretention to be also informed about the Hungarians' and Transylvanians' intentions. *Documente istorice slavo-române din Țara-Românească și Moldova privitoare la legăturile cu Ardealul 1346–1603*, ed. Grigore Tocilescu (București, 1931), nos 193–94, pp. 184–86.

Therefore, seen from Basarab's perspective, the Wallachian ruler had three reasons for supporting the idea of a new crusade: (1) he was an illegitimate ruler; therefore, he *had* to gain legitimation not by blood, but through his deeds, demonstrating to all his critics that, by combating the infidels, he was fully deserving of the epithets in his princely title, 'most faithful and orthodox lord'. (2) Basarab was also aware that Selim I would take the first opportunity to depose him from the Wallachian throne;[15] therefore, he had to do something, all the more so that Selim and his troops were, at that moment, busy in Anatolia with the Shiite Safavid state and, after that, in North Africa with the war against the Mamluks. (3) Basarab, like all his predecessors, was a convinced enemy of the Ottomans.

Nevertheless, he had to be careful: this is why one of his first actions as prince of Wallachia was to travel to Constantinople to renew the tribute contract with Selim.[16] Negotiating skilfully, Basarab convinced the sultan to recognise his rule and to confirm him on the throne by conferring upon him the insignia of authority: kaftan, sanjak and drum. He had, however, to increase his tribute in order to achieve this, which demonstrates that Selim was also prepared to make some concessions, and negotiate with an antipathetic partner, in order to secure peace on the northern borders, given that he was preoccupied with the army in the empire's southern provinces. Basarab also consciously accepted a double vassal relation, to the Ottoman Turks on the one hand, and to the Hungarians on the other hand. In this politicking, we recognise the Machiavellian principle that a ruler should be clever like a fox and resolute like a lion.[17]

A first step on the path to a possible crusade was for Basarab to transform his country into a platform for diplomatic networks and the exchange of information. He reported regularly to the Hungarian crown on the Ottomans' actions, a fact confirmed in a 1513 letter of King Vladislas II.[18] On the other hand, the Hungarians attempted to mediate between the Danubian principalities of Moldavia and Wallachia, which were at war with each other, since these countries were the best transit route to the Balkans in the eventuality of a major movement of forces south of the Danube.[19] Neagoe Basarab was aware of the geostrategic position of his principality, laying on the path of Hungarian and Polish embassies to Constantinople and back.[20] Therefore, the Wallachian prince insisted that all foreign legations passing through provide an account of their business in the Ottoman

---

15 DIR 2/3, no. 55, p. 47: *Vojevoda namque Transalpinus [...] Selimbegk timet*.
16 *Documents Concerning Romanian History (1427–1601), Collected from the British Archives*, ed. Eric D. Tappe (The Hague, 1964), no. 6, pp. 20–21. See also Manole Neagoe, 'Politica externă a lui Neagoe Basarab', *Studii: Revistă de istorie* 19 (1966), 745–64 (here 747).
17 Grigore, *Neagoe Basarab*, p. 97.
18 *Documente istorice*, no. 270, pp. 260–61.
19 DIR 2/3, nos 65–66, pp. 60–61.
20 See for instance the letter of Vladislas II to Neagoe Basarab, biding him to take care of his ambassador to the Ottomans, who was supposed to cross the Wallachian territory, in *Acta et epistolae relationum Transylvaniae Hungariaeque cum Moldavia et Valachia*, ed. Andreas Veress, 1 vol. (Budapest, 1914), 1, no. 81, pp. 105–6. See also the report from 1515 of the Ragusan Felix Petanius — diplomat

capital, as was the case, for instance, with the Polish ambassador Jerzy Krupski (1472–1548), who crossed Wallachia in 1513 on his way to Constantinople and had to make use of the hospitality of Neagoe Basarab for several days.[21]

The capital city of Wallachia, Târgoviște, became a meeting point for diplomatic routes from the European courts on the way to or from the Sublime Porte. There are accounts that different legations planned to meet in Târgoviște to agree a common strategy towards the sultan.[22] However, Neagoe Basarab was not merely an intermediary between the great powers. He himself was often the purpose of secret legations, for example that of the same Polish legate mentioned above, Jerzy Krupski, in 1514 or of the Hungarian embassy of Malm Horvath in 1520, who informed the Wallachian ruler of the imminent plans for an anti-Ottoman offensive.[23]

Planning the Crusade

On 1 February 1518, Neagoe Basarab's ambassador, Jeronim Matijević, arrived in Venice. During his stay, he discussed the possibility of organising a united Christian front against the Ottoman Empire. The Ottomans had recently harmed Venetian interests in the Eastern Mediterranean by conquering Syria and Egypt. The ambassador handed over a gift sent by Neagoe Basarab, a gilded silver cup, and in return Matijević received the accolade from the doge (*per il Serenissimo Principe nostro fato cavalier*), together with a garment worth 100 ducats (*una vesta di panno d'oro, in la qual non si spendi più di ducati 100*).[24] After two months in Venice, the same legate appeared again as Basarab's ambassador in the republic of Ragusa. We do not know what his business there was — Jeronim Matijević was born a Ragusan — but it is not impossible that he approached the Ragusan authorities in the anti-Ottoman matter.

In January 1519, the princes of Wallachia and Moldavia, Neagoe Basarab and Stephen IV the Younger (r. 1517–27), sent a common embassy to Rome, which demonstrates the common interests of both countries in the matter of the crusade.[25] This was led by the Greek diplomat Antonios Paikalas and approached Pope Leo X about his crusading plans. Paikalas delivered the firm commitment of the Wallachian and Moldavia lords that they and their successors would offer all the military power at their disposal in the event of a new crusade. They were ready to join the Christian *expeditio* against the Ottomans (*Principum christianorum*

---

at Vladislas II's court and author of *Historia Turcica* (1502) — on the diplomatic routes through Wallachia in *Acta et epistolae relationum Transylvaniae* 1, no. 85, pp. 110–11.

21 *DIR* 2/3, no. 83, p. 79.
22 *DIR* 2/3, nos 139–40, pp. 151–53.
23 *DIR* 2/3, no. 136, p. 147.
24 *Archiva istorică a României*, ed. Bogdan Petriceicu Hașdeu, 5 vols (București 1865–67), 1.1: 284.
25 Eugen Denize, *Țările Române și Veneția. Relațiile politice (1441–1541)* (București, 1995), p. 186.

sancta adversus Selinum Turcarum tyrannum expeditio) and promised that they would not sign any armistice or peace treaty with the sultan without the pope's consent (*sanctae sedis licentia*). In return — as Paikalas said to the pope — the princes were expecting to receive a part of the re-conquered territories on the Balkans.[26]

Pope Leo X had already started organising a new crusade as early as 1513, when he delegated Archbishop Thomas of Esztergom to preach the new enterprise around Poland, Hungary, and Wallachia (*ad sumendam at faciendam in Turcos et Tartaros sanctam et imprimis necessariam expeditionem*).[27] It seems that Neagoe Basarab, who was ardently Orthodox, did not hinder the high Roman prelate from preaching the crusade in his country. After 1517, the pope intensified his efforts for a new crusade and Neagoe Basarab was very receptive of this.[28] He saw a good opportunity for a quick and efficient reconquest, since Sultan Selim I was with his army in Egypt.[29] Pope Leo, who was very well informed about Selim's wars in Persia and Egypt, thought the same.[30] The pope imagined the Moldavians and Wallachians being joined by the expeditionary corps of Sigismund the Jagiellonian, king of Poland and grand duke of Lithuania, and engaging the Ottomans on the lower Danube. This could not be defended by the Ottomans, since their armies had only just conquered the Mamluk possessions and were about to conquer new territories in Asia.[31]

---

26 *DIR* 2/3, no. 224, pp. 307–9.
27 *DIR* 2/3, no. 119, p. 113.
28 Neagoe, 'Politica externă', p. 757.
29 For Selim's Egyptian wars against the Mamluks, see Mustafa M. Ziada, 'The Mamluk Sultans 1291–1517', in *The Fourteenth and Fifteenth Centuries*, ed. Harry W. Hazard, HC 3 (Madison, 1975), pp. 486–512 (here 511); Michael Winter, 'The Ottoman Occupation', in *The Cambridge History of Egypt*, ed. Carl F. Petry and M. W. Daly, 2 vols (Cambridge, 1998), 1: 498–516 (here 498–502); Gábor Ágoston, 'Selim I', in *Encyclopedia of Ottoman Empire*, ed. Gábor Àgoston and Bruce Masters (New York, 2009), pp. 511–13 (here 512–13); Michael Winter, 'The Conquest of Syria and Egypt by Sultan Selim I, According to Evlya Celebi', in *The Mamluk-Ottoman Transition*, ed. Stephan Conermann and Gül Sen (Bonn, 2017), pp. 127–43 (here 131–42).
30 Carl Göllner, *Tvrcica: Die europäischen Türkendrücke des XVI. Jahrhunderts*, 3 vols (Bucureşti, 1961–78), 1: no. 84, p. 64.
31 *Négociations de la France dans le Levant ou correspondances, mémoires et actes diplomatiques des ambassadeurs de France à Constantinople et des ambassadeurs, envoyés ou résidents à divers titres à Venise, Raguse, Rome, Malte et Jérusalem, en Turquie, Perse, Géorgie, Crimée, Syrie, Égypte, etc., et dans les états de Tunis, d'Alger et de Maroc*, ed. Ernest Charrierè, 4 vols (Paris, 1848–60), 1: 59: *Et, his tribus nationibus Scytharum, Moldavie ac Valahie copiis exercitibus suis adjectis, poterit Polonie rex predictam suam expeditionem Modram versus et Chiliam oppidum dirigere.* […] [Q]uam *Turcharum tyrannus non ad eas regiones sed potius ad conservandam Syriam, Arabiam et Africam, quas nuper suae ditioni subjecit, aut versus alias partes Asie animum intendet.* 'And joining with the forces of these three Scythic nations to Wallachia's and Moldavia's armies, the king of Poland will be able to lead the mentioned expedition towards Modra and [further] to Chilia. Because the tyrant of the Turks will not [come] to those regions, but will rather preserve the provinces Syria, Arabia and Africa, which he newly conquered, or will dedicate his attention to other territories in Asia'.

The new impetus in the papal policy for a new crusade could be felt all around the Latin world: numerous reports on the situation of the fight against the Ottoman Empire, reports on the deeds and actions of the Ottomans, and chronicles on the history, culture, and religion of the Ottoman Turks etc. all reveal a new mood, which Pope Leo took over and intensified.[32] In 1518, Leo felt that the time had finally come to proclaim the crusade. In the late Middle Ages and the early modern period, this idea was far from dead, and both Innocent VIII (r. 1484–92) and Alexander VI (r. 1492–1503) had already tried to organise a major expedition against the *infideles*.[33] The final session of the Fifth Lateran Council on 16 March 1517 was dedicated to the war against the Ottoman Empire.[34] The following year, on 6 March 1518, Leo organised great processions and ceremonies in Rome to celebrate the *pernecessaria contra catholice fidei hostes expeditio* ('very necessary expedition against the enemies of the Catholic faith', which means in fact the crusade) against the 'unbelievers', proclaimed by the bull *Considerantes ac animo revolventes* ('Thoughtful and coming back to sense').[35]

All the classical criteria to confer the status of crusade upon this military expedition were in place: (1) the Roman pontifex promulgated the expedition at an (ecumenical) council. (2) The canonical mechanism of indulgences granted the crusaders the *remissio peccatorum* ('absolution of all sins').[36] (3) A general truce or a *Pax Dei* among Christian princes (*pax inter eos aut treugae*) — reinforced by a so-called *militia pacis* ('peace militia') and by symbolic penalties of excommunication and anathema — preceded the promulgation of the crusade.[37] (4) The crusade claimed the goal of the liberation of the holy sites (i.e. Jerusalem). (5) The salvation of the souls of the participants in the crusade was promised. (6) The crusaders were understood to be a *militia Christi*.[38] It is only the idea of the crusade as a form of pilgrimage which is not present, as well as the

---

32 Göllner, *Tvrcica* 1: 46–52. See also Hans Joachim Kissling, 'Türkenfurcht und Türkenhoffnung im 15.–16. Jahrhundert', *SOF* 23 (1964), 1–18.
33 Jacob Ter Meulen, *Der Gedanke der Internationalen Organisation in seiner Entwicklung 1300–1800* (Haag, 1917), pp. 29–30; Nicolae Iorga, *Notes et extraits pour servir à l'histoire des croisades au XVe siècle*, 6 vols (Paris, 1899–1916); Mihail Berza, 'Der Kreuzzug gegen die Türken ein europäisches Problem', *Revue Historique du Sud-Est Européen* 19 (1942), 48–62; Göllner, 'Zur Problematik der Kreuzzüge', pp. 1–2; Georg Wagner, 'Der letzte Türkenkreuzzugsplan Kaiser Maximilians I. aus dem Jahre 1517', *MIÖG* 77 (1969), 314–53 (here 314–19).
34 Wagner, 'Der letzte Türkenkreuzzugsplan', p. 325; Charrierè, *Négociations*, pp. 65, 67. The proclamation of the five years truce in the bull *Ac animo considerantes* has been confirmed in a separate treaty from 2 October 1518, *Tractatus et Confoederatio generalis Pacis et Concordiae*, where a *quinquennalis treuga*, a five year-truce, was promulgated (Ter Meulen, *Gedanke*, p. 138).
35 Charrierè, *Négociations*, p. 64. See also Göllner, *Tvrcica* 1, no. 86, p. 64.
36 Göllner, *Tvrcica* 1, nos 87–88, 90, pp. 66–67.
37 Wagner, 'Der letzte Türkenkreuzzugsplan', p. 325; Charrierè, *Négociations*, pp. 65, 67. The proclamation of the five years truce in the bull *Ac animo considerantes* has been confirmed in a separate treaty from 2 October 1518, *Tractatus et Confoederatio generalis Pacis et Concordiae*, where a *quinquennalis treuga*, a five year-truce, was promulgated (Ter Meulen, *Gedanke*, p. 138).
38 The exactly term was *fraternitas Sanctae Cruciatae* (Wagner, 'Der letzte Türkenkreuzzugsplan', p. 322). For the criteria of crusade, see Mihai-D. Grigore, *Ehre und Gesellschaft: Ehrkonstrukte und soziale Ordnungsvorstellungen am Beispiel des Gottesfriedens (10. bis 11. Jahrhundert)* (Darmstadt, 2009), p. 356.

idea of the crusade as a form of mission seeking to convert infidels to the true faith. All of these elements conferred upon Leo's proclamation the credibility and authenticity of a real crusade, locating it within the high medieval crusading tradition, started by Pope Urban II at Clermont and refined in the twelfth and thirteenth centuries.[39]

On the other hand, Pope Leo X was also convinced of the important role which Wallachia and Moldavia could play in the war. In 1516, King Vladislas II of Bohemia and Hungary had already pointed out the major importance of Wallachia and Moldavia for the crusade in the correspondence with his younger brother, Sigismund of Poland and Lithuania.[40] He alluded that no crusade would be possible without these countries, so they — said the king — must *not* be lost to the Ottomans, because they 'are forewalls put in front of us' (*antemuralia praeposita sunt*) and their fall would also mean the fall of Central Europe.[41] The Ottomans themselves were also aware of the role played by Wallachia and Moldavia in the Christian anti-Ottoman coalition, as is revealed by the Tartar incursions into Moldavia in 1518, intended to punish Prince Stephen the Young for his participation in the anti-Ottoman alliance.[42] Furthermore, the importance of Wallachia for the crusade is revealed by the fact that the pope enfeoffed Neagoe Basarab *ante factum* with Balkan territories, i.e. before they had even been re-conquered from the Ottomans.[43]

The pope's plans had already been made: together with the Poles, the Hungarians, and the Wallachians, the Holy Roman Empire was to attack the Balkan provinces of the Ottoman Empire. At the same time, French and Italian troops were to land in Epirus and attempt to march from there on Constantinople, while the Germans and their allies pinned down the Ottoman army in Rumelia. The direct assault on the city was to be made by English, Portuguese and Spanish expeditionary corps.[44]

---

39 For a general overview, see Paul Srodecki, 'Crusading on the Periphery in the High Middle Ages: Main Debates, New Approaches', in *The Expansion of the Faith: Crusading on the Frontiers of Latin Christendom in the High Middle Ages*, ed. Srodecki and Norbert Kersken (Turnhout, 2022), pp. 29–52; Nikolas Jaspert, *Die Kreuzzüge*, 6th edn (Darmstadt, 2013), pp. 12–13 (crusade as just war to bring martyrdom and redemption), pp. 16–18 (crusade and peace/truce of God), pp. 19–21 (crusade and pilgrimage), pp. 29–31 (crusade and indulgences); Jean Richard, 'La Croisade l'évolution des conceptions et des stratégies', in *From Clermont to Jerusalem: The Crusades and Crusader Societies 1095–1500*, ed. Alan V. Murray (Turnhout, 1998), pp. 3–25 (especially 4–5).
40 Horia I. Ursu, *Moldova în contextul politic european (1517–27)* (București, 1972), p. 22.
41 *DIR* 2/3, no. 193, pp. 246–47.
42 Ursu, *Moldova*, pp. 29–32.
43 *Documents Concerning Romanian History*, no. 6, pp. 20–21. To offer Ottoman territories not yet conquered was a general policy of the papacy and of the Western princes. It was maybe a way to motivate the participation at the crusade. See Ter Meulen, *Gedanke*, pp. 129, 132, 135.
44 Martinus Crusius, *Germano-Graeciae Libri Sex* (Basel, 1585), p. 156: *Caesar cum Germanis, Vngaris, Polonis in Bossinam & Thraciam descenderet; Gallus, Itali, Veneti, Heluetij, in Epeirum è Brundusio traijicerent: & et in Graeciam, Christianis refertam, desecturam, irruerent: Hispaniae veró, Lusitaniae, & Angliae Reges, CC. nauibus, per Callipolitanum fretum Constantinopolin contenderent.* 'The emperor

Given that Neagoe Basarab had committed to provide Pope Leo X with all the military assistance at his disposal, it might be worth considering how powerful Wallachia really was at the beginning of the sixteenth century. In a letter from 26 April 1520, Neagoe Basarab informed the city council of Kronstadt (mod. Brașov, Romania, Hung. Brassó) that they might announce to their king — i.e. King Louis II of Bohemia and Hungary (r. 1516–26) — that he was ready: on the pretext of inspecting his army, he was able to assemble forty thousand soldiers.[45] The same was true in Moldavia which, at the beginning of the sixteenth century, was able to raise at least thirty-five thousand soldiers. In 1518, Stephen the Young of Moldavia was able to crush a Tartar host of c. 25,000 men, which suggests that the Moldavians must have been able to deploy at least thirty thousand, a force summoned — *nota bene* — in an extremely short period of time.[46]

However, Leo X's crusading plans vanished definitively with Luther and the onset of the Reformation.[47] The Christian princes were reluctant to support Leo's crusading project in any case and had an equivocal attitude towards it. This is not to mention their tendencies to come to good terms with the sultan on their own account, rather than combatting him together.[48] These plans were unrealistic anyway, if one considers the quarrels and discord among the European Christian powers, which hindered the coagulation of an anti-Ottoman front. In September 1520, Sultan Selim I, who had had no major policies in Europe, died. He was replaced by the worst enemy Europe could have expected: Suleiman the Magnificent (r. 1520–66). Neagoe Basarab died a year later, in September 1521, but not before the bitter experience of the fall of Belgrade on 28 August 1521, the strategic key to Europe. Finally, Pope Leo X also died in December 1521. In 1522, Suleiman the Magnificent conquered Rhodes from the Hospitallers and, in 1526, crushed the Hungarians at Mohács. Three years later, the Ottomans were at the gates of Vienna. Any crusading plans were now definitely dead, and the Europeans' only aim now was to survive the war which the 'infidels' brought *to* them, in their very own home.

---

should descend with the Germans, Hungarians, Poles towards Bosnia and Thracia; the French, Italians, Venetians, Helvetians should push forward in Epirus going form Brundisi; but the kings of Spain, Portugal and England should make haste on Constantinople, via the strait of Gallipoli, with their 200 ships'. See also Wagner, 'Der letzte Türkenkreuzzugsplan', p. 322. Furthermore (pp. 324–27), Wagner shows that such detailed crusade plans of the pope, emperor, king of France, etc., were plenty. However, their realisation remained a desideratum.

45 Iorga, *Scrisori*, no. 14, p. 185.
46 Mihai Adauge, 'Invazia tătarilor în vara anului 1518 și lupta de la Ștefănești. Reconstituire', *Revista militară* 2 (2012), 70–87 (here 78–79).
47 Ter Meulen, *Gedanke*, p. 30. Protestant propaganda saw in the pope's money collection for the crusade only a pretext to impoverish the German lands, without really to intend an expedition against the Ottomans. See, for instance, Göllner, *Tvrcica* 1, no. 100, p. 70; Ehrenfried Hermann, 'Türken und Osmanenreich in der Vorstellung der Zeitgenossen Luthers' (unpublished doctoral dissertation, Albert Ludwig University of Freiburg, 1961), p. 6; Göllner, 'Zur Problematik der Kreuzzüge', pp. 6–7, 12.
48 Ter Meulen, *Gedanke*, pp. 128–29, 133, 137; Göllner, 'Zur Problematik der Kreuzzüge', pp. 3–4.

Conclusions

I attempted to show how, in fact, diplomatic networks aiming to organise a crusade break this dichotomy between a 'core' and a 'periphery' in the crusading phenomenology. In the later Middle Ages, important players were present in Western, Central and South-Eastern Europe. The most dynamic impulses on the path to the late crusades actually came from East-Central and South-Eastern European rulers: Mircea I and Vlad Dracul of Wallachia, the Transylvanian voivode John of Hunyad, and Stephen the Great of Moldavia, not to mention the Polish and the Hungarian kings. As a result of their proximity and vassal status in relation to the Turks, the Wallachian and Moldavian princes were necessarily cautious in their anti-Ottoman policies, leading to elaborate diplomatic relations with the major Western actors involved in the crusade project. The crusade against the 'infidels' was not only a strong legitimation of their rule in front of their subjects, it also offered a form of European integration within a common project, therefore serving as a form of legitimation as an actor on the international stage. Although devoted to their Eastern Orthodox faith, the Wallachian princes did not consider the doctrinal differences between Eastern and Western Christianity to pose an obstacle to their participation in this joint European undertaking of 'all' Christians. At the same time, the papacy sought to play down all allusions to the 'schismatic' situation of the South-Eastern Europeans. The 'confessional' differences were therefore replaced by common Christian beliefs which, in the 'crusade', saw the justified modality of combatting the 'infidels' on all levels, religious, symbolical, military, and propagandistic. Following the Ottoman conquest of Constantinople, the new target of the crusade narrative became the liberation of the imperial city of Constantinople, which thus replaced in the imagery Jerusalem, the 'classical' centre of crusading efforts, following its final loss to the Muslims in 1244.

Part II

Chivalry and Nobility

DALIBOR JANIŠ

The Bohemo-Moravian Nobility and the Baltic Crusades of the Bohemian Kings Ottokar II Premislas and John of Luxemburg in the Thirteenth and Fourteenth Centuries*

Introduction

Czech historiography has not paid a great deal of attention to the history of the crusades to the Baltics. Only a few authors have discussed this issue, starting with the Czech historian and expert on the Middle Ages, Jaroslav Goll, one of the founders of critical historiography in the Czech lands. In 1897, he published a comprehensive monograph on Bohemia and Prussia in the Middle Ages in which, on the basis of the available sources, he attempted to provide a critical viewpoint on the crusades of the Czech sovereigns to the south-eastern Baltic Sea region in the thirteenth and fourteenth centuries.[1] Later, the issue of the crusades to Prussia was mentioned repeatedly in the monographs dedicated to the Přemyslid and Luxemburg dynasties. The older comprehensive works of Václav Novotný and Josef Šusta, or the 1994 biography of John of Bohemia by Jiří Spěváček are also worthy of note.[2] However, these works do not provide a comprehensive overview of the participation of Czech nobles in the crusades to Prussia in the thirteenth

---

* This study was developed within the project *Norms and Values in the Medieval Society*, Reg. nr. SGS 08/FF/2018–19, University of Ostrava, the Czech Republic.

[1] Jaroslav Goll, *Čechy a Prusy ve středověku* (Praha, 1897). For a recent and wider analysis of historiographical issues, see Sven Ekdahl, 'Crusades and Colonisation in the Baltic: A Historiographic Analysis', in *The North-Eastern Frontiers of Medieval Europe: The Expansion of Latin Christendom in the Baltic Lands*, ed. Alan V. Murray (Farnham, 2016), pp. 1–42.

[2] Václav Novotný, *Rozmach české moci za Přemysla II. Otakara (1253–71)* (Praha, 1937), pp. 22–29, 151–62; Josef Šusta, *Král cizinec* (Praha, 1939), pp. 462–70; Josef Šusta, *Karel IV: Otec a syn* (Praha, 1946), pp. 236–54, 430–38; Jiří Spěváček, *Jan Lucemburský a jeho doba 1296–1346: K prvnímu vstupu českých zemí do svazku se západní Evropou* (Praha, 1994), pp. 441–47, 530–32, 557–58. Recently Tomáš Borovský, 'John the Blind of Bohemia, Charles IV and Lithuania', in *Svět tajemných Baltů / The World of the Mysterious Balts*, ed. Libor Jan, Petr Kostrhun and Zdeňka Nerudová (Brno, 2013), pp. 131–39; Wojciech Iwańczak, *Jan Lucemburský: Dějiny bouřlivého života a hrdinné smrti českého krále a lucemburského hraběte v jednadvaceti obrazech* (Praha, 2018), pp. 155–65.

The Defence of the Faith, Outremer: Studies in the Crusades and the Latin East, 15 (Turnhout: Brepols, 2024), pp. 127–140
BREPOLS PUBLISHERS 10.1484/M.OUTREMER-EB.5.136531

and fourteenth centuries. In contrast to these earlier works, this paper will offer a focused analysis of the involvement of Bohemian and Moravian nobility and kings in the crusades to Prussia within a given period, and will offer new interpretations concerning the identification of the nobles and their origin and relationship to the Czech monarch. Finally, attention will also be paid to the circumstances and reasons behind the participation of Bohemian kings in the crusades.

Bohemian Kings and Their Support of the Teutonic Order

The crusades to the Baltics are connected with the names of two Czech sovereigns — Ottokar II Premislas (d. 1278) and John (d. 1346), the first Bohemian king from the Luxemburgian dynasty. Greater attention in the literature has been paid to the crusades led by the former. The last Přemyslid generation significantly supported the Teutonic Order which settled in the Czech lands at the turn of the twelfth and thirteenth centuries, and enjoyed the support of Ottokar I of Bohemia (d. 1230) and his brother Vladislas Henry, margrave of Moravia (d. 1222).[3] King Wenceslas II, Ottokar's son, also had close ties to the order. It is not known whether he carried out a crusade to the Baltics, but this is related to the fact that he led an active military policy in Poland, with the support of the Teutonic Order, which culminated in him gaining the Polish crown (coronation 1300).[4]

The first settlements of the Teutonic Order in the Czech lands were established in Prague and Opava, with others following in the first half of the thirteenth century. Alongside members of the Přemyslid dynasty, members of the Bohemian and Moravian nobility also donated property to the order.[5] Bruno of Schauenburg (d. 1281), bishop of Olomouc, was also an important supporter of the Teutonic Knights and some of their members served him.[6] The bailiwick in Bohemia and Moravia was established in the 1230s and became an important part of the structure of the order: its position was crucial, since it lay on the route between the Italian ports in the Mediterranean (with Venice being the order's headquarter

---

3 Martin Wihoda, 'Příchod řádu německých rytířů do českých zemí', *Časopis Slezského zemského muzea* 41 (1992), 7–10; Wihoda, 'Marchio Morauie, domus vestre fundator: Přemyslovská dynastie a počátky řádu německých rytířů', *Sborník prací Filozofické fakulty brněnské univerzity* 48 (1999), 5–15; Wihoda, 'The Přemyslid Dynasty and the Beginnings of the Teutonic Order', in *The Crusades and the Military Orders: Expanding the Frontiers of Medieval Latin Christianity*, ed. Zsolt Hunyadi and József Laszlowszky (Budapest, 2001), pp. 337–47; Libor Jan, 'Řád německých rytířů v Čechách a na Moravě (1204–1411)', in *Němečtí rytíři v českých zemích*, ed. Jan and František Skřivánek (Praha, 1997), pp. 11–60.
4 See Robert Antonín, *Zahraniční politika krále Václava II. v letech 1283–1300* (Brno, 2009), pp. 114–47; Libor Jan, *Václav II. Král na stříbrném trůnu 1283–1305* (Praha, 2015), pp. 289–95.
5 Libor Jan, 'Böhmische und mährische Adelige als Förderer und Mitglieder der geistlichen Ritterorden', in *The Crusades and the Military Orders*, pp. 303–17.
6 Miloš Kouřil, 'Der Olmützer Bischof Bruno von Schauenburg und der Deutsche Orden', in *Acht Jahrhunderte Deutscher Orden in Einzeldarstellungen*, ed. Klemens Wieser (Bad Godesberg, 1967), pp. 143–52.

from 1291 to 1309) and the Baltic lands. The land commander for Bohemia and Moravia was directly subordinate to the Prussian land master (the latter office being united with that of the grand master in 1309).[7]

Enemies at the Borders: The Prussian Crusades of King Ottokar II Premislas

The Teutonic Order settled in Chełmno Land (Ger. Kulmer Land) around 1230 at the initiative and with the support of Duke Conrad I of Masovia (d. 1247). It soon went from a defensive to an offensive position and managed to conquer a large part of Prussia. After the suppression of the First Prussian Uprising in the 1240s, the order began to focus on the Sambia Peninsula, which it was able to conquer thanks to the assistance of Ottokar II of Bohemia, who organised two crusades to the south-eastern Baltic Sea region.[8]

These two crusades have received quite a lot of attention in both Czech and foreign contemporary sources. The first crusade (1254–55) was preceded by the visit of Bishop Anselm of Warmia to Moravia in 1253 and that of Grand Master Poppo of Osterna to Bohemia one year later. Bruno of Schauenburg also participated in the crusade and he is considered to be one of the crucial persons who made the crusade possible.[9] The course and the results of the crusade have been interpreted many times. The main reason for the participation of the Bohemian king in the Prussian crusade was to reinforce his political significance, particularly in relation to the papal court. Ottokar's correspondence with Pope Innocent IV proves that the Bohemian king styled himself as an important protector of Christianity and considered his kingdom a barrier to the pagans and schismatics of Eastern Europe.[10]

---

7 Jan, 'Řád německých rytířů', pp. 17–18; Libor Jan, 'České země a řádový stát v Prusku na konci 13. a v první polovině 14. století', *Památková péče na Moravě — Monumentorum Moraviae tutela* 9 (2005), 9–12 (here 9).
8 Libor Jan, 'The Role of the Czech Lands in the Building of the Domain of the Order of the Teutonic Knights in Prussia', in *Svět tajemných Baltů*, pp. 99–115; Jan, 'České země a řádový stát v Prusku', pp. 9–12. On a wider context particularly Tiina Kala, 'The Incorporation of the Northern Baltic Lands into the Western Christian World', in *Crusade and Conversion on the Baltic Frontier 1150–1500*, ed. Alan V. Murray (Aldershot, 2001), pp. 3–20. See also the anthology *The North-Eastern Frontiers of Medieval Europe: The Expansion of Latin Christendom in the Baltic Lands*, ed. Alan V. Murray (Farnham, 2016).
9 David Sychra, 'The Role Played by Bishop Bruno of Olomouc in the Prussian Crusades of the Bohemian king Ottokar II Premislas', in *The Expansion of the Faith: Crusading on the Frontiers of Latin Christendom in the High Middle Ages*, ed. Paul Srodecki and Norbert Kersken (Turnhout, 2022), pp. 147–63.
10 Recently Robert Antonín, 'The Rhetoric of the Crusades and Anti-Paganism in the Political Propaganda of Ottokar II Premislas of Bohemia', in *The Expansion of the Faith*, pp. 291–302; Jan, 'The Role of the Czech Lands', pp. 109–11; Jiří Knap, 'Dvě křížové výpravy Přemysla Otakara II do Prus', in *Drugie polsko-czeskie forum młodych mediewistów: Materiały z konferencji naukowej, Gniezno 25–28*

Crusaders from Bohemia, Moravia and Austria campaigned alongside the Bohemian king. In Wrocław, other participants from the West joined the crusade. According to Peter of Dusburg's *Chronica terrae Prussiae* (finished in 1326), the army allegedly had almost 60,000 soldiers. However, there is only one source which documents the actual composition of the participants from Bohemia: the charter of Ottokar II, issued in Elbing (mod. Elbląg, Poland) on 17 January 1255, in which he confirmed the property and rights of the Teutonic Order in the countries under his rule. The list of witnesses includes prominent members of the royal company and the Bohemo-Moravian nobility. In addition to Bishop Bruno of Olomouc, the charter also includes the names of Vítek of Hradec, Boreš of Rýzmburk, Jaroš of Schlieben, Vok of Rožmberk, Smil of Lichtenburk, Boček of Zbraslav and his brothers (Smil of Střílky, Kuna of Zbraslav), Smil of Bílkov, Jenec and Hartleb of Deblín, Markvard of Dunajovice, Idík of Švábenice, Ondřej of Všechromy, Beneš of Cvilín, and the brothers Kadold Orphan and Siegfried Orphan (Germ. *Waisen*).[11] All were members of leading Bohemian and Moravian noble families, some of whom supported the Teutonic Order in the Czech lands. The first of the noblemen mentioned above, Vítek of Hradec, is particularly worthy of mention. At the end of 1255 he confirmed all the property given to the Teutonic Order by his father, Henry. The order commandery in the southern Bohemian Jindřichův Hradec (Germ. Neuhaus) was also supported by following generations of the family.[12] It is quite certain that Bruno's vassals, settled at the episcopal manors in Moravia, campaigned alongside the bishop. Many of them came to Moravia from Saxony and Westphalia, together with Bruno, in the mid-1240s. In particular, members of the Stange family, who were also engaged in the Baltic crusades, worked in Bruno's service in Moravia (Heinrich Stange, the commander of Christburg [mod. Dzierzgoń, Poland] from 1249, and probably

---

września 2007 roku, ed. Józef Dobosz, Jakub Kujawiński and Marzena Matla-Kozłowska (Poznań, 2009), pp. 83–111; Jiří Knap, 'Křížové výpravy Přemysla Otakara II. do Prus v kontextu dobového vnímání a moderní historiografie' (unpublished master thesis, Masaryk University Brno, 2007), pp. 42–53; Vratislav Vaníček, *Velké dějiny zemí Koruny české*, 15 vols (Praha, 1998–2013), 3: 68–71; Josef Žemlička, *Přemysl Otakar II. Král na rozhraní věků* (Praha, 2011), pp. 97–101; Marian Biskup and Roman Czaja, *Państwo zakonu krzyżackiego w Prusach: Władza i społeczeństwo* (Warszawa, 2009), pp. 79–80, 87–88. From older works, see Josef Šusta, 'První výprava Přemysla Otakara II. do Prus', in *Z dějin východní Evropy a Slovanstva: Sborník věnovaný Jaroslavu Bidlovi profesoru Karlovy university k šedesátým narozeninám*, ed. Miloš Weingart, Josef Dobiáš and Milada Paulová (Praha, 1928), pp. 220–28; Novotný, *Rozmach české moci*, pp. 22–29.

11 *CDEB* 5.1, no. 39, pp. 81–83.

12 Jan, 'Řád německých rytířů', pp. 20–21; Luděk Jirásko, 'Die Deutschordenskommende Neuhaus im Mittelalter', in *Sankt Georg und sein Bilderzyklus in Neuhaus/Böhmen (Jindřichův Hradec): Historische, kunsthistorische und theologische Beiträge*, ed. Ewald Volgger (Marburg, 2002), pp. 6–33; Miroslav Novotný, 'Páni z Hradce a jindřichohradecké konventy', in *Ve stopách sv. Benedikta*, ed. Libor Jan and Petr Obšusta (Brno, 2002), pp. 159–71 (here 165).

the best-known figure in that family, was killed in a battle with the Sambians in 1252).[13]

Another great uprising in Prussia broke out in 1260 and lasted until 1283, with the Teutonic Order losing some of their bases. Therefore, a series of crusades were directed to the Baltics to help the order, and the Bohemian ruler was also asked to arrange a new crusade to the region. Ottokar II organised his second campaign at the turn of 1267 and 1268, and this was closely related to promoting the Olomouc bishopric to an archbishopric. The new church capital was to be in charge of the newly conquered territories in the south-eastern Baltic Sea region. However, Pope Clement IV denied this request at the beginning of 1268, and only awarded Bishop Bruno with temporary pastoral care in specific areas. The crusade, which could have transformed relations in the Baltics, ended prematurely due to a change in the weather (the rise of temperature made it impossible for the army to move in the marshland) and the army retreated.[14] The sources do not state the actual names of the Bohemian and Moravian noblemen who participated in Ottokar's second crusade to Prussia. Vok of Rožmberk, a significant Czech nobleman who also participated in the first Bohemo-Moravian crusade, considered taking part. In 1262, he drew up a will, offering thirty silver talents to anyone who would participate in the Prussian campaign to save his soul. It is likely that Vok was worried he would not live to see the crusade, and he did indeed die shortly after the will was written.[15]

King Ottokar's two Prussian crusades were also reflected in the work of court poets. The poet Meister Sigeher stayed at the Ottokar's royal court from about 1251 and probably accompanied the king on the first Prussian campaign, and perhaps even in both crusades. Sigeher's two surviving poems (written in German) describe the Bohemian king as the protector of Christianity, and highlight the significance of the military ventures under the sign of the cross to Prussia and their parallels to the Holy Land crusades. Styling Ottokar as the crusader king par excellence, the poet compares the deeds and heroism of the Přemyslid ruler with those of Alexander the Great. The character of Alexander later played an important role in the literary celebration of the Bohemian rulers (the poet Ulrich

---

13 On Bruno's vassals, see Dalibor Janiš, 'Milites ac famuli episcopi Olomucensis: Feudal System of the Bishopric of Olomouc and Military-service Relations in the Medieval Czech Lands in the 13th century', in *Ecclesia et bellum: Kościół wobec wojny i zaangażowania militarnego duchowieństwa w wiekach średnich*, ed. Radosław Kotecki and Jacek Maciejewski (Bydgoszcz, 2016), pp. 256–71; Dalibor Janiš, 'Ke skladbě dvora olomouckých biskupů ve 13. století', in *Dvory a rezidence ve středověku II. Skladba a kultura dvorské společnosti (Mediaevalia Historica Bohemica, Supplementum 2)*, ed. Dana Dvořáčková-Malá and Jan Zelenka (Praha, 2008), pp. 347–62; Max Eisler, 'Geschichte Brunos von Schauenburg', *Zeitschrift des deutschen Vereines für die Geschichte Mährens und Schlesiens* 8 (1904), 239–95; 9 (1905), 335–84; 10 (1906), 337–93; 11 (1907), 95–116, 344–80; 12 (1908), 187–96; Libuše Hrabová, *Ekonomika feudální državy olomouckého biskupství ve druhé polovině 13. století* (Praha, 1964).
14 Jan, 'The Role of the Czech Lands', pp. 111–12; Knap, *Křížové výpravy Přemysla Otakara II.*, pp. 54–64; Novotný, *Rozmach české moci*, pp. 151–61.
15 CDEB 5.1, no. 335, pp. 496–99. See Knap, *Křížové výpravy Přemysla Otakara II.*, p. 58.

of Etzenbach created the epic *Alexandreis* written in German for King Ottokar).[16] The theme of the Prussian crusades was thus probably preserved in the literary memory of the Prague royal court, which could thus mediate them to later generations of the nobility. Similarly, memories of noble participation in the Prussian crusades of the thirteenth century may have encouraged the participation of the nobility in further *Preussen-* and *Litauerreisen*, i.e. the military expeditions of Western and Central European nobility to the Baltics. Conducted sporadically in the thirteenth century, the *Reisen* developed into a significant phenomenon among the European nobility in the fourteenth century and lasted well into the early fifteenth century, when the Christianisation of Lithuania gradually deprived the order of the legitimate basis for further campaigns under the sign of the cross.[17]

Reisen of the Bohemo-Moravian Nobility to the Baltics

The first records of the participation of the Czech nobility in the late medieval *Reisen* come from the 1320s. According to the chronicle of a Sambian minor canon, there was a campaign in 1316 in which two Bohemian noblemen participated, alongside nobility from Rhineland: one of them, called *Plisk*, was said to have killed a Lithuanian in a battle. This crusader was Plichta of Žerotín-Adlar, who is described by the Czech sources as a brave warrior and a participant in many jousting events abroad.[18] The name of the other Czech knight remains unknown. Plichta's participation in the Prussian campaign is also mentioned in the aforementioned chronicle of Peter of Dusburg. Older literature identifies both pieces of information as referring to 1322. However, it is likely that Plichta of Žerotín-Adlar participated in two crusades. In 1322, there were also Bohemian lords and other knights and men-at-arms involved (*cum multis militibus et armigeris venerunt ad terram Prussie*) in addition to several knights (including the

---

16 Heinrich Peter Brodt, *Meister Sigeher* (Breslau, 1913); Václav Bok, 'Zu dichterischen Aufgaben und Intentionen mittelhochdeutscher Autoren im Dienst der letzten Přemyslidenkönige', in *Böhmen und seine Nachbarn in der Přemyslidenzeit*, ed. Ivan Hlaváček and Alexander Patschovsky (Ostfildern, 2011), pp. 437–56; David Sychra, 'Středohornoněmecká lyrika a epika na dvoře posledních Přemyslovců jako pramen k interpretaci panovnického ideálu 13. století v českých zemích', *Historica: Revue pro historii a příbuzné vědy* 8 (2017), 1–19; *Moravo, Čechy, radujte se! (Němečtí a rakouští básníci v českých zemích za posledních Přemyslovců)*, ed. Václav Bok and Jindřich Pokorný (Praha, 1998), pp. 25–27, 38–39; Žemlička, *Přemysl Otakar*, pp. 100–1.

17 See Werner Paravicini, *Die Preussenreisen des europäischen Adels*, 4 vols (Sigmaringen, 1989–2023). On the participation of the Czech nobility, see Tomáš Baletka, 'Účast české a moravské šlechty na "pruských jízdách" ve 14. století', in *Sto let od narození profesora Jindřicha Šebánka*, ed. Kateřina Smutná (Brno, 2000), pp. 79–88.

18 'Canonici Sambiensis epitome gestorum Prussie', ed. Max Toeppen, in *SRP* 1: 272–90 (here 286); Peter of Dusburg, 'Chronicon terrae Prussiae', ed. Max Töppen, in *SRP* 1: 21–219 (here 182); Šusta, *Král cizinec*, pp. 290–91; *Staročeská kronika tak řečeného Dalimila*, ed. Jiří Daňhelka et al., 2 vols (Praha, 1988), 2: 576–77; Paravicini, *Preussenreisen* 1: 54; 2: 135.

Silesian duke Bernard of Świdnica).[19] As well as Plichta, one of his brothers also participated in the crusade (*Phligt cum fratre suo de Bohemia*) — it is known that Plichta had two brothers, Jaroslav and Habart. Plichta died in the same year after returning from the crusade (1321/1322), at the Battle of Mühldorf (28 September 1322) while fighting along King John who supported the Romano-German king Louis IV the Bavarian against the anti-king Frederick of Habsburg. Dusburg's chronicle also mentions the *dominus de Lichtenbergk*, that is, a member of the prominent Bohemian family of Lichtenburk. This was Henry of Lichtenburk (d. after 1356), whose grandfather Smil had participated in the first Bohemian crusade to Prussia, led by the Bohemian king, in 1254–55. Both noblemen, Plichta and Henry, belonged to a close aristocratic Bohemian circle around King John of Bohemia. Henry of Lichtenburk later participated in a crusade led by the Bohemian king in 1337.[20]

The participation of the aforementioned nobles in the *Reisen* most likely had an impact on both the self-perception and the cultural environment of the Bohemian and Moravian nobility. The older crusades from the time of Ottokar II of Bohemia could also be kept as a tradition or memory within prominent noble families whose members had participated in the crusades. It is clear that other prominent members of the Bohemian and Moravian nobility organised a crusade to Prussia the following year (1323). The chronicler Peter of Dusburg mentions a campaign managed by a nobleman from Cimburk and a nobleman from Egerberg, with the attendance of other noblemen from Bohemia and the Rhineland (*dominus de Cinnenbergk et dominus de Egerbergk cum multis nobilibus de Bohemia et Reno fuerunt in terra Prussie*).[21] The first of these two noblemen can be identified as Bernard of Cimburk, who was also one of the close courtiers of John of Bohemia — he is mentioned in 1318 as a royal sword keeper (*ensifer*) and vice-chamberlain (*subcamerarius*) in the margraviate of Moravia, where he owned some estates.[22] In the 1320s, he was in the diplomatic service of King John. In 1330, he participated in a meeting in Luxembourg at the behest of John's son, Prince Charles. This meeting was about donating Pomerelia to the Teutonic Order, which was represented by Grand Master Werner of Orseln.[23] The second

---

19 Dusburg, 'Chronicon terrae Prussiae', p. 186.
20 Dusburg, 'Chronicon terrae Prussiae', p. 186; Jan Urban, *Lichtenburkové: Vzestupy a pády jednoho panského rodu* (Praha, 2003), pp. 173–74; August Sedláček, 'Z Žirotína', in *Ottův slovník naučný* 27 (1908), 844–45. On the aristocratic circle around King John, see Zdeněk Žalud, 'Čeští šlechtici u dvora Jana Lucemburského', *Husitský Tábor* 15 (2006), 177–207; Zdeněk Žalud, 'Dvůr Jana Lucemburského a česká šlechta', in *Lesk královského majestátu ve středověku: Pocta Prof. PhDr. Františku Kavkovi k nedožitým 85. narozeninám*, ed. Lenka Bobková and Mlada Holá (Praha, 2005), pp. 143–52.
21 Dusburg, 'Chronicon terrae Prussiae', pp. 186–87; Goll, *Čechy a Prusy*, p. 59.
22 See Dalibor Janiš, 'Cimburk', in *Höfe und Residenzen im spätmittelalterlichen Reich: Grafen und Herren*, ed. Jan Hirschbiegel, Anna Paulina Orlowska and Jörg Wettlaufer, 2 vols (Ostfildern, 2012), 2: 284–90 (here 284–85, 288).
23 *CDEM* 6, no. 264, pp. 200–2; 7, no. 273, p. 860. See Spěváček, *Jan Lucemburský a jeho doba*, p. 477.

noblemen in the 1323 campaign can be identified as either Vilém of Egerberk or his brother Frick. Their father, Vilém of Hustopeče, held some estates in Bohemia and Moravia. However, they sold their estates in Moravia in 1322. Vilém of Egerberk was one of the important people around the Bohemian nobleman Henry of Lipá.[24]

Other prominent noblemen participated in the following Prussian campaign of 1324. Peter of Dusburg states that this was a campaign of many knights and noblemen particularly from the Rhineland and Alsace. He mentions John and Philip, counts of Sponheim, and two participants from Bohemia, namely Peter of Rožmberk and his uncle Heřman (of Miličín).[25] Peter of Rožmberk (d. 1347) was a member of one of the most prominent Bohemian families, with a red rose as his coat-of-arms insignia. Peter held the office of the high chamberlain of the kingdom of Bohemia (*summus camerarius terrae*) for many years. He lost this office temporarily in 1319–23 having joined the noble opposition to the king. His campaign to the Baltics is undoubtedly related to his testament, which he had drawn up in 1324 (the actual date is not stated in the copy of the original document). However, the campaign proved unsuccessful as a result of the warm winter: rivers and marshes did not freeze, meaning that the army lacked its usual convenient means of travelling quickly across the country.[26]

King and Knight: Three Baltic Crusades of John of Bohemia

Both the aforementioned noblemen, Bernard of Cimburk and Peter of Rožmberk, also participated in the first crusade organised by John of Bohemia in 1328/29. In 1325, in what at the time was more a diplomatic move than a statement of real intent, the Bohemian king committed himself to Pope John XXII to participate in a crusade to the Holy Land.[27] In order to fulfil his crusade vows, King John decided to support the Teutonic Order in its religious warfare in the nearby south-eastern Baltic Sea region. The crusade venture started in winter 1328 and, after the army had gathered in Silesia's historical capital Wrocław, as they had during Ottokar II's first Prussian campaign in 1254, they set off to Königsberg (mod. Kaliningrad, Russia). Besides various nobles from the Czech lands, the large-scale campaign included further imperial nobility, some of the Silesian

---

24 Zdeněk Pokluda, 'Kapitoly z dějin Zlína (I–VIII)', *Gottwaldovsko od minulosti k současnosti* 9 (1987), 63–188 (here 70–71); Šusta, *Král cizinec*, pp. 445, 464; *CDEM* 6, nos 202, 220, pp. 152–53, 162.
25 Peter von Dusburg, 'Chronicon terrae Prussiae', p. 189.
26 Valentin Schmidt, 'Testament Peters v. Rosenberg vor seinem Zuge gegen die Preußen 1324', in *Mitteilungen des Vereines für Geschichte der Deutschen in Böhmen* 47 (1909), 62–65; Anna Kubíková, *Petr I. z Rožmberka a jeho synové* (České Budějovice, 2011), pp. 19–28; Jan, 'České země a řádový stát', p. 11; Žalud, 'Čeští šlechtici', pp. 197–98; Baletka, 'Účast české a moravské šlechty', p. 79.
27 Spěváček, *Jan Lucemburský a jeho doba*, pp. 387, 400; Borovský, 'John the Blind of Bohemia', pp. 131–32.

dukes and knights from England. In addition to the two noblemen mentioned above, other participants included Henry jr. of Lipá, Vilém of Landštejn, Thimo of Colditz and Otto of Bergow.[28] Guillaume de Machaut, a French poet, also participated in the campaign, and he described the course of the campaign in the desolate northern lands in his poem, *Le confort d'ami*.[29]

The whole crusade was coordinated with the Teutonic Order under the command of Grand Master Werner of Orseln, and was aimed at the north-western part of the Lithuanian lands (Samogitia).[30] The Christian army first conquered four castles, and later laid siege to and conquered the Lithuanian castle of *Medwaglen* (or *Medewage* according to Peter of Dusburg). Several thousand prisoners of war were baptised at the request of King John and his knights. The grand master agreed with this. Through this crusade, John (who was also the titular king of Poland) reinforced his position not only in relation to the Teutonic Order, but also in relation to his rival, the Polish king Vladislas I the Elbow-High, especially with regard to the disputed Silesian lands.[31]

Organised with his son Charles, the margrave of Moravia and later Holy Roman emperor, John's second Lithuanian crusade (started in late 1336) took a similar course. In January 1337, they stayed in Wrocław with their company, where a series of charters were issued. The lists of witnesses document the participation of Bohemian and Moravian noblemen in the crusade. Several noble guests from the West were also present. In addition to Jan Volek, the bishop of Olomouc, the crusade was attended by Hynek Berka of Dubá, Jan of Lipá, Thimo of Colditz, Oldřich Pluh of Rabštejn, Vilém of Landštejn, Otto of Bergow, Ješek of Michalovice, Henry of Lichtenburk, Vaněk of Vartenberk, Hynek of Dubá, Ješek of Boskovice, Smil of Bítov and Jan of Klingenberg. Some of them had taken part in King John's first crusade.[32] This venture was not as successful since, as in the 1328/29 crusade, a warm winter ensured that the unfrozen and thus wet ground

---

28 *RDBM* 3, nos 1532–33, pp. 600–1; Johannes Voigt, *Geschichte Preußens von den ältesten Zeiten bis zum Untergange der Herrschaft des Deutschen Ordens*, 9 vols (Königsberg, 1827–39), 4: 426–35; Spěváček, *Jan Lucemburský a jeho doba*, p. 445; Borovský, 'John the Blind of Bohemia', p. 132; Goll, *Čechy a Prusy*, pp. 59–63.
29 Šusta, *Král cizinec*, pp. 464–46; Comte de Puymaigre, 'Une campagne de Jean de Luxembourg, roi de Bohême', *Revue des Questions Historiques* 42 (1887), 168–80.
30 For the Teutonic Order's Samogitian crusades, see Gregory Leighton, 'Crusading and Holy War in the Teutonic Order's Struggle for Žemaitija: Written and Visual Perspectives', *Acta Historica Universitatis Klaipedensis* 41 (2020), 25–52; William L. Urban, *The Samogitian Crusade* (Chicago, 1989).
31 Wigand of Marburg, 'Chronik', ed. Theodor Hirsch, in *SRP* 2: 429–662 (here 462–63); Spěváček, *Jan Lucemburský a jeho doba*, p. 445; Baletka, 'Účast české a moravské šlechty', pp. 79–80. Recently Lenka Bobková, *Jan Lucemburský: Otec slavného syna* (Praha, 2018), pp. 198–205. See Axel Ehlers, 'The Crusade of the Teutonic Knights against Lithuania Reconsidered', in *Crusade and Conversion*, pp. 21–44.
32 *RDBM* 4, no. 366, 370, 386, pp. 148, 154–57.

hampered the army's movements. Moreover, King John and his son Charles both fell ill during the campaign.[33]

The third and final of John of Bohemia's holy war campaigns to Lithuania took place at the turn of 1344/1345. In January 1345, the Bohemo-Moravian crusaders again met in Wrocław.[34] In addition to many Western and West Central European barons, in particular from France and Germany, Louis I of Hungary also participated, as did John's son, Margrave Charles of Moravia. The joint crusader host gathered in Insterburg (mod. Chernyakhovsk, Russia) close to the Lithuanian border. According to Wigand of Marburg's chronicle, *200 domini terrarum*, i.e. 200 members of the 'landed nobility', participated in the crusade.[35] Duke Peter I of Bourbon took 300 horses; Count William of Holland-Hainaut took 400. There were about 1,600 horses in the crusade, as recorded in the report of the grand master.[36] However, the participation of the Bohemian nobility is not documented. John and Charles issued a series of charters during their stay in Wrocław, but these either do not contain any lists of witnesses, or these are only made available in brief regesta.[37] The crusade aimed to strengthen Czech interests in Silesia in relation to the Polish king Casimir III. Grand Master Ludolf König of Wattzau led the crusaders to Lithuania, but false reports on the movement of the enemy led to the withdrawal of the Christian army back to Prussia. Again, the warm winter made it impossible to travel on ice.[38] Towards the end of the crusade, the Polish king attempted to capture Margrave Charles, who managed to escape. As a result, the Bohemian army raided Poland all the way to Cracow in the summer of 1345.[39]

Miles christianus: The Baltic Crusades and the Knightly Culture in the Czech Lands

It is difficult to trace the influence of the crusades to the Baltics on the knightly culture in the Czech lands due to a lack of 'private' sources. One of the few preserved sources is the gallery of coats-of-arms accompanying the legend of St George. The narrative is depicted in the form of a cycle of wall paintings in one

---

33 Baletka, 'Účast české a moravské šlechty', p. 80; Spěváček, *Jan Lucemburský a jeho doba*, pp. 530–31; Iwańczak, *Jan Lucemburský*, pp. 162–63; Borovský, 'John the Blind of Bohemia', pp. 133–34; Šusta, *Král cizinec*, p. 239; Goll, *Čechy a Prusy*, pp. 68–9; Paravicini, *Preussenreisen* 1: 185; Biskupa and Czaja, *Państwo zakonu krzyżackiego*, pp. 108, 111–14.

34 Šusta, *Karel IV.*, p. 434; Borovský, 'John the Blind of Bohemia', pp. 134–35; Spěváček, *Jan Lucemburský a jeho doba*, pp. 557–58; Iwańczak, *Jan Lucemburský*, pp. 163–64.

35 Wigand, 'Chronik', p. 504.

36 Urban, *The Samogitian Crusade*, p. 124.

37 Šusta, *Karel IV.*, pp. 433–35.

38 Goll, *Čechy a Prusy*, pp. 74–76; Baletka, 'Účast české a moravské šlechty', p. 81; Spěváček, *Jan Lucemburský a jeho doba*, pp. 557–58; Iwańczak, *Jan Lucemburský*, pp. 163–64.

39 Spěváček, *Jan Lucemburský a jeho doba*, p. 558; Šusta, *Karel IV.*, pp. 435–42; Borovský, 'John the Blind of Bohemia', pp. 134–35.

of the rooms in the old palace at the castle complex of Jindřichův Hradec, South Bohemia.[40] The original castle used to be the residence of the lords of Hradec, one of the most important aristocratic families in the Czech lands. Vítek I of Hradec, as mentioned above, participated in the first crusade of Ottokar II to Prussia, and the lords of Hradec supported the Teutonic Order. The murals were uncovered in 1838 and restored. The paintings include inscriptions documenting that the gallery of coats-of-arms was painted in 1338, when the castle belonged to Oldřich III of Hradec (d. about 1348), which is one year after the end of the second crusade of John of Bohemia to the Baltics.[41]

The gallery contains nineteen coats-of-arms, of which eleven belong to noble families whose members demonstrably participated in the crusades to the Baltics. The coats-of-arms are painted below the paintings with descriptions in the following order: the families of Velhartice, Kasejovice, Miličín, Rýzmberk, Házmburk, Šternberk, Litice, Valdek, one of Ronov, Landštejn, another one of Ronov, Ústí, one damaged (illegible) coat-of-arms, Michalovice, Vartenberk, Strakonice, Cimburk, Klingenberg and, again, Šternberk.[42] The coat-of-arms of the Hradec family (a golden rose in a blue field) is not included among them. However, it is not missing from the gallery, since it is painted on the cloak of the person who represents Oldřich III of Hradec. St George represented an important symbol in medieval knightly culture and the Teutonic Order also worshipped him. According to a fifteenth century report, the order banner with St George was reserved for the military group formed by warriors who came from various parts of Europe.[43] St George is usually depicted with a coat-of-arms with a red cross in a white field. However, the banner has a black cross, which explicitly refers to the coat-of-arms of the Teutonic Order. St George is depicted as a member of the order and, figuratively, as a crusader — a member of the Baltic crusades. The symbolism of the whole room thus refers to the important attributes of knightly culture — St George, military campaigns, and the close bond to the Teutonic Order, which had its commandery in Jindřichův Hradec. Jindřichův Hradec was already an important centre of this knightly culture during the life of Oldřich II of Hradec (d. before 1312), who hosted many minnesingers at his court.[44]

The preserved room with the coats-of-arms and the legend could have served as a meeting room for noblemen unified by the ideas mentioned there, but it could also have been a room that served the brotherhood of St George. The priests from the order's commandery could have provided spiritual services to the members — knights there. The room with the depicted legend was next to

---

40 See Michal Konečný et al., *Hrad Jindřichův Hradec* (České Budějovice, 2017).
41 Rostislav Nový, 'Jindřichohradecká znaková galérie z r. 1338', *Acta Universitatis Carolinae, Philosophica et historica* 3–4 (1971), 179–97; Rostislav Nový, 'Die Wappengalerie auf Schloß Neuhaus aus dem Jahre 1338', in *Sankt Georg und sein Bilderzyklus*, pp. 34–47.
42 Nový, 'Jindřichohradecká znaková galérie', pp. 183–87; Jan P. V. Hájíček, 'Heraldická výzdoba jindřichohradeckého hradu z doby Lucemburků', *Heraldika a genealogie* 32 (1999), 3–22.
43 Nový, 'Jindřichohradecká znaková galérie', p. 189.
44 Nový, 'Jindřichohradecká znaková galérie', p. 192; Jan, 'Řád německých rytířů', pp. 20–21.

the Chapel of the Holy Spirit and the two rooms were connected by a door, leading to the chapel gallery. The connection to the Teutonic Order commandery is also clearly indicated by the second figure (alongside the figure from the legend), which is a counterpart to Oldřich of Hradec — as the fragments of the inscription around the figure show, this is the commander in Jindřichův Hradec, Herman. It is assumed that the initiative to commission such a work came from the surroundings of the commandery in Jindřichův Hradec, and that the unknown artist was probably a member of the order.[45]

In the second half of the fourteenth century, the interest of the Bohemian and Moravian nobility in the Prussian campaigns cooled off significantly. One of the main reasons for this was probably the lack of interest of the Bohemian monarchs (Charles IV and his son Wenceslas IV) in the south-eastern and eastern Baltic Sea region. The recorded history only states a few names of Bohemian and Moravian noblemen who were likely to have participated in the Prussian campaigns. The sources also document that a lot of foreign noblemen passed through the Czech lands at that time on their way to the north, to the Baltics (for example John II of Blois-Châtillon in 1363, Duke Leopold III of Austria in 1371–72, Duke Albert III of Austria in 1377, Earl Henry of Derby in 1392).[46] The third campaign of King John and his son Charles was the end of the crusades of the Bohemian rulers to Prussia and Lithuania. However, the king of Bohemia and Holy Roman emperor Charles IV (d. 1378) did lead an active policy in relation to Lithuania, albeit only on the diplomatic level. His interest in the affairs of the Teutonic Order in the Baltics was very limited and he did not include this area in his active policies.[47]

Conclusion

The participation of the Bohemian and Moravian nobility in the Prussian battles was thus closely bound to the campaigns of the two Bohemian kings, Ottokar II and John of Bohemia. The Prussian crusades were related to their policies in relation to the pope, the Teutonic Order and Poland. An important element in the case of both of these Bohemian rulers was the active creation of the image of an ideal king, protecting Christians and fighting pagans and enemies of the faith. After all, the participation of court poets in these military expeditions is

---

45 Nový, 'Jindřichohradecká znaková galérie', pp. 188–97; Peter Dinzelbacher, 'Mögliche Funktionen des Raumes mit dem Georgszyklus', in *Sankt Georg und sein Bilderzyklus*, pp. 64–68; Jirásko, 'Die Deutschordenskommende Neuhaus', pp. 27–32; Borovský, 'John the Blind of Bohemia', p. 134; Jan, 'České země a řádový stát', p. 11.
46 See Baletka, 'Účast české a moravské šlechty', pp. 81–84; Paravicini, *Preussenreisen*, 1: 140–41, 212, 229, 317. See Francis R. H. du Boulay, 'Henry of Derby's Expeditions to Prussia 1390-1 and 1392', in *The Reign of Richard II: Essays in Honour of May McKisack*, ed. Francis R. H. du Boulay and Caroline M. Barron (London, 1971), pp. 153–72.
47 See recently Borovský, 'John the Blind of Bohemia', pp. 135–38; Jan, 'České země a řádový stát v Prusku', pp. 10–11.

characteristic. Their task was to record and relate the glorious deeds of the kings. The idea of a Christian knight (*miles christianus*) was then part of the knightly culture and strongly influenced Bohemian and Moravian nobles. There are also records from the first decade of the fourteenth century documenting individual journeys by prominent Bohemian and Moravian noblemen to the Baltics as an important part of the knightly culture of the period. Czech and Moravian warriors again visited the northern battlefields in the fifteenth century, usually as mercenaries serving the Polish kings or the Teutonic Order, two opponents fighting each other.[48] That, however, belongs to a different chapter.

---

48 See Goll, *Čechy a Prusy*, pp. 83–313; Václav Štěpán, 'Účast žoldnéřů z českých zemí (zejména Slezska a severní Moravy) ve "velké válce 1409–11" zachycená prameny z velmistrovského archivu řádu německých rytířů', *Časopis Slezského muzea, série B — vědy historické* 39 (1990), 1–15; Eva Barborová, 'Češi a Moravané jako účastníci válek Polska s řádem německých rytířů v letech 1410 a 1414', *Sborník Matice moravské* 86 (1967), 191–201.

BENJÁMIN BORBÁS

How to Uphold a Dying Institution

English Support for the Teutonic Order's Baltic Crusades in the Early Fifteenth Century

There were only a few countries whose nobility did not take part in the campaigns of the Teutonic Order against the Lithuanians, the so-called *Reisen*.[1] The popularity of these military actions reached its zenith in the second half of the fourteenth century. The kingdom of England — thanks to its significant contribution to the campaigns — surpassed other participants, and its close cooperation with the Teutonic Order was not simply confined to military actions. England sought to support the military order, and thus the cause of Christianity in the Baltics, by offering different means of help: military, diplomatic and financial. The purpose of this essay is to answer the following questions: what factors led to the significant participation of the English nobility in the Lithuanian campaigns? Can we speak of a continuous and unchanging assistance? It is also interesting to investigate what benefits England sought to gain from this support and how the Teutonic Order profited from the cooperation. Finally, what were the possibilities for continuing this cooperation after the battle of Tannenberg/Grunwald/Žalgiris (15 July 1410), and how could the Teutonic Order utilise the diplomatic assistance of its former supporter? The primary goal of this paper, however, is to follow the course of the diplomatic relationship between the two parties after 1410, especially from a Teutonic point of view.

Introduction

The first contacts between the Teutonic Order and the kingdom of England can be traced back to the early crusades. Thanks to the excellent diplomatic and organisational skills of Herman of Salza, grand master of the Teutonic Order from 1210 to 1239, the young military order was an active participant in the Fifth Crusade

---

1 I am indebted to Helen Nicholson for her comments on the paper, especially on the initiation of the English rent and on the period of Henry III of England. I am also very thankful to John Kee, Ph.D. Candidate in Byzantine Studies at the Harvard University, for his comments and suggestions. These were valuable and very helpful for revising and improving the manuscript.

The Defence of the Faith, Outremer: Studies in the Crusades and the Latin East, 15 (Turnhout: Brepols, 2024), pp. 141–154
BREPOLS ❧ PUBLISHERS   10.1484/M.OUTREMER-EB.5.136532

(1217–21). Thereafter, as a result of personal contacts established during the campaign and the growing fame of the order, English kings started to support the young institution financially, and, from the fourteenth century on, also militarily.[2] Interestingly, in contrast with former English undertakings, military actions led by members of the royal family in the 1390s became popular.[3] This phenomenon was partially the result of internal English conflicts as well as financial considerations.[4] However, after 1394, significant English participation came to an end: besides two nobles from 1408 and 1409, and the English crusaders mentioned in connection with the battle of Tannenberg, no Englishman took part in the Baltic campaigns of the Teutonic Order.[5] Although English military assistance did not arrive in Prussia from overseas, the Teutonic Order did not give up the hope of gaining financial or diplomatic support from its old ally. In the following, I will focus on these efforts and some of their results after 1410.

English Rent

Teutonic requests for English support even after 1410 cannot be understood without a brief overview of the so-called 'English rent'. This financial assistance preceded the military one, and was also in place during the *Litauenreisen* of English nobles. It is not at all surprising, therefore, that after the end of English participation in these campaigns in 1394, the Teutonic Order sought above all to ensure the continuous flow of the annual rent paid by the English kings. Our very first information on English financial support is connected to King Henry III (r. 1216–72) who, in 1235, ordered that the exchequer pay an annual rent of 40 marks to the order for his own soul and the soul of his predecessors.[6] On 2 March,

---

2 Werner Paravicini, *Die Preussenreisen des europäischen Adels*, 4 vols (Sigmaringen, 1989–2023), 1: 88–104, 115–35.
3 These were the successful (1390–91) and unsuccessful (1392) campaigns of Henry, earl of Derby, and the aborted venture of his uncle, Thomas of Woodstock, duke of Gloucester. The importance of personal contacts established during the *Reisen* is proved by the fact that several persons in the retinue of Henry contributed to the stabilisation of the Lancaster dynasty (Hugh Waterton, John Norbury and Thomas Erpingham became royal councillors). Christopher Tyerman, *England and the Crusades, 1095–1588* (Chicago, 1988), p. 271. We can see a similar example in the case of William Esturmy, who was rewarded by Henry IV for his legation and other activities performed in Prussia and Germany. *Henry IV*, ed. Henry C. Maxwell Lyte, CPR, 4 vols (London, 1903–9), 4: 138.
4 Henry and his uncle also preferred to leave the country for a period rather than getting involved in internal conflicts any further. In contrast to earlier periods, English nobles set sail to Prussia in a company of magnates so as to divide and reduce the costs of the expensive journey. Tyerman, *England and the Crusades*, p. 270.
5 Paravicini, *Preussenreisen* 1: 127. Their exact number is not known, see 'Die Ältere Hochmeisterchronik', ed. Max Töppen, in *SRP* 3: 519–729 (here 724).
6 Hans Koeppen, 'Die englische Rente für den Deutschen Orden', in *Festschrift für Hermann Heimpel zum 70. Geburtstag am 19. September 1971*, ed. Josef Fleckenstein, Sabine Krüger und Rudolf Vierhaus, 3 vols (1971–73), 2: 402–21 (here 413–14). As a mark was two thirds of a pound, 40

he issued a document which guaranteed that that amount would be paid by Easter of the following year. He added that this should be maintained 'till we or our successors provide an appropriate territory in England for the same Herman [of Salza], his brethren and their successors'.[7] Generally, the rent was paid every year before Easter; only two exemptions are known from this period.[8]

In order to identify the motives behind the initiation of the English rent, there are perhaps two different events we have to bear in mind. First, it is necessary to turn our attention to the Damietta Crusade (1218–21). We know that English crusaders were also present in Damietta, alongside Grand Master Herman of Salza and his knights.[9] It is therefore plausible to regard the donation of Henry III as an act of gratitude towards the order for its previous service during the Fifth Crusade.[10] The bond between the Teutonic Order and England might have been strengthened after the crusade of the Holy Roman emperor Frederick II, since both Herman of Salza and numerous English crusaders took part in this undertaking. Furthermore, the grand master — together with the bishops of Winchester and Exeter — witnessed the oath of the emperor during the ratification of a treaty with al-Kāmil Muḥammad al-Malik, sultan of Egypt (r. 1217–38), on 18 February 1229.[11] However, it seems more likely that the donation was linked to the marriage of Henry III's sister Isabella to Frederick II in 1235, the same year that Henry set up this regular payment. It appears that two Teutonic Knights were in the delegation which came from Frederick II to Henry III's court in February 1235 to negotiate the marriage: the St Albans chronicler Roger of Wendover recorded that two Templars were in this delegation, but it is much more likely that they were Teutonic Knights and that Roger's informant had mistaken their white mantles for Templar mantles.[12] Roger's successor at St Albans, Matthew Paris, corrected Roger's account to *duo Hospitalarii Theutonicorum*, i.e. two Teutonic Knights.[13]

---

marks was equal to 26 pounds, 13 shillings and 4 pence. This amount of money corresponded roughly to the legal income of an English knight at the time. Paravicini, *Preussenreisen* 1: 115–16.

7 'Privilèges octroyés aux Teutoniques', ed. Paul Riant, in *Archives de l'Orient Latin*, ed. Ernst Leroux, 2 vols (Paris, 1881–84), 1: 416–22 (here no. 2, p. 418): [...] *donec nos vel heredes nostri eisdem fratri Hermanno et fratribus et successoribus sui providerimus in aliqua certa terra competenti in Anglia*.

8 Koeppen, 'Die englische Rente', p. 403.

9 Herman of Salza was the leader of that Teutonic expedition group which helped to capture the city of Damietta in the December 1218. He and his order were active participants in the successes and the final failure of the Fifth Crusade. See Koeppen, 'Die englische Rente', p. 405.

10 This assumption is supported by the fact that Adolf IV, count of Berg, similarly donated his property in Dieren (near Arnheim, Netherlands) to the order during the siege of Damietta in 1218. Later this donation served as the foundation for the Teutonic commandery in Dieren. See Koeppen, 'Die englische Rente', p. 405.

11 Willy Cohn, *Hermann von Salza* (Breslau, 1930), pp. 23–33.

12 Roger of Wendover, *The Flowers of History*, ed. Henry G. Hewlett, RS 84.1–3 (London, 1886–89), 3: 108.

13 Matthew Paris, *Chronica Majora*, ed. Henry Richards Luard, 7 vols, RS 57.1–7 (London, 1872–83), 3: 318.

The more than two-hundred-year history of the English rent encapsulates the changing relationship between England and the order. The payment was suspended for the first time in 1262, during the reign of Henry III. The cause was that the English monarchy was bankrupt. King Henry's aim to secure the Sicilian crown for his younger son, Edward, put a heavy burden on the English treasury since Henry had promised the papacy to pay 135,541 marks in 1254 to achieve this goal. This, together with the conflict with Welsh as well as with the financial and human sacrifices to pacify Gascony in 1253–54 caused serious expenses. Henry was forced to take out serious loans from different creditors, both domestic and foreigners. One of the most important creditors of the crown was Simon of Montfort, the future leader of the baronial revolt against King Henry. From 1258, the baronial reformers who took control of Henry III's financial affairs cancelled unnecessary expenditure, and when Henry temporarily recovered power in 1261, he did not reinstate the rent.[14]

All cash donations to military religious orders were suspended during the late 1250s and early 1260s: an annual cash donation of 50 marks per annum to the Templars ceased in 1259, and an annual cash donation of 40 marks per annum to the Order of St Lazarus ceased in 1257 (both of these had been initiated by King Henry II, and were restored by Edward I).[15] The annual cash payment to the Teutonic Order continued longer, the last payment being in 1261 (this was likewise re-established by Edward I).[16] Payments in kind also continued: an annual gift of brushwood to the Hospitaller sisters of Buckland in Somerset continued until the battle of Evesham in 1265, one of the main events of England's Second Baron's War, and an annual gift of venison to the Templars, instituted by King John, continued until Henry III's death in 1272, although an annual gift of wine was stopped in 1246.[17] However, in 1279, his son Edward I granted his permission for the annual payment of the 40 marks offered to the Teutonic Knights to be continued.[18] This was apparently paid without interruption until 1357. With this said, it seems quite clear, that the reason behind suspending the annual rent to the Teutonic Order was a financial one, the crown's indebtedness at

---

14 For the actions of the baronial reformers in England during this period, see Nick Barratt, 'Crisis Management: Baronial Reform at the Exchequer', in *Baronial Reform and Revolution in England, 1258–67*, ed. Adrian Jobson (Woodbridge, 2016), pp. 56–70; H. W. Ridgeway, 'What Happened in 1261?', in *Baronial Reform*, pp. 89–108.

15 *CLR* 4: 370, 482.

16 *CLR* 5: 36.

17 Thomas Hugo, *The History of Mynchin Buckland Priory and Preceptory, in the County of Somerset* (London, 1861), p. 18; *Henry III*, ed. Henry C. Maxwell Lyte, 14 vols, CCR (London, 1902–38), 5: 422; 14: 501.

18 We learn from the charter of Edward I that *ex certa causa* Henry III had previously cancelled the payment. Bruno Schumacher, 'Der Deutsche Orden und England', in *Altpreussische Beiträge: Festschrift zur Hauptversammlung des Gesamtvereins der deutschen Geschichts- und Altertums-Vereine zu Königsberg Pr. vom 4. bis 7. September 1933*, ed. Bruno Schumacher et al. (Königsberg, 1933), p. 12, n. 9.

that time, to be precise, not a change in attitude towards the Teutonic Knights or other military orders.

Of course, there were years where the payment failed to arrive in time. In these cases, the grand master of the Teutonic Order sought to receive payment for the preceding years all together. For example, in 1359, Grand Master Winrich of Kniprode (r. 1351–82) sought to receive payment for three years.[19] The positive response of Edward III also offers us an insight into the past of Teutonic-English relations. The king granted the request of the grand master for his honouring of the Blessed Virgin and as gratitude 'for all the kindness and support, well known to us, that the grand master and his brethren often provided to our people heading to Prussia, and what was offered to them with pleasure and benevolence'.[20] Here, for the first time, a concrete cause for the payment was provided: the participation of English crusaders in the fight against the Lithuanians, and the military and diplomatic cooperation connected with the *Reisen*. The aforementioned quotation proves that the previous travels of English crusaders in Prussia positively influenced the decision of the ruler, or, at least, that they were considered an important enough phenomenon to serve as the reason for the confirmation of the payment.

The popularity of the *Reisen* at the end of fourteenth century is revealed by the fact that, at the request of the grand masters Conrad Zöllner of Rotenstein (r. 1382–90) and Conrad of Jungingen (r. 1393–1407), the successors of Edward III, both Richard II (r. 1377–99) and Henry IV (r. 1399–1413), confirmed the privilege of 1235 without any further hesitation (in 1390 and 1401).[21] This is worth emphasising, since there was a serious commercial rivalry developing from the 1380s onwards between English merchants, expanding their influence in the Baltic Sea region, and the Hanseatic League, seeking to protect its share of trade with the support of the grand masters of the Teutonic Order.[22] In matters of this kind, the English kings and the grand masters were always intent on coming to a conclusion and recovering the losses of the other party. When, in 1359, the Teutonic legate returned to Marienburg (mod. Malbork, Poland) from his mission with arrears of twenty marks, he also handed over the letter of the English king. In this, Edward III made a promise that payment of the rent would be guaranteed, but emphasised his desire to replace this financial support with a *beneficium* of great value in England.[23] During the reign of Richard II, payment of the rent

---

19 Koeppen, 'Die englische Rente', p. 408.
20 'Privilèges octroyés aux Teutoniques', no. 5, p. 421.
21 *Richard II*, ed. Henry C. Maxwell Lyte, CPR, 6 vols (London, 1895–1902), 4: 74; 'Privilèges octroyés aux Teutoniques', no. 7, p. 422.
22 Several cities belonging to the Hanseatic League were located in the territory of the Teutonic Knights, and the grand masters were always seen as the highest secular protectors of the league. Terrence H. Lloyd, *England and the German Hanse, 1157–1611: A Study of Their Trade and Diplomacy* (Cambridge, 1991), p. 51.
23 'Privilèges octroyés aux Teutoniques', no. 5, p. 421.

depended almost entirely on the extent of current mercantile rivalry. In the year after the conclusion of a commercial agreement in 1388, the king of England once again confirmed the payment.[24]

The Continuing Demand for English Support after the Battle of Tannenberg

In the following sections, primary sources relating to the contacts between England and the Teutonic Order after 1410 will be presented and divided into different groups. In analysing these documents, I will focus on answering two major questions: (1) what possibilities were there for reviving the former cooperation after Tannenberg? (2) In which political matters could the Teutonic Order rely upon the diplomatic support of England?

a. Demands to Revive the English Rent

As the participation of English nobles came to an end after 1394, so did the payment of the annual rent.[25] The last confirmation of the rent is dated to 1401, with the grant of Henry IV.[26] From a document of 1435 we learn that, by this time, the rent had not been paid for a long time, and the reigning grand master also dissuaded the commander of Koblenz from making a complaint about it to the English king. He argued that it was not worth the trouble; furthermore, there would be no real chance of success.[27] Despite all this, Deputy Grand Master Henry Reuss of Plauen made a last attempt in 1468 to win financial support from the king.[28] The fact that Reuss of Plauen did solicit the rent from Edward IV (r. 1461–83) in 1468 sheds some light on the meagre financial resources of the order soon after the Thirteen Years' War (1454–66). The Teutonic Order was in great need of every kind of income, even the relatively small amount of 40 marks.[29]

b. The Possibilities for Military Support

After the battle of Tannenberg, the positive relationship between the English and the Teutonic Knights continued, and the latter, along with the Hanseatic League, were well aware of the current position and financial possibilities of England. On the basis of their former cooperation, potential financial and military support was always present in the following years, testifying to the importance of the earlier

---

24 *Richard II* (CPR) 4: 74.
25 Hans Koeppen, 'Das Ende der englischen Preußenfahrten', *Preußenland* 8 (1970), 49–52.
26 'Privilèges octroyés aux Teutoniques', no. 7, p. 422.
27 The letter of the grand master is quoted by Koeppen, 'Die englische Rente', pp. 420–21.
28 *SVDOP* 3, no. 416, pp. 20–22.
29 *SVDOP* 3, no. 416, pp. 20–22.

participation of English crusaders in the *Reisen*. The bitterness that the Teutonic Order felt towards the termination of English participation at the turn of the fourteenth and fifteenth centuries is very evident in the correspondence of the grand masters. I have already mentioned some complaints about the non-payment of the annual English rent. At the same time, we also have some primary sources at our disposal which, besides documenting continuing demands for diplomatic assistance, cast light on the great popularity of and appreciation for English longbowmen in Prussia.

The content of two letters written by Grand Master Henry of Plauen (r. 1410–13) attests to the importance of longbowmen in the Lithuanian campaigns. These soldiers had made a very positive impression on the Teutonic leaders in earlier *Reisen*, as the excerpts of some documents from that time testify.[30] In the first, the grand master reported on the military preparations of the Poles and the Lithuanians and asked for a hundred longbowmen from the English king to help the Teutonic Order. He wished, furthermore, that Henry IV would placate Sigismund of Luxemburg, king of Hungary from 1387 and king of the Romans from 1411, since Plauen had made peace with the enemy without the consent of the latter. The grand master also tried to seek the help of Henry IV in another diplomatic matter. He wanted the king to plead the order's cause with the pope and other secular princes. He tried to gain the Polish king's consent to extend the payment deadline of the third part of the indemnity imposed on the Teutonic Order and to remit the fourth part entirely. In his second letter, he pleaded with the English king once again, and urged him to send the hundred longbowmen to Prussia.

References to the war waged against the Poles and the Lithuanians occur quite frequently in the correspondence.[31] In July 1413, the grand master informed Henry IV on the events of the 'Great War'. According to his letter, Vladislas II Jogaila, king of Poland (r. 1386–1434), and Vytautas, grand duke of Lithuania (r. 1392–1430), were preparing to attack the order with great forces, and their intention was utterly to destroy it with the help of their Mongol/Tatar and other heretical allies. Referring to the benevolences of Henry's predecessors, Plauen urged him to send his support to the order in its difficult situation and asked him — if the payment of the usual sum would not be possible — to send one thousand selected archers for six months at his own cost instead.[32]

---

30 *VPUB* 1411.07.17.a, 1411.08.10.
31 *VPUB*, JH I 1247 (on the good-will and commitment of the English king); 1282 (letter of complaint to European princes, including the king of England, against Jogaila and Vytautas); 1411.00.00.c (report to Henry IV on the peace concluded with Jogaila).
32 GStA PK, XX. HA, OF 6, pp. 289–90.

c. Diplomatic and Financial Assistance

The outcome of the 'Great War' (1409–11) placed serious burdens on the Teutonic Order. The enormous amount of money that the order had to pay for the return of its castles and captives almost caused its bankruptcy.[33] The delay in paying the indemnity threatened to cause Jogaila to restart the war. In order to avoid this outcome, the Teutonic Order put all of its diplomatic resources and connections among the powerful European princes into play, exhorting them to intervene in favour of the order. First of all, they sought to utilise the pope's influence in order to achieve their primary goals: firstly, to force the Polish king to keep the regulations of the peace, and secondly to modify the conditions of the indemnity's payment. On this occasion the leaders of the Teutonic Order could once again count on the support of their loyal ally, the English king.[34] This information is also confirmed by other sources. According to the anonymous continuator of John of Posilge's chronicle, both the French and the English king interceded with the pope in favour of the order at the turn of 1411–12.[35] Furthermore, in February 1412, the procurator of the order serving in the papal curia informed the grand master that Henry IV had, through his legate, proclaimed his commitment to the order before the Holy See. According to the statement of the envoy, his lord would be more than willing to take part in the fighting, if he had not been laid low with sickness.[36]

The great need caused by the war is also apparent in a further document from May 1411: in a letter addressed to Henry IV, Grand Master Henry of Plauen tried to ensure that compensation for the losses which Hanseatic merchants had suffered at the hands of Englishmen would arrive before 29 September.[37] He added that payment of the next amount was due by 2 February 1412.[38] It is likely that he rendered his thanks for this money to the king in October 1412, informing

---

33 Through the First Peace of Thorn (mod. Toruń, Poland) made on 1 February 1411, the Teutonic Order was obliged to pay an indemnity of 100,000 *Schocks* (150,000 Prussian marks) to the Polish king for the return of some castles and the release of captives held in Poland and Lithuania. Sven Ekdahl, 'The Teutonic Order's Mercenaries during the "Great War" with Poland-Lithuania (1409–11)', in *Mercenaries and Paid Men: The Mercenary Identity in the Middle Ages. Proceedings of a Conference Held at University of Wales, Swansea, 7th–9th July 2005*, ed. John France (London, 2008), pp. 345–62 (here 355).
34 GStA PK, XX. HA, OBA 1585, fol. 1r–v.
35 Johann von Posilge, 'Chronik des Landes Preussen', ed. Ernst Strehlke, in *SRP* 3: 79–388 (here 328).
36 *BGDO* 1, no.68, p. 140: *Und der bobst frogte, ap dem konige ouch ernst were. Do sprach der ambasiator, das dem konige also ernst dorczu were; und were her gesunt gewest, her welde lange in eigener persone do sin gewest, uff das der orden nicht vortube. Also was der bobst den tag gar gnedig vor den orden.* As I mentioned earlier, Henry IV (at that time as the earl of Derby) travelled to Prussia twice in the 1390s to participate in the Lithuanian campaigns of the Teutonic Knights.
37 *VPUB* 1411.05.17.
38 According to the excerpt of a document found in the patent rolls from 16 May 1412 this was a compensation paid for the Hanseatic merchants who had been in captivity. *Henry IV* (CPR) 4: 400.

him that agents of the order had received the 2,000 nobles.[39] However, for our purposes, it is more significant that Plauen informed him about the current state of affairs and the order's present stance towards the Polish king. We also learn that the grand master had not yet sent his envoy to Henry IV, since he wanted to wait for the results of negotiations taking place at the court of Sigismund of Luxemburg.

The serious involvement of the English king is also supported by the content of a report sent from Prussia to England, which was intended to provide a comprehensive account of events since 1409, the beginning of the 'Great War'.[40] It was meant to be a kind of overview and summary, presenting the course of events from a Teutonic point of view in order to persuade its supporter to offer further assistance. Indeed, assistance — above all financial — was sorely needed: from a document we learn that, at the beginning of 1411, the Teutonic Knights were forced to take out a loan from several rulers in order to pay the sum of the indemnity demanded by the Polish king. From the addressees of the letters, we learn that agents authorised to accept the money were sent to Henry IV of England and to Charles VI of France. In addition, we also find several English towns (Lynn, Hull, London) and even the mayor of London amongst the names of creditors.[41]

From the instructions of the agents sent to the duke of Burgundy and the kings of England and France, we learn that the grand master entrusted his emissaries to complain about the acute financial crisis that had befallen the order as a result of the extravagant demands of the Polish king.[42] Plauen commanded his agents to do their best to acquire these lords' help in collecting the necessary sum. This was more than urgent as, in his letter addressed to his envoys in England, the grand master reported that, despite increasing taxes significantly, the order had been unable to pay its debts completely.[43] Therefore, the grand master had been forced to take out a loan which had shattered the economy of the country. He asked his deputies to provide an account of the present situation to the dukes and lords of England and to leave no stone unturned in order to avoid a repeat of the situation.

The death of Henry IV (March 1413), a patron of the Teutonic Knights, represented a serious blow to the cause of the order. It is telling that the order was very well-informed about the health of the king: in a letter to the master of Livonia the grand master already mentioned in February that the desperately ill Henry was close to death and expected to die soon.[44] After Henry V's accession to

---

39 *VPUB* 1412.10.05.a. A noble was a gold coin used in England from the middle of the fourteenth century. Its value was approximately equal to half a mark.
40 *VPUB*, JH I 1737.
41 It is more than probable that the Hanseatic League had a leading role in arranging the loan between the parties, since it had close connections with the English port towns.
42 *VPUB* 1412.11.12.
43 *VPUB* 1413.01.30.
44 *LUB* 1/4, no. 1932, pp. 837–40.

the throne, the grand master immediately informed him about the previous events and sought to gain the new king's support for the cause of the Teutonic Knights.[45] However, in the second half of the 1410s, correspondence between the two countries was confined to commercial matters. One reason for this phenomenon might have been that most of the issues between the order and the Polish king had been settled at the Council of Constance. Furthermore, after fighting had been renewed between England and France, the cause of the Teutonic Order faded into the background at the English court.

Nevertheless, the order strove to maintain its close relationship with the king of England, and tried to keep up to date on the progress of the Hundred Years' War. The motives behind these efforts could have been a desire to remain fully informed about the actual situation in order to identify opportunities for soliciting the financial or diplomatic help of the English king at the right time.[46] Moreover, to ensure the safety of maritime trade, the Hanseatic cities were also interested in receiving the latest and most precise information on the Anglo-French conflict. The letter of the citizens of Riga (10 December 1415), one of the most important cities in the Hanseatic League at this time, demonstrates the importance of receiving intelligence on the possibilities of trading and shipping:

> Also, dear grand master, we desire indeed that you be so gracious as to write us the news once again, how it is between the English and the French; does the war still rage or not? We would like to know this because of money, namely, whether we are free to send money to our Lord Archbishop of Riga from his revenues? Would it be safe now in the sea? We would like to be informed about these matters.[47]

At this time, the archbishop was staying in Narbonne, and the safety of the sea routes between the Baltic Sea and Occitania depended greatly upon the successes or misfortunes of the English in France.[48] For example, grain-carrying ships sent from Prussia were crucial for the provision of certain English footholds in

---

45 *VPUB* 1414.06.28.a.
46 It seems that, by this time, the order had abandoned its plan to get direct military support from England.
47 *BGDO* 2, no. 135, p. 283: *Ouch, lieber her meister, bitten wir euch zcu more begerlich, daz ir uns widder geruchet schreiben zcitunge, wi is ste czwisschen den Engilsschen und den Frantsoyern, ob die krig noch ste odir nicht. Want uns macht daran is zcu wißen ume des geldes willen, daz wir unserm heren erczbisschoffe von Rige uz dem lande von syme stiffte senden sollen, ob daz nu^e unfelig uff der zee were. Darnoch wolden wir uns richten.* At this time the archbishop of Riga was John of Wallenrode (r. 1393–1418). At the command of Sigismund of Luxemburg, he and Miklós Garai, palatine of Hungary, were on a diplomatic mission to extend the period of the armistice signed at Strasburg (mod. Brodnica, Poland) between the Teutonic Order and the kingdom of Poland on 7 October 1414. In this, the two parties agreed that they would settle their differences at the Council of Constance. See *BGDO* 2, no. 143, p. 297.
48 *BGDO* 2, no. 143, p. 296.

France.⁴⁹ However, despite the prospective profit of selling these goods to the English, Prussian merchants were occasionally loathed to risk the voyage due to the dangers of war, or were forbidden from exporting grain from Prussia in a period of necessity.⁵⁰

The Hundred Years' War is mentioned many times in the correspondence. At the beginning of 1413, the French king made a request to the grand master for an escort who would guide his envoy to Prussia in order to inform him of the peace made with the English.⁵¹ Again, one and half decades later, the grand master received the latest news on the Anglo-French war: in 1429, Nicholas of Redwitz, advocate of Stuhm (mod. Sztum, Poland), reported on the defeat of the English at Orléans, and wrote about its expected consequences:

> Also, your grace, we received intelligence that the cardinal of England withdrew due to a defeat the English had suffered at Orléans, and it is to be feared that from this year on there will not be real opportunities to take action against the heretics.⁵²

In fact, the war against the Hussites was the last major military cooperation between the Teutonic Order and England.⁵³ Despite the cardinal's departure from the region, the grand master asked Henry Beaufort to recruit English longbowmen even after the siege of Orléans. These were to be used in the fighting against the Hussites.⁵⁴ A further document referring to the Hundred Years' War is dated to December 1444. We learn from this that Henry VI informed the grand master about the peace made with the French through a knight called Gilbert of Alneto, who was present during the negotiations.⁵⁵

---

49 *VPUB*, JH I 7157 (the cardinal of England asks the help of the grand master to supply the soldiers of Calais; around 1436).
50 *VPUB* 1417.05.14 (Grand Master Michael Küchmeister refuses the request of Henry V to send grain to the English due to the needs of the people in Prussia).
51 *VPUB*, DH 178.
52 GStA PK, XX. HA, OBA 5245, fol. 1r: *Item meynen herrn gnaden ist zu wissen worden das der Cardinal von Engelandt durch einen niderlag willen der Englischen vor Oriens geschen wird czuruken geczogen ist und ist zu besorgen das aber von disem jar kein felt nach merklichen handel wider dy keczer ich gesche sind.* Henry Beaufort, half-brother of Henry IV, was a cardinal from 1426. He also functioned as the papal legate of Germany, Hungary and Bohemia from 1427, and took part in the Hussite Wars. George A. Holmes, 'Cardinal Beaufort and the Crusade against the Hussites', *EHR* 88 (1973), 721–50 (here 726).
53 A few years before, Beaufort had asked the citizens of Lübeck to send two ships full of timber for the making of longbows. Beaufort ordered these materials at his own cost. He remarked that he was hoping to overcome the Hussites with the help of the Catholic European rulers and the participation of English longbowmen. *Codex diplomaticus Lubecensis: Urkundenbuch der Stadt Lübeck*, ed. Johann Friedrich Böhmer and Friedrich Techen, 12 vols (Lübeck, 1843–1932), 7: no. 41, pp. 36–37.
54 *VPUB*, JH I 5248. Beaufort did recruit certain contingents, but they were eventually deployed in France.
55 GStA PK, XX. HA, OBA 8632, fol. 1r. Gilbert was not the first time involved in these negotiations: already in 1421, the grand master recommended him to the council of Thorn when he was carrying the letter of the kings of England and France, as well as the duke of Burgundy. *VPUB* 1421.06.13.

Conclusion

Although we do not have any information regarding the payment of the annual rent or crusaders sent from England after 1410, the Teutonic Order did not stop placing confidence in the English king. It still hoped for military or financial support in the future. However, it seems that, by the first third of the fifteenth century, the annual rent had already lost its relevance from the English point of view, and the matter was also dropped once and for all by the Teutonic Knights after 1468. Paradoxically, at the zenith of English participation in the *Reisen* (at the turn of the 1380s and 90s), there was a commercial rivalry between England and Prussia which led to strained relations and later to a temporary estrangement. English merchants' attempts to gain a larger share of Baltic trade naturally led to increased tensions with the Hanseatic League, which sought to protect its monopolies in the region.[56] By the end of the fourteenth century things had worsened, and there was a poor relationship between English and Hanseatic merchants. The latter demanded financial recompense several times for losses caused by the English.[57] The two parties sought to settle their dispute through negotiation (1388 and 1409) and Prussian merchants were compensated for their losses with more than 3,500 pounds from the exchequer.[58]

---

56 In 1373, John Swerd, a bowyer from York, received a royal approval on his plan to establish a workshop in Prussia. *Edward III*, ed. Henry C. Maxwell Lyte, CPR, 16 vols (London, 1891–1916), 15: 264. In 1374, Walter Brown from Norwich was granted permission to ship fourteen tuns of Spanish wine from Yarmouth to Prussia which, because of 'its weakness and age [...] may not advantageously be sold in England'. *Edward III*, ed. Henry C. Maxwell Lyte, CCR, 14 vols (London, 1896–1913), 14: 11. By 1390, English merchants had settled down in Danzig (mod. Gdańsk, Poland) and Königsberg (mod. Kaliningrad, Russia) and became aware of the Gotlandic harbours. These sources were used by Tyerman, *England and the Crusades*, pp. 272–73.

57 For commercial rivalries and negotiations, see *Foedera, conventiones, litterae, et cujuscunque generis acta publica, inter reges Angliae et alios quosvis imperatores, reges, pontifices, principes, vel communitates, ab ineunte saeculo duodecimo, viz. ab anno 1101. ad nostra usque tempora, habita aut tractata: ex autographis, infra secretiores archivorum regiorum thesaurarias per multa saecula reconditis, fideliter exscripta*, ed. Thomas Rymer, 10 vols, 3rd edn (Den Haag, 1739–45.), 3.4: 26 (1388 — commission to English envoys to negotiate with the grand master on commercial matters), 30 (1388 — negotiation on the damages and inequities committed by the English), 48–49 (1389 — immunity for Teutonic envoys travelling back to Prussia), 66–67 (1391– controversies between English and Prussian merchants); *Henry V*, ed. Henry C. Maxwell Lyte, CPR, 2 vols (London, 1910–11), 1: 64 (1 June 1413 — plundering of a Prussian ship); 2: 205 (15 Nov 1418 — seizure of an English ship); *Henry VI*, ed. Maxwell Lyte, CPR, 6 vols (London, 1901–10), 2: 201 (26 May 1432 — goods of Hanseatic merchants washed up on English shore), 274 (27 January 1433 — seizure of goods of Hanseatic merchants); 3: 74 (June 1437 — ratification of a former agreement), 214 (1 August 1438 — seizure of a Prussian ship), 409 (20 February 1440 — plundering of a Prussian ship). Furthermore: *VPUB* 1412.05.01 (1412 — plundering of a Prussian ship), 1412.10.05 (1412 — financial claims of Prussian and Livonian cities), JH I 1682 (compensation of 1,600 nobles sent to the Livonian cities), 1415.01.12 (1415 — compensation for damages suffered by Prussian merchants), JH I 7837 (1417 — increasing English customs).

58 Tyerman, *England and the Crusades*, pp. 272–73.

Reviewing the correspondence between the two countries after 1410, one can state that, except in the immediate aftermath of Tannenberg/Grunwald/Žalgiris, most of this was confined to commercial matters. The majority of letters dealt with the following issues: the shipment of grain to England (a subject of strategic importance during the Hundred Years' War); damages suffered by Prussian or English merchants and ships; and complaints made by the concerned party about the violation of privileges enjoyed in Prussia or England. It is worth noting that, after the frequent correspondence of the 1410s, there is a significant decline in the 1420s, and communication livened up again in the second half of the 1430s exclusively as a result of commercial matters. It is telling that, while previous wars and fighting are often commented in the aforementioned collection, there is no reference to the events of Thirteen Years' War or the so-called Rider's War (1519–21). This result coincides with the conclusion drawn by the termination of the annual English rent: England was no longer interested in the wars of the Teutonic Order or, at least, it did not expect to make much profit from supporting an institution of now questionable legitimacy.[59] An article by the Hungarian historian Attila Bárány supports the idea that this mutation was a consequence of the order's problems of legitimacy, and not of a change in the attitude of English rulers towards crusading enterprises.[60] Bárány presents in detail how Henry VIII of England had a keen interest in representing himself as a *defensor fidei* in European politics through planned financial support of the Hungarian king in his fight against the Ottomans. A similar motivation might have persuaded earlier English rulers to support the Teutonic Order's campaigns against then-pagan Lithuania. However, after the Christianisation of Lithuania, this territory lost its importance from this point of view. The crusading enterprises of English soldiers in other parts of Europe from the end of the fourteenth century lend further credence to this line of reasoning. By this time, military undertakings against the increasing Ottoman military threat in the Mediterranean and the Balkans, not to mention the Arabic one in the Iberian Peninsula, seemed far more justifiable from a crusading point of view than did the Lithuanian campaigns.

---

59 With the exception of the Hussite Wars, which were morally justifiable from a Catholic point of view. Therefore, both England and the Teutonic Order took part in the actions.
60 Attila Bárány, 'Magyarország és a külső segítség 1526-ban', in *"Nekünk mégis Mohács kell…": II. Lajos rejtélyes halála és különböző temetései*, ed. Gábor Farkas, Zsolt Szebelédi and Bernadett Varga (Budapest, 2016), pp. 35–54.

Score	Date	Sender	Addressee	Topic
VPUB, JH I 1247	20 January 1410	Dederick of Legendorf	Ulrich of Jungingen	• Polish agitation against the order • Henry IV's positive attitude to the order • grain shipment to England
VPUB, JH I 1282	20 May 1410	Ulrich of Jungingen	Holy Roman emperor; German princes; kings of Denmark, England, France; Dutch princes	• letter of complaint against Jogaila and Vytautas
VPUB 1411.07.17.a	17 July 1411	Henry of Plauen	Henry IV	• military preparations of the enemy • request for 100 longbowmen • payment of indemnity.
VPUB 1411.08.10	10 August 1411	Henry of Plauen	Henry IV	• repeated request for 100 longbowmen
GStA PK, XX. HA, OBA 1585	24 November 1411	Henry IV	pope (Gregory XII [?])	• peace negotiations between the order and the Polish king • apology in defence of the order • order's treasury is empty • asks the pope to force king Jogaila to keep to the peace agreement • extend the deadline of payment for the rest of the indemnity imposed on the Teutonic Order or to remit the sum entirely
VPUB 1411.00.00.c	1411	Henry of Plauen	Henry IV	• report to Henry IV on the peace concluded with Jogaila • request for support
VPUB 1412.10.05	5 October 1412	Henry of Plauen	Henry IV	• current state of affairs • order's present stance toward the Polish king • Teutonic envoys and negotiations at the court of Sigismund of Luxemburg • envoys sent to England
VPUB 1412.11.12	12 November 1412	Henry of Plauen (?)	Agents of the order sent to the sent to the duke of Burgundy and the kings of England and France	• acute financial crisis • request for collecting the necessary sum of indemnity
VPUB 1413.01.30	30 January 1413	Henry of Plauen	Teutonic envoys in England	• inability of the order to pay its debts despite increasing taxes • loan • shattered economy • request for the help of English lords
GStA PK, XX. HA, OF 6, pp. 289–90	July 1413	Henry of Plauen	Henry IV	• military preparations of the enemy • reference to his former deputies who had reported on the events • praise for the benevolence of former English kings toward the order • request for financial help • request for 1000 elected longbowmen (if financial help is not an option)
VPUB 1414.06.28.a	28 June 1414	Michael Küchmeister	Henry V	• summary of previous events • response to the charges of Polish king • request for continued support
VPUB, JH I 5248	1429	Paul of Rusdorf	Henry Beaufort, (English cardinal)	• Hussite Wars • request for longbowmen
GStA PK, XX. HA, OBA 8632	24 December 1444	Henry VI	Conrad of Erlichshausen	• peace concluded with the king of France

Tbl. 1. Non-trade-related correspondence between the Teutonic Order and England in the 1410s.

DARIUS BARONAS

Lithuanian Participation in the Crusading Movement in the Long Fifteenth Century

Kenneth Setton's monumental edition of *A History of the Crusades* represents the most comprehensive treatment of the crusades, from their inception to their zenith, final demise and legacy.[1] However, it contains no evidence to suggest that medieval Lithuanians may also be viewed as crusaders of a sort. This is quite understandable. For almost two centuries, it was the pagan Lithuanians who were on the receiving end of crusading activities in North-Eastern Europe. By the time of their conversion to Roman Catholicism in the late fourteenth century, the best days of crusading were well over, and Lithuanians seem to have missed the golden opportunity to sport their crusading credentials, as many other European nations had done at one time or another. However, this is not the whole story. A sustained interest in the phenomenon of the late crusades, and a closer look at what the first Christian Lithuanian rulers said and wrote, and what courses of action they took, allow us to advance the thesis that, following their conversion, the Lithuanians were not left beyond the pale of the pan-European enterprise that was the crusades, despite their fairly late entry to the most respectable club of proud European Catholic nations.[2] In a word, they were not merely victims of the

---

1 *A History of the Crusades*, ed. Kenneth M. Setton, 6 vols (Madison, 1969–89). The best single monograph dealing with the Northern crusades remains Eric Christiansen, *The Northern Crusades: The Baltic and the Catholic Frontier, 1100–1525*, (London, 1980 [2nd edn 1997]). The war of the Teutonic Order against the Baltic pagans has been covered by William Urban, *The Baltic Crusade* (DeKalb, 1975); Urban, *The Livonian Crusade* (Washington, 1981); Urban, *The Prussian Crusade* (Chicago, 2000); Anti Selart, *Livonia, Rus' and the Baltic Crusades in the Thirteenth Century*, trans. Fiona Robb (Boston, 2015). To date, the results of international cooperation on the Northern crusades are most readily available in *Crusade and Conversion on the Baltic Frontier, 1150–1500*, ed. Alan V. Murray (Aldershot, 2001); *The Clash of Cultures in the Medieval Baltic Frontier*, ed. Alan V. Murray (Farnham, 2009); *The North-Eastern Frontiers of Medieval Europe: The Expansion of Latin Christendom in the Baltic Lands*, ed. Alan V. Murray (Farnham, 2014). On all these issues, see also the various chapters in the most recently published selected work *The Expansion of the Faith: Crusading on the Frontiers of Latin Christendom in the High Middle Ages*, ed. Paul Srodecki and Norbert Kersken (Turnhout, 2021).
2 Besides the introductory chapter in this volume, the recent historiography of fifteenth-century crusading is also discussed in Norman Housley, *Crusading and the Ottoman Threat, 1453–1505*

crusades,[3] for some time they were also participants in the movement.[4] Further research is needed in order to fill out the full picture of Lithuanian participation in the crusading movement, and this chapter provides one more step in this direction.

The most promising avenue for this kind of research has been opened up by the pluralistic school of thought in the study of crusades, as represented by Jonathan Riley-Smith, Norman Housley, Alan V. Murray, and others.[5] This approach provides us with a flexibility that is most necessary in an attempt to capture the phenomenon of crusades in all its variegated manifestations and on virtually every front of medieval Christendom. As far as is reasonably possible, it enables us to understand medieval men on their own terms. As a point of departure, therefore, I take a view current in medieval Prussia and Livonia that the crusades were a spiritually meritorious form of warfare directed against the enemies of the Church, a war that could be equally well employed both in the defence of the Church and in the expansion of Christian dominions.[6] With regards to medieval Lithuanians, one may safely assume that, following their conversion to Christianity, their elite felt quite at home within the late medieval world, permeated as it was with chivalric practices and crusading ideals.[7] This change, however, was not as abrupt as the theological opposition between pagan and Christian would have us believe, nor as deep as the received wisdom on a chasm between enemy and friend would imply.

(Oxford, 2013). See also *Reconfiguring the Fifteenth-Century Crusade*, ed. Housley (London, 2017); *The Crusade in the Fifteenth Century: Converging and Competing Cultures*, ed. Housley (New York, 2017).

3 William Urban, 'Victims of the Baltic Crusade', *JBS* 29 (1998), 195–212.

4 Stephen C. Rowell, 'Lietuva — krikščionybės pylimas?: Vienos XV a. ideologijos pasisavinimas', in *Europos idėja Lietuvoje: Istorija ir dabartis*, ed. Darius Staliūnas (Vilnius, 2002), pp. 17–32; Stephen C. Rowell, 'Naujieji kryžiaus žygiuotojai: LDK ir Bizantijos santykiai XIV–XV a. sandūroje: Ar Vytautas Didysis buvo Lietuvos kryžiaus žygių prieš turkus bei totorius pradininkas?', in *Kryžiaus karų epocha Baltijos regiono tautų istorinėje sąmonėje*, ed. Rita R. Trimonienė and Robertas Jurgaitis (Šiauliai, 2007), pp. 181–205; Rita R. Trimonienė, 'Kryžiaus karų idėja XV a. II pusėje ir Lietuvos Didžioji Kunigaikštystė', in *Kryžiaus*, pp. 223–34; Darius Baronas, 'Byzantium and Lithuania: North and South look at each other', in *Byzantium, New Peoples, New Powers: The Byzantino-Slav Contact Zone, from the Ninth to the Fifteenth Century*, ed. Milijana Kaimakamova et al. (Kraków, 2007), pp. 310–17.

5 Different approaches are discussed by Norman Housley, *Contesting the Crusades* (Oxford, 2006), pp. 2–13.

6 Axel Ehlers, *Die Ablasspraxis des Deutschen Ordens im Mittelalter* (Marburg, 2007), pp. 54–59.

7 Darius Baronas and Stephen C. Rowell, *The Conversion of Lithuania: From Pagan Barbarians to Late Medieval Christians* (Vilnius, 2015).

Pagan-Christian Interface

Therefore, it is advantageous to turn our attention to the pagan-Christian interface at the time when the *Litauerreisen* were at their most intense.[8] The Teutonic Order provided opportunities for Western European nobles to display their Christian virtues and chivalric way of life in the fight against the 'Saracens' of the North.[9] These 'Saracens' proved to be a tough nut to crack, and it was therefore almost inevitable that certain peaceful modes of communication would arise. The most usual means of communication was to conduct negotiations over the exchange of prisoners of war, and these became quite frequent from the second half of the fourteenth century on.[10] Such negotiations must have involved some informal talk about the period of time when martial activities were supposed to come to a standstill.[11] It is no accident that the pagan Lithuanian prince who communicated most actively was Duke Kęstutis of Trakai (grand duke of Lithuania in 1381–82), the man who was in charge of relations with Lithuania's western neighbours. He and the Teutonic Knights had personal conversations on at least six occasions and, thanks to such contacts, he seems to have picked up a smattering of German.[12] In exceptional cases he managed to enter into personal relations with some of his adversaries. The prime example in this regard is supplied by the commander of Brandenburg (mod. Ushakovo), Gunter of Hohenstein, who acted as godfather to Danutė when her father Kęstutis handed her in marriage to Duke Janusz I of Masovia.[13]

The *Litauerreisen* did not constitute an all-out war of destruction and annihilation. The continuation of business as usual in the background may be exemplified by making reference to the trade treaties concluded between Lithuanian and Livonian authorities in 1338 and 1367.[14] The parties sought to ensure that their

---

8 Werner Paravicini, *Die Preussenreisen des europäischen Adels*, 4 vols (Sigmaringen, 1989–2023).
9 Paravicini, *Preussenreisen* 3; Alan V. Murray, 'The Saracens of the Baltic: Pagan and Christian Lithuanians in the Perception of English and French Crusaders to Late Medieval Prussia', *JBS* 41 (2010), 413–29; Loïc Chollet, *Les Sarrasins du Nord: Une histoire de la croisade balte par la littérature (XIIe–XVe siècle)* (Neuchâtel, 2019).
10 Sven Ekdahl, 'The Treatment of Prisoners of War during the Fighting between the Teutonic Order and Lithuania', in *The Military Orders: Fighting for the Faith and Caring for the Sick*, ed. Malcolm Barber (Aldershot, 1994), pp. 263–69; Alvydas Nikžentaitis, 'Belaisviai Lietuvoje ir Vokiečių Ordino valstybėje (1283–1409)', in *Lietuvos valstybė XII–XVIII a.*, ed. Zigmantas Kiaupa et al. (Vilnius, 1997), pp. 507–27; Antanas Petrilionis, 'Belaisviai Lietuvos Didžiosios Kunigaikštystės ir Vokiečių ordino karuose (XIV–XV amžiai)' (unpublished doctoral dissertation, Vilnius University, 2022).
11 *Kodex dyplomatyczny Litwy*, ed. Edward Raczyński (Wrocław, 1845), p. 69.
12 Darius Baronas, 'Lietuvių ir vokiečių taikaus bendravimo bruožai XIV a. karo sūkuryje', *Lituanistica* 56 (2010), 7–9.
13 Jan Tęgowski, *Pierwsze pokolenia Giedyminowiczów* (Poznań, 1999), p. 218; Rimvydas Petrauskas, 'Litauen und der Deutsche Orden: Vom Feind zum Verbündeten', in *Tannenberg-Grunwald-Žalgiris 1410: Krieg und Frieden im späten Mittelalter*, ed. Werner Paravicini, Rimvydas Petrauskas and Grischa Vercamer (Wiesbaden, 2012), pp. 238–40.
14 *Chartularium Lithuaniae res gestas magni ducis Gedeminne illustrans = Gedimino laiškai*, ed. Stephen C. Rowell (Vilnius, 2003), pp. 258–60; *LUB* 1/2, no. 1041, cols 772–73; Rasa Mažeika,

Fig. 13. Seal of Duke Kęstutis of Trakai from 1379. Courtesy of Edmundas Rimša.

merchants could carry on with trading even in the thick of military activities. To achieve this on the Riga–Vilnius route was not plain sailing, and brigands roaming far and wide presented a nuisance to merchants from both sides. In order to contain the brigands within certain limits, both the Lithuanian and Livonian authorities took it upon themselves to ensure safe-conduct all the way to Vilnius or Riga, but no wider than one could throw a spear. One step further afield and a merchant could be killed or spoiled of his goods without provoking any legal repercussions. What is important to note is that the Teutonic Knights took care to ensure good behaviour on the part of 'their' brigands in territories deep into Lithuania, while Lithuanian nobles must have been authorised to look after 'their' brigands almost to the outskirts of Riga.[15]

Military confrontation with Western crusaders, raids, spying, and occasional peaceful contacts with the Teutonic Knights not only facilitated the flow of military know-how in both directions, but also brought the modes of knightly self-expression closer to the hearts of Lithuanian nobles.[16] It also needs to be admitted that pagans constituted an exotic thing for Western European nobles, evoking in them a blend of emotions ranging from hatred and disdain to interest and respect. The joy of taking part in the indiscriminate killing of the pagans, the desire to obtain slaves of pagan origin, the curiosity of paying a visit to a pagan prince — all these strands come together to form a multi-faceted picture of pagan-Christian relations and contacts at the height of the *Litauerreisen*.[17] The experience of this

---

'Of Cabbages and Knights: Trade and Trade Treaties with the Infidel on the Northern Frontier, 1200–1390', *Journal of Medieval History* 20 (1994), 71–76.

15 Darius Baronas, 'Działalność paramilitarnych band rozbójniczych na pograniczu krzyżacko-litewskim w XIV wieku', *RL* 1 (2015), 7–17.

16 Darius Baronas, 'Der Kontext der litauischen Kriegskunst des 13. Jahrhunderts und die militärischen Innovationen von der zweiten Hälfte des 14. Jahrhunderts bis zum Beginn des 15. Jahrhunderts', in *Tannenberg-Grunwald-Žalgiris 1410*, pp. 159–73; Rimvydas Petrauskas, 'Knighthood in the Grand Duchy of Lithuania from the Late Fourteenth to the Early Sixteenth Centuries', *LHS* 11 (2006), 39–66. On early Lithuanian heraldry, see Władysław Semkowicz, 'Braterstwo szlachty polskiej z bojarstwem litewskim w unji horodelskiej 1413 roku', in *Polska i Litwa w dziejowym stosunku*, ed. Wojciech Baranowski (Kraków, 1914), p. 414; Edmundas Rimša, *Heraldry: Past to Present*, trans. Vijolė Arbas (Vilnius, 2005), pp. 58–76 and 119–21.

17 *Peter Suchenwirts Werke aus dem vierzehnten Jahrhunderte: Ein Beytrag zur Zeit- und Sittengeschichte*, ed. Alois Primisser (Vienna, 1827), lns 257–62: *In ein lant, daz haist Sameyt, / Da vand man einew*

pagan-Christian interface was not lost on the first generation of Lithuania's Christian rulers. In order to denounce the grand master of the Teutonic Order in the eyes of King Sigismund of Hungary, Vladislas II Jogaila found it opportune to recall that, even in his pagan days, he had not been exposed to such nasty behaviour at the hands of the Teutonic Knights as was the case now he had become king of Poland.[18]

Even though relations between the Teutonic Order and their pagan Lithuanian adversaries were the most intense, they were far from being the only ones. Poland was another East-Central European polity whose rulers assumed the role of defenders of the faith and sought to stylise their realm as the shield or bulwark of Christendom, exposed as it was to continual attacks from Mongols/Tatars, Ruthenians, and Lithuanians.[19] These enemies had to be dealt with by making recourse to crusading for the sake of extending the limits of the Christian faith. This drama was played out most intensively in the lands of Volhynia, Galicia and Podolia, where Polish, Hungarian, Mongol/Tatar, and Lithuanian interests intersected.[20] It was also in the region of Podolia that the first Lithuanian crusader was produced — Duke Alexander Karijotaitis. After consolidating his power there, he became ever more assertive vis-à-vis the Mongols/Tatars. In 1378, Pope Gregory XI granted him full remission of sins as he was about to launch a campaign against the Golden Horde in defence, as he believed, of the Roman Catholic Church.[21] Fighting them, he died sometime around 1380.[22] In his capacity as crusader, Duke Alexander was exceptional among his Lithuanian kith and kin, but as far as the other general qualities of a Christian prince are concerned, he falls in line with his brothers George, Boris, Constantine, Theodore and Basil. Based in Podolia, these Karijotid princes entered into close relations with their Hungarian and Polish neighbours and became either Roman Catholic or Greek Orthodox Christians. In a sense, they may be regarded as harbingers of what was to come in the wake of the conversion of Grand Duke Jogaila and his accession to the Polish throne. Poland proved to be the main vehicle for the establishment of a Roman Catholic church organisation in Lithuania, but it was the Teutonic Order, however, whose initial impact was most decisive in forming the more militant Christian attitudes among the Lithuanians.

---

hochtzeit; / Di gest chomen ungepeten! / Ein tantz mit haiden wart getreten, / Daz ir wol sechtzig bliben tot; / Dar nach daz dorf mit vewr rot; Paravicini, *Preussenreisen* 2: 105–10; Petrauskas, 'Litauen', p. 241.

18 *CEV*, no. 713, p. 376.
19 Paul Srodecki, *Antemurale Christianitatis: Zur Genese der Bollwerksrethorik im östlichen Mitteleuropa an der Schwelle vom Mittelalter zur Frühen Neuzeit* (Husum, 2015), pp. 110–11.
20 *On the Frontier of Latin Europe: Integration and Segregation in Red Ruthenia, 1350–1600*, ed. Thomas Wünsch and Andrzej Janeczek (Warsaw, 2004); Sven Jaros, *Iterationen im Grenzraum: Akteure und Felder multikonfessioneller Herrschaftsaushandlung in Kronruthenien (1340–1434)* (Berlin, 2021).
21 *VMPL* 1, no. 1015, pp. 748–49.
22 Baronas and Rowell, *The Conversion*, pp. 238–40.

Teutonic Knights' Tutorial for Lithuanian Princes

Relations between the Teutonic Order and the Lithuanian dukes became significantly more diversified and intense following the accession of Jogaila to the grand ducal throne in 1377. A sign of the times is the series of treaties concluded between the Teutonic Order and the Lithuanian rulers from 1379 on.[23] Their formulaic expressions reveal the influence of the Teutonic Order's chancery and, taken on their own, they may seem to have nothing to do with crusading ideology. However, we need to look at them in closer detail. Grand Master Conrad Zöllner of Rotenstein's promise, made in 1384, to support Prince Vytautas against the enemies of the Christian religion, stands in stark contrast to earlier documents.[24] The fight for the recovery of the patrimony of Vytautas could thus be presented as some sort of struggle on behalf of Christianity, even if the object was so mundane, and the enemies, Grand Duke Jogaila and Duke Skirgaila, could only be portrayed as enemies of the Christian faith by means of a very loose interpretation. That such a view had little to do with the actual adherence to paganism or Christianity is clear from the fact that Vytautas' brother Sigismund was still technically pagan, but was evidently not considered to be an enemy of Christianity.[25] Opprobrium could be heaped on somebody depending on the political circumstances and the intended audience. The Teutonic Order's habit of depicting its adversaries as enemies of the Church and Christianity had a long pedigree.[26] The Knights and their guests taking part in the so-called *Litauerreisen* believed this to be true.[27] It was a one-size-fits-all means of attracting support for a noble cause. The first Lithuanian prince who picked up this ideological weapon was none other than Vytautas himself. This is not to say that Vytautas or his kin, the Lithuanian grand ducal family, were novices requiring instruction in the ways of late medieval realpolitik from their Teutonic masters. However, it is my contention that the very idiom of deciding who was on the right side and who was on the wrong was borrowed and internalised initially as a result of their dealings with the Teutonic Order. Lithuanian dukes were quite adroit in exploiting the divide between Christian and non-Christian for their own ends. When, in 1402, in a bid to undo the power of Vytautas, the regular troublemaker prince Švitrigaila and his Teutonic allies

---

23 The treaty of 29 September 1379: *CDP* 3, no. 134, pp. 180–82; the treaty of 31 May 1380: *LUB* 1/3, no. 1153, cols 362–63; the three treaties concluded at Dubysa on 31 October 1382: *LUB* 1/3, no. 1185, cols 394–95. For a detailed analysis of these, see Oleg Litskevich, 'Орденский экземпляр договора о четырехлетнем перемирии и военной помощи между Великим Княжеством Литовским и Тевтонским Орденом (31 октября 1382 г.)', *Istorijos Šaltinių Tyrimai* 5 (2014), 215–32; Sergey V. Polekhov, 'Układ litewsko-krzyżacki o odstąpieniu Żmudzi z 1382 roku — kwestia autentyczności tekstu', *RL* 8 (2022), 7–25.
24 *CEV*, no. 15, p. 5.
25 *CEV*, no. 16, pp. 5–6.
26 Marcus Wüst, *Studien zum Selbstverständnis des Deutschen Ordens im Mittelalter* (Weimar, 2013), pp. 82–83, 276–77.
27 Loïc Chollet, *Les Sarrasins du Nord*, pp. 60–71, 114–21, 199–214.

launched deep raids into newly-converted Lithuania, their avowed promise not to attack Christian lands posed no real problems since it was up to them to decide where the line between true and false Christians ran.[28] One and the same person could be described in starkly contrasting terms, but this did not make him or her a pariah. The best example of this is Vytautas's daughter Sophia, who had been given in marriage to the Muscovite prince Vasily back in 1391.[29] In a general appeal addressed to a Roman Catholic audience in 1409, Polish king Vladislas II Jogaila depicted her as the 'most cruel hater' of the Roman Catholic faith, filled with rage even against her own parents.[30] This about-face was attributed to the Teutonic Knights who were given credit for engineering this marriage in order to have a schismatic Muscovy as an ally in an attempt to suppress the Catholic faith. Four years later, however, in the legal battle against the Teutonic Order, the good offices of this same Sophia were most welcome to both Jogaila and Vytautas.[31] It must be stressed that high-flown rhetorical devices stressing stark opposition between a true and a false religion were most frequently employed by the royal or grand ducal chancery in their correspondence with Western powers. The situation on the ground was much more diverse and dependent on ever changing pattern of relations between all the sides concerned.

The fight against the infidel Ottoman Turks and Mongols/Tatars of the Golden Horde was one of the earliest tasks presented to the newly-converted Lithuanian rulers by their Roman Catholic spiritual masters and allies.[32] In view of Lithuania's traditionally deep involvement in Rus and Mongol/Tatar-related affairs, Vytautas did not need much prompting to act.[33] Having made good his claims to grand ducal power in 1392, Vytautas was proving time and again that he was up to the task, even in the far-away steppes. In 1397 and 1398, he led victorious campaigns to the shores of the Black Sea, capturing and resettling the

---

28 *CEV*, no. 249, p. 82.
29 Jarosław Nikodem, *Witold wielki książę litewski (1354 lub 1355–27 października 1430)* (Kraków, 2013), pp. 119–20, 136.
30 *CEV*, no. 425, p. 196.
31 GStA PK, XX. HA, OF 7, pp. 64, 200–1. See also *Lites* 2/2, no. 29, p. 83 (28 January 1413). For more detail on these negotiations, see Wiesław Sieradzan, *Misja Benedykta Makraia w latach 1412– 13: Z dziejów pokojowych metod rozwiązywania konfliktów międzypaństwowych w Europie Środkowo-Wschodniej* (Malbork, 2009), pp. 55–78; Adam Szweda, 'Zakon Krzyżacki wobec Polski i Litwy w latach 1411–1414', *PH* 141 (2014), 538–42.
32 At the request of Jogaila, Pope Urban VI granted remission of sins to those who would take part in the fight against the Ottomans and Tatars, 1 April 1388: *CESDQ* 2, no. 13, p. 17.
33 On Tataro-Lithuanian relations, see Darius Baronas, 'The Lithuanians and the Tatars: Confrontation from a Safe Distance and Vested Interests in the Common Ground', in *The Routledge Handbook of the Mongols and Central-Eastern Europe: Political, Economic, and Cultural Relations*, ed. Alexander V. Maiorov and Roman Hautala (London, 2021), pp. 311–20; Vladyslav Gulevych, 'Expansion of the Grand Duchy of Lithuania in the Middle and the Second Half of the Fourteenth Century and Its Relations with the Horde', in *The Routledge Handbook of the Mongols*, pp. 340–67; Gulevych, 'The Grand Duchy of Lithuania, the Kingdom of Poland, and the Tatar World in the Fifteenth Century', in *The Routledge Handbook of the Mongols*, pp. 368–88.

Tatar prisoners of war on Lithuanian soil. The best proof that these campaigns were linked to crusading ideology was the castle built in 1398 on the lower reaches of the River Dnieper and given the aptly chosen name of St John.[34] To extend his clout and stabilise his rule over Kiev, Vytautas had to come to terms with the Teutonic Order. A mutual desire for cooperation was in the air, as may be inferred from the fact that a number of Teutonic Knights joined Vytautas in his campaigns of 1397 and 1398. The prospect of availing themselves of prisoners of war was not lost on them. It is therefore not by chance that there is a clause in the 1398 Treaty of Salinas (Ger. Salinwerder) which stipulates that both sides should enjoy equal rights over their prospective prisoners of war.[35] However mundane such struggles may appear, they had to be clad in the garb of a righteous war. To find yourself on the right side brought not only a sense of self-satisfaction, it also meant getting involved in the difficult task of spreading the Christian faith. This phrase was still relevant to the politics of the day — the Teutonic Order took much care to have this clause inscribed in the Treaty of Salinwerder.[36] After much talk and preparation Vytautas led an international host under the sign of the cross, only to suffer a debacle on the banks of the River Vorskla.[37] The best proof that this campaign was connected with crusading ideology is to be seen in the indulgence granted by Pope Boniface IX, albeit too late to make a difference, to the international Christian army, supplemented by Tatars allied to Vytautas who, this time, happened to be on the right side, if not the winning one.[38]

Lithuanian Neophytes Come of Age

The defeat at Vorskla was a bitter blow for Vytautas, and one from which he drew his lesson by becoming less rash and more circumspect. It is therefore not surprising that, in dealing with their own Orthodox subjects, Lithuanian rulers avoided the use of harsh language that might alienate them — circumspection was advisable. However, where matters related to international politics and substantial gains seemed to be within easy reach, a crusade-style idiom could still

---

34 Johann von Posilge, 'Chronik des Landes Preussen', ed. Ernst Strehlke, in *SRP* 3: 79–388 (here 222).
35 *SVDOP* 2: 11; Klaus Neitmann, *Die Staatsverträge des Deutschen Ordens in Preußen 1230–1449: Studien zur Diplomatie eines spätmittelalterlichen deutschen Territorialstaates* (Köln, 1986), pp. 150–53; Sebastian Kubon, *Die Außenpolitik des Deutschen Ordens unter Hochmeister Konrad von Jungingen (1393–1407)* (Göttingen, 2016), pp. 66–123. For slave trade in the region under consideration, see Danuta Quirini-Popławska, *Włoski handel czarnomorskimi niewolnikami w późnym średniowieczu* (Kraków, 2002), pp. 219–22.
36 Kubon, *Außenpolitik*, p. 99.
37 The sources on the battle of Vorskla are discussed by Stephen C. Rowell, 'Ne visai priminitnos kautynės: ką byloja šaltiniai apie 1399 m. mūšį ties Vorsklos upe', *Istorijos Šaltinių Tyrimai* 1 (2008), 67–89. For more on the battle, see Bertold Spuler, *Die Goldene Horde: Die Mongolen in Rußland 1223–1502* (Leipzig, 1943), pp. 136–40; Robert Frost, *The Oxford History of Poland-Lithuania*, 2 vols (Oxford, 2015), 1: 85–86.
38 *VMPL* 1, no. 1041, pp. 769–71.

be employed. When relations with their Muscovite neighbours were approaching the point of military confrontation in 1406, both King Vladislas II and Grand Duke Vytautas requested that the pope grant Holy Land plenary indulgences to all warriors who would come to their aid against the infidels or schismatics. The same remission of sins was requested for all those whose bodily strength did not allow them to proceed in person, but who could nevertheless contribute to the common cause in other ways.[39]

The matter was an urgent one. The royal and grand ducal supplicants admitted that they were fighting a defensive war for the sake of the Christian faith but, exposed to the innumerable multitude of the infidels, they were in sore need of strenuous warriors. If Poland and Lithuania failed, God forbid, then all the Christian lands in those parts could easily be destroyed or subjected to perpetual slavery. Thus, the supplication of 1406 pro-

Fig. 14. An early-fifteenth-century depiction of Vladislas II Jogaila, king of Poland and grand duke of Lithuania, as a defender of the faith from the Holy Trinity Chapel in Lublin Castle, Poland. Photo by Darius Baronas.

vides one of the earliest instances of both Poland and Lithuania acting as a bulwark of Christendom. In their eagerness to enlist foreign aid, Vladislas II Jogaila and Vytautas were following in the footsteps of the Teutonic Knights. Furthermore, of course, they were also quite prepared to cooperate with the order. Early in 1407, news arrived that German 'noble guests' were coming to join Vytautas in his campaign to the Rus lands and the grand duke asked the order's marshal to inform them that he had sent guides to meet them and show them the best way to catch up with his troops should they arrive in Vilnius after his departure to the east.[40] In the end, however, the Teutonic Order came to see all this flurry of activity as in competition with its own enterprise. When the pope inquired as to whether the requested indulgences would jeopardise its privileges, the procurator of the order, unsurprisingly, gave an affirmative answer, and the required grace was withheld.[41] This, of course, did not stop the campaign from taking place anyway.

---

39 GStA PK, XX. HA, OBA 861, fol. 2r.
40 *CEV*, no. 357, p. 140 (= GStA PK, XX. HA, OBA 962, fol. 2r).
41 *BGDO* 2, no. 31, pp. 89–60 (14 May [1407]); Ehlers, *Ablaspraxis*, pp. 66–67, 74.

The confrontation between Vytautas of Lithuania and his son-in-law Vasily I of Moscow in 1406–8 was by no means a clear-cut encounter, but resembled rather a knightly tug of war in an attempt to clarify spheres of influence in Smolensk, Chernihiv, Ryazan and the upper reaches of the River Oka.[42]

Following the Battle of Tannenberg, Poland and Lithuania reached the pinnacle of their power and prestige on the European stage, while the Teutonic Order was forced into a defensive position.[43] In 1411, Grand Master Henry of Plauen informed Western potentates of his anxiety about the Ottoman and Golden Horde envoys who had come to negotiate with Jogaila and Vytautas.[44] Sometime later, a papal legate and the envoys of King Sigismund arrived in Vilnius.[45] In the same year Polish and Lithuanian rulers mounted a triumphal progress across their Ruthenian dominions to drive home the message of their power and military might.[46] Tensions between Poland, Lithuania and the Teutonic Order were again on the rise. It was perhaps not merely a rhetorical flourish on the part of the Teutonic Knights when they depicted the dire straits they found themselves in by expressing their fears over the upcoming *Reyse* from the east. The grand master was alarmed that Vytautas could not only bring together all the Ruthenians against his Order, but could also call on 'guests' to support him.[47] The good working relationships which Vytautas enjoyed with Orthodox Christians and mostly Islamised Mongols/Tatars of the Golden Horde could hardly have impinged negatively on his authority and fame. Like Vladislas II, Vytautas took care to have a papal permit for the mass to be celebrated even when Orthodox believers were in attendance.[48] This was meant to be beneficial for the increase in the numbers of faithful believers. Vytautas also took care to be allowed to have mass celebrated in his presence even before dawn, thus receiving the same privilege which the Teutonic Order had obtained long ago to meet the spiritual needs of its troops wading through the lands of pagans and schismatics.[49]

One of the biggest public fora in the later Middle Ages was provided by the Council of Constance (1414–18). This provided a good occasion for both Jogaila and Vytautas, for Poles and Lithuanians alike, to present their Christian credentials in the best possible light. They strove to show that they could succeed where

---

42 On the war of 1406–8, see Roman A. Bespalov, 'Литовско-московские отношения 1392–1408 годов в связи со смоленской, черниговской и рязанской политикой Витовта и Василия I', *Средневековая Русь* 12 (2016), 129–82; Nikodem, *Witold*, pp. 229–42.
43 William Urban, *Tannenberg and After: Lithuania, Poland and the Teutonic Order in Search of Immortality* (Chicago, IL, 2002).
44 *CEV*, no. 477, pp. 223–24.
45 *LUB* 1/4, no. 1888, cols 779–80.
46 Giedrė Mickūnaitė, *Making a Great Ruler: Grand Duke Vytautas of Lithuania* (Budapest, 2006), pp. 31–33.
47 *CEV*, no. 543, p. 262 (May, 1413); *LUB* 1/4, no. 1938, cols 848–49 (1 May 1413).
48 Permission granted to Jogaila: AAV, RA 122A, fol. 50v (06 November 1404). Further copies have been preserved in RA 119, fols 178v, 183v, 189v. Permission granted to Vytautas: AAV, RS 116, fol. 212v. Published in part in *BP* 4, no. 327, p. 60 (27 August 1418).
49 *CDP* 3, no. 96, pp. 126–27 (1368).

the Teutonic Order had failed, namely in the conversion of the Samogitians, who inhabited the last pagan enclave in Europe, surrounded on all sides by Christian dominions. However, the issue of reclaiming Samogitia into the Lithuanian fold was subordinated to far greater concerns, namely the union between the Latin and Greek Church. In this light, both Jogaila and Vytautas could be seen as significant players on the international stage, where the necessity of stemming the Ottoman tide and bringing about a union between Christians of the Latin and Greek rites were burning issues. At this time their influence could be felt from Moscow to Constance and from Constance to Constantinople.[50]

Both of them seemed to be concerned over the fate of Constantinople, where the grand-daughter of Vytautas, Anna, was married to the heir-apparent John Palaiologos.[51] In 1415, King Vladislas II Jogaila sent a shipment of grain to the impoverished city at the Bosporus.[52] The efforts of Jogaila and Vytautas to play an active role did not go unnoticed. Council fathers urged them to fight against the infidel Ottoman Turks and Golden Horde Tatars and the heretical Bohemians.[53] In 1417, Sigismund of Luxemburg, as king of Hungary (since 1387) and king of the Romans (since 1411), asked for Jogaila's mediation to determine whether a truce could be concluded with the Ottoman Empire.[54] In 1418, Pope Martin V reconfirmed his papal blessing for the military actions if they were to be undertaken by Vladislas II or Vytautas against the 'barbaric tribes' for the sake of the propagation of the Christian faith.[55] Soon afterwards, both of them were accorded the dignity of vicars general *in temporalibus* of the Holy See in the Rus lands of Novgorod and Pskov.[56]

Something serious was clearly afoot in 1420–21, when the Franco-Flemish knight Ghillebert of Lannoy, acting as Anglo-French ambassador, was crisscrossing the lands of Eastern Europe and the Middle East, and when the map of Constantinople made by the Italian scholar and traveller Cristoforo Buondelmonti was dispatched to Vytautas.[57] In 1420, the Byzantine envoy Manuel

---

50 Baronas and Rowell, *The Conversion*, pp. 328, 366–78. On church union, see also Darius Baronas, 'King Ladislas II Jogaila of Poland, Grand Duke Vytautas of Lithuania and the Roman Catholic and Greek Orthodoc Church Union', in *Unions and Divisions: New Forms of Rule in Medieval and Renaissance Europe*, ed. Paul Srodecki, Norbert Kersken and Rimvydas Petrauskas (London, 2023), pp. 237–47.
51 Oskar Halecki, 'La Pologne et l'Empire Byzantin', *Byzantion* 7 (1932), 51–53; Igor P. Medvedev, 'Русская княжна на византийском троне', *Вопросы Истории* 2 (1995), 144–47; Baronas and Rowell, *The Conversion*, pp. 366–77.
52 Jan Długosz, *Annales seu cronicae incliti regni Poloniae*, ed. Jan Dąbrowski et al., [11 vols] (Warszawa, 1964–2005), [8]: bk 11, pp. 54–55.
53 BP 3, nos 1477, 1481–84, p. 236–37. Jorg K. Hoensch, *Kaiser Sigismund: Herrscher an der Schwelle zur Neuzeit, 1368–1437* (München, 1996), pp. 241–42.
54 CESDQ 1, no. 48, pp. 42–43; Hoensch, *Kaiser Sigismund*, pp. 241–42.
55 BP 4, nos 272–73, p. 50 (4 May 1418).
56 VMPL 2, no. 25–26, pp. 20–22 (13 May 1418).
57 Oskar Halecki, 'Gilbert de Lannoy and His Discovery of East Central Europe', *Bulletin of the Polish Institute of Arts and Sciences in America* 2 (1944), 324–29; Giuseppe Ragone, 'Il 'Liber insularum

Philantropenos attended the court of Vytautas in Novgorodok (mod. Navahrudak, Belarus) at the same time that the Moscow-based Metropolitan Photius of Kiev and All Rus was also present.[58] The following year, King Vladislas II asked the pope to grant indulgences for a *passagium generale* against the Ottoman Turks and Tatars of the Golden Horde.[59] Before anything tangible could be put into effect, however, Murad II laid siege to Constantinople in 1422. Outside help was not forthcoming, and the Greeks attributed their deliverance to the intervention of the Blessed Virgin Mary.[60] As the imminent danger evaporated, so too did the immediate cause for contemplating a crusade to save Constantinople.

Even though the capital of the Byzantine Empire and the Black Sea coast remained within the sphere of vested interests of Vytautas, his final years were absorbed by concerns closer to hand.[61] The years 1426–28 witnessed distant campaigns towards Pskov, Ryazan, and Novgorod.[62] The grand duke of Lithuania strove to attract volunteer knights, mostly Poles and Germans, to his expeditions.[63] The campaign of summer 1427 amounted essentially to a demonstration of power — visiting the easternmost lands within his reach, Vytautas would accept homage and gifts from Ruthenian dukes based in the upper reaches of the River Oka. The following year he achieved a logistical feat when his troops penetrated deep into the Novgorodian marshland and lay siege to the town of Porkhov. To rescue the situation, the townspeople and their Novgorodian masters had to pay a substantial contribution, just as the Pskovians had done in 1426. Vytautas left, but memories of the campaigns lingered on and, more than a century later, it was still possible to find crosses erected during his campaigns to Novgorod and Moscow on the banks of the Western Dvina (Latv. and Latg. Daugava).[64] In Lithuania, such crosses appeared to underline the Christian character of a newly-converted country.[65] Those on the way to Novgorod and Moscow may have served as signs of a Roman Catholic host reaching out to their schismatic enemy. However, it may also be that the papal blessing of 1418 was then still in force.

---

archipelagi' di Cristoforo dei Buondelmonti: filologia del testo, filologia dell'immagine', in *Humanisme et Culture Géographique à l'Époque du Concile de Constance: Autour de Guillaume Fillastre*, ed. Didier Marcotte (Turnhout, 2002), pp. 211–14.

58 'Супрасльский список', in *PSRL* 17: 58–59; 'Уваровский список', in *PSRL* 17: 109; Oskar Halecki, *From Florence to Brest (1439–1596)* (Rome, 1958), pp. 30–35; John W. Barker, *Manuel II Palaeologus (1391–1425): A Study in Late Byzantine Statesmanship* (New Brunswick, 1969), p. 338.

59 *BP* 4, no. 879, p. 163.

60 *Ioannis Canani de Constantinopolitana obsidione relatio*, ed. Andrea Massimo Cuomo (Boston, 2016), pp. 39–42. For the geneal context, see Nevra Necipoğlu, *Byzantium between the Ottomans and the Latins: Politics and Society in the Late Empire* (Cambridge, 2009), esp. pp. 184–232.

61 On the expedition of Vytautas to the Black Sea coast in February 1427, see Darius Baronas, 'Vytautas — žvejys: Simbolinės komunikacijos reikšmės politiniam procesui klausimu', *Istorijos šaltinių tyrimai* [upcoming volume — in print].

62 Nikodem, *Witold*, pp. 245–49.

63 *CEV*, no. 1235–36, pp. 732–34; Petrauskas, 'Knighthood', p. 48.

64 *LM* 37, p. 182.

65 *Lites* 2/2, no. 32, p. 154.

The Ebb and Flow of Religious Fervour

Back in 1415, both Vladislas II Jogaila and Vytautas were seeking to create a sense of urgency by sharing with the fathers of the Council of Constance their apprehension that their successors might lose religious fervour.[66] They proved to have been largely correct, even if they could not have foreseen future events. Following the death of Vytautas and the troublesome reign of Jogaila's brother Švitrigaila (1430–32), the country was plunged into an internecine war between Sigismund Kęstutaitis (r. 1432–40), brother of Vytautas, and the dethroned Švitrigaila.[67] Lithuanian participation in the crusading movement was therefore out of the question. Even after the accession of Casimir, son of Vladislas II Jogaila, to the grand ducal throne (1440–92), these kinds of activities still had to wait for a good while.[68] In 1445, looking back to the time of Jogaila and Vytautas, Bishop Zbigniew Oleśnicki of Cracow came close to referring to it as a golden age.[69] The time when Polish and Lithuanian rulers could threaten the Ottoman Empire with reprisals was well and truly over. When Catholic Europe sprang into hectic action following the fall of Constantinople, seeking to find a way to stop the advance of the Ottomans, the new king of Poland Casimir IV (r. 1447–92) certainly fell in line with the rest by demonstrating his full appreciation of the necessity of reconquering Constantinople and redeeming the shame inflicted on the Christians. At the same time, however, he was frank enough to admit that he did not have enough resources to stand up to the dual enemy — the Ottoman Turks and the Tatars.[70] The popes proved much more enthusiastic, and their initiatives to stir Christians into action also reached the Lithuanian Catholics.[71] Pope Sixtus IV called on King Casimir IV and his subjects to contribute their share to the beleaguered Knights of Rhodes in 1479–80 and to join the anti-Ottoman

---

66 BAV, Vat. Lat. 4178 I, fols 264v–267v (17 October 1415); *CEV*, no. 651, p. 332 (18 October 1415).
67 The most comprehensive treatment of the troubled period of the 1430s is provided by Sergey V. Polekhov, Наследники Витовта: Династическая война в Великом Княжестве Литовском в 30-е годы XV века (Moskva, 2015).
68 The participation of individual knights from the grand duchy of Lithuania in the struggle against the Ottoman Turks and Golden Horde Tatars should not be excluded outright. The 1440s brought forth the first, and thus far only known person originating from the vast lands of the grand duchy of Lithuania in the fifteenth century to have explicitly been granted the epithet 'knight of God' — the Volhynian nobleman Peter of Kremenets: *LM* 3, p. 63. The title 'Божий рытер' may signify either crusading or pilgrimage to the Holy Land: Petrauskas, 'Knighthood', p. 53.
69 *CESDQ* 1.1, no. 5, pp. 10–11 (to Bishop Matthew of Vilnius, 1445).
70 *CESDQ* 1.2, no. 137, pp. 150–51 (oration of Jan Lutkowic z Brzezia at the 1454 diet in Ratisbon).
71 *VMPL* 2, no. 156, p. 113 (Pope Callixtus III to the archbishop of Gniezno and the bishops of Chełmno and Vilnius, 4 April 1457), no. 239, p. 219 (papal injunction to Friars Minor in the province of Poland to preach *cruciatam* against the Turks, 7 November 1482), no. 243, p. 220 (Bartholomew of Camerino commended to the king to preach *sanctam cruciatam*, 10 December, 1482), no. 262, pp. 234–40 (brief of the crusade against the Turks and Tatars, 5 July 1486), no. 360, pp. 327–29 (papal exhortation to join the crusade against the Turks, 28 July 1509): Rita R. Trimonienė, 'Kryžiaus karų idėja', pp. 224–32.

crusade after Otranto had been liberated in 1481.[72] The popes urged Casimir and his son Alexander, grand duke of Lithuania (1492–1506) and king of Poland (1501–06), to send their envoys to discuss the crusade against the Ottomans in 1484, 1489, and 1499.[73] In the end it was not so much the popes, but the ever increasing pressure of the Ottoman Empire in the Black Sea region that prompted resistance and the revival and spread of crusading modes of communication.

One of the earliest examples provided by the Lithuanian nobility is strange. Safely ensconced some eighty kilometres north of Vilnius, the lord lieutenant of Kaunas, Stankus Sudivojaitis, re-founded the parochial church in his patrimonial village of Deltuva. He requested and was granted an indulgence of seven years for visitors to the church. Perhaps in order to smooth the path for obtaining this grace he had not only depicted his milieu as heavily infested with Tatars and pagans, but also confessed himself to be a fresh convert who *pro fide christiana continue fortiter debellat.*[74] The younger son and namesake of King Casimir and future Catholic saint, Prince Casimir (1458–84) was clear about the need to do battle with the Ottomans and held his royal uncle Vladislas of Varna in high esteem.[75] In 1484, the captain of Samogitia, Jonas Kęsgailaitis, declared his readiness to join the Teutonic Order in the fight against the infidels since he was alarmed at how badly Christendom had recently been weakened.[76] A curious example of the Lithuanian interest in the pan-European phenomenon of crusades is a 1465 letter from the Georgian king Constantine II to Queen Isabella of Castile — its translation into Ruthenian was included in 1496 among the files of the grand ducal archive.[77]

The Lithuanian ruling elite proved to be active in 1495 when plans to retake the Moldavian ports of Cetatea Albă (mod. Bilhorod-Dnistrovskyi, Ukraine; Turk. Akkerman) and Chilia (mod. Kiliya, Ukraine; Turk. Kilya) from Ottoman rule were being hatched.[78] However, although Grand Duke Alexander, after expelling the Tatars from southern Volhynia at the end of July and later moving to Izyaslav and Vinnytsya in August and September 1497, manoeuvred with his army not far away from the Moldavian border, the majority of Lithuanian troops did not join the simultaneous Polish campaign against the Moldavian voivode Stephen III the Great. Warned by the Muscovite grand prince Ivan III who, through his diplomats, emphasised the 'unity' between Moscow and Suceava due to dynastic connections, Alexander contented himself with sending smaller

---

72 *EFE* 64, no. 60, pp. 35–36 (21 October 1479), no. 63, pp. 38–39 (18 October 1480), no. 66, pp. 41–42 (18 September 1481), no. 105, pp. 57–58 (10 January 1483).
73 *VMPL* 2, no. 282, p. 251 (7 December 1489), no. 295, pp. 266–67 (1499). Papal-Polish relations at the time are analysed in detail by Janusz Smołucha, *Papiestwo a Polska w latach 1484–1526: Kontakty dyplomatyczne na tle zagrożenia tureckiego* (Kraków, 1999), pp. 28–90.
74 *Kodeks dyplomatyczny katedry i diecezji wileńskiej*, ed. Jan Fijałek and Władysław Semkowicz, 1 vol. (Kraków, 1932–48), p. 301 (4 March 1469); Baronas and Rowell, *The Conversion*, p. 413.
75 Rowell, 'Lietuva — krikščionybės pylimas?', p. 23.
76 Petrauskas, 'Knighthood', p. 53.
77 *LM* 5: 397–98; Rowell, 'Lietuva — krikščionybės pylimas?', pp. 28–29.
78 Trimonienė, 'Kryžiaus karų idėja', p. 229.

contingents of a few thousand volunteers under the command of Stanislovas Kiška, the later grand Lithuanian hetman, in the autumn of the same year. They arrived too late to make any difference in the Polish defeat in the battle of Cosmin Forest 26 October 1497.[79] Defence became the top priority, rather than aggressive campaigning abroad. Starting from the last decade of the fifteenth century, Lithuania found herself exposed to a war of attrition conducted by the Crimean Tatars and the ever more self-assertive Muscovy. Despite huge territorial losses culminating in the Muscovite capture of Smolensk in 1514, the Lithuanian political nation eventually managed to stand its ground.[80] The resounding victory of the allied forces of the grand duchy of Lithuania and the kingdom of Poland achieved at the Battle of Orsha (8 September 1514) was not only exploited to the full by the Jagiellonian dynasty's Europe-wide propaganda to drive home the message about the danger posed by schismatic Muscovy, but also served as a source of jubilation for those Orthodox believers to whom the grand duchy of Lithuania was their only native country.[81] The crusading idiom expressed in terms of fighting the infidel and schismatic alike had a share in the process of bringing Lithuanian Roman Catholic and Rus Orthodox closer together without doing away with their differences or putting aside differences of opinion.

Concluding Thoughts

The reigns of Jogaila and Vytautas represent the period when Lithuanians came to be seen as an integral part of Western Christendom. The transformation from being crusaded against to joining the crusader movement can well be demonstrated through recourse to Philippe de Mézières: in one part of his *Le songe du vieil pelerin* Lithuania is still described as a porch of Tartary but, later on, the Lithuanian ruler's conversion is depicted as having brought 'much fame to the Christian faith' and that his forces may participate in the salvage operation of Constantinople.[82] The late medieval Lithuanian military campaigns never ventured overseas or to faraway lands. Lithuanian rulers and their noble elite were almost exclusively concerned with affairs closer to home and with what they perceived to be the genuine interests of their grand duchy. Their crusading was a short-range

---

79 Natalia Nowakowska, 'Poland and the Crusade in the reign of king Jan Olbracht, 1492–1501', in *Crusading in the Fifteenth Century: Message and Impact*, ed. Norman Housley (Basingstoke, 2004), pp. 128–47; Fryderyk Papée, *Jan Olbracht* (Kraków, 2006), pp. 125–46.
80 The process of social and political integration in the face of Muscovite aggression has been analysed by Mikhail M. Krom, *Меж Русью и Литвой: Пограничные земли в системе русско-литовских отношений конца XV — первой трети XVI в.* (Moskva, 1995, 2nd edition 2010).
81 Mintautas Čiurinskas, 'Karas ir kultūra Lietuvos Didžiojoje Kunigaikštystėje: 1514 metai', *Senoji Lietuvos Literatūra* 31 (2011), 127–58; Stephen C. Rowell, 'War and Piety in the Grand Duchy of Lithuania in the Late Middle Ages', *RL* 2 (2016), 13–14.
82 Philippe de Mézières, *Le Songe du Vieil Pelerin*, ed. George W. Coopland, 2 vols (Cambridge, 1969), 1: 235, 2: 100, 427.

affair. In their appropriation of the political language of the time, Lithuanians and their rulers proved to be capable learners. They were masters of the art of politics to the point of being able to take even the pope aback, as was the case in 1422 when Martin V expressed his dismay at Vytautas' claim that it was on the orders of the pope that he had dealings with ... Bohemian heretics![83] In many other cases they would tell their intended audience (Western crusade-minded nobility) what they wanted to hear. In the end, all this political activity and real military enterprise brought much fame to Lithuania under Vytautas. In 1429, Francesco de Comitibus Aquae Vivae heaped praise on Vytautas by declaring that he could not only overwhelm the Ottoman Turks but also liberate Jerusalem itself.[84] Sigismund of Luxemburg claimed that Vytautas must be crowned king of Lithuania in recognition of his role in defence of the Christian faith — his country being held up as a shield of the Christians.[85] Even though such full-blown rhetoric never seems to have been repeated from abroad, Lithuanians did gain great fame for their military prowess and as potential crusaders, and this state of affairs can be illustrated by reference to the post-Byzantine historian Laonikos Chalkokondyles. In his eyes, 'this race seems to be the greatest among the peoples around this land and the most courageous, and they fight against Prussians, Germans, and Poles regarding the boundaries of their country. This race too has adopted the customs and way of life of the Romans but its dress is similar to that of the Russians. It borders for the most part on Moldavia and fights against its people'.[86] This was put down in writing in the 1460s, long after the days of Lithuanian military glory were over, but the image remained. And as we all know, it is the image that often carries more weight than down-to-earth statements and conclusions.

---

83 *UBGH* 1, no. 186, pp. 203–4 (Pope Martin V to King Sigismund of Luxemburg, 21 May 1422).
84 *CEV*, no. 1894, p. 881; Rowell, 'Lietuva — krikščionybės pylimas?', p. 22.
85 Srodecki, *Antemurale*, pp. 128–29.
86 Laonikos Chalkokondyles, *The Histories*, trans. Anthony Kaldellis, 2 vols (Cambridge, MA, 2014), 1: 218. See Baronas, 'Byzantium and Lithuania', pp. 310–14.

PART III

From Expansion to Defence

PAUL SRODECKI

The Crusade of Nicopolis and Its Significance for the Western Image of the Ottoman Turks around 1400[*]

Although in no way comparable to the vast research on the crusades of the high medieval period, and despite the large number of still open questions, the crusade of Nicopolis (mod. Nikopol, Bulgaria) can without a doubt be considered one of the better-researched crusades of the later Middle Ages, with modern historiographical discussion of this undertaking reaching well back into the nineteenth century.[1] In comparison to other campaigns carried out under the sign of the cross

---

[*] This chapter was written as part of the research project 'The Construction of the Other in Medieval Europe' (IRP), which was conducted by the Department of History and Centre for Research in Medieval Society and Culture VIVARIUM, Faculty of Arts, University of Ostrava, from 2018 to 2020. It is a translated, modified and further developed version of the author's earlier work on this topic, in particular the following two works: Paul Srodecki, '"Contre les ennemis de la foy de Dieu": Der Kreuzzug von Nikopolis und das abendländische Türkenbild um 1400', in *Das Bild des Feindes: Konstruktion von Antagonismen und Kulturtransfer im Zeitalter der Türkenkriege. Ostmitteleuropa, Italien und Osmanisches Reich*, ed. Eckhard Leuschner and Thomas Wünsch (Berlin, 2013), pp. 33–49; Srodecki, 'Kreuzzugsbewegung und ritterliches Heer im Spätmittelalter im Spiegel der Schlacht von Nikopolis 1396' (unpublished M.A. thesis, Albert Ludwig University of Freiburg, 2008).

1 The most important and influential monographs and articles on the Nicopolis Crusade include: Alois Brauner, *Die Schlacht bei Nikopolis 1396* (Breslau, 1876); Ferdo Šišić, 'Die Schlacht bei Nicopolis (25. September 1396)', *Wissenschaftliche Mittheilungen aus Bosnien und der Hercegovina* 6 (1899), 291–327; Gustav Kling, *Die Schlacht bei Nikopolis im Jahre 1396* (Berlin, 1906); Aziz S. Atiya, *The Crusade of Nicopolis* (London, 1934); Radu Rosetti, 'Notes on the Battle of Nicopolis (1396)', *The Slavonic and East European Review* 15 (1937), 629–38; Henry L. Savage, 'Enguerrand de Coucy VII and the Campaign of Nicopolis', *Speculum* 14 (1939), 423–42; Mihály Benkő, *Csata Nikápolynál* (Móra, 1987); *Nicopolis, 1396–1996: Actes du colloque international*, ed. Jacques Paviot and Martine Chauney-Bouillot (Dijon, 1997); Veszprémy László, 'A nikápolyi hadjárat és értékelése', *Iskolakultúra* 7 (1997), 48–59; Kelly R. DeVries, 'The Battle of Nicopolis', *Medieval History Magazin* 2 (2003), 22–27; Bertrand Schnerb, '1396: Bataille de Nicopolis', in *Histoire du monde au XVe siècle*, ed. Patrick Boucheron (Paris, 2009), pp. 295–98; Cristea Ovidiu, 'La croisade de Nicopolis (1396): Controverses autour d'une bataille', in *Church Union and Crusading in the Fourteenth and Fifteenth Centuries*, ed. Christian Gastgeber et al. (Cluj-Napoca, 2009), pp. 31–56; Dražen Nemet, 'Križarski pohod i bitka kod Nikopola 1396. Godine', *Radovi: Zavod za Hrvatsku Povijest* 41 (2009), 55–113. See also László Veszprémy, 'Some Remarks on Recent Historiography of the Crusade of Nicopolis (1396)', in *The Crusades and the Military Orders: Expanding the Frontiers of Medieval*

in the fourteenth century, the abundance of sources here is highly significant. Due to the international character of the venture in particular, several insightful French or German eyewitness accounts have been preserved, such as Johannes Schiltberger's *Reisebuch* or the biographical *Livre des fais du bon messire Jehan le Maingre*, and there are also numerous further contemporary written records based on participants' reports or other first-hand sources.[2]

In this chapter, I will examine an aspect of this crusade which has received less attention, namely the question of the influence of the Christian defeat near Nicopolis on the slowly developing Western image of the Turks and its significance for the later perception of the so-called Ottoman threat in the fifteenth and in particular the sixteenth and seventeenth centuries. Before I address this latter issue, let me briefly outline in a few paragraphs (also as a prelude to Attila Bárány's following chapter) the events which led to the anti-Ottoman crusade in 1396, the planning, organisation and composition of the crusader army and finally the (in)famous battle of Nicopolis.

Anti-Turkish Crusades before Nicopolis

Although the Ottoman Sultanate, as one of the Anatolian successor principalities of the Seljuk Sultanate of Rum, had been incorporating one European territory after another into its dominion from the early 1350s, it was initially perceived by the Latin West only as a marginal phenomenon in the South-Eastern European balance of power.[3] In the fourteenth century, occasional campaigns under the sign

---

Latin Christianity — In Memoriam Sir Steven Runciman (1903–2000), ed. Zsolt Hunyadi and József Laszlovszky (Budapest, 2001), pp. 223–30.

2 See Craig Taylor, *A Virtuous Knight: Defending Marshal Boucicaut (Jean II Le Meingre, 1366–1421)* (Woodbridge, 2019); Andrei Pippidi, 'O versiune italiana a bataliei de la Nicopol', *Studii si materiale de istorie medie* 35 (2017), 17–24; Marie-Gaëtane Martenet, 'Le Récit de la bataille de Nicopolis (1396) dans les Chroniques de Jean Froissart: De l'échec à la gloire', *Questes: Revue pluridisciplinaire d'études médiévales* 30 (2015), 125–39; Marie-Gaetane Martenet, 'Le Récit de la bataille de Nicopolis (1396) dans les Chroniques de Jean Froissart: de l'échec à la gloire', *Questes* 30 (2015), 125–40; Ilker Evrim Binbas, 'A Damascene Eyewitness to the Battle of Nicopolis: Shams al-Din Ibn al-Jazari (d. 883/1429)', in *Contact and Conflict in Frankish Greece and the Aegean, 1204–1453: Crusade, Religion and Trade between Latins, Greeks and Turks*, ed. Nikolaos G. Chrissis and Mike Carr (Farnham, 2014), pp. 153–76; Marko Šuica, 'Битка код Никопоља у делу Константина Философа', *Историјски часопис* 58 (2009), 109–24; Cristea Ovidiu, 'Bătălia de la Nicopol în viziunea surselor occidentale: mentalitate cavalerească și mentalitate ecleziastică', *Revista Istorică* 9 (1998), 431–41; Élisabeth Gaucher, 'Deux regards sur une défaite: Nicopolis (d'après la Chronique du Religieux de Saint-Denis et le Livre des faits de Boucicaut)', in *Croisades et idée de croisade à la fin du Moyen Âge*, ed. Michel Balard (Paris, 1996 [= CRM 1]), pp. 93–104; Toma G. Bulat, 'La croisade de Nicoplis dans la littérature du temps', in *Mélanges d'histoire générale*, ed. Constantin Marinescu, 2 vols (Cluj, 1927–38), 1: 101–23.

3 For an overview of the early Ottoman expansion and the rise of the Ottoman Emirate (later sultanate) to an empire in the fourteenth century, see Douglas A. Howard, *A History of the Ottoman Empire* (Cambridge, 2017), pp. 8–38; Dimitris J. Kastritsis, 'Conquest and Political Legitimation in

of the cross into western and southern Asia Minor gradually brought the Anatolian Turks into Latin Christendom's broader field of view, making 'the Eastern question slowly [...] a Turkish one'.[4] During this period of the predominantly 'merchant crusaders', as pointedly exaggerated in a recent study, Latin Christians, especially the maritime republics of Venice and Genoa, were able to demonstrate their superiority at sea.[5] In 1344, for example, a naval league consisting of Venice, the Holy See, Cyprus and the Hospitallers succeeded in taking the major part of the city of Smyrna (mod. Izmir, Turkey) from the Turkish beylik of Aydin, including the strategically important sea port but not, however, the citadel.[6] The ideological basis for this enterprise had already been prepared a year earlier with the bull *Insurgentibus contra fidem catholicam*, in which Pope Clement VI had, for the first time, explicitly called for a crusade against the 'tribes of those unbelieving pagans, called in the vernacular the Turks, who thirst for the blood of Christian people and seek destruction of the Catholic faith'.[7] In 1347, the crusading army in

---

the Early Ottoman Empire', in *Byzantines, Latins, and Turks in the Eastern Mediterranean World after 1150*, ed. Jonathan P. Harris, Catherine J. Holmes and Eugenia Russell (Oxford, 2012), pp. 221–46; Paul Wittek, *The Rise of the Ottoman Empire: Studies in the History of Turkey, Thirteenth–Fifteenth Centuries* (London, 2012); Colin Imber, *The Ottoman Empire, 1300–1650* (Basingstoke, 2000), pp. 4–26: *The Ottoman Emirate (1300–1389): Halcyon Days in Crete I: A Symposium Held in Rethymnon 11–13 January 1991*, ed. Elizabeth A. Zachariadou (Rethymnon, 1993); Halil İnalcık, 'The Rise of the Ottoman Empire', in *A History of the Ottoman Empire to 1730*, ed. Michael A. Cook (London, 1976), pp. 10–53; İnalcık, *The Ottoman Empire: The Classical Age 1300–1600* (London, 1973), pp. 3–16. For the origins of the Ottoman Turks and the Seljuk legacy, see M. Fuad Köprülü, *The Origins of the Ottoman Empire*, trans. and ed. Gary Leiser (New York, 1992).

4 Anthony Luttrell, 'Latin Responses to Ottoman Expansion before 1389', in *The Ottoman Emirate (1300–89)*, pp. 119–34 (here 121). See Antun Nekić, 'Europske predodžbe o "turskoj" prijetnji (14.–16. stoljece)', *Povijesni prilozi* 43 (2012), pp. 81–118; Halil İnalcık, 'The Ottoman Turks and the Crusades, 1329–1451', in *The Impact of the Crusades on Europe*, ed. Harry W. Hazard and Norman P. Zacour, HC 6 (Madison, 1989), pp. 222–75 (here 222–54); Oskar Halecki, 'The Last Century of the Crusades — from Smyrna to Varna (1344–1444)', *Bulletin of the Polish Institute of Arts and Sciences in America* 3 (1944/45), 300–7. On high medieval Latin Christian campaigns under the sign of the cross against the Seljuks, see Giovanni Curatola, 'Die Seldschuken — ein türkischer Kreuzzug', in *Die Zeit der Kreuzzüge: Geschichte und Kunst*, ed. Roberto Cassanelli (Stuttgart, 2000), pp. 175–93.

5 Mike Carr, *Merchant Crusaders in the Aegean 1291–1352* (Woodbridge, 2015). See Georg Christ, 'Kreuzzug und Seeherrschaft: Clemens V., Venedig und das Handelsembargo von 1308', in *Maritimes Mittelalter: Meere als Kommunikationsräume*, ed. Michael Borgolte and Nikolas Jaspert (Ostfildern, 2016), pp. 261–82; Liviu Pilat and Ovidiu Cristea, *The Ottoman Threat and Crusading on the Eastern Border of Christendom during the 15th Century* (Leiden, 2015), pp. 32–49; Kate Fleet, 'Turks, Mamluks, and Latin Merchants: Commerce, Conflict, and Cooperation in the Eastern Mediterranean', in *Byzantines, Latins, and Turks*, pp. 327–44.

6 Carr, *Merchant Crusaders*, pp. 74–78; Kenneth M. Setton, *The Papacy and the Levant (1204–1571)*, 4 vols (Philadelphia, 1976–84), 1: 163–94. On the kingdom of Cyprus's prominent position in the fourteenth century crusades in the Eastern Mediterranean, see Peter W. Edbury, *The Kingdom of Cyprus and the Crusades 1191–1374* (Cambridge, 1994), pp. 141–79; Łukasz Burkiewicz, *Polityczna rola królestwa Cypru w XIV wieku* (Kraków, 2013), pp. 108–285.

7 Bull from 30 September 1343, *VMHH* 1, no. 986, pp. 660–62. English translation in *Documents on the Later Crusades, 1274–1580*, ed. and trans. Norman Housley (Basingstoke, 1996), no. 22, pp. 78–80. On papal crusading activity under Clement VI, see Philippe Genequand, 'Prédication et politique à

Smyrna gained support from Humbert II de la Tour-du-Pin, dauphin of Vienne, whose small French crusader host helped to hold the conquered city.[8] Smyrna remained in Latin Christian (Hospitaller) hands until 1402, when a mighty Mongol-Turkic army under Timur sacked it again for the Muslims.[9]

The first significant plans for an explicit anti-Ottoman crusade were discussed in the mid-1350s, when the Byzantine emperor John V Palaiologos asked Pope Innocent VI for military support in exchange for the long-sought union of the churches. Following several years of diplomatic exchange and negotiations between the Holy See and the Byzantines, the Carmelite friar and papal legate Peter Thomas finally brought a small crusading host consisting of Hospitallers, Venetians, Genoese and English soldiers to Constantinople in the autumn of 1359. According to Philippe de Mézières, and as confirmed in an Ottoman report, the crusaders, together with Byzantine troops, managed to capture and burn Lampsakos (mod. Lampseki, Turkey).[10] Although the joint Christian forces were

---

la cour d'Avignon: Pierre Roger (Clément VI) et la croisade', in *Preaching and Political Society: From Late Antiquity to the End of the Middle Ages* (Turnhout, 2013), pp. 203–26; Alain Demurger, 'Le pape Clément VI et l'Orient: ligue ou croisade?', in *Guerre, pouvoir et noblesse au Moyen Âge, Mélanges en l'honneur de Philippe Contamine*, ed. Jacques Paviot and Jacques Verger (Paris, 2000), pp. 217–14.

8 See Constantinos Georgiou, 'Ordinavi armatam sancte unionis: Clement VI's Sermon on the Dauphin Humbert II of Viennois's Leadership of the Christian Armada against the Turks, 1345', *Crusades* 15 (2016), 157–75; Mike Carr, 'Humbert of Viennois and the Crusade of Smyrna: A Reconsideration', *Crusades* 13 (2014), 237–51; Setton, *The Papacy and the Levant* 1: 195–223; Elizabeth A. Zachariadou, *Trade and Crusade: Venetian Crete and the Emirates of Menteshe and Aydin (1300–1415)* (Venice, 1983), pp. 41–62; Paul Lemerle, *L'Emirat d'Aydin, Byzance et l'occident: recherches sur 'La geste d'Umur pacha'* (Paris, 1953), pp. 180–203.

9 Anthony Luttrell, 'Timur's Capture of Hospitaller Smyrna (1402)', in *Von Hamburg nach Java: Studien zur mittelalterlichen, neuen und digitalen Geschichte. Festschrift zu Ehren von Jürgen Sarnowsky*, ed. Jochen Burgtorf, Christian Hoffarth and Sebastian Kubon (Göttingen, 2020), pp. 337–48; Michel Balard, 'Les Hospitaliers et Smyrne (1344–1402)', in *Entre Deus e o rei: O mundo das Ordens Militares*, ed. Isabel Cristina Ferreira Fernandes, 2 vols (Palmela, 2018), 2: 747–54; Jean Richard, 'Les Marchands génois de Famagouste et la défense de Smyrne', in *Oriente e Occidente tra medioevo ed età moderna: Studi in onore di Geo Pistarino*, ed. Laura Balletto, 2 vols (Genova, 1997), 2: 1059–71; Jürgen Sarnowsky, 'Die Johanniter und Smyrna 1344–1402', *Römische Quartalschrift für christliche Altertumskunde und Kirchengeschichte* 86 (1991), 215–51, 87 (1992), 47–98; Joseph Delaville Le Roulx, 'L'occupation chrétienne à Smyrne (1344–1402)', in *Florilegium ou recueil de travaux d'érudition dédiés à Monsieur le Marquis Melchior de Vogüé à l'occasion du quatre-vingtième anniversaire de sa naissance* (Paris, 1909), pp. 177–86. See also Michele Bernardini, 'Tīmūr and the "Frankish" Powers', in *The Crusade in the Fifteenth Century: Converging and Competing Cultures*, ed. Norman Housley (London, 2017), pp. 109–19. Smyrna was once again to become the target of a crusade venture in the early 1470s. See Reinhard Klockow, 'Beutezüge im Zeichen des Kreuzes: Der venezianisch-päpstliche Überfall auf Smyrna im Herbst 1472', in *'Ja muz ich sunder riuwe sin': Festschrift für Karl Stackmann zum 15. Februar 1990*, ed. Wolfgang Dinkelacker, Ludger Grenzmann and Werner Höver (Göttingen, 1990), pp. 36–50.

10 *Documents on the Later Crusades*, no. 25, pp. 83–84; *Die altosmanischen anonymen Chroniken*, ed. Friedrich Giese, 2 vols (Breslau, 1922–25), 1: 18. See Zachariadou, *Trade and Crusade*, pp. 63–66; Frederick J. Boehlke, *Pierre de Thomas: Scholar, Diplomat, and Crusader* (Philadelphia, 1966), pp. 156–80. See Oskar Halecki, *Un Empereur de Byzance à Rome: Ving tans de travail pour l'union des églises et pour la défense de l'empire d'orient, 1355–75* (Warszawa, 1930).

said to have fled and narrowly escaped a massacre following the arrival of an Ottoman army, this episode marks the first anti-Ottoman crusade venture in history.[11] Two years later, Peter Thomas joined another anti-Turkish crusade, this time led by King Peter I of Cyprus, who set sail to the Mediterranean coast of southern Anatolia and conquered Adalia (mod. Antalya, Turkey), one of the centres of the beylik of Hamid.[12]

In 1366, a good five years after the Adalia campaign, Amadeus VI, count of Savoy, succeeded in capturing Gallipoli (under Ottoman rule since March 1354) with the help of a predominantly French crusader army.[13] As the first explicit campaign conducted under the sign of the cross against the Ottoman Turks on European soil, this so-called Savoyard Crusade was part of wider crusade operations in the mid-1360s: alongside the annual *Reisen* of the Teutonic Order in the south-eastern and eastern Baltic Sea region, various crusader armies also fought against the schismatic Bulgarians on the lower Danube (1365), against the Muslim Mamluks in northern Egypt (1365) and against the pagan Lithuanians in Volhynia (1366).[14] After the count's success, a joint crusade against the Ottomans

---

11 İnalcık, 'The Ottoman Turks and the Crusades', pp. 235–38.
12 *Documents on the Later Crusades*, no. 25, p. 85. See Özge Bozkurtoğlu Özcan, 'Lusignanların 1361 Yılında Antalya'yı Adalia İşgalinin Ardında Yatan Sebepler', *Cedrus: The Journal of MCRI* 5 (2017), 397–409.
13 See Matteo Magnani, 'The Crusade of Amadeus VI of Savoy between History and Historiography', in *Italy and Europe's Eastern Border, 1204–1669*, ed. Iulian Mihai Damian et al. (Frankfurt am Main, 2012), pp. 215–36; Zachariadou, *Trade and Crusade*, pp. 69–71; Setton, *The Papacy and the Levant* 1: 285–326; Lionel Eugene Cox, *The Green Count of Savoy: Amadeus VI, and Transalpine Savoy in the Fourteenth century* (Princeton, NJ, 1967), pp. 204–39.
14 In addition to the introductory chapter as well as Andrzej Marzec's and Sven Jaros's essays in this volume, see also Tamás Ölbei, 'Crusading Companies in the 1365th Year of Our Lord', *East Central Europe* 47 (2020), 67–88; Georg Christ, 'Non ad caudam sed ad caput invadere: the Sack of Alexandria Between Pride, Crusade and Trade Diplomacy (1365–70)', in *Rapporti mediterranei, pratiche documentarie, presenze veneziane: le reti economiche e culturali (XIV–XVI secolo)*, ed. Gherardo Ortalli and Alessio Sopracasa (Venezia, 2017), pp. 153–82; Łukasz Burkiewicz, *Aleksandria 1365* (Warszawa, 2014); Jo Van Steenbergen, 'The Alexandrian Crusade (1365) and the Mamluk Sources: Reassessment of the Kitab al-Ilmam of an-Nuwayri al-'Iskandarani (d. 1372 AD)', in *East and West in the Crusader States: Context — Contacts — Confrontations, III. Acta of the Congress Held at Hernen Castle in September 2000*, ed. Krijnie Ciggaar and Herman Teule (Leuven, 2003), p. 123–37; Guillaume de Machaut, *The Capture of Alexandria*, trans. and ed. Janet Shirley and Peter W. Edbury (Aldershot, 2001); Norman Housley, 'King Louis the Great of Hungary and the Crusades, 1342–82', *The Slavonic and East European Review* 62 (1984), 192–208; Vasil T. Gjuzelev, 'La guerre bulgaro-hongroise au printemps de 1365 et des documents nouveaux sur la domination hongroise du royaume de Vidin (1365–69)', *Byzantinobulgarica* 6 (1980), 153–72; Gjuzelev, 'Beiträge zur Geschichte des Königreiches von Vidin im Jahre 1365', *SOF* 39 (1980), 1–16; Harry Luke, 'The Kingdom of Cyprus, 1291–1369', in *The Fourteenth and Fifteenth Centuries*, ed. Harry W. Hazard, HC 3 (Madison, 1975), pp. 340–60 (here 352–60); Setton, *The Papacy and the Levant* 1: 258–84; Boehlke, *Pierre de Thomas*, pp. 234–94; Georgius Johannes Capitanovici, *Die Eroberung von Alexandria (Iskanderîje) durch Peter I. von Lusignan, König von Cypern 1365: Mit einer Karte von Alexandrien* (Berlin, 1894). For the *Reisen* to Prussia and Lithuania, see Werner Paravicini, *Die Preussenreisen des europäischen Adels*, 4 vols (Sigmaringen, 1989–2023).

became an increasing concern for the Latin Christian princes: in the year of the Savoyard Crusade, John V Palaiologos visited Buda and discussed the formation of a broader anti-Ottoman alliance with the Hungarian king Louis the Great — the latter having been an eager champion of the crusade idea who led himself various campaigns in the name of the cross not only in the Balkans but also in Lithuania.[15] Ultimately, however, a coalition against the Ottomans did not materialise.[16] In the 1370s, the idea of an anti-Ottoman crusade was eagerly discussed at the court of Pope Gregory XI and the curia constantly promoted propaganda in this direction.[17] However, a large-scale crusade undertaken by various occidental forces, such as in the heyday of the crusades in the high Middle Ages, was hardly feasible, particularly in the 1370s and 1380s. There were two main reasons for this: on the one hand, the two most powerful monarchies of late medieval Europe, England and France, were locked in a seemingly never-ending conflict. On the other, following the death of Gregory XI in 1378, a schism caused by the election of two popes had also split the West.[18]

The quickly expanding Ottoman Sultanate, which by that time had already grown well beyond its origins as a petty local Anatolian frontier beylik and risen to be a significant regional power and an intercontinental empire of vassal principalities straddling the Balkans and Anatolia, finally came into the greater focus of Latin Christianity around 1390. Concerned about the rapid increase in Ottoman power and the first Turkish incursions into southern Hungary, King Sigismund from the house of Luxemburg began to solicit support in the West for a crusade against the Ottomans.[19] The late 1380s and early 1390s were crucial for

---

15 On the Hungarian Angevins' crusading efforts, see, most recently, Attila Bárány, 'The Hungarian Angevins and the Crusade: King Charles I (1301–1342)', in *Zwischen Ostsee und Adria: Ostmitteleuropa im Mittelalter und in der Frühen Neuzeit. Politische, wirtschaftlichen, religiöse und wissenschaftliche Beziehungen*, ed. Bárány, Roman Czaja and László Pósán (Debrecen, 2023), pp. 41–80; László Pósán, 'Die Feldzüge des ungarischen Königs Ludwig I. von Anjou nach Litauen', in *Zwischen Mittelmeer und Baltikum: Festschrift für Hubert Houben zum 70. Geburtstag*, ed. Udo Arnold, Roman Czaja and Jürgen Sarnowski (Ilmtal-Weinstraße, 2023), pp. 383–404.

16 See Ioan-Aurel Pop, 'The Religious Union of Buda (1366) in the Context of the Religious Offensive of Hungarian King Louis I of Anjou against the "Schismatics"', *Revue roumaine d'histoire* 49 (2010), 109–24; Joseph Gill, 'John V Palaeologus at the court of Louis I of Hungary (1366)', *Byzantinoslavica* 38 (1977), 30–38; Peter Wirth, 'Die Haltung Kaiser Johannes' V. bei den Verhandlungen mit König Ludwig I. von Ungarn zu Buda im Jahre 1366', *Byzantinische Zeitschrift* 56 (1963), 271–72.

17 Paul R. Thibault, 'Pope Gregory XI (1370–78) and the Crusade', *Canadian Journal of History* 20 (1985), 313–36. See also Norman Housley, *The Avignon Papacy and the Crusades, 1305–78* (Oxford, 1986).

18 See Ovidiu Cristea, 'Razboiul de 100 de ani si cruciada', in *National si Universal in istoria românilor: Studii oferite prof. dr. Serban Papacostea cu ocazia împlinirii a 70 de ani*, ed. Cristea and Gheorghe Lazăr (București, 1998), pp. 329–42; Francoise Autrand, 'La paix impossible: Les négociations franco-anglaises à la fin du 14e siècle', *Annales de Bourgogne* 68 (1996), S. 11–22; Christiane Deluz, 'Croisade et paix en Europe au XIVe siècle: Le rôle du cardinal Hélie de Talleyrand', in *Croisades et idée de croisade*, pp. 53–64.

19 In a letter to Count Ladislas of Temes from 14 August 1390, Sigismund mentions the Ottoman incursions *in Machouiensi, Sirimiensi, Crassouiensi et Temesiensi antefato districtibus et comatitatibus*, i.e.

the Balkan policy of the Hungarian crown. Whereas Louis the Great (r. 1342–82) pursued a very offensive policy which aimed to build a vast empire stretching from the Adriatic to the Black seas, and with all the Danube principalities of Bosnia, Serbia, Wallachia, Moldavia and Bulgaria reduced to the role of Hungarian vassals, Sigismund had to face the changed real political conditions of the time.[20] Consequently, there was a remarkable shift in the diplomatic language at the court in Buda (as there also was in Rome and Venice) and the formula of a defensive struggle to save Europe from the Ottoman Turks was increasingly emphasised.[21]

This became particularly significant following the Serbian defeat at the Battle of Kosovo Field in 1389, the Ottoman reduction of the two Bulgarian tsardoms of Tarnovo and Vidin to a state of vassalage in 1388, and the final annexation of almost the whole of Bulgaria between 1393 and 1395 (Vidin was still an Ottoman vassal state when the Nicopolis Crusade started).[22] The northern borders of the Ottoman Empire now lay on the right bank of the lower Danube, making Hungary and the two Romanian voivodeships of Wallachia and Moldavia its immediate neighbours. From then on, Sigismund significantly increased his

---

the banate of Macsó and the counties of Syrmia, Krassó and Temes: *Documenta historiam Valachorum in Hungaria illustrantia*, ed. Imre Lukinich et al. (Budapest, 1941), no. 356, p. 396. See also Pál Engel, 'A török-magyar háborúk első évei. 1389–1392', *Hadtörténelmi Közlemények* 111 (1998), 561–77; János M. Bak, 'Sigismund and the Ottoman Advance', in *Sigismund von Luxemburg: Ein Kaiser in Europa*, ed. Michel Pauly and François Reinert (Mainz, 2006), pp. 89–94.

20 On Louis's expansionist Balkan policy, see Pop, 'The Religious Union of Buda'; Housley, 'King Louis the Great'. For Sigismund's Ottoman policy, see Mark Whelan, 'Dances, Dragons and a Pagan Queen: Sigismund of Luxemburg and the Publicizing of the Ottoman Turkish Threat', in *The Crusade in the Fifteenth Century*, pp. 49–63; Pál Engel, 'Ungarn und die Türkengefahr zur Zeit Sigismunds (1387–1437)', in *Das Zeitalter König Sigismunds in Ungarn und im Deutschen Reich*, ed. Peter Gunst and Tilmann Schmidt (Debrecen, 2000), pp. 55–71; Gustav Beckmann, *Der Kampf Sigismunds gegen die werdende Weltmacht der Osmanen 1392–1437: Eine historische Grundlegung* (Gotha, 1902).

21 On the Ottoman issue in Venice's Mediterranean policy in the late fourteenth century, see Max Silberschmidt, *Das orientalische Problem zur Zeit der Entstehung des türkischen Reiches nach venezianischen Quellen: Ein Beitrag zur Geschichte der Beziehungen Venedigs zu Sultan Bajezid I., zu Byzanz, Ungarn und Genua und zum Reiche von Kiptschak (1381–1400)* (Leipzig, 1923).

22 On the battle of Kosovo (1389), see Stanisław Rek, *Kosowe Pole 1389* (Warszawa, 2016); Anna di Lellio, *The Battle of Kosovo 1389: An Albanian Epic* (London, 2009); James E. Held, 'The Legend of the Fall, 1389: The Battle of Kosovo', *Medieval History Magazin* 5 (2004), 32–37; Selami Pulaha, 'Die Albaner und die Schlacht am Amselfeld 1389', *Dardania* 4 (1995), 61–85; Stephen W. Reinert, 'From Niš to Kosovo Polje: Reflections on Murād I's Final Years', in *The Ottoman Emirate*, pp. 169–211; Thomas A. Emmert, *Serbian Golgotha Kosovo, 1389* (Boulder, 1990). For an overview on the early Ottoman tributary and vassal system, see İnalcık, *The Ottoman Empire*, pp. 9–16. For the following centuries: *Tributaries and Peripheries of the Ottoman Empire*, ed. Gábor Kármán (Leiden, 2020); *The European Tributary States of the Ottoman Empire in the Sixteenth and Seventeenth Centuries*, ed. Gabor Kármán and Lovro Kunčević (Leiden, 2013); Radu G. Păun, 'Conquered by the (S)word: Governing the Tributary Principalities of Wallachia and Moldavia (16th–17th Centuries)', in *The Ottoman Orient in Renaissance Culture: Papers from the International Conference at the National Museum in Krakow, June 26–27, 2015*, ed. Robert Born and Michał Dziewulski (Kraków, 2015), pp. 19–40. On the Ottoman conquest of Bulgaria, see (with further references) Jake Ransohoff, 'Ivan Šišman and the Ottoman Conquest of Bulgaria (1371–95): A Reconsideration', *Palaeobulgarica* 37 (2013), 89–100.

diplomatic efforts to win the support of the West for a joint crusade against the expansive Ottomans, depicting various horror scenarios of an upcoming Ottoman conquest of the Latin hinterland. Parallels can be drawn here to the 1240s, when Sigismund's predecessor on the Hungarian throne, the Arpad king Béla IV, dramatically emphasised the alleged imminent extinction of Latin Christianity in his numerous calls for Western help against the Mongols.[23] This rhetoric was fuel for the Western European crusade propagandists of the time, who, having received comparable reports of the Turkish threat from the Byzantines for several decades by then, now started to call for an anti-Ottoman crusade.[24] Following two less fruitful delegations in 1393 and 1394, it was the embassy in 1395 under the leadership of the archbishop of Gran and chancellor of Hungary, János Kanizsai, and supported by the papal legate John of Gubbio and the French chronicler Philippe de Mézières that was to have success at the European courts.[25]

Pride Comes before a Fall

Unlike the 1370s and 1380s, the omens were now considerably better. The Hungarian diplomats succeeded not only in winning over the two popes who, with the usual indulgences, had the cross preached in their respective obediences. Sigismund also benefited from the ceasefire between the French and English, which meant that the Hungarians were able to secure the support of the French knighthood. The duchy of Burgundy, in particular, agreed to send a large contingent of crusaders to south-east Europe.[26] As at the peak of the high medieval crusades, the knights came from almost all parts of the West: there are reports

---

23 See with further references Paul Srodecki, 'Fighting the "Eastern Plague": Anti-Mongol Crusade Ventures in the Thirteenth Century', in *The Expansion of the Faith: Crusading on the Edges of Latin Christendom in the High Middle Ages*, ed. Srodecki and Norbert Kersken (Turnhout, 2021), pp. 303–27; Nora Berend, 'Hungary, "the Gate of Christendom"', in *Medieval Frontiers: Concepts and Practices*, ed. David Abulafia and Berend (Aldershot, 2002), pp. 195–215. See also Katharina Schmidt, *Trauma und Erinnerung: Die Historisierung der Mongoleninvasion im mittelalterlichen Polen und Ungarn* (Heidelberg, 2013).
24 See Jonathan Harris, 'Byzantine Refugees as Crusade Propagandists: The Travels of Nicholas Agallon', in *The Crusade in the Fifteenth Century*, pp. 34–46; Judith R. Ryder, 'Byzantium and the West in the 1360s: The Kydones Version', in *Byzantines, Latins, and Turks*, pp. 345–66; István Baán, 'Die Beziehungen zwischen Sigismund und Byzanz', in *Sigismundus rex et imperator: Kunst und Kultur zur Zeit Sigismunds von Luxemburg 1387–1437*, ed. Zsombor Jékely et al. (Budapest, 2006), pp. 438–41.
25 Hektor Mülich, 'Chronik 1348–1487', ed. Matthias Lexer, in *CDS* 22: 1–376 (here 41); Denis Lalande, *Jean II le Meingre, dit Boucicaut (1366–1421): Étude d'une biographie héroïque* (Genève, 1988), p. 57. On the crusade agenda in the works of Philippe de Mézières, see Kiril Petkov, 'The Rotten Apple and the Good Apples: Orthodox, Catholics, and Turks in Philippe de Mézières' Crusading Propaganda', *Journal of Medieval History* 23 (1997), 255–70; Nicolae Iorga, *Philippe de Mézières, 1327–1405, et la croisade au XIVe siècle* (Paris, 1896).
26 See Jaques Paviot, *Les ducs de Bourgogne, la croisade et l'Orient (fin XIVe–XVe siècle)* (Paris, 2003).

of English, Lombard, Venetian, Flemish, Bohemian and Polish contingents.[27] The main burden, however, was borne on the one hand by the Franco-Burgundian armed forces under the leadership of Count John of Nevers (later better known under the epithet of the 'Fearless'), the son of Duke Philip the Bold of Burgundy, and by the numerous German knights who joined them on their route through Swabia, Bavaria and Austria to Buda, where they were received by King Sigismund.[28] Naturally, as the initiator of the enterprise, he himself contributed the second significant group of combatants to the crusader army. The Wallachian voivode Mircea the Old, as Sigismund's vassal, also declared his willingness to join the anti-Ottoman venture and to meet with the main crusader host on the lower Danube.[29] Additionally, the Venetian republic, which also saw the Ottomans as posing a growing threat to its interests in the region, agreed to send a fleet of up to twenty-five galleys to prevent the Ottoman troops stationed in Anatolia from crossing the Sea of Marmara.[30]

The crusaders who met in Buda disagreed about the aims of the campaign. Sigismund, who, as discussed earlier, saw in the crusade enterprise a means to an end, that is as the fulfilment of his foreign policy goals and the strengthening of his internal position in his own kingdom, pleaded for a defensive strategy in the fight against the Ottoman Turks and their Sultan Bayezid I the Thunderbolt. He wanted to provoke the enemy with an incursion into Serbia or Bulgaria, in order to lure them north. Then, nearer to the Hungarian sphere of influence,

---

27 On the international character of the Nicopolis Crusade, see Michael C. E. Jones, 'Breton Soldiers from the Battle of the Thirty (26 March 1351) to Nicopolis (25 September 1396)', in *The Soldier Experience in the Fourteenth Century*, ed. Adrian R. Bell (Woodbridge, 2011), pp. 157–74; Bertrand Schnerb, 'Le contingent franco-bourguignon à la croisade de Nicopolis', *AB* 68 (1996), 59–75; Adrian R. Bell, 'England and the Crusade of Nicopolis, 1396', *Medieval Life* 4 (1996), 18–22; Jerzy Grygiel, 'Udział rycerstwa polskiego w walce z Turkami w czasach panowania Władysława Jagiełły i Zygmunta Luksemburskiego', in *600-lecie bitwy na Kosowym Polu*, ed. Krzysztof Baczkowski (Kraków, 1992), pp. 75–85; Charles L. Tipton, 'The English at Nicopolis', *Speculum* 37 (1962), 528–40.

28 Attila Bárány, 'King Sigismund of Luxemburg and the Preparations for the Hungarian Crusading Host of Nicopolis (1389–96)', in *Partir en croisade à la fin du Moyen Âge: Financement et logistique*, ed. Daniel Baloup and Manuel Sánchez Martínez (Toulouse, 2015), pp. 153–78; Fawzi Sahili, 'La croisade de Nicopolis: Problèmes financiers et idéal chevaleresque' (unpublished Ph.D. thesis, Paris Diderot University, 1986).

29 Károly Kranzieritz, 'Havasalföld szerepe az 1396-os keresztes hadjárat elokészítésében és végrehajtásában', *Hadtörténelmi közlemények* 129 (2016), 3–26. See Tasin Gemil, *Romanians and Ottomans in the XIVth–XVIth Centuries* (Bucharest, 2009).

30 Ovidiu Cristea, 'Considérations sur la participation vénitienne à la croisade de Nicopolis', *Quaderni della Casa Romena di Venezia* 2 (2003), pp. 95–10; Cristea, 'Venetia si cruciada de la Nicopol', *Studii si materiale de istorie medie* 21 (2003), 106–18. On Venice's Ottoman policy in the fourteenth and fifteenth centuries in general, see Cristea, 'Venice: the Balkan Policy of Hungary and the Rise of the Ottoman Empire', *RESEE* 40 (2002), 179–94; Stefan K. Stantchev, 'Venice and the Ottoman Threat, 1381–1453', in *Reconfiguring the Fifteenth-Century Crusade*, ed. Norman Housley (London, 2017), pp. 161–205; Danuta Quirini-Popławska, 'Wenecja a sytuacja we wsochdniej części Morza Śródziemnego w dobie ekspansji tureckiej (II połowa XIV wieku)', in *600-lecie bitwy na Kosowym Polu*, pp. 45–60.

he would meet the Ottoman troops, tired from a long march, in battle, thus keeping a quick retreat open even in the event of an unfavourable outcome. The Hungarian king had considerable experience of the troublesome enemy from the south and knew them well. Although the struggles with the Ottomans for hegemony in the Balkans had increased significantly during Sigismund's reign, the Hungarian composite monarchy was still a long way from seeing the Ottomans as an existential and imminent threat, as they would later in the later fifteenth and sixteenth centuries. At the end of the fourteenth century, the conflict with the Ottoman Empire was more about areas of influence in the so-called buffer zone of various smaller protectorates. Every year (and sometimes several times a year), from the late 1380s onwards, Sigismund carried out numerous campaigns in Bosnia, Serbia, Bulgaria, Walachia and Moldavia, where his Hungaro-Croatian armies clashed repeatedly with Ottoman troops in smaller skirmishes and battles, with varying degrees of success.[31] One can therefore reasonably assume that the tactics and fighting power of the Ottomans were well known to the Hungarians.

The Western European crusaders, above all the Franco-Burgundian contingents, preferred an offensive war that would hit the enemy deep in his own lands, and their goals were set significantly higher: according to the crusade doctrine of the fourteenth century, the fight against the Ottomans could only mean a first step, a *passagium particulare*, on the crusaders' way to the liberation of the Holy Land (*passagium generale*), the 'promised land' (*terre de promission*), from the Muslims. The conquest of Bulgaria was to be followed by the capture of the Ottoman capital at Edirne, in order to drive the Ottomans from mainland Europe to Asia Minor and then, finally, to press on to Palestine. Situated at the Wallacho-Bulgarian border, as a preliminary goal of the crusade, Nicopolis represented a compromise between Sigismund's defensive strategy and the more offensive plans of the Frenchmen and Burgundians, since the capture of the heavily fortified city would allow control of northern Bulgaria and prepare the ground for further operations against Thrace and Thessaly. Neither was Nicopolis a random choice: one year earlier, Sigismund had already sent a Hungarian expeditionary force to the lower Danube as part of a Hungaro-Byzantine alliance against the Ottomans. Supported by Wallachian troops, attempts had been made to secure the most important fortresses as starting points for further operations, but these efforts had proved unsuccessful.[32]

At the start of August 1396, the united crusader army left Buda for the south, heading down the left bank of the Danube.[33] They were accompanied by a mighty transport and provisions fleet, which, according to Hektor Mülich, carried food for sixteen months and, as reported in the *Annals of Vienne*, consisted of more

---

31 Bárány, 'King Sigismund', pp. 163–64, table 1.
32 See Dan Ioan Muresan, 'Avant Nicopolis: La campagne de 1395 pour le contrôle du Bas-Danube', *Revue internationale d'histoire militaire* 83 (2003), 115–32.
33 On the crusader army's journey from Buda to Nicopolis, see Károly Kranzieritz, 'A Nikápolyhoz vezető út: A keresztes hadak útvonalai a Magyar Királyság területén', *MM* 4 (2015), 157–74.

than seventy ships.[34] With their help, the crusaders crossed the Danube near the Iron Gates and, for the first time, set foot on land that belonged to the Ottoman sphere of influence. Ivan Sratsimir, tsar of Bulgaria-Vidin and an Ottoman vassal since 1388, willingly opened the gates of his capital to the crusaders and allowed them to subdue the Ottoman garrison. Oryahovo, about one hundred kilometres further down the Danube and occupied by a stronger contingent of Ottoman troops, also surrendered in the face of military superiority of the Latin Christians. This time, however, the crusaders not only executed the Ottoman occupation, but also carried out a massacre of the city's Orthodox population. At the beginning of September 1396, the crusade host finally reached the gates of the heavily fortified Nicopolis. The city was completely encircled by the crusaders, both from the landward side and from the Danube side, but after sixteen days it was still holding out when the Ottomans arrived with the relief army under Bayezid.

The battle that followed before Nicopolis on 25 September 1396 was a clash between two armies which could not have been more different in terms of their composition and tactics. On the Christian side was an offensively minded knightly army of 10,500–12,000 men, whose tactics consisted of riding down the enemy with the sheer force of their heavy but cumbersome cavalry.[35] Due to their heavy armour, the Western knights were hindered in their movements and thus were primarily interested in close combat. In the Ottoman Turks, however, the Christians found an opponent who only accepted 'close combat, with lance, sword, and mace [...] when a decisive advantage had been gained'.[36] The more lightly-armed and quicker, 18,500–23,000 strong Ottomans overcame their supposed disadvantage by combining their agility and speed with a sophisticated tactic. Bayezid, who recognised the advantages of the defensive in combat, led an army into the field in which foot soldiers and archers constituted independent formations, a separate tactical body and a particularly well-organised core. His battle plan was an optimal combination of defensive and offensive tactics and, at the same time, made ideal use of the terrain. In addition, discord and a lack of discipline also weakened the crusader army. Mostly driven by arrogance and their demand to lead the fight, the Franco-Burgundian contingents were the first to reach the battlefield and, after being lured into an ambush by an apparently fleeing Ottoman vanguard of lightly mounted Akinci, were completely wiped out by the elite janissaries and sipahis. The rest of the mostly Hungaro-German crusader army offered a more even fight, but the intervention of the approximately

---

34 Mülich, 'Chronik 1348–1487', p. 42; *Wiener Annalen von 1348–1404*, ed. Joseph Seemüller, MGH DC 6: 231–42 (here 237). See also Johann von Posilge, 'Chronik des Landes Preussen (nebst Fortsetzungen)', ed. Ernst Strehlke, in *SRP* 3: 79–388 (here 208); 'Annales Mellicenses', ed. Wilhelm Wattenbach, in *MGH SS* 9: 484–535 (here 514).
35 On Christian and Ottoman numbers in the battle, see Srodecki, '"Contre les ennemis"', p. 35.
36 Andrew Ayton, 'Arms, Armour, and Horses', in *Medieval Warfare: A History*, ed. Maurice Keen (Oxford, 1999), pp. 186–208 (here 193).

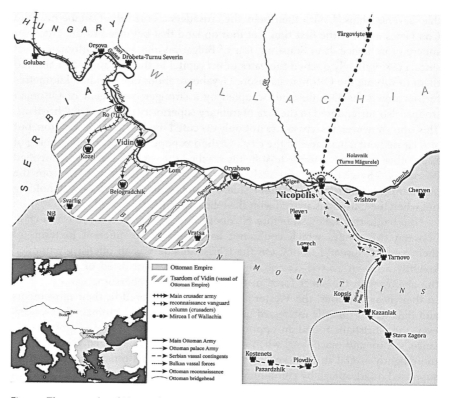

Fig. 15. The crusade of Nicopolis, 1396. Reproduced and reworked by Paul Srodecki from *Danube Crusade and Battle of Nicopolis*, map by Kandi, available online at <https://w.wiki/6i9y> [accessed 21 September 2023], licence CC BY-SA 4.0

1500-strong Serbian auxiliary force under the despot Stefan Lazarević, the sultan's brother-in-law, who arrived in the late afternoon, finally decided the battle in favour of the Ottomans.

Explaining the Defeat

The debacle near Nicopolis was to have a fundamental impact on the Western image of the Ottoman Turks around 1400, since it caused a major stir in large parts of the West and increased interest in the hitherto little-known Muslim enemy originating from western Anatolia. Furthermore, the unsuccessful crusade also required a historiographical and literary appraisal. In contrast to victorious campaigns, medieval depictions of defeats — where they were not simply passed over in silence by the historiographers — were usually more intense and far-reaching.

Contemporary writers interpreted the historical context of events from a deep religiosity, in which they believed God's will to be revealed both in war and in all other life situations. Therefore, while the victory of one's own side was accepted as a triumph of a righteous cause, a defeat required a detailed interpretation of a divine judgment, especially when (ignoring the fact that Serbians fought on the Ottoman side) Christians were defeated by non-Christians.[37]

The cantor at the abbey of Saint-Denis near Paris, Michel Pintoin, addressed the Christian defeat in several chapters of his *Chronica Karoli Sexti*. He attributed the failure of the crusade to the sinfulness of the crusaders, especially the French. According to Pintoin, the proud Christians were brought down by decadent feasts paired with a dissolute and unrestrained lifestyle, massacres of the local Orthodox population, greed for ransom and booty, discord in their own ranks and, ultimately, an overweening arrogance. As is common for medieval descriptions of a fiasco, even before the departure from Buda, bad omens in the sky could not portend anything good for the undertaking.[38] Here, Pintoin's depiction of the Ottomans is of particular interest. They serve the chronicler 'as a mirror to show the deplorable behaviour of Christians'.[39] The cantor recounts an anecdote in which the Turkish prisoners who were lucky enough not to have been slaughtered following the sack of Oryahovo were said to have shaken their heads in amazement at the elegant shoes of the crusaders, a fad of the late fourteenth century, decorated with a point two feet or more in length. The pomposity of the French, which manifested itself in brightly decorated tents, also met with the incomprehension of the Muslim hostages. The Ottomans are not only shown as non-materialistic in Pintoin's portrayal, but are also depicted as godly and pious fighters, whose leaders, after the victory over the Christians, were the first to call on the army to thank God for their luck in battle.[40]

Deeply impressed by the defeat of the Christian crusaders at Nicopolis, the early humanist Coluccio Salutati also talked about the Ottoman Turks in detail in a letter sent in August 1397 to Margrave Jobst of Moravia, the later Romano-German king. He presented the Ottomans not as *Turchi* but as *Teucri*, defending his choice of words by paying less attention to their (from his point of view) supposed original home in the Caucasus than to the fact that, when he wrote the letter, they dominated the ancient area around Troy, which Salutati referred

---

37 See Martin Clauss, 'Vae Victoribus? Deutungen von Kriegsniederlagen im Mittelalter', in *Niederlagen und Kriegsfolgen — Vae Victis oder Vae Victoribus? Vom Alten Orient bis ins europäische Mittelalter*, ed. Lena Meier and Oliver Stoll (Berlin, 2016), pp. 139–53; Clauss, *Kriegsniederlagen im Mittelalter: Darstellung — Deutung — Bewältigung* (Paderborn, 2009); Clauss, 'Von spitzen Schuhen und ungehörten Helden: Zum Umgang der mittelalterlichen Historiographie mit Kriegsniederlagen am Beispiel der Schlacht von Nikopolis', *Arbeitskreis Militärgeschichte e.V.: Newsletter* 10 (2005), 15–18.
38 Michel Pintoin, *Chronica Karoli Sexti*, ed. Louis Bellaguet, 6 vols (Paris, 1839–52), 2: bk 17.22–27, pp. 480–515.
39 Clauss, 'Von spitzen Schuhen', p. 16.
40 Pintoin, *Chronica* 2, bk 17.24–28, pp. 496–517.

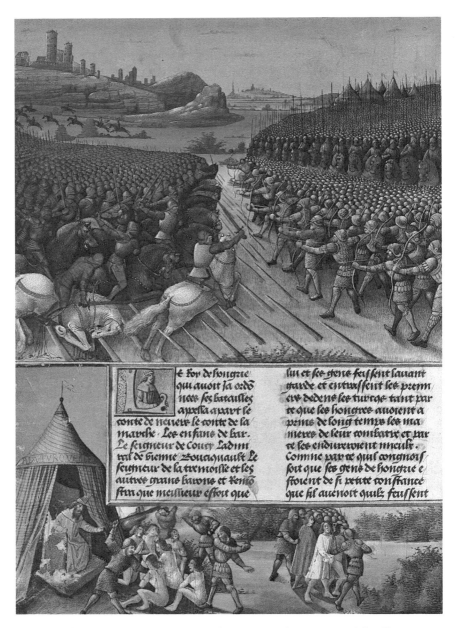

Fig. 16 The battle of Nicopolis, 25 September 1396 (top); execution of the Christian prisoners by the Ottoman Turks (bottom) — both pictures by Jean Colombe, 1474. Taken from Sébastien Mamerot, *Les passages faiz oultremer par les Roys de france et autres princes et seigneurs francois contre les turcqs et autres sarrazins et mores oultre marins* (s. l., 1474), Bibliothèque nationale de France, Paris, Département des Manuscrits, Fr. 5594, fol. 263v, available online at <https://w.wiki/3UAC> [accessed 21 September 2023], licence public domain

to as *Teucria*.[41] The Italian humanist had already chosen a similar depiction as early as 1389 when, in a letter to King Stephen Trvtko I of Bosnia, he called the Turkish troops 'Trojan infidels'.[42] This account should be placed in the context of a wider discourse among Western intellectuals of the late fourteenth century on the origins of the Turks.[43] The main representative here may well be Philippe de Mézières, who, in his work *Le songe du vieil pelerin* (1389) repeatedly underlined the supposed Trojan origins of the Turks.[44] Both Salutati and Mézières drew upon the early medieval tradition of the *Chronicle of Fredegar*, which describes three groups of refugees who fled Troy after its capture by the Greeks: the first under *Friga* is said to have fled to Macedonia, the second under *Franchio* to the Rhine, and the third under a certain *Turchot* is said to have remained in Asia Minor. Salutati saw the last group as the progenitor of the Turks, thus connecting them with another ancient people, namely the Romans. This connection to the ancient model was intended to underline the military and organisational efficiency of the Ottomans, who through their 'customs, life and habits' reminded the humanist of 'the rites and customs of the bravest Romans'.[45] As a result, Salutati dedicated

---

41 Coluccio Salutati, *Epistolario*, ed. Francesco Novati, 4 vols (Roma, 1891–1911), 3, bk 10, no. 4, p. 208: *Videtis Teucros; sic enim appellare potius libet quam Turchos, postquam apud Teucriam dominantur, licet fama sit ipsos a monte Caucaso descendisse*.
42 Salutati, *Epistolario* 3, p. 208, n. 1. See Nancy Bisaha, *Creating East and West: Renaissance Humanists and the Ottoman Turks* (Philadelphia, 2004), p. 215, n. 86. The notion that the Turks were descended from the Trojans persisted among Italian humanists well into the fifteenth century. Representatively, in his work *Historiae de varietate fortunae* (1444), Gian Francesco Poggio Bracciolini still uses both terms synonymously. Nevertheless, from the second half of the fifteenth century, more and more doubts about this idea began to emerge. Some time later, the same Poggio, for instance, questioned his view of the Trojan origins of the Turks in a letter to a friend. Gian Francesco Poggio Bracciolini, *Historiae de varietate fortunae libri quatuor*, ed. Giorgi Domenico (Paris, 1723); Bracciolini *Epistolae*, ed. Tonelli, 3 vols (Florence, 1832–61), 3: bk 12, no. 3, p. 129. The most important and influential rejection of this depiction, however, was provided by Enea Silvio Piccolomini in his work *Asia*, published in 1461/62. For Piccolomini, the Turks were not descended from the ancient Trojans, the noble opponents of Homer's Greeks, but rather from the barbaric Scythians of the Inner Asian steppes. This description is in keeping with the spirit of the times and other treatises from the mid-fifteenth century. Shocked by the heavy defeats of the Christians at Varna and Kosovo in the 1440s and, above all, by the loss of Constantinople in 1453, defamatory descriptions of the Ottomans were intended to animate Latin Christianity to launch a pan-European crusade against the 'worst enemy of faith'. Enea Silvio Piccolomini, *La Dicrittione de l'Asia, et Europa [...] e l'Historia de le cose memorabilia tutte in quelle, con l'aggionta de L'Africa, secondo diversi scrittori, con incredibile brevità e diligenza* (Vinegia, 1544), fols 14r–28v, 172r–73v. See Giampiero Bellingeri, 'Turchi e Persiani fra visioni abnormi e normalizzazioni, a Venezia (secoli XV–XVIII)', *RILUNE — Revue des littératures européennes* 9 (2015), 14–89 (here 26–29).
43 Steve Runciman, 'Teucri and Turci', in *Medieval and Middle Eastern Studies in Honour of Aziz Suryal Atiya*, ed. S. Hanna (Leiden, 1972), pp. 344–48.
44 Philippe de Mézières, *Le songe du vieil pelerin*, ed. George William Coopland, 2 vols (Cambridge, 1969).
45 Salutati, *Epistolario* 3, bk 10, no. 4, p. 209: *Credite michi: genus hoc hominum, quorum cum mores, vitam et instituta percipio, fortissimorum Romanorum ritum consuetudinesque recordor [...]*.

much space in his writing to the warlike characteristics of the Ottomans. He discussed the tactical behaviour of the Turks as well as their organisational skills, but focused his attention primarily on the individual strengths and the strict training of the Ottoman warriors, who were 'cultivated in the art of war by their princes' from the age of 'ten or twelve' and lived their lives for war alone.[46]

As with Pintoin, the Ottomans served Salutati as a mirror. For him, Nicopolis symbolised the unity and strength of the Turks, while the Christian crusader army in its poor organisation, prejudiced arrogance and the discord resulting from particular interests, symbolised the disastrous political conditions of the Catholic West, such as the papal schism, which had now lasted for a good twenty years, and the Anglo-French conflict. Again, as with Pintoin, Salutati also underlined the orthodoxy and piety of the Ottomans. Therefore, even if the Ottomans did not believe in the one true Christian God, Salutati could not hide his respect for the zeal with which the Ottomans fought for their faith:

> Indeed, they are not barbarians to the extent that they do not believe in the existence of God or a future life and glory; but they consider it a certainty that fighters for the Lord or his perpetual law are received into glory. To the extent that they believe more firmly, they live more simply and less learnedly.[47]

However, his letter was anything but a eulogy of the Turks. Rather, it had an appellative character. Despite all their virtues, Salutati considered the Ottomans to be a cruel and violent people, and their determination and organisational skills made them the greatest possible threat to Christianity:

> The Turks are an extremely ferocious race of men with high expectations. Do not ignore what I mention here. They trust and believe that they will erase the name of Christ throughout the world and they say that it is in their fates to devastate Italy until they reach the city divided by a river, which they interpret as Rome, and they will consume everything by fire and sword.[48]

Michel Pintoin shared Salutati's opinion. As an instrument of God, the Ottomans were the most inexorable enemy of all Christianity and cruel oppressors of the Balkan Christians. Year after year they devastated South-Eastern Europe, subjugating more and more of the Orthodox peoples.[49] The French poet Jean Froissart, probably the best-known chronicler of the Hundred Years' War, painted a similar picture of the Ottoman danger in his *Chronicles*. Froissart reported on an exchange of letters between Sigismund of Luxemburg and the French king Charles VI, which took place in the run-up to the Nicopolis Crusade, and in which the

---

46 Salutati, *Epistolario* 3, bk 10, no. 4, pp. 208–9.
47 Salutati, *Epistolario* 3, bk 10, no. 4, p. 209. English translation by Nancy Bisaha, *Creating East and West*, p. 57.
48 Salutati, *Epistolario* 3, bk 10, no. 4, p. 208. English translation by Nancy Bisaha, *Creating East and West*, p. 56.
49 Pintoin, *Chronica* 2, bk 17.3, pp. 424–26.

Hungarian king again outlined Sultan Bayezid's supposed provocations; these had not only revealed the Ottomans' aims of conquest, but had also specifically aimed to insult religious symbols of the Christians. The Turkish sultan is portrayed as a rabid barbarian who brags about having his warhorse eat oats from the altar in St Peter's Basilica in Rome at the end of his conquests.[50] Whether Bayezid actually challenged the West with such harsh words remains unclear due to the lack of existing letters from the sultan to the Hungarian king. Sigismund's correspondence with Charles VI has also not been preserved. Froissart's report, however, testifies to the chronicler's endeavours to win over Western Christianity for the struggle against the Ottomans by portraying a Turkish threat that appears to be omnipotent and dedicated to the annihilation of all Christianity.

The defeat of the Christians at Nicopolis prompted Philippe de Mézières to make similar gloomy predictions for Christianity. In his pessimistic elegy *Epistre lamentable et consolatoire*, written immediately after the battle, he described the Christian discord and contrasted it with the Ottomans' unity, power and hunger for conquest.[51] He called on the Christians to found a new order of knights, the *Ordre de la Passion*, because this was the only way to overcome the Ottoman threat.[52] Mézières had already expressed the idea of an all-Christian order of knights dedicated to the reconquest of the Holy Land as early as 1367. This vision of the approaching downfall of the Christian world was not a literary novelty reserved to the French. As early as 1389 in the allegorical representation *Le songe du vieil pelerin*, Mézières, visibly moved by the news of the Ottoman victory at Kosovo Field, described the Ottoman expansion as one of the greatest threats to Latin Christianity: if a divided and chronically discordant Christendom did not come to an agreement, it would take less than ten years for the Ottomans, who had been sent as God's tools to punish the sinful Christians, to reach Apulia and,

---

50 *Oeuvres de Froissart: Chroniques*, ed. Josep Kervyn de Lettenhove, 25 vols (Bruxelles, 1867–77), 15: 216–18. See also the *Relation de la croisade de Nicopoli* (*Oeuvres de Froissart: Chroniques* 15: 439–508 [here 439–40]), published anonymously at the court of Count Guy II of Blois (d. 1397), which is, to all intents and purposes, a copy of Froissart's accounts.

51 Philippe de Mézières, *Une epistre lamentable et consolatoire adressée en 1397 à Philippe le Hardi, duc de Bourgogne, sur la défaite de Nicopolis (1396)*, ed. Philippe Contamine and Jacques Paviot (Paris, 2008). See Charles-Louis Morand Metivier, 'Creation and Union through Death and Massacre: The Crusade of Nicopolis and Philippe de Mézières' Epistre lamentable et consolatoire', in *Trauma in Medieval Society*, ed. Wendy J. Turner and Christina Lee (Leiden, 2018), pp. 298–319.

52 Philippe de Mézières, *Nova religio passionis*, publ. in Atiya, *The Crusade of Nicopolis*, pp. 136–38. See Philippe Contamine, 'L'ordre de la Passion de Jésus-Christ de Philippe de Mézières: Une utopie de chevalier Angleterre', in *Élites et ordres militaires au Moyen Âge: Rencontre autour d'Alain Demurger*, ed. Philippe Josserand, Luís Filipe Simões Dias de Oliveira and Damien Carraz (Madrid, 2015) pp. 125–34; Contamine, '"Les princes, barons et chevaliers qui a la chevalerie au service de Dieu se sont ja vouez": Recherches prosopographiques sur l'ordre de la Passion de Jésus-Christ (1385–95)', in *La noblesse et la croisade à la fin du Moyen Âge: Piété, diplomatie, aventure: Actes du colloque de Prague (26–27 octobre 2007)*, ed. Martin Nejedlý and Jaroslav Svátek (Toulouse, 2009), pp. 43–68; Abdel Hamid Hamdy, 'Philippe de Mézières and the New Order of the Passion', *Bulletin of the Faculty of the Arts (Alexandria University)* 18 (1964), 45–54.

following the subjugation of Germany, the gates of France. Then the West could expect the same fate that had befallen the Balkan Christians.[53]

Alongside the news of the crushing defeat of the crusaders, the reports of the atrocities committed by the Ottomans against the captured Christians immediately after the battle at the instigation of Bayezid caused the greatest grief and a storm of indignation among Latin Christians.[54] Johannes Schiltberger, who took part in the crusade as a squire of the Bavarian knight Leonhard Reichartinger, described the bloody events which took place immediately after the battle in great detail in one of the most famous and most widely received German travelogues of the fifteenth century. According to Schiltberger, Bayezid had John of Nevers brought to him so that he could witness at first hand the vengeance that the Ottomans wanted to exact on Christian prisoners for the high blood toll that the crusader army had caused in their ranks. The sultan had the majority of the crusaders beheaded before the eyes of the Burgundian prince. Schiltberger reports that the 'bloodshed lasted from morning to evening' and that the number of the executed 'was estimated at 10,000 men'.[55]

According to Pintoin, some of the Ottoman leaders who had taken part in a post-battle council pleaded for the captive Christians to be sold into slavery or ransomed. However, Sultan Bayezid preferred to take revenge for the crimes committed by the crusaders on their way to Nicopolis, because the Christians had shown no mercy towards the Turkish prisoners taken at Oryahovo and had massacred them in cold blood. Pintoin backs Schiltberger's accounts by stressing that John of Nevers, as the nominal leader of the Franco-Burgundian contingents, was only spared in order to witness the humiliation of the execution of thousands of Christians.[56] How many prisoners were actually executed is very difficult to reconstruct. Around 6000 crusaders, the entire French leadership included, were probably captured by the Ottomans as a result of the Christian defeat, but only about 300 of them succeeded in returning home by paying an enormous ransom of more than 200,000 ducats, about half the annual income of the duke of

---

53 Mézières, *Le songe du vieil pelerin* 1: 251, 256–57. See Marie Radkovska, 'Le Songe du Vieil Pelerin: l'idée de croisade rêvée et vécue chez Philippe de Mézières', in *La noblesse et la croisade*, pp. 31–42.
54 Charles-Louis Morand Metivier, 'Narrating a Massacre: The Writing of History and Emotions as Response to the Battle of Nicopolis (1396)', in *Affective and Emotional Economies in Medieval and Early Modern Europe*, ed. Andreea Marculescu and Charles-Louis Morand Métivier (Cham, 2018), pp. 195–210; Kelly R. DeVries, 'The Effect of Killing the Christian Prisoners at the Battle of Nicopolis', in *Crusaders, Condottieri and Cannon: Medieval Warfare in Societies around the Mediterranean*, ed. Donald J. Kagay and L. J. Andrew Villalon (Leiden, 2003), pp. 157–72; Nicole Chareyron, 'Le sang des croisés de Nicopolis', in *Le sang au Moyen Âge: Actes du quatrième colloque international de Montpellier, Université Paul-Valéry (27–29 novembre 1997)*, ed. Marcel Faure (Montpellier, 1999), pp. 321–30; Daniel Dereck, 'Un seigneur de Roisin victime de la bataille de Nicopolis (1396)', *Annales du Cercle d'histoire et d'archéologie de Saint-Ghislain et de la région* 8 (2000), 243–62.
55 Johannes Schiltberger, *Reisebuch*, ed. Valentin Langmantel (Tübingen, 1885), p. 6.
56 Pintoin, *Chronica* 2, bk 17.28, pp. 516–21.

Burgundy in the 1390s.[57] While on his knees, John of Nevers was said to have asked that some of his companions' lives be spared, including that of Marshal Jean II Le Maingre (also known as Boucicaut), the French crusader par excellence of the late fourteenth century. This was a motif that was subsequently reproduced not only in literature but also in various allegorical depictions over the following decades.[58]

The outcry of grief and indignation which the Ottoman massacre of the Christian captives caused in the West is described by Michel Pintoin in a chapter of his chronicle dedicated specifically to the event: on 9 January 1397, by order of Charles VI, funeral services were held in all Paris churches and many other churches across France followed this example. The grieving for the fallen assumed the proportions of a national mourning.[59] In the eyes of the West, the execution of prisoners was an act of barbarism, since the imprisonment of captured enemies as hostages for the extortion of ransom was part of the knightly habitus in the bellicose late Middle Ages.[60] The residents of the captured Oryahovo had of course painfully discovered that this procedure was reserved for wealthy aristocrats and burgesses since, with the exception of around 1000 captives considered rich enough to pay the ransom, all the others were slaughtered by the Latin Christians.[61]

---

57 See Jean Richard, 'Les prisonniers de Nicopolis', AB 68 (1996), 75–83; Atiya, *The Crusade of Nicopolis*, 94–97; Setton, *The Papacy and the Levant* 1: 355–56; Richard Vaughan, *Philip the Bold: The Formation of the Burgundian State* (London, 1962), pp. 71–78, 226–36; Barthélemy Pocquet du Haut-Jussé, 'Le retour de Nicopolis et la rançon de Jean sans Peur: Compte inédit de maître Oudart Douay pour le duc de Bourgogne 1397–1398', AB 9 (1937), 296–302.
58 *Le Livre des fais du bon messire Jehan le Maingre, dit Bouciquaut, mareschal de France et gouverneur de Jennes*, ed. Denis Lalande (Genève, 1985), pp. 110–11; *Oeuvres de Froissart: Chroniques* 15: 323–27. See Jacques Paviot, 'Boucicaut et la croisade (fin XIVe–début XVe siècle)', in *La noblesse et la croisade*, pp. 69–84; Norman Housley, 'Le Maréchal Boucicaut à Nicopolis', AB 68 (1996), 85–99.
59 Pintoin, *Chronica* 2, bk 17.29, pp. 520–22. There is also a similar report in *Le Livre des fais*, 118–20. On the commemoration of the Nicopolis Crusade, see Christoph Brachmann, 'The Crusade of Nicopolis, Burgundy, and the Entombment of Christ at Pont-à-Mousson', *Journal of the Warburg and Courtauld Institutes* 74 (2011), 155–90.
60 See Rémy Ambühl, *Prisoners of War in the Hundred Years War: Ransom Culture in the Late Middle Ages* (Cambridge, 2013); Hannelore Zug Tucci, 'Kriegsgefangenschaft im Mittelalter: Probleme und erste Forschungsergebnisse', in *Der Krieg im Mittelalter*, ed. Hans-Henning Kortüm (Berlin, 2001), pp. 123–40; Karl Heinz Ziegler, 'Kriegsrechtliche Literatur im Spätmittelalter', in *Der Krieg im Mittelalter und in der Frühen Neuzeit: Gründe, Begründungen, Bilder, Bräuche, Recht*, ed. Horst Brunner (Wiesbaden, 1999), pp. 57–71; Volker Schmidtchen, 'Ius in Bello und militärischer Alltag — Rechtliche Regelungen in Kriegsordnungen des 14. bis 16. Jahrhunderts', in *Der Krieg im Mittelalter*, pp. 25–56; Maurice Keen, *The Laws of War in the Late Middle Ages* (London, 1965), pp. 137–88.
61 Pintoin, *Chronica* 2, bk 17.24, pp. 494–95.

Fig. 17. The massacre of the Christians by the Ottomans after the battle of Nicopolis as a revenge for the preceding Rahova by the crusaders as depicted in a late-fifteenth-century (s. l., c. 1470) version of Jean Froissart's *Chronicles*. Bibliothèque nationale de France, Paris, Département des Manuscrits, Fr. 2646, fol. 255v. Reproduced by Paul Srodecki from <https://w.wiki/777U> [accessed 21 September 2023], licence public domain

A Distorted Image

One might think that the newly discovered interest of the West in the Ottomans after the Nicopolis Crusade, mirrored in the various written records of the time, would also have led to a differentiated picture of the Ottomans, their manners and customs, and their political, religious and social organisation. This was, however, only partially the case. In most reports, the picture remains very fragmentary and even quite distorted. Some writers of the late fourteenth century described the Ottomans as polytheists. In his chronicle, Jean Froissart has Bayezid and his entourage thanking various deities for their victory over the Christians.[62] According to Michel Pintoin, the ancient god Apollo appeared to Murad I in a dream, with thirteen European princes paying homage to him with a crown adorned with gold and precious stones, which Turkish proponents were said to interpret as signalling the coming subjugation of Western Christianity by the Ottomans. In German sources, the expression *Türkenheiden*, which is very much in the tradition of the high medieval crusades — in which the followers of the Mohammedan faith were equated with heathens — is a very common name for the Ottomans. These misrepresentations can be traced back to ignorance, but they may well also be the result of old thought patterns, built upon constructions of alterity and alienity, which contrasted the Christian world of belief with the non-Christian world of unbelief.[63]

The ethnic differences among Muslims were also little known to Latin Christians. No real detailed distinction was made between the Ottomans and the Seljuks. The Ottoman Turks were often seen as one of many Arab tribes or simply thrown together into the synecdochical hodgepodge of Christianity's 'Saracen' enemies.[64] Demonyms well-known to one's own readership were used as synonyms for other foes of their own cultural circle, meaning, for example, that the Iberian Moors appear as Tatars in sources of the Teutonic Order or that the pagan Balts are perceived as Saracens in English and French sources of the fourteenth and even fifteenth centuries.[65] But even with regard to an umbrella term for the Muslims there can be no question of consistency in the Western sources. The anonymous author of the *Chronique des quatre premiers Valois*, written at the end of the fourteenth century, sometimes distinguishes between the 'Turks' and the 'Saracens', but sometimes — even in the same paragraph — the term 'Saracens' is again used as superordinate. Additionally, the chronicler saw the Ottoman Turks under Bayezid not only as the undisputed rulers of Asia Minor, which was alternately referred to as *Turquie* or *Tartarie*, but also as exceptionally well-connected with all the important Muslim powers.[66]

Indeed, the defeat at Nicopolis increased the number of reports of those in the West who liked to exaggerate Bayezid's actual power and military capabilities and,

---

62 *Oeuvres de Froissart: Chroniques* 15: 321: *Amourath prinst trèsgrant plaisance au regarder, et entra dedens à moult grant gloire et magnificence, et se gloriffoit en son cuer de la belle victoire que il avoit eue sur les crestiens, et en regracioit les dieux et les déesses selon sa loy où il créoit et que les paiens croient.*

63 Representatively, see Hilmi Kaçar and Jan Dumolyn, 'The Battle of Nicopolis (1396), Burgundian Catastrophe and Ottoman Fait Divers: The Relevance of "Other" in State Ideologies', *Revue Belge de Philologie et d'Histoire* 91 (2013), 905–34.

64 See with further references Krzysztof Baczkowski, 'Turcy Osmańscy w piśmiennictwie francuskim drugiej połowy XIV wieku', in *600-lecie bitwy*, pp. 61–74.

65 Paul Srodecki, 'Playing the Crusade Card: Rhetorical References to Outremer and Iberian Crusades in the Conflict between the Teutonic Order and the Crown of Poland in the Early Fifteenth Century', in *The Defence of The Faith: Crusading on the Frontiers of Latin Christendom in the Late Middle Ages*, ed. Srodecki and Norbert Kersken (Turnhout, 2024), pp. 314–38.

66 *Chronique des quatre premiers Valois*, ed. Siméon Auguste Luce (Paris, 1862), pp. 319, 326.

in one fell swoop, declare the Ottomans to be the dominant player in the Islamic world — be it in the Levant, Northern Africa or even on the Iberian Peninsula.[67] It may therefore not be surprising that, in some French portrayals of the battle of Nicopolis, Persians, Arabs, Syrians, Tatars and even Lithuanians took to the field alongside the Ottomans.[68] In keeping with this, the Ottomans were even considered to be the leaders — or at least the party to follow — of the entire world of unbelief! The listing of different peoples in the enemy's camp is characteristic of this medieval form of reporting. In the absence of more detailed information on what actually happened, all factual and potential enemies of one's own cultural and religious circle were often combined into a single unit, even if this meant that, in the Western imagination, the pagan Lithuanians from North-Eastern Europe fought alongside the monotheistic Ottomans on the banks of the lower Danube.[69] Jean Brandon (d. 1428), abbot of the Cistercian convent in Dunes, may serve as another example for this increased depiction of the Ottoman threat in the run-up to the Nicopolis Crusade. In his chronicle, Bayezid is posed to conquer not only the whole of South-Eastern Europe but also Northern Italy and Germany (*Romania, Longobardia et Alemania*)![70] Here we can already see the first signs of later anti-Turkish crusade rhetoric of the ilk of Enea Silvio Piccolomini, according to which Europe was in a permanent state of siege in the face of overwhelming Ottoman power and thus had to fear for its very existence.[71]

The Christian writers were variously well informed with regard to Bayezid's name: Michel Pintoin alternately refers to the Ottoman sultan as *Basit* or *Lamorat Baxin*; the anonymous author of the *Chronique des quatre premiers Valois* writes of an *Amoral Bakin, amiral Baquin* or *Bakan*; Jean Brandon calls him *Lamourach Bahy* or *Bacquin sive Basach*; and, in Froissart's depiction, he appears

---

67 Srodecki, '"Contre les ennemis"', pp. 42–44.
68 See with further references Baczkowski, 'Turcy Osmańscy', p. 65; Srodecki, '"Contre les ennemis"', pp. 42–43.
69 On this issue, see representatively Zeynep Kocabiyikoglu Çeçen, 'The Use of "The Saracen Opinion" on Knighthood in Medieval French Literature: L'Ordene de Chevalerie and L'Apparicion Maistre Jehan de Meun', *The Medieval History Journal* 19 (2016), 57–92; Alan V. Murray, 'The Saracens of the Baltic: Pagan and Christian Lithuanians in the Perception of English and French Crusaders to Late Medieval Prussia', *JBS* 41 (2010), 413–29; Antonio Donato Sciacovelli, 'Turchi, arabi mori, saraceni: la fedeltà allo stereotipo dell'infedele nella letteratura italiana medievale', *I Turchi, gli Asburgo e l'Adriatico*, ed. Gizella Nemeth and Adriano Papo (Duino, 2007), pp. 21–34.
70 *Chroniques des religieux des Dunes, Jean Brandon — Gilles de Roye — Adrien de But*, ed. Kevryn de Lettenhove (Bruxelles, 1870), p. 24.
71 Paul Srodecki, *Antemurale Christianitatis: Zur Genese der Bollwerksrhetorik im östlichen Mitteleuropa and der Schwelle vom Mittelalter zur Frühen Neuzeit* (Husum, 2015), pp. 151–62; Johannes Helmrath, 'Pius II. und die Türken', in *Europa und die Türken in der Renaissance*, ed. Bodo Guthmüller and Wilhelm Kühlmann (Tübingen, 2000), pp. 79–138; Jürgen Blusch, 'Enea Silvio Piccolomini und Giannantonio Campano: Die unterschiedlichen Darstellungsprinzipien in ihren Türkenreden', *Humanistica Lovaniensia: Journal of Neo-Latin Studies* 28 (1979), 78–138; Rigomera Eysser, 'Papst Pius II. und der Kreuzzug gegen die Türken, in *Mélanges d'histoire* 2: 1–134.

as 'King *Basaach* called *l'Amourath Bacquin*'.⁷² These and similar names for Bayezid (*Weyasit[t]*, *Wayser*, *Amorat*, *Waysant*) can also be found in contemporary and later German sources.⁷³ In particular the phonetic proximity between *Murad* and *Amorat* or *Amourath* could lead one to the conclusion that the Christian scribes confused son and father. However, as Herbert Adams Gibbons pointed out over a century ago, this might instead be traced back to the distinction between name and office, with *l'Amourath Bacquin* a corruption of *l'émir-pacha* ('emir-pasha').⁷⁴ Nevertheless, later humanist chroniclers and writers of the renaissance period such as Niccolò 'Secundinus' Sagundino, Donado da Lezze, Enea Silvio Piccolomini or Paolo Giovio often confused Murad I and his son and successor Bayezid, resulting in the two Ottoman rulers becoming merged into a single person.⁷⁵ This Western ignorance with regard to the degree of kinship within the house of Osman persisted well into the fifteenth century: even several decades after the battle of Nicopolis, for instance, Duke Philip the Good of Burgundy believed his contemporary on the Ottoman throne, Mehmed II the Conqueror, to be the son of the sultan who defeated Philip's father when, in reality, Mehmed was Bayezid's great-grandson.⁷⁶

Where a distinction is made between Bayezid and his father Murad, the chroniclers paint an ambiguous picture. In Michel Pintoin's chronicle, for example, Murad is described as a moderate, wise and just ruler who, despite his desire for conquest, always behaved graciously and generously towards those he subjugated, never exploiting them nor oppressing them in their faith so long as they acknowledged Ottoman rule and did not act against Muslim laws or customs.⁷⁷ Bayezid, by contrast, is continuously portrayed as a cruel and vengeful despot.⁷⁸ Philippe de Mézières painted a similar picture of Bayezid in his *Epistre lamentable et consolatoire*. Here, the Ottoman ruler appears as a 'strong and horrible tyrant' who, in his bloodlust and cruelty (especially against Christians), could only be compared to 'Attila and Totila, the kings of the Huns, Vandals and Goths'. The historical reference here is clear: as in the case of Attila, 'the scourge of God', Bayezid's task was to punish the Christians for their vices and sins. Schiltberger,

---

72 Pintoin, *Chronica* 1, bk 14.13, pp. 113–14, bk 18.8, pp. 558–59; 2, bk 17.3, pp. 424–26. 2, bk 17.22–28, pp. 480–521; *Chronique des religieux des Dunes*, pp. 24, 34, 36–37, 49; *Oeuvres de Froissart: Chroniques* 15: 217.

73 Schiltberger, *Reisebuch*, 2, 4–14, 30; Ulman Stromer, 'Püchel von meim geslechet und von abentewr', ed. Karl Hegel, in CDS 1: 1–312 (here 49); Jacob Twinger von Königshofen, 'Chronik 1400 (1415)', ed. Karl Hegel, in CDS 8: 230–498; 9: 499–917 (here 9: 855); Mülich, 'Chronik 1348–1487', p. 43.

74 See with further references on the sources Herbert Adams Gibbons, *The Foundation of the Ottoman Empire: A History of the Osmanlis up to the Death of Bayezid I (1300–1403)* (Oxford, 1916), p. 213, n. 2.

75 Gibbons, *The Foundation of the Ottoman Empire*, p. 213, n. 2.

76 Erich Meuthen, 'Der Fall von Konstantinopel und der lateinische Westen', *Historische Zeitschrift* 237 (1983), 1–35 (here 21–22, n. 66); Armand Grunzweig, 'Philippe le Bon et Constantinople', *Byzantion* 24 (1954), 47–61 (here 48); Vaughan, *Philip the Bold*, pp. 59–78.

77 Pintoin, *Chronica* 1 bk 12.2, pp. 708–9.

78 *Chronique des religieux des Dunes*, pp. 24, 34, 36–37 and 49.

who served at the Ottoman court after Nicopolis up until Bayezid's defeat by Timur at Ankara in 1402, also pictured the sultan as a determined and vindictive ruler, unpredictable in his outbursts, who did not shrink from brute force in order to achieve his goals.[79] Froissart, by contrast, emphasised the magnanimity of Bayezid in his treatment of the captured French elite. The sultan was said to have spared no luxury or expense in the accommodation of his noble hostages and reportedly showed great decency and courtesy in bidding farewell to those released. In his chronicle, the French writer even went a step further and sought to portray the Turkish sultan as an adversary on a par with the French in terms of his chivalrous behaviour: for example, when John of Nevers was set free, Bayezid not only waived an oath that would forbid the duke's son from fighting the Ottomans again. Rather, according to Froissart, the sultan assured the Valois that he was willing to face him again in the field at any time.[80]

Concluding Thoughts

In conclusion, it can be stated that the Nicopolis Crusade led to the first comprehensive depictions of the Ottoman Turks in the West. While the latter were almost indistinguishable from other Anatolian Turks or even Muslim peoples before the crusade, with the victory over the Christians at the gates of Nicopolis the Ottomans muscled their way into the public consciousness of the West. This was at least the first expression of an increased interest in their alien culture from a Western perspective. However, the newly awakened attention concentrated largely on a discussion of the military characteristics of the Ottomans, and knowledge about their social, political and economic organisation, their religion, customs and traditions remained very fragmentary. An exception to this is certainly Johannes Schiltberger's very detailed *Reisebuch*, the archetype of the vast number of all European travel reports on the Ottoman Empire to follow. This work, however, was written after his return from the east to Bavaria in 1427 and only became popular in Europe after its first printing in the second half of the fifteenth century. Nevertheless, the 1396 crusade can be considered a milestone in Western literature on the Ottoman Turks, since it initiated what would later become an early form of scholarship and expertism in the Ottomans and the so-called *Turcica* collections at pre-modern European courts.[81]

---

79 Schiltberger, *Reisebuch*, 2, 4–14, 30.
80 *Oeuvres de Froissart: Chroniques* 15: 216–26, 242–46, 249–53, 262–69, 307–60.
81 On early modern depictions of and scholarship on the Ottoman Turks, see, for example, Pál Ács, 'Pro Turcis and contra Turcos: Curiosity, Scholarship and Spiritualism in Turkish Histories by Johannes Löwenklau (1541–94)', *Acta Comeniana: International Review of Comenius Studies and Early Modern Intellectual History* 25 (2011), 25–46; Almut Höfert, 'Turcica: Annäherung an eine Gesamtbetrachtung repräsentativer Reiseberichte über das Osmanische Reich bis 1600', in *Text und Bild in Reiseberichten des 16. Jahrhunderts: Westliche Zeugnisse über Amerika und das Osmanische Reich*,

In summary, two supposedly contrary currents can be identified in the type of reporting, which mostly even appear in the same accounts: on the one hand, the rudeness and inhumane cruelty of the Ottomans, their barbaric behaviour, the pagan customs and manners and the constant urge to expand are continuously emphasised. On the other hand, respect, recognition and even admiration can be read in the sources, as virtues such as discipline, abstinence, piety, diligence and ambition are ascribed to the Ottomans. The fact that the Christian reports combine contradictions is nothing unusual for the medieval way of portraying mighty non-Christian rulers (one has only to think of Saladin), whose political and military power was a source of fear and dislike and at the same time that of attraction and intriguingness. Characterising the Ottoman sultans as barbarian and yet noble, as cruel and yet quixotic would remain a rhetorical constant up until the early modern times, when, in the wake of developing exotism and orientalism, the so-called *Türkenfurcht* went hand in hand with the *Türkenfaszination*.[82] Paired with a significant level of wanderlust, this fascination with the exotic was probably one of the most important driving forces behind Western adventurers travelling to the Ottoman Empire.[83] Ultimately, however, both narratives served as mirrors and memoranda, to show the mistakes and misconduct in the Latin Christians' own camp. Based on the domino theory, the exaggeration of the Ottoman danger became particularly popular with the humanists of the fifteenth and sixteenth centuries and served them as an important argumentative component of the anti-Turkish speeches and crusade calls.[84]

---

ed. Ulrike Ilg (Venezia, 2008), pp. 38–94; Carl Göllner, *Tvrcica: Die europäischen Türkendrücke des XVI. Jahrhunderts*, 3 vols (Bucureşti, 1961–78).

[82] See *Imagined, Embodied and Actual Turks in Early Modern Europe*, ed. Bent Holm and Mikael Bøgh Rasmusen (Wien, 2021); Natalia Królikowska-Jedlińska, 'Between Fear, Contempt and Fascination — the Ottoman Empire in Polish Renaissance Writing', in *The Ottoman Orient in Renaissance Culture*, pp. 119–35; Pál Ács, 'The Changing Image of Ottoman Turks in East-Central European Renaissance Culture', in *The Ottoman Orient in Renaissance Culture*, pp. 161–92; Wolfgang Neuber, 'Grade der Fremdheit: Alteritätskonstruktion und "experiential"-Argumentation in deutschen Turcica der Renaissance', in *Europa und die Türken*, pp. 249–66.

[83] These adventurers included Jacques de Helly from Picardy, who was reported to have once travelled to the court of Sultan Murad, where he served in the Ottoman army for about three years. Helly fought at Nicopolis and was chosen by Bayezid as a plenipotentiary to bring the news of the Christian defeat and demands for ransom to the French king. His knowledge of Turkish was said to have saved his life. See Philippe Gardette, 'Jacques de Helly, figure de l'entre-deux culturel au lendemain de la défaite de Nicopolis', *Erytheia* 24 (2003), 111–24.

[84] See Srodecki, *Antemurale Christianitatis*, pp. 149–62; Karoline Döring, 'Rhetorik und Politik im 15. Jahrhundert: Die Türkenreden und ihre Verbreitung im Druck', in *Rhetorik in Mittelalter und Renaissance: Konzepte — Praxis — Diversität*, ed. Georg Strack and Julia Knödler (München, 2011), pp. 429–53; Dieter Mertens, 'Europa, id est patria, domus propria, sedes nostra ...: Zu Funktionen und Überlieferung lateinischer Türkenreden im 15. Jahrhundert', in *Europa und die osmanische Expansion im ausgehenden Mittelalter*, ed. Franz-Reiner Erkens (Berlin, 1997), pp. 39–57.

ATTILA BÁRÁNY

Hungary and the *passagium particulare* after Nicopolis (1396–1437)

Sigismund of Luxemburg, king of Hungary (1387–1437), has frequently been blamed for his defeats at the hand of the Ottomans (Nicopolis 1396, Golubac 1428) and for not leading large-scale expeditions into the Balkans in the style of the Angevins.[1] However, his defence system withstood Ottoman invasion for nearly a century, and prevented bloodshed in a pitched battle. Nicopolis demonstrated that the era of the offensive *passagium generale* ('great crusade') enterprises was over. Here I will be investigating the king's efforts at limited-scope enterprises, *passagia particulare* ('smaller, partial crusades'). Hungary realised that the Ottoman state and people were not like the many other warlike emirates in Asia Minor, but possessed a completely different quality in terms of their statecraft and the organisation of their army. Since there was now no chance to halt the Ottomans, the crusade would have to take the form of small-scale campaigns, constant borderline warfare, and the fortification of castles. Christendom had to be protected in Europe, in *Kleinkrieg* ventures along its southern borders.

In the early 1390s, Sultan Bayezid I laid out a new programme of systematic conquest in the Balkans and reached out for territories across the Danube. Key strongholds such as Golubac (Hun. Galambóc) and Orshova (Rom. Orşova, Hun. Orsova) fell to the Ottomans, and from 1391–92, during the campaigns in Temes (mod. Timiş, Romania), Transylvania and Szerémség (mod. Srem, Serbia) were heavily plundered.[2] The Ottomans ratcheted up the pressure, and Hungarian charters refer repeatedly to recurrent incursions, and to thousands being taken captive, especially in the years following the Nicopolis debacle.[3]

---

1 Martin Kintzinger, 'Sigismond, roi de Hongrie, et la croisade', *Annales de Bourgogne* 68 (1996), 23–33.
2 Pál Engel, 'A török-magyar háborúk első évei, 1389–1392', *Hadtörténelmi Közlemények* 111 (1998), 561–77 (here 581); Engel, *The Realm of St. Stephen: A History of Medieval Hungary, 895–1526*, (London, 2001), pp. 202–8.
3 *ZsO* 1, nos 4471, 4497, 5030, 5502, 6049, pp. 494–95, 498, 556–57, 607, 670; *OT* 1, no. 154, p. 263; MNL DL 70706; *A Magyarország és Szerbia közötti összeköttetések oklevéltára 1198–1526*, ed. Lajos Thallóczy and Antal Áldásy (Budapest, 1907), p. 40; *PCsL*, no. 206, pp. 121–22.

The Defence of the Faith, Outremer: Studies in the Crusades and the Latin East, 15 (Turnhout: Brepols, 2024), pp. 199–218

Contemporaries felt they 'had been suffering severe damage for a long time'.[4] In 1400, Pope Boniface IX preached a crusade against the Ottoman Turks 'who were now endeavouring to occupy Hungary'.[5] Sigismund, although faced with a critical situation after Nicopolis, raised armies and led several campaigns to the frontier. In 1401, Ottoman forces plundered the surroundings of Kronstadt (mod. Braşov, Romania, Hung. Brassó).[6] They took a great amount of booty but, on their way back, were defeated by the Hungarians, together with Voivode Mircea of Wallachia.[7] This is an early example of a coordinated *passagium particulare*. The advance of the Ottomans was held back for a period: Bayezid suffered defeat at the hands of Timur Lenk in 1402 at Ankara, and the empire became enmeshed in civil strife. However, even after Ankara 'the warriors of half the Balkans raided Hungary to kidnap people'.[8]

Buffer State Doctrine

Although Ottoman power weakened as a result of the internal crisis which followed Timur's victory, Hungary still had to face attacks from the tribute-paying Balkan warlords. The charters emphasise that assaults were made not only by the Ottomans but also by their allies, *aliarum scismaticarum gencium* ('by other schismatic nations'), mostly Serbians.[9] Sigismund had to fight in the political sphere.[10] In a *cordon sanitaire* system, pushed forward to the south, the king aided pro-Christian claimants and drew them into the anti-Ottoman struggle as satellites, rewarding them with lands in Hungary and providing military assistance against their pro-Ottoman opponents where it was needed. Despot Stefan Lazarević, in return for denouncing his homage to the sultan, was granted huge wealth. In 1426, Sigismund agreed that his successor Đurađ Branković should retain these properties, with Hungary obtaining Serbian fortresses (e.g. Belgrade, Golubac) in exchange, thus contributing much to the defence of the realm up to 1521.[11]

---

4 MNL DF 220288; *ZsO* 1, no. 5683, pp. 627–28; *Acta Anni* 1, no. 238, p. 312: [...] *a multis retrolapsis temporibus*.
5 1400: *ZsO* 2.1, nos 293, 507, pp. 38, 62; *MVHH* 1/4, no. 284, p. 229.
6 *ZsO* 2.1, no. 1925, p. 228; *MVHH* 1/4, no. 522, p. 460.
7 1402: *ZsO* 2.1, no. 1486, p. 176.
8 1403: Pál Fodor, 'Introduction', in *Ransom Slavery along the Ottoman Borders (Early Fifteenth — Early Eighteenth Centuries)*, ed. Géza Dávid and Pál Fodor (Leiden, 2007), pp. xi–xx.
9 MNL DL 8283 (transc. 1406); DF 220288; *ZsO* 1, nos 5102, 5683, pp. 565, 627–28; *Acta anni* 1, no. 238, p. 312; *MVHH* 1/4, no. 284, p. 229 (*Turchos perfidos et infideles Rasscianos*).
10 János M. Bak, 'Sigismund and the Ottoman Advance', in *Sigismund von Luxemburg: Ein Kaiser in Europa*, ed. Michel Pauly and François Reinert (Mainz, 2006), pp. 89–94.
11 Engel, *Realm*, p. 232; Elemér Mályusz, *Kaiser Sigismund in Ungarn, 1387–1437* (Budapest, 1990), pp. 146–47.

Bosnia

Most important military bridgeheads were guarded by Bosnian valleys. In the early 1400s, Sigismund was faced with a pretender to his throne, Ladislas of Naples, who was backed by a baronial league. The Angevin anti-king landed in Dalmatia in 1403 in order to take possession of the throne. The kings of Bosnia had already allied with the Neapolitan party in the 1380s, revolted against Sigismund, and occupied Hungarian territories. Although a truce was agreed in the mid-1390s, since Bosnia was in practice controlled by Grand Voivode Hrvoje Vukčić Hrvatinić, who gave refuge to the Angevin partisans, Hungary faced an ever-present threat on this front. Castles close to the Slavonian border 'sheltered disloyal vassals'.[12] After Nicopolis, Hrvoje was now free to betray the truce, proclaim his support for Ladislas and devastate Hungary — first in Dubica county in 1398 — with the help of Ottoman auxiliaries.[13] Sigismund made a failed attempt to seize the castles of Vrbas and Dubica.[14] Ladislas 'gave his word to marry Bayezid's daughter, since the sultan chose to promote him for the throne of Hungary on condition that the Ottomans provide him with help against Sigismund'.[15] A number of Bosnian barons were 'created kings' with Ottoman assistance, and the sultan 'subjected to their authority a certain part of Bosnia, it pleased to him to establish a new king' in this land, whom he 'named as king of Bosnia'.[16] Even though the tragedy of Ankara shocked the Ottoman Turks, Hungary still had to ward off almost constant onslaughts, mainly from Bosnia, since the Rumelian forces maintained their 'partnership', and sources still report that Hungary had to fight against *Thurcos et eis colligatos ac adherentes* ('Turks and their allies and auxiliaries').[17]

In 1403–4, Hrvoje became the *de facto* ruler as he put his claimant, Tvrtko II on the throne. Sigismund's attempts failed: the buffer state did not function without military intervention, and the king now sought to force a conclusion through the use of arms. The Hungarians staged an invasion every year up to 1410, with the monarch himself present on five occasions. He gained a decisive victory in 1408, and took radical measures, having 120 Bosnian nobles executed

---

12 Johannes de Thurocz, *Chronica Hungarorum*, ed. Erzsébet Galántai, Gyula Kristó and Elemér Mályusz, 3 vols (Budapest, 1985–88), 1: cap. 199, p. 208: [...] *castrum, suos quod tutabatur infideles.*
13 *Magyarország történelmi kronológiája*, 4 vols, ed. Kálmán Benda and László Solymosi (Budapest, 1983), 1: 235.
14 Pál Engel, 'Zur Frage der bosnisch-ungarischen Beziehungen im 14–15. Jahrhundert', *SOF* 56 (1997), 27–42 (here 36); *IRR*, p. 75; Vrbas: *ZsO* 1, no. 5433, p. 598; Dubica: *ZsO* 1, no. 5437, p. 599.
15 Johannes de Thurocz, *Chronica* 1, cap. 207, p. 220: [...] *ad cesarem Thurcorum* [...] *filiamque* [...] *Ladislao, quem inducere conabatur,* [...] *contra Sigismundum adiumento fieret, iugo matrimonali ducere spopondisse.*
16 Johannes de Thurocz, *Chronica* 1, cap. 213, p. 226: [...] *quandam partem* [...] *superiorem Boznam suo subdidisset dominio, placuit ill, ut novum terra in hac regem crearet* [...] *hominem* [...] *regem* [...] *denominavit.*
17 *DRH* 1: 418.

and forcing Hrvoje to surrender.[18] Certain key fortresses were garrisoned and placed under the rule of Hungarian barons.[19] The king did not crush Hrvoje's power, but rather granted him possessions in Hungary. Sigismund hoped this conciliatory attitude would provide him with a faithful pillar of protection against the Ottomans. However, the 'seditious' Hrvoje soon betrayed Sigismund again: with Ottoman aid he led an enterprise against Hungary in 1413.[20] He plundered Slavonia with Ottoman auxiliaries and captured numerous castles.[21] Some sources even report that Ottoman forces invaded Hungary proper.[22]

By the mid-1410, the Ottomans had recovered from their crisis and set out to play an active part in Bosnian politics again. They did not wish to surrender the recently seized and strategically important bridgeheads. An Ottoman-Bosnian army defeated a formidable Hungarian force in 1415 on the banks of the Lašva.[23] By 1413–14, the Bosnian defence line was on the verge of collapse, and the path into Hungary was open. Although Hrvoje died in 1416, the re-emergence of Ottoman power in the Balkans meant that Sigismund now had to face even stronger adversaries in Bosnia, supported every year by increasingly numerous Ottoman auxiliaries. However, although it seemed that the most of the buffer zone was ineffective for almost a decade, certain parts did hold out under Hungarian control, and the system had been reinstated by the 1430s, albeit only partially. Several castles fell, but Vranduk held out until 1418, and in Toričan, Vesela Straža and Dubočac Hungarian control only came to an end in 1414.[24] It was also a success that a particularly formidable fortress, Srebrenik, with the district of Usora and the strongholds of Brčko and Grabovac, remained in Hungarian hands.[25] One small-scale mission saw the safeguarding of Srebrenik — deep behind enemy lines — with expeditionary forces in 1417.[26] The preservation of this outlying post until 1443 (!) was a true *passagium particulare*.

---

18 Engel, *Realm*, p. 234.
19 Engel, 'Zur Frage', pp. 38–39.
20 Johannes de Thurocz, *Chronica* 1, cap. 211, p. 223: [...] *ante hec regi fidelis* [...] *protervie stimulo* [...] *in perfidiam* [...] *Hungariae* [...] *ingentia Thurcorum agmina conduxit* [...] *Boznensis regi subiectis* [...] *predo fuit*. '[...] had formerly been faithful to the king [...] urged by his wantonness [...] perfidiously [...] hired large numbers of Turks in his pay [...] plundered the territories of Bosnia under the king's rule'. *ZsO* 4, nos 768, 801, 941, 964, 1117, pp. 194, 199, 225, 228, 263. See Engel, 'Zur Frage', p. 38.
21 Slavonia: *ZsO* 4, nos 296, 1750, 2244, pp. 105, 407, 514. With 20,000 Turks charged against Senj: *ZsO* 4, no. 2407, p. 547. The Turks remained there, causing further peril: *ZsO* 4, no. 2373, p. 540.
22 Giovanni Francesco Poggio Bracciolini, 'Vita di messer Filippo Scolari', *Archivio Storico Italiano* 4 (1843), 163–84; Hungarian translation in Bracciolini, 'Filippo Scolari, ragadványnevén Spano úrnak, firenzei polgárnak az élete', ed. and trans. István Vigh and Magda Jászay, in *Ozorai Pipo emlékezete*, ed. Ferenc Vadas (Szekszárd, 1987), pp. 13–23 (here 18).
23 Károly Kranzieritz, 'A Lašva környéki csata 1415-ben', *Hadtörténelmi Közlemények* 125 (2012), 959–86.
24 *ZsO* 4, no. 1652, p. 388; 6, no. 1669, p. 442; 11, no. 869, pp. 357–58; *MVA* 1: 282, 445, 457. See Engel, 'Zur Frage', pp. 38–39.
25 1422: *ZsO* 9, no. 734, p. 235; 1430: MNL DL 43837; Engel, 'Zur Frage', p. 39.
26 1417: *ZsO* 6, no. 1106, p. 318.

Sigismund stressed the importance of the Bosnian front in his 1432–33 Siena military regulations (see below). He was particularly concerned since 'the Bosnians have afflicted many insults and injuries on the kingdom and inhabitants of Hungary'.[27] The Hungarian control was strengthened again in 1422 when Tvrtko II came to a rapprochement with Sigismund. By the 1430s, even though Tvrtko had agreed to pay tribute to the sultan, certain parts of the Northern Bosnian defensive belt had been restored and fortresses had been re-garrisoned with Hungarians. The 'Sigismundian' frontier was still able to withstand the attacks. Sigismund placed several strongholds — Srebrenik (1430), Komotin, Bočac (1434), and for a time, Jajce (1434–49) — under the *pro honore* control of the Tallóci/Talovac brothers, who succeeded in halting the Ottomans at least dozens of miles from the Hungarian border.[28] It is not our task to provide an overview of the enormous accumulation of offices granted to the family in the 1430s.[29] In a way, the Bosnian frontier had a part to play, indirectly, in John of Hunyad's successes, since he was able largely to focus on the fronts east of Belgrade. And, Belgrade, under the control of one of Sigismund's 'creations', Ivan Tallóci/Jovan Talovac survived a considerable Ottoman siege in 1440.

Wallachia

In the mid-1390s Sigismund managed to detach Mircea the Old, voivode of Wallachia (r. 1386–1418), from Ottoman vassalage, and he helped in warding off onslaughts from Transylvania. Mircea was standing up firmly to the menace, but this resistance was being undermined in the late 1410s as Mehmed I consolidated Ottoman power. The Ottomans re-emerged in the Balkans: in the late 1410s they occupied and established Giurgiu as a base for further assaults, and also took hold of Szörény (mod. Turnu Severin, Romania), an outpost on the Hungarian banks of the Danube. In 1418–19, the Temesköz (a part of mod. Banat), and Kronstadt were sacked. Although Szörény was re-captured in an offensive in Bulgaria in 1419, following Mircea's death in 1418 the south-eastern frontiers saw the re-intensification of an ever-present peril.[30] In the early 1420s, Murad II re-awakened the spirit of conquest and occupied the eastern part of Serbia and the south of Bosnia. Faced with a new campaign of systematic conquest, Hungary had to face again the every-day reality of possible inroads into their territory. Wallachia

---

27 DRMH 2: 148: *[...] Boznensis multis insolentiis et iniuriis affecerunt.*
28 MNL DL 13137: *Castra et honores apud Mathkonem banum et fratres suos pro honore: Consignatio castrorum pro honore Sigismundi regis datorum.* 'Castles and honour offices under Ban Matthias [Talovac] and his brothers as honour office holders. Proof of the castles in honour offices dated under the rule of Sigismund'. Pál Engel, *Királyi hatalom és arisztokrácia viszonya a Zsigmond-korban (1387–1437)* (Budapest, 1977), pp. 203–4; 1435, Jajce, Vranduk, Bočac: MNL DL 34067; MVA 1, pp. 282, 332, 463.
29 Elemér Mályusz, 'A négy Tallóci fivér', *Történelmi Szemle* 23 (1980), 531–76.
30 ZsO 7, nos 529, 1111, pp. 164, 273.

was subjected to Ottoman suzerainty several times under puppet-princes, who also ravaged Transylvania. From time to time, new pro-Hungarian candidates asked for assistance and, though mostly restored for a time through costly interventions, they were not able to stabilise their rule. The protégés could not stop Ottoman assaults, were soon deposed and fled to Hungary, with the pro-Turkish claimant being re-instated. As John of Thurocz (Lat. Johannes de Thurocz, Hung. Thuróczy János, Slk Ján z Turca) encapsulated, 'there were two competing princes, each striving to be sole ruler'. One 'sought the help of the Turks, and forced the other side to flee', who 'requested Hungarian aid'.[31]

The mid-1420s saw a series of long-term Hungarian operations, several with considerable armies. From July to October 1423, Filippo Scolari, sheriff (*ispán*) of Temes, conducted a campaign *contra Turcos [...] in subsidium [...] Dan wayvode* ('against the Turks in assistance of Voivode Dan'), defeated the Ottomans and deposed Radu II the Bald.[32] The successes were short-lived however. In 1425–26, three Hungarian ventures were led, with numerous forces, to stabilise the position of Sigismund's voivode. In the autumn of 1425, the voivode of Transylvania led an offensive which aimed at putting Dan back on the throne.[33] However, within a few months, Scolari had to confirm his rule again.[34] What is more, in November, Sigismund was forced to deploy yet further troops on the front.[35] However, the situation became even more acute the following year, with the king conducting two campaigns himself and spending more than two years on the frontier.[36] By contrast, the Ottoman Turks were making inroads into Transylvania. In 1421, Transylvania suffered a major blow when Ottomans forces broke deep into the country, hundreds of miles behind the frontier zone, and defeated the entire Transylvanian army at Hátszeg (mod. Hațeg, Romania). In the 1430s, they advanced even deeper, plundered Kronstadt, Nagyszeben (mod. Sibiu, Romania) and the whole Bârsa Land (named after the eponymous river, Rom. Țara Bârsei, Hung. Barcaság, Ger. Burzenland), and reached the Székely

---

31 Johannes de Thurocz, *Chronica* 1, cap. 212, p. 224: *[...] in illis terra in hac duo principes, [...] uti dominio laborabant [...] Daan suas partes debilitari agnovit, preceps Thurcorum quesivit subsidium, et illo potitus partem alteram coegit in fugam. Merche vero, cum vires suas ad arcendum extraneum hostem debiles sensit, regis Sigismundi petivit auxilium.* '[...] in this country there were two princes, [...] both aspired for power [...] Dan noticed that his league had weakened, hurried to the Turks to ask for aid, and as he got it, made the other league flee. But Mircea, as he felt that his forces were weak to ward off external enemy, applied for Sigismund's help'.
32 1423: *ZsO* 10, nos 595, 829, pp. 254, 346; (MNL DF 210668); prorogation, 1423: *ZsO* 10, nos 435, 732, 736, 776, 781, 1086, pp. 201, 310, 311, 321, 322–23, 434; donation, 1427: MNL DL 102971, *ZsO* 14, no. 620, pp. 275–76. See Norbert C. Tóth, 'Zsigmond király tisztségviselőinek itineráriuma I. (Uralkodásának elejétől az 1420-as évekig)', *Századok* 138 (2004), 465–94 (here 486).
33 *ZsO* 12, no. 1144, p. 441; DRRR, no. 199, pp. 309–12; 1425: *ZsO* 12, no. 1036, p. 403.
34 *Prorogatio*: 1426: *ZsO* 13, nos 312, 672, 749, 765, pp. 141, 251, 274, 278; campaign in 1426: *ZsO* 13, no. 685, p. 255. See Tóth, 'Zsigmond', p. 487.
35 1426: *ZsO* 13, no. 1280, p. 421.
36 1427: MNL DL 38515, *ZsO* 14, no. 459, pp. 218–19; MNL DL 92715, *ZsO* 14, no. 580, pp. 261–62; MNL DL 92726, *ZsO* 14, no. 980, p. 390.; 1428: MNL DL 30431.

HUNGARY AND THE *PASSAGIUM PARTICULARE* AFTER NICOPOLIS 205

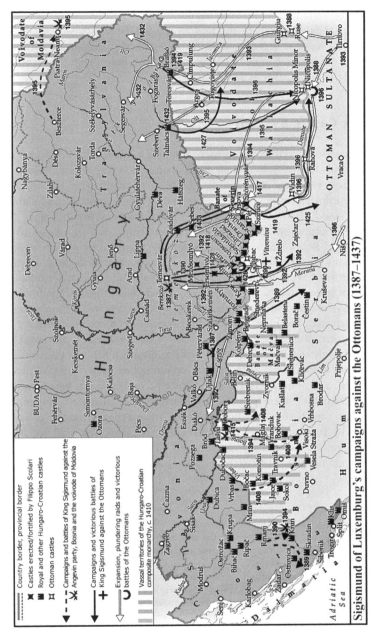

Fig. 18. Anti-Ottoman campaigns of Sigismund of Luxemburg, 1387–1437.
Map by Béla Nagy.

Land (Hung. Székelyföld, Ger. Szeklerland, Rom. Ținutul Secuiesc or Secuimea), taking thousands captive.[37] In the mid-1430s, the Temesköz was ravaged again, and in 1437 Murad II was preparing for a large-scale campaign.[38] Although the Hungarians did have a couple of successes, on the whole, Sigismund was not able to organise the principality as a safe buffer zone.

Frontier Castle System

Sigismund underlined that castles inevitably had a role to play in *tutela et defensio* ('tutelage and defence'), and their maintenance was important.[39] However, up to the 1410s, very few strongholds had been fortified: Törcsvár (mod. Bran, Romania), Talmács (mod. Talmaci, Romania), Haram (mod. Nova Palanka, Serbia), Keve (mod. Kovin, Serbia), Szörény, Bitva, Kölpény (mod. Kulpin, Serbia). An advance outpost in Serbia, the district of Belin, with its castles of Debrc, Nepričava and Belastena, was taken under royal control in 1389, meaning that the Ottomans could not reach the border.[40] Logistical bases and supply lines, with the crown having to supply the frontier garrisons amidst Ottoman forays, had still not been established. Nevertheless, there were signs of the formation of a defence system: the sources differentiate *metae et confinia*, ('the border zones, the southern marches'), i.e. a borderline zone, with territorial military control over areas surrounding the castles. The castles were also to be protected by field forces, since only the core of the garrisons was arranged for on a permanent basis. Captains were appointed with special commissions (*per regiam deputatorum*, 'assigned by royal mandate'), and were allotted a share of royal revenues. Baronial *banderia* ('retinues') were paid for by mortgaged or alienated lordships. Field armies were paid with sums directly issued from tax returns, the collection of which had been entrusted to army leaders. In 1394, János Kanizsai, archbishop of Esztergom, raised his *banderia* and received its *quid pro quo* from the royal tax.[41] Captains were licensed to seize their wages in salt or linen, or often got the whole

---

37 Counter-action: 1432: MNL DL 54796.
38 1436: MNL DL 102460; counter-actions by the voivode in 1436: MNL DL 59185; attacks in 1437: MNL DL 61528–29, 65044; invasion into Temes in 1437: MNL DL 55083; Murad II's large-scale campaign in 1437: MNL DL 88122.
39 1399: MNL DL 70750 (transc. 1405): […] *ex edificatione et constructione castrorum et fortalitiorum regnum quodsumque maioris efficitur potestatis et regnicole in maiori et uberiori pacis tranquillitate* […] *vivere possint.* '[…] every country will be more powerful with the construction of castles and strongholds, and the people could live in a greater peace and tranquility'. *ZsO* 1, no. 6111, p. 680; *PCsL*, no. 215, p. 125; *DRMH* 2: 21: […] *de bono et tranquillo statu ac restauratione confiniorum*. '[…] for the proper and peaceful condition and restoration of our border regions'.
40 *ZsO* 1, no. 1626, p. 183; MNL DL 7768: […] *pro conseruacione et vberiori tuicione* […] *in confiniis terre rasciensis*. *ZsO* 1, no. 2421, p. 265; *Documenta historiam Valachorum in Hungaria illustrantia*, ed. Antal Nagy Fekete and László Makkai, (Budapest, 1941), p. 394–95.
41 *ZsO* 1, no. 3380, p. 375.

census of a city (e.g. Esztergom).[42] The kingdom had recourse to extraordinary subsidies and war taxes.

The military districts were labelled as *partes inferiores* ('southern territories') referring to their peculiar wartime privileges.[43] Beyond the banates of Macsó (mod. Mačva, Serbia) and Szörény, the county of Temes was categorised as a defence zone under the supervision of its sheriff, who had authority over a cluster of castles, spreading over several counties (Keve, Krassó).

Filippo Scolari

The defence system was established by the Florentine Filippo Scolari — also known as Pipo of Ozora —, who was appointed sheriff of Temes (1404) and received exclusive rights over the royal revenues of the adjacent territories. First, he was made sheriff of the salt chambers, and then was 'entrusted with the defence of the Istros', upon becoming sheriff of several contiguous counties (Csanád, Krassó, Keve, Arad, Zaránd and Csongrád).[44] The king had his relatives installed in church offices (Carninaus, archbishop of Kalocsa, 1421–22; Andrea, bishop of Zagreb, 1407–09, and of Várad [mod. Oradea, Romania], 1409–26), and he also governed ecclesiastical dignities kept in vacancy (e.g. the archbishopric of Kalocsa in 1419–21).[45] Scolari was the sole lord of the south-eastern border region. He was responsible for chairing the *generalis congregatio* ('general assembly of nobles') and for summoning the levy. With authority over military affairs, he established the frontier from Orshova to Belgrade. Up to his death in 1426 he had control over thirteen (and probably a further three) castles, eleven of which he had a decisive role in erecting, fortifying and preparing for siege warfare: Dombó (mod. Dubovac, Serbia), Pozsezsin (mod. Pojejena, Romania), Tornistye, Szinice (mod. Svinița, Romania), Drankó (mod. Drencova, Romania), Librazsd (mod. Liborajdea, Romania). The number of castles built to withstand the Ottomans grew to at least twenty, and some held out for decades. Scolari laid a great stress on logistics, and the castles were well maintained in arms, ammunition and victuals. He could control the most important bridgeheads, meaning that the 'smaller troops of the Turks could only sneak in secret paths'.[46] The Tuscan humanist Giovanni Francesco Poggio Bracciolini emphasised in his *Vita di messer Filippo Scolari*, that 'on the banks of the Danube, all along the routes, ferries and fords wherever one could cross, he [Filippo Scolari] built strongholds, [...] so that it was hardly possible to pass without much loss'.[47]

---

42 *ZsO* 1, no. 4779, p. 527.
43 1436: MNL DL 92853; 1438: MNL DL 57679.
44 Bracciolini, 'Filippo Scolari, ragadványnevén Spano úrnak', p. 19.
45 *MVA* 1: 65, 77, 80.
46 Johannes de Thurocz, *Chronica* 1, cap. 233, p. 246: [...] *ubicumque Thurcorum quevis turma particularis consuetam regni in depredationem quovis occulto tramite se ingerebat.*
47 Bracciolini, 'Filippo Scolari, ragadványnevén Spano úrnak', p. 19.

Tactical Innovations — Small-Scale Operations

This defence was *active*: it had to be founded on actions of a shorter radius and a limited range. The fortification system in itself would not protect the kingdom, and Ottoman incursions could only be effectively repulsed with counter-attacks.

The blueprint of this limited range enterprise had already been in place before Nicopolis. A 'classic example' of this could be seen when Sigismund moved forward up to Ždrelo (mod. Serbia) and forced Bayezid himself to withdraw in 1392.[48] Local forces also took retaliation on several occasions, and in 1396 the voivode of Transylvania advanced into Wallachia.[49] When marauders attacked the Bârsa Land with its 'capital' Kronstadt in 1421, and with the king occupied in Bohemia, the voivode of Transylvania attacked the withdrawing troops.[50]

This limited range campaigning was also developing in Bosnia between 1404 and 1416. Sigismund moved forward, step by step, and occupied strongholds protecting strategic deployment routes. After 1398, Sigismund had wooden *castella* erected along the Sava against Hrvoje and his Ottoman adherents, and after 1404 key fortresses — Sokol, Vranduk, Duboćac, Toričan, Vesela Straža, Bočac, Ostrožac, Srebrenik and Bobovac — were garrisoned and put under Hungarian rule.[51] The construction of a bridge-head at Duboćac on the banks of the Sava in 1404 can also be seen as a small-scale new *passagium*.[52] In 1408, it also served as a crossing point (*in portu Zawe*), a base to host the camp.[53] Each campaign had a consciously designed range and direction. In 1404, the ban of Macsó invaded along the Bosna, captured and garrisoned Bobovac and Srebrenik. This was a short-term action of two months, and the Hungarians did not move any further.[54] An even shorter, classic *Kleinkrieg* manoeuvre saw the castellans of Srebrenik storm several *castra et castella* ('castles and smaller, probably wooden fortifications') in the neighbouring territory and seize Vranduk.[55] In 1405, Sigismund pushed forward into the central Hrvatinić lands, along the valleys of the Vrbas and the Una, and seized Sokol, Bihać and Ostrožac.[56] In 1408, the Hungarians took

---

48 *ZsO* 1, nos 2529, 2543, 2544, pp. 276, 278.
49 *ZsO* 1, no. 4509, p. 499.
50 *ZsO* 8, no. 637, p. 187.
51 1402: MNL DF 288086: [...] *in expugnatione castelli seu bastite Neboyze* [...] *occupati*. '[...] besieging the castle or fortress of Neboyze [...] occupied it'. See Engel, 'Zur Frage', p. 37; 1409: MNL DL 50282; *ZsO* 2.2, no. 7211, p. 302: *in conservatione castri Babowch* ['in the upkeep of the castle of Babowch']. See *MVA* 1, pp. 282, 306, 385, 412, 435, 445.
52 Engel, 'Zur Frage', p. 38.
53 MNL DL 9449; *ZsO* 2.2, nos 6347, 6349, p. 173; *MVA* 1, p. 306.
54 *ZsO* 2.1, nos 3227, 3231, pp. 382, 383. Bobovac was retaken in 1406, *ZsO* 2.2, no. 5721, p. 84; Pál Engel, 'Ozorai Pipo', in *Ozorai*, pp. 53–88 (here 65, 82).
55 *ZsO* 2.2, no. 6496, p. 194; *OT* 1, no. 246, p. 398, Gusztáv Wenzel, 'Okmánytár Ozorai Pipo történetéhez I–IV', *Történelmi Tár* 32 (1884), 1–31, 220–47, 412–37, 613–27 (here 220); Engel, 'Zur Frage', p. 37.
56 *IRR*, p. 84; *ZsO* 2.2, nos 4168, 4170; *Acta Anni* 2, no. 121, p. 365; Ostrožac: Engel, 'Zur Frage', p. 30; *ZsO* 2.1, no. 4448, p. 510; *MVA* 1, pp. 280, 385, 412.

Dobor, and moved up to Maglaj, and in 1410, the king campaigned in the Drina valley in Eastern Bosnia and seized Kličevac and Srebrenica.[57] It was a small-scale success that, through an agreement with Hrvoje, Sigismund took control of several castles surrounding Srebrenica — Susjed, Brodar, Kušlat –, which contributed much to the 'shield' of Northern Bosnia.[58] Large parts of Bosnia were pacified through a series of small-scale operations.

Nevertheless, although the shock of Ankara did impact upon Ottoman rule in the Balkans, and for years, at least from 1402 to 1407, the Hungarian sources do not speak of Ottoman auxiliaries in Bosnia, from 1407 onwards Ottoman power was being reorganised in the region.[59] In 1407, the Turks 'return' to the sources, and wars are again fought *contra Turcos et Boznenses* ('against Turks and Bosnians').[60] In 1407, Sigismund asked Pope Gregory XII to license his venture against 'the Bosnians and their Turkish supporters' with the sign of the cross. The pope duly gave plenary indulgence to those taking up arms.[61]

Sigismund and Scolari mounted a campaign to Serbia in 1409, aimed expressly against the Ottoman Turks, and moved forward to Prizren.[62] Certain Serbian castles far from the frontier were garrisoned with Hungarians. In 1413, expeditionary forces under a Hungarian castellan protected Novo Brdo, an outpost hundreds of miles ahead.[63] In 1414, Scolari staged an assault into Bosnia, again expressly against the Ottoman Empire.[64] When numerous magnates were taken into captivity near the Lašva in 1415, the sources make it clear that the enemy were Ottoman Turks.[65] Although most *passagia* in Bosnia from the late 1410s onwards were defensive — e.g. the protection of Vrbas Castle in 1415 — the frontier warfare did also include offensive assaults.[66] The Siena regulations (see below) stipulated that the barons and prelates were to be 'deployed in the defence of the kingdom and to attack the enemies of Bosnia'.[67]

---

57 ZsO 2.2, nos 5724, 6111, 6133, 6134, 6333, 6335, 6347, 6349, 7965, 7969, 7974, 7984, 7994, 8013–15, 8019–20, pp. 84, 137, 139, 171, 173, 421–22, 423, 424–25, 426, 428–29; *A leleszi konvent statutoriae sorozatának 1387–1410 közötti oklevelei*, ed. Norbert C. Tóth (Nyíregyháza, 2006), no. 174, p. 96; IRR, p. 91. See Tóth, 'Zsigmond', p. 483; Engel, 'Zur Frage', p. 38.
58 ZsO 2.2, nos 8099, p. 442; 1425: ZsO 12, no. 995, p. 385; MVA 1, p. 416; Engel, 'Zur Frage', p. 39.
59 1404: MNL DL 78590; ZsO 2.1, no. 3231, p. 383: *[…] ad partes Boznenses*.
60 ZsO 2.2, nos 5552, 5593, 5706, 5793, 6111, 6122, pp. 56, 65, 82, 92, 137, 138.
61 ZsO 2.2, no. 5798, p. 82.
62 ZsO 2.2, nos 6567, 6576, 6583, pp. 207, 204, 205; 4, no. 521, p. 146; Wenzel, 'Ozorai', p. 226; Tóth, 'Zsigmond', p. 483.
63 1413: ZsO 4, no. 914, p. 219; MVA 1, p. 377. In the service of Lazarević: ZsO 4, no. 916, p. 219.
64 1414: MNL DL 79212: *[…] contra immanissimos turcas versus Boznam*. '[…] against the most savage Turks into Bosnia'. ZsO 4, no. 2379, p. 541. See Tóth, 'Zsigmond', p. 484. In arms in October: ZsO 4, no. 2528, p. 574; Wenzel, 'Ozorai', p. 245; ZsO 4, no. 2741, p. 616.
65 MNL DL 43338 : *[…] per paganos et Turcos infideles captos*. '[…] captured by pagan and infidel Turks'. ZsO 5, no. 2255, pp. 599–600. 1418: ZsO 6, no. 1791, p. 463.
66 1428: MNL DF 265596; Hungarian castellan, 1417: ZsO 6, no. 337, p. 136; MVA 1, p. 381; Engel, 'Zur Frage', p. 40.
67 DRMH 2: 148: *[…] prelatos, barones et nobiles […] sui ordine […] divisit […] contra Boznam […] pro regni defensione et hostium offensione habere teneantur*.

The small-scale campaign technique was further refined along the lower Danube in the 1410s and 1420s by the tactical innovator Filippo Scolari, 'the new Belisarius', as highlightened in another anonymously written vita from the fifteenth century devoted to the Tuscan general in services of the Hungarian crown.[68] Interestingly, the reforms in leadership, strategy and reconnaissance characteristically assigned to Hunyadi can sometimes be found in Scolari's 'style' of waging war. The Florentine did not lie in wait for Ottoman onslaughts but forged ahead instead. He 'was occupied' in Ottoman territory, *in confinibus seu partibus Razcie* ('on the frontiers or border parts of Serbia'), and awaited the moment to force a clash.[69] As a battle-seeking strategist he sought to bide his time, waiting for most advantageous time and place. Domenico Mellini, another Tuscan humanist writer, would later recall in his *Vita di Filippo Scolari* (1570): 'Slowly retreating [...] he lured the Turks' into 'steep valleys and narrow gorges before engaging in combat' where they could not prevail through their numerical advantage.[70] Scolari did not allow his forces to become entangled in large-scale enterprises, which would have consumed much of the energy of the country, and sought to prevent open-field close-quarter combat, preferring instead 'ambushes in secret'.[71]

Of his '18 campaigns', most were short-term actions protecting the border fortresses.[72] He carefully selected his targets in order to gain control over strategic operation routes (e.g. crossings) — then sought to preserve his positions and would not allow his foes to 'cross the river'.[73] His goal was to 'force the Turks to leave his borders', and push them and their radius of mobilisation back as far as possible, 40–50 miles.[74] He aimed to 'block' their preparations for making inroads, and 'drove them away from their own borders'.[75] Scolari consciously staged counter-offensives, and also laid waste to enemy territory and took considerable booty. In 1419, he ravaged deeply into Bulgaria, and in the autumn of 1425 routed up to Vidin.[76]

Scolari coordinated the activities of field and fortification armies, running offensives from behind a line of strongholds, and moving back strategically when necessary. Castles were not only there to provide passive shelter, but their garrison

---

68 'La vita di messer Philippo Scolari', ed. Filippo Polidori, *Archivio Storico Italiano* 4 (1843), 151–62; Hungarian translation in 'Filippo Scolari úr élete', ed. and trans. István Vigh and Magda Jászay, in *Ozorai*, pp. 5–11 (here 10).
69 1413: MNL DL 61325, ZsO 4, no. 1255, p. 297.
70 Domenico Mellini, *Vita di Filippo Scolari, volgarmente chiamato Pippo Spano* (Fiorenza, 1570); Hungarian translation in Mellini, 'Filippo Scolarinak, ismertebb nevén Pippo Spanonak élete', ed. and trans. István Vigh and Magda Jászay, in *Ozorai*, pp. 25–52 (here 50).
71 'Filippo Scolari úr élete', p. 10.
72 Engel, 'Ozorai', 66.
73 Mellini, 'Filippo Scolarinak', p. 50.
74 'Filippo Scolari úr élete', p. 9.
75 'Filippo Scolari úr élete', p. 9.
76 Sept–Nov 1419: ZsO 7, no. 938, p. 247.

forces were actively involved in field service. Scolari did not treat castles as mere defensive posts or ammunition depots but had them integrated organically into field administration, entrusted with covering withdrawals or as relocation centres. Field troops were also actively involved in garrison service. When the fortification of Szörény was required, Scolari allocated his men-at-arms to work on the construction.[77] When the king laid siege to Golubac, both 'the garrisons along the borders of Serbia and field armies' were mobilised.[78]

Scolari was a 'master of mounting and continuing wars'.[79] He took the initiative, and not only excelled in battle but could also pursue his actions to a successful end. He could organise an entire operation in terms of logistics, supply and finances.

Autumn and Winter Offensives

Scolari was also a master of timing and radius. His troops swarmed out of his castles unexpectedly. Decades before the 1443–44 winter campaign of King Vladislas the Jagiellonian and John of Hunyad, Scolari realised that, because of the traditional mobilisation patterns, Ottoman armies returned to winter quarters after *ruz-ı Kasım* (26 October) and the core forces were disbanded after early November. The capacities of the Ottoman machinery therefore ranged only up to the end of October, and no great offensives with the main bulk of the sultan's forces were to start before April. This is why Scolari attacked as 'winter was coming'.[80]

Scolari's 1416 Bosnian operation was of limited range, in the late autumn, in November.[81] In 1420, he led an action in late September and October.[82] In 1423, 1424 and 1425, he also started military activities in the late autumn.[83] He consciously started to re-fortify the stronghold of Szörény in September and November 1424, and invaded enemy territory, thus blocking attempts to prevent the building works.[84] He did not even start the works before mid-August and, as this was necessary, he summoned more troops at the end of September.[85] There were a series of clashes around Szörény in October and November, and Scolari was forced to recruit yet further troops, but he did finally earn a few

---

77 MNL DL 48752, *ZsO* 11, no. 1160, pp. 472–73: [...] *pro constructione, reformatione ac restauratione castri nostri Zewriniensis et aliorum fortalitiorum*: '[...] for the construction, repair and restoration of our castle Szörény and other strongholds'.
78 Mellini, 'Filippo Scolarinak', p. 49.
79 Mellini, 'Filippo Scolarinak', p. 38.
80 'Filippo Scolari úr élete', 10.
81 Nov 1416: *ZsO* 5, no. 2421, p. 649; Wenzel, 'Ozorai', p. 419.
82 *ZsO* 7, no. 2206, p. 502, Tóth, 'Zsigmond', p. 486.
83 Tóth, 'Zsigmond', p. 487.
84 Engel, 'Ozorai', p. 66.
85 MNL DL 102028; *ZsO* 11, nos 961, 1091, pp. 395–96, 451. See Tóth, 'Zsigmond', p. 487.

months' respite in order to re-construct the castle.[86] Between September and early November 1425, Scolari staged an offensive into Serbia, and in 1426 he was still fighting in Wallachia in November.[87]

Nevertheless, the autumn offensive was not only Scolari's congenial idea: those who had had experience fighting the Ottomans were also aware of the characteristics of the Turkish military machinery. The Transylvanians soon adapted to this type of warfare, and launched campaigns throughout wintertime. In 1421, Deputy Voivode Loránd Lépes invaded Ottoman territories in mid-January.[88] In February 1431, the captain of Belgrade summoned the nobles of Keve to the Danube ferry since the Ottoman Turks had already crossed the river,[89] and the *exercitus* was again raised in the county the following winter.[90] In mid-November 1433, the Temesvár garrison were preparing against a Turkish onslaught.[91]

These small-scale operations also included 'non-combatant' defence: there were times when Sigismund positioned himself with all his forces *circa confinia regni* ('around the borders of the kingdom'), in order to control the key crossing points, sometimes even without unsheathing a sword, and spent two to three months in arms *in descensu nostro campestri* ('in our field lodging'), expecting an assault any minute. In 1394, Sigismund led a campaign into Bosnia against the allies of the Ottoman Empire,[92] then moved on to the Serbian front and Temesköz.[93] What is more, he did not leave the Temes–Szeged region, but conducted his preparations in Transylvania, close to the front, and launched a campaign into Moldavia next January, not returning until the end of March. Furthermore, he spent only a few weeks in the country afterwards, and in June 1394 campaigned into Wallachia, not leaving the frontier again until October.[94] This was an inevitable defensive technique, of territorial control and strategic cover, though not in the style of a victorious *passagium generale*.

Scolari consciously called upon his forces to plunder the Ottoman frontier regions. '[...] his army strengthened through pillaging and from the treasures of the enemy'. To prevent him from 'moving further into the inner territories to get riches, [...] the Turks offered him gifts and asked for his right hand'.[95]

---

86 MNL DL 11587: '[...] *gentes exercituantes* [...] *Zewrinii accedere debentes in* [...] *comitatu Themesiensi ad presens dispon*[...] *asseritur et illac destinare*. '[...] men at war [...] are obliged now to come to the county of Temes [...] assigned to maintain the defence'. OT 1, no. 381, p. 588; ZsO 11, nos 1148, 1346, pp. 469, 535–36. See Tóth, 'Zsigmond', p. 487.
87 ZsO 12, nos 660, 683, 1144, pp. 249, 257, 441; vol. 13, nos 1192–95, 1367, pp. 393–95, 449; DRRR, no. 199, pp. 309–12. See Tóth, 'Zsigmond' p. 487.
88 ZsO 8, no. 49, p. 41.
89 MNL DL 54737.
90 MNL DL 54781.
91 MNL DF 264657.
92 IRR, p. 68.
93 ZsO 1, no. 5101, p. 565.
94 ZsO 1, no. 3823, p. 418; IRR, pp. 70–71.
95 That is, the Turks asked him to come to a compromise with them. 'Filippo Scolari úr élete', p. 10.

Scolari had exclusive authority in military affairs. If necessary, calling upon the royal revenues under his control, his armies were supplemented with further baronial *banderia*. In the 1423 Wallachian campaign, he was accompanied by the retinues of the sheriff of the Székely and the bishop of Transylvania.[96] In 1426, even more retinues were allotted to him: those of the sheriff of Bihar and Szolnok,[97] of the bishops of Pécs,[98] and Várad,[99] and those of the archbishop of Esztergom.[100] When necessary, infidels were pardoned on condition that they join the Temes army.[101]

It was partly under Scolari's influence that John of Hunyad further refined the small-scale offensives, which he then developed into a superior *Kleinkrieg* tactics. Scolari 'ardently desired to attack the enemy rather than be attacked by them and pursued [them] right to the borders'.[102] The Bosnian and Wallachian ventures, of the 1410s and 1420s respectively, laid the foundations for Hunyadi's counter-incursions into Ottoman territory. It was essential not to engage in open combat with the Janissaries but to retreat to safe bases.

The success of Scolari's system was justified by the fact that the frontier between Szörény and Belgrade did not witness a Turkish assault until the late 1430s. Scolari's work was to be continued by the Tallóci/Talovac brothers. From the mid-1430s, most of 'his' castles were put under their governance: e.g. Szörény, Görény, Orshova, Miháld (mod. Mehadia, Romania), Sebes (mod. Turnu Ruieni, Romania), Halmás (mod. Almaș, Romania), Ilyéd (mod. Ilidia, Romania).[103] In allocating strategic financial, military, secular and ecclesiastical offices to the brothers, in some ways Sigismund was following Scolari's 'master plan'.[104]

---

96 *ZsO* 10, nos 595, 829, 1086, pp. 254, 346, 434; 13, nos 652, 689, pp. 245, 256–57.
97 *ZsO* 13, nos 236, 671, 1338, pp. 112, 251, 439–40.
98 *ZsO* 13, no. 724, pp. 667–68.
99 *ZsO* 13, no. 826, pp. 293.
100 *ZsO* 13, no. 436, pp. 186.
101 *ZsO* 2.2, nos 6924, 6941–42, pp. 259–60, 263.
102 Johannes de Thurocz, *Chronica* 1, cap. 233, p. 247: [...] *quam invadi ab illo peroptans viribus et numero impar illarum partium usque ad extremum persecutus est illum*.
103 Engel, *Királyi hatalom*, pp. 202–4; *MVA* 1, pp. 305, 320, 324, 331, 367, 407, 427.
104 Offices (together with appurtenant castles) under their control, Matko, 1429–35: sheriff of Keve and Krassó; 1429–35: captain of Belgrade; 1430–31; sheriff of Csanád; 1433–38: governor of the bishopric of Zagreb; 1434: governor of the bishopric of Várad; 1434–39: governor of the priory of Vrana; 1435–45: ban of Slavonia; 1436–45: ban of Dalmatia and Croatia; Frank(o): 1429–40: captain of Belgrade; 1429–39: sheriff of Keve and Krassó; 1432: sheriff of Csanád; 1433–36: governor of the archbishopric of Kalocsa; 1436–39: ban of Szörény; 1444–46: ban of Slavonia, Dalmatia and Croatia; 1445: governor of the bishopric of Várad; Petar/Petko: 1436–38: governor of the bishopric of Zagreb; 1437–52: ban of Dalmatia and Croatia; Ivan/Jovan, 1438–40: captain of Belgrade; 1438–45: prior of Vrana.

The Exception: Golubac, 1428

There is an 'odd one out' which requires discussion here, namely the enterprise of Golubac in 1428, where Sigismund made a final experiment and put all his efforts into a large-scale *passagium*. To be clear, this was not an 'old-style' *passagium generale*, since it was siege warfare and the king's major goal was to seize Golubac, rather than become embroiled in open field warfare. It is not the task of this article to discuss the campaign in depth, not least because the siege has recently been investigated in detail.[105] In brief, Sigismund set out with an army of about 15–20,000, together with several Lithuanian and Polish knights sent particularly by Grand Duke Vytautas of Lithuania and a 6,000-strong force from Wallachia. However, the king did not assign a great role to men-at-arms but rather to the siege engines and artillery transported in galleys. He also erected a *contra-castrum* ('counter-fortress') over the Danube, Szentlászlóvár (mod. Pescari, Romania), from which he also hoped to attack with his cannons. Sigismund failed, since the Rumelian troops appeared sooner than he might have expected and forced a pitched field battle with the besieging army. However, the failure of this campaign did justify the legitimacy of small-scale enterprises.[106]

Defence Legislation

The country was simply not able to withstand the threat through the traditional defence system. As the 1397 decree put it: 'our strength and that of all of our gentlemen of the realm appear to have declined'.[107] Although Sigismund experimented with summoning the general levy, they were of no use in practice, as he himself complained of their inefficiency: 'they appear on crutches rather than with arms, more like beggars than warriors'.[108] Still, as the injuries became 'intolerable',[109] he was bound to summon the *generalis exercitus* ('general levy of nobles') on several occasions.[110]

At the Diet of Temesvár (mod. Timișoara, Romania) in 1397, the king took radical measures. One of the noble privileges, i.e. the liberty not to wage war outside the borders, was suspended. 'All the gentlemen must rise with us' in soldierly

---

105 László Veszprémy, 'King Sigismund of Luxemburg at Golubac (Galamboc) 1428', *Transylvanian Review* 18 (2009), 291–308.
106 Summons: MNL DL 92743; *prorogatio*: MNL DL 103523; campaign: MNL DL 30431; 1430: MNL DL 65941; details of the siege: 1428: MNL DL 59120; donation: MNL DL 11983, 67774.
107 DRMH 2: 21: [...] *regnicolarum potentia diminuta esse* [...] ('[...] the strength of the nobles of the realm appears to have declined [...]').
108 DRH 1, p. 408: [...] *aut paupertate aut senio aut alia impotentia constricti potius baculis, quam armis fulciti verius mendicitati, quam militie actu vacaverunt.* (Eng. transl. DRMH 2: 141.)
109 DRMH 2: 21.
110 ZsO 1, nos 2516, 4187, 4511, 5568, 5583, 5794, 5833, pp. 275, 459, 499, 613, 614, 642, 645. Very few times later, 1428: MNL DL 92743; 1437: MNL DL 88122.

fashion, 'in time of great need'.[111] The decree of 12 March 1435 went even further: the wording 'during the present war with the heathen', meant, in practice, 'as long as the king sees it necessary'.[112] The diet introduced a quota system of recruitment in accordance with the number of tenant holdings (5 mounted archers per 100) — for which the term *militia portalis* ('army raised upon the number of tenant holdings') was 'created' in historiography. The 12 March 1435 decree reduced the number of mounted archers (3 per 100 tenants), but the counties were to recruit them through a register, to be set up on conscriptions.[113]

The 1397 decree freely interpreted what 'the enemy' was, and the 1432–33 Siena regulations summoned the nobles against 'all enemies attacking from any direction'.[114] What is more, the 12 March 1435 decree — 'against foreign invaders' — gave the ruler an even wider authority.[115] The *metae et confinia regni* ('the border zones, the southern marches of the country') were also to be interpreted widely, and fighting on Wallachian or Bosnian soil was legitimised.

Be that as it may, it is only on very few occasions that the quota system was in fact applied, at least in part.[116] There is no unequivocal evidence for the deployment of just such a force, and the *portalis* army proved to be too cumbersome and disorganised to resist a major Ottoman attack.

Military Regulations

Sigismund experimented with defensive schemes founded, to a large extent, on paid armies. In 1415–17 and 1432–33, he elaborated two military *dispositiones contra Turcos* ('arrangement'), in which he issued detailed *propositiones* ('propositions, scheme not enacted into a decree'), and set a *divisio* ('assignment for division') for forces allocated on the frontiers. Although the proposals had not become law, they did serve in one way or another as a basis for the 12 March 1435 decree.[117]

In the 1415–17 system, dignitary holders were expected to raise a fixed number of troops for a year, whose wages were to be paid by the king. The bulk —

---

111 DRMH 2: 22: [...] *tempore maxime necessitatis*.
112 DRMH 2: 22: [...] *durante duntaxat presenti guerra paganorum*. In the 1432–33 propositions: DRMH 2, p. 143: [...] *tamdiu, quosque domino regi* [...] *necessarium fore videtur*.
113 Early examples, 1398: ZsO 1, no. 5683, p. 627; Acta anni 1, no. 238, p. 312; 1399: ZsO 1, no. 6049, p. 670.
114 DRMH 2: 141: [...] *contra omnes inimicos ex quacunque parte* [...] *regnum insultantes*.
115 DRMH 2: 77: [...] *ab extraneis invasoribus*.
116 1398: ZsO 1, no. 5583, p. 614.
117 1415–17: *Constitutio prelatis et baronibus regni Hungariae destinatarum* ('Ordinance for the assignment of the prelates and barons of Hungary'); MNL DL 56715; DRH 1, pp. 397–404; *Propositiones*, 1432–33: *Circa modum et formam defensionis totius regni Hungariae* ('On the means and methods defending the whole kingdom of Hungary'); Orszàgos Széchényi Library, MS Fol. Lat. 4355; DRH 1, pp. 405–29; DRMH 2: 141–52.

2,200 lances — were sent to Transylvania and the Lower Danube (the regulations were most probably triggered by the invasions in Wallachia in 1416–17), and smaller forces (450 lances) were assigned to the *medium regni* ('central, politically important region of the kingdom').[118]

The 1432–33 propositions, drafted while the monarch was staying in Siena, distributed forces along the whole frontier, divided into zones, the control of which was handed to both lay and ecclesiastical office-holders, who were obliged to raise a fixed number of soldiers, with the levies of adjacent counties.[119] The system was logical, and the zones were assigned to those who held offices close to the given territories. Furthermore, the criteria of the division were also determined by the given military situation, that is from where, in which direction, an invasion was expected. The *divisio* was constantly being modified and re-arranged. The propositions allotted substantial numbers to Bosnia in particular, from where Ottoman assaults were most likely at the time. Furthermore, thirteen counties — beyond those that were territorially responsible — were ordered *contra Boznenses* ('against Bosnians')[120]

It is possible to make calculations about army numbers on the grounds of these propositions. The total of the 1415–17 regulations is 2,650 lances, that is, around 8,000 men altogether.[121] It is quite reasonable to doubt that these numbers are real, however. In principle, rather, they reflect expectations, or obligations. If one starts out from the wages, the total sum for an army like that, counted with an average *stipendium* ('wage') of one lancea per month, i.e. 10 golden florins, would have been over 380,000 florins a year, which exceeded the total annual income of the whole kingdom. The 1432–33 regulations propose a more substantial army. It allocates at least 4,000 horsemen to the defence of Bosnia alone![122] On top of that, the proposals state that the soldiers were to receive wages for the whole campaign.[123] The regulations laid out that there were 'means from the revenues which are to be assigned' *pro defensione confiniorum* ('for the defence of the border zones'), 'which should be disbursed in a given way'.[124] The only way to meet even a portion of these expenses was to transfer rights for royal revenues. Nevertheless, these propositions should not be taken as a possible scheme, but rather as a total that may be raised *in principle*.

---

118 E.g. Nicolaus de Gara palatinus ad lanceas [IIc] L^ta. MNL DL 56715; DRH 1, p. 399.
119 DRMH 2: 141, 148: *[…] prelati, barones […] declarent […] de locis et terminis per totum circuitum regni, […] contra inimicos exercitus deberet, sicut tenetur, ingruente necessitate proficisci atque stare.*
  '[…] prelates, barons […] should define places and borders along the circumference of the whole kingdom, […] to which the general levy has to go, and how long it has to stay there to defend the kingdom against enemies, when necessary'.
120 DRH 1: 399.
121 DRH 1: 398.
122 DRH 1: 418, 422, 429.
123 DRMH 2: 143–44: *[…] ad unam integram exercituationem […]* ('[…] for an entire campaign[…]').
124 DRMH 2 : 144: *[…] de proventibus regalibus sunt disponenda, et hac vice disponant.*

There is a *Supplementum*, which is assumed to be an appendix to the 12 March 1435 decree, although its date is debated.[125] It might be another version of the regulations, drafted after a discussion of the Siena propositions with the counties. This fixes the number of horsemen a county was expected to recruit. The lowest values are around 100 and the highest one is 600.[126] It lists 55 counties, from which a total county force of 10,000 — most probably light cavalry — can be calculated.

However, neither the 1415–17 dispositions nor the 1432–33 regulations were enacted in the 1435 decree. The decree does stipulate, in general, that a baron or a prelate is expected to raise troops, but it does not make clear either to which territories they are allocated or what forces they are expected to raise. One might feel, however, that according to 'the spirit of the law', a system much like the Siena one might have been in place on certain occasions. The law pronounces that 'barons and prelates [...] have been *ordered* to protect this frontier region with their *banderia* [...] according to the arrangements made and customarily observed in this matter'. This may imply that there had previously been some arrangements with the king, and the lords had been rendered previously in terms of a system very much like the Siena dispositions.[127] It does state that the nobles are to repel any attack 'according to the rules of the general levy'.[128] The rules of the *exercitus* ('noble levy') had changed, customarily, in other words, and the *mode* of the recruitment and enforcement of the levy had been modified in Siena (*per modum generalis expeditionis exercitualis*, 'by means of the general campaign of the levy'). These 'previous' modifications could reflect a measure from *before* 1435. The decree also declares that the sheriffs are 'designated to defend frontier regions', though there is no arrangement, or list, stating who is to go to war where.[129] However, all this imply that a system similar to the Siena one might have been in place, according to which the noble forces might have been divided along the frontier zones, on the grounds of their designation to the sheriffs of the counties, where their estates lay.[130]

Although we do not have any evidence as to whether this system actually worked at all, we might deduce that a system like this could have been in place in certain parts, in the territories of the Bosnian or Temes region, and in 'special military zones'.

---

125 *DRH* 1: 425–30. Eötvös Loránd University Library, Budapest, MS G. 39 (Cod. Nádasdy), fols 190v–92v.
126 *DRH* 1: 427.
127 *DRMH* 2: 77: [...] *prelati deputati pro defensione* [...] *partium* [...] *iuxta dispositionem de ipsis factam et observari consuetam.* '[...] those prelates who have been ordered to protect [...] border parts [...] according to the arrangements made and customarily observed in this matter'.
128 *DRMH* 2: 77.
129 *DRMH* 2: 77: [...] *comites* [...] *pro earundem partium vel aliarum gwerras habere contingentium defensione* [...] *deputatorum.* '[...] county sheriffs [...] designated to defend that border region or to repel any attack'.
130 *DRMH* 2: 77.

Conclusion

Sigismund was a *modern* crusader, not at all in the style of the chivalrous heroes of the past. Amadeus VI, the 'green' count of Savoy, or Peter I of Lusignan, king of Cyprus, would perhaps not accept him as a fellow *crucesignatus* ('crusader'). However, he wished to open the eyes of Christendom to the fact that there was no longer any point in organising *passagia* like Adalia (mod. Antalya, Turkey) or Alexandria. It was no longer Jerusalem whose *recuperatio* formed the goal of the struggle, but rather Christendom itself which was under assault. The *voyage de Turquie* could now mean service at a Hungarian frontier garrison.

The defence programme was to be founded upon dependent states, a shield of strategically located strongholds, and a safe hinterland, from the cover of which preventive campaigns could be launched. The *passagium particulare* involved the provision and upkeep of castles. The king tackled the down-to-earth work of organising recruitment, finances and supplies. Although most of Sigismund's defensive regulations were not put into practice, the system was able to ward off the Ottomans for decades after 1437.

NEVYAN MITEV

The Last Crusades in the Balkans from 1443–44 or the Union between Central and South-Eastern Europe against the Ottoman Invasion

In the late 1430s, almost the entirety of the Balkan Peninsula was captured by the Ottomans. Byzantium itself was reduced to the city of Constantinople and its hinterland, and memories of its former greatness were long gone. The Byzantine emperor John VIII Palaiologos (1392–1448) was seeking help from the West whilst, on the other hand, Pope Eugene IV (r. 1431–47) was looking for different ways of strengthening the shaken authority of the papacy. He envisaged a future crusade against the Turks as one means of doing so which, along with other benefits, would also raise the authority of the Holy See in the European southeast. It was decided that Byzantium and the Western world would sign a union. Initially, the council during which this unification was to be signed opened in Ferrara in 1438, before later moving to Florence where, on 6 July 1439, the Byzantine officials recognised the pope's authority. The consequence of this treaty, after a delay caused by civil war in Hungary, was the organisation of the crusades of 1443–44. The aim of this study is to present the military campaigns as the attempt to establish a union between vast parts of East-Central and South-Eastern Europe against the Ottoman invasion.

Considerable research has been conducted into this campaign, thanks to its importance for all of Europe. The authors with most important contributions are the Polish historians Jan Dąbrowski and Oskar Halecki, and the Bulgarian researchers Hermengild and Karel Shkorpil, Bistra Tsvetkova and Hristo Kolarov.[1] In recent years, Western historiography has also developed an interest in the topic, with two general overviews being published by Colin Imber and John Jefferson.[2]

Joint Forces against the Ottomans

The signing of the church union was a disappointment both for the Eastern priests and for Western church dignitaries. Despite stubborn resistance on the part of the Byzantine clergy, John VIII Palaiologos saw in the treaty the only means of salvation, since it provided for military assistance from the papal state against the invaders. Although most of the leading rulers of Western Europe, who were still caught up in the conflict between the papacy and the Council of Basle, did not take part in the convocation, the union was a moment of success in negotiations between the East and the West.[3] The Bulgarians also participated at the Council of Florence.[4] Thus, a united Christian Europe could now organise a new crusade.

In May 1440, only several months after the death of Albert of Habsburg (1397–1439), king of Germany, Bohemia and Hungary, a personal union was signed, which saw the Polish king Vladislas III the Jagiellonian (1424–44) also elected as Hungarian king. In Vladislas, the pope identified the ideal figure to lead the campaign against the Turks. Two years earlier, Eugene IV had revealed his support for Vladislas's claims on the Hungarian throne. In the second half of December 1437, a few days after the death of King Sigismund of Luxemburg (1368–1437), the pope sent a message to the papal ambassadors in Austria, Bohemia and Hungary testifying his actions.[5] The papal legate in Hungary, Cardinal Giuliano Cesarini, was assigned the task of defending the pope's interests in the dual monarchy, as well as providing substantial support to the young king. On the other hand, the aristocracy in Hungary, headed by John of Hunyad (Hunyadi), voivode of Transylvania, also insisted on declaring war on the Ottomans. The

---

1 Jan Dąbrowski, *Władysław I Jagiellończyk na Węgrzech (1440–44)* (Kraków, 1922); Oskar Halecki, *The Crusade of Varna: A Discussion of Controversial* (New York, 1943); Hermengild and Karel Škorpil, *Владислав Варненчик 1444–1923* (Varna, 1923). The Škorpil brothers were Czechs who lived in Bulgaria for the majority of their lives. They conducted a great degree of research in the fields of Bulgarian history and archaeology, including into the battle of Varna from 10 November 1444. See also Bistra Tsvetkova, *Паметна битка на народите (Европейският Югоизток и османското завоевание — края на XIV и първата половина на XV век)* (Varna, 1979); Hristo Kolarov, "'Дългият поход" от 1443–44 г. на полско-унгарския крал Владислав III Ягело (Варненчик) на Балканите' (unpublished doctoral dissertation, Veliko Tarnovo University, 1971).
2 Colin Imber, *The Crusade of Varna, 1443–45* (Ashgate, 2006); John Jefferson, *The Holy Wars of King Wladislas and Sultan Murad: The Ottoman-Christian Conflict from 1438–44* (Leiden, 2012).
3 Joseph Gill, *The Council of Florence* (Cambridge, 1959); Khristo Matanov and Rumyana Mikhneva, *От Галиполи до Лепанто* (Sofia, 1998), pp. 143–45.
4 Ivan Tyutyundzhiev, 'Митрополит Игнатий Търновски (?–†1464) е Съборът във Ферара — Флоренция (1438–39)', *Црквене студије: Годишњак Центра за црквене студије* 2 (2005), 229–44.
5 *CESDQ* 2, no. 246, pp. 358–64.

Serbian leader Đurađ Branković had the same attitude. In 1440, the invaders conquered Smederevo and thus found themselves very close to Hungarian territory. All this contributed to the completion of the crusade prepared by Eugene IV. The outbreak of civil war in Hungary slowed down the course of events. The coalition supporting Vladislas the Jagiellonian was forced to fight on two fronts: on the one hand, to the north, against the camp of Elizabeth of Luxemburg (1409–42), widowed queen consort of Germany, Bohemia and Hungary and mother of the newly born Ladislas the Posthumous (1440–57), for whom Elizabeth was determined to contend for the patrimony; on the other, to the south, against the Ottoman Turks. In those turbulent days, the figure of John of Hunyad stood out, who, through his military-tactical approach, managed to win victories on both fronts.

John of Hunyad's successes against Elizabeth's army resulted in Vladislas consolidating his position on the Hungarian throne. At the same time, the Transylvanian voivode also defeated the Ottoman army several times, destroying the myth of the invincibility of the Ottoman Turks. Hunyadi quickly became a hero of Latin Christianity, and, through his actions, managed to convince the Western public that the Ottoman army was not invulnerable and that the time for the long-awaited crusade had come.[6] With the sudden death of Elizabeth of Luxemburg at the end of 1442 in Győr, and with several of her supporters going over to Vladislas's side, all the political and military energy of the kingdom could now be concentrated at one point — against the Ottoman Empire.[7] It was because of this lengthy preparation period from 1439 to 1443 that this military offensive earned the nickname the 'Long Campaign'.

Despite the favourable conditions for conducting the campaign, the international environment was far from calm, and not all countries unanimously accepted the idea of a crusade against the Turks. The Holy Roman emperor Frederick III (1415–93), a legal guardian of the under-age Ladislas the Posthumous, was not willing to take part in the crusade, due to the Habsburgs' struggle against the Jagiellons for the Hungarian crown. Two of the most prominent historians of the period, Enea Silvio Piccolomini, the later pope Pius II (r. 1458–64), and Jan Długosz, were convinced that Frederick feared Vladislas's possible success in the anti-Ottoman campaign, since this would undoubtedly raise the authority of the young king and turn him into a powerful neighbour who might oppose Habsburg rule in the future.[8] Długosz provides us with information about Cardinal Cesarini's negotiations with different European rulers and about the refusals of

---

6 Tsvetkova, *Паметна битка на народите*, pp. 235–37.
7 Hristo Kolarov, 'Някои въпроси от подготовката в Унгария на първия антитурски поход на Владислав Варненчик от 1443–44 г.', *Трудове на Висшия педагогически институт "Братя Кирил и Методий"* 7 (1969–70), 75–107.
8 Jovan Radonić, *Западна Европа и балкански народи према турцима у првој половини XV века* (Novi Sad, 1905), p. 129–38. See Tsvetkova, *Паметна битка на народите*, p. 260; Enea Silvio Piccolomini, *De Europa*, ed. Adrianus van Heck (Civitas Vaticana, 2001), p. 44.

Fredrick III and the grand master of the Teutonic Order, Conrad of Erlichshausen, to grant their support.[9]

In Western Europe, the Hundred Years' War between England and France had not yet come to an end at the time of preparations for the crusade. Faced with their own problems and far from the Ottoman threat, the two great powers were not related to the events of 1443–44.

Interestingly, Poland disapproved of the campaign. The leading aristocratic circles, headed by Cracow's bishop Zbigniew Oleśnicki, did not consider Poland's intervention to be necessary, given that the enemy did not directly threaten the Polish kingdom. On the other hand, the later cardinal Oleśnicki also supported the Council of Basle, which supported the opposition party in Hungary.[10]

Despite the death of Elizabeth and the recognition of Vladislas's rule by the majority of the Hungaro-Croatian aristocracy, there was still a degree of unrest within the dual monarchy. The most active anti-Jagiellonian opponents were the leaders of the Czech mercenaries in several northern Hungarian towns, Jan Jiskra of Brandýs and the ban of Mačva, László Garai. This situation was further complicated by King Vladislas's desire for a crusade, the possible success of which would further consolidate his position on the throne. As for Byzantium, it was desperate for assistance from the West, without which Emperor John VIII Palaiologos feared the end of his country.

The pope's negotiations to secure a naval support of the upcoming crusade were difficult and painful. Despite numerous discussions, the Venetians agreed to participate in the campaign, whereas Genoa and Ragusa (mod. Dubrovnik, Croatia) opted not to engage actively. Negotiations with the Neapolitan king Alfonso V of Aragon (1396–1458) were the most successful. He provided a positive answer, excited by the speech of Cyriacus of Ancona, made in 1443 at Ascoli. The king assured Cyriacus and the Byzantine envoy that he would supply the Byzantines with a fleet.[11] In a contract, he undertook to deliver six ships and also to support the pope against his Sforza opponents. In return, Eugene IV agreed to recognise his royal title. Despite the assurance that he would help the Christian navy, Alfonso V did not particpate in the campaign because of the war that he was involved in with Milan.[12] The duke of Burgundy was also very active in the international negotiations and committed himself to participating in the campaign. In a letter he sent to the senate, which was in fact a response to another letter addressed earlier to the senate, the duke highlighted his desire for the salvation of the Christian world and of the holy city of Constantinople.[13]

---

9 Jan Długosz, *Roczniki czyli kroniki sławnego Królestwa Polskiego*, ed. Jan Dąbrowski et al., [11 vols] 2nd edn (Warszawa, 1962–2006), [9]: bk 12, p. 314.
10 Tsvetkova, *Паметна битка на народите*, p. 259.
11 Francisk Pall, *Ciriaco d'Ancona e la Crociata contro i Turchi* (Valenii de Munte, 1937), p. 14.
12 Francisk Pall, 'Le condizioni e gli echi internazionali della lotta anttiottomana del 1442–44, condotta da Giovanni di Hunedoara', *RESEE* 3–4 (1965), 433–63 (here 449).
13 *Венециански документи за историята на България и българите от XII–XV век*, ed. Vasil Gyuzelev (Sofia, 2001), no. 103, pp. 266–69.

Vlad Dracul, voivode of Wallachia, also agreed to participate in the fight against the Ottoman Turks. On more than one occassion, his soldiers had been part of Hunyadi's army which had managed to inflict several defeats upon the enemy.[14]

There were several major supporters of the crusade against the Ottomans. Pope Eugene IV was the administrative heart of the campaign, and his political activity, conducted with the help of his legate in Hungary, Cardinal Giuliano Cesarini, was of paramount importance for its organisation and conduct. On 1 January 1443, the pope pronounced a papal bull to all Christianity, calling for the preparation of a crusade against the Turks. In two of his letters from 18 February to the papal nuncio in France and to the papal legate in Poland, Eugene promised to finance the preparation of the campaign. In another letter, he informed King Vladislas that he would provide him with a considerable sum of money for the upcoming campaign.[15] The Serbian despot Đurađ Branković was seeking to regain his lost homeland whereas John of Hunyad yearned for new victories over the Turks. Led by the youthful king Vladislas and the experienced military leader Hunyadi, the united Christian army seemed well prepared and ready for success in such an initiative. This was also proved by the chronicler John of Thurocz (c. 1435–88/89), who wrote:

> When the king was at rest under the high roof of the royal chapels of the Buda Castle, John inspired him and encouraged him to fight against the Turks and send them off because of their numerous injustices towards the Hungarian kingdom. That is why, in the third year of his reign, King Vladislas personally, with a great and costly army, together with Voivode John himself and many princes of the kingdom, with Đurađ, despot or king of the Rashka kingdom, who at that point of his rule had been expelled from his possessions, crossed the Danube and entered Rashka.[16]

The Long Campaign

In the spring of 1443, the Ottoman state was shaken by internal unrest. In Asia Minor, Ibrahim II, bey of Karaman, had conquered several cities and sought

---

14 Iorga, *Histoire des Roumains et de la romanité orientale*, 10 vols (Bucarest, 1937–45), 4: 89.
15 Hristo Kolarov, 'Антитурските походи от 1443–44 г на полско-унгарския крал Владислав III Ягело (Варненчик) (обзор на изворите)', *Трудове на Висшия педагогически институт "Братя Кирил и Методий"* 6 (1968–69), 43–104 (here 52–54).
16 John of Thurocz, 'Унгарска хроника', ed. Ilia Iliev, Krasimira Gagova and Hristo Dimitrov, in *Латински извори за българската история*, ed. Iliev, Gagova and Dimitrov, 5 vols (Sofia, 1958–2001), 5.1: 101–19 (here 113): *Cum igitur rex ipse regalium atriorum altis sub tectis in Budensi quietus resideret, dominus Iohannes wayuoda illum ad iferendum Thurcis bellum ad propulsandasque per ipsos crebris vicinus Hungarie illatus iniuraius animavit et induxit. Quare ipse rex Wladislaus tertio sui regni anno grandi et sumptuoso egregiorum militum conflato exercitu una cum ipso domino Iohanne wayuoda pluribusque sui regni principibus et Georgio regni Rascie dezpoto sive rege, is enim ad tunc sui principatus de dominio eiectus erat, Danubium transiens pervent in Rasciam.*

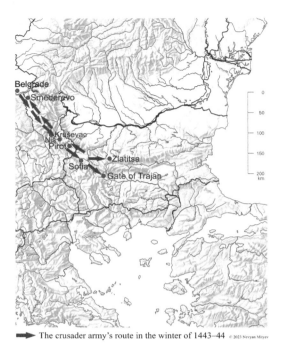

➤ The crusader army's route in the winter of 1443–44 © 2023 Nevyan Mitev

Fig. 19. The Long Campaign of 1443-44. Map by Nevyan Mitev

to expel Murad II from these lands. Two Muslim historiographs, Aşıkpaşazade (also known as Devish Ahmet Âşıkî) and Mehmed Neşri, would later write that emissaries of the emir were sent to the Hungarian king with a proposal for general military action against the Ottomans. Aşıkpaşazade recalled: 'Let us attack, you from there, I from here. Rumelia to be yours, and Anatolia to be mine. We will even give Valkoglu his vilayet'.[17] The same passage, slightly modified, can also be found in Neşri's work.[18] In the end, these plans did not work out, and Ibrahim Bey was defeated by the Ottomans at a decisive battle of Konya.

The long preparation did not hamper the undertaking, and the favourable situation allowed the army of Vladislas and Hunyadi to enter the Ottoman territories. A decision was taken to follow the Belgrade-Nish-Pirot-Sofia-Plovdiv-Edirne road. The ultimate goal was to capture the Ottoman capital Edirne and to expel the Ottomans from the Balkans. The Christian army was composed mainly of Hungarians, Poles, Czechs and Wallachians. The size of the army is quite debatable in the scientific literature. According to some sources, it numbered 14,000, whereas others number it at around 25,000. The army included 600 carts of the Czech Hussite mercenaries, under the leadership of Jan Čepek from San, and there were also volunteers from Germany. The army gathered near Belgrade. As Cardinal Giuliano Cesarini noted, 8,000 Serbian horsemen, infantrymen and a group of about 600–700 Bosnian soldiers, led by Voivode Petar Kovać,

---

17 Aşıkpaşazade, 'История на османската династия', ed. Ibrahim Tatarla and Bistra Tsvetkova, in *Варна 1444: Сборник от изследвания и документи в чест на 525-та годишнина от битката край Варна*, ed. Marin Mihov et al. (Sofia, 1969), pp. 401–9 (here 406).

18 Mehmed Neşri, 'Книга за описанието на света', ed. Ibrahim Tatarla and Bistra Tsvetkova, in *Варна 1444: Сборник*, pp. 413–19 (here 415).

joined the army.[19] According to Bistra Tsvetkova, the army was divided into two corps. The first one had two units, one of which consisted of 12,000 people and was under the command of John of Hunyad, while the other, which consisted of Serbian and Bosnian soldiers, was commanded by Đurađ Branković. A little further behind was the second corps, which consisted of 20,000 soldiers and was under the leadership of the nominal commander of the whole crusade, King Vladislas. At the head of the army, with a cross in his hand, was Cardinal Giuliano Cesarini.[20] John of Thurocz wrote:

> There, King Vladislas stopped at a permanent camp and decided to send forward John of Hunyad as a chief commander of his army. These lands were under the control of the Turkish state. Then he divided his whole expeditionary army into two parts and one of them, which was better armed and equipped, was personally entrusted to the voivode. The voivode himself had a number of units from his army, whose experience in battle made the enemy run away from the battlefield.[21]

Two Italian humanists occupationally engaged at East-Central European courts in the second half of the fifteenth century, Filippo 'Callimachus' Buonaccorsi and Antonio Bonfini, provided different information about the start of the campaign. In his panegyrical *Historia de rege Vladislao*, Buonaccorsi drew his informations from first-hand participant reports.[22] Bonfini mainly adopted Buonaccorsi's accounts and wrote representatively for both:

> Around May, the king left Buda and crossed the Danube, and settled in a camp after the long road, so that those who were not there could easily gather together. Initially, he headed for River Timish (Rom. Timiş, Hung. Temes, Serb. Tamish) and from there gradually assembled the army, settling down for three days on the banks of the Timish to allow those who followed him to catch up. After crossing the river, he went down to *Dacia* and following the left bank of the Danube, no longer turned off. Then, when he realised that he had reached Bulgaria, he crossed [...] the Danube at Slankamen and led the army, which had been enforced by auxiliary soldiers from the delayed units on the way, directly to Sofia, which was six days away from the Danube and in the first part of Bulgaria. The Danubian despot united his army with the royal one. Others said that the king had three armies. Corvinus [John of Hunyad] and the despot went forward with the two of them and he himself followed them at a distance of one day.[23]

---

19 Nicolae Iorga, *Notes et extraits pour servir à l'histoire des croisades au XVe siècle*, 6 vols (Paris, 1899–1916), 3: 109.
20 Tsvetkova, *Паметна битка на народите*, p. 266.
21 Thuróczy, 'Унгарска хроника', p. 113.
22 Filippo Buonaccorsi, *Historia de rege Vladislao*, ed. Irmina Lichońska (Warszawa, 1961).
23 Antonio Bonfini, 'История на унгарците', ed. Ilia Iliev, Krasimira Gagova and Hristo Dimitrov, in *Латински извори за българската история* 5.1: 120–69 (here 146). For the minor differences

In his poem specially dedicated to the late crusader king Vladislas, Michael Beheim conveyed the events briefly as follows:

> The king, knowing this,
> has reconciled
> and gave the order
> that everyone had to come to Varadin on time,
> he gathered with his army
> he succeeded in gathering fourteen thousand
> with the help of the Hungarians.
> These were almost all good, valuable people.
> They passed Urbar –
> Tutterib is its name
> towards the Danube that is opposite
> Bulgaria; that was their way.[24]

The army having now gathered, the campaign could begin. Guided by Đurađ Branković, who was familiar with the area, the crusaders headed southwards for Krushevats. Being the most significant participant from among the Balkan nations, the Serbian soldiers were used by John of Hunyad as shock troops. The Transylvanian voivode placed great trust in the Serbs by including them alongside his elite Transylvanian units in the advanced guard during the crusade's offensive. At Kunovitsa, for instance, the Serb forces managed to hold back the Ottoman army until Hunyadi's arrival.

The military actions during this campaign have been extensively discussed in the academic literature, and I will not go into them in greater detail here, since that is not the purpose of this study. To shorten things up, a brief overview of the most important events: after entering Bulgaria, the crusaders managed to take such important cities as Nish, where an Ottoman army under Kasim Pasha, the beylerbey of Rumelia, and his co-commander Turahan Bey was defeated in early November 1443, and Sofia. In mid-December, the Christian offensive eventually stalled in the battle of Zlatitsa, where the victorious Ottomans as well as the harsh winter forced the crusaders to turn back. During their retreat home, however, the Christians heavily defeated a pursuing Ottoman force at the afore-mentioned Kunovitsa (early January 1444), where Mahmud Bey, son-in-law of Sultan Murad II and brother of Grand Vizier Çandarlı Halil Pasha, was taken prisoner. This

---

between Bonfini and Buonaccorsi with regard to the route of the 1443-crusade, see Florio Banfi, 'Two Italian Maps of the Balkan Peninsula', *Imago Mundi* 11 (1954), 17–34 (here 19–24).

24 Michael Beheim, 'Von dem kung pladislau wy der mit den türken strait', ed. Theodor G. v. Karajan, in *Quellen und Forschungen zur vaterländischen Geschichte, Literatur und Kunst* (Wien, 1849), pp. 35–46 (here p. 30, lines 27–38): *Da der kung daz vername, / da rihtet er fich mit den hern / und schraib ain heruart. in den mern / gen wardein er da kame. / Er samelt sich mit seinem her, / uirczehentausent man praht er / mit hilff der unger zamen. / Daz warn gut werlich leut all gar. / sie furen vber daz uruar, / haist tutenrib mit namen, / Auff der tunaw, hy gegen / der pulgarei, da waz ir pfat.*

last victorious encounter gave the crusaders the feeling of having carried out an all-round successful campaign against the allegedly invincible Ottoman Turks. Although it did not achieve its ultimate goal, the crusade from 1443–44 did also give confidence to the Orthodox peoples in the Balkans that they could liberate themselves from their conquerors. The victories of the crusaders inspired the Balkan peoples, and led to mass uprisings against the enslavers. The Albanian resistance under the leadership of Gjergj Kastrioti Skanderbeg was a key example. He managed to conquer a number of strongholds in his homeland and to establish an independent territory, thus allowing Albanians, if only for a short time, to reject foreign rule.

Besides the Serbs, the participation of the Bulgarians was also substantial for the crusade. The crusading army was reinforced by locals who took an active part in the anti-Turkish campaign. The Orthodox in the Balkans could see a hope for liberation, as was testified in several written records. In a letter from Hunyadi dated 9 November 1443, only six days after the Nish battle, the following was mentioned: 'Our army is well, waiting impatiently for a fight and enlarging every day with Bulgarians, Bosnians, Albanians, Serbs joining us with gifts and rejoicing at our arrival'.[25] In a letter from Cardinal Cesarini from 4 December 1443 we can read the following:

> Serbs and Bulgarians came to me and assured me on their behalf and on behalf of others that many Turks were captured or killed when they ran away after the battle, it was believed that the enemies had suffered no less losses at the hands of the local population in their escape after the battle, than during the battle [...].[26]

Turkish chroniclers also document the mass support for the crusaders among the local population. *The Holy Wars of Sultan Murad, Son of Sultan Mehmed Khan* mentions that Hunyadi formed a Bulgarian detachment as a rearguard of the Christian army. These were Bulgarians who had joined the army after the battle of Nish and during the crossing of Dragoman pass.[27] This is what Filippo Buonaccorsi wrote:

> Most of the Bulgarian cities, guided by hatred for Muslim godlessness and at the same time motivated by eagerness of the Christian faith and because of the

---

[25] *DIR* 2/1.2, no. 581, p. 688: *Verum exercitus noster adhuc integer est est et animosus, de die in diem augetur; venient enim ad regiam Maiestatem multi homines, Bulgari, Bosnenses, Albani et Rasciani cum muneribus, gaudent et laetantur de adventu nostro [...].*

[26] Iorga, *Notes et extraits*, 3: 109–10: *Post scriptas has litteras advenerunt mihi ex Rassianis ac Bulgaris, asserentes, Iam a se quam ab aliis multos ex Turcis, post conflictum, dum fugerent, fore captos et interfectos; putatur non minus damnum accepisse hostes post conflictum in fuga a circumstantibus populis quam in conflictu a nostris.*

[27] *Писание за верските битки на султан Мурад, син на Мехмед хан*, trans. and ed. Maria Kalitsin (Sofia, 1992), pp. 42–43.

common language and the same origin with the Poles as being expelled from the Turkish garrisons, join the king's army.[28]

Jan Długosz also reported that the Turkish garrisons from the fortresses were expelled with the help of the Bulgarian population.[29] Later, Bonfini wrote almost the same:

> Once the soldiers left, wherever they appeared, they captured the Bulgarian cities partly by force, and partly because they surrendered, because of the common Christian faith as well as the abominable cruelty of the Turks, and the great similarity of language, and it was obvious that there was a great opportunity for the spirit of the population to be fermented. Because the Bulgarians and Poles came from Slavic roots and used the same language, as soon as they approached any fortress with their cavalry it surrendered immediately.[30]

Reports on the welcome reception of the Christian army and on the participation of the Bulgarians in the army can also be found in the chronicles of the sixteenth-century Polish humanists — Bernard Wapowski and Marcin Kromer.[31] In his letter to his friend Giovanni Campisio, Enea Silvio Piccolomini wrote: *It was said that those who escaped from death were killed by the locals.*[32] It is undoubtable that the Bulgarian population supported the crusaders, in which the population could see a liberator from the Ottoman oppression. Vasil Gyuzelev considers that the army of Vladislas and Hunyadi included Bulgarians in their ranks. These were Bulgarians who relocated to Slankamen and made up a 4,000-strong cavalry.[33] John of Hunyad wrote to the citizens of Kronstadt (mod. Braşov, Romania, Hung. Brassó) that the Ottomans had withdrawn to the sea and could

---

28 Buonaccorsi, *Historia de rege Vladislao*, p. 138: *Post eam uictoriam pleraque Bulgarorum oppida simul odio Musomanicae impietatis simul affectu Christianae professionis pellecta, tum etiam linguae commercio et quod eadem cum Polonis primordial generis haberent, eiectis Turcorum praesidiis, ad regem defecere [...]*.

29 Długosz, *Roczniki* [9], bk 12, p. 316.

30 Bonfini, 'История на унгарците', 148: *Proinde motis castris, quecunque occurrunt, Bulgarie oppida patim vi, partim per deditionem capiunt, qua quidem in re haud parvo adiumento fuit consimilitudo Christiane professionis, abominabilis Turci feritas lingueque magna cognatio, que ad conciliandos hominum animos potissima videtur esse magistra. Nam, cum Poloni Bulgarique a Sclavonico genere oriundi eandem linguam servent, ad nullum oppidum Polonus equitatus accessit, quin se continuo dediderit.*

31 Bernard Wapowski, *Dzieje Korony Polskiéj i Wielkiego Księstwa Litewskiego od roku 1380 do 1535*, ed. Mikołaj Malinowski (Wilno, 1847), p. 438; Macin Kromer, *Kronika Polska*, ed. and trans. Marcin Błażowski (Sanok, 1857), p. 982.

32 *Извори за средновековната история на България (VII–XV в.) в австрийските ръкописни сбирки и архиви*, ed. Vasil Gyuzelev, 2 vols (Sofia, 2000), 2: no. 111, pp. 133–34: *Reliqui, quos fuga morti eripuerat, incolarum insult periise dicuntur.*

33 Vasil Gyuzelev, '"Дългият поход" на полско-унгарския крал Владислав III Ягело от 1443–1444г. и българите', in *550 години от похода на Владислав Ягело (Варненчик) с Януш Хуняди (1443–1993 г.)*, ed. Atanas Hrischev (Belovo, 1993), pp. 3–18 (here 10–11).

no longer stop the crusaders. The voivode noted that the Bulgarians maintained a friendly attitude towards the army.[34]

In addition to the crusaders' victories at Nish and Kunovitsa, the emerging anti-Ottoman rebellions among the Balkan peoples as well as the simultaneaous destabilising riots in Asia Minor, led by Ibrahim of Karaman, forced Murad II to negotiate peace with the Christians. Talks between the Christian Coalition and the Ottoman sultan began in the spring. In the summer of 1444, the Edirne-Szeged peace treaty was concluded, the greatest beneficiary of which was Đurađ Branković. His sons were returned to him and Serbia was granted autonomy. This is why Serbs did not take part in the second campaign from the autumn of 1444.

The Crusade of Varna

On the other hand, the Balkan peoples were ready for new military actions. Hunyadi's successes excited the people, and that excitement was reflected in the afore-mentioned strong Albanian and Bosnian resistance, with the two countries succeeding in gaining their independence from the sultan. Whereas the Serbian despot patiently awaited the return of his territory and his two sons, King Vladislas and John of Hunyad yearned for further successes against the Ottoman Turks and finally to achieve the goal of expelling the invaders from the European continent. The papacy was also interested in the continuation of the military actions since, as has already been mentioned, it was only in this way that it could impose its power over the Eastern Orthodox peoples and solve its internal problems. The Byzantine emperor once again turned to the West for help. He realised that the end of the Byzantine Empire was near. Poland's position is quite interesting, as it had already expressed its negative attitude towards an anti-Turkish offensive before the start of the 'Long Campaign'. The disapproval of another organised anti-Ottoman crusade among leading Polish circles was expressed in a letter dated 1 July 1444 from Zbigniew Oleśnicki to King Vladislas, requesting that he withdraw from the leadership of the campaign and return to Poland, where urgent concerns awaited his attention.[35] Organising the fleet was also an agonising task. Venice agreed to participate, encouraged by papal promises. Evidence for this can be found in three letters from the senate: the first was from 4 July to Cardinal Cesarini concerning eight or more galleries that would go to Nicopolis along the Danube;[36] the second one was to Francesco Condulmer, cardinal of Venice and papal vice chancellor, notifying him about the same, and the third was to the admiral of the papal navy about a voyage to Nicopolis along the Danube.[37] In fact, the goal would change and the papal fleet would have to block the straits

---

34 *DIR* 2/15.1, no. 48, p. 29.
35 Dąbrowski, *Władysław I Jagiellończyk*, p. 146.
36 *Венециански документи*, no. 104, pp. 270–72.
37 *Венециански документи*, no.105, pp. 272–77.

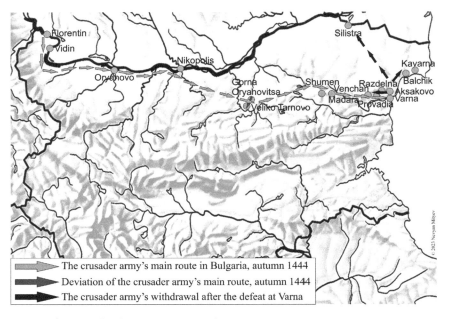

Fig. 20. The crusade of Varna, 1444. Map by Nevyan Mitev

between Asia Minor and Europe and prevent them being crossed by the Ottoman Anatolian army. In the summer of 1444, the fleet, made up of papal, Venetian, Genoese, Ragusan and Burgundian ships, was ready to fight with the Turks.

Again, the organisation of the second march was delayed, but this time only for a few months. Fewer soldiers were involved in the new military initiative under the flags of King Vladislas. A piece of information, recorded by Giuliano Cesarini, about the aid which would be provided by the local population, further encouraged the new military campaign. He received assurances from the rulers and the people of Bulgaria, Albania and Byzantium, that they would support the crusaders. John of Thurocz has written: 'And many Christian rulers promised to send to Bulgaria, Albania and Thrace, and to the glorious imperial city of Constantinople weapons and large military assistance. The people and the leaders of those countries also promised the same'.[38] At the same time the papal fleet headed towards the straits, aiming to establish itself in the Hellespont and thus obstruct the passage of the Ottoman army from Asia Minor to Europe. Bonfini provides us with interesting information about the organisation of the fleet:

---

38 Thuróczy, 'Унгарска хроника', p. 116: *Multos enim Christianorum principles eisdem armorum ferre opem pollicebatur, de Bulgariaque ac de Albania et de Tratia, necnon et de illa famosissima imperiali urbe Constantinopolitana magna militum subsidia ipsis venire dicebat. Id ipsumque et principles idem ac dictorum regnorum incole promittebant.*

With the onset of spring, Vladislas and Corvinus [John of Hunyad] found it appropriate to remind all princes with their legates to assist the expedition with a fleet, and they promised help and money, so initially they distinguished themselves with their promises; at first they informed the emperor of Constantinople, who was with his army in Thrace and Macedonia, to stand there with the auxiliary troops; they also informed Pope Eugene, the Venetians, Genoese and other allies to prepare the fleet and send it into the Hellespont; this was done by them.[39]

The time for the conduct of a new crusade was favourable, since military operations in Asia Minor had flared up again, and a large part of the Ottoman army was directed against the beylik of Karaman.

One can find a number of different opinions about the number and ethnical diversity of the soldiers who took part in the campaign which eventually became known as the Varna Crusade. Bistra Tsvetkova claims that the Christian army numbered around 16,000 soldiers and 2,000 wagons.[40] According to the fifteenth-century Ottoman historian Oruç Bey (also known as Oruç bin Âdil) the army consisted of 16,000 men and 400 artillery wagons;[41] and the number of 300,000 soldiers can be found in *The Holy Wars of Sultan Murad, Son of Sultan Mehmed Khan*.[42] However, the number of the Christian soldiers have been exaggerated later by the Ottoman writers so that they could justify the heavy losses. The Ottoman sources show that Germans, Austrians and Bosnians also participated in the 1444-crusade. Of course, these informations should also be treated with scepticism. The Holy Roman Empire and Bosnia officially did not participate in this military campaign, and the only German soldiers in the army were mercenaries. It is likely that Hans Maugest, the informant of Michael Beheim, was one of them. Bosnia, just like Albania, was stopped by Serbia.[43]

The army of King Vladislas headed to Varna (on the Black Sea coast) going through Northern Bulgaria aiming at reaching Edirne. The reasons for choosing this route were the participation of Hussite battle wagons meaning it would be difficult to cross the mountains and the fact that the Serbian despot Đurađ

---

39 Bonfini, 'История на унгарците', p. 151: *Ingruente iam vere Wladislao Corvinoque placuit per legatos omnis principles admonere, qui in salutary hac expedition classem, auxilia pecuniasve ultro promiserant, uti in primo tempore promissis prestarent; imprimis Constantinopolitanum imperatorem, ut, cum se in Thracie Macedonieve finibus cum exercitu esse sentiret, presto quoque ipse cum auxiliaribus copiis afforet; insuper Eugenium pontificem maximum, Venetos et Genuenses ceterosque socios, qui comparande classis negotium ultro susceperant, ut in Hellespontum eam mitterent; quod et impigre ab illis factum est.*
40 Tsvetkova, *Паметна битка на народите*, p. 299.
41 Oruç Bey, 'История на Османската династия', ed. Ibrahim Tatarla and Bistra Tsvetkova, in *Варна 1444: Сборник*, pp. 389–93 (here 391).
42 *Писание за верските битки на султан Мурад*, p. 82.
43 For a more detailed examination of Bosnian attitudes towards these crusades, see Emir O. Filipović, 'Exurge igitur, miles Christi, et in barbaros viriliter pugna …: The Anti-Ottoman Activities of Bosnian King Stjepan Tomaš (1443–61)', in *Holy War in Late Medieval and Early Modern East-Central Europe*, ed. Janusz Smołucha, John Jefferson and Andrzej Wadas (Kraków, 2017), pp. 201–42.

Branković this time did not take part in the military campaign. The absence of the despot led to the prohibition of the crusader army to pass through Serbian territory.[44]

In the autumn of 1444, the final stage of the military campaign against the Ottomans commenced. The crusaders crossed the Danube near Orshova around 20 September. In *The Holy Wars of Sultan Murad, Son of Sultan Mehmed Khan* it is mentioned that the army entered the 'Saradzh eli' region. Plamen Pavlov and Ivan Tyutyundzhiev suppose that this term refers to the 'land of Stratsimir', named after the former tsar Ivan Stratsimir, the last independent Bulgarian ruler (1356–96) before the Ottoman conquest. The anonymous Ottoman chronicler continues:

> And the rayah, seeing the situation, had fully obeyed the miserable infidels, and Kumüllogu, who was a sanjak bey in this area, was walking around and thinking about what to do. One night the rayah from this land attacked him and robbed all his banners, flags and tents. Kumüllogu escaped and reached the town called Ivrajaya (Vratsa). He found Feris Beyoglu and explained the situation to him in detail [...].[45]

Once they had conquered the fortress, they moved eastwards, conquering Kladovo and Florentin after that. We should highlight two important facts which occur from the sources. Firstly, that the local population helped the crusaders, and secondly that, despite this assistance, the local population was still plundered by the crusaders. They then besieged the strong fortress of Vidin and Michael Behaim mentions that they conquered it on the seventh day and that the Turkish leaders were killed. The crusaders were helped by the locals and proof for this can be seen in the information found in registers from fifteenth century concerning unrest in northwest Bulgaria.[46] The army then headed down the Danube, passing by the fortress of Oryahovo, which probably was also conquered, and besieged the 'main city' of Bulgaria, Nicopolis.[47] The latter was besieged for several days and, as Beheim wrote:

---

44 Nevyan Mitev, 'Походите на Владислав Варненчик и Янош Хуняди от 1443–44 г. в записките на един еничар', *Исторически преглед* 3–4 (2014), 176–85.
45 *Писание за верските битки на султан Мурад*, p. 83. See Plamen Pavlov and Ivan Tyutyundzhiev, *Българите и османското завоевание (краят на XIII–средата на XV в.)* (Veliko Tarnovo, 1995), p. 135.
46 Tsvetkova, *Паметна битка на народите*, pp. 300–1; Hristo Kolarov, 'Два малко известни извора за битката на народите на 10 ноември 1444 г. при Варна', *Известия на Народния музей — Варна* 6 (1970), 171–93 (here 180).
47 It is very interesting that Długosz, Buonaccorsi, Wapowski and several other European writers mention Nicopolis as the capital of Bulgaria. The chroniclers themselves find it doubtful because the city lacks the appearance of a former medieval capital. The mistake among the Western historians is probably derived from the fact that it was the last residence of Tsar Ivan Shishman.

Inside there were many Greeks [Orthodox Christians]
and also, a lot of Turks.
The Greek [Orthodox Christians] jumped down the walls
and went to the Hungarians.
Then, on the fifth day, the city was
captured and burned down immediately
and completely destroyed.[48]

The Bulgarians from Nicopolis willingly joined the Christian army, which was additionally strengthened by the Wallachian voivode Vlad II Dracul who joined the crusaders with 4,000 horsemen. He advised the crusaders to return to their lands in order to gather together a larger army and then to attack the Ottoman Turks.[49] Perhaps due to pressure from Cardinal Cesarini, his advice was not followed by the commanders of the campaign.

There is one very interesting moment in Jan Długosz's description of events during the march from Nicopolis to Shumen. The chronicler also describes the outrages commited upon the local population by the crusaders, and emphasises that they behaved worse than the Turks. This is also mentioned by Andrea Palacio in a letter written soon after the campaign's failure.[50] As stated above, this behaviour was also evident during the crossing of north-western Bulgaria. If we believe the sources, it can be suggested that the Bulgarians were very reserved towards the Christian forces. However, most of the sources show us that the local people did look upon the crusade as bringing the chance of deliverance from Ottoman rule, and were joining the army. This is supported by a letter from Enea Silvio Piccolomini to the duke of Milan, Filippo Maria Visconti, dated 13 December 1444. Piccolomini confirms the participation of Bulgarians and Wallachians in the Christian army.[51] The army besieged the fortress of Shumen which was conquered on the third day, then took the strongholds of Madara and Venchan and reached Ovech, called by the Ottomans Tash Hisar (mod. Provadiya, Bulgaria). The crusaders plundered a lot of clothes and treasures and

---

48 Beheim, 'Von dem kung pladislau', p. 39, lines 367–73: *Darynn vil kriechen waren / vnd ach vil turken vngeheur. / dy kriechen vieln über dy meur, / zu den vngern sie faren. / Am funfften tag da wart dy statt / gewunnen vnd verprennet drat / und gancz geprachen nider.*
49 Buonaccorsi reports in detail on the events that took place around Nicopolis and on the meeting between Vlad Dracul and the crusaders. See Kolarov, 'Хрониката на Калимах', 244–46. Andrea Palacio writes that the crusader army did not capture the fortresses of Orshova, Vidin and Nicopolis, and the author reports that the crusaders plundered and burned all the houses outside of the cities. Milko Mirchev, 'Андреас де Палацио: Писмо за поражението при Варна, изпратено до кардинал Людовик', *Известия на Варненското археологическо дружество* 15 (1964), 85–95 (here 88).
50 Mirchev, 'Андреас де Палацио', 89.
51 *Извори за средновековната* 2, no. 112, pp. 135–38: *Ajunt omnes nuntii uno ore, regem Polonie cum cardinali sancti Angeli multisque Hungaris sed pluribus Walachis et Bulgaris atque Ruthens in Romaniam usque profectos tot belando successus habuisse, ut non longe ab Adrianopoli castra posuerint.* See Tsvetkova, *Паметна битка на народите*, pp. 300–1.

that made King Vladislas order everything to be burned.[52] On 7 November, the army reached the fortress of Petrich and conquered it with difficulties. Filippo Buonaccorsi describes that many knights made their reputation during the attacks against the strongholds of Petrich and Shumen, among them Jan Tarnowski and Leszek Bobrzycki.[53] The garrisons from the strongholds of Kavarna, Kaliakra and Makropolis (mod. Evksinograd, Bulgaria) had left, and the Bulgarians opened their gates to the crusading army.

Meanwhile the king was handed a letter informing him that the Ottoman army led by Sultan Murad II had been transported to the European shore.[54] It is very difficult to determine precisely how the Ottomans crossed the straits. There are two main statements: the first says that someone took a bribe but who, Venetians, Genoese, Byzantines? It is a question which is difficult to answer; the second statement claims that it is the small Christian fleet which should be blamed, since it could not provide a reliable defence and most probably the Ottomans succeeded in finding a gap through which they could cross the Straits. No matter which of these statements sounds more plausible, the question remains open.[55]

After leaving Petrich, on 8 November the crusaders managed to take over the fortress of Mihalich (above now-days town of Aksakovo, Bulgaria). According to Michael Beheim, the king continued his way to the east the next day and arrived at Varna on 9 November.[56] In the meantime, the Ottoman army was able to reunite, reaching about 60,000 people. Sultan Murad led his huge forces north of Edirne, to the mountain passes of the eastern Balkan Mountains.[57] Thus, on 9 November, the Ottomans arrived at Varna Fortress, taking the crusaders by surprise. Despite receiving notice of the Muslim army's passage through the straits, the Christian command did not expect the enemy troops to appear on their rear, in front of Varna.

Among the descriptions of various authors of the composition of the army during the battle of Varna, the names of various participants can be found, above all, of course, senior noblemen and clergymen. The army consisted of three main parts, the left wing comprising five banners (units) — 4,000 men, predominantly

---

52 Kolarov, 'Два малко известни извора', 182.
53 Kolarov, 'Хрониката на Калимах', 247.
54 For the majority of sources and the historiography on this issue, see Nevyan Mitev, 'При коя крепост кръстоносната армия на Владислав III Варненчик (1434–44) получава писмото, което я известява за преминаването на османската войска през Проливите през есента на 1444г.?', Журнал за исторически и археологически изследвания 1 (2013), 81–84.
55 For the various opinions on this issue, see Nevyan Mitev, 'Как е преминала войската на Мурад II (1421–51) през Проливите в есента на 1444г.?', Електронен вестник по музеология и военна история 1 (2013), 29–31.
56 Kolarov, 'Два малко известни извора', 186.
57 For more details about the passing of the Ottoman army in the eastern Balkan Mountains, see Stefan Nedev, 'Пътищата на Владислав III и Мурад II към Варна през 1444 година', in Варна 1444: Сборник, pp. 208–33; Tsveta Raychevska, 'Походът на Мурад II от 1444 г. срещу кръстоносците според османския извор "Писание за верските битки на султан Мурад хан"', Известия на Националния исторически музей 16 (2006), 157–66.

Hungarians under the command of Hunyadi's brother-in-law — Mihály Szilágyi. The king occupied the centre of the army with his personal guards. There were five banners in the right wing, located behind the centre of the army. Four of the banners were Hungarians and the last one comprised of papal crusaders, led by Cardinal Giuliano Cesarini. The Wallachians were behind the main wings as reserve. There is no information about the exact location of the Bulgarians.[58]

It seems highly likely that the last Bulgarian ruler, Fruzhin, son of Tsar Ivan Shishman, took part in the Varna Crusade. A charter from 6 September 1444 says that Fruzhin sold his estate Faydash in the Zaránd area to the ban of Mačva, László Maróti. The same ban had earlier given him this estate as a present. According to Petŭr Petrov, the sale of the property might be related to the campaign of Vladislas the Jagiellonian and he even reaches the conclusion that the Bulgarian ruler took part in the military campaign.[59] On the eve of the campaign, King Vladislas promised Bulgaria to Hunyadi as a future possession. On the one hand, this fact shows the importance of the country for the crusaders, but on the other hand the reservations of Fruzhin (earlier referred to as 'ruler of Zagora') are quite understandable.[60]

On 10 November, the crucial battle against the Ottoman forces took place near Varna. Initially, the crusaders had difficulties on their right flank. Hunyadi and Vladislas, along with the two royal detachments and the Wallachian cavalry, came to their rescue. The Ottoman left wing was destroyed and its commander Karaca Bey was killed. Attacks of the Rumelian sipahis against the crusaders' left wing followed. John of Hunyad rushed again to the rescue, advising the king to wait for his return and not to attack the Ottoman centre alone. The Transylvanian voivode succeeded to scatter the entire right wing of the Turks and many of them fled back to Thrace. In the meantime, the young Polono-Hungarian ruler, most likely after listening to his advisors, decided to charge the enemy square of 10,000 janissaries with only 500 heavily armoured horsemen. Initially, the attack managed to kill many enemies, but eventually Vladislas was knocked down from his horse and killed. We learn from the Ottoman sources that the janissary Koca Hizir cut off his head. The death of the king severely demoralised the crusaders and they began to flee. Janos Hunyadi tried to restore some order in their ranks, but to no avail. Thus, ended the 'memorable battle of the nations', as Bistra Tsvetkova called it, dooming the Balkan people to remain under foreign rule for centuries.[61]

During the aftermath of the battle of Varna a naval campaign of Waleran of Wavrin in 1445 took place. He entered the Danube with a fleet, joined his forces with the Wallachians of Vlad Dracul, took the fortresses of Silistra, Tutrakan,

---

58 Tsvetkova, *Паметна битка на народите*, pp. 306–8.
59 Petŭr Petrov, 'Фружин и походът до Варна през 1444г.', in *Варна 1444: Сборник*, pp. 272–83.
60 Pavlov and Tyutyundzhiev, *Българите и османското завоевание*, p. 128.
61 Tsvetkova, *Паметна битка на народите*, p. 310–11.

Giurgiu and Ruse and finally withdrew upon hearing about a huge Ottoman army heading towards him. As a result, the naval campaign in search of the fallen king was brought to an end.[62]

Concluding Thoughts

King Vladislas the Jagiellonian and John of Hunyad's two crusades in 1443–44 were some of the final attempts of Latin Christianity to halt the Ottoman expansion in South-Eastern Europe. In the following years there was much talk about organising new military campaigns on a such a large scale, but these would never be realised. Hungarians, Wallachians, Bulgarians, Poles, Czechs, Croats, and Ruthenians all took part in both campaigns, and there was also a unit of papal crusaders under the leadership of Cardinal Giuliano Cesarini. However, the initiative never gained meaningful support from the most important countries of the Catholic West, England, France and the Holy Roman Empire. Internal political problems in Poland at that time also prevented it from taking an active part. Thus, to return to the question raised at the beginning of this essay: the article clearly shows that many potentates both of Central and of South-Eastern Europe effectively did not join the crusading initiatives or the actual campaigns. Nevertheless, despite their small number, the Polish knights who took part in both crusades were amongst the most battle-hardened soldiers. Zdzisław Pentek compiled a list of Polish participants in the Varna Crusade and came up with the names of just over one hundred people, including the king himself, and historiography seems to agree that they did not exceed 500, the personal guards of King Vladislas.[63] The papal fleet most likely betrayed the crusading army. The spontaneous attack of the young king determined the fate of South-Eastern Europe for centuries. The short-sighted policy of the Serbian despot Đurađ Branković, who prevented Skanderbeg's fighters from taking part in the battle of Varna, also contributed to the subsequent development of events. Less than a century later, the Ottomans had conquered the entire Balkan Peninsula, and even Hungary was under their authority.

---

62 For more on the naval campaign of 1445, see Jehan de Wavrin, 'Extract from the Anciennes Chroniques d'Angleterre', ed. Colin Imber, in *The Crusade of Varna, 1443–45*, pp. 107–66.
63 Zdisław Pentek, 'Полските участници във Варненската битка', in *Варна 1444. Действителност и традиции* (Varna, 2005), pp. 109–24.

EMIR O. FILIPOVIĆ

Converting Heretics into Crusaders on the Fringes of Latin Christendom

Shifting Crusading Paradigms in Medieval Bosnia

The small land-locked country of Bosnia can be considered a textbook example of a state and society on the very outer edges of the medieval Christian West. Throughout the Middle Ages it belonged neither fully to the Catholic World, nor to the Orthodox one. Instead, it remained on the peripheries of both. Its political and religious reality was shaped by the fact that it was located between the two dominant cultural forces of East and West, where it served as a border region separating these two great civilisational spheres. This almost unique geographical position left Bosnia open to influences from all sides, and in turn created a specific religious, political and cultural environment which has come to define the history of the state and its inhabitants.

This distinctiveness and peculiarity also resulted in an unconventional ecclesiastical development which had an impact on the way that the country was perceived by contemporary elites of the medieval West. Namely, in the eyes of Latin Christians, Bosnia, its ruler and his subjects, were irrevocably tarnished with the stain of heresy ever since the first allegations of their religious malpractice reached the papal curia by the end of the twelfth century. These accusations were swiftly turned into a convenient justification for the launching of several crusade campaigns with the aim of eliminating heretics. However, the failure of these crusades either to materialise or to achieve their stated goals meant that Bosnia continued to be seen by Westerners as a cradle of heresy, and the idea of initiating a new crusade continued sporadically to reappear at times when it seemed appropriate.

During the fifteenth century, however, the situation changed dramatically with the rising Ottoman tide, which began slowly to erode the borders of the Bosnian kingdom. In such circumstances the erstwhile heretics came to be seen as potential partners in Christendom's struggle with the Ottoman Turks, and the papacy increased its efforts to convert them into crusaders. In fact, the whole kingdom was expected to fully embrace Catholicism as a precondition before receiving any meaningful military or financial assistance from the West. The last kings of Bosnia duly obliged and converted, placing themselves on the frontline of crusade. They were forced to maintain a careful balancing act in an attempt to preserve the fragile religious and political unity of their kingdom whilst ideologically framing their official state policy in the rhetoric of holy war. Despite everything, the slow diplomatic process proved to be too little too late, the expected help never arrived and the anti-Ottoman crusade campaign in Bosnia failed miserably in a trail of false hopes and broken promises.

This work will seek to elaborate further on these two distinct phases in crusading history regarding Bosnia. It will initially concentrate on the background and repercussions of the crusader discourse directed against the Bosnian heretics throughout the thirteenth century, and then, with a particular focus on the powerful *topos* of conversion, it will attempt to show how the crusading paradigm had evolved by the 1400s, when the attention of the papacy turned towards the struggle of creating a united front against the Ottoman Turks and generating a sense of crusading identity on the diminishing borders of Christendom in the Balkans.

***

The first reliable sources that connect Bosnia to accusations of heresy can be dated to the final years of the twelfth century. By then, Bosnia had grown from modest and humble origins into a relatively stable political structure. It had its own rulers who bore the title of 'ban' and were under the influence of the Hungarian kings, while maintaining a great degree of independence in matters of trade, economy, military and religion.[1] However, it is precisely in light of this burgeoning Bosnian autonomy that, in 1199, its ruler Ban Kulin was denounced and accused by one neighbouring lord of receiving and protecting heretics in his realm. Vukan, the lord of Duklja to the southeast, wrote a letter to the pope stating that heresy blossomed in Bosnia — which was a 'land of the king of Hungary' — and that this movement had grown to such an extent that Ban Kulin himself, together with his wife, sister and numerous other relatives, had inducted more than 10 000 Christians into this heresy.[2] Alarmed by these claims, Pope Innocent III subsequently wrote to the king of Hungary urging him to take swift and decisive military action against the insubordinate Bosnian ruler.[3]

Protesting his innocence in the whole matter, hoping to avert the involvement of the king and believing also that the accused heretics were actually faithful Christians, Kulin allowed them to be investigated by a papal emissary.[4] The assignment was entrusted to chaplain John, a monk from the Cistercian Abbey of Casamari, who managed to extract an admission and promise from the leaders of the group that, in the future, they would abstain from the sins that they had committed in the past. According to the text of their statement which was composed at

---

[1] As of yet there is no modern, scholarly, detailed and reliable account of early Bosnian history published in English or German. A very brief encapsulation of the major events and processes up to 1198 is given by John V. A. Fine, *The Late Medieval Balkans* (Ann Arbor, 1994), pp. 17–21.
[2] *VMSM* 1, no. 10, p. 6.
[3] *VMSM* 1, no. 20, pp. 12–13.
[4] *VMSM* 1, no. 25, p. 15.

the time, and which has survived in the registers of the Vatican Apostolic Archive, it is evident that this was a specific community whose heterodox beliefs and organisation cannot easily be explained.[5] The Bosnian Christians were accused of heresy and schism, but it is still not completely clear whether they were a monastic order, whether their group existed in Bosnia alongside the Catholic bishopric, or whether they had in fact taken over a neglected diocese which had lost contact with Rome and retained the practice of celebrating liturgy in the Slavonic vernacular. Furthermore, it also seems that contemporaries were not fully aware what the proper character of their religion was. In 1203, chaplain John of Casamari claimed that he solved the affairs with the 'former Patarenes',[6] and the pope himself called them 'Patarenes' in one letter,[7] whereas in a different letter he asserted that they were strongly suspected of following the 'cursed Cathar heresy'.[8] On the basis of available evidence it is difficult to determine for sure whether they had any connections to these heretical movements or whether their teachings resembled Catharism in any way.[9]

When everything settled down, the papal chaplain who was tasked with resolving this issue wrote a brief report to the pope in which he effectively identified the root of the problem. Namely, he noticed that there was only one bishopric on the territory of the whole of Bosnia and that the episcopal see was vacant since the previous bishop had recently passed away. He thought that the longevity and success of the whole mission could be ensured through the ecclesiastical reorganisation of Kulin's state, so he suggested to the pope that a foreigner who knew the Latin service should be invested as bishop, and he also recommended the establishing of three or four new bishoprics in the state, since Bosnia encompassed a territory that extended for more than ten days of walking.[10] His farsighted proposals were not considered, as both sides were content with the compromise. The written declaration was ultimately confirmed by the Hungarian king Emeric in 1203 and the whole issue seemed to have been settled without much fuss.[11] Judging on the basis of subsequent developments, however, it appears that the coerced renunciation did not drastically alter the unusual religious situation.

---

5 The most recent critical edition of the text is: Pejo Ćošković, 'Interpretacija Kniewaldovog kritičkog izdanja bilinopoljske izjave', *Prilozi* 32 (2003), 75–117. An English translation is provided in: *Christian Dualist Heresies in the Byzantine World, c. 650–c. 1450*, ed. and trans. Janet Hamilton, Bernard Hamilton and Yuri Stoyanov (Manchester, 1998), pp. 257–59. For more on the mission of chaplain John of Casamari in Bosnia, see Ivan Majnarić, 'Giovanni de Casamaris e l'abiura di Bilino Polje 1203 — Guidice delegato papale in Bosnia', *Review of Croatian History* 13 (2017), 29–44.
6 *VMSM* 1, no. 34, p. 19.
7 *VMSM* 1, no. 20, p. 12.
8 *VMSM* 1, no. 25, p. 15.
9 A recent attempt to join all the threads connecting heterodox movements in the West with those in the East is Bernard Hamilton, 'Cathar Links with the Balkans and Byzantium', in *Cathars in Question*, ed. Antonio Sennis (Woodbridge, 2016), pp. 131–50.
10 *VMSM* 1, no. 34, p. 19.
11 *VMSM* 1, no. 38, p. 22.

Believing that the problem was solved, the papacy lost all contact with Bosnia for almost two decades. This gap could best be explained, perhaps, by the multitude of hectic and urgent events at the time which took precedence at the Roman curia and forced Bosnian issues into the background. But, neglecting to deal with the concern promptly and properly meant that, in this intervening period, the Roman Church lost any authority it might have had in this land. When the pope became aware of this in 1221, his reaction had to be swift and severe.[12] Having heard how heretics were received and accommodated in Bosnia where they fed their young like *lamias* with open breasts, 'publicly spreading the folly of their wickedness to the great detriment of the Lord's flock', Pope Honorius III advised his legate Acontius from Viterbo to act with papal authority and encourage the king of Hungary, as well as the archbishops and bishops of that kingdom, to whom he had also sent letters, to proceed against these heretics and their collaborators 'manly and powerfully'.[13]

Regrettably, the letter to King Andrew II has not been preserved, but we do have the text of a letter that Pope Honorius III sent on 5 December 1221 to the archbishop of Esztergom and the other prelates of Hungary. He urged each and every single one them to apply all diligence and effort in abolishing this pestilence in Bosnia, exhorting them to engage their subjects in this endeavour by offering them remissions for their sins.[14]

Considering that the letters were composed at the beginning of December, that it must have taken them a while to reach their destination and that, when they did, it was winter — during which not much could be done to achieve the stated goals — we can safely assume that no concrete action was undertaken until spring time. In fact, we have a kind of a confirmation of this in Pope Honorius III's letter sent on 12 March 1222 to the cathedral chapter of Ragusa, warning them to choose a new archbishop who would then have a special task of assisting legate Acontius in his struggle against the pirates from Dalmatia and the heretics in Bosnia.[15] This letter can be taken as proof that Acontius' action had either failed to occur by March 1222, or that it had not been as easy as was initially anticipated, since the legate required additional assistance from the archbishop of Ragusa in fulfilling his mission.

As has already been emphasised, these letters are the first pieces of any kind of information we have about Bosnia for a long time, making it very difficult to place

---

12 On relations between the Holy See and Bosnia in the first half of the thirteenth century, see Jaroslav Šidak, '"Ecclesia Sclavoniae" i misija dominikanaca u Bosni', *Zbornik Filozofskog fakulteta u Zagrebu* 3 (1955), 11–40; a more recent article by Gábor Barabás, 'Heretics, Pirates, and Legates: The Bosnian Heresy, the Hungarian Kingdom, and the Popes in the Early 13th Century', *Specimina Nova Pars Prima Sectio Mediaevalis* 9 (2017), 35–58.
13 *VMHH* 1, no. 61, p. 31. The legate's life and activities are discussed in more detail by: Ivan Majnarić, 'Papinski poslanik Akoncije u Dalmaciji i Hrvatskoj 1219.–1223. godine', in *Humanitas et litterae: Zbornik u čast Franje Šanjeka*, ed. Lovorka Čoralić and Slavko Slišković (Zagreb, 2009), pp. 79–98.
14 *VMHH* 1, no. 62, p. 31.
15 *CDH* 7.5, no. 111, pp. 229–30.

them in a specific context. From their content it is obvious that the previous papal mission of 1203 eventually ended up not being successful, that the suggested reforms were not implemented and that additional steps needed to be taken in order to align the religious situation in Bosnia with the rest of Latin Christendom. There is no way of knowing what it was precisely that changed in 1221, provoking such a strong response from the pope, who issued a comprehensive call to action to the king, nobles and prelates of Hungary. The tone and message of the letters inferred a full-scale military intervention in the form of a crusade, even entailing the remission of sins for those who took part, but explicit crusading terminology was evidently missing.

Despite the direct messages contained in the papal correspondence, the available sources do not provide us with substantial evidence that any kind of campaign was initiated or that Acontius ever reached his intended destination. Even if he had managed to visit Bosnia, which is less than likely,[16] anything he might have undertaken there to suppress heresy certainly had no long-lasting consequences.

This example therefore clearly illustrates the many problems of researching heresy and crusade in thirteenth-century Bosnia. Almost all of the surviving documents containing crusading discourse from that time stem from the papal chancery, leaving us with an overly one-sided, one-dimensional and incomplete picture of events. Historians often fill these vast gaps in our knowledge with diverse, sometimes even diametrically opposing interpretations. This has obviously contributed to many misunderstandings and different explanations of various key issues from that period in historiography, making it difficult to deliver a more balanced assessment. Since the accusations of heresy and calls for crusade can even be construed as politically motivated attempts to suppress the existing ecclesiastical organisation in Bosnia and, in so doing, also to overpower its increasingly independent secular rulers, some scholars recently began disputing that any actual crusading campaigns had taken place.[17] For the present topic, however, it is not of crucial importance whether the threats and warnings from the sources ever properly transpired, since the crusading terminology and language undoubtedly contributed to the stereotyping of Bosnia as a land of heretics and deviants, and a rightful object of crusade, leaving a legacy that extended well into the fifteenth century.

The other noticeable thing is that, despite all the enthusiasm that the papacy demonstrated for the eradication of heresy, the Hungarian king and nobles who were entrusted with the crusade effort as the secular arm of the Church in the matter remained rather reluctant to actively engage their military potential for the common cause. Furthermore, while the disinterested king and ruling elites of

---

16 Only one unreliable source claims that the legate travelled to Bosnia: Archdeacon Thomas of Split, *History of the Bishops of Salona and Split*, ed. and trans. Olga Perić et al. (Budapest, 2006), p. 190.
17 Nada Klaić, *Srednjovjekovna Bosna* (Zagreb, 1989), pp. 111–48. See Mladen Ančić, '"Križarske vojne" XIII stoljeća', *Radovi Hrvatskog društva za znanost i umjetnost* 4 (1996), 12–35.

Hungary hesitated in committing fully to resolving the issue, the clergy of that country did offer their services.

After a couple of years of calm, Bosnia appears in the written records again in 1225. Trying to get rid of the obligation to lead a long, difficult and uncertain armed campaign which promised very limited benefits in return, King Andrew II provisionally presented the Bosnian territories to Ugrin, the archbishop of Kalocsa in Hungary, if he agreed to clean these lands of heresy. Ugrin sent the deed to the pope and implored him to confirm this donation made by the king of Hungary who permanently gave Bosnia, Soli and Usora, which were infected with heretical wickedness, as a pious donation to his church, committing him to purge those areas.[18] The pope duly obliged and confirmed this donation in 1225 but, in another letter sent on the same day, he encouraged the archbishop to persevere in his efforts, authorising him to preach the cross and exhort with efficacy the faithful against the unfaithful, naming those who took or would take part in the prosecution of those who subvert Catholic purity as *crucegignatos vel crucegignandos*. In the case that any of them had previously been excommunicated, he was permitted to absolve them of their sins, because their merits for the Apostolic See would far outweigh their earlier misdemeanours.[19]

The archbishop unquestionably did set about organising the crusade but he met numerous unexpected difficulties along the way. Transferring this crusading 'hot potato' to a third party, he gave 200 marks of silver to John Angelos, son of Byzantine emperor Isaac II and the nephew of Hungarian king Andrew II, who took the sign of the cross and, in turn, vowed to organise a military campaign 'against the heretics of Bosnia'.[20] However, as he refrained from honouring his commitment, despite the archbishop reminding him to do so on many occasions, the pope reprimanded him in January 1227 and threatened him with punishment if he refused to fulfil his promise and immediately join the expedition against those heretics, together with the aforementioned archbishop, so that Christ may bestow his grace upon him in the present and glory in the future.[21] Pope Honorius III died soon after, on 18 March 1227, the envisaged crusade never took place, and almost a decade had passed in empty correspondence without any concrete action.

It took some time before Bosnian issues were brought back once again into the limelight and the attention of the papacy. The topic was revived in the first half of 1232 when news reached Rome that the man occupying the Bosnian episcopal see had acquired his post through simony, was apparently ignorant of the Holy Christian rites, could not speak a word of Latin and was a shameless defender of heretics. It was alleged that he lived in a village among heretics

---

18 *VMHH* 1, no. 119, pp. 55–56.
19 *VMHH* 1, no. 118, p. 55.
20 *VMHH* 1, no. 149, p. 72.
21 *VMHH* 1, no. 149, p. 72.

and that his own brother was a heresiarch.[22] Following a short investigation, conducted by the papal legate Giacomo Pecorara from Piacenza,[23] the wayward cleric was quickly replaced by a Dominican friar from Westphalia in Germany — John of Wildeshausen — while his diocese was removed from the metropolitan jurisdiction of the archbishop of Ragusa and placed under direct papal authority.[24] However, since the new bishop was incapable of introducing any real change, Bosnia remained, in the words of Pope Gregory IX from 1234, a deserted land 'covered with thorns and nettles — a lair of dragons and pasture for ostriches'.[25] Therefore, the papacy once more turned to a military solution. The pope sent the prior of the Carthusian monastery of St Bartholomew in Trisulti as his appointed legate to Bosnia, ordering that whoever accepted the sign of the cross from his hands would be absolved of sins and be granted the same privileges as those given to crusaders in the Holy Land.[26]

Furthermore, in mid-October 1234, the pope sent a series of letters to various destinations hoping to get the campaign under way, offering spiritual protection and aid in the crusade against the heretics.[27] An invitation was extended to Andrew II's son Coloman, the duke of Slavonia, to lead the war effort.[28] To this end the king granted the possession of Bosnia to Coloman, and Pope Gregory IX confirmed the donation on 9 August 1235.[29] Even though the preparations for this military campaign were much more serious than in the previous cases where crusades had been proclaimed against Bosnia, not many traces of its outcome have survived in the official documents. In one charter issued by King Béla IV on 29 October 1244, the king claims that he confirmed all possessions to his brother

---

22 *CDAC* 1, no. 181, pp. 298–99.
23 *VMHH* 1, no. 191, p. 113. On the legation of Giacomo Pecorara in Hungary, see Tibor Almási, 'Egy ciszterci bíboros a pápai világhatalom szolgálatában: Pecorari Jakab magyarországi legációja', *Magyar egyháztörténeti vázlatok* 5 (1993), 129–41.
24 See Nedim Rabić, 'Im toten Winkel der Geschichte: Johannes von Wildeshausen als Bischof von Bosnien 1233/34–1237', in *Die deutschen Dominikaner und Dominikanerinnen im Mittelalter*, ed. Sabine von Heusinger et al. (Berlin, 2016), pp. 53–69. The earliest history of the Catholic Bosnian diocese has not yet been subjected to serious scholarly study. The few existing works that treat the topic do not do so extensively: Ivan Jablanović, 'Bosanska biskupija u srednjem vijeku do Kulina bana', *Vrhbosna* 46.7 (1932), 175–79; Danko Dujmović and Vjekoslav Jukić, 'Počeci bosanske biskupije', *Vjesnik Arheološkog muzeja u Zagrebu* 43 (2010), 127–33; Bálint Ternovácz, 'A bosznai latin püspökség története 1344-ig', *Micae Mediaevales* 5 (2016), 215–28.
25 *VMHH* 1, no. 207, p. 123.
26 *VMHH* 1, no. 207, p. 123.
27 *VMHH* 1, no. 221, p. 129.
28 *VMHH* 1, no. 218, pp. 128–29. A recent biography of Duke Coloman was published by: Márta Font and Gábor Barabás, *Coloman, King of Galicia and Duke of Slavonia (1208–1241): Medieval Central Europe and Hungarian Power* (Leeds, 2019). For an approach that focuses more on the relations between the duke and Pope Gregory IX, see Gábor Barabás, 'Kálmán szlavón herceg és IX. Gergely pápa', *Aetas: Történettudományi folyóirat* 32.3 (2017), 36–51.
29 *VMHH* 1, no. 229, p. 133.

Coloman at that time when he 'assumed the sign of the cross and went against the Patarenes to the lands of Bosnia and Rama in Christ's name'.[30]

However, much like in earlier instances, the fruits of these military endeavours are extremely difficult to identify. This was probably because, in seeking to reform the Bosnian church, the papacy relied on the help of nobles and prelates from Hungary, rather than on the compliant secular authorities in Bosnia, where the introduction of Latin Christianity gradually came to be associated with the establishment of greater Hungarian political and cultural influence. This process was clearly opposed by the domestic Bosnian elites who considered the Hungarian and Catholic advances as foreign, strange and potentially destructive to the autonomous position they had enjoyed thus far.

The lack of cooperation with the ruler and the aristocracy of Bosnia prevented the papacy from achieving any effective control over the issue, which was now almost completely in the hands of the Hungarian prelates. In 1238, they managed to convince the pope to name Pósa, a Dominican friar from Hungary, as the new bishop of Bosnia, thus initiating the process which would irreversibly bind the Bosnian diocese to the Hungarian ecclesiastical structure.[31] As the earlier crusades did not reap the expected results, a new campaign was proclaimed soon after and, by December 1238, Duke Coloman was urged to continue his good work in Bosnia.[32] At the same time, the pope sent letters to the prelates of Hungary to collect crusaders and place them at the disposal of the Bosnian bishop.[33] He also reassured the recently appointed bishop, praised him for his conscientious activities in clearing the land of heresy, named him as his legate in the Bosnian diocese, and exhorted him to encourage the faithful in Hungary to fight the heretics by granting them remissions for sins.[34]

It is not completely clear whether a crusading army commanded by Duke Coloman ever descended on Bosnia, but papal documents only speak of glorious victories and have words of praise for the duke.[35] No other reliable sources confirm these successes which feature so prominently in the papal correspondence of the time.

Furthermore, even if the 1238 crusade did end successfully, the triumph was certainly short-lived since it would have been almost completely wiped out with the Mongol invasion in 1241–42, during which both Archbishop Ugrin and Duke Coloman lost their lives.[36] It took a while for the Hungarian nobility

---

30 *CDAC* 7, no. 109, p. 167.
31 *VMHH* 1, no. 289, pp. 162–63.
32 *VMHH* 1, no. 301, p. 168.
33 *VMHH* 1, no. 303, p. 169.
34 *VMHH* 1, no. 306, pp. 169–70.
35 *VMHH* 1, no. 310, p. 172.
36 For the Mongol invasion of Hungary, see Peter Jackson, *The Mongols and the West, 1221–1410* (London, 2005), pp. 58–86. Cf. Paul Srodecki, 'Fighting the "Eastern Plague": Anti-Mongol Crusade Ventures in the Thirteenth Century', in *The Expansion of the Faith: Crusading on the Edges of Latin Christendom in the High Middle Ages*, ed. Srodecki and Norbert Kersken (Turnhout, 2021), pp. 303–

and clergy to regroup and, in August 1245, Pope Innocent IV again called for a crusade against Bosnia. He informed Bishop Pósa that he had authorised the archbishop of Kalocsa as his legate in the Bosnian diocese and instructed him to preach the crusade.[37] In another letter, Pope Innocent IV ordered the prior of the Hungarian Dominicans to elect appropriate friars who could preach the cross throughout the kingdom of Hungary, giving all those who answered their call the usual indulgences and privileges.[38] The pope called upon the archbishop of Esztergom and his suffragan bishops to rise up and join the crusade in return for the remission of sins.[39] King Béla IV was likewise invited to take up the 'flag of the living cross' and begin work on the eradication of heretics. After cleaning Bosnia from heresy, he was then advised to give the purged land over to the faithful.[40]

In 1246, Pope Innocent IV sent the sign of the cross to the new archbishop of Kalocsa, but once again nothing came out of the whole matter.[41] Moreover, in the following year, the pope finally admitted that the Bosnian diocese had lapsed so deeply into sin and heretical wickedness that it could no longer be considered a part of the Roman Church.[42] Since there was no hope that the land of Bosnia would voluntarily return to the righteous faith, King Béla IV suggested to the pope that better results could be achieved if the Bosnian diocese was subjected to the metropolitan see of Kalocsa.[43] The pope obliged and thus inadvertently sealed the fate of Catholicism in Bosnia.

Soon after these events, the archbishop of Kalocsa organised the removal of the bishop and his chapter from Bosnia, transferring them to Đakovo in Slavonia and incorporating them fully into the episcopal network of Hungary.[44] By displacing the see of the diocese he had hoped to exert greater political and religious control over Bosnia, but his project backfired spectacularly. Instead of reaffirming Hungarian influence and Latin Christianity in Bosnia, this seemingly insignificant landlocked state remained outside of the firmer reach of the Hungarian kings and its doors were firmly shut to institutional Catholicism. It would take more than six

---

27; Felicitas Schmieder, *Europa und die Fremden: Die Mongolen im Urteil des Abendlandes vom 13. bis in das 15. Jahrhundert* (Sigmaringen, 1994), pp. 73–77.
37 Jaroslav Šidak, 'Nova građa o akciji Rimske kurije u Bosni 1245', *Historijski zbornik* 27–28 (1974–75), 319–29 (here 325–26).
38 Šidak, 'Nova građa o akciji Rimske kurije u Bosni 1245', p. 327.
39 Šidak, 'Nova građa o akciji Rimske kurije u Bosni 1245', p. 328.
40 Šidak, 'Nova građa o akciji Rimske kurije u Bosni 1245', p. 328.
41 *VMHH* 1, no. 373, p. 202.
42 *VMHH* 1, no. 382, p. 204.
43 *VMHH* 1, no. 382, p. 204.
44 See Đuro Basler, 'Ungarn und das bosnische Bistum (1181/85–1247)', *Ungarn-Jahrbuch* 5 (1973), 9–15; Srećko M. Džaja, 'Bosansko srednjovjekovlje kroz prizmu bosanske krune, grba i biskupije', *Jukić* 15 (1985), 81–102.

centuries until regular Catholic hierarchy was reintroduced in Bosnia in the late 1800s.[45]

The Bosnian elites quickly replaced the dislocated Bosnian diocese by establishing a sort of national church, which was in essence a fusion of the old monastic order accused of heretical practices with the remnants of the ecclesiastical institution which had existed there previously. This Church had its own local bishop of Bosnian origin, its own hierarchy, its own liturgy performed in the Slavonic language, its own distinct religious teaching, influenced by western Christianity, but even more so by eastern monastic traditions, and was considered schismatic and heretical by both the Catholic and Orthodox churches. Members of this Bosnian Church called themselves 'Christians' and considered their Church a continuation of the old dislocated bishopric which protected their Slavic language and identity.[46]

It was precisely this framework which enabled the unimpeded development, progress and expansion of the Bosnian state throughout the fourteenth century, when its borders stretched out towards the sea. In such circumstances, talk of crusade resurfaced once again in 1337, when the nobles of Croatia acquired papal blessing for an envisaged campaign against the Bosnian ruler Ban Stephen II Kotromanić,, accusing him and his nobles of protecting heretics.[47] However, it is assumed that King Charles Robert of Hungary ultimately thwarted their plans by preventing any attack against the ruler of Bosnia, who was his cousin and close ally. Bosnia was also mentioned as a potential target of crusade some twenty years later,[48] and then again in 1391, when Pope Boniface IX blessed the campaign of King Sigismund of Luxemburg against 'Turks, Manicheans, heretics and other enemies of the Lord's name' in neighbouring lands, as well as against the 'schismatics residing in Bosnia', granting it the status of a crusade war.[49]

By this time the expanding power of the Ottoman Turks had become a major threat both for the smaller Balkan states and for the kingdom of Hungary itself.[50] The Bosnian nobility initially sought to ally themselves with the Turks in order to execute joint attacks on the Hungarian lands to the north, but this alliance was short-lived. During the second decade of the fifteenth century the Ottoman

---

45 Berislav Gavranović, *Uspostava redovite katoličke hijerarhije u Bosni i Hercegovini 1881: godine* (Beograd 1935). See also Srećko M. Džaja, 'Katoličanstvo u Bosni i Hercegovini od Kulina bana do austro-ugarske okupacije', *Croatica Christiana periodica* 30 (1992), 153–78.
46 The extant literature on the Bosnian Church is vast, presenting diverse and often even conflicting interpretations. The most authoritative works published thus far are: Jaroslav Šidak, *Studije o "Crkvi bosanskoj" i bogumilstvu* (Zagreb, 1975); Franjo Šanjek, *Bosansko-humski krstjani i katarsko-dualistički pokret u srednjem vijeku* (Zagreb, 1975); John V. A. Fine, *The Bosnian Church: A New Interpretation* (New York, 1975); Pejo Ćošković, *Crkva bosanska u XV. stoljeću* (Sarajevo, 2005).
47 *VMHH* 1, no. 925, pp. 616–17.
48 *VMSM* 1, no. 327, p. 240.
49 *Bullae Bonifacii IX. P.M.*, ed. Vilmos Fraknói, 2 vols (Budapest, 1886–89), 1: no. 203, pp. 178–79.
50 See Ferenc Szakály, 'Phases of Turco-Hungarian Warfare before the Battle of Mohács (1365–1526)', *Acta Orientalia Academiae Scientiarum Hungaricae* 33 (1979), 65–111; Tamás Pálosfalvi, *From Nicopolis to Mohács: A History of Ottoman-Hungarian Warfare, 1389–1526* (Leiden, 2018).

Turks managed to gain a strong foothold in Bosnia and began to exert greater political control over the king and his nobles. It was only then that the Bosnians realised they could not get rid of nor deal with the Ottoman military pressure without external aid. Nevertheless, decades of fighting at the end of the fourteenth and beginning of the fifteenth century, during which alliances in the region were constantly reshuffled, meant that the enduring stereotype of Bosnia as a heretical land persisted even when the Bosnian king openly accepted Catholicism and co-operation with Hungary. In 1435, for instance, King Tvrtko II of Bosnia attended a state diet with King Sigismund in Pressburg where he publicly submitted himself and all the sects of his kingdom to the Hungarian ruler,[51] and even this was clearly not enough, since Sigismund considered the Bosnians, alongside the Turks and Hussites, to be one of the three major sources of threat for his kingdom.[52] Even though Hungary and Bosnia were essentially faced with the same problem, it is clear that the Hungarian king did not perceive Bosnia as an equal partner in the joint struggle against a mutual enemy.

Throughout the 1440s and 1450s the rulers of Bosnia initiated and maintained contacts with the pope, repeatedly proclaiming their allegiance to the common cause. In September 1443, King Tvrtko II even sent a special envoy to Rome where, in his name and in the name of the whole kingdom, the representative renounced the 'Manichean heresy and accepted the Roman faith'.[53] His successor, King Stephen Thomas, who converted upon ascending to the throne, continued these same policies, constantly professing his Catholic faith and appealing to the pope for support.[54] Apparently, the papal legate bishop of Hvar (Ven. and Ital. Lesina) Thomas Tommasini worked tirelessly to convert both the Bosnian king and queen, as well as numerous other barons of the kingdom.[55] Pope Nicholas V claimed that Stephen Thomas was the 'first among the Bosnian kings to accept the

---

51 Gustav Beckmann, 'Tagebuchaufzeichnungen zur Geschichte des Basler Konzils 1431–35 und 1438', in *Concilium Basiliense V*, ed. Gustav Beckmann, Rudolf Wackernagel and Gulio Coggiola (Basel, 1904), p. 118. For the stay and activities of the Bosnian king in Hungary during 1435, see Emir O. Filipović, 'Boravak bosanskog kralja Tvrtka II Tvrtkovića u Beču tokom 1435. godine', *Radovi Filozofskog fakulteta (Historija, Historija umjetnosti, Arheologija)* 2 (2012), 229–45.
52 *DRH* 1: 418. English translation in: *The Laws of the Medieval Kingdom of Hungary 2: 1301–1457*, trans. and ed. János M. Bak, Pál Engel and James Ross Sweeney (Salt Lake City, 1992), p. 148. See Petar Rokai, 'Poslednje godine balkanske politike kralja Žigmunda (1435–37)', *Godišnjak Filozofskog fakulteta u Novom Sadu* 12 (1969), 89–109.
53 *VMSH* 1: 1591–92. For the dating of the letter, see Pejo Ćošković, *Bosanska Kraljevina u prijelomnim godinama 1443–46* (Banja Luka, 1988), p. 182.
54 Emir O. Filipović, '"Exurge igitur, miles Christi, et in barbaros viriliter pugna…": The Anti-Ottoman Activities of Bosnian King Stjepan Tomaš (1443–61)', in *Holy War in Late Medieval and Early Modern East-Central Europe*, ed. Janusz Smołucha, John Jefferson and Andrzej Wadas (Kraków, 2017), pp. 201–42.
55 *VMSM* 1, no. 565, p. 396. See *VMHH* 2: no. 427, p. 264. For the career of Thomas Tommasini, with particular attention given to his legation in Bosnia, see Stjepan Krasić, 'Toma Tomasini: Hvarski biskup, teolog i diplomat (1429–62.)', *Starine HAZU* 63 (2005), 91–162.

holy Catholic faith',[56] even praising him in 1445 for maintaining his kingdom 'pure and uncontaminated by heresy'.[57]

However, one of the key obstacles to the institutional affirmation of Catholicism in Bosnia was the strong and unwavering position of the Bosnian church. The king might have converted to the Roman faith, as did the majority of his nobles, but, in the eyes of the Holy See, most of his subjects were still heretics. Furthermore, Stephen Thomas did not want to disturb the frail political balance he managed to establish in the first couple of years of his reign. Therefore, soon after he had sorted out his relations with the curia in 1445, the king was accused of maintaining close ties with the heretics and their leaders. Stephen Thomas then had to defend himself to the pope, arguing that specific conditions had forced him to show courtesy to the heretics, and that he had only done so out of political necessity because they were numerous and powerful in his kingdom. He also assured the pontiff that he would make them accept Catholicism or leave his country when the suitable time arrived.[58] Similar news reached the pope in 1448 when he was informed that the king had strayed from the true path, and that his kingdom was still full of those who were 'infected with heresy', including some nobles who had initially converted but then returned to their fallacy for a second time.[59]

It seems that, rather than focusing on the internal problem of heresy, and with the Ottoman burden growing bigger by the day, the king and the nobility had far more pressing issues to think about, and were impatient to embark upon a crusade. In June 1450, the pope finally conferred upon Stephen Thomas and his army all the privileges that were usually given to crusaders fighting against heretics and infidels but, in the given circumstances, the letter remained just a hollow manifestation of support and was not followed by an armed conflict.[60] Obviously, the pope saw things somewhat differently and considered that the issue of the Bosnian Church had to be solved first before dealing with the external Turkish menace. However, conversion was not a quick or easy process since it would entail the disintegration of an established and centuries-old ecclesiastical system which was deeply embedded in Bosnian society. This is why there are so many confusing and contradictory reports on its development. One of these accounts is that sent by the bishop of Hvar to John of Capestrano in 1451, which claims that King Stephen Thomas and the greater part of his kingdom had accepted Catholicism, that the king supported the Franciscans in their work, that he had already built several monasteries, and that the heretics were disappearing

---

56 *VMHH* 2, no. 395, p. 237.
57 *VMSM* 1, no. 555, p. 388.
58 Daniele Farlati, *Illyricum Sacrum IV* (Venetiis, 1769), p. 257.
59 Giuseppe Simone Assemani, *Kalendaria Ecclesiae Universae V* (Romae, 1755), p. 84.
60 *VMHH* 2, no. 417, p. 255.

before the Franciscans like 'wax before the flame'.[61] Completely contradicting him, however, is the testimony of a Dominican friar who met with the Bosnian king shortly before the siege of Belgrade in 1456. According to his letter, sent to Cardinal Juan Carvajal, King Stephen Thomas was ready to act upon the pope's wishes, but needed assistance because the 'Manicheans', who made up a great deal of his kingdom, preferred the Turks to the Christians.[62]

This negative assessment was soon replaced by naïve enthusiasm following the wave of optimism after the victory in Belgrade.[63] The deaths of a number of established crusaders, who all died by the end of 1456, confirmed Stephen Thomas as one of the senior figures in the region able to assume leadership of the crusade. In March 1457, Stephen Thomas dispatched his messengers to Rome asking for the crusading flag against the Turks. The request was promptly granted, and he was exhorted to endure in his 'noble, pious and holy intention'.[64] Cardinal Carvajal was instructed to travel to Bosnia, where he would negotiate with the king about the upcoming war, as well as to do all that was necessary for the campaign to succeed. The king received the cardinal and expressed his eagerness to commence the battle.[65] Following the meeting, Stephen Thomas also attempted to gather broader international assistance, so he issued a letter of credence to his messenger, who was supposed to visit the pope and other rulers of the West in order to encourage them to support the Bosnian war against the Turks.[66] The messenger managed to reach Venice, Milan and Rome, but no traces of his missions to Naples and Burgundy survive, even though both were on his itinerary.

In June 1457, Pope Callixtus III wrote to Cardinal Carvajal, notifying him that the messengers of King Stephen Thomas had credibly presented his case at the curia. They had apparently convinced the pope that the king was steadfast in his resolution to proceed against the Turks, and that he even ceased to pay the customary tribute to the Ottoman sultan, asking for the sign of the cross and the apostolic flag which would legitimate his campaign. Nevertheless, in order to be fully assured of the king's good will, the pope urged Carvajal to consider

---

61 *Annales Minorum seu Trium Ordinum a sancto Francisco institutorum*, ed. Luca Wadding, 19 vols (Romae, 1731–45), 12: no. 53, p. 112: [...] *evanscunt haeretici sicut cera a facie ignis* [...].
62 Lajos Thallóczy, *Studien zur Geschichte Bosniens und Serbiens im Mittelalter* (München, 1914), pp. 415–16.
63 On the siege of Belgrade, see Kenneth M. Setton, *The Papacy and the Levant (1204–1571)*, 4 vols (Philadelphia, 1976–84), 2: 161–95; Norman Housley, 'Giovanni da Capistrano and the Crusade of 1456', in *Crusading in the Fifteenth Century: Message and Impact*, ed. Norman Housley (New York, 2004), pp. 94–115.
64 *VMHH* 2, no. 456, p. 291.
65 Vilmos Fraknói, 'Kardinal Carvajal u Bosni 1457', *Glasnik Zemaljskog muzeja* 1 (1890), 9–12; Fraknói, 'Carvajal János bíbornok Magyarországi követségei: 1448–1461', *Értekezések a Történeti Tudományok köréből* 14 (1889), 3–88.
66 Thallóczy, *Studien zur Geschichte Bosniens und Serbiens im Mittelalter*, p. 413. See also Neven Isailović, 'Akreditivno pismo kralja Stefana Tomaša za poslanika Nikolu Testu', *Stari srpski arhiv* 7 (2008), 175–86.

the resources at his disposal, and, if Stephen Thomas's devotion and faith proved to be true, the cardinal could grant him the requested symbols.[67] The Bosnian king justified the trust invested in him and, a month later, the pope wrote to the Venetian doge, advising him to join the crusade and to transfer the money collected for crusade in Dalmatia to the king of Bosnia for his campaign.[68] The pope also commanded the Franciscan Mariano from Siena to preach the crusade in Hungary, Bosnia and Serbia, to collect tithes for the crusade in those parts, and to consign all collected money to the Bosnian king. The enthusiastic pope soon wrote to Stephen Thomas about his decision to grant him these funds, lauding his decision to march against the Turks the following September, and exhorting him with the words: 'Rise up, Knight of Christ, and bravely fight the barbarians, whose slaughter will bring you, with God's will, glorious victory….'[69]

Even though Stephen Thomas was expected to lead a full-scale crusade against the Ottomans, by the beginning of September the Bosnian king had undertaken no military action, and it seems that the main cause of his inaction was primarily a lack of finances. By the beginning of August, news had reached Italy about an Ottoman attack on Albania and, in order to offset the damage incurred in those parts, Pope Callixtus III had rearranged the funds collected for the crusades, dividing it into three parts; one for the Hungarian king, the other for Gjergj Kastrioti, known as Skanderbeg, in Albania, and the third for the king of Bosnia.[70] This had a profound impact on the preparations of the Bosnian army because the king did not receive the money which had previously been promised to him, not even a third of it. Consequently, he sent a messenger to Venice in September to enquire about the collected tithes but received only a typically blunt answer that the funds taken from Venetian subjects on the account of the crusade would be used exclusively for the arming of a future fleet.[71]

Evidently disappointed by these developments, the crusading ambitions of the Bosnian king came tumbling down, and as soon as April 1458 Stephen Thomas, 'not being able to carry such a fury on his back', as one contemporary account puts it, made peace with the Turks and paid the required tribute.[72] He died in 1461 and, two years later, his son Stephen Tomašević, the last king of Bosnia, was beheaded on the orders of Sultan Mehmed II, an event which had huge repercussions and the results of which are still relevant today.[73]

---

67 *VMHH* 2, no. 464, pp. 296–97.
68 *VMHH* 2, no. 465, p. 297.
69 *VMHH* 2, no. 468, pp. 298–99.
70 *VMSM* 1, no. 604, p. 427. See *VMHH* 2, no. 473, p. 304.
71 *Listine o odnošajih izmedju južnoga Slavenstva i Mletačke republike*, ed. Šime Ljubić, 10 vols (Zagreb, 1868–91), 10: no. 117, p. 114.
72 *MHSM* 2: 115: *Re de Bossina ha fatto et confermato lo pace con el Turchc, dandoli el tributo ordenato, per non poter far altro et per non haver tanta furia ale spale.*
73 See Emir O. Filipović, 'Historiografija o padu Bosanskog kraljevstva', in *Stjepan Tomašević (1461–63.) — slom srednjovjekovnoga Bosanskog Kraljevstva*, ed. Ante Birin (Zagreb, 2013), pp. 11–28.

Concluding Remarks

By juxtaposing comparable sources from two different periods of Bosnian history I have tried to demonstrate how events from the mid-thirteenth century might have had a direct impact on the anti-Ottoman crusading of the 1400s. The overriding and enduring perception of Bosnian Christians as irreversible heretics, which persisted well into the late Middle Ages, was forged in the heat of the military campaigns waged by Hungarian nobles and prelates in the name of holy war throughout the first half of the thirteenth century. Irrespective of whether their motives were primarily political in nature, they nevertheless sought to legitimise their actions and to sanctify them by employing the sentiment, terminology, and symbols of crusade. As a result, Bosnia gained an explicitly negative reputation in the Catholic West and its inhabitants were given various and numerous derogatory names, such as: 'infidels', 'schismatics', 'Manicheans', 'Patarenes', 'enemies of the Cross of Christ', etc. This excluded the Bosnians ideologically and pushed them further away from the Roman Church, almost permanently alienating Bosnia from Latin Christianity in the process.

The specific physical features of Bosnia, the inhospitable and rugged terrain, along with its geographic location on the very outskirts of both Catholicism and Orthodoxy, allowed the rulers and inhabitants of that land to develop their religious and ecclesiastical policy independently of foreign influence. In this, they were helped by the fact that, for most of the fourteenth and beginning of the fifteenth century, the papacy was faced with problems of its own. The situation changed drastically by the mid-1400s when Bosnia was again brought back into the focus of Western powers because of the perceived threat posed by the advancing Ottoman armies, not only to Bosnia but also to Christianity in general. The resurgent papacy reactivated its interest in Bosnian affairs and attempted to perform a turnaround in the traditional modes of ecclesiastical communication. On the other side they found a cooperative ruler and elite who were enticed to convert to Catholicism by promises of concrete military and financial support in their struggle against the Ottoman Turks. However, the stumbling block in these seemingly positive initial steps were the Bosnian Christians, who rejected the new religious and political course of the country's leadership. Attempts to convert them to Catholicism and turn them into crusaders merely increased tensions, disrupting the internal cohesion of Bosnian society and further weakening the defensive capabilities of the kingdom.

The papal insistence on prioritising the fight against the heretics over the fight against the Turks, and a general lack of understanding of the specific and precarious position that Bosnia was in at the time, made it extremely difficult for the Bosnian king to direct his focus onto the Ottoman wars. He did his best to employ *antemurale* rhetoric by framing his messages in crusading vocabulary and trying to convince the Christian centre of his perilous position on the periphery, but he received very little in return. On the frontline, the king of Bosnia needed money, soldiers and weapons, not blessings, indulgences and apostolic flags.

The crusading paraphernalia, although important, was obviously not motivation enough for the recent converts. The label and stain of heresy that had been attached to them during the crusades of the thirteenth century, and reaffirmed subsequently, proved to be a crucial impediment in any dealings they might have had with the papacy, meaning that the misunderstanding and mistrust between the two sides was far too great to guarantee any realistic success. And while the Bosnians waited in vain for the promised external assistance and the launching of a crusade, the tangible Ottoman danger kept growing relentlessly, eventually destroying both the Bosnian kingdom and the Bosnian Church.

RIMVYDAS PETRAUSKAS

Ziel oder Ausgangsort?

Das Großfürstentum Litauen als verlängerter Arm der Kreuzzugsbewegung vom Ende des 14. bis zum Beginn des 16. Jahrhunderts

Im Jahre 1484 hat der Hauptmann von Samogitien Jonas Kęsgailaitis in einem Brief an den Hochmeister des Deutschen Ordens seine Bereitschaft geäußert, an dem vom Hochmeister organisierten Kriegszug gegen die „Heidenschaft" persönlich teilzunehmen, da *dy kristenheit leider genuck gswecht wirt und man sy nicht forder dorften swechen*.[1] Diese Angelegenheit, zu deren Kontext die mehrmals angestrebte aber nie verwirklichte Durchführung eines gesamtabendländischen Kreuzzugs gegen die Türken gehörte,[2] veranschaulicht eine Entwicklung, die im späten 15. Jahrhundert bereits seit einigen Jahrzehnten angedauert hatte. Samogitien — eine westliche Region des Großfürstentums Litauen und das letzte heidnische Land Europas, das erst 1417 endgültig christianisiert wurde[3] — sah sich nach einem halben Jahrhundert im Kreise der christlichen Völker gezwungen, in die Phalanx der Vertreter des rechten Glaubens einzureihen. Die Zeiten haben sich geändert, die Söhne und Enkel der heidnischen litauischen Adligen (der Vater des erwähnten Hauptmanns wurde noch zweifelsohne als Heide geboren)[4] haben ihre Herkunft verdrängt und sich zum christlichen Rittertum bekannt. Dieses einleitend gewählte Beispiel führt gleich zu unserem Thema: Litauen als Ziel- und Ausgangsort der Kreuzzugsbewegung.

Zum Ziel der Kreuzzüge wurde Litauen selbst in der ersten Hälfte des 13. Jahrhunderts. Allerdings wurde das von den christlichen Herrschaftsmittelpunkten im Ostbaltikum entfernte Land lange Zeit in päpstlichen Bullen explizit nicht

---

1 GStA PK, XX. HA, OBA 17114.
2 Über die Kreuzzüge des 15. Jahrhunderts: *Crusading in the Fifteenth Century: Message and Impact*, hg. v. Norman Housley (Basingstoke, 2004); *Reconfiguring the Fifteenth-Century Crusade*, hg. v. Norman Housley (Basingstoke, 2016); *The Crusade in the Fifteenth Century: Converging and Competing Cultures*, hg. v. Housley (London, 2017).
3 Vgl. Darius Baronas and Stephen C. Rowell, *The Conversion of Lithuania: From Pagan Barbarians to Late Medieval Christians* (Vilnius, 2015).
4 Zum litauischen Hochadel vgl. Rimvydas Petrauskas, *Lietuvos diduomenė XIV a. pabaigoje–XV a.: sudėtis — struktūra — valdžia* (Vilnius, 2003); Rimvydas Petrauskas, 'Lithuanian Nobility in the Late-Fourteenth and Fifteenth Centuries: Composition and Structure', *LHS* 7 (2002), 1–22.

erwähnt.[5] Nachdem der litauische Herrscher Mindaugas 1251 den christlichen Glauben angenommen hatte, hat Papst Innozenz IV. ihm und seinem Land den Schutz des Heiligen Stuhles zugesichert und umgekehrt zu weiteren kriegerischen Handlungen gegen die Heiden angeregt.[6] Wie in manchen anderen Fällen durfte somit ein neues christliches Königtum (die Krönung von Mindaugas erfolgte im Jahre 1253) die politische Expansion mit dem Argument der Erweiterung des Christentums bekräftigen; dieselbe Situation werden wir in Litauen noch einmal nach anderthalb Jahrhunderten wiederfinden. Wie auch die Tatsache, dass die Grenze zwischen dem Ziel- und Ausgangsort sehr nahe liegen und sich sehr schnell verschieben konnte.

Das christliche Königtum hat in Litauen nur wenige Jahre existiert, Mindaugas und seine direkten Nachkommen fielen einer Verschwörung zum Opfer (1263), die politische Elite wurde für längere Jahre wiederum heidnisch. Erst jetzt, beinahe einhundert Jahre nach dem ersten Kreuzzugzug im östlichen Baltikum und siebzehn Jahre nach der oben zitierten Bulle Innozenz' IV., hat Papst Klemens IV. 1268 Litauen zum Ziel eines Kreuzzuges erklärt. In einem Schreiben an Ottokar II. Premislaus hat der Papst den böhmischen König beauftragt, den litauischen Königsstuhl wiederherzustellen, wie es zur Zeit des „Königs Mindaugas seligen Gedächtnisses" (*clare memorie Mindota*) gewesen war.[7]

Diese Bulle fand keine Fortsetzung. Im 14. Jahrhundert haben die Päpste mit geringen Ausnahmen nicht mehr Ablässe für die Teilnahme an den Kreuzzügen ins Ostbaltikum verkündet. Vielmehr war es der Deutsche Orden selbst, der nun Ablässe für den Heidenkrieg ausstellte. Es gibt Belege dafür, dass vor und nach einer Preußenreise in den Rekrutierungsgebieten Ablässe schriftlich ausgeteilt wurden.[8] Dem Orden ist es auf jeden Fall auch ohne direkte päpstliche Kreuzzugsmandate gelungen, die Heidenfahrt nach Litauen als den Kampf *pro fidei protectio et defensione* darzustellen und damit breite Resonanz im Abendland zu erreichen. Während des 14. Jahrhunderts avancierte Litauen von einem fast unbekannten Land an der europäischen Peripherie zu einer wichtigen Bühne des abendländischen Adels, als die „Preußen- bzw. Litauerreisen" zu einem wesentlichen Element

---

5 Zu den Anfängen und dem Verlauf der Kreuzzüge im Ostbaltikum siehe Eric Christiansen, *The Northern Crusades: The Baltic and the Catholic Frontier, 1100–1525* (Minneapolis, 1980); *Crusade and Conversion on the Baltic Frontier, 1150–1500*, hg. v. Alan V. Murray (Aldershot, 2001); *The North-Eastern Frontiers of Medieval Europe: The Expansion of Latin Christendom in the Baltic Lands*, hg. v. Murray (Farnham, 2014); Edvardas Gudavičius, *Kryžiaus karai Pabaltijyje ir Lietuva XIII amžiuje* (Vilnius, 1989); Iben Fonnesberg-Schmidt, *The Popes and the Baltic Crusades, 1147–1254* (Leiden, 2007).
6 Schreiben des Papstes Innozenz IV. an Mindaugas vom 17. Juli 1251, *VMPL* 1, Nr. 102, S. 49. Zu Mindaugas vgl. Edvardas Gudavičius, *Mindaugas* (Vilnius, 1998).
7 *VMPL* 1, Nr. 152, S. 79.
8 Axel Ehlers, *Die Ablaßpraxis des Deutschen Ordens im Mittelalter* (Marburg, 2007), S. 64, 72–75; Werner Paravicini, 'Prasmingas švaistymas: žygiai į Prūsiją ir Lietuvą Pierre Bourdieu kapitalų teorijos požiūriu', *Lietuvos istorijos studijos* 26 (2010), 9–21.

adliger Kultur in ganz Europa wurden.[9] Diese Fahrten haben die Ziele und die Art der Kriegsführung im Ostbaltikum nachhaltig verändert. Sowohl im Deutschordensstaat als auch im Großfürstentum Litauen bildeten sich neue Formen der Kriegsideologie wie auch -ökonomie heraus. Die Leitung des Ordens vermochte es, eine gut funktionierende Wirtschaftsbürokratie zu entwickeln, von der die Organisation und finanzielle Durchführung der Heidenfahrten entschieden profitierte. Aber auch die litauischen Großfürsten haben politische und ökonomische Lösungen gefunden, indem sie die Kriegswirtschaft mit der territorialen Ausdehnung nach Osten zu verbinden verstanden.[10]

Trotz des tradierten Bildes eines ständigen Krieges zwischen den Christen und Heiden Ostbaltikum können wir in den spärlichen Quellen doch ziemlich deutlich erkennen, wie die herrschende Elite Litauens sich durch eine schrittweise Adaption der ritterlichen Kultur Westeuropas in ihren Bräuchen wie auch ihrer Ethik sowohl im Krieg als auch im Frieden mehr und mehr den Deutschrittern und ihren adeligen Unterstützern aus den verschiedenen Teilen des Abendlandes anglich. All dies schuf neue komunikative Kriegs- und Friedensformen, deren Ziel darin bestand, ein System von Regeln zu bilden, die beide Seiten verpflichten sollten: der ritterliche Kampf, der Umgang mit Gefangenen, das Abschließen von Waffenstillständen und Friedensverträgen, Handelsbedingungen usw. Dieser kriegsbedingte Kulturaustausch veränderte insbesondere die litauische Oberschicht, die immer mehr Elemente der ritterlich–höfischen Kultur des Westens übernahm.[11] Die in der Epoche des Krieges stattgefundenen Wandlungen im Bewusstsein der litauischen Aristokratie spiegeln sich in ihren adligen Zeichen wider: Am Ende des 14. Jahrhunderts enthielten sowohl das Wappen des Großfürsten Kęstutis, als auch die der litauischen Adligen die Stilistik westlicher ritterlicher Heraldik. Ein gutes Beispiel dieser schrittweisen Angleichung der ritterlich-christlichen Sitten und Bräuche bietet uns ein Gesuch des in Podolien regierenden litauischen Fürsten Alexander Karijotid, eines Vetters des Großfürsten Jogaila und Mitglieds des mächtigen Gediminidengeschlechts. Nachdem er dem ungarischen König Ludwig von Anjou einen Lehnseid geleistet hatte, bat Alexander Ende des Jahres 1377 Papst Gregor XI., ihm eine Absolution *in mortis articulo* zu erteilen, da er *contra perfidos Tartaros* aufbrechen wolle — es handelte sich hierbei wohl um die erste Initiative dieser Art bei den litauischen Fürsten.[12]

Die Personalunion zwischen Polen und Litauen 1385–86 unter dem Gediminiden Jogaila (fortan als polnischer König auch unter dem Namen Władysław II.

---

9 Grundlegend: Werner Paravicini, *Die Preussenreisen des europäischen Adels*, 4 Bde. (Sigmaringen, 1989–2023).
10 Stephen C. Rowell, *Lithuania Ascending: A Pagan Empire within East-Central Europe, 1295–1345* (Cambridge, 1994).
11 Rimvydas Petrauskas, 'Litauen und der Deutsche Orden: Vom Feind zum Verbündeten', in *Tannenberg — Grunwald — Žalgiris 1410: Krieg und Frieden im späten Mittelalter*, hg. v. Werner Paravicini, Petrauskas und Grischa Vercamer (Wiesbaden, 2012), S. 237–51.
12 Schreiben des Papstes Gregors XI. vom 30. Januar 1378 an *nobili viro Alexandro de Litwania domino de Camnicz Ruscie*, VMPL 1, Nr. 1015, S. 748–49.

Jagiełło bekannt) und die darauffolgende Christianisierung Litauens Ende des 14. Jahrhunderts markieren rückwärts betrachtet eine folgenträchtige Wende in der Geschichte der ganzen Region. Der offizielle Übertritt der Litauer zum Christentum lateinischer Prägung hinderte allerdings den Deutschen Orden nicht daran, eine Zeit lang weiterhin den Heidenkrieg im Abendland zu propagieren, um neue Feldzüge gegen die vermeintlich immer noch heidnischen Litauer durchführen und sich nach außen wie nach innen als *fredeschilt cristen geloubens* darstellen zu können.[13] Ungeachtet dieser offen gegen die Litauer gerichteten Diplomatie des Ordens und seiner exkludierenden Rhetorik lassen sich zur gleichen Zeit jedoch auch Anstrengungen der Deutschritter feststellen, die das Eingehen friedlicher Beziehungen mit den litauischen Herrschern zum Ziel hatten. Zwar beklagte der Hochmeister des Deutschen Ordens Konrad von Jungingen[14] noch in seinen Briefen von 1395 und 1397 an den Pfalzgrafen bei Rhein und den skandinavischen Unionskönig Erich VII. offen das Bündnis der livländischen Bischöfe mit den Litauern und den Völkern der Rus,[15] ein Jahr später (1398) aber schloss derselbe Hochmeister in Salinwerder einen „ewigen Frieden" mit dem litauischen Großfürsten Witold.[16] In dieser Form der „ewigen" Vereinbarung, die für die Beziehungen zwischen Litauen und Orden neu war, verpflichteten sich beide Seiten *in allen unsern landin und luten, das wir breiten wellen den cristenthum noch unserm vermoegen und czu thuen der heiligen Romischen Kirchen und dem Romischen Riche, was andere cristene frie konige und frie fursten pflichtig sin czu thun.*[17]

Dass eine solche Formulierung keine rhetorische Floskel war, erwies sich schon im nächsten Jahr, als eine von dem Ordensgebietiger Marquard von Salzbach, einem „persönlichen Freund" Witolds, angeführte Schar von Ordensrittern den Großfürsten in dessen unglücklichen, mit der Niederlage an der Worskla (August 1399) endenden Kreuzzug gegen die Tataren unterstützte. Witold, der zwei insgesamt fast fünf Jahre dauernde Aufenthalte im Deutschordensland hinter sich hatte und bestens mit der Rhetorik und Organisation der Heidenfahrten vertraut war, versuchte geschickt die Abwehr gegen die Tataren mit

---

13 Karl Heinl, *Fürst Witold von Litauen in seinem Verhältnis zum Deutschen Orden in Preußen während der Zeit seines Kampfes um sein litauisches Erbe 1382–1401* (Berlin, 1925); Harro Gersdorf, *Der Deutsche Orden im Zeitalter der polnisch-litauischen Union: Die Amtszeit des Hochmeisters Konrad Zöllner von Rotenstein (1382–90)* (Marburg, 1957). Zum Deutschen Orden als Pionier der Bollwerksrhetorik siehe Paul Srodecki, *Antemurale Christianitatis: Zur Genese der Bollwerksrhetorik im östlichen Mitteleuropa an der Schwelle vom Mittelalter zur Frühen Neuzeit* (Husum, 2015), S. 62–72, 105–18.

14 Kürzlich ausführlich hierzu: Sebastian Kubon, *Die Außenpolitik des Deutschen Ordens unter Hochmeister Konrad von Jungingen (1393–1407)* (Göttingen, 2016).

15 Srodecki, *Antemurale Christianitatis*, S. 69–70.

16 Klaus Neitmann, 'Vom „ewigen Frieden": Die Kunst des Friedensschlusses zwischen dem Deutschen Orden und Polen-Litauen 1398–1435', in *Tannenberg — Grunwald — Žalgiris 1410: Krieg und Frieden im späten Mittelalter*, hg. v. Werner Paravicini, Rimvydas Petrauskas und Grischa Vercamer (Wiesbaden, 2012), S. 201–9. Vgl. auch Neitmann, *Die Staatsverträge des Deutschen Ordens in Preußen 1230–1449* (Köln, 1986).

17 Vertrag von Salinwerder (12.10.1398), *SVDOP* 1: 10–12.

der heilgeschichtlich-repräsentativen Haltung eines christlichen Herrschers zu vereinbaren. Seit 1397 organisierte er mehrere Kriegszüge gegen die Tataren Richtung Schwarzes Meer, die in einem „wirklichen" Kreuzzug größeren Umfangs gipfeln sollten.[18] Dank der Vermittlung der polnischen Gesandten hat Papst Bonifatius IX. im Mai 1399 allen Christen, die nach Polen und Litauen kommen und den Kampf gegen die heidnischen Türken und Tataren aufnehmen würden, einen Kreuzzugsablass gewährt.[19] Obwohl dieses Schreiben, wie Stephen C. Rowell bereits in einer früheren Studie gezeigt hat, zu spät verabschiedet worden war und den Gang des Kriegsunternehmens nicht hätte beeinflussen können, verdeutlicht diese Geschichte doch die Absicht von Witold und Jogaila, sich der herkömmlichen Praktiken des Heidenkrieges zu bedienen. Sie folgten dabei der Aufforderung des Papstes Urban VI., der in seinen Briefen an den „christlichsten Fürsten" (*princeps christianissimus*) Jogaila im Jahre 1388 nicht nur zur Annahme des christlichen Glaubens gratulierte[20], sondern letzteren auch zum gemeinsamen Kampf gegen Türken und Tataren ermahnte.[21]

Trotz der Niederlage von 1399 hat Witold eine Zeit lang weiterhin die Pläne neuer Tatarenfahrten geschmiedet. Noch im selben Jahr hat er mit dem Hochmeister über den nächsten Zug gegen die Goldene Horde verhandelt.[22] Letztere Waffenbruderschaft sollte in Analogie zu einer anderen gemeinsamen militärischen Aktion des Deutschen Ordens und des Großfürstentums Litauen stehen, nämlich des tatsächlich durchgeführten Feldzugs in das gegen den Deutschen Orden rebellierende Samogitien, welches sich erst seit wenigen Jahren unter der Ordensherrschaft befand.[23] In seinem Brief an Witold lobte der Hochmeister die rege Teilnahme an dem Unternehmen gegen die Samogiten, schrieb in diesem Zusammenhang von *vil erbar geste*, die zu der Heidenreise erschienen seien, darunter unter anderem die Herzöge von Geldern und Lothringen.[24] Um die Wende vom 14. zum 15. Jahrhundert befanden sich die litauischen Länder also in einer merkwürdigen Situation — zum einen als Ziel und zum anderen als Ausgangsort der „Heidenfahrten".

Allerdings änderten sich die Politik und die Prioritäten von Witold so rasch, dass immer wieder neue Kriegsziele beziehungsweise Kriegsgegner ausgerufen wurden. Mit den Tataren hat der Großfürst ziemlich schnell einen *modus vivendi* gefunden. So wußte der Komtur von Dünaburg 1419 seinem Vorgesetzten zu berichten, dass Witold einen Frieden mit dem „tatarischen Kaiser" geschlossen

---

18 Dazu Stephen C. Rowell, 'Naujieji kryžiaus žygiuotojai: LDK ir Bizantijos santykiai XIV–XV a. sandūroje: Ar Vytautas Didysis buvo Lietuvos kryžiaus žygių prieš turkus bei totorius pradininkas?', in *Kryžiaus karų epocha Baltijos regiono tautų istorinėje savimonėje*, hg. v. Rita Regina Trimonienė und Robertas Jurgaitis (Šiauliai, 2007), S. 181–205.
19 VMPL 1, Nr. 1041, S. 769.
20 CDECDV 1: 24.
21 CESDQ 2: 17–19.
22 CEV, S. 60.
23 CDPr 6: 98–99. Vgl. Kubon, *Die Außenpolitik des Deutschen Ordens*, S. 124–32.
24 CEV, S. 64–65.

habe, der ihm einen „ganz freundlichen Brief samt einem sehr großen Tier, genannt Dromedar", geschickt habe.[25] Der litauische Herrscher griff dabei zunehmend auf die im Westen bereits seit Jahrhunderten erprobte Taktik zurück, für seine politischen Ziele nicht die Kreuzzüge an sich, sondern eher ein aus der Tradition der Kreuzzüge entliehenes organisatorisches Muster „des Zuges gegen die Ungläubigen" mit allen dazugehörenden Begrifflichkeiten und rhetorischen Floskeln einzusetzen. So benachrichtigte Witold im Jahre 1406 den Ordensmarschall über *die Gäste*, die mit ihm in die ruthenischen Länder *reisen* wollten.[26] Unter ihnen waren mit Sicherheit auch zwei Herolde aus Holland und Burgund, deren Zwischenstopp in Marienburg im Treßlerbuch des Ordens notiert worden war.[27] Im Jahre 1426 wandte sich der Großfürst *umb ritterschafft adir umbe andir sachin wellen* an den livländischen Meister mit der Bitte, allen willigen *ritter[n] und knechte[n]* aus Livland die Beteiligung an einem Feldzug gegen Pleskau zu genehmigen.[28] Dass zu diesen Fahrten auch die Ritter aus ferneren Ländern dazu stoßen konnten, zeigt das Beispiel des deutschen Adligen Friedrichs von Flersheim, der im Juli von 1428 im von Witold veranstalten Kriegszug gegen Nowgorod teilnahm und danach zutiefst sein Bedauern kundtat, andere Verpflichtungen hätten ihn an einer Weiterfahrt zum Lucker Monarchen-Treffen im Januar 1429 gehindert.[29] Es ist leider aus den Quellen nicht ersichtlich, ob mit diesen Ereignissen auch die Ankunft des weitgereisten und durch die ritterlichen Interessen bekannten Herzogs von Liegnitz und Brieg Ludwig II. verbunden war, der auch im selben Jahr den großfürstlichen Hof besuchte.[30]

Ein anderes Feld der Anwendung der Kreuzzugsrhetorik war mit dem Wettkampf um eine Deutungshoheit verbunden. Bald nach der Schlacht bei Tannenberg (15. Juli 1410) lud der römische König Sigismund von Luxemburg die christlichen Herrscher und Ritter ein, dem Deutschen Orden, den er als „Verteidigungsschild" (*clipeus defensionis*) gegen die heidnischen Litauer und Samogiten bezeichnete, zur Hilfe zu eilen.[31] Kurz danach (1412) gab jedoch Sigismund den Kurfürsten bekannt, dass die polnischen und litauischen Herrscher ihm die Unterstützung gegen die Türken zugesagt hätten. Im gleichen Jahr hat *Allexander alias Witowdus* in einem Brief an den am 28. Juni 1412 zum König von Aragon

---

25 *CEV*, S. 443.
26 GStA PK, XX. HA, OBA 962.
27 Hartmut Boockmann, 'Alltag am Hof des Deutschordens-Hochmeisters in Preußen', in *Alltag bei Hofe: 3. Symposion der Residenzen-Kommission der Akademie der Wissenschaften in Göttingen vom 28. Februar bis 1. März 1992 in Ansbach*, hg. v. Werner Paravicini (Sigmaringen, 1995), S. 137–48.
28 *CEV*, S. 732.
29 *Die Flersheimer Chronik*, hg. v. Otto Waltz (Leipzig, 1874), S. 20, 30.
30 Eine im Oktober 1429 im Namen Witolds ausgestellte Urkunde führt Herzog Ludwig II. an erster Stelle in der Zeugenliste, *Vitoldiana: Codex privilegiorum Vitoldi magni ducis Lithuaniae 1386–1430*, hg. v. Jerzy Ochmański (Warszawa, 1986), S. 102. Zu Ludwig II. von Liegnitz und Brieg siehe Werner Paravicini, 'Von Schlesien nach Frankreich, England, Spanien und zurück: Über die Ausbreitung adliger Kultur im späten Mittelalter', in *Adel in Schlesien: Herrschaft — Kultur — Selbstdarstellung*, hg. v. Jan Harasimowicz und Matthias Weber, 2 Bde. (München, 2010), 1: 150–71.
31 *SRP* 3: 403. Vgl. auch seinen Brief aus dem Jahre 1412: *Lites* 2/2: 33–34.

ausgerufenen Ferdinand dasselbe Motiv angewandt, die der Orden lange Zeit für sich beanspruchte (Außengrenze der *christianitas*), indem er auf die Gemeinsamkeit zweier sich an der Peripherie der christlichen Welt befindenden Länder (also Litauen und Kastilien) im Kampf gegen *hostem sancte fidei* anspielte.[32]

Obwohl Witold nach 1399 keine Feldzüge mehr gegen die Tataren und schon gar nicht gegen die Osmanen durchführte, ist es ihm ganz offensichtlich gelungen, das feste Renommee eines Bekämpfers der Ungläubigen zu erwerben. 1422 drückte der römische König Sigismund von Luxemburg seine Freude aus, dass Witold ihm Hilfe gegen die Hussiten und Türken versprochen habe, was der litauische Großfürst umgekehrt allerdings unmissverständlich an des Luxemburgers Zugeständnisse in der Angelegenheit des Deutschen Ordens knüpfte.[33] 1429 rühmte der Frühhumanist Franziskus de Comitibus Witold als einen waffenerprobten christlichen Fürsten, der nicht nur die Osmanen besiegen, sondern gar Jerusalem für die Christen zurückerobern könnte.[34] Einige Jahre später klagte der spanische Reisende Pero Tafur, dass „die Tataren insbesondere seit dem Tode Witolds, der in Litauen und der Rus geherrscht hat, umliegende christliche Völker verwüsten" würden.[35] Und schließlich erscheint in einem Entwurf der Krönungsurkunde, die 1430 in der Kanzlei von Sigismund von Luxemburg hergestellt wurde, Litauen gar als *clipeus contra gentiles insultus coadiutores*, was zugleich die argumentative Grundlage für die königliche Rangerhöhung von Witold darstellen sollte.[36]

---

32 Werner Paravicini, 'Fürschriften und Testimonia: Der Dokumentationskreislauf der spätmittelalterlichen Adelsreise am Beispiel des kastilischen Ritters Alfonso Mudarra 1411–1412', in *Studien zum 15. Jahrhundert: Festschrift für Erich Meuthen*, hg. v. Johannes Helmrath und Heribert Müller, 2 Bde. (München, 1994), 2: 903–26 (hier 925).
33 CEV, S. 573 (der Brief von Sigismund an den Hochmeister vom 1. Oktober 1422: Gesandtschaft von Jogaila und Witold). Vgl. auch den Brief des Großfürsten aus dem Jahre 1428 an den Hochmeister, in dem er bedauernd über die Niederlage Sigismunds gegen die Türken bei Belgrad berichtet (S. 800). Dazu auch Rowell, 'Naujieji kryžiaus žygiuotojai', S. 200.
34 CEV, Nr. 1411, 881: *posse Theucros superare, sed Jerusolimam sanctam, diu exigentibus nostris demeritis et peccatis in infidelium manibus devolutam, recuperari posse*.
35 Pero Tafur, *Странствия и путешествия*, hg. v. Masiel' Sančes Lev Karlosovič (Moskva, 2006). Zum Autor: Mike Burkhardt, 'Fremde im spätmittelalterlichen Deutschland — Die Reiseberichte eines unbekannten Russen, des Kastiliers Pero Tafur und des Venezianers Andrea de Franceschi im Vergleich', *Concilium Medii Aevi* 6 (2003), 239–90.
36 CESDQ 2: 246: *sed solum ut cristianorum in illis finibus clipeus contra gentiles insultus coadiutores persistatis*. Dasselbe Motiv wird auch in der Instruktion des römischen Königs an den Gesandten an den Hof Witolds wiederholt, wo Litauen zusammen mit Ungarn als *ianitor et clipeus* des Christentums bezeichnet werden (S. 250). Vgl. auch den Brief von Sigismund an den Herzog von Mailand von 1429, in dem der römische König behauptet, dass er die Krönungsidee von Witold nur zum Wohl und Schutz der Christen sowie zur Abschreckung vor den Ungläubigen und Heiden unterstützt (CEV, S. 876). Vgl. Rimvydas Petrauskas, 'Korona Witolda: niedoszła koronacja i jej późniejsza legenda historyczna', in *Tradycja — metody przekazywania i formy upamiętnienia w państwie polsko-litewskim, XV — pierwsza połowa XIX wieku*, hg. v. Urszula Augustyniak (Warszawa, 2011), S. 13–23; Přemysl Bar, 'Der „Krönungssturm": König Sigismund von Luxemburg, Großfürst Witold von Litauen und das gescheiterte politische Bündnis zwischen beiden Herrschern', *RH* 83 (2017), 65–101.

Somit wurde schrittweise das Bild von Litauen und seiner Großfürsten als einem festen Bestandteil des Kampfes gegen die Ungläubigen und demzufolge der Kreuzzugsbewegung verankert. Solche Vorstellungen finden wir zum Beispiel in einer fiktiven Episode des „Kaiser Sigismunds Buches" von Eberhard Windeck. Der deutsche Autor erzählt von einer Seeschlacht Švitrigailas, Witolds Nachfolgers auf dem großfürstlichen Thron, der mit Hilfe der Deutschordensritter an einem nicht näher genannten Ort in Ungarn die Türken verheerend geschlagen habe.[37] Zu dieser Zeit erscheinen in Frankreich und Burgund Ritterromane, deren Helden ihren Damen gegenüber Gelübde ablegen, sich im Gefolge des polnischen Königs und des litauischen Fürsten in das Preußenland aufzumachen, um dort gegen die Sarazenen zu kämpfen.[38] Zumindest in dieser fiktiven Welt des abendländischen Rittertums könnten litauische Fürsten und Adlige zu einem verlängerten Arm der Kreuzzugsbewegung gezählt werden.

Die historische Realität sah allerdings anders aus. Für eine litauische Beteiligung an der Kreuzzugsbewegung in der zweiten Hälfte des 15. Jahrhunderts gibt es nur sehr wenige tatsächliche Zeugnisse.[39] Ein Hauptgrund dafür war (neben einer relativ langen Friedenszeit ohne längere größere Konflikte) zweifelsohne das Fehlen des monarchischen Herrschaftsmittelpunktes in Wilna während der langen Regierungszeit Kasimirs des Jagiellonen, der in Personalunion auf den Thronen Polens und Litauens herrschte (1447–92).[40] Erst nach der für das Großfürstentum Litauen schmerzhaft empfundenen Verwüstung von Kiew durch die Tataren im Jahre 1480 hat Papst Sixtus IV. eine Kreuzzugsbulle gegen die Türken und ihre krimtatarischen Vasallen ausgestellt, deren Abschriften unter anderem an litauische Hochadlige, so beispielsweise an die Woiwoden von Wilna und Trakai Alekna Sudimantaitis und Martynas Goštautas sowie an die Bischöfe von Wilna und Kiew, gerichtet wurden.[41] Die polnisch-litauische Diplomatie hat in der päpstlichen Kurie immer wieder die „türkische Frage" mit der „tatarischen" verknüpft (so wurden zum Beispiel unter den Tataren, die 1480 Kiew geplündert

---

37 Eberhard Windecke, *Imperatoriaus Zigmanto knyga. XV a. Lietuvos valdovų portretai*, hg. v. Jūratė Kiaupienė und Rimvydas Petrauskas (Vilnius, 2015), S. 336–37 (mit Illustration). Dieses Sujet knüpft wohl an die Beziehungen zwischen Švitrigaila und Sigismund von Luxemburg nach dem Tod von Witold an, als der neue litauische Großfürst dem römischen König seine (*mit seiner eigen person*) Hilfe gegen „Türken und anderen Feinden" zugesichert hat (GStA PK, XX. HA, OBA 5542). Vgl. Sergei V. Polekhov, *Наследники Витовта. Династическая война в Великом Княжестве Литовском в 30-е годы XV века* (Moskva, 2015).
38 Erich Maschke, 'Burgund und der preussische Ordensstaat. Ein Beitrag zur Einheit der ritterlichen Kultur Europas im späten Mittelalter', in Maschke, *Domus Hospitalis Theutonicorum: Europäische Verbindungslinien der Deutschordensgeschichte. Gesammelte Aufsätze aus den Jahren 1931–63* (Bonn, 1970), S. 15–34 (hier 30–33).
39 Rita Regina Trimonienė, 'Kryžiaus žygių idėja XV a. II pusėje ir Lietuvos didžioji Kunigaikštystė', in *Kryžiaus karų epocha Baltijos regiono tautų istorinėje savimonėje*, hg. v. Trimonienė und Robertas Jurgaitis (Šiauliai, 2007), S. 223–34.
40 Historische Zusammenhänge: Robert Frost, *The Oxford History of Poland Lithuania, vol. 1: The Making of the Polish-Lithuanian Union, 1385–1569* (Oxford, 2015).
41 EFE 64: 52.

haben, auch türkische Truppen „entdeckt").[42] Deswegen erlaubte der Papst mehrmals den Polen und Litauern, einen Teil der Annaten für den Kampf gegen die Tataren beziehungsweise zum Wiederaufbau der zerstörten Städte und Kirchen zu benutzen.[43] Somit wurde die Auseinandersetzung mit den Tataren, die für Litauen viel aktueller war als der Kampf gegen geographisch weitentfernte Osmanen, auf die gleiche Ebene wie die Türkenkreuzzüge gesetzt.[44] Noch vielmehr als bei den Polen, war die Frage eines genuin gegen das Osmanische Reich gerichteten Feldzugs für die litauischen politischen Eliten eher zweitrangig. Das Großfürstentum Litauen hat nicht aktiv an der militärischen Unternehmung Kasimirs des Jagiellonen teilgenommen, die im Jahre 1485 die Unterstützung des moldauischen Woiwoden Stefans des Großen gegen die Türken zum Ziel hatte.[45] Die ausführliche und umfangreiche Beschreibung dieses Kriegszuges in der in den 1520er Jahren verfassten sogenannten „Litauischen Chronik" (auch als Chronik von Bychowiec bekannt), in der zugleich die Präsenz (in der Tat nur weniger) litauischer Truppen akzentuiert wird, könnte als ein Indiz dafür dienen, dass man die Ereignisse an der südlichen Grenze des Großfürstentums dennoch sehr aufmerksam beobachtete.[46] Abgesehen aber von diesen episodenhaften litauischen Überschneidungen mit der Kreuzzugsbewegung des 15. Jahrhunderts blieb das Großfürstentum Litauen insgesamt für mehrere Jahrzehnte im Schatten polnischer Diplomatie und erschien in der ziemlich ausgedehnten europäischen Kreuzzugskorrespondenz nur sehr selten als ein aktiver Akteur.[47]

Diese Situation änderte sich an der Wende vom 15. zum 16. Jahrhundert, als in Litauen zur Zeit Alexanders des Jagiellonen (Großfürst 1492–1506, seit 1501 auch König von Polen) ein großfürstlicher Hof erneuert wurde.[48] Litauen hat seine Politik auf der internationalen Ebene wesentlich ausgeweitet, was sich auch in der Sache des „Heidenkampfes" widerspiegelte.[49] So weilte beispielsweise im Jahre 1496 in Wilna ein Gesandter des georgischen Königs Konstantin II. von Kartlien, der auf der Suche nach Unterstützung gegen die Osmanen sich auf einer Reise bis nach Spanien befand. Dass es ihm gelang, am litauischen Hof Gehör zu finden, zeigt eine im litauischen Kanzleiarchiv überlieferte ruthenische

---

42 Stephen C. Rowell, 'War and Piety in the Grand Duchy of Lithuania in the Later Middle Ages', RL 2 (2016), 7–21 (hier 17–18).
43 Rowell, 'War and Piety', S. 16–17.
44 Krzysztof Baczkowski, 'Argument obrony wiary w służbie dyplomacji polskiej w XV wieku', in Baczkowski, Polska i jej sąsiedzi za Jagiellonów (Kraków, 2012), S. 171–92.
45 Dazu: Krzysztof Baczkowski, 'Państwa Europy Środkowo-Wschodniej wobec antytureckich projektów Innocentego VIII (1484–92)', in Baczkowski, Polska i jej sąsiedzi za Jagiellonów, S. 265–94.
46 Lietuvos metraštis: Bychovco kronika, hg. v. Rimantas Jasas (Vilnius, 1971), S. 146. Vgl. Trimonienė, 'Kryžiaus žygių idėja', S. 226–27.
47 Ausführlich: Srodecki, Antemurale Christianitatis, S. 217–44.
48 Rimvydas Petrauskas, 'The Court of Alexander Jagiellon and His Account Books', in Lietuvos didžiojo kunigaikščio Aleksandro Jogailaičio dvaro sąskaitų knygos (1494–1504), hg. v. Darius Antanavičius und Rimvydas Petrauskas (Vilnius, 2007), S. xxvii–xlviii.
49 Diese Ausrichtung entsprach auch der breiteren zeitgenössischen Tendenz, vgl. Srodecki, Antemurale Christianitatis, S. 247–62.

Übersetzung eines Briefes des georgischen Herrschers an die kastilische Königin Isabella, in der sie aufgefordert wird, „ein Kreuz gegen die heidnischen Türken aufzunehmen".[50] 1495 hat der litauische Gesandte Stanislovas Kiška in Polen über einen gemeinsamen Kriegszug gegen die Tataren und Türken verhandelt. Ziele der Unternehmung sollten wie bereits in den Jahren zuvor die Unterstützung der Moldauer in ihrem Kampf gegen das Osmanische Reich und die Befreiung der Hafenstädte Cetatea Albă (türk. Akkerman, das heutige Bilhorod-Dnistrovks'kij in der Ukraine) und Chilia (türk. Kili, das heutige Kilija in der Ukraine) sein.[51] Zu einem wirklich aktiven diplomatischen Handeln hat die litauische Elite allerdings ein anderer Konflikt gezwungen. Seit dem Ende des 15. Jahrhunderts war Litauen in einen Krieg mit dem aufstrebenden Großfürstentum Moskau verwickelt. Während eines Feldzugs gegen Moskau ließ der litauische Großfürst Alexander im Juli 1500 eine offene Proklamation an alle abendländische Fürsten und Adlige verlauten: Unter der Berufung auf die altbewährte Kreuzzugsformel vergangener Zeiten, wonach nicht nur Litauen, sondern vielmehr das ganze Abendland von *der Turcke, Tatern und heyden und andere unglaubige, [...] verfolger cristliches bluts* bedroht sei, forderte Alexander den Rest der Lateinischen Christenheit auf, *ein ritterliche bruderschafft* mit den Litauern einzugehen und sich am Kampf gegen die *untugentsamen fursten aus der Moskaw und ander unglaubigen* zu beteiligen. Um diesen Appell zu untermauern, sollten aus Wilna aus an alle Höfe des Westens Boten entsandt werden, um für einen Feldzug gegen Moskau zu werben.[52] Damit ist wohl auch die gleichzeitige Gesandtschaft Alexanders an seinen Bruder, den böhmisch-ungarischen König Wladislaus II., verbunden gewesen. den er nicht nur „aufgrund brüderlicher Liebe", sondern vielmehr „wegen des heiligen christlichen Glaubens" um Hilfe bat.[53]

Im denselben Monat brach aus Wilna eine andere Gesandtschaft des Großfürsten auf, diesmal nach Rom zu Papst Alexander VI. In seiner Rede, die noch in gleichem Jahr (1501) in Rom gedruckt wurde, hat der großfürstliche Schreiber Erazm Ciołek ausführlich die Lage und Geschichte des Großfürstentums dargestellt.[54] Hier finden wir den Höhepunkt der spätmittelalterlichen litauischen Kreuzzugsideologie. Der litauische Gesandte hat die Verdienste der litauischen Herrscher seit Witold *in defendendo ab hostibus* geschildert und die Bereitschaft des damaligen Großfürsten erklärt, sich an einem Bündnis der christlichen Länder gegen die Türken zu beteiligen, allerdings mit dem deutlichen Hinweis, dass

---

50 *LM* 5: 294.
51 *LM* 5: 94–95; Trimonienė, 'Kryžiaus žygių idėja', S. 229. Vgl. Inhalt einer anderen Botschaft aus dem Jahre 1499, wo es um eine gemeinsame Abwehr des mutmaßlichen Zuges der Türken Richtung Kiew handelt (S. 288).
52 Jacob Caro, *Geschichte Polens*, 6 Bde. (Hamburg, 1840–1915), 5.2: 1022–24. Vgl. Rimvydas Petrauskas, 'Knighthood in the Grand Duchy of Lithuania from the Late Fourteenth to the Early Sixteenth Centuries', *LHS* 11 (2006), 39–66.
53 *LM* 5: 185.
54 Sigitas Narbutas, 'Vilniaus prepozito Erazmo Vitelijaus kalba popiežiui Aleksandrui VI: tekstas ir komentarai', in *Lietuvos didysis kunigaikštis Aleksandras ir jo epocham* (Vilnius, 2007), S. 210–19.

man auch auf die Gefahr seitens der Tataren und Moskowiter achten sollte.[55] In seiner Antwort hat der Papst erstmals den Ausdruck *antemurale et propugnaculum christianitatis* in Bezug auf Litauen (neben Polen und Ungarn) gebraucht[56] und dem Gesandten eine große Zahl an Reliquien mitgegeben, die unter anderem der Stärkung des Geistes in der Abwehr der tatarischen Einfälle dienen sollten.[57] Zur militärischen Bekräftigung hingegen wurde ein spezieller Ablass bestimmt, der eine Kampagne zur Sammlung von Geldmitteln vorsah, die im Kampf *contra Turcos, Tartaros et alios infideles* verwendet werden sollten.[58] Die wachsende Wahrnehmung der jagiellonischen Dynastie spiegelt auch der Brief des Kardinals Bernardino López de Carvajal aus Rom an den litauischen Großfürsten Alexander im Mai desselben Jahres wider. Der Autor verband mit der *domus Iagiellonica* die Hoffnung für die Ausweitung der christlichen Religion und bezeichnete die jagiellonischen Länder gleichzeitig als ein „Schild gegen die Tataren und Türken".[59]

Die Taktik, eine reale oder potentielle Tataren-bzw. Türkengefahr zu eigenen Zwecken und Bedürfnissen zu instrumentalisieren, haben interessanterweise auch einzelne Vertreter des litauischen Hochadels übernommen. Im Jahre 1469 warb der litauische Hofmarschall Stanislovas Sudivojaitis mit Erfolg beim Papst um siebenjährige Ablässe für eine Pfarrkirche seines Patronats mit dem Argument, dass diese Kirche unter den „Tataren und Heiden" steht, sowie mit der rhetorischen Überbetonung seiner persönlichen *vita* als eines frischen Neophyten.[60] In Wirklichkeit handelte es sich hierbei um eine Kirche, die sich mitten im „sicheren" litauischen Kernland befand und um eine Person, die mindestens in dritter Generation bereits ein Christ gewesen war.[61] 1518 wurden im Diplom des Kaisers Maximilian I. für Mikalojus Radvila die Verdienste des letzteren für die *respublica christiana* im Kampf *contra christiani nominis hostes* als Hauptgrund für die außergewöhnliche Standeserhöhung zum Fürsten des Heiligen Römischen Reiches herausgehoben.[62]

***

Zusammenfassend lässt sich Folgendes festhalten: 1402–3 fanden die letzten Reisen des Ordens nach Litauen statt. Im 1403 Jahr hat Papst Bonifatius IX.

---

55 *VMPL* 2, Nr. 299, S. 279.
56 Narbutas, 'Vilniaus prepozito Erazmo Vitelijaus kalba popiežiui Aleksandrui VI', S. 217.
57 Stephen C. Rowell, 'Procesy rozwoju i zaniku kultu świętych na Litwie i w Polsce w drugiej połowie XV wieku', *ZH* 70 (2005), 11.
58 *CDECDV* 1: 587–91.
59 *LAPM*, Nr. 55, S. 57. See Srodecki, *Antemurale Christianitatis*, S. 252.
60 *CDECDV* 1: 301–2.
61 Genealogie: Krzysztof Pietkiewicz, *Kieżgajłowie i ich latyfundium do połowy XVI wieku* (Poznań, 1982).
62 Karol Fryderyk Eichhorn, *Stosunek xiążęcego domu Radziwiłłów do domów xiążęcych w Niemczech* (Warszawa, 1843), S. 64. Dazu Rimvydas Petrauskas, 'Fürsten und Grafen des Heiligen Römischen Reiches: Die litauischen Hochadligen und ihre römischen Titel im Kontext des Wiener Fürstentags', in *Das Wiener Fürstentreffen von 1515. Beiträge zur Geschichte der habsburgisch-jagiellonischen Doppelvermählung*, hg. v. Bogusław Dybaś und István Tringli (Budapest, 2019), S. 213–24.

dem Orden Kriegszüge gegen Litauen untersagt.[63] Aber damit ging keinesfalls die Epoche der Kreuzzüge im Ostbaltikum zu Ende. Sie haben nur neue Richtungen eingeschlagen, wurden ideologisch umgedeutet. Die litauischen Herrscher haben sich des Motivs des heiligen Krieges bedient und seit dem Ende des 14. Jahrhunderts ihre Feldzüge gegen die Tataren, Nowgorod oder später allem voran gegen Moskau als Unternehmungen der christlichen Ritterschaft manifestiert. Im Jahre 1407 behauptete der polnische König Wladislaus II. in einem Brief an den Papst Gregor XII., dass seine sowie des Großfürsten Witold Länder an den 'stärksten schismatischen und barbarischen Völkern' grenzten und somit den christlichen Glauben verteidigten.[64] Im ähnlichen Geist wurde über das Bistum Wilna („belagert von Ruthenen wie ein Lamm von gierigen Wölfen") noch am Anfang des 16. Jahrhunderts geschrieben.[65]

Der Kreuzzugsdiskurs war aber in Litauen ins Stocken geraten und erst später kam der Versuch die Bedrohung seitens der Tataren und Moskau als eine europäische Angelegenheit zu internationalisieren. Mit Witolds Tod 1430 verengte sich der Horizont litauischer Diplomatie, weshalb im Westen vor allem Polen (wie auch Ungarn) die Stellung des Bollwerks der *respublica christiana* eingenommen haben. In Litauen sah man dies natürlich etwas anders. Im Jahre 1529 hat ein führender Vertreter der litauischen Oberschicht, Kanzler des Großfürstentums und Woiwode von Wilna Albertas Goštautas, in einer Streitschrift die institutionellen Unterschiede zwischen Litauen und Polen auch mit dem Hinweis auf die spezifische Lage seines Landes untermauert: Während Polen doch fast nur von den christlichen Nachbarn umgeben sei, habe Litauen Moskau und die Tataren gegen sich.[66] In der diplomatischen Korrespondenz der litauischen Kanzlei wurde in Analogie zum im östlichen Mitteleuropa weitverbreiteten Bollwerksmotiv ein neues Attribut für das Großfürstentum Litauen entdeckt: Das Großfürstentum wurde nun zu „einem Tor zur ganzen Christenheit" stilisiert.[67]

---

63 *CDPr*, 5, S. 186–92.
64 *CESDQ* 1: 31: *cum fortissimis scissmaticorum et barbarorum nationibus fines teneo ac ab eorum iucursibus christianam fidem [...] defendo*. Mit einer gewissen Übertreibung stellte dann der Papst in einem Brief vom 16. Januar 1408 an Mikołaj Gorzkowski, den Bischof von Wilna, fest (*CDECDV* 1: 74), dass „die Kathedrale von Wilna inmitten der Schismatiker und Ungläubigen stehe" (*in medio scismaticorum et infidelium consistit*).
65 Jan Sakran, *Elucidarius errorum ritus Ruthenici* (Cracoviae, 1501): *In Lithuania Vilnensi sedi vigilantissime presidens, tumultuante turba Ruthenorum tue Romaneque ecclesie infensissimorum hostium circumseptus, velud agnus inter rapaces lupos*. Zitiert nach Stephen C. Rowell, 'LDK ir totorių santykiai Katalikų Bažnyčios akimis: prielaidos ir poveikis', in *Viduriо Rytų Europa mūsio prie Mėlynųjų Vandenų metu*, hg. v. Vytas Jankauskas und Vitaliy Nagirnyy (Kaunas, 2013), S. 228.
66 'Raciones Gastoldi, cur judices in Lithuania non sint constituendi, ut in Polonia', in *AT* 11, Nr. 214, S. 163–64.
67 'Das Großfürstentum ist ein Tor zum ganzen Christentum' (Великое Князьтво есть ворота всему хрестиянству) — so bezeichneten die litauischen Herren ihr Land im Schreiben an die polnischen Standesgenossen im Jahre 1514, *LM* 7: 295. Der Vertreter des böhmisch-ungarischen Königs Wladislaus hat im selben Jahr Ungarn und Polen als „Tore der Christenheit" gerühmt (Srodecki, *Antemurale Christianitatis*, S. 301). Man kann hier nur am Rande anmerken, dass

So wichtig für die litauische Selbstdarstellung die Kreuzzugsrhetorik auch sein konnte, die litauischen Hochadligen waren sich dennoch im Klaren darüber, dass die Entscheidung über Krieg und Frieden mit den andersgläubigen Nachbarn zum großen Teil auch in ihren eigenen Händen lag. Diese außenpolitische Pragmatik spiegelt sich ganz gut in einem Brief Kasimirs des Jagiellonen an den Hochmeister des Deutschen Ordens aus der Mitte des 15. Jahrhunderts wider: Kasimir prahlt hierin, er habe erst kürzlich den tatarischen Khan mit dem Gedanken an seinem Hofe aufgenommen, letzteren zum gesamttatarischen Khan zu machen, *als denn das unsere vorfare eyn gewonheyt gehat haben*.[68] Ein Kreuzzug gegen die Tataren wäre also mit Sicherheit gut gewesen, aber den „eigenen Khan" am Hofe zu haben — viel besser.

---

man die „Tore-Metapher" auch umgekehrt verwenden konnte, bezeichnete man doch noch im Deutschordenslande in der Mitte des 15. Jahrhunderts ausgerechnet Polen als *eyne phorte [...] der heiden in dy cristenheit*. 'Die Ältere Hochmeisterchronik', ed. M. Töppen, in SRP 3: 540–709 (hier 611).
68 Brief vom 26. August 1449 aus Trakai: GStA PK, XX. HA, OBA 10038.

ADAM SZWEDA

Fighting Pagans and Relations between Poland and the Teutonic Order after 1466[*]

Introduction: The Teutonic Order and the Kingdom of Poland towards the Fight against Pagans

The Teutonic Order, like other knightly orders, was established to defend and protect Christianity — originally in the Middle East, in the Holy Land, and then in its subordinate territories, i.e. in the Bârsa Land (named after the eponymous river, Rom. Țara Bârsei, Hung. Barcaság, Ger. Burzenland) in south-eastern Transylvania and in Prussia. Here, its task was to fight pagan Prussian tribes; following the completion of their conquest in the early 1280s, the main opponent of the order became pagan Lithuania, with whom persistent battles were fought until the end of the fourteenth century. These circumstances made the Teutonic Knights pioneers in the use of rhetoric about being the fortress and bulwark of Christendom.[1] The crucial moments (although their importance in this respect was not immediately recognised at the time) were the Polono-Lithuanian Union of Kreva (1385), the coronation of the grand duke of Lithuania, Jogaila, as the king of Poland (1386), and the following Christianisation of Lithuania.[2] The significance of its commitment to the defence of Christianity in legitimising the actions of the order is emphasised by Herman of Wartberge's *Chronicon Livoniae* written in the late 1370s. According to this chronicle, the Lithuanian rulers Algirdas and

---

[*] The text was created as a part of the project Królewscy lennicy: W poszukiwaniu modelu relacji królów Polski z władcami zależnymi w późnym średniowieczu (II połowa XIV–początek XVI w.) ['Royal Vassals: In Search of a Model of Relations between Polish Kings and Dependent Lords, Second Half of the Fourteenth to the Early Sixteenth Centuries'] founded by the National Science Centre, Poland (project no. 2018/29/B/HS3/00793).

[1] Paul Srodecki, *Antemurale Christianitatis: Zur Genese der Bollwerksrhetorik im östlichen Mitteleuropa an der Schwelle vom Mittelalter zur Frühen Neuzeit* (Husum, 2015), pp. 57–72.

[2] These issues are discussed widely in *Państwo zakonu krzyżackiego w Prusach: Władza i społeczeństwo*, ed. Marian Biskup and Roman Czaja (Warszawa 2008); Klaus Militzer, *Die Geschichte des Deutschen Ordens*, 2 edn (Stuttgart 2012), pp. 91–114, 144–57; Hartmut Boockmann, *Johannes Falkenberg, der Deutsche Orden und die polnische Politik: Untersuchungen zur politischen Theorie des späten Mittelalters* (Göttingen 1975), pp. 50–58.

The Defence of the Faith, Outremer: Studies in the Crusades and the Latin East, 15 (Turnhout: Brepols, 2024), pp. 267–280

BREPOLS PUBLISHERS   10.1484/M.OUTREMER-EB.5.136539

Kęstutis declared their willingness to accept baptism and conducted talks with the envoys of Emperor Charles IV. During the negotiations, they also proposed that the order be moved to the wild areas between Ruthenia and the Tatar lands so as to defend the Ruthenians against pagans.[3] We can therefore claim that pagan Lithuania was well aware of the reasons for the presence of the Teutonic Order in the Baltic Sea region and were able to capitalise on these in order to achieve their own political goals.[4]

Polish diplomacy also had a tradition of using motifs related to Christianity for its own purposes. As early as the reigns of King Vladislas the Elbow-High and, especially, King Casimir the Great, religious arguments were used to obtain papal support for the eastern policy of the last rulers of the Piast dynasty. Here the terms as *scutum* or *clipeus* were first used to a large extent in relation to a Poland which was meant to protect the Christian world of the West against pagans and schismatics.[5] This trend was accelerated following the ascension of King Vladislas III of Poland to the Hungarian throne in 1440; in this new role, the monarch initiated a confrontation with the Ottomans.[6]

It is not surprising, therefore, that these motifs were very evident in the propaganda struggle between Poland and Lithuania and the Teutonic Knights in the international arena. The terms of the Peace of Thorn (mod. Toruń, Poland) of 1411 included an obligation for both parties — and therefore also for the order — to spread Christianity among their subjects. The admission that there still were many pagans among the Prussian population so long after the conquest was a blow to the prestige of the grand master and the Order, and laid the grounds for an ideological clash during the Council of Constance.[7] The momentum of fighting and converting pagans formed one of the key points in the dispute between Poland, Lithuania and the Teutonic Order in 1414–18, as shown in Paul Srodecki's chapter on this issue in this volume.[8] In this, the assignment of

---

3 Hermann von Wartberge, 'Chronicon Livoniae', ed. Ernst Strehlke, in *SRP* 2: 21–116 (here 79–80).
4 See Rimvydas Petrauskas, 'Die Außenwelt der Gediminiden: Formen und Möglichkeiten internationaler Politik der heidnischen Großfürsten Litauens in der zweiten Hälfte des 14. Jahrhunderts', in *Akteure mittelalterlicher Außenpolitik: Das Beispiel Ostmitteleuropas*, ed. Stephan Flemmig and Norbert Kersken (Marburg, 2017), pp. 53–67.
5 Srodecki, *Antemurale Christianitatis*, pp. 73–103 (on the very early origins of this phenomenon), and Andrzej Marzec in this volume.
6 Krzysztof Baczkowski, 'Argument obrony wiary w służbie dyplomacji polskiej w XV wieku', in *Ludzie, Kościół, wierzenia: Studia z dziejów kultury i społeczeństwa Europy Środkowej*, ed. Wojciech Iwańczak and Stefan K. Kuczyński (Warszawa, 2001), p. 205; Paul Srodecki, 'Władysław III and the Polish-Hungarian Bulwark *topoi* against the Background of the Ottoman Threat in the 15th Century', in *Hungaro-Polonica: Young Scholars on Medieval Polish-Hungarian Relations*, ed. Dániel Bagi, Gábor Barabás and Zsólt Máté (Pécs, 2016), pp. 327–56.
7 Sławomir Jóźwiak et al., *Wojna Polski i Litwy z zakonem krzyżackim w latach 1409–1411* (Malbork, 2010), pp. 715, 718, 720.
8 On this issue, see also Krzysztof Ożóg, *Uczeni w monarchii Jadwigi Andegaweńskiej i Władysława Jagiełły (1384–1434)* (Kraków, 2004), pp. 206–17; László Pósán, 'Der Konflikt zwischen dem Deutschen Orden und dem polnisch-litauischen Staat uf dem Konstanzer Konzil', in *Das Konzil*

new tasks to the Teutonic knights was an issue which was not only raised by their political opponents. The king of Hungary and the Romans, Sigismund of Luxemburg, and his entourage considered the possibility of using the military potential of the order in other parts of Europe, above all against the Ottoman Turks. This resulted, among other things, in several knightly brothers being sent to southern Hungary in 1429. They managed to establish their headquarters there, but the forces involved were too few, and this initiative soon collapsed. Later in life, Sigismund, the then Holy Roman emperor, propagated the idea of the complete relocation of the order from Prussia to the Hungaro-Ottoman border in order to strengthen its defensive potential.[9]

Polono-Teutonic Relations after the Thirteen Years' War

The fall of Constantinople in 1453 led to the revival of crusading sentiment across Europe. Almost simultaneously, in 1454, the Thirteen Years' War broke out between Poland and the Teutonic Order, and both sides utilised crusading arguments in their diplomatic conflicts. The ways in which they did so were not very sophisticated: the Teutonic Knights indicated to the king the progress of the Ottoman Turks and, at the same time, accused him of fighting against Christians and, for his part, the king criticised the order for not fulfilling its mission of fighting pagans, and additionally of engaging Polish forces and thereby preventing Poland from fighting against the Ottomans.[10] During bilateral negotiations in 1463, the Poles put forward the idea of relocating the order from Prussia to Podolia so that it could fight the Turks there.[11]

In October 1466, the war was brought to an end. The grand master became 'the counsellor of the king and kingdom', obliged to give an oath of allegiance to the Polish king. He also had to provide military assistance if the situation

---

von Konstanz und Ungarn, ed. Attila Bárány and Balázs A. Bacsa (Debrecen, 2016), pp. 65–83; Paul Srodecki, 'Murus et antemurale pollens et propugnaculum tocius christianitatis: Der Traktatenstreit zwischen dem Deutschen Orden und dem Königreich Polen auf dem Konstanzer Konzil', *Schweizerische Zeitschrift für Religions- und Kulturgeschichte* 109 (2015), 47–65; Srodecki, *Antemurale Christianitatis*, pp. 111–17; Přemysl Bar, 'Eine (un)genutzte Gelegenheit: Die Polnisch-litauische Union und der Deutsche Orden auf dem Konstanzer Konzil (1414–18)', in *Der Deutsche Orden auf dem Konstanzer Konzil: Pläne-Strategien-Erwartungen*, ed. Helmut Flachenecker (Ilmtal-Weinstraße, 2020), pp. 33–54.

9 Matthias Thumser, 'Eine neue Aufgabe im Heidenkampf? Pläne mit dem Deutschen Orden als Vorposten gegen die Türken', in *Europa und die Türken in der Renaissance*, ed. Bodo Guthmüller and Wilhelm Kühlmann (Tübingen, 2000), pp. 139–76 (here 142); Liviu Pilat and Oliviu Cristea, *The Ottoman Threat and Crusading on the Eastern Border of Christendom during the 15th Century* (Leiden, 2018), pp. 97–102.

10 Bolesław Stachoń, *Polityka Polski wobec Turcji i akcji antytureckiej w wieku XV do utraty Kilii i Białogrodu (1484)*, 2 edn (Oświęcim, 2015), p. 104.

11 Thumser, 'Neue Aufgabe', p. 143.

required it.[12] However, King Casimir IV Andrew the Jagiellonian issued a separate document under which he released the order from the duty of military assistance for the period of twenty years; this decision was caused by the destruction of Prussia during the lengthy conflict. There was one situation, however, where this exemption from the obligation to provide military assistance was not supposed to be effective: in the case of 'what God could reverse' — as it was stipulated in the text of a relevant provision, i.e., if the Ottomans invaded the Polish kingdom, principalities and lands subordinate to it. For his part, Grand Master Louis of Erlichshausen released his own subjects from military obligations for the period of twenty-five years, but again with the proviso that this would not apply to a situation when the Ottoman Turks or Tatars were to attack Poland because 'nobody can be exempt from fighting them as enemies of faith'.[13] The document supplementing the so-called Second Peace of Thorn of 1466, which is mentioned here, presents two issues: firstly, the issue of the Ottoman threat had become important in Polish politics on a permanent basis; secondly, from the very beginning, the fight against this threat and the struggle to defend Christianity became one of the central issues in Polono-Teutonic relations in the period under study.

The Turkish Issue at the Thorn Assembly in 1485

The Ottoman threat was on the rise, and further warning signals for Poland were the loss of Caffa (mod. Feodosia, Ukraine [de jure] / Russia [de facto]) in Crimea (1475), and especially the fall of Chilia (mod. Kiliya, Ukraine) in the Danube Delta and of Cetatea Albă (mod. Bilhorod-Dnistrovskyi, Ukraine) at the mouth of the Dniester in 1484. In 1482, the Tatars also invaded the grand duchy of Lithuania and burnt down Kiev.[14] The loss of the Black Sea ports, subordinate to the authority of the Polish vassal, Voivode Stephen of Moldavia, forced the king

---

12 *SVDOP* 2, no. 403, pp. 273–75. See Adam Szweda, '"Princeps et consiliarius Regni Poloniae": Król i wielki mistrz w latach 1466–1497', in *Od traktatu kaliskiego do pokoju oliwskiego: Polsko-krzyżacko-pruskie stosunki dyplomatyczne w latach 1343–70*, ed. Almut Bues et al. (Warszawa, 2014), pp. 241–60 (here 242); Klaus Neitmann, 'Von der Herrstellung und Sicherung des "ewigen Friedens": Der II. Thorner Friede von 1466 im Rahmen der Landfriedens Vereinbarungen und Friedensschlüsse des Deutschen Ordens in Preußen mit seinen Nachbarmächten im 15. Jahrhundert', in *Erbeinungen und Erbverbrüderungen im Spätmittelalter und Früher Neuzeit: Generationsübergreifende Verträge und Strategien im europäischen Vergleich*, ed. Mario Müller, Karl-Heinz Spieß and Uwe Tresp (Berlin, 2016), pp. 173–210 (here 186); Adam Szweda, 'Das Verhältnis zwischen den Königen von Polen und abhängigen Herrschern: Auf der Suche nach einem Modell', in *Zwischen der Geschichte von Ereignissen, Phänomenen und Prozessen: Länder, Regionen und Städte und ihre weltlichen und geistlichen Einwohner:innen [sic!]*, ed. Renata Skowrońska (Göttingen, 2023), pp. 283–299 (here 293-296).
13 *CDPL* 4, no. 126, p. 176. See also *SVDOP* 2, no. 407, p. 292.
14 Ilona Czamańska, *Mołdawia i Wołoszczyzna wobec Polski, Węgier i Turcji w XIV i XV wieku* (Poznań, 1996), pp. 149–50; Janusz Smołucha, *Papiestwo a Polska w latach 1484–1525: Kontakty dyplomatyczne na tle zagrożenia tureckiego* (Kraków, 1999), p. 31; Alexandriu Simon, 'The Ottoman-Hungarian Crisis of 1484: Diplomacy and Warfare in Matthias Corvinus' local and regional Politics', in *Matthias and*

to consider military solutions. On the international stage he shared the crusading intentions of Pope Innocent VIII and began to prepare a set of actions. The Ottoman issues were widely considered during a meeting of the states in Thorn in the spring of 1485 (6 March — 19 April).[15] The monarch, representatives of the states of Royal Prussia, and the grand master of the Teutonic Order, Martin Truchsess of Wetzhausen, accompanied by his retinue, all participated in this event. At this point, the grand master had to consider a request to provide military support to the king, since it concerned the Ottoman Empire; moreover, the twenty-year period of release from this duty was gradually coming to an end.

During talks with representatives of the states in the town hall in Thorn on 12 March 1485, the archbishop of Gniezno, Zbigniew Oleśnicki, who spoke on behalf of the king, outlined the situation in the Danubian principalities and emphasised that the king had come to Thorn to consult the states and to seek the advice of the grand master 'as His Grace and counsellor'. The king, through Oleśnicki speaking in German, also addressed his Prussian subjects and asked them to express their opinion as to what kind of assistance he should demand from the grand master.[16] Martin Truchsess was expected in Thorn in two days' time, and it was therefore urgent to decide exactly how to tell him about the Ottoman threat and the military assistance required: *Seyne ko. gnade mochte wissen, wie mit ym derhalbenn zcu reden were*.[17] The talks were prolonged since the representatives of Royal Prussia were not overly enthusiastic about the king's plans. They were predominantly interested in realising their own political demands, defending the privileges of the province and determining the model of relations between Royal Prussia and the monarch, which led to a conflict. These factors resulted in the meeting between the king and the delegation of the order not being held until the third day after their arrival in Thorn.

Finally, on 17 March 1485, after another exchange of views between the king and the bishop of Warmia, Nicholas of Tüngen, Grand Master Martin Truchsess appeared before the king, and Zbigniew Oleśnicki presented the development of the situation in the Danube region and the resultant threat. Truchsess initially avoided taking an explicit stance. He claimed that he did not have sufficient knowledge to advise the king on matters concerning areas so far away from Prussia. The archbishop replied that, in the case of such a specific enemy, the procedure was quite simple — one should fight. Oleśnicki emphasised: 'Your Grace is obliged to fight such an enemy because of the [mission] of your order'.[18] In the first place, therefore, religious arguments and the reminder about the mission

---

His Legacy: Cultural and Political Encounters between East and West, ed. Attila Bárány and Attila Györkös (Debrecen, 2009), pp. 405–36; Pilat and Cristea, *Ottoman Threat*, pp. 192–222.
15 This congress is discussed by Beata Możejko, 'Odległe pogranicze: Stanowisko stanów Prus Królewskich, a zwłaszcza Gdańska, wobec problemu zagrożenia tureckiego w latach 1485–1488', *Średniowiecze polskie i powszechne* 7 (2011), 151–70 (here 153–59).
16 Szweda, 'Princeps et consiliarius', p. 250.
17 *ASPK* 1, no. 200, p. 289.
18 *ASPK* 1, no. 200, p. 304.

of the order, i.e., the fight against pagans, were used. In the following sentence, the primate mentioned the grand master's duty to advise the king. The order's superior did not react too enthusiastically to the king's explanation, pointing at the plague, his financial obligations, and the uncertain situation in relations with the archbishop of Riga (an eternal rival in the Livonian branch of the Teutonic Order) and with Novgorod. In 1478, Novgorod was subordinated to Moscow, which did not change the fact that schismatics were at stake, and thus also 'pagan' Ruthenians, which provided a certain counterbalance to the religious arguments advanced by the Poles. For these reasons the order requested exemption from the duty of providing assistance, and the grand master appealed to the king not to hold any grievance because of these excuses.[19]

The response to the master's request was discussed with the representatives of Royal Prussia. First of all, the document of 1466 releasing the grand master and the order from the obligation of military assistance for twenty years was recalled and read out loud. The voivode of Marienburg (mod. Malbork, Poland), Nicholas of Baysen (Pol. Mikołaj Bażyński), preferred to ensure that the invasion of the Ottoman Turks into Moldavia would also result in the order's military assistance. This demonstrates the lack of orientation among the elites of Royal Prussia (which had only been under the authority of the Polish king for twenty years) with regards to developments in the Danubian principalities, which were also a subject of rivalry between Poland and Hungary, something the elites were possibly aware of. Archbishop Oleśnicki explained that Moldavia was subordinated to the Polish crown, since its coat of arms appears on the banners of the king (*das wopen der Walachie ist eyn ochsenhaupt myt eym rade und ist yn des hern konigs herzceichen*).[20]

After these explanations, the grand master was called, and his excuses were addressed. Oleśnicki simply referred to the 'eternal peace', expressing a conviction that the grand master wanted to maintain this under the oath taken. On behalf of the superior of the order, a judge (*Landrichter*) from the Vistula lagoon district of Brandenburg (mod. Ushakovo, Russia), Daniel of Kunheim, responded following a discussion. Kunheim, rather than denying the obligations arising from the treaty, asked for a one-time release of the order from them, repeating the arguments mentioned above.[21] This position led the Polish side to reconsider their

---

19 *ASPK* 1, no. 200, pp. 304–6. See Szweda, 'Princeps et consiliarius', pp. 250–53. The issue of relations between the Teutonic Order (mainly its Livonian branch) and Moscow has been more comprehensively discussed by Maike Sach, *Hochmeister und Grossfürst: Die Beziehungen zwischen dem Deutschen Orden in Preussen und dem Moskauer Staat um die Wende zur Neuzeit* (Stuttgart, 2002).
20 *ASPK* 1, no. 200, p. 307. See Adam Szweda, 'Zur Abhängigkeit der moldauischen Fürsten von den polnischen Königen im Spätmittelalter' in *Zwischen Ostsee und Adria: Ostmitteleuropa im Mittelalter und in der Frühen Neuzeit. Politische, wirtschaftliche, religiöse und wissenschaftliche Beziehungen*, ed. Attila Bárány, Roman Czaja and László Pósán (Debrecen, 2023), pp. 95–116 (here 110–11); Szweda, 'Das Verhältnis', pp. 290–93.
21 *ASPK* 1, no. 200, pp. 305–6. See Szweda, 'Princeps et consiliarius', p. 253; Pilat and Cristea, *Ottoman Threat*, pp. 223–24.

negotiation strategy and to define the understanding of treaty obligations in this specific situation. The archbishop noted that the peace had been concluded by the predecessors of the current negotiators, and that it should now be specified how it should function at this particular moment. It should be given a new beginning, 'to make the grand master take his yoke upon him forever'. It is no coincidence that, on the margins of the document, these words were marked as 'words of great importance'. When Martin Truchsess arrived at the meeting room with his entourage, the parties repeated their arguments, and Oleśnicki emphasised the necessity of the order fulfilling the provisions of the Second Peace of Thorn and the necessity for the grand master to participate in person in fights, if the king decided to take this step. In turn, the grand master, stressing his willingness to help the monarch, emphasised that, in order to obtain a potentially definitive answer, he had to appeal to his subjects in Prussia; conversations in this tone were also held on the next day. Over the following days, the main issues discussed concerned economics, which does not mean, however, that there were no tensions as to the understanding of the provisions of 'eternal peace'. Finally, on 29 March 1485, the order's delegation was bid farewell by the king and the princes and offered generous gifts. On its departure, Zbigniew Oleśnicki set out what Poland expected from the order: the estates of Teutonic Prussia were to be informed about the situation, but only to comply with the provisions of the 'eternal peace'. The archbishop's statement was addressed to the Brandenburg Castle commander and representatives of the knights and towns of East Prussia.[22]

The Thorn negotiations of 1485 demonstrate that, from the outset, King Casimir IV Andrew the Jagiellonian and his entourage did not have a ready formulated idea as to how solve the problem of turning to the order for military assistance in practical terms. This was a new situation, which had only theoretically been outlined in the treaty concluded nineteen years earlier. Even if we take into account that the king's manner of conducting negotiations was in part the implementation of his intentions towards the elites of Royal Prussia, there is still clearly some uncertainty in the approach of the Polish royal court towards the grand master. This state of affairs also resulted in the Poles reaching for arguments related to crusader ideology. These could have served as a sort of a common denominator for both the king and the grand master of the order. It was not necessary to refer to the duties of the superior of the order resulting from the treaty and the document supplementing it. Paradoxically, the king and his advisers were facilitated in their task by the very assertive attitude of Martin Truchsess, who sought to avoid fulfilling his obligations whilst confirming them verbally. This attitude gave rise to the Polish royal court abandoning the 'general Christian' rhetoric or 'crusade' rhetoric and underlining the necessity of fulfilling the provisions of the Second Peace of Thorn pursuant to the oath taken by the grand master.

---

22 *ASPK* 1, no. 200, pp. 311–13; GStA PK, XX. HA, OF 18a, pp. 155–58; Szweda, 'Princeps et consiliarius', p. 254.

It should be added that the king managed to achieve this goal — shortly after the meeting of the states the envoys of the grand master appeared before him with an explicit promise of military assistance, although without the grand master's personal participation. However, the monarch did not agree to this solution, and Martin Truchsess eventually took to the battlefield; his troops reached Neidenburg (mod. Nidzica, Poland), where he was informed by the monarch to cancel the further march, because certain settlements had already been made, with Hospodar Stephen of Moldavia paying homage in Kolomyia and with the victorious battle at Lake Cătlăbuga.[23]

The Turkish Issue at the 1488 Sejm in Piotrków

The problem of relations with the Ottoman Empire returned in 1488 during the Sejm (general assembly) in Piotrków. In response to earlier Polish missions, the envoy of Sultan Bayezid II appeared at this assembly, and the grand master was also present. He had come to Piotrków to pursue a completely different matter, but this time was also called upon to advise the king. This concerned the decision as to whether to adopt the course of peace, or whether to make such a step dependent upon the sultan's resignation of Chilia (Turk. Kilya) and Cetatea Albă (Turk. Akkerman). Martin Truchsess pointed out that his knowledge of the kingdom's affairs was not extensive, but did finally express his opinion, which demonstrated that he was not overwhelmingly enthusiastic about fighting pagans. He claimed that the use of war could be more effective and profitable, but that it might be a completely unpredictable path, and thus uncertain. The grand master's advice was as follows: 'Therefore, I advise Your Majesty to resolve the matter peacefully, and not through war'.[24] It is worth noting that, during the discussions over the response to the Ottoman delegate, members of the Teutonic delegation were presented with the credentials of the sultan's envoy, written in Italian, in gold-coloured ink, and authenticated with a tughra, i.e. the sultan's monogram painted on an empty field at the beginning of the document. The order's report covered the content of this document, but it was translated into Latin by the Polish chancellery.[25] During the assembly in Piotrków, the grand master received a special kind of 'bonus' for the attitude he had manifested three years earlier. The king referred warmly to the fact that he went on a military expedition and, when bidding farewell to the representatives of the states of Royal Prussia in Piotrków,

---

23 Szweda, 'Princeps et consiliarius', p. 255. See also Czamańska, *Mołdawia i Wołoszczyzna*, pp. 151–53; Thumser, 'Neue Aufgabe', pp. 146–47.
24 Adam Szweda, 'Odprawa posłów tureckich (Piotrków, 1488)', in *Inter Regnum et Ducatum: Studia ofiarowane Profesorowi Janowi Tęgowskiemu w siedemdziesiątą rocznicę urodzin*, ed. Piotr Guzowski, Marzena Liedke and Krzysztof Borodo (Białystok, 2018), pp. 565–75 (here 571).
25 Szweda, 'Odprawa posłów', pp. 569–70.

he also criticised their attitude (they were still refusing to give advice), contrasting this with the stance of the grand master.

At the end of the reign of King Casimir IV Andrew the Jagiellonian, between 1489 and 1491, the Poles tried to obtain the military support of the Teutonic Order against the Tatars. In this respect, the authorities in Königsberg (mod. Kaliningrad, Russia) declared their general readiness to act 'in accordance with their possibilities', whilst stipulating that these possibilities were limited. In the end, no Teutonic troop were sent to the south.[26]

Plans to Transfer the Teutonic Order to Podolia (1493–95)

Relations between Casimir IV Andrew's successor on the Polish throne, King John I Albert, and the Grand Master John of Tiefen were far from ideal, and tension was present from the very beginning of their relationship. This tension derived from a dispute over whether the grand master should swear an oath of loyalty to the new Polish king, since Tiefen had already done so to John I Albert's father. Finally, the king made the grand master take the oath.[27] It is not surprising, therefore, that open conflict broke out shortly thereafter. Its cause, or pretext, was the issue of fighting the Ottomans. In this context, the idea of transferring the order to Podolia so as to fight pagans, returned. This idea had already been floated for the first time in 1493, and was also related to dynastic issues. In this situation, John I Albert's younger brother, Sigismund (the future King Sigismund I the Old), would govern Teutonic Prussia and reside in Königsberg. This was most likely one of the problems discussed at the meetings of the Jagiellons in Levoča (Hung. Lőcse; Ger. Leutschau) in 1494, in which John I Albert, his brother Vladislas II of Hungary and Bohemia, Prince Sigismund and their brother-in-law, the Hohenzoller Frederick V, margrave of Brandenburg, all took part. This idea was to obtain international support, especially from the Romano-German king Maximilian I, the princes of the *Reich* and Pope Alexander VI. However, it appears that no binding decisions regarding Podolia were taken in Levoča.[28]

Nevertheless, this issue was soon to become the focus of Polono-Teutonic relations thanks to the bishop of Warmia, Lucas Watzenrode the Younger, who was in a conflict with Grand Master John of Tiefen concerning the bishop's jurisdiction over the Teutonic clergy. In this matter, the order's superior referred to the earlier papal privileges of the order. Watzenrode argued that, since the Teutonic Knights were not fighting pagans overseas, the legal validity of their exemption from the bishop's authority had also ceased to function. This marked

---

26 Thumser, 'Neue Aufgabe', pp. 148–50.
27 Szweda, 'Princeps et consiliarius', pp. 256–57.
28 Fryderyk Papée, *Jan Olbracht*, 2 edn (Kraków, 1999), pp. 66–69; Marian Biskup, *Polska a Zakon Krzyżacki w Prusach w początkach XVI w.: U źródeł sekularyzacji Prus Krzyżackich* (Olsztyn, 1983), p. 47.

the beginning of the so-called privilege conflict (*Privilegienstreit*), which had numerous echoes of crusade ideology in the background. The main argument of the bishop of Warmia in questioning the special legal status of the order was the fact that the knights did not fulfil their basic task. Watzenrode, together with the royal diplomat Filippo 'Callimachus' Buonaccorsi and with the support of John I Albert, continued to push this concept in Rome. As early as April 1495, in his instructions to his envoy to Livonia, the grand master claimed that the bishop of Warmia, together with his canons, had told the king that the order's duty was to fight pagans, and since the Teutonic Knights were not doing so, they should be removed from Prussia and transferred to Podolia to fight against the Ottomans. John of Tiefen stressed that gaining the favour of the European rulers for the order in this matter would be neither easy nor cheap.[29]

However, it was necessary, in the context of John I Albert's actions, who (according to Tiefen's account given to the order's procurator in the Roman curia in August 1495) was to apply for the papal mandate *obir uns alhir von hynnen zürer niemen inholl unsers ordens fundacion in die Padolien wedir die ungloubigen streiten sollen*.[30] He also declared his intention to fight these plans. The order's countermove resulted in the approval of its privileges by King Maximilian I. The latter also intervened with the cardinals to block the Podolia plans in consideration of the wellbeing of the German nobility which served as the recruitment base for the order. After its possible relocation 'to a certain ravaged land, which they call Podolia', the relations of the order and the *Reich* would be discontinued simply because of the considerable distance.[31]

The reluctance of the order's authorities to relocate to Podolia was so strong that, in 1494, John of Tiefen even persuaded the German land master, Andrew of Grumbach, to help 'with pagan Ruthenians', who were to planning to attack Livonia. Providing such assistance would satisfy the obligations arising from the foundations of the order and would silence the rumours that the Teutonic Knights were no longer fighting pagans.[32] This would allow the Teutonic Knights to refute the accusations that they were not fighting pagans. Although ties between the Prussian and Livonian branches of the order were very loose at that time, the authorities in Königsberg were keen to mention the threat from the schismatic Rus, and when addressing the Ruthenians, whether from Pskov or Moscow, the same rhetoric was used as in the case of the Ottomans. In 1495, the order attempted to dismiss the danger resulting from the actions of the bishop of Warmia, when King John I Albert requested the grand master to provide military assistance against the duke of Masovia, Conrad the Red. The order's authorities were aware that they could not avoid satisfying this request. However, they claimed that it was not possible to take military action while the dispute with Lucas Watzenrode was still

---

29 *LUB* 2/1, no. 181, pp. 139–40.
30 *LUB* 2/1, no. 256, pp. 192–93.
31 Biskup, *Polska a Zakon*, p. 50.
32 *SVDOP* 3, no. 510, pp. 162–63.

unresolved. The expedition to Masovia quickly lost its relevance, and therefore failed to stop the Podolia-related plans of the bishop of Warmia.[33] His position in the curia expired as late as in 1496, when the succeeded in persuading Bishop Lucas Watzenrode's representative in Rome to take its side.[34]

John of Tiefen and the Moldavia Expedition of 1497

This did not mean, however, that the issue of fighting the Ottoman Empire disappeared from Polono-Teutonic relations. An anti-Ottoman expedition appeared on the horizon, prepared by the king, the planned course of which was initially discussed during the aforementioned meeting in Levoča. In August 1496, the grand master and Prussian states responded to the Polish mission calling for the order to participate in the anti-Ottoman expedition. Essentially, John of Tiefen voluntarily declared that he would fulfil his duties to provide help 'against pagan Turks and Tatars', as his predecessor had done for the father of the present king. However, the conflict with the bishop of Warmia was still ongoing, and the resolution of this conflict was largely in the king's hands. Another urgent task was the protection of Livonia 'from pagan rebels Ruthenians and Muscovites [*Moschkowiten*] who did great damage to the Christian countries'. The grand master asked, due to 'impossibility' (*unmogenheit* — probably because of illness), not to have to participate in the expedition himself, claiming however that, if the king wished Tiefen's personal participation, he would even get on the cart and go so that he would not infringe the eternal peace, but make amends.[35] It is characteristic that both parties in this particular case referred to the obligations on the grand master and the order arising from the terms of the Second Peace of Thorn of 1466. However, the duty of the order to fight pagans and defend Christianity was not addressed.

From that moment on, the issue of the next anti-Ottoman expedition was constantly present in the order's diplomatic contacts. When Maximilian I attempted to extend the *Reich*'s supremacy over the whole of Prussia (both Royal and Teutonic) and demanded that they pay taxes, in his refusal of November 1496, the grand master mentioned the 'attack of rebel Ruthenians' and the need to fulfil his obligations to the king of Poland.

In turn, in a letter to King Maximilian I from May 1497, John of Tiefen asked that the order's bailiwicks in the *Reich* be release from their obligation to pay taxes. He gave the necessity of helping Livonia against Ruthenians and fighting against the Ottoman Empire as the main reasons for doing so. The grand master declared: '[I want] to fulfil my order's duty against pagan Turks to the best of all

---

33 Adam Szweda, 'Starania Jana Olbrachta o krzyżacką pomoc przeciwko księciu mazowieckiemu Konradowi III Rudemu w 1495 roku', *RH* 82 (2016), pp. 187–95.
34 Biskup, *Polska a Zakon*, p. 48.
35 *SVDOP* 3, no. 511, pp. 163–64.

my abilities'.[36] Interestingly, this time, in his argumentation, the order's superior preferred to mention the traditional duties of subordinate knights.

The course of the originally anti-Ottoman expedition of 1497, which in the end turned into a campaign against Voivode Stephen III of Moldavia, is primarily known through one source — a diary written by the grand master's secretary Liborius Naker.[37] His narration is certainly not objective, but it does accurately reflect the poor relationship between the master and the king. In one of the instructions for the envoys to the king, reported on by Naker, John of Tiefen sourly states that he was not asked for his advice before going on the expedition, even though he was the 'prince and counsellor of the crown' (eventually, the monarch was never presented with this provision). However, as a Christian ruler, he would stand against the pagans, even if he was not bound by the provisions of the eternal peace of 1466. He expressed concern that, as the head of the entire order, he had left the Livonian land master alone in the struggle against schismatics.[38] The illness and death of the grand master in Lwów (mod. Lviv, Ukraine) before the end of the expedition were undoubtedly symbolic moments.[39] Nevertheless, the remaining commanders of the Teutonic contingent sought to use these dramatic circumstances in order to obtain royal permission to return, with the entire Teutonic expedition, to Prussia.

In his letter to John I Albert, the commander of the northern Prussian town of Holland (mod. Pasłęk, Poland), Simon of Drahe, provided an account of the events related to the death of the grand master, but also presented the Ruthenian danger threatening Livonia. At this particular moment the fears of 'pagan Ruthenians' were formulated in a slightly exaggerated manner, which is evidenced by the fact that, in a letter by the same official to the regent of the order, William of Isenburg, written almost simultaneously, no mention is made of this threat.[40]

The order tried to take advantage of the circumstances after Tiefen's death in order to improve its situation. In a letter from the order's authorities to an unknown addressee (most likely Michael Sculteti, the procurator of the order in Rome), it was emphasised that the order went to war against the Ottomans voluntarily (*sponte*) as *christiane fidei defensor*.[41] The regent, William of Isenburg, stressed in a letter to the Romano-German king that the order was 'a tower and a wall against pagan Turks, Tatars and Ruthenians', thus increasing the Teutonic

---

36 *LUB* 2/1, no. 535, p. 391.
37 Liborius Naker, 'Tagebuch über den Kriegszug des Hochmeisters Johann von Tiefen gegen die Türken im Jahre 1497', ed. Max Töppen, in *SRP* 5: 289–314. On King John I Albert's unfortune anti-Moldavian campaign in 1497, see Czamańska, *Mołdawia i Wołoszczyzna*, pp. 167–84; Smołucha, *Papiestwo a Polska*, pp. 59–70; Pilat and Cristea, *Ottoman Threat*, pp. 243–51.
38 Naker, 'Tagebuch', p. 297. Thumser aptly summarises — 'Neue Aufgabe', p. 163 — that, according to the accounts of Liborius Naker, the Teutonic contingent's expedition was plagued with 'failures and unpleasant events'.
39 Naker, 'Tagebuch', pp. 308–9.
40 Naker, 'Tagebuch', pp. 309–10. See Thumser, 'Neue Aufgabe', p. 165.
41 *SVDOP* 3, no. 512, p. 164.

Knights' chances of gaining help, since there were fears in Prussia that the Ottoman Empire would seek revenge for the participation of the Teutonic knights' contingent in the Polish expedition.[42]

After Tiefen's death in August 1497, Frederick of Saxony became the new grand master — his election, according to the concept of the previous grand master, was to strengthen the position of the Teutonic Knights in Prussia, especially in relation to the king of Poland.[43] In a letter to the new grand master's brother — George the Bearded, duke of Saxony — in the tense situation following the election, John I Albert expressed his hope that, in the person of Frederick, he would gain a loyal helper in the fight against the Tatars.[44]

Conclusion

The intensity of use of the struggle-for-faith rhetoric, however, was decreasing, although crusading arguments did appear in Polono-Teutonic diplomatic disputes up until the end of the Teutonic rule in Prussia, as a consequence of the Treaty of Cracow and Prussian Homage in 1525. Interestingly, in the 1530s, within the *Reich*, the first duke of Prussia (former grand master) Albert of Hohenzollern referred to the order's past as *propugnaculum adversus ethnicos et scysmaticos*, i.e. 'a bulwark against heathens and schismatics".[45]

After 1466, crusade ideology and argumentations about the struggle to defend the faith were used in two ways in Polono-Teutonic relations. On the one hand, Kings Casimir IV Andrew and John I Albert used them to strengthen the pressure on the order when military assistance was expected from it. On the other hand, the grand masters Martin Truchsess and John of Tiefen tried to strengthen their position in Western Europe by using these arguments, or by indicating the Rutheno-Muscovite threat, so as to have a justification to give the king for their lack of enthusiasm for his demands. The struggle against the Ottomans and the extent of involvement of the Teutonic Order in it was, for both parties, one of the measures of the Second Peace of Thorn of 1466 and one of the key aspects in mutual relations between the king and the grand master, who was a vassal of the Polish monarch and his counsellor.

Such an instrumental approach to crusades was typical of the complicated world of European politics in the late fifteenth century when no one either questioned the real and growing Ottoman threat, or gave up the pursuit of their individual political strategies and the implementation of state and dynastic goals.

---

42 Biskup, *Polska a Zakon*, p. 63; Thumser, 'Neue Aufgabe', p. 168.
43 Biskup, *Polska a Zakon*, pp. 58–60, 64–67.
44 CESDQ 3, no. 437, p. 456. See Biskup, *Polska a Zakon*, p. 74.
45 Srodecki, *Antemurale Christianitatis*, pp. 146–47.

PART IV

Legitimation and Propaganda

ANDRZEJ MARZEC

Infideles et perfidi schismatici

Crusades and Christianisation as Political Tools of the Polish Kings in the Fourteenth Century

Introduction

Following the deaths of the Přemyslid kings Wenceslas II and his son Wenceslas III who, as well as their Bohemian home lands, also ruled Poland in personal union between 1300 and 1306, the Cuyavian duke Vladislas the Elbow-High initiated actions to recover the Polish lands, and in particular the region of Lesser Poland with Cracow, from Bohemian hands.[1] He had no difficulty in securing the endorsement of the knighthood and official elites in these endeavours, but the support of the urban communities required a special policy.[2] The problem lay not only in gaining the support of metropolitan Cracow, but also that of the burghers of the majority of Polish towns, where the dominant class had clear German sympathies. The Polono-German cultural clash was particularly strong at the time, and similar enmities could also be observed in many town communities in other adjacent monarchies, for example in Bohemia. The most serious incident which threatened the power of the Cuyavian duke was Mayor Albert's revolt in Cracow in the years 1311–12, which spread beyond the boundaries of the city and into

---

1 Edmund Długopolski, *Władysław Łokietek na tle swoich czasów* (Wrocław, 1951), pp. 57–105; Janusz Kurtyka, 'Das wiedervereinigte Königreich Polen unter Ladislaus Ellenlang (1304/05–33) und Kasimir dem Grossen (1333–70)', in *Die 'Blüte' der Staaten des östlichen Europa im 14. Jahrhundert*, ed. Marc Löwener, (Wiesbaden, 2004), pp. 107–42; Andrzej Marzec, 'Wenceslas II Přemyslid and Louis of Anjou: Two Personal Unions of the Polish Kingdom in the Fourteenth Century', in *Unions and Divisions: New Forms of Rule in Medieval and Renaissance Europe*, ed. Paul Srodecki, Norbert Kersken and Rimvydas Petrauskas (London, 2023), pp. 197–209.
2 Janusz Bieniak, *Wielkopolska, Kujawy, ziemie łęczycka i sieradzka wobec problemu zjednoczenia państwowego w latach 1300–06* (Toruń, 1969); Andrzej Marzec, *Urzędnicy małopolscy w otoczeniu Władysława Łokietka i Kazimierza Wielkiego 1306–70* (Kraków, 2006), pp. 21–47; Andrzej Marzec, 'Die Amtsträgerelite im Königreich Polen unter Władysław Ellenlang und Kasimir der Grossen (1305–70)', in *Studien zum Adel im mittelalterlichen Polen*, ed. Eduard Mühle (Wiesbaden 2012), pp. 311–20.

many smaller towns in Lesser Poland.[3] Likewise, there were also skirmishes with German burghers in Greater Poland, which became subordinated to his power in 1314. These enmities were a reflection of the international conflict between the Poles and the Teutonic Knights who, not without controversy, as pointed out by various contemporary reports, took over Pomerelia in the years 1308-9. The result was a heightened anti-German attitude among the Polish knighthood, while in Greater Poland the policies of the margraviate of Brandenburg under the Ascanian and Wittelsbach dynasties aimed against the Polish presence in Pomerelia was still vividly remembered.[4] Another field of political tensions at the time were the claims of John of Luxemburg, the new Bohemian king, to the Polish throne.[5] Against the background of this complex setting of competing power constellations and changing alliances in fourteenth-century East-Central Europe, the appeal to faith-defending motifs was one of the main rhetorical devices of international relations. In the following, I will address the momenta of crusading and Christianisation as political tools within Polish diplomacy, with a particular focus on the last two Piast kings.

Fighting the 'Infidels' as a Political Tool of the Polish Kings

In 1318, against all odds, an all-Polish congress took place in Sulejów. Here the decision was taken to send a diplomatic mission to Avignon with a request for the crown for Vladislas the Elbow-High. The mission was headed by Gerward of Ostrów, the bishop of Włocławek.[6] John XXII, in his papal bull of 20 August 1319, granted the crown to the Elbow-High, with the proviso, however, that the interests of the Luxemburgs should not suffer.[7] The most interesting passage in the bull is the main argument which finally decided upon the papal decision and

---

3 Edmund Długopolski, 'Bunt wójta Alberta', *Rocznik krakowski* 7, (1905), 135-86; Adam Kłodziński, 'Jeden czy dwa bunty wójta Alberta', in *Studia historyczne ku czci Stanisława Kutrzeby*, 2 vols (Kraków, 1938), 2: 339-59; Tomasz Pietras, *Krwawy wilk z pastorałem: Biskup krakowski Jan zwany Muskatą* (Warszawa, 2001), pp. 87-118.
4 Błażej Śliwiński, *Pomorze Wschodnie w okresie rządów księcia polskiego Władysława Łokietka w latach 1306-09* (Gdańsk, 2003), pp. 317-580.
5 Bronisław Nowacki, *Czeskie roszczenia do korony polskiej 1290-1335* (Poznań, 1987).
6 Janusz Bieniak, 'Wiec ogólnopolski w Żarnowie 3-7 czerwca 1319 a geneza koronacji Władysława Łokietka', PrzH 64 (1973), 469-81; Maciej Maciejowski, *Orientacje polityczne biskupów metropolii gnieźnieńskiej 1283-1320* (Kraków, 2007), pp. 343-51.
7 Władysław Abraham, 'Stanowisko kurii papieskiej wobec koronacji Łokietka', in *Księga pamiątkowa Uniwersytetu Lwowskiego ku czci 500 rocznicy fundacji Jagiellońskiej Uniwersytetu Krakowskiego* (Lwów, 1900), pp. 3-34; Jarosław Nikodem, 'Krakowska koronacja Władysława Łokietka', in *Gnieźnieńskie koronacje królewskie i ich środkowo-europejskie konteksty*, ed. Józef Dobosz, Marzena Matla and Leszek Wetesko (Poznań, 2011), pp. 273-84; Tomasz Jurek, 'Od dziedzica królestwa do króla', in *Władztwo Władysława Łokietka: 700 lecie koronacji królewskiej*, ed. Wojciech Fałkowski and Paweł Tyszka (Warszawa, 2022), pp. 87-117.

which seems to be repeated after the text of the Polish supplication. The passage in question states that the greatest misfortune faced by Poland after the death of King Premislas were the wars and threats from 'Tatars, Lithuanians, Ruthenians'.[8] The point is that this argument, based on the well-used Polish crusade rhetoric of the twelfth and thirteenth century, which depicted Poland as a crusading frontier country of Latin Christianity surrounded by enemies of the Catholic faith, is proof of the conscious propaganda and strategy of Polish diplomacy at the time.[9]

A great deal happened between the death of King Premislas and the coronation of Vladislas the Elbow-High, but the raids of the Mongolian/Tatar and Lithuanian 'infidels' and Ruthenian schismatics were marginal in the first quarter of the fourteenth century. Why then should precisely these have become the decisive argument? The answer is to be found in the experience that the Polish elites had gained in the lawsuit of the Gniezno archbishop Jakub Świnka against the Cracow bishop Jan called Muskata in the first decade of the fourteenth century. As the court files prove, the bishop of Cracow promoted the German element and asked for German help in the struggle against Vladislas.[10] Archbishop Świnka had strong anti-German sentiments, as is demonstrated in the chronicle of Peter of Žitava.[11] However, the papal court did not understand the concerns of the anti-German policy and the suit presented on these grounds was lost. Therefore, the attempts to gain the crown for the Elbow-High were constructed on entirely different grounds. Here, the crusade argument about the necessity of fighting the infidels and the schismatics proved to be the most effective.

Following Vladislas's coronation in 1320, the eastern policy of the state grew in strength, even though the Polono-Teutonic and Piast-Luxemburg relations had not been resolved and continued to bring problems to the royal court in Cracow.[12] The newly crowned Polish king opened up a long-term process of

---

8 *VMPL* 1, no. 226, pp. 146–48.
9 On the perception and adaptation of the crusade idea by Polish elites in the high Middle Ages, see Darius von Güttner-Sporzyński, 'The Periphery of Europe and the Idea of Crusade: Adaptation and Evolution of Crusader Ideology in Poland under the Piast Dynasty (1100–47)', in *The Expansion of the Faith: Crusading on the Frontiers of Latin Christendom in the High Middle Ages*, ed. Paul Srodecki and Norbert Kersken (Turnhout, 2021), pp. 69–88; Paul Srodecki, 'Fighting the "Eastern Plague": Anti-Mongol Crusade Ventures in the Thirteenth Century', in *The Expansion of the Faith*, pp. 303–27.
10 *AV*, no. 121, pp. 78–95.
11 'Petra Žitavského kronika zbraslavská', ed. Josef Emler, in *FRB* 4, pp. 1–337 (here 82); *Cronica Aulae Regiae*, ed. Anna Pumpova and Libor Jan, MGH SS 40 (Wiesbaden, 2022), p. 133.
12 Antoni Prohaska, 'Stosunki Krzyżaków z Giedyminem i Łokietkiem', *KH* 10 (1896), 1–66; Jan Dąbrowski, 'Z czasów Łokietka: Studium nad stosunkami polsko-węgierskimi w XIV wieku', *Rozprawy Akademii Umiejętności: Wydziału filozoficzno-historycznego* 59 (1916), 278–326; Stanisław Zajączkowski, *Polska a Zakon Krzyżacki w ostatnich latach Władysława Łokietka* (Lwów, 1929); Henryk Paszkiewicz, 'Polska a Wittelsbachowie w pierwszej połowie XIV wieku', in *Prace historyczne w 30-lecie działalności profesorskiej Stanisława Zakrzewskiego* (Lwów, 1934), pp. 43–111; Janina Gładyszówna, 'Ludwik Wittelsbach margrabia brandenburski wobec Polski (czasy Władysława Łokietka)', *RH* 9 (1933), 1–45; Stanisław Nowogrodzki, *Między Luksemburgami, Wittelsbachami a Polską (Pomorze Zachodnie a Polska w latach 1323–70)* (Gdańsk, 1936); Janusz Kurtyka, *Odrodzone*

political rapprochement with the grand duchy of Lithuania, which grew in importance over time. Although there is no way of proving the continuous character of this process between Vladislas's reign and the Union of Kreva (Pol. Krewa, Lith. Krėva) in 1385, it is evident that an understanding of the advantages of a better and closer relationship with Lithuania became quite strong. The first visible and important sign was the Polono-Lithuanian treaty of 1325, crowned with the marriage of Prince Casimir Aldona (baptised as Anne), the daughter of Grand Duke Gediminas.[13] Lithuanian participation in the Polish wars with the Teutonic Knights in the late 1320s became the subject of relatively strong attacks aimed at the Elbow-High from the house of Luxemburg, who portrayed Vladislas as an illegal Polish king, contemptuously referring to him as 'the Cracow king' and depicting him as an ally of the pagans whose raids harassed Christian territories. In a suit before the papal court in 1339, the Teutonic Knights also used the latter argument against the Polish kingdom.[14] What is worth noting, though, is the fact that, until the death of Aldona in 1339, the Polish kingdom did not suffer any destructive Lithuanian raids.

With the reign of Casimir the Great and the beginning of expansion into Ruthenia, relations with the pagans and schismatics changed and led to long-lasting conflicts with the Lithuanian dukes.[15] After 1340 and after the first Polish military expedition against Galicia, the dynamics of the conflicts with the Lithuanian princes, both those who were Orthodox and those who were pagan, intensified, as did those with the Golden Horde Tatars. The anti-Polish alliances kept changing, with the most frequent ones, however, bringing together the Lithuanians and Tatars against the Poles. In 1341, Lesser Poland suffered from a Tatar raid in which the voivode of Cracow Mścigniew Czelej was killed.[16] This immediately led to the king placing a strong emphasis on engaging in fighting the infidel and schismatic world under the sign of the cross, particularly in his relations with the Roman curia. It became Casimir's main argument in securing church funds for the expensive wars. In this regard, the papacy met the Polish king with benevolence: while granting the same indulgences as for the Levant ventures, Pope Benedict XII, for instance, explicitly called for a crusade against

---

królestwo: Monarchia Władysława Łokietka i Kazimierza Wielkiego w świetle nowszych badań (Kraków, 2001), pp. 37–42.

13 Kazimierz Jasiński, Rodowód Piastów małopolskich i kujawskich (Poznań, 2001), p. 167; Bronisław Włodarski, 'Między Polską, Litwa a Zakonem Krzyżackim', Zapiski Towarzystwa Naukowego Toruńskiego 16 (1950), 5–21; Grzegorz Błaszczyk, Dzieje stosunków polsko-litewskich od czasów najdawniejszych do współczesności, 2 vols (Poznań, 1998–2007), 1: Trudne początki, pp. 111–13.

14 Andrzej Feliks Grabski, Polska w opiniach Europy Zachodniej XIV–XV w. (Warszawa, 1968), pp. 149–67.

15 On the context of the Polono-Lithuanian wars, see Henryk Paszkiewicz, Polityka ruska Kazimierza Wielkiego (Warszawa, 1925); Sven Jaros, Iterationen im Grenzenraum: Akteure und Felder multikonfessioneller Herrschaftsaushandlung in Kronruthenien (1340–1434) (Berlin, 2021).

16 'Annales Posnaniensis I (929–1341)', ed. Gerard Labuda, in MPH n. s. 6, pp. 127–34 (here 130); 'Annales Sanctae Crucis', ed. Anna Rutkowska-Płachcińska, in MPH n. s. 12, pp. 62–63; John of Czarnków, 'Chronicon Polonorum', ed. Jan Szlachtowski, in MPH 2, pp. 599–756 (here 622).

'the perfidious tribe of the Tatars' in summer 1340.[17] Three years later, the Polish king obtained consent to use tithes to fund the war with the Lithuanians and the Golden Horde Tatars from Benedict's successor, Pope Clement VI.[18] Further Tatar raids in the early 1350s led the same pope to call for a crusade against the Golden Horde in May 1352.[19]

In the intensive contacts with the pagan world, however, Christianisation through proselytisation still seems to have been much more important than wars against the 'infidels' from the east and forced conversion. The royal court in Cracow was confident that good relations with Lithuania would help to keep the Ruthenian territories in Polish hands in the long term. Apart from these political calculations, the ambition to become the dominant power in the process of the Christianisation of the grand duchy of Lithuania also lay behind the royal policy. A good example is the 1351–52 war between Poland, Lithuania and Hungary. By 1349 the Polish king had gained control over Galicia and Volhynia, defeating the Lithuanian grand prince up to the borders of Podolia.[20] The result was that Louis the Great of Hungary developed an interest in the Polish expansion. Ever since the first half of the thirteenth century, the Arpads had had claims on the thrones of Galicia and Volhynia (*rex Galiciae et Lodomeriae*); the Angevin dynasty inherited that appetite.[21] Furthermore, crusading at the Lithuanian frontier was nothing new for the Hungarian ruler: only two years after ascending the throne, the Angevin took part in the campaign of King John of Bohemia, who joined forces with the Teutonic Knights against the pagan Lithuanians at the end of 1344.[22] Seven years later, Louis willingly rushed with an army across the Carpathians to help his uncle Casimir in his fight against the Lithuanians and Tatars. The campaign was accompanied by crusade preaching throughout Poland, Hungary and Bohemia and the Holy See granted both rulers a four-year tithe for the defence of Latin Christianity.[23] The joint Polono-Hungarian army set out towards Ruthenia, but got stuck at Lublin because the Polish king fell so seriously ill that there were fears he might die.[24]

---

17 *VMHH* 1, no. 958, pp. 637–38.
18 *BP* 1, no. 1895–97.
19 *VMPL* 1, no. 713, pp. 539–40.
20 Paszkiewicz, *Polityka ruska*, pp. 111–19.
21 Bronisław Włodarski, *Polska i Ruś 1194–1340* (Warszawa, 1966), pp. 31–90; Witalij Nagirnyj, *Polityka zagraniczna księstw ziem halickiej i włodzimierskiej w latach 1198–1264* (Kraków, 2011), pp. 147–225.
22 Norman Housley, 'King Louis the Great of Hungary and the Crusades, 1342–82', *The Slavonic and East European Review* 62 (1984), 192–208 (here 193–95).
23 *VMPL* 1, no. 713, pp 539–40; *VMHH* 1, no. 1249, pp. 815–16.
24 *Chronicon Dubnicense*, ed. Flórián Mátyás, HHFD 3, pp. 160–63.

Changing Alliances

Seeing that Casimir was no longer a participant in the political manoeuvres, Louis the Great, instead of continuing a military campaign against the Lithuanian duke Kęstutis of Trakai, started negotiations to convince the latter to enter a political union with Hungary on condition of accepting baptism. The Hungarian efforts, as described in detail in *Chronicon Dubnicense*, clearly demonstrate their sense. The proposition was that Kęstutis would be baptised into the Catholic Church in Hungary, in return obtaining the papal grant of the royal crown and consent to create an independent church province in Lithuania. Poland and Hungary were to help Lithuania in fighting the Teutonic Knights. The agreement would lead to Louis's unquestioned prerogative in the western parts of Ruthenia. Two events came to hinder Louis's success in this instance. First, on his way to Hungary, Kęstutis proved treasonous, and second, Poland helped him betray his faith to Louis. Kęstutis had no desire to remain faithful to the treaty with Louis and, winning the Polish escort over to his side (*quod Poloni custodiam adhibuissent*), managed to return to Lithuania.[25] If we accept the truth of the Polish hand in this betrayal, then we may claim this as evidence of competition between the kings of Poland and Hungary over the control of the Christianisation process in Lithuania.

Casimir the Great finally recovered from his illness and showed no intention of giving up his plans for domination in the east. On the contrary, Polish troops led various minor and bigger campaigns against Poland's eastern neighbours in the following years. After two campaigns in 1352 and 1353, the Piast king sent one of his finest diplomates to the Golden Horde, Jan Pakosławic, who managed to make peace with the Tatars under favourable conditions for the Poles in the winter of 1353–54. According to the Italian contemporary historian Matteo Villani (*c.* 1290–1363), shortly after the Polono-Tatar peace was arranged, Louis of Hungary renewed his military efforts in this region and moved against the Golden Horde in April 1354, reportedly this time with a larger army.[26] Then, in 1356, Polish forces moved against the Lithuanians once again, defeating them heavily.[27] As in the past, Casimir again petitioned the Holy See for renewed crusade preaching against the Lithuanians, Tatars and Ruthenians — something Pope Innocent IV granted without hesitation as proven by his crusade bull from November 1354.[28]

The next important event which demonstrates the position of Christianisation in Casimir's political plans was the attempt to convince the Lithuanian prince

---

25 See previous footnote; Antoni Prochaska, 'W sprawie zajęcia Rusi przez Kazimierza Wielkiego', *KH* 6 (1892), 1–33; Paszkiewicz, *Polityka ruska*, pp. 125–30; Henryk Paszkiewicz, 'Z dziejów rywalizacji polsko-węgierskiej na terenie Rusi halicko-włodzimierskiej w XIV wieku: Traktaty z lat 1350–1352', *KH* 38 (1924), 281–310; Andrzej Marzec, *Pod rządami nieobecnego monarchy: Królestwo Polskie 1370–82* (Kraków, 2017), pp. 44–45.
26 Gyula Kristó, *Az Anjou-kor háborúi*, pp. 134, 269; Housley, 'King Louis', p. 194.
27 Housley, 'King Louis', p. 194.
28 *VMHH* 2, no. 18, pp. 10–11.

to accept baptism in the late 1350s, together with the proposed marriage of a Lithuanian princess (Grand Duke Algirdas's daughter Kenna, baptised as Joan) to Casimir's grandson (i.e., the son of Bogislas V of Pomerania and Elizabeth, the daughter of the Polish king). After the Ruthenian campaigns led under the sign of the cross in the years 1351–56, Polish domination of Galicia became solidified and the king returned to the idea of securing lasting relations with Lithuania.[29] The proposed marriage was to be the main guarantee of good relations, irrespective of the Lithuanian acceptance of Christianity. At this time, most probably also thanks to Algirdas's widespread diplomatic range of actions, the question of the Lithuanian baptism also became the object of attention at the court of Charles IV, the first king of Bohemia to become Holy Roman emperor in 1355. Algirdas must have realised that the Polish king alone could not guarantee relief from the military and political pressure caused by the Teutonic Knights' *Litauerreisen*. However, building on old imperial traditions from the Hohenstaufen era, since when the Romano-German rulers had seen themselves as protectors of the Order, Charles IV had no intention, of course, of forcing the Teutonic Knights to move from the south-eastern and eastern Baltic Sea region to southern Ruthenia in order to help fight the Tatars, as the Lithuanians wished, nor was he in any position to do so. Although the emperor's mission returned from Lithuania with no result sometime in the late spring and early summer of 1358, it remains an interesting episode of the first Lithuanian plans to instrumentalise — and thus redirect from their own country — the Teutonic Knights and the crusaders travelling to Prussia for their fight against the Golden Horde.[30] These attempts foreshadowed Grand Duke Vytautas's Vorskla campaign of 1399, led under the sign of the cross and with not insignificant support from the Order.

Back in the 1350s, Casimir the Great increased his diplomatic efforts in Lithuania's Christianisation process and in 1357 he sent letters to Avignon asking the pope to help convince the emperor and Louis the Great to become involved in the negotiations. At the same time, he tried to secure the supremacy of the Polish church over the future Christian province in Lithuania.[31] Casimir's real achievement, though, was safeguarding a few years of peace on the Polono-Lithuanian border. The marriage of the Pomeranian prince Casimir (his mother was a

---

29 Paszkiewicz, *Polityka ruska*, pp. 190–95.
30 The Lithuanian dukes promised to come to the imperial court to be baptised, but they did not do so. Władysław Abraham, 'Polska a chrzest Litwy', in *Polska i Litwa w dziejowym stosunku: Ku uczczeniu 500-setniej rocznicy unii horodelskiej*, ed. Wojciech Baranowski (Warszawa 1914), pp. 8–9; Jadwiga Karwasińska, 'Złote bulle Karola IV w sprawie chrztu Litwy', in *Cultus et cognition: Studia z dziejów średniowiecznej kultury*, ed. Stefan Krzysztof Kuczyński (Warszawa, 1976), pp. 233–49; Jerzy Wyrozumski, 'Litwa w polityce Piastów', *Acta Universitatis Nicolai Copernici*, 26 (1992), 63–65; Alvydas Nikžentaitis, 'Die friedliche Periode in den Beziehungen zwischen dem Deutschen Orden und dem Grossfürstentum Litauen (1345–60) und das Problem der Christianisierung Litauens', *JGO NF* 41 (1993), 1–21 (here 18).
31 Władysław Abraham, *Powstanie organizacyi kościoła łacińskiego na Rusi* (Lwów, 1904), pp. 367–68; Błaszczyk, *Dzieje stosunków* 1: 174–75.

granddaughter of Prince Gediminas) and Algirdas's daughter Joan did not last long, however, since she died in 1368.[32] Nevertheless, Casimir's policy with regard to Lithuania was an important milestone in the Polono-Lithuanian reproachment, which demonstrated the extent to which the king was able to look towards the future, even though we can of course only guess how far and in what way he might have planned the Polono-Lithuanian alliance. Doubtless, if Algirdas had accepted Christianity, and the marriage with Casimir's grandson had lasted long enough, the position of Poland in Ruthenia would have positively grown in strength while the Teutonic Order state in Prussia and Livonia would have evidently become weaker. Bearing in mind that Casimir later tried to secure the Polish throne for his grandson, one can understand the momentous significance of the king's actions in the period between 1357–58.[33] However, the Christianisation of Lithuania did not take place. Quite the contrary, rather than retain the peaceful path of Christianisation through diplomacy, the Lithuanians were soon once again relocated to the camp of the enemies of the Catholic faith. Like his predecessors, Pope Urban V called for a crusade against 'Lithuanians, Tatars and other unbelievers and schismatics' and granted indulgences to all Christians who were willing to take the cross and help Poland in the summer of 1363.[34] Casimir did indeed lead a campaign under the sign of the cross against the Lithuanians in 1366, defeating them in Volhynia. In response, Masovia and the kingdom of Poland were once again raided by Lithuania in 1368. As soon as the king died in November 1370, the Gediminid prince Liubartas seized back the castle of Volodymyr in Volhynia without much effort.[35]

It is worth offering a further proof of Casimir the Great's elastic diplomacy here. In the years before his activity connected with the Christianisation of Lithuania, the king sought to arrange a settlement with the Golden Horde and sent a diplomatic mission there under Jan Pakosławic of Strożyska, which must have been successful, judging by the considerable estate in Ruthenia he later received from the king.[36] The burgesses of Wrocław/Breslau knew about Jan's

---

32 Jan Tęgowski, 'Małżeństwo Kaźka Bogusławowica z Kenną Olgierdówną i jego rola w politycznych planach Kazimierza Wielkiego', in *Homines et societas*, ed. Tomasz Jasiński, Tomasz Jurek and Jan M. Piskorski (Poznań, 1997), pp. 125–33.
33 Kazimierz Jasiński, 'Małżeństwa i koligacje polityczne Kazimierza Wielkiego', *Studia Źródłoznawcze: Commentationes* 32–33 (1990), 67–76; Joachim Zdrenka, 'Pomorze Zachodnie w świetle polityki dynastycznej Kazimierza', in *Europa Środkowa i Wschodnia w polityce Piatów*, ed. Zofia Zielińska-Melkowska (Toruń, 1997), pp. 159–71; Janusz Bieniak, 'Jan (Janek) z Czarnkowa: Niedokończona kronika polska z XIV wieku', *Studia Źródłoznawcze*, 47 (2009), 121–24.
34 *VMPL* 1, no. 833, pp. 618–19. See Srodecki, 'Fighting the "Eastern Plague"'.
35 John of Czarnków, 'Chronicon Polonorum', pp. 631 and 643–44; *CDM* 3, no. 105; Paszkiewicz, *Polityka ruska*, pp. 231–48; Anna Supruniuk, *Mazowsze Siemowitów (1341–1442): Dzieje polityczne, struktury władzy* (Warszawa, 2010), pp. 28.
36 Paszkiewicz, *Polityka ruska*, pp. 171–72; Janusz Kurtyka, 'Krąg rodowy i rodzinny Jan Pakosławica ze Strożyska i Rzeszowa (ze studiów nad rodem Półkoziców w XIII i XIV wieku)', *Przemyskie zapiski historyczne* 6–7 (1988–89), 7–12; Maciej Wilamowski, 'Magnate Territories in Red Ruthenia in the Fourteenth and Fifteenth Centuries: Origin, Development and Social Impact', in *On the Frontier*

mission and informed Emperor Charles IV — not without evident exaggeration — that the Polish king was allegedly looking for a wife there.[37] The effect of the mission was to free Poland from the threat of the Golden Horde, therefore allowing for the military successes in Ruthenia in 1356 as well as subsequent attempts at negotiating Christianisation with Lithuania.

Louis the Great, as king of Poland from 1370, did not undertake any further attempts to use the Christianisation of Lithuania as a tool in strengthening his political position in Eastern Europe. He subjected Galicia to the authority of the Hungarian Crown and controlled it by means of his tributary, the Piast duke Vladislas II of Opole (a former provincial governor of Hungary). Until his death in 1382, Louis was much more interested in strengthening and stabilising church structures in this region.[38] As a result, in the papal bull *Debitum pastoralis officii* of 1375, Pope Gregory XI endorsed the new church province under the archbishop of Halych, consisting of the dioceses of Peremyshl (mod. Przemyśl, Poland), Kholm (mod. Chełm, Poland) and Volodymyr.[39] However, the duke of Masovia, Siemowit III, sent his chancellor Dobrogost of Nowy Dwór to the pope to negotiate help in obtaining Louis the Great's support for his efforts at bringing Lithuania into Christian Europe.[40]

The next stage in the process of Polono-Lithuanian rapprochement began during the interregnum which followed Louis's death. The Polish elites were unable to negotiate any kind of settlement with the widowed Queen Elisabeth of Bosnia and therefore saw a chance for political stabilisation in the person of Grand Duke Jogaila.[41] This meant that the idea of the Christianisation of Lithuania was no longer part of royal policy, but rather a political aim of the Polish elites who were trying to secure a new king for the country.

Concluding Thoughts

The themes of crusades and Christianisation in the late Middle Ages were by no means less exploited than at the heyday of the crusades. They became a useful

---

of *Latin Europe: Integration and Segregation in Red Ruthenia 1350–1600*, ed. Thomas Wünsch and Andrzej Janeczek (Warszawa, 2004), p. 92.
37 *Correspondenz der Stadt Breslau mit Karl IV in der Jahren 1347–55*, ed. Colmar Grünhagen (Wien, 1865), p. 365.
38 Jerzy Sperka, 'Territorial Powers, System of Administration and the Inner Circle of Duke Władysław Opolczyk (†1401)', *QMAN* 14 (2009); Marzec, *Pod rządami nieobecnego monarchy*, pp. 70–76, 83–96.
39 Abraham, *Powstanie organizacyi*, pp. 288–315.
40 *VMPL* 1, nos 934–36, pp. 694–96; Jan Pakulski, *Nałęcze wielkopolscy w średniowieczu: Genealogia, uposażenie i rola polityczna* (Warszawa, 1982), pp. 146–49.
41 Oskar Halecki, *Dzieje unii jagiellońskiej*, 2 vols (Kraków, 1919–20), 1: 113–66; Henryk Paszkiewicz, *O genezie i znaczeniu Krewa* (Warszawa, 1938); Jan Tęgowski, 'Bezkrólewie po śmierci Ludwika Węgierskiego a geneza unii Polski z Litwą', in *Studia historyczne z XIII–XV wieku*, ed. Józef Śliwiński (Olsztyn, 1995), pp. 87–110; Marzec, 'Pod rządami nieobecnego monarchy', pp. 211–28.

tool in achieving incisive political aims, as was the case, for example, in the Polish kingdom in the fourteenth century, when the argument of the threat posed by the non-Latin Christian eastern neighbours was used to obtain the royal crown for Vladislas the Elbow-High, as well as to secure the success of the expansive policies in Ruthenia. The policy of peaceful Christianisation was used as a tool in strengthening and stabilising the position of the Polish monarchy in East-Central Europe, and also as a major argument in discrediting the existence of the state of the Teutonic Knights in Prussia and Livonia. There is yet another aspect to the problem which is interesting in cultural terms. The crusades offered an ideal image of the monarch as a Christian knight which was still valid in the fourteenth century, as a pattern of the monarch-knight who challenges the infidels and pagans. This was exploited not only in the realisation of political plans, but also in political propaganda.

A good example is the famous assembly of the Central European monarchs in Cracow in 1364. This event, organised by Casimir the Great as a solemn celebration of the end of enmities between Charles IV and Louis the Great, made the Polish king one of the arbiters in the eponymous feud. The king of Cyprus, Peter, who at the time was travelling from one kingdom to the next looking for support in fighting the Ottoman Turks, came to Cracow together with the Emperor Charles IV. He was greeted as an honorary guest, and the Cracow Assembly therefore became the occasion at which all the monarchs present could publicly declare their readiness to engage in the crusade against the eternal enemy of Christianity.[42] The assembly thus acquired a new and extremely attractive shape as a meeting of crusaders. Although it is difficult to imagine that Casimir the Great was truly interested in fighting the Muslims, one should still be careful not to interpret the whole event as a display of political cynicism. The example of Duke Vladislas the White of Gniewkowo, a member of the Cuyavian line of the Piast dynasty and second half-nephew of the Polish king, proves an honest if not particularly swashbuckling attitude to crusades. Vladislas left his small duchy on the northern border of the Polish kingdom to Casimir the Great and, with a group of Polish knights, set off for the Holy Land.[43]

The geographical position of the Polish kingdom placed it at the point of contact of four different worlds: Western Christianity, Eastern Christianity, Mongol/Tatar Islam, and Lithuanian paganism. As a result, the themes of Christianisation and crusading were always present as not insignificant leitmotifs in the political and ideological programmes construed at the royal court. There was nothing new about this because, ever since the baptism of Mieszko I in 966, confrontation with the non-Latin Christian neighbours had been a constant element of the political reality of the Polish lands, and was thus mirrored in the fast

---

42 Stanisław Szczur, 'Krakowski zjazd monarchów z 1364 roku', *RH* 64 (1998), 35–58.
43 John of Czarnków, 'Chronicon Polonorum', pp. 661–63; Józef Śliwiński, *Władysław Biały (1327/1333–20 luty 1388): Ostatni książę kujawski, największy podróżnik wśród Piastów* (Kraków, 2011), pp. 38–46.

Fig. 21. Contemporary royal seals of the Polish kings Vladislas the Elbow-High (top) and his son Casimir III the Great (bottom) as used in the late 1320s and the second half of the 1330s respectively. Reproduced by Paul Srodecki from Teofil Żebrawski, *O pieczęciach dawnéj Polski i Litwy* (Kraków, 1865), figs 30 and 32.

adaptation of the high medieval crusade idea and rhetoric of fighting the enemies of the faith and defending the Catholic West at its eastern frontiers. However, if the policy was hardly coordinated during the period of fragmentation of the Piast lands in the thirteenth century, when the duchy of Masovia was mainly responsible for fighting the Lithuanians, the eastern policy took on a new shape at the moment of the unification of the country. The updated royal and political ambitions of Vladislas the Elbow-High, and then those of his son, dictated new and more nuanced activities in respect to the problem of Christianisation. The political propaganda based on the idea of crusades had also become more sophisticated and dynamic. I believe that this served, perhaps unconsciously, to lay out a definite political direction which led to the Union of Kreva (Pol. Krewa, Lith. Krėva) between the kingdom of Poland and the grand duchy of Lithuania in 1385.

SVEN JAROS

Against *Tartari, Rutheni et Litfani, hostes fidei*

The Role and Ambivalence of the Crusading Idea in the Integration of Ruthenia into the Polish Crown in the Second Half of the Fourteenth Century

In the summer of 1340, the kingdom of Poland sent a call for help to the curia of Pope Benedict XII in Avignon. The Polish king Casimir III informed the pope that his realm was threatened by the 'treacherous tribes of the Tatars', who 'walked in darkness, missing the light of Catholic truth'. In this Polish realm, lying 'on the outer borders of Christianity', the pope announced a crusade against the Tatars (*crucis Christi signaculo [...] duximus concedam*) on 1 August. Furthermore, this crusade was also to be preached in the kingdom of Bohemia and the lands of the Hungarian crown. Finally, to motivate potential crusaders, those who took up the fight against the Tatars were promised the same indulgences granted to those fighting in the Holy Land.[1]

Following this rhetoric, the importance of the fight against the Tatars equalled that of the struggle against the Muslims in the Holy Land. As the other contributions in the preceding book *The Expansion of the Faith: Crusading on the Frontiers of Latin Christendom in the High Middle Ages* as well those in this volume have shown, the fight against non-Christians outside the Levante became a trans-European phenomenon from the twelfth century onwards and lasted well into the later Middle Ages.[2] In this chapter, I would like to challenge this crusade rhetoric and ask: how much of the crusading idea can we find when examining the situation at the frontier between Central and Eastern Europe in the fourteenth century?

---

1 Given the fact that the papal letters presented in the following article are often printed in several editions, I have tried to align them as completely as possible. For 1 August 1340, the situation is the following: *BP* 1, nos 1895–96 (those letters are falsely listed under 1 July), see *VMHH* 1, nos 958–59, p. 637.
2 For the high medieval peripheral crusades, see, with further references, Paul Srodecki, 'Crusading on the Periphery in the High Middle Ages: Main Debates, New Approaches', in *The Expansion of the Faith: Crusading on the Frontiers of Latin Christendom in the High Middle Ages*, ed. Paul Srodecki and Norbert Kersken (Turnhout, 2022), pp. 29–52. For an overview of the late medieval crusade movement with further references, see this volume's introductory chapter.

At the time, this border region was the scene of a battle for supremacy between the Teutonic Order, the grand duchy of Lithuania, the western Ruthenian principalities, the Golden Horde and the kingdoms of Hungary and Poland.[3] There are many aspects underlying this rivalry, one of which was the expansion of both Poland and Lithuania into the former principality of Galicia-Volhynia between 1340 and 1366.[4] The western Ruthenian lands conquered by the kingdom of Poland have several designations, the one most frequently used in Polish

---

3 As a general overview for the political entities mentioned above, see *Die 'Blüte' der Staaten des östlichen Europa im 14. Jahrhundert*, ed. Marc Löwener (Wiesbaden, 2004); *Akteure mittelalterlicher Außenpolitik: Das Beispiel Ostmitteleuropas*, ed. Stephan Flemmig and Norbert Kersken (Marburg, 2017). On the diplomatic relations between the Teutonic Order and the kingdom of Poland, see, for instance, Adam Szweda, 'Polen und der Deutsche Orden — Botenwesen und friedliche Verhandlungen', in *Tannenberg — Grundwald — Zalgiris 1410: Krieg und Frieden im späten Mittlealter*, ed. Werner Paravicini, Rymvydas Petrauskas and Grischa Vercamer (Wiesbaden, 2012), pp. 223–36. On the Golden Horde, see Bertold Spuler, *Die Goldene Horde: Die Mongolen in Rußland. 1223–1502* (Leipzig, 1943); Peter Jackson, *The Mongols and the West: 1221–1405* (London, 2005). On diplomatic relations between those entities, see especially Christian Lübke, 'Außenpolitik im östlichen Mitteleuropa: Expansion und Hegemonie am Beispiel Polens und des Landes Halič-Volyn' (bis 1387)', in *Das Reich und Polen: Parallelen: Interaktionen und Formen der Akkulturation im hohen und späten Mittelalter*, ed. Thomas Wünsch (Ostfildern, 2003), pp. 21–58. Sven Jaros, *Iterationen im Grenzraum: Akteure und Felder multikonfessioneller Herrschaftsaushandlung in Kronruthenien (1340–1434)* (Berlin, 2021).

4 The classic works concerning the Polish expansion are Henryk Paszkiewicz, *Polityka ruska Kazimierza Wielkiego* (Warszawa, 1925), and Gotthold Rhode, *Die Ostgrenze Polens: Politische Entwicklung, kulturelle Bedeutung und geistige Auswirkungen im Mittelalter bis zum Jahre 1401* (Köln, 1955). Later research has focused on more detailed social or legal aspects of the expansion: Andrzej Janeczek, 'Udział szlachty w kolonizacji Rusi Koronnej: Migracje rodów i ich nowa własność (XIV–XV w.): Próba ujęcia syntetycznego', in *Rody na Śląsku, Rusi Czerwonej i w Małopolsce: Średniowiecze i czasy nowożytne. Stan badań, metodologia, nowe ustalenia*, ed. Wioletta Zawitkowska and Anna Pobóg-Lenartowicz (Rzeszów, 2010), pp. 59–91; Janeczek, 'New Authority, New Property, New Nobility: The Foundation of Noble Estates in Red Ruthenia during the Fourteenth and Fifteenth Centuries', QMAN 7 (2002), 77–125; Janeczek, *Osadnictwo pogranicza polsko-ruskiego: Województwo Bełskie od schyłku XIV do początku XVII w.* (Warszawa, 1993); Olga Kozubska-Andrusiv, '... propter disparitatem linguae et religionis pares ipsis non esse ...: Minority Communities in Medieval and Early Modern Lviv', in *Segregation, Integration, Assimilation: Religious and Ethnic Groups in the Medieval Towns of Central and Eastern Europe*, ed. Derek Keene, Balázs Nagy and Katalin Szende (Farnham, 2009), pp. 51–66; Kozubska-Andrusiv, 'German Law in Medieval Galician Rus' (Rotreussen)', *Rechtsgeschichte: Zeitschrift des Max-Planck-Instituts für europäische Rechtsgeschichte* 13 (2008), 25–46. A comparative perspective is offered by Christian Lübke, '"Germania Slavica" und "Polonia Ruthenica": Religiöse Divergenz in ethno-kulturellen Grenz- und Kontaktzonen des mittelalterlichen Osteuropa (8.–16. Jahrhundert)', in *Grenzräume und Grenzüberschreitungen im Vergleich: Der Osten und der Westen des mittelalterlichen Lateineuropa*, ed. Klaus Herbers and Nicolas Jaspert (Berlin, 2007), pp. 175–89. Jan Orzechowski's essay is in many ways an intriguing but also problematic synthesis: 'Okcydentalizacja Rusi Koronnej w XIV, XV i XVI w.', in *Państwo, naród stany w świadomości wieków średnich: Pamięci Benedykta Zientary 1929–83*, ed. Aleksander Gieysztor and Sławomir Gawlas (Warszawa, 1990), pp. 215–43. The best introduction in English to this topic is by far *On the Frontier of Latin Europe: Integration and Segregation in Red Ruthenia, 1350–1600*, ed. Thomas Wünsch and Andrzej Janeczek (Warszawa, 2004).

historiography — which I also prefer — being 'Crown Ruthenia'.[5] After 1434, this region had become a regular voivodship within the kingdom of Poland.[6]

To succeed in incorporating the region of the Galicio-Volhynian Rus into the Polish crown, Polish diplomacy applied the rhetoric of *antemurale christianitatis* in order to gain international support, as Paul Srodecki has argued convincingly.[7] Andrzej Marzec and other Polish scholars have cast a revealing new light on the reign of Casimir III, the last Polish king of the Piast dynasty and conqueror of the Rus lands to become Crown Ruthenia.[8] Rather than presenting newly found material, this paper is dedicated to a detailed examination of the papal correspondence during the years of the Polish conquest of this region, particularly between 1340 and 1358.

For this paper, I will focus on six of these letters, dating from 1341, 1343, 1351–52 and 1356–57 (highlighted in bold in table 1). This material seems to be the most helpful in answering the following questions: first, which aspects of crusading are mentioned? Second, what information about the Polish expansion can be deduced from the papal correspondence? Third, which rhetorical strategies can be discerned when addressing the pope? And finally, how well informed was the Roman curia about political, religious and diplomatic developments during this conquest?

In a following step, I will seek to compare my findings on these aspects with the results of my analysis of royal charters for Crown Ruthenia. In a final paragraph, I will compare this conquest during the reign of Casimir with the reincorporation of Crown Ruthenia following the coronation of Jogaila in the mid-1380s.

---

5 The term *Crown Ruthenia* is a literal translation of the Polish term 'Ruś koronna', which has become popular in Polish research. This term is used as an alternative to *Red Ruthenia* (Germ. 'Rotreußen', Pol. 'Ruś Czerwona') because it is much more specific and bypasses any anachronistic connotation. On the emergence of the term 'Red Ruthenia', see Christophe von Werdt, *Stadt und Gemeindebildung in Ruthenien: Okzidentalisierung der Ukraine und Weißrusslands im Spätmittelalter und in der frühen Neuzeit* (Wiesbaden, 2006), p. 21.

6 The year 1434 marks the end point of the long process of establishing Polish law and administrative structures in Crown Ruthenia, see Werdt, *Stadt und Gemeindebildung*, p. 62; Maciej Wilamowski, 'Powstanie i początki hierarchii urzędów ziemskich województwa ruskiego i Podola', *RH* 64 (1998), 105–27.

7 Paul Srodecki, *Antemurale Christianitatis: Zur Genese der Bollwerksrhetorik im östlichen Mitteleuropa an der Schwelle vom Mittelalter zur Frühen Neuzeit* (Husum, 2015). For our context, see especially Paul Srodecki, '"Scutum inexpugnabile": The Use of the "Christian Outpost" Propaganda to Legitimise the Conquest of Galicia-Volhynia under the Two Last Piast Kings of Poland, 1323–1370', in *Principalities in Lands of Galicia and Volhynia in International Relations in the 11th–14th Centuries*, ed. Vitalyj Nagirnyj (Kraków, 2012), pp. 114–20.

8 See, for instance, Andrzej Marzec, *Urzędnicy małopolscy w otoczeniu Władysława Łokietka i Kazimierza Wielkiego, 1305–70* (Kraków, 2006); *Król w Polsce XIV i XV wieku*, ed. Andrzej Marzec and Maciej Wilamowski (Kraków, 2006); Janusz Kurtyka, *Odrodzone Królestwo: Monarchia Władysława Łokietka i Kazimierza Wielkiego w świetle nowszych badań* (Kraków, 2001). See also the German synopsis by Janusz Kurtyka, 'Das wiedervereinigte Königreich Polen unter Ladislaus Ellenlang (1304/5–1333) und Kasimir dem Großen (1333–70)', in *Die 'Blüte' der Staaten*, pp. 107–42.

Date	Content	Pope	Published in
1 August 1340	Pope Benedict announces the crusade in the kingdoms of Poland, Bohemia and Hungary against the Tatars.	Benedict XII	*BP* 1, nos 1895–96 (those letters are falsely listed under 1 July); *VMHH* 1, nos 958–59, p. 637.
29 June 1341	Papal letter concerning the treaty with Dmytro Detko.	Benedict XII	*BP* 1, no. 1913, p. 338; *VMPL* 1, no. 566, p. 434; *DPRHU* 1, no. 42, pp. 65–66.
1 December 1343	Bulls with papal tithe for fighting *Tartari, Rutheni et Litfani*	Clement VI	*BP* 2, nos 105–6, pp. 20–21; *VMPL* 1, nos 604–5, pp. 468–70; *ACA* 1, nos 214–15, pp. 424–32.
16–19 September 1349	Letter concerning the conversion of the Lithuanians	Clement VI	*BP* 2, nos 440–42, p. 73; *VMPL* 1, nos 691–93, pp. 525–27.
14 March 1351	Second bull with papal tithe	Clement VI	*BP* 2, no. 518, p. 85; *VMPL* 1, no. 702, pp. 531–33; *DPRHU* 1, no. 43, pp. 69–71; ACA, 2, no. 80, pp. 52–54.
15 May 1352	Letter to Polish bishoprics concerning the announcement of the crusade	Clement VI	*BP* 2, no. 607, p. 99; *VMPL* 1, no. 713, pp. 539–40; *Acta Clem. VI*, no 180, pp. 281–84.
27 July 1352	Letter concerning the confirmation of the indulgence	Clement VI	*BP* 2, no. 627, p. 102; *AV*, no. 347, pp. 340–41.
10 and 22 November 1354, 12 February 1355	Third papal tithe	Innocent VI	*BP* 2, nos 724, 728, 732, pp. 118–20; *VMHH* 2, no. 18, pp. 10–11; *Acta Inn. VI*, no. 52, pp. 97–99 (there falsely under 4 November 1354); *VMPL* 1, nos 739, 742, pp. 556–59; *ACA* 2, nos 110, 113, pp. 73, 75–77.
17 September 1356	Papal protest against the Teutonic Order aiding the Lithuanians.	Innocent VI	*BP* 2, no. 801, pp. 130–31; *VMPL* 1, no. 769, pp. 577–78; *CDPr* 3, no. 85, pp. 109–10.
24 January 1357	Papal protest against Casimir's treaties with Tatars and Lithuanians	Innocent VI	*BP* 2, no. 813, p. 133; *VMPL* 1, no. 776, p. 581; *Acta Inn. VI*, no. 101, pp. 188–89.
17 December 1357	Second Letter concerning the conversion of the Lithuanians	Innocent VI	*BP* 2, no. 845, p. 138; *AV*, no. 375, pp. 357–59.
8 July 1363	Casimir demands broader support for his fight *contra Litwanos, Tartaros et alios infideles ac scismaticos*	Urban V	*BP* 2, no. 1209, p. 198; *VMPL* 1, no. 833, pp. 618–19; *Acta Urb. V*, no. 29a, pp. 47–48.

Tbl. 2. Papal correspondence concerning the eastern politics of Casimir III, 1340–63.

Conquest and Rhetoric

The Polish policy of expansionism towards the western Ruthenian lands started when the last duke, George II Boleslas, was murdered by an Orthodox boyar opposition, who constituted the noble elite of the principality.[9] As far as can be deduced from the scattered source material, we can assume that preparations for a military campaign into western Rus had been made long beforehand.[10] Following the success of the expedition, Casimir turned to the papal court in Avignon in 1341.[11] We can reconstruct his letter from the papal response, which is characteristic for the curia's correspondence with Latin Europe in the late medieval period.[12] Before going into details, I should also point out that, for

---

9   A detailed overview of the sources is provided by Rhode, *Die Ostgrenze Polens*, p. 175; Knoll, *The Rise of the Polish Monarchy*, p. 141; Paszkiewicz, *Polityka ruska Kazimierza Wielkiego*, pp. 41–45. On the principality and its elites in the thirteenth century, see Dariusz Dąbrowski, *Daniel Romanowicz król Rusi (ok. 1201–64): Biografia polityczna* (Kraków, 2012); Adrian Jusupović, *Elity ziemi halickiej i wołyńskiej w czasach Romanowiczów (1205–69): Studium prozopograficzne* (Kraków, 2013). In the fourteenth century, the main land for boyar families seems to have been Peremyshl: Sergei Pashyn, *Перемышльская Шляхта: второй половины XIV– начала XVI века. Историко-генеалогическое исслудование* (Tyumen, 2001). Because of the small amount of sources and the longstanding nationally-motivated quarrels between Polish, Russian or Ukrainian scholars, it is hard to generalise about the position and function of boyars inside the principality. See on this topic Janeczek, 'Udział szlachty w kolonizacji Rusi Koronnej', pp. 62–67; Janeczek, 'New Authority, New Property, New Nobility', pp. 83–86; Maciej Wilamowski, 'Magnate Territories in Red Ruthenia in the Fourteenth and Fifteenth Century: Origin, Development and Social Impact', in *On the Frontier of Latin Europe*, pp. 81–118 (in particular 85–88).
10 This interpretation was already put forward by the aforementioned Rhode, Knoll and Paszkiewicz. However, they overlooked the papal bull from August 1340 announcing the crusade against the Tatars in the kingdoms of Poland, Bohemia and Hungary. See *BP* 2, nos 1895–97; Stanisław Szczur, 'W sprawie sukcesji andegaweńskiej w Polsce', *RH* 75 (2009), 61–102 (here 83–85). A recent synthesis of the Ukranian and Polish research concerning the Polono-Lithuanian struggle over succession in the Galicio-Volhynian Rus is provided by Stanislav Kelembet, 'Фінал "Королівства" Русі: боротьба за галицько-волинські землі б 1340–1351 pp.', *Ruthenica* 16 (2020), 75–111.
11 Norman Housley, *The Avignon Papacy and the Crusades: 1305–78* (Oxford, 1986), p. 68; Housley, *The Later Crusades: From Lyons to Alcazar 1274–1580* (Oxford, 1992), pp. 346–47. For the papacy in Avignon in general, see the classic study by Yves Renouard, *The Avignon Papacy 1305–1403*, trans. Denis Bethell (London, 1970), and Joëlle Rollo-Koster, *Avignon and Its Papacy 1309–1417* (New York, 2015).
12 Already in the thirteenth century, supplications to the curia were written in a certain *stilis curie* which allowed the papal chancery to maintain its wording while conceptualising the papal letter. After the expedition, the supplications — now useless — were destroyed, which is why they are seldomly preserved, see Peter Herde, *Beiträge zum päpstlichen Kanzlei- und Urkundenwesen im 13. Jahrhundert*, 2nd edn (Kallmünz, 1967), pp. 155, 161. This phenomenon even led to the assumption that the curia was more or less passive in the issuing of letters and bulls, especially when it came to the peripheries of Latin Europe. See Matthias Thumser, 'Ernst Pitz wiedergelesen: Päpstliche Urkundenausstellung und die Mission in Livland', in *Livland — eine Region am Ende der Welt? Forschungen zum Verhältnis von Zentrum und Peripherie im späten Mittelalter*, ed. by Anti Selart and Matthias Thumser (Köln, 2017), pp. 209–36. Concerning the Polish supplications towards the curia, see Stanisław Szczur, 'Supliki Kazimierza Wielkiego', *RH* 59 (1993), pp. 43–91.

practical reasons, I will use terms like 'Casimir' and 'the pope' as generalised expressions, bearing in mind that an up-to-date understanding of rulership tries to cope with the often-complex melange of a large number of people involved in the interactions and communication processes that are discussed here, regardless of whether they take place at the royal or the papal court.[13] Wherever possible, however, I will attempt to link a certain situation with a concrete actor.

In his letter, Casimir informed the curia that the last duke of Galicia-Volhynia, George II Boleslas — his kinsman! (*ipsius Regis consaguineum germanum*) — had been murdered and that he had had to enter the adjacent Ruthenian territories with his army.[14] The captain of the Ruthenians, Dmytro Dedko, escaped to the khan of the Golden Horde, who was the legitimate suzerain of this land.[15] As we know from other sources, Casimir was able to defeat the Mongolo/Tataro-Ruthenian forces in the spring of 1341 and to force Dmytro into an agreement.[16] This agreement is also presented in the letter: Casimir promised the Ruthenians that they could continue practising their rites, laws, and customs. Finally, Casimir asked the pope to be released from this promise. This argumentation seems rather odd. Paul Knoll states that Casimir 'contemplated future plans for Ruthenia' and

---

13 See Bernd Schneidmüller, 'Konsensuale Herrschaft: Ein Essay über Formen und Konzepte politischer Ordnung im Mittelalter', in *Reich, Regionen und Europa in Mittelalter und Neuzeit: Festschrift für Peter Moraw*, ed. Paul-Joachim Heinig and Sigrid Jahns (Berlin, 2000), pp. 53–87; Wolfgang Huschner, 'Einleitung', in *Originale — Fälschungen — Kopien: Kaiser- und Königsurkunden für Empfänger in "Deutschland" und "Italien" (9.–11. Jahrhundert) und ihre Nachwirkungen im Hoch- und Spätmittelalter (bis c. 1500)*, ed. by Nicolangelo D'Acunto, Wolfgang Huschner and Sebastian Roebert (Leipzig, 2017), pp. 7–14. For an overview on the papal court, see in particular *Das begrenzte Papsttum: Spielräume päpstlichen Handelns. Legaten — delegierte Richter — Grenzen*, ed. Klaus Herbers, Alsina López and Frank Engel (Berlin, 2013). See also the publications of the research network group Stilus Curiae: *Stilus — modus — usus: Regeln der Konflikt- und Verhandlungsführung am Papsthof des Mittelalters*, ed. Jessica Nowak and Georg Strack (Turnhout, 2019); a second volume is in preparation. Following recent approaches, 'courts' are not only understood as the actual spaces of meetings between rulers and elites but rather virtually as 'nodal points of communication'. See Marc von der Höh, Nikolas Jaspert and Jenny Rahel Oesterle, 'Courts, Brokers and Brokerage in the Medieval Mediterranean', in *Cultural Brokers at Mediterranean Courts in the Middle Ages*, ed. Höh, Jaspert and Oesterle (Paderborn, 2013), pp. 9–32 (here 11).
14 *VMPL* 1, no. 566, p. 434.
15 Jackson, *The Mongols and the West*, p. 210; Rhode, *Die Ostgrenze Polens*, pp. 179–80; Sven Jaros, 'Between East and West: Crown Ruthenia between the Golden Horde and the Rising Power of the Polish Kingdom', in *Rus' and the World of the Nomads (the Second Half of the 9th–16th c.)*, ed. Vitaliy Nagirnyy (Kraków 2017), pp. 281–90 (here 283). Dmytro uses the title of *provisor seu Capitaneus terre Russie* in his letter to the merchants of Thorn, see *CDPr* 3, no. 61, p. 83. See on him also Janusz Szyszka, *Formowanie i organizacja dóbr monarszych w ziemi lwowskiej od połowy XIV do początku XVI wieku* (Kraków, 2016), p. 72; Miroslav Voloshchuk, 'Проблема васальної залежності Дмітра Детка від угорського короля Людовіка І', *Княжа доба: Історія і культура* 6 (2012), 269–79.
16 John of Czarnków, 'Chronicon Polonorum', ed. Jan Szlachtowski, in *MPH* 2, pp. 599–756 (here 621–22); see Rhode, *Die Ostgrenze Polens*, p. 180; Srodecki, '"Scutum inexpugnabile"', p. 116; Srodecki, *Antemurale Christianitatis*, pp. 82–83.

by this 'realised that he had promised too much to Dedko and the other boyars'.[17] Gotthold Rhode also argues that, following his return from Ruthenia, Casimir feared that he made too far-reaching concessions to Dmytro and the boyars and had therefore asked to be released from his oath.[18]

This interpretation seems highly problematic, since it is based on the controversial debate surrounding the status of Dmytro Dedko as *capitaneus terre Russie*.[19] This is not the place to go into this debate in detail, but it should be pointed out that the central problem here is an anachronistic understanding of medieval 'statehood' and 'power': even if the source material for the time between 1341 and 1349 is generally not very helpful, there is no evidence to suggest that Casimir changed his policies towards Ruthenia after 'being released from his oath'.[20] Given the fact that royal influence and capacities in those first years must have been somewhat limited, the largely independent dominion of Dmytro Dedko over large parts of Ruthenia, with only a formal subordination to the kingdoms of Poland and Hungary, was probably the only possible solution, given the threat of counter attacks by the Lithuanians, who also wanted their share of the spoils.[21] Under these circumstances, it could be argued that Casimir made the request to be released from his oath primarily for strategic reasons. As we will see later on, agreements with non-Latin Christian powers were unacceptable for the curia.[22] It might therefore have been a rhetoric strategy to inform the pope about such an agreement by simultaneously begging for invalidation. With the prospect of Lithuanian attacks, papal support was still needed, as can be seen in the request for the papal tithe that was granted to Casimir in December 1343 from all Polish dioceses except Wrocław/Breslau, which, although under the archbishopric of Gniezno, had, as capital of Silesia, been an official subject of the crown of Bohemia since the Visegrád Treaty of 1335.[23] In contrast to the bull of 1341,

---

17 Paul W. Knoll, *The Rise of the Polish Monarchy: Piast Poland in East Central Europe, 1320–70* (Chicago, 1972), p. 134.
18 Rhode, *Die Ostgrenze Polens*, p. 181.
19 Voloshchuk, 'Проблема васальної залежності Дмітра Детка', pp. 272–73; Rhode, *Die Ostgrenze Polens*, p. 180, n. 44; Knoll, *The Rise of the Polish Monarchy*, p. 134; Paszkiewicz, *Polityka ruska Kazimierza Wielkiego*, pp. 79–85.
20 Rhode, *Die Ostgrenze Polens*, p. 182.
21 This was already the interpretation offered by Rhode, *Die Ostgrenze Polens*, p. 181; Stephen C. Rowell, *Lithuania Ascending: A Pagan Empire within East-Central Europe 1295–1345* (Cambridge, 1994), p. 269, attributes a more active role to Dmytro and thinks that he 'maintained his own policy between Poland and Lithuania' and 'managed to play off the Poles, Lithuanians and the Tatars for some time'. According to recent Polish studies on the subject, the majority of the newly conquered territories immediately became part of the royal demesne, see Szyszka, *Formowanie i organizacja dóbr monarszych*, pp. 68–69; Wilamowski, 'Magnate Territories in Red Ruthenia', p. 87. However, the very limited number of charters issued during Casimir's reign shows that the ability to dispose of those territories by granting them to others needed to be established over time.
22 This is also palpable in Casimir's apology to the pope and his explanation for not being able to continue his battle against the *scismaticis*: VMPL 1, no. 628, pp. 483–84; Rhode, *Die Ostgrenze Polens*, p. 183, n. 62.
23 VMPL 1, no. 605, pp. 468–70.

there is no mentioning of newly conquered territories. Rather, Poland is described as being repeatedly under attack from *Tartari, Rutheni et Litfani*, 'enemies of the Christian faith', and Casimir is granted the papal tithe 'for the defence of his realm'. We have no knowledge of any military campaign in 1344.[24] On the contrary: the first Polish royal charters and a letter from Louis the Great to Dmytro Dedko indicate that Casimir and his Hungarian ally tried to stabilise the relationship with the Ruthenian lands and to strengthen the trading ties between them.[25]

The political situation changed some time after May 1344, when Dmytro died and the Lithuanians attacked the lands of the western Rus again, bringing almost all of them under their control.[26] It took Casimir a while to react but, in 1349, he launched a new military campaign, annexing almost the entire territory of the former principality.[27] Following Lithuanian counter attacks, Casimir now turned to Avignon, seeking to gain more financial support by stressing the constant danger posed to his newly conquered territories: 'With God's help, but not without great losses' Casimir had been able to conquer the principality from 'the infidel Ruthenians'. At this point, Casimir emphasised, it would be possible 'to found seven bishoprics and one archbishopric' and thereby to convert the Ruthenians to the Catholic faith. However, this prospect was endangered because the former lords, 'the Tatars, enemies of Christ's name', who were in alliance with the Lithuanians, kept invading the country. Therefore, the king requested support from the pope, who granted the papal tithe in March 1351.[28]

Notable here is the prospect presented by the Polish delegation under Wojciech of Opatowiec, which claimed that seven bishoprics and one metropolitan church could be founded in the conquered Ruthenian lands. The number of bishoprics was based on the traditional Orthodox eparchies in western Rus.[29] The canonistic interpretation saw those eparchies as the illegally occupied seats of

---

24 Knoll, *The Rise of the Polish Monarchy*, p. 135; Rhode, *Die Ostgrenze Polens*, p. 183.
25 *ZDM* 6, no. 1830a, pp. 449–50; *CDPM* 1, no. 218, pp. 258–59; *CDH* 9.1, no. 95, p. 209; Knoll, *The Rise of the Polish Monarchy*, p. 135. On the trading policy of Casimir, see Anna Orlowska, 'W sprawie Polityki Handlowej Kazimierza Wielkiego', *Z dziejów średniowiecznej Europy środkowo-wschodniej: Zbiór studiów*, ed. Jan Tyszkiewicz (Warszawa, 2007), pp. 153–65.
26 Knoll, *The Rise of the Polish Monarchy*, pp. 137, 139; Rhode, *Die Ostgrenze Polens*, pp. 184–85.
27 Knoll, *The Rise of the Polish Monarchy*, p. 141; Rhode, *Die Ostgrenze Polens*, pp. 185–86.
28 *VMPL* 1, no. 702, pp. 531–33; Srodecki, '"Scutum inexpugnabile"', p. 117; Srodecki, *Antemurale Christianitatis*, p. 84.
29 See Szczur, 'Dyplomaci Kazimierza Wielkiego w Awinionie', *Nasza Przeszłość: Studia z dziejów kościoła i kultury katolickiej w Polsce* 66 (1986), pp. 43–105 (here 62); Stanisław Krzyżanowski, 'Poselstwo Kazimierza Wielkiego do Awinionu i pierwsze uniwersyteckie przywileje', *Rocznik Krakowki* 4 (1990), pp. 1–112 (here 20–21); Jan Fijałek, 'Średniowieczne Biskupstwa Kościoła Wschodniego na Rusi i Litwie: Na Podstawie źródeł greckich', *KH* 10 (1898), 487–521 (here 488); Housley, *Avignon Papacy and the Crusades*, p. 96.

Latin bishops, which therefore needed to be re-established.[30] The prospect of such an expansion would have sounded very promising to the papal curia.

With this renewed support, a military campaign was launched in the spring of 1351, together with Louis of Hungary.[31] The latter assumed control of the joint forces after Casimir had been forced to stay in Lublin due to a severe illness.[32] The results of this campaign were long-lasting, but when Louis returned to Hungary, the Polish king once again turned to the curia for support. In 1352, Clement VI expanded the tithe of 1351 with another bull.[33] For the large part adopting the same wording as the bull of 1340, he announced a crusade for the western Rus lands: by applying the *antemurale* rhetoric, Poland is described as lying 'at the outer borders of Christianity'. To fight the Tatars, the pope ordered to preach the crusade against those barbarians in the kingdoms of Poland, Bohemia and Hungary.[34] Furthermore, the same indulgence that was usually given to crusaders in the Holy Land was also applied to this crusade.

However, the financial support seems to have been insufficient, since Casimir searched for other ways to gain more resources for his military campaigns.[35] Those efforts were not in vain, and he was able to secure the position of the Polish kingdom in the western Ruthenian lands until 1355, to the great dismay of the Teutonic Order.[36] In this very complex and ever-changing diplomatic kaleidoscope, the order even supported the Lithuanians against Poland.[37] Casimir complained to the pope and Innocent VI sent a harsh letter to the order, criticising their policies: the Teutonic Knights, the pope underlined, not only supported the Lithuanians and their armies.[38] Furthermore, the pope also complained about the order's attacks on and occupation of Masovia, a Polish royal fiefdom. This shows how well informed the curia was, given the fact that Masovia had only

---

30 Krzysztof Stopka, 'Odpust bocheński z 1354 roku i jego ormiański kontekst', in *Polska i jej sąsiedzi w późnym średniowieczu*, ed. Krzysztof Ożóg und Stanisław Szczur (Kraków, 2000), pp. 55–79 (here 76–77).
31 This is not the place to discuss the complex matter of the Hungarian succession in the kingdom of Poland. For a detailed discussion of the historiography, see the article by Stanisław Sczczur, 'W sprawie sukcesji andegaweńskiej w Polsce', who comes to the conclusion that the devolution of the crown was a gradually unfolding matter of debate between Louis of Anjou and the Polish elites, in particular those from Lesser Poland. For relations between Hungary and the papal curia concerning crusading, see Housley, *Avignon Papacy and the Crusades*, pp. 71–73.
32 Rhode, *Die Ostgrenze Polens*, pp. 189–90; Knoll, *The Rise of the Polish Monarchy*, p. 149.
33 *VMPL* 1, no. 713, pp. 539–40.
34 For Hungary, the bull was issued with more or less the same wording two years later, in 1354, *VMHH* 2, no. 18, pp. 10–11.
35 Rhode, *Die Ostgrenze Polens*, p. 191; Housley, *Avignon Papacy and the Crusades*, p. 69.
36 Rhode, *Die Ostgrenze Polens*, pp. 191–97.
37 Knoll, *The Rise of the Polish Monarchy*, pp. 159–60. The short episode of Polono-Teutonic alliance against the Lithuanians seemed already forgotten, see Jaros, 'Between East and West', p. 284.
38 *VMPL* 1, no. 769, pp. 577–78.

became a feudal fiefdom of the Polish crown in December 1355.[39] The diplomatic response was not long in coming: in 1357 the Teutonic Order beat Poland at their own game, complaining for their part that Casimir had come to an agreement not only with the Lithuanians but also with the Tatars, to whom he had agreed to pay a tribute.[40]

From both letters, it is clear that agreements with non-Christian powers were not looked upon kindly by the curia. The only possible justification was to provide a prospect of future Christianisation which, in the case of the Lithuanians, was raised again in December 1357, albeit without any long-lasting results.[41] As the circumstances in Poland and in Avignon were changing, the intensity of papal correspondence declined significantly after 1357.[42] As table 1 shows, there is only one single request for papal aid against 'Lithuanians, Tatars and other infidels and schismatics' from Casimir's later reign. However, this letter has to be set into a broader European context.[43]

Summarising the information gathered from the papal correspondence, one has to admit that they contain more than mere rhetoric about fighting pagans and spreading the Christian belief. On the contrary, they deliver numerous insights into the circumstances and developments of Polish policies in the east. From them, we learn about the boyar opposition that murdered the last prince of Galicia-Volhynia, George II Boleslas, and about the Tatar supremacy over the Ruthenian lands. The new fiefdom of Masovia is mentioned, as are the diplomatic agreements that Casimir reached with the Lithuanians and the Golden Horde.

---

39 Knoll, *The Rise of the Polish Monarchy*, p. 206; Rhode, *Die Ostgrenze Polens*, pp. 206–19. See also Aleksander Swieżawski, 'Polityka mazowiecka Kazimierza Wielkiego', in *Mazowsze i Ruś Czerwona w średniowieczu: Wybór prac* (Częstochowa, 1997), pp. 60–72.

40 *VMPL* 1, no. 776, p. 581. The agreement mentioned here was the result of the diplomatic mission of Jan Pakosławic.

41 Robert Frost, *The Oxford History of Poland-Lithuania, vol. 1: The Making of the Polish-Lithuanian Union, 1385–1569* (Oxford, 2015), p. 27; on the attempts to convert the Lithuanians, see Zdzisław Kaczmarczyk, *Monarchia Kazimierza Wielkiego*, 2 vols (Poznań, 1946), 2: 122–26. The only Lithuanian duke baptised during Casimir's reign was Alexander Karijotaitis, the ceremony having maybe already taken place in 1351. He became a close ally to Casimir in the following years, see Rhode, *Die Ostgrenze Polens*, p. 200; Vitaliy Mykhaylovskiy, *European Expansion and the Contested Borderlands of Late Medieval Podillya, Ukraine* (Leeds, 2019), p. 53. In this context, see also the paper of Andrzej Marzec in this volume.

42 As Szczur, 'Dyplomaci Kazimierza Wielkiego', pp. 67–68, pointed out, the situation for Polish delegations changed during the last decade of Casimir's reign, given the fact that a constant Polish procurator was established around 1360.

43 In 1363, Pope Urban V launched a Europe-wide campaign to support King Peter I of Cyprus in his crusading attempts. See Housley, *The Later Crusades*, pp. 192–94; Housley, *Avignon Papacy and the Crusades*, pp. 247–50. King Peter even accompanied Emperor Charles IV to Cracow in 1364 in order to promote his campaign. See Stanisław Szczur, 'Krakowski zjazd monarchów w 1364 roku', *RH* 64 (1998), 35–58 (here 54–55). One might argue that, in this context, Casimir intended to be seen as quite occupied with his own affairs against the enemies of the Christian faith. However, his support for Cyprus was again requested in 1366 (*BP* 2, no. 1527, p. 255). See Stopka, 'Odpust bocheński', p. 74, n. 93.

This may seem unsurprising, given that most of these pieces of information are taken from the letters written to the pope, either from the Polish court or the Teutonic Order. However, this information is not given neutrally, but is set within a certain line of argumentation.[44] As we have seen in the second bull concerning the papal tithe from 1351, the prospect of future Christianisation was a promising argument when addressing the pope. Accusations about agreements with non-Christian powers, however, were equally powerful in discrediting one's rivals, as we have seen in the last two examples.

It is my hypothesis that this was one of the reasons why the curia was not addressed to the same extent after 1357. It seems as if papal support could only be gained by presenting a clear picture of true Christians fighting infidels and schismatics beyond their own borders. The realities, however — both for the kingdom of Poland and for the Teutonic Order — were far more complex. A degree of 'realpolitik' was required: to stabilise his control over large parts of Ruthenia, Casimir needed to reach agreements with Lithuania and the Golden Horde, and he succeeded in doing both.[45] Besides the agreement with the Golden Horde reached by Jan Pakosławic in the winter of in 1353–54, several treaties with the Lithuanians followed, most importantly in 1358, as well as the defining treaty from 1366, which sealed the division of the Galicio-Volhynian Rus between Lithuania and the kingdom of Poland.[46]

To bring this first section to an end: which crusade characteristics can be found during the conquest of the principality of Galicia-Volhynia? As we have seen, the pope gave his consent to the fight against pagans and non-Latin Christians, and he even granted an indulgence for those who fought for the Roman cause. However, the expansion towards the western Ruthenian lands lacked the supranational character that is so often described as an important element of the high and late medieval 'classic' crusades.[47] Besides such large scale campaigns under the sign of the cross as the unfortunate Vorskla campaign of the Lithuanian grand duke Vytautas against the Golden Horde in 1399, in which several Western crusaders and not insignificant numbers of Teutonic Knights also took part, the fight against *Tartari, Rutheni et Litfani* remained more or less a regional phenomenon.[48] In the overall correspondence between the papal curia and the kingdom of Poland, the question of crusading in Ruthenia was not even the

---

44 For more examples of specific crusading rhetoric and reasoning, see Housley, *Avignon Papacy and the Crusades*, pp. 96–98.
45 Knoll, *The Rise of the Polish Monarchy*, pp. 157 and 174–77.
46 CDP 1, no. 119, pp. 209–11; Rhode, *Die Ostgrenze Polens*, pp. 192 and 198; Srodecki, '"Scutum inexpugnabile"', p. 117. I will not focus here on the still unresolved question of whether Poland agreed to pay a tribute only for Podolia or (as is more likely) for the whole of Ruthenia. See Jaros, 'Beween East and West', p. 284, n. 17, with further literature.
47 See, for instance, Robert Bartlett, *The Making of Europe: Conquest, Colonization, and Cultural Change 950–1350* (London, 1993), pp. 260–61; Michael Mitterauer, *Warum Europa? Mittelalterliche Grundlagen eines Sonderweges* (München, 2004), p. 203.
48 Jackson, *The Mongols and the West*, p. 215.

most pressing concern. Relations with the Teutonic Order, the struggle with the kingdom of Bohemia over Silesia or the foundation of Cracow University were all discussed far more frequently.[49]

Allow me here to add a rather postcolonial consideration: it is particularly remarkable, that — with the exception of the first letter concerning the treaty with Dmytro — the Ruthenians were presented as a passive and subaltern group.[50] Lithuanians and Tatars were well established images of alien and cruel enemies, against whom *antemurale* rhetoric was often used, and therefore were much more popular when addressing the pope.[51] The Ruthenians, however, were only considered when it came to their possible conversion to Latin Christianity. One might add that this very same prospect was used as a threat towards the patriarch of Constantinople in order to achieve the constitution of a new Orthodox church province for Crown Ruthenia in 1370.[52] This proved to be successful, as we know from the founding of the Metropolitan Church in Halych in 1371![53] The liminal

---

49 As quantitative orientation for the papal letters to Poland, see Irena Sułkowska-Kuraś and Stanisław Kuraś, 'La Pologne et la Papauté d'Avignon', in *Aux origines de l'Etat moderne: Le fonctionnement administratif de la papauté d'Avignon. Actes de la table ronde organisée par l'Ecole française de Rome avec le concours du CNRS, du Conseil général de Vaucluse et de l'Université d'Avignon (Avignon, 23– 24 janvier 1988)* (Rome, 1990), pp. 113–33 (here 127, 130). The main articles about the Polish delegation in Avignon also give much more space to these matters than to the question of crusading: Krzyżanowski, 'Poselstwo Kazimierza Wielkiego do Awinionu'; Szczur, 'Dyplomaci Kazimierza Wielkiego w Awinionie'.

50 For an overview of the adaptation of postcolonial theories to medieval research, see Jeffrey Jerome Cohen, *The Postcolonial Middle Ages* (New York, 2001).

51 Jaros, 'Between East and West', pp. 282, 289; Srodecki, '"Scutum inexpugnabile"'. The importance of bearing in mind the recipients' expectations and perspectives when describing the peripheries of Latin Europe is also stressed by Anti Selart, 'Sie kommen, und sie gehen: Zentrale Orte, Randgebiete und die Livländer im Mittelalter', in *Livland — eine Region am Ende der Welt?*, pp. 27–60 (here 30).

52 As Casimir wrote in his letter to the Patriarch: 'The princes of Rus were our relatives, but these princes left Ruthenia and the country was widowed. Henceforth I, king of Poland, took over the land of Rus. And now, o Holy Father, patriarch of the ecumenical councils, we request from you [...] consecrate Anthony as a metropolitanate. [...] As if the grace of God and your blessing are not bestowed upon that man, do not complain against us afterwards. We will be forced to baptise the Ruthenians into the faith of the Latins, if there is no metropolitan in Rus, for the land cannot remain without law'. This English translation is based on: John Meyendorff, *Byzantium and the Rise of Russia: A Study of Byzantino-Russian Relations in the Fourteenth Century* (Cambridge, 1981), p. 287; the original text in Old Greek is printed in: *Acta patriarchatus Constantinopolitani MCCCXV–MCCCCII e codicibus manu scriptis Bibliothecae Palatinae Vindobonesis*, ed. Franz Miklosich and Joseph Müller, 2 vols (Wien, 1860–62), 1: no. 318, pp. 577–88. See also *Les regestes des actes du patriarcat de Constantinople*, ed. Venance Grumel, Vitalien Laurent and Jean Darrouzès, 7 vols (Paris, 1932–79), 1.5: no. 2622.

53 See Rhode, *Die Ostgrenze Polens*, pp. 274–75; Johannes Preiser-Kapeller, 'Zwischen Union, Konversion und Konfrontation: Polen, Litauen und die byzantinische Kirche im 14. und 15. Jahrhundert', *Jahrbuch des Wissenschaftlichen Zentrums der Polnischen Akademie der Wissenschaften in Wien* 3 (2010–12), 93–113 (here 98); Sophia Senyk, *A History of the Church in Ukraine*, 2 vols (Roma, 1993–2011), 2: 55–56; Andrzej Gil and Ihor Skochylyas, *Kościoły wschodnie w państwie polsko-litewskim w procesie przemian i adaptacji metropola kijowska w latach 1458–1795* (Lublin, 2014), pp. 74–75.

status of the western Ruthenian lands for both Western and Eastern Christianity was a powerful argument for regional rulers in their communication with the two highest ecclesiastical authorities.

From Occupation to Integration

This image of Casimir as the great converter of the Ruthenians, who expanded the borders of Latin Christianity, can be found not only in the papal bull of 1351 alone. It is also well established in historiography and beyond: in his famous cycle on the decisive moments of Polish civilisation, the nineteenth-century history painter Jan Matejko presented the Piast king as the founder of the Catholic cathedral in Lviv (fig. 22).[54]

However, the picture gained from analysing the royal charters is quite different. Firstly, the royal presence in Crown Ruthenia was limited to several visits during the military campaigns. As a result, only about twenty percent of the royal charters concerning the newly won territories in the east were issued there. The overwhelming majority of the documents were drawn in Lesser Poland.[55] When we look at the objects of those charters, it becomes clear that the policy of Casimir was limited to the western parts of the former Galicio-Volhynian principality (fig. 23). Most documents concern the fortified centres — in particular the old Ruthenian *volosti*, i.e. the administrative-territorial units — and their immediate surroundings such as Syanik (Pol. Sanok), Korosno (Pol. Krosno), Ryashiv (Pol. Rzeszów), Peremyshl (Pol. Przemyśl) and of course Lviv (Pol. Lwów) which all received privileges.[56] The land of Halych, lying further to the east, received only

---

54 See, for instance, the classic study by Karl Reifenkugel, 'Die Gründung der römisch-katholischen Bistümer in den Territorien Halicz und Wladimir: Ein Beitrag zur Geschichte dieser Territorien im 14. Jahrhunderte', *Archiv für österreichische Geschichte* 52 (1875), pp. 401–74, which presents a very idealised picture of Casimir's attempts at church organisation. For a full description of the painting, see Ewa Suchodolska and Marek Wrede, *Jana Matejki Dzieje cywilizacji w Polsce* (Warszawa, 1998), pp. 58–64. It can be considered a typical trait of Matejko's style to condense complex historical processes into a single, more or less fictional situation. See Jarosław Krawczyk, *Matejko i Historia* (Warszawa, 1990), p. 47. Despite their often chaotic and fictional character, his pictures are somewhat unique as canonised visualisations of Polish national mythology, see Maria Poprzęcka, 'Jan Matejko: Schlacht bei Tannenberg (Bitwa pod Grunwaldem). Vom Nachleben eines Gemäldes', in *Tür and Tür: Polen — Deutschland. 1000 Jahre Kunst und Geschichte. Ausstellungskatalog*, ed. Małgorzata Omilanowska (Berlin, 2011), pp. 110–15 (here 110).
55 The best overview for the charters issued by Casimir III remains Antoni Gąsiorowski, 'Itinerarium króla Kazimierza Wielkiego: Materiały 1333–1370', *RH* 64 (1998), pp. 175–208. For a detailed analysis of the charters concerning Crown Ruthenia, see Jaros, *Iterationen im Grenzraum*.
56 Szyszka, *Formowanie i organizacja dóbr monarszych*, p. 62; Andrzej Janeczek, 'System grodowo-terytorialny Rusi halickiej w źródłach późnego średniowiecza', in *Lokalne ośrodki władzy państwowej w XI–XII wieku w Europie Środkowo-Wschodniej*, ed. Sławomir Mozdzioch (Wrocław, 1993), pp. 143–58. See also Wilamowski, 'Magnate Territories in Red Ruthenia', pp. 89–93. This policy has to be interpreted as a defensive strategy to fortify the newly conquered territory against attacks from Tatars and Lithuanians. See John of Czarnków, 'Chronicon Polonorum', pp. 626–27. The recipients of the

Fig. 22. The Re-Occupation of Ruthenia: Wealth and Education (painting by Jan Matejko, 1888). Muzeum Narodowe in Warsaw, Poland. Reproduced by Paul Srodecki from <https://t1p.de/ca13d> [accessed 22 November 2023], licence public domain.

three charters, and only at the end of Casimir's reign. This image of a very limited royal presence during the first years after the conquest is also evident if we look at the content of the charters.[57] Charters with different content only became a stable reality after the treaties with Lithuania in 1358 and in 1366 (see tbl. 3).

What is most striking when examining the contents and recipients of these royal charters is the lack of ecclesiastical content. The picture of Casimir as a great promoter of the Catholic faith clashes here with the reality. Despite some attempts to found bishoprics and promote mendicant orders, Crown Ruthenia remained more or less outside the Latin obedience during his reign.[58] It was only gradually

---

charters were obliged to defend their property as well, see Paszkiewicz, *Polityka ruska Kazimierza Wielkiego*, p. 252.

[57] The image gained from analysing the charters seems to be hardly compatible with the fact that most parts of the newly conquered territory became *de iure* part of the royal demesne immediately after the Polish conquest. Considering recent approaches towards the configuration of rulership as communicative process, this contrast seems more comprehensible.

[58] The classical study for the history of church organisation in Ruthenia remains Władysław Abraham, *Powstanie organizacyi kościoła łacińskiego na Rusi* (Lwów, 1904). A good overview over the relatively unsuccessful attempts of church foundations during Casimir's reign can be found in Rhode, *Die Ostgrenze Polens*, pp. 273–86. Recent Polish research stresses the weak position of the Latin Church,

and step by step that royal authority spread throughout Crown Ruthenia. In the long run, the privileged migrations of members of Polish noble families, the allegiance of some Ruthenian boyars and the application of Magdeburg Law by the newly founded cities and villages formed a society that was loyal to the crown and supported Polish influence in the Ruthenian lands.[59]

This is perhaps the most important difference when comparing this expansion with the reincorporation of the region under Queen Hedwig and King Vladislas II Jogaila in 1387–88.[60] After Casimir's death, Louis of Hungary was crowned Polish king, but rarely entered his Polish kingdom.[61] In the western Ruthenian lands, which now were incorporated into

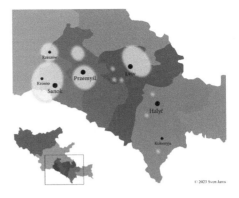

Fig. 23. Crown Ruthenia within the crown of Poland (including the duchy of Masovia as a Polish fiefdom as well as temporarily dependent territories such as Chełm, Bełz and Western Podolia) and the localisation of objects in Casimir's charters concerning Crown Ruthenia (1340–70).

the crown of Hungary, he ruled through a more or less autonomous governor, the Silesian duke Vladislas of Opole, until 1378.[62] This governor was succeeded by a number of Hungarian incumbents, who sought to tie Ruthenia more firmly to the Hungarian crown. When Louis died in 1382, the succession of his daughter Mary was denied by the opposition of nobles from Lesser Poland.[63] Two years later, Hedwig — another yet unmarried daughter of Louis — was crowned Polish

---

which persisted until the late fourteenth century, see Gregorz Klebowicz, *Organizacja parafialna diecezji przemyskiej obrządku łacińskiego w XIV–XVI wieku* (Lublin, 2013), pp. 70–78.

59 Janeczek, 'Udział szlachty w kolonizacji Rusi Koronnej', p. 90.

60 For an overview, see Rhode, *Die Ostgrenze Polens*, pp. 305–8; Oskar Halecki, *Dzieje unii jagiellońskiej*, 2 vols (Kraków, 1919–20), 1: 122–30.

61 On the reign of Louis in Poland, see Andrzej Marzec, *Pod rządami nieobecnego monarchy: Królestwo Polskie 1370–82*, 2nd edn (Kraków, 2021) (Kraków, 2017); Dániel Bagi, *Az Anjouk Krakkóban: Nagy Lajos lengyelországi uralmának belpolitikai kérdései* (Pécs, 2014).

62 The most important recent research about Duke Vladislas of Opole was conducted by Jerzy Sperka, *Władysław Książę Opolski, Wieluński, Kujawski, Dobrzyński: Pan Rusi, Palatyn Węgier i Namiestnik Polski* (Kraków, 2013); Sperka, 'Territorial Powers, System of Administration, and the Inner Circle of Duke Wladyslaw Opolczyk (†1401)', *QMAN* 14 (2009), 361–88.

63 See Dariusz Wróbel, 'The Polish Magnates as the Sovereign Subject of Foreign Politics during Interregnum and Minority of Rulers (1382–86, 1434–38)', in *Akteure mittelalterlicher Außenpolitik*, pp. 197–210; Kurtyka, *Tęczyńscy*, pp. 610–11.

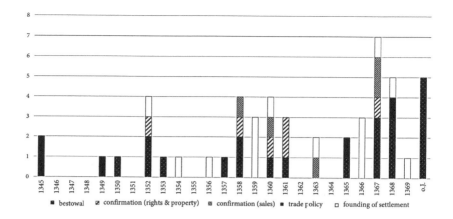

Tbl. 3. Subjects of the Polish king Casimir the Great's charters concerning Crown Ruthenia (1340–70).

queen and, in 1386, was married to the Lithuanian grand duke Jogaila, who became Polish king.[64] Soon afterwards, the project of reincorporating the western

---

64 It is often stressed that Hedwig was crowned Polish *king* following the phrase *in regem coronata*, see, for instance, 'Kalendarz katedralny krakowski', in *Najdawniejsze Roczniki Krakowskie i Kalendarz*, ed. Zofia Kozlowska-Budkowa (Warszawa, 1978), pp. 107–96 (here 178); Julia Burkhardt, 'Handeln und Verhandeln: Außenpolitische Dimensionen polnischer und ungarischer Reichsversammlungen im Spätmittelalter', in *Akteure mittelalterlicher Außenpolitik*, pp. 169–96 (here 178); Piotr Węcowski, 'Jadwiga Andegaweńska w opinii prawniczej z końca XV w. Przyczynek do późnośredniowiecznych wyobrażeń na temat władzy monarszej', in *Ecclesia regnum fontes: Studia z dziejów średniowiecza. Prace ofiarowane Profesor Marii Koczerskiej*, ed. Sławomir Gawlas et al. (Warszawa, 2014), pp. 250–57 (here 255). For a detailed overview on the sources concerning the coronation, see Jerzy Wyrozumski, *Królowa Jadwiga: Między epoką piastowską i jagiellońską* (Kraków, 1997), pp. 83–86. This formulation is often overinterpreted, as if gender was more important than legitimacy based on bloodline, see, for instance, Marianne Sághy, 'Jadwiga', in *Women and Gender in Medieval Europe: An Encyclopedia*, ed. Margaret Schaus (New York, 2006), p. 421. Even Halecki speaks of a 'diarchy' of two crowned kings after 1386, see Oskar Halecki, *Jadwiga of Anjou and the Rise of East Central Europe* (New York, 1991), p. 155. The picture gained from pragmatic documents is far less prosaic: from the very beginning the *intitulatio* in Hedwig's charters was formulated as *Heduigis dei gracia Regina Polonie*, see *CDPM* 1, no. 369, pp. 438–39. That formulation was not meant to impair her reputation as crowned head of the kingdom until her marriage. After Vladislas II Jogaila was crowned king, the royal seal and the royal chancellor changed into his entourage. Hedwig received her own seal and chancellor, see Jadwiga Krzyżaniakowa, *Kancelaria królewska Władysława Jagiełły: Studium z dziejów kultury politycznej polski w 15 wieku*, 2 vols (Poznán, 1972), 2: 14. See for the queen's charters Grażyna Rutkowska, 'Itinerarium królowej Jadwigi 1384–1399', in *Dzieło Jadwigi i Jagiełły: W sześćsetlecie chrztu Litwy i jej związków z Polską*, ed. Wojciech Biliński (Warszawa. 1989), pp. 204–25. For a pragmatic overview on the issue of legitimising royal succession in the kingdom of Poland in the fourteenth century, see Sławomir Gawlas, 'Das Erb- und Wahlrecht des Herrschers in Polen im 14. Jahrhundert', in *Die Goldene Bulle: Politik — Wahrnehmung — Rezeption*, ed. Ulrike Hohensee

Ruthenian lands into the Polish crown began.[65] The circumstances differed greatly from those during the expansion of Casimir in the 1340s and 1350s, since the social changes of Casimir's integration were irreversible and had endured the Hungarian episode. From the 1350s onwards, Polish noble families accumulated property in the Galicio-Volhynian Rus, as did Ruthenian families in Poland.[66] When looking at the factors motivating the reincorporation, it becomes quite clear that those actors and their networks were of the greatest importance.[67]

A further major difference concerns the role of Lithuania. During Casimir's campaigns, the Lithuanians had been the strongest rivals to Polish expansion. Now the nominal Lithuanian grand duke was also the Polish king. The fact that Vytautas and Jogaila conquered the last Hungarian fortress Halych in October 1387 with joint forces is in itself proof of how much the situation differed from the 1340s.[68] Given the context of this volume, the most important difference might be that the crusading idea was most likely not applied during the military campaign of the late 1380s. At least we do not have any knowledge of any such plans, considering the fact that the papal correspondence of 1387–88 has not been preserved.[69] With regards to church organisation, it should be mentioned

---

(Berlin, 2009), pp. 665–712. On the meaning of the so called Kreva Act, which stood at the beginning of the long process of building the Polono-Lithuanian Union, see Frost, *The Oxford History of Poland-Lithuania* 1: 47–57.

65 In contrast to Halecki, *Jadwiga of Anjou*, pp. 174–75, Hedwig and her troops were not welcomed enthusiastically by everyone. This can be seen by the two letters of consignment that Hedwig and the nobles of Lesser Poland issued to the city and citizens of Lviv in order to ensure the safe passage of the city's delegation to negotiate the handover of the city, see *Akta grodzkie i ziemski z czasów Rzeczpospolitej Polskiej z Archiwum tak zwanego bernardyńskiego w Lwowie*, 25 vols (Lwów 1868–1935), 3: nos 40–41, pp. 74–75. Hedwig's expedition in spring 1387 was followed by a second campaign, led by Vytautas and Jogaila in autumn 1387, which brought the east of Galicia-Volhynia with the castle of Halych under Polish control, see Jan Tęgowski, 'Nieznane nadanie Władysława Jagiełły dla Benedykta, węgierskiego kasztelana Halicza, i jego braci: Przyczynek źródłowy do dziejów Rusi Halickiej', in *Narodziny Rzeczypospolitej studia z dziejów średniowiecza i czasów wczesnonowożytnych*, ed. Waldemar Bukowski and Tomasz Jurek, 2 vols (Kraków, 2012), 2: 1341–47 (here 1346–47); ZDM 6, no. 1529, pp. 25–26. For an overview on the charters issued by Jogaila during the reincorporation, see Antoni Gąsiorowski, *Itinerarium krola Władysława Jagielły 1386–1434* (Warszawa, 2015), pp. 37–40, as well as Jaros, *Iterationen im Grenzraum*, pp. 117–25, 317–25.

66 Such a Ruthenian boyar was, for instance, Dmytro of Goraj. See Andrzej Marzec, 'Kariery polityczne na Rusi Czerwonej za panowania Kazimierza Wielkiego (1340–70)', СОЦІУМ 4 (2004), pp. 9–18 (here 16–17); Franciszek Sikora, 'Krąg rodzinny i dworski Dymitra z Goraja i jego rola na Rusi', in *Genealogia — Kręgi zawodowe i grupy interesu w Polsce*, ed. Jan Wroniszewski (Toruń, 1989), pp. 55–89.

67 Janusz Kurtyka, *Tęczyńscy: Studium z dziejów polskiej elity możnowładczej w średniowieczu* (Kraków, 1997), pp. 212–13; Renata Trawka, *Kmitowie: Studium kariery politycznej i społecznej w późnośredniowiecznej Polsce* (Kraków, 2003), pp. 70–71.

68 See Jarosław Nikodem, *Witold: Wielki Książę Litewski (1354 lub 1355–27 października 1430)* (Kraków, 2013), p. 109; Andrii Fedoruk, 'Облога Галича 1387 р. у світлі вітчизняної історіографії', ГАЛИЧ 2 (2017), pp. 194–206; Rhode, *Die Ostgrenze Polens*, p. 307.

69 See the small note in *BP* 3, p. 18.

that Hedwig and Jogaila built upon the foundations of Casimir's reign, as well as those from the reign of King Louis and Duke Vladislas of Opole.[70] Nevertheless, Polish clerics complained about the multitude of 'infidels and schismatics' in their provinces until the 1390s.[71] Undoubtedly, this mélange of beliefs, ethnicities, laws, customs, and languages soon became characteristic for Crown Ruthenia and, to some degree, for the entire Polono-Lithuanian commonwealth of the following centuries.[72] Whereas the reality of such a crosscurrent of cultures eludes simplifying polarisations, the use of the crusade momentum against the longstanding triad of the *Tartari, Rutheni et Litfani, hostes fidei* as a well-proven rhetorical strategy — used by the Poles at least since the early 1240s — to gain urgently needed financial support came to an abrupt end as the Polish control over the western Ruthenian lands was established at the end of the fourteenth century.

---

70 Klebowicz, *Organizacja parafialna diecezji przemyskiej*, pp. 78–84; Abraham, *Powstanie organizacyi kościoła łacińskiego na Rusi*, pp. 288–341. See also Tadeusz M. Trajdos, *Kościół katolicki na ziemiach ruskich Korony i Litwy za panowania Władysława II Jagiełły 1396–1434* (Wrocław, 1983). The latter book has to be approached with care, given the number of complaints by Polish scholars. See Ireneusz Wysokiński, 'Review of *Kościół katolicki* by Tadeusz M. Trajdos', Przegląd Historyczny 76 (1985), 547–61; Stopka, 'Odpust bocheński', p. 79, n. 114.

71 In 1372, Bartholomew of Alverna, vicar of the Franciscan Order, complained: *Non erant Ecclesiae Cathedrales & Parochiales (illo videlicet tempore) in Russia, nec Rectores earum, quibus cura immineret animarum, & tamta multitudo infidelium, & schmismaticorum, ut paucae personae reputarentur fideles respectu multitudinis errantium.* 'There were no cathedral and parish churches in Ruthenia at that time, nor masters of these, to whom the care of souls would be entrusted, and [there was] such a great number of unbelievers and schismatics that only few persons could be counted as believers, given the mass of erring people'. See *Vita archiepiscoporum Haliciensium et Leopoliensium*, ed. Jacób Skrobiszewski (Lviv, 1628), cap. 6. And still in 1390, Bishop Eric (aka Henry) of Przemyśl described his arrival as follows: *Advenientes multo et laborisso itinere ad hanc nostram sponsam et ecclesiam Prem., ex eo; quiam cum ipsa nullus unquam ante nos personaliter catholicus sponsus, scil. pontifex habitavit, penitus deformatam et desolatam, quasi viduam et dolentem vid:mus, et omni decentia et bonore ecclesiae cathedr. destitutam. Et quamvis ecclesiam ipsam jam dudum a multis retro temporibus fuisse et esse cathedralem [...] plene constat, nos tamen eandem cum multis suis possessionibus a schismaticis reperimus occupatam.* 'After a long and exhausting journey, we arrived at our "bride", the church of Przemyśl. Since there was never an Orthodox spouse namely bishop living with her, we saw her totally misshapen and desolated, virtually a mourning widow, and deprived from all decency and honour of a cathedral church. And although it is absolutely certain that, since long times ago, she has been and still is a cathedral, we nevertheless found herself and many of her belongings occupied by the schismatics'. See: *Premislia sacra, sive series et gesta episcoporum r. l. premisliensium*, ed. Francziczek Pawłowski (Kraków, 1869), pp. 60–61, n. 4.

72 *On the Frontier of Latin Europe*; Christophe von Werdt, 'Halyč-Wolhynien — Rotreußen — Galizien: Im Überlappungsgebiet der Kulturen und Völker', *JGO* 46 (1998), 69–99; *Lviv: A City in the Crosscurrents of Cultures*, ed. John Czaplicka (Havard, 2005); Moshe Rosman, 'How Polish Is Polish History', in *Imaginations and Configurations of Polish Society: From the Middle Ages through the Twentieth Century*, ed. Yvonne Kleinmann et al. (Göttingen, 2017), pp. 19–34 (here 26).

PAUL SRODECKI

Playing the Crusade Card

Rhetorical References to Outremer and Iberian Crusades in the Conflict between the Teutonic Order and the Crown of Poland in the Early Fifteenth Century

The late fourteenth century brought profound changes in the power constellation of East-Central, Eastern and North-Eastern Europe. The signing of the Union of Kreva (Pol. Krewo, Lith. Krėva) between the crown of Poland and the grand duchy of Lithuania in 1385 created a powerful conglomerate of lands under the rule of the new-founded Jagiellonian dynasty, which reached from the vast steppes of the northern Black Sea coasts and the Carpathian Mountains in the south to Greater Poland in the northwest and Lithuania in the northeast.[1] The Polono-Lithuanian union had far-reaching consequences not only for the two partners, but also for the adjacent countries, above all for the state of the Teutonic Order in Prussia and Livonia, for whom the union was dangerously challenging in two respects: on the one hand, the order was now surrounded by a mighty political and military alliance. The first effects of this power shift away from the Teutonic Knights were noticeable in the so-called 'Great War' of 1409–11 and the crushing defeat of the order at Tannenberg/Grunwald/Žalgiris in July 1410. On the other hand, even though it still required several decades to Christianise the majority of the Lithuanians (not counting their Orthodox subjects in the conquered Rus territories), the grand duchy's official conversion to Latin Christendom meant that the Teutonic Order state in effect lost both its existential and its functional legitimacy.[2] Since their arrival in Prussia in the 1220s, the Teutonic Knights had

---

1 For an overview on the Union of Kreva and the beginning of the various personal unions between the kingdom of Poland and the grand duchy of Lithuania under the Jagiellonians from the fourteenth to sixteenth centuries which eventually led to the singing of a real union in Lublin in 1569, see, with further references, Robert Frost, *The Oxford History of Poland-Lithuania, vol. 1: The Making of the Polish-Lithuanian Union, 1385–1569* (Oxford, 2015).

2 See Darius Baronas, 'Christian in Late Pagan, and Pagans in Early Christian Lithuania: The Fourteenth and Fifteenth Centuries', *LHS* 19 (2014), 51–81; Michał Giedroyć, 'The Arrival of Christianity in Lithuania: Baptism and Survival (1341–87)', in *The North-Eastern Frontiers of Medieval Europe: The Expansion of Latin Christendom in the Baltic Lands*, ed. Alan V. Murray (Farnham et al., 2014), pp. 155–78; Darius Baronas, 'Christians in Late Pagan, and Pagans in Early Christian Lithuania: The Fourteenth and Fifteenth Centuries', *LHS* 19 (2014), 51–81; Baronas,

Fig. 24. *The Battle of Grunwald* (painting by Jan Matejko, 1878), Muzeum Narodowe, Warsaw, Poland. Reproduced by Paul Srodecki from <https://w.wiki/76vF> [accessed 29 September 2023], licence public domain

been justifying, with papal benevolence, their conquest of the pagan Baltic tribes with the defence and spreading of the faith and comparing it to the crusades in the Holy Land. These central pillars within the order's self-perception now appeared to have become obsolete. However, interestingly enough, it was actually during the political and military decline of the following years that the Teutonic diplomats began to use the arguments of crusading and defending the faith more forcefully than ever before. The Polish side also quickly adopted this strategy and reversed it against the order.

The diplomatic dispute between the two parties in the first half of the fifteenth century has already received a great deal of academic attention in the past, not to mention the considerable research conducted into military aspects. In this chapter, I will focus on the rhetorical instrumentalisation of the crusade movement and the simultaneous drawing of parallels to the religious warfare in Outremer and Iberia for their own purposes by both the Teutonic and Polish diplomacy — issues largely unheeded or only marginally examined in the historical research so far.

'Die Hintergründe für Litauens späte Annahme des Christentums', *Annaberger Annalen* 14 (2006), 6–13; Marceli Kosman, 'Początki i rozwój chrystianizacji Litwy', *Nasza przeszłość* 112 (2009), 5–53, 113 (2010), 5–65; *Die Christianisierung Litauens im mitteleuropäischen Kontext: Materialien zur internationalen wissenschaftlichen Konferenz, gewidmet dem 750. Jubiläumsjahr der Taufe des Mindaugas, König von Litauen, Vilnius, Museum für Angewandte Kunst, am 26. und 27. September 2001*, ed. Vydas Dolinskas (Vilnius 2005); *La cristianizzazione della Lituania: Atti del Colloquio internazionale di storia ecclesiastica in occasione del VI centenario della Lituania cristiana, Roma, 24–26 giugno 1987*, ed. Pontifico Comitato di scienze storiche (Città del Vaticano, 1989).

Defending the Faith as a Central Pillar in Self-Perceptions

The ideological foundations which were fundamental for the self- and external perception of the Teutonic Knights as defenders of the faith can only be understood in the context of the high-medieval crusades and the crusader movement.[3] The connection between the clerical and the militaristic formed the nucleus of their faith-defending self-image. Founded in the Holy Land in the wake of the siege of Acre (1189–91), the Teutonic Order was originally established as a monastic brotherhood with its primary obligations mainly in nursing care and in the service of the sick.[4] In its earliest years, the organisation was therefore largely inspired by the statutes of the Hospitallers.[5] At the end of the twelfth century however, during and after the so-called 'German Crusade' initiated by emperor Henry VI in 1197,[6] the Teutonic Knights increasingly began to adopt the rules of the Templars in the sense of a faith-defending protective force in the Holy Land, coming to regard the latter as their role model par excellence.

Presenting themselves as the 'new Maccabees' and the 'shield' or the 'walls of the faith', from a propaganda point of view, the Teutonic Knights knew how advertise their indispensability for religious warfare. Neither topoi were new: already in the twelfth century, the Templars had been compared to the biblical Hebrew warriors who fought the polytheistic Seleucids and who were regarded as warrior-martyr models for the crusading movement in the Middle Ages.[7] Furthermore, it was also the Templars who had styled themselves, and were styled by others, as the protective outpost of Christianity.[8] What was new with regard to the Teutonic Knights was the extent of this rhetorical self-perception, since they continuously emphasised this status in various correspondences with the papacy and the Latin Christian rulers as well as in historiographical works such as the chronicles of

---

3 On the subject matter of the following five paragraphs, see, with further references, Paul Srodecki, *Antemurale Christianitatis: Zur Genese der Bollwerksrhetorik im östlichen Mitteleuropa an der Schwelle vom Mittelalter zur Frühen Neuzeit* (Husum, 2015), pp. 57–87.

4 For the order's twelfth commitments in the Levante, see Nicholas Morton, *The Teutonic Knights in the Holy Land, 1190–1291* (Woodbridge, 2009).

5 On this issue, see, most recently, Bernhart Jähnig, 'Die älterene geistlichen Ritterorden in ihren Anfängen im Vergleich mit dem Deutschen Orden', in *Zwischen Mittelmeer und Baltikum: Festschrift für Hubert Houben zum 70. Geburtstag*, ed. Udo Arnold, Roman Czaja and Jürgen Sarnowski (Ilmtal-Weinstraße, 2023), pp. 242–66.

6 For Holy Roman emperor Henry VI's role in the founding process of the Teutonic Order, see, most recently, Arno Mentzel-Reuters, 'Heinrich VI. und der Deutsche Orden', in *Zwischen Mittelmeer und Baltikum*, pp. 304–31.

7 For a general overview, see with further references Julian Yolles, 'The Maccabees in the Lord's Temple: Biblical Imagery and Latin Poetry in Frankish Jerusalem', in *The Uses of the Bible in Crusader Sources*, ed. Elizabeth Lapina and Nicholas Morton (Leiden, 2017), pp. 421–39; Morton, 'The Defence of the Holy Land and the Memory of the Maccabees', *Journal of Medieval History* 36 (2010), 275–93.

8 Nicholas Morton, 'Walls of Defence for the House of Israel: Ezekiel 13:5 and the Crusading Movement', in *The Uses of the Bible*, pp. 403–20.

Peter of Dusburg, Nicholas of Jeroschin or John of Posilge.[9] In the early thirteenth century, the faith-defending tasks of the Teutonic Knights were extended from the Holy Land, through their short-lived intermezzo in the Bârsa Land (named after the eponymous river, Rom. Țara Bârsei, Hung. Barcaság, Ger. Burzenland) in south-eastern Transylvania, and into their new commitments in the southern and eastern Baltic Sea region in particular.[10] Various papal crusade bulls from the 1220s onwards declared the raids of the Teutonic Order against the Prussians as campaigns *pro defensione catholice fidei* and equated them with the crusades to the Holy Land. Again, this rhetorical argumentation was not new, since granting the same indulgences to those combatants who joined non-Holy Land campaigns under the sign of the cross became quite common papal practice from the second half of the twelfth century.[11] However, it was the Teutonic Order in particular that, in its extremely skilful diplomatic networking and propagandistic activity, turned the fight against paganism (Germ. *Heidenkampf*) in East-Central and North-Eastern Europe into a substitute for the Palestine crusades in the broader public perception, thus making it an attractive proposition for the wider European knighthood from the thirteenth to early fifteenth centuries.[12]

The increased popularity of the order's military commitment in Prussia, Livonia and later Lithuania ultimately led to another phenomenon which distinguished the struggle in the Baltic Sea region from those in other areas and which, beyond the Levant, could only be compared with the anti-Muslim *frontera* in Iberia: what was new was the increased scale of the campaigns which — carried out annually — gained the character of a constant holy war in which a vast part of Latin Christian nobility participated.[13] This, as well as the full support of the papacy for the *Reisen*, demonstrate certain key similarities to the Holy Land crusades. Assigned numerous papal privileges (especially under Innocent IV and

---

9 Torben Kjersgaard Nielsen, 'Providential History in the Chronicles of the Baltic Crusades', in *The Uses of the Bible*, pp. 361–402; Marcus Wüst, *Studien zum Selbstverständnis des Deutschen Ordens im Mittelalter* (Weimar, 2013); Janusz Trupinda, *Ideologia krucjatowa w kronice Piotra z Dusburga* (Gdańsk, 1999).

10 On these issues, see, most recently, Udo Arnold, 'Ansätze zur Territorialisierung des Deutschen Ordens: Hochmeister Hermann von Salza und mögliche Einsatzorte in der ersten Hälfte des 13. Jahrhunderts. Das ungarische Burzenland als Teil eines übergreifenden Konzepts', in *Zwischen Ostsee und Adria: Ostmitteleuropa im Mittelalter und in der Frühen Neuzeit. Politische, wirtschaftlichen, religiöse und wissenschaftliche Beziehungen*, ed. Bárány, Roman Czaja and László Pósán (Debrecen, 2023), pp. 14–40.

11 On this topic, see, with further references, the various chapters in the essay collection *The Expansion of the Faith: Crusading on the Edges of Latin Christendom in the High Middle Ages*, ed. Paul Srodecki and Norbert Kersken (Turnhout, 2021).

12 For a general overview, see Werner Paravicini, *Die Preussenreisen des europäischen Adels*, 4 vols (Sigmaringen, 1989–2023).

13 For the increased popularity of the Teutonic Order's crusades in the southeastern and eastern Baltic Sea regions, see Paravicini, *Preussenreisen*; Nicholas Morton, 'In Subsidium: The Declining Contribution of Germany and Eastern Europe to the Crusades to the Holy Land, 1221–91', *German Historical Institute Bulletin* 33 (2011), 33–66.

Fig. 25. (1) *The Defence of the Thorn Tree Castle in 1231* (painting by an anonymous artist, c. 1600), Stadtmuseum in Sterzing, Italy. Reproduced from <https://w.wiki/6hv8> [accessed 21 September 2023], licence public domain; (2) *The Burning of a Teutonic Knight by Prussian Pagans* (painting by Joseph Anton Baumann, c. 1740). Commandery of the Teutonic Order in Lengmoos, Italy. Photo by Paul Srodecki.
Showing conspicuous references to contemporary *Türkenkriege* and the widespread bulwark *topoi*, in the allegorical painting on the top the besieging Prussian pagans are portrayed as Ottoman Turks and the Teutonic Order as Latin Christianity's firmest outpost in the fight against the hostile outer-groups of unbelievers. Another early-modern motif was that of the Teutonic Knights as pious martyrs who willingly and self-sacrificingly gave up their lives for the defence of Christian faith. The bottom painting shows the burning of Teutonic Knight by Prussian pagans who in the depiction of their clothing again show strong similarities to early modern Ottoman Turks.

his successor Alexander IV), which continuously extended the order's scope of action and finally gave its clergymen the right to preach the cross, to recruit crusaders and to grant indulgences, the Teutonic Knights now led 'a more or less privatised, eternal crusade', as Christopher Tyerman once splendidly put it.[14] This represented a significant increase in power for the order, since it no longer required further papal crusade proclamations, and could therefore invite the European chivalry to join the crusades against the Baltic infidels at any time.[15]

In this context, the pagan Balts were often presented synecdochically as Saracens, whereas, in reverse, the 'Saracens' (e. g. Moors) of Iberia were even portrayed as 'Tatars' to the Teutonic brothers in Prussia and the German lands, as shown for instance in Peter of Dusburg's *Chronicle of the Prussian Land*.[16] This almost obligatory amalgamation of various non-Christian peoples to form a hodgepodge of enemies was used not only to familiarise mostly unknown regions and enemies of the faith to the respective audiences; it also testifies to the supra-regional awareness in the ranks of the Teutonic Order of their being part of a larger crusading and faith-defending movement. In sum, following the end of the Latin Christian Levant in the early 1290s, alongside the anti-Muslim fronts in Iberia and the Balkans, the south-eastern and eastern Baltic Sea areas formed 'established sites' of crusading for a not insignificant part of the Western knighthood and were seen by them as constituting 'one large unity' of the faith defending movement.[17]

---

14 Christopher Tyerman, *The Invention of the Crusades* (Basingstoke, 1998), p. 41.
15 See with further references Axel Ehlers, *Die Ablasspraxis des Deutschen Ordens im Mittelalter* (Marburg, 2007), pp. 24–76.
16 Peter von Dusburg, 'Chronicon terrae Prussiae', ed. Max Töppen, in SRP 1: 21–219 (here lib. 4, p. 195): *De occisione multorum Tartarorum in Hispania. Hoc eciam tempore Almimolinus imperator Sarracenorum venit cum infinita multitudine in Hispaniam, et indixit bellum omnibus adorantibus crucifixum. Quem reges Hispanie aggredientes in bello vicerunt, et facta fuit tanta strages, ut rivi sanguinis de occisis fluerent Sarracenis.* The term *Almivolus* is most probably a corruption of the term used for the Caliph al-Nasir in the Spanish chronicles — "miramamolin" — and Almohad, the dynasty of the leaders of the Muslim Berbers'. See *The Chronicle of Prussia by Nicclaus von Jeroschin: A History of the Teutonic Knights in Prussia, 1190–1331*, ed. and trans. Mary Fischer (Farnham, 2010), p. 39, fn. 2. From today's perspective, it is difficult to answer whether this title was chosen on purpose or due to ignorance (or whether Dusburg simply made a mistake). Conforming to the zeitgeist, in the following entry the chronicler speaks of the Saracens and their defeat. In this context, one should remember that the addressees of Dusburg's work and similar chronicles were mainly the Teutonic Knights themselves. From this perspective, equating the terms Saracens and Mongols/Tatars (the latter being an enemy of the order on their own doorstep) appears as an additional rhetorical finesse to underline the pan-European holy war on the Christian periphery and to strengthen the feeling of togetherness. For the depiction of the pagan Balts as Saracens in Western sources, see with further references Alan V. Murray, 'The Saracens of the Baltic: Pagan and Christian Lithuanians in the Perception of English and French Crusaders to Late Medieval Prussia', *JBS* 41 (2010), 413–29. For the Teutonic Order's participation in the anti-Mongol/Tatar crusades, see Paul Srodecki, 'Fighting the "Eastern Plague": Anti-Mongol Crusade Ventures in the Thirteenth Century', in *The Expansion of the Faith*, pp. 303–27.
17 Hartmut Boockmann, *Johannes Falkenberg, der Deutsche Orden und die polnische Politik: Untersuchungen zur politischen Theorie des späteren Mittelalters: Mit einem Anhang: Die Satira des*

As for the Poles, even if their participation in the Levant crusades was rather episodic compared to that of the French, Germans, English or Italians, there was nevertheless also a lively reception of the crusade idea in Poland, whose princes and knights had already gained some peripheral crusading experience when the Teutonic Knights arrived in Prussia in 1225.[18] The numerous campaigns of the Piast dukes against the Pomeranians, Prussians and Yotvingians in the twelfth and early thirteenth centuries were legitimised by the Holy See as *bella iusta* in the cause of the cross.[19] Furthermore, even after the Teutonic Knights set foot in Prussia, the Poles were still considered in Rome as one of the first addressees for a crusade against the Prussians, although papal crusade appeals were admittedly now increasingly sent primarily to the German nobility.[20] Due to its peripheral position and the ongoing conflicts with the aforementioned pagan Pomeranians and Balts as well as the Mongols/Tatars and the schismatic Ruthenians — many of them carried out as crusades — the Polish elites, like the Teutonic Order, were able to establish the image of a Christian bulwark in the rest of Europe. This was especially the case with the last two Piast kings on the Polish throne, Vladislas the Elbow-High and his son Casimir the Great, as well as under their successor Vladislas II Jogaila.[21]

Fighting the Baltic Saracens

All in all, to return to the point of departure in the title, both the Teutonic Order state and the kingdom of Poland had achieved a certain reputation by around 1400 as faith-defending border countries of the Catholic West. References to

---

Johannes Falkenberg (Göttingen, 1975), p. 123, n. 319; Erich Maschke, 'Burgund und der preußische Ordensstaat: Ein Beitrag zur Einheit der ritterlichen Kultur Europas im Spätmittelalter', in *Syntagma Friburgense: Historische Studien Hermann Aubin dargebracht zum 70. Geburtstag am 23.12.1955* (Lindau, 1955), pp. 147–72 (here 164).

18 For a general overview on the Polish crusading movement, see Darius von Güttner-Sporzyński, *Poland, Holy War, and the Piast Monarchy, 1100–1230* (Turnhout, 2014); Mikołaj Gładysz, *The Forgotten Crusaders: Poland and the Crusader Movement in the Twelfth and Thirteenth Century* (Leiden, 2012). For Polish participation in the Holy Land crusades, see Zdzisław Pentek, 'Why Did So Few Crusaders from East-Central and Eastern Europe Participate in the Crusades to the Holy Land?', in *The Expansion of the Faith*, pp. 55–67; Agnieszka Teterycz-Puzio, *Polscy krzyżowcy: Fascynująca historia wypraw Polaków do Ziemi Świętej* (Poznań, 2017); Marcin Wołoszyn, 'Vor Władysław von Warna: Polen und die Kreuzfahrerstaaten. Ein archäologischer Beitrag', in *Eurika: In honorem Ludmilae Donchevae-Petkovae*, ed. Valeri Grigorov, Metodi Daskalov and Evgeniya Komatarova-Balinova (Sofiya, 2009), pp. 157–69.

19 See with further references Darius von Güttner-Sporzyński, 'The Periphery of Europe and the Idea of Crusade: Adaptation and Evolution of Crusader Ideology in Poland under the Piast Dynasty (1100–47)', in *The Expansion of the Faith*, pp. 69–88; Srodecki, *Antemurale Christianitatis*, pp. 73–79.

20 On the involvement of the Piasts in the Prussian crusades of the 1230s, see Gładysz, *The Forgotten Crusaders*, pp. 227–52.

21 Besides Andrzej Marzec and Sven Jaros's chapters in this book, see Srodecki, *Antemurale Christianitatis*, pp. 80–87.

these external depictions and self-perceptions mixed with crusade motifs were important parts of the diplomatic rhetoric in the long-lasting conflict between both players in the first half of the fifteenth century, especially at the councils in Constance (1414–18) and Basle/Ferrara/Florence (1431–49).[22] In this dispute, the Teutonic Knights were diplomatically supported by various German princes, of whom the Hungarian and (since 1411) Romano-German king Sigismund of Luxemburg, as the order's 'advocate' (although this role was not undisputed), was without doubt among the most popular figures.[23]

Perhaps the best known, and simultaneously most infamous, treatises (*Satira* and *Liber de doctrina*, published in 1412 and 1416 respectively) for the Teutonic side were written by the Pomerania-born Dominican friar Johannes Falkenberg. The latter summarised the allegations made by the order and its supporters in recent years, according to which Poland, for the sake of her own striving for power and to the detriment of the whole of the Catholic West, had strayed from the path of true faith by allying with the admittedly baptised but, in truth, still pagan Lithuanians, the Muslim Tatars and the schismatic Ruthenians. However, Falkenberg even went a radical step further and, in view of the allegations raised, called not only for the murder of the Polish king Vladislas II Jogaila but also for the extermination of all Poles and pagans — demands which, from the post-World War II perspective, triggered Stanisław F. Bełch to name Falkenberg as 'the first writer to formulate the argument in justification of genocide'.[24] An essential core of Falkenberg's arguments was the appeal to holy war: fighting incessantly under the sign of the cross against infidels and fallacious Christians (in this case: the Poles) was an 'indispensable' duty for every Latin Christian ruler and knight.

Similar arguments can also be found in a memorandum most likely written by the order's procurator general at the Roman curia, Peter of Wormditt, and presented at the council in early 1415. Using the domino effect theory so typical of crusade rhetoric, the importance of the Teutonic Knights was emphasised whilst, at the same time, the allegedly reprehensible actions of the Poles were de-credited: if the Order state in Prussia, with all its well-fortified and 'strong houses, castles and cities', raised solely 'for the protection of Christianity', was to fall, then no one could prevent 'the enemies of Christ's cross' from further storming the Catholic West. The document concludes with an appeal to the pope, the participants of the council and, last but not least, to Sigismund of Luxemburg to protect the Teutonic Order's territories in the south-eastern and eastern Baltic

---

22 See Paul Srodecki, 'Schilt der Cristenheite i Scutum christianitatis — spory polsko-krzyżackie a retoryka przedmurza/tarczy na początku XV wieku', in *Unia w Horodle na tle stosunków polsko-litewskich: Od Krewa do Zaręczenia wzajemnego Obojga Narodów*, ed. Sławomir Górzyński (Warszawa, 2015), pp. 147–63.
23 See Paul Srodecki, 'Mediating Actors in the Conflict between the Teutonic Order and the Kingdom of Poland in the Early Fifteenth Century', in *Der Deutsche Orden auf dem Konstanzer Konzil: Pläne — Strategien — Erwartungen*, ed. Helmut Flachenecker (Ilmtal-Weinstraße, 2020), pp. 15–33.
24 Stanislaus F. Belch, *Paulus Vladimiri and His Doctrine Concerning International Law and Politics*, 2 vols (London, 1965), 1: 713.

Sea region, which had now been defending Christendom and in particular the Holy Roman Empire from the eastern threats for nearly two hundred years.[25] The effectiveness of this propaganda among the literary Western European elites around 1400 is shown by several non-German reports in which, in addition to the image of the Teutonic Order as the Christian shield par excellence, the Poles were repeatedly defamed as cynical allies of 'non-believers' (*mescréans*) and 'Saracens' (*sarrasins*), as pointed out, for instance, by the Franco-Flemish knight Gilbert of Lannoy in his widely received travel reports.[26] The cantor at the Saint-Denis Monastery near Paris, Michel Pintoin, even went so far in his *Chronica Karoli Sexti* as to depict the Teutonic defeat at Tannenberg as a defeat for all Christianity at the hands of the 'Turks', the latter being led by the 'king of Cracow [i.e. Vladislas II Jogaila]' and 'his brother, the king of the Saracens [i.e. Vytautas the Great]'.[27]

I have already discussed the Polish charges against the Teutonic Order in the early fifteenth century in general and at the Constance Council in particular in detail elsewhere.[28] To summarise briefly: on the one hand, the Poles sought to refute the defamations of the order. After the outbreak of the Great War in 1409, Jogaila was praised as an eager 'pupil of the Catholic faith and son of the Roman Church' who would not only defend the Christian faith, but would also zealously spread it in the manner of a pious *athleta Christi*. The non-Christians in his army were only his and his cousin, the Lithuanian Grand Duke Vytautas's, subordinates (*servientes nationes*). Calling upon pagans or schismatics for military services, whether as vassals (as in the case of the Ruthenians and Moldavians) or allies (as in the case of the Mongolo-Tatarian contingents under the later Golden Horde khan Jalal al-Din), was a practice which Sigismund of Luxemburg as well

---

25 SSDOP 1, no. 2, pp. 65–111. See Srodecki, *Antemurale Christianitatis*, pp. 114–15.
26 *Oeuvres de Ghillebert de Lannoy, voyageur, diplomate et moraliste*, ed. Charles Potvin (Louvain, 1878), pp. 20 and 26. See Oscar Halecki, 'Gilbert de Lannoy and His Discovery of East Central Europe', *Bulletin of the Polish Institute of Arts and Sciences in America* 2 (1944), 324–29.
27 Michel Pintoin, *Chronica Karoli Sexti*, ed. Louis Bellaguet, 6 vols (Paris, 1839–52), 4, bk 31.13, pp. 334–35. For more examples of anti-Polish rhetoric among a not insignificant part of the Western European elites against the background of the Teutonic-Polish conflict in the early fifteenth century, see Andrzej Feliks Grabski, *Polska w opiniach Europy Zachodniej XIV–XV w.* (Warszawa, 1968), pp. 253–301, 348–81.
28 Paul Srodecki, '"Murus et antemurale pollens et propugnaculum tocius christianitatis": Der Traktatenstreit zwischen dem Deutschen Orden und dem Königreich Polen auf dem Konstanzer Konzil', *Schweizerische Zeitschrift für Religions- und Kulturgeschichte* 109 (2015), 47–65; Srodecki, *Antemurale Christianitatis*, pp. 132–42; Srodecki, 'Schilt der Cristenheite'. See also Tomasz Graff, 'Servants of the Devil or Protectors of Christianity and Apostles among Pagans? Shaping the Image of Poland and Poles in the Context of Steps Taken by Wladyslaw II Jagiello's Diplomacy against 'Satira' by John Falkenberg', *Folia Historica Cracoviensia* 23 (2017), 143–76; Jürgen Miethke, 'Die Polen auf dem Konstanzer Konzil: Der Konflikt um den Dominikaner Johannes Falkenberg', in *Das Konstanzer Konzil 1414–18: Weltereignis des Mittelalters: Essays*, ed. Karl-Heinz Braun (Stuttgart, 2013), pp. 106–10; Krzysztof Ożóg, 'Udział Andrzeja Łaskarzyca w sprawach i sporach polsko-krzyżackich do soboru w Konstancji', in *Polska i jej sąsiedzi w późnym średniowieczu: Profesorowi Jerzemu Wyrozumskiemu — uczniowie*, ed. Ożóg and Stanisław Szczur (Kraków, 2000), pp. 159–86.

as the Teutonic Knights had also used in the past.[29] Falkenberg's afore-mentioned infamous demands were met with the sharpest protests on the Polish side (and were even not undisputed among the Teutonic Knights themselves), which had incessantly been calling for Falkenberg's conviction for heresy and his burning at the stake at the council in Constance.[30] The accusation of heresy had also been raised a good century earlier, during the annihilation of the Templar Order — a historical precedent which caused alarming headaches in internal correspondence between the order's procurator general Peter of Wormditt and the Grand Master Henry of Plauen.[31]

On the other hand, the Poles themselves raised heavy criticisms against the order by portraying the latter as the real aggressor, who had long since ceased to be a faith-defending 'shield of Christianity'. Rather, by shedding Christian blood and spreading the Christian faith by fire and the sword, the Teutonic Order state had turned into a coldly calculating territorial power, acting only for its own benefit and for whom human lives meant nothing. Since their arrival in Prussia in the 1220s, the Teutonic Knights had been striving — first secretly and now, after Falkenberg's revealing and eye-opening treatises, openly — for the 'final extinction' (*finale excidium*) of Poland and her Christian inhabitants.[32] It was self-evident that the deliberate killing of people (even pagans) would be contrary to Christ's teachings. Pagans should only be converted by proselytisation and not by force. Anyway, through the official adoption of Christianity by the Lithuanians, the Teutonic Order forfeited its right to exist in the south-eastern Baltic Sea region. Rather, its services would be needed on other fronts of Christendom, above all in the fight against the Golden Horde in Eastern and the Ottoman Turks in South-Eastern Europe. The Polish deputies emphasised that a relocation of the Teutonic Knights was therefore inevitable.[33] Like the Teutonic propaganda, albeit to a lesser extent, the viewpoints and charges raised on the Polish side in the conflict with the order also found some support in other Western Christian countries. A more or less critical position towards the Teutonic Knights was taken, for instance, by the Benedictine monk Thomas Walsingham in his *Ypodigma*

---

29 *CESDQ* 3, app. 2, p. 499; *SRP* 3, pp. 427–29. See Boockmann, *Johannes Falkenberg*, pp. 90–91; Srodecki, '"Murus et antemurale"', pp. 56–61.
30 The Council of Constance as well as the Dominican Order eventually declared Falkenberg's works as scandalously reprehensible and libellous, but acquitted him of the charge of heresy. For a general overview on the controversy around Falkenberg's treatise, see Norman Housley's recent article 'A Crusade against the Poles? Johannes Falkenberg's "Satira" (1412)', in *The Templars, the Hospitallers and the Crusades: Essays in Homage to Alan J. Forey*, ed. Helen J. Nicholson and Jochen Burgtorf (London, 2020), pp. 183–98.
31 *BGDO* 2, no. 84, p. 182.
32 *CESDQ* 3, app. 2, p. 499.
33 *CEV*, no. 38, p. 1017. In secret negotiations between Jogaila and the Danish king in 1418, the proposal was even raised to move the order to Cyprus or Rhodes: *BGDO* 2, p. 576, n. 5. See Matthias Thumser, 'Eine neue Aufgabe im Heidenkampf? Pläne mit dem Deutschen Orden als Vorposten gegen die Türken', in *Europa und die osmanische Expansion im ausgehenden Mittelalter*, ed. Franz-Reiner Erkens (Berlin, 1997), pp. 139–76.

Neustriæ.[34] In his chronicle, the Augustinian friar John Capgrave even openly accused the order of turning from good to evil and blamed them of having acted in a non-Christian manner in bringing war upon the newly baptised Jogaila and the Lithuanians:

> The Kyng of Cracow [Vladislas II Jogaila] was baptised in the name of the Trinite. Alle thei that were Sarasines laboured eythir to perverte him, or ells to distroye him; therfor he disposed him to gete help of Cristen me, and supposed that the heres of Pruse schuld best help. Thei, seing that his frendis were turned fro him, set upon him on the other side, only to distroye him. Behold what zelatouris thei were of oure Feith! Her religion was ordeyned to defense the Feith; and now covetise stereth hem to distroye it. The Kyng that was newly Cristis child thoute it was best first to fite ageyn these religious renegatis. He faute with hem, and put hem to flite, and conqwered al the cuntre, suffering hem to use her eld lawes and customes.[35]

These allegations weighed heavily, and it was not easy to argue against them. In this context, Falkenberg and the other deputies of the order gained help, above all, from Germany, the order's country of origin. It is therefore hardly surprising that, in particular, the crusade image of the Teutonic Order as *the* faith-defending Christian bulwark, besieged by the Poles in conjunction with pagan auxiliaries and in urgent need of help, enjoyed great popularity in the *Reich*. The strong bonds between the German-speaking lands and the order were also evident in the widespread outrage over Sigismund's erratic policy in the conflict between the Teutonic Knights and Poland and Lithuania, which was regarded as a demonstration of support for enemies of the faith as well as an affront to the order and, by extension, the Holy Roman Empire. Evidence of this is provided by numerous letters of the imperial princes to Sigismund, to the council in Constance and later, to Pope Martin V, in which the Teutonic Knights were praised as crusaders par excellence, and as most honourable 'fighters and defenders' of the Catholic Church and in which, in turn, Vladislas II Jogaila and his cousin Vytautas were repeatedly defamed as allies of the 'Saracens and pagan peoples'.[36]

The Teutonic Knights also received support from non-German sympathisers, who still considered the order to be one of the most important faith-defending institutions of Latin Christianity. Since these have been discussed by other historians in numerous treatises, again I do not wish to recount the numerous arguments put forward in this context, but rather to focus solely on the crusade momentum in the apologias of the order's non-German supporters and — later — on the references connecting the order's Baltic crusades to the religious warfare in the

---

34 John Capgrave, *The Chronicle of England*, ed. Francis Charles Hingeston, RS 1 (London, 1858), p. 298. See Grabski, *Polska w opiniach*, pp. 283–84.

35 Thomas Walsingham, *Ypodigma Neustriae*, ed. Henry Thomas Riley, RS 28.7 (London, 1876), pp. 431–32; Walsingham, *Historia Anglicana*, ed. Riley, 2 vols, RS 28.1.1–2 (London, 1863–64), 2: 282–85.

36 For this paragraph, see with further references Srodecki, 'Mediating Actors'.

Levant and Iberia. Inspired by their eagerness to carry out a pan-European crusade against the various enemies of the Catholic faith (especially the Ottomans), a not insubstantial number of the council participants backed Falkenberg's crusade arguments against the Polish attacks.[37] Among them were such renowned and rhetorically skilled theologians as Giacomo Belardi Arrigoni, bishop of Lodi, the Benedictine Jean de Vincelles, procurator of the Cluny abbey and later abbot of Saint-Oyend-de-Joux (mod. Saint-Claude, France), or the Portugal-born André Dias de Escobar (also known as Díaz, Didaci, de Lisboa, de Rendufe or simply Hispanus), bishop of Ciudad Rodrigo.[38]

It was especially the latter who took side for the Teutonic Order in Constance by setting the crusader motif at the centre of his explanations. The Iberian was a passionate advocate of the conciliar movement, with his works among the most widely received theological texts of the fifteenth century.[39] Dias de Escobar was assigned the task of writing a tract for the order's defence by the afore-mentioned Peter von Wormditt. His positive image of Germany and the Germans and his open sympathies for the Holy Roman Empire in general and the Teutonic Order in particular may have had various roots. As a young man, Dias de Escobar studied

---

37 Even before the council, both Antipope John XXIII and King Sigismund of Luxemburg announced, in various writings, that the achievement of general unity through the settlement of the so-called Western Schism and the numerous disputes between the respective actors of Latin Christianity would only serve one higher goal, namely the implementation of a *passagium generale*, a great crusade in a high medieval manner. See *ACC* 1, pp. 15, 169, 236–37. For the crusade issue at the church councils in the first half of the fifteenth century, see recently Norman Housley, 'Crusade and Reform, 1414–49: Allies or Rivals?', in *Reconfiguring the Fifteenth-Century Crusade*, ed. Norman Housley (London, 2017), pp. 45–83.

38 *SSDOP* 1, nos 3 and 16, pp. 112–17, 391–413; *ACC* 4, no. 443, pp. 370–73. See Boockmann, *Johannes Falkenberg*, p. 269.

39 At the Council of Constance this was very true for the catalogue *De scismatibus*, which — written in 1409 — listed and described twenty-four schisms. In 1414/1415, Dias de Escobar published *Gubernaculum conciliorum* which served the participants of the council as a welcome guidebook. Some scholars also consider him to be a co-author of the important council book *De modis uniendi et reformandi ecclesiam in concilio universali*, which was published in 1410 (*SSDOP* 1, p. 392). See Johann Baptist Sägmüller, 'Der Verfasser des Traktats "De modus uniendi ac reformandi ecclesiam in concilio universali" vom Jahre 1410', *Historisches Jahrbuch* 14 (1893), 562–82 (here 562). In contrast to this, André Dias de Escobar's participation in *De modis uniendi et reformandi ecclesiam in concilio universali* had been already denied as early as in 1901 by Ludwig Walters in his doctoral dissertation 'Andreas von Escobar, ein Vertreter der Konziliaren Theorie am Anfange des 15. Jahrhunderts' (unpublished Ph.D. thesis, University of Münster, 1901), pp. 27–34. Michael Milway, 'Forgotten Best-Sellers from the Dawn of the Reformation', in *Continuity and Change: The Harvest of Late-Medieval and Reformation History: Essays Presented to Heiko A. Oberman On His 70th Birthday*, ed. Robert J. Bast and Andrew C. Gow (Leiden, 2000), pp. 113–42 (here 117, 130 and 141–42), lists André Dias de Escobar as one of the best-selling authors of the second half of the fifteenth century. For an overview, see António Domingues de Sousa Costa, *Mestre André Dias de Escobar, figura ecuménica do século XV* (Roma and Porto, 1967); Sousa Costa, 'Posizione di Giovanni di Dio, Andrea Dias de Escobar e altri canonisti sulla funzione sociale delle decime', in *Proceedings of the Fourth International Congress of Medieval Canon Law, Toronto, 21–25 August 1972*, ed. Stephan Kuttner (Città del Vaticano, 1976), pp. 411–66 (here 433–45).

in Vienna, where he became *magister theologiae* in 1393. He surely also knew the Teutonic Order from its Spanish possessions in La Mota near Zamora which were situated close to his bishopric in Ciudad Rodrigo.[40] Born in the homeland of the *Reconquista*, where fighting the Muslim Moors had already been a pillar of the faith-defending self-identity for centuries, the Iberian theologian naturally had quite a positive attitude towards the Teutonic Order's fight against the heathens. In his homeland, the Teutonic Order was also well known, and was supported by various Iberian rulers with several letters of safe-conduct, especially with regards to the acquisition of funds through trading indulgences for the order's religious warfare against the 'Saracens' in the south-eastern and eastern Baltic Sea region.[41] Important for the provenance of his pro-order apologia in Constance was also Dias de Escobar's proximity to Pope Martin V, who never denied his affinity for the Teutonic Knights.[42]

Written most probably in November 1417, Dias de Escobar's treatise opened by repeating all the well-known arguments of the order and accusations against the Polish side repeatedly levelled by Falkenberg, Wormditt et al. in the preceding years: he demanded justice and support for the Teutonic Order in their conflict against the Polish king who, with the help of 'schismatics, heretics, Saracens and pagans', would fight 'against the catholic faith and against all justice'.[43] In the following *narracio*, André Dias de Escobar praised the nature of the Teutonic Order as a military-religious order. In this regard, references to the crusade movement are omnipresent: founded in the Holy Land in the late twelfth century, from the very beginning, the main task of the Teutonic Knights was double-edged. On one hand, they had been instructed with the 'defence of the faith' (*pro defensione fidei*); on the other hand, they had been charged by various papal and imperial privileges with spreading the frontiers of Latin Christianity.[44] Outside Germany, too, the order had become a welcome destination for numerous Christian knights in their pursuit of participation in the holy war against infidels and, at the same

---

40 See Manuel Fuertes de Gilbert, 'La Orden Teutónica en España: la encomienda de Santa María de Castellanos (1222–1556)', in *Congreso Internacional Arte y Patrimonio de las Órdenes Militares de Jeruslaén en España*, ed. Amelia López-Yarto Elizalde (Zaragoza, 2010), pp. 467–82; Nikolas Jaspert, 'Der Deutsche Orden auf der Iberischen Halbinsel', in *España y el "Sacro Imperio": Procesos de cambios, influencias y acciones recíprocas en la época de la "europeización" (siglos XI–XIII)*, ed. Julio Valdeón (Valladolid, 2002), pp. 273–98.
41 Axel Ehlers, Die Ablasspraxis des Deutschen Ordens im Mittelalter (Marburg, 2007), p. 329.
42 The tract must have been finished shortly after the election of Oddone Colonna as Martin V in November 1417, since Dias de Escobar often addresses it to Martin as the new pope in later parts (whereas in the introducing chapters he only refers to the 'emperor' and the secular princes). See *SSDOP* 1: 391–92; Paul Srodecki, 'Quia inter vos stabilita concordia est valde opportune: Zu den vermittelnden Kräften im Konflikt zwischen dem Deutschen Orden und dem Königreich Polen im frühen 15. Jahrhundert', *Biuletyn Polskiej Misji Historycznej* 11 (2016), 321–58 (here 341–43); Lisbeth Nitschmann, *Die Stellung Martins V. zum deutschen Ritterorden in der preussisch-polnischen Frage von 1418–24* (Königsberg, 1919).
43 *SSDOP* 1, no. 16, p. 395.
44 *SSDOP* 1, no. 16, p. 397.

time, it had received a lot of help and support from various countries, mostly from France, Spain and England. Fighting infidels, schismatics and allegedly false Christians at the edges of Latin Christianity could therefore in no way be considered reprehensible.

Here, André Dias de Escobar built his argumentation on the points raised by the Italian consistorial lawyer and later cardinal Ardicino della Porta in early 1417. In his treatise, the Novara-born della Porta defended the right of the pope and the emperor to entrust the Teutonic Order and other Christian crusaders with anti-pagan warfare in the Baltic Sea region. The Teutonic Knights owed the special privileges, repeatedly granted, confirmed and extended by the two highest powers of Latin Christendom, above all to their achievements and commitments in defending the faith which had made them 'the wall and forewall and bulwark of the whole of Christianity'. Della Porta also referred to the other two great military orders, since the Hospitallers and, in the past, the Templars had also been granted the same privileges for the same reasons. As with the explanations of André Dias de Escobar, by skilfully making the connection to the Holy Land crusades, the Italian lawyer raised his arguments to a higher level of legitimacy.[45] By throwing 'three hundred years of crusades into the weighing pan',[46] some months later, the Franciscan vicar general Jean Roques (also known as la Roque or de Rocha) refined Ardicino della Porta's theses and raised the following question: if the campaigns against infidels and the associated necessity of killing them without legal sanction did not meet the requirements of a just war, would this not then mean that generations of Latin Christian crusaders — among them such illustrious kings and princes as Louis IX of France, Godfrey of Bouillon or Baldwin I of Jerusalem — as well as the innumerable members of military orders had acted in an un-Christian manner in the past while fighting the Saracens and Moors, thus taking a great burden of guilt upon themselves?[47]

Initially, the astonished Polish side, with its chief-advocate Paweł Włodkowic, was unable to resolve the dilemma presented by this argument, which — if affirmed — would have turned the self-image of the entire Christian (e.g. also Polish) chivalry on its head. Indeed, in his 52 *Conclusiones ad tractatum de potestate pape et imperatoris etc.* (published before 27 June 1416), even Włodkowic had to recognise the crusades into the Levant and Iberia as legitimate. Referring to such authorities in both canon and civil law as Oldrado da Ponte (died in the mid-1330s), however, the Polish lawyer underlined that the morally disgraceful fight of the Teutonic Knights against the Balts could in no way be compared to the legitimate crusades against the Saracens in the Holy Land or Spain. The former fought an unjust war against peaceful infidels and conquered lands which had never before belonged to Christianity, whereas the Levant and Iberian crusades served a just cause, since their goal had been to reconquer previously Christian

---

45 *SSDOP* 1, no. 9, pp. 231–39.
46 Boockmann, *Johannes Falkenberg*, p. 271. See Housley, 'Crusade and Reform', p. 62.
47 *ACC* 4, no. 449, p. 409.

lands which had been conquered by force by the Muslims — 'the homeland of which we were violently despoiled', as emphasised by Oldrado da Ponte in the first half of the fourteenth century.[48] Thus, the support of the order by Christian crusaders 'to combat peaceful pagans' was an 'error' which 'could not be accepted under any condition, [...] since impiety should not be done under the pretext of piety'.[49]

Nevertheless, this line of argument did not prevent the order's supporters from accusing Włodkowic of inconsistency, since, in their view, it was irrelevant on which fronts the Christian knighthood would confront the enemies of the faith, thus meaning that the same legitimising conditions as in the Levant and Iberia should also apply to the holy war in the Baltic Sea region.[50] Ardicino della Porta emphasised that the pagans were given their land by God only as a fief, and that it was therefore also a divine right to take them from them again — if necessary by force, and under the sign of the cross. For the Italian, however, there was still a hierarchy of crusading goals: in the end, della Porta continued, the expansion of the Latin Christian borders in general and in the eastern Baltic Sea region in particular, as well as the associated additional incomes from church tithes, would strengthen the Catholic West and serve a higher goal, namely the recapture of the Holy Land from the 'Saracens, who have detained and occupied it to this very day'. Since the Teutonic Knights, as well as all the crusaders who supported and still support them, waged war against the pagans and Saracens on papal commands, they were excused in their actions. However, those (i.e. the Poles) who criticised the order's crusading ventures were in opposition to the Holy See, and thus showed not only their 'ignorant', 'ill-disposed' and 'non-Catholic' nature, but might even be deemed downright 'heretical'.[51]

Turning the Rhetorical Tables

The *de facto* end of the Western Schism with the election of Oddone Colonna — taking the name Martin V — as the sole pope accepted by all (with the exception of Aragon) at the Constance Council in 1417 increased the pressure on the Teutonic Order and Poland finally to end their long-standing conflict. For Martin, a peace between the two opponents was indispensable for the further tasks which Latin Christianity still had to solve in this region of Europe. Alongside the Ottoman threat, the pope identified the Hussite movement as posing the

---

48 Jews and Saracens in the Consilia of Oldradus de Ponte, ed. N. P. Zacour (1990), p. 49.
49 SSDOP 1, no. 5, pp. 138 and 144.
50 SSDOP, nos 10 and 14, pp. 261–62, 322–23 and 365. See Boockmann, *Johannes Falkenberg*, p. 272.
51 SSDOP 1, no. 9, pp. 243–47.

greatest danger to Latin Christianity.[52] The defeats of the Catholic armies at Kutná Hora (Ger. Kuttenberg) and Deutschbrod (mod. Havlíčkův Brod, Czechia), as well as the related failure of the Third Hussite Crusade in early 1422, reinforced Martin's view that a reconquest of Bohemia for the Catholic Church would be only possible with the combined efforts of the Central European powers and, above all, with the support of both Poland and the Teutonic Order. Like the pope, Sigismund of Luxemburg, after succeeding his half-brother Wenceslas as king of Bohemia in 1419, was also particularly interested in an early termination of the Hussite heresy. However, both papal and royal attempts at intervention were ultimately unsuccessful. By the summer of 1422, renewed tensions between the Polono-Lithuanian union and the Teutonic Order had culminated in a new war after almost eight years of ceasefire. Once again, the order could not withstand the joint Polono-Lithuanian forces and was forced to concede its first major territorial losses in the Peace Treaty of Lake Melno on 27 September 1422.[53] In these years, Poland's diplomacy with foreign envoys in Polish services such as the restless Milanese Jacopo de Paravesino (also Paravicino) was trying hard to win papal favour.[54] Like Sigismund, who once again changed sides, in the following years, the order intensified its efforts on the diplomatic level to break up the Polono-Lithuanian union. The support of the newly enthroned Lithuanian grand duke Švitrigaila, who was striving for complete independence from his brother Jogaila following the death of Vytautas in 1430, led to a new war between the order and Poland, the so-called Lutsk War.

As in the 1410s, a new council, which had been meeting in Basle since 1431, offered the two conflicting parties a diplomatic platform for resolving their dispute. By and large, the order's arguments resembled those presented at the Council of Constance: (1) since its initiation in the twelfth century, the Teutonic Order state in Prussia and Livonia had been a solid shield of the Catholic faith and one of the few faith-defending outposts comparable only to the high medieval crusader states in the Levant and the Christian kingdoms on the Iberian *frontera*; (2) the order's crusades against paganism served the good of all Christianity; (3) Poland would ally itself with the latter's enemies (this time with

---

52 Antonín Kalous, 'Papal Legates and Crusading Activity in Central Europe', in *The Crusade in the Fifteenth Century: Converging and Competing Cultures*, ed. Norman Housley (London, 2017), pp. 75–89.

53 On the 1422 war between the Teutonic Order and Poland-Lithuania and the Treaty of Lake Melno, see Sven Ekdahl, 'Der Krieg zwischen dem Deutschen Orden und Polen-Litauen im Jahre 1422', *ZfO* 13, 614–51.

54 On this very interesting figure of early-fifteenth-century diplomacy, see, most recently, Werner Paravicini, 'Jacobus de Paravesino: Krakau, Mailand und die Kurie zu Beginn des 15. Jahrhunderts', in *Zwischen Mittelmeer und Baltikum*, pp. 360–82. For Polish diplomacy at the court of Pope Martin V, see Jan Drabina, *Papiestwo–Polska w latach 1384–1434* (Kraków, 2003), pp. 65–116, 129–184; Monika Dudka, 'Dyplomaci Władysława Jagiełły w Stolicy Apostolskiej', *Our Past: Studies in the History of the Church and Catholic Culture in Poland* 128 (2017), 5–39.

the heretical Hussites).[55] The Poles countered the order's allegations with tried and tested arguments from Constance, by extolling Poland as the true defender of Latin Christianity and King Vladislas II Jogaila as a firm defender of the faith.[56] Interestingly, this time, the Polish diplomacy also adopted the crusade rhetoric used by the order in previous years by setting Poland's centuries-long experience in peripheral crusading on an equal level to the Mediterranean crusades and describing her as an antipole to the Iberian Peninsula. The most obvious example of this is a document, most probably written during the second half of 1435, by the Polish diplomat and early humanist Mikołaj Lasocki. As a member of the Polish delegation at the Basle Council, Lasocki was sent to the Congress of Arras, at which a peace between France, England and Burgundy was negotiated with the facilitation of both the council and Pope Eugene IV. The Polish humanist arrived in Artois in July 1435 and presented his memorandum to the representatives of the Castilian king John II.[57]

Lasocki started with a description of Poland's geographical situation. Located 'at the frontiers of the Christians', the Polish kingdom had long since faced various enemies of the faith. This tactic of familiarisation was intended to bring Poland closer to the Castilians as well as to win their sympathies. Here, in his description of Poland's neighbours, Lasocki adopted the alienity concept built upon strategies of inclusion and exclusion and well-known from the biblical bulwark rhetoric: following a strictly antagonistic self- and other-image, the Polish humanist very clearly divided the surrounding countries into Christian ones, i.e. an 'own' cultural community including Poland (*pars Christianorum*), and an opposing and evil world of the unbelievers (*pars infidelium*). Despite its heterogenic composition, Lasocki described the latter as united, in essence and in its goals, since all the pagans, schismatics, Muslims etc. existed solely to destroy the Christian West. Once, Lasocki emphasised, the Lithuanians had also been amongst Poland's infidel neighbours, but now they had been loyal Christians for several years.[58]

Just like the Castilians, the Poles were not only deeply pious in their faith, but also eager and ready to defy 'the wildest enemies'. As warden of the eastern flanks of Latin Christianity, Poland's crusading task was to repel the Ottomans, Tatars and Ruthenians. To emphasise the Polono-Castilian parallels even more firmly, Lasocki referred to the efforts and accomplishments of the Polish combatants in their long-standing fight against the 'millions' of Mongols/Tatars. Since the latter had largely been Islamised for a long time by the middle of the fifteenth century, in referring to them, Lasocki styled Poland as the eastern mirror image of Castile which, for her part, had for centuries been the Christian spearhead against the Islamic al-Andalus. The description of the Tatar menace was intended to highlight

---

55 See with further references Srodecki, *Antemurale Christianitatis*, pp. 128–32.
56 See with further references Srodecki, *Antemurale Christianitatis*, pp. 137–42.
57 On the dating of the memorandum, see Kurt Forstreuter, 'Eine polnische Denkschrift auf dem Konzil in Basel', *ZfO* 21 (1972), pp. 684–96 (here p. 689, n. 7).
58 Forstreuter, 'Eine polnische Denkschrift', p. 693.

Poland's importance to the rest of Latin Christianity, since the various victories of Polish knights, fighting under the sign of the cross against the Tatar Muslims, those 'cruel and inhuman' enemies of the faith, had preserved the Christian hinterland from devastations and destructions such as those experienced during the great Mongol raids into East-Central Europe in the thirteenth century.[59]

Like his diplomatic predecessors at the Council of Constance, Lasocki also emphasised the merits of the recently deceased Vladislas II Jogaila, praising him as the *athleta Christi* and crusader king par excellence. The latter had led numerous campaigns against the Tatars in the name of the Holy Cross and had even built various fortifications beyond the eastern Polish frontier for better control over the enemies of the faith.[60] Lasocki played here on the ignorance of his Castilian audience regarding the situation on the eastern periphery of Latin Christianity: having more or less cordial relations with the Golden Horde during his whole reign as Polish king, Jogaila's allegedly anti-Tatar campaigns were in fact the raids of his cousin Vytautas against the so-called *magna Tartaria*.[61] Nevertheless, in Lasocki's speech, it was Poland alone that stood against the Tatars and — in another rhetorical parallel to the *Reconquista* and the geographical conditions of the Iberian peninsula — only Polish crusaders could expel the Tatar infidels 'over the sea' (*ultra mare*) from Europe. However, if this was ever to happen, 'other Christian princes, who always were hostile to this kingdom', would have to stop preventing Poland from fulfilling its faith-defending duty — a clear side-swipe at the Teutonic Knights and Sigismund of Luxemburg. Only then could Latin Christianity be safe on its eastern flank.[62]

In another speech, given to the Burgundian duke Philip the Good in May 1435, Lasocki advocated peace as quickly as possible between the conflicting parties of the Hundred Years' War gathered in Arras. The Polish diplomat drew the picture of a pan-European crusade movement that had to take up the cross and confront the 'Turks, Tatars and Saracens' on all fronts. It was now time to take seriously the fear that these enemies of the Catholic faith would expand their borders further to the west and despoil Christian land after Christian land, subjugating them to vassalage or tributary status. This is what once happened to the Holy Land, and what had recently happened to the kingdom of Cyprus.[63] Self-evidently, with such statements Lasocki was charging at an open door in Arras, since the demand for a pan-European crusade, especially against the Ottomans, increased again noticeably.[64]

---

59 Forstreuter, 'Eine polnische Denkschrift', p. 694. See Srodecki, 'Fighting the "Eastern Plague"'.
60 Forstreuter, 'Eine polnische Denkschrift', p. 694.
61 See Józef Skrzypek, Południowo-wschodnia polityka Polski od koronacji Jagiełły do śmierci Jadwigi i bitwy nad Worsklą, 1386–99 (Lwów, 1936).
62 Forstreuter, 'Eine polnische Denkschrift', p. 694.
63 The speech was printed in Karolina Grodziska, 'Mikołaja Lasockiego apel o pokój na kongresie w Arras w 1435 r.', *Studia Historyczne* 35 (1992), 241–51 (here 245–51).
64 See Franco Cardini, 'Le concile de Ferrare et la croisade', *CRM* 1 (1996), 45–52. For Iberian interest in such a venture, see Mark Aloisio, 'Alfonso V and the Anti-Turkish Crusade', in *The Crusade in*

Crusading Motifs after 1450

References to the images of faith-defending 'shields' and 'bulwarks' and crusading frontier states also continued to be recurring arguments in the diplomatic struggle between the Teutonic Order and Poland after the church councils of the first half of the fifteenth century. Nearly three-quarters of a century after the first union between Poland and Lithuania and the latter's official conversion to Latin Christianity, the order still portrayed the conflict with Poland in the best crusading fashion as a fight against false and evil Polish Christians and their 'Saracen' allies, i.e. the Lithuanians and Tatars. In this context, the reports that the order's representatives sent to Western Europe prove to be very interesting for the subject under discussion. In 1438, for instance, the French king Charles VII had given five friars under the leadership of the Beauvoir commander, John of Frankfurt, permission to propagate the holy war on the Lithuanian front in his kingdom and to collect money for the defence of Christianity in the distant Baltic Sea region by granting indulgences. Similar letters of recommendation were issued in France after the outbreak of the so-called Thirteen Years' War (1454–66), for example by the Orléans bishop Thibault d'Aussigny in 1455. Although the collections were only marginal sources of income for the order, the examples listed and the support offered to the order by the French elites show the persistent virulence of the faith-defending self- and external image of the order, clearly based on its crusading roots.[65]

Regardless of this, the order's starting position in its dispute with Poland had changed by the years 1454–66, since the war arose from a conflict between the Prussian Confederation established by a sizable number of the Prussian nobility and cities in 1440 in order to protect their interests against the ruling Teutonic Knights.[66] This time, too, the order invoked its exposed position as a shield of

---

the *Fifteenth Century*, pp. 64–74; David S. H. Abulafia, 'Aragon versus Turkey-Tirant lo Blanc and Mehmed the Conqueror: Iberia, the Crusade, and Late Medieval Chivalry', in *Byzantines, Latins, and Turks in the Eastern Mediterranean World after 1150*, Jonathan P. Harris, Catherine J. Holmes and Eugenia Russell (Oxford, 2012), pp. 291–312; Rafael Beltrán Llavador, 'Des emblèmes du pouvoir d'Alphonse V d'Aragon à la récupération de Constantinople: croisade historique et utopie littéraire dans Tirant lo Blanc', in *Histoires et mémoires des croisades à la fin du Moyen Âge*, ed. Martin Nejedlý and Jaroslav Svátek (Toulouse, 2012), pp. 293–304.

65 See Karol Polejowski, 'The Teutonic Order's Propaganda in France during the Wars against Poland and Lithuania (Fifteenth Century)', in *Die geistlichen Ritterorden in Mitteleuropa: Mittelalter*, ed. Karl Borchardt and Libor Jan (Brno, 2011), pp. 233–42.

66 For a general overview on the dispute between the Teutonic Order and the Prussian Confederation and the Thirteen Years' War, see Wiesław Długolecki, 'Zur Geschichte der Führungsschichten in Königsberg und Marienburg in der Zeit des Dreizehnjährigen Krieges: Ein Beitrag zum Austausch der städtischen Machteliten', ZH 82 (2017), 55–70; Klaus Neitmann, 'Die preußischen Stände und Außenpolitik des Deutschen Ordens bis zum Abfall des Preußischen Bundes (1411–54): Formen und Wege ständischer Einflussnahme', in *Ordensherrschaft, Stände und Stadtpolitik: Zur Entwicklung des Preußenlandes im 14. und 15. Jahrhundert*, ed. Udo Arnold (Lüneburg, 1985), pp. 27–80; Marian Biskup, 'Der preußische Bund 1440–54: Geschichte, Struktur, Tätigkeit und Bedeutung

Christianity and underlined, albeit less often, its past crusading services in the defence of the Christian West as well as in the Christianisation of Prussia, Livonia, Samogitia and Lithuania. The main opponent in the Thirteen Years' War, however, was the rebellious Prussian Confederation and most of the order's accusations were directed against its members. Contemporary chroniclers loyal to the order such as Laurentius Blumenau, humanist and councillor of the grand master, preferred to criticise the rebels of the Prussian Confederation as faithless traitors as well as defiant and greedy subjects (*plebs novarum rerum cupida*), who were revolting against the divine order, rather than to revive old arguments about being the shield of Christianity.[67] The confederation itself was nothing more than a union proclaimed 'in the name of the devil, who is an instigator and augmenter of war', and thus directed 'against God and the liberty of the Holy Church'.[68]

By contrast, the order now had to refrain from turning its tried and tested self-portrayal against itself. In this respect, the negotiations in Kobelgrube on the Vistula Spit (1465) in the run-up to the Second Peace of Thorn (1466) offer an interesting anecdote. Stibor of Baysen (Pol. Ścibor Bażyński), one of the leaders of the Prussian secessionists and partisan of the Polish king and Lithuanian grand duke Casimir Andrew, spoke openly to the representatives of the order, stating that the latter should be subordinated to the Polish crown. The Polish king, in turn, was to be the order's supreme protector from then on and, in return, would include its leaders in his royal council. Baysen lent his proposal rhetorical emphasis by referring to the political zeitgeist, since the same procedure could also be found 'in other lands' with crusading traditions tied to the defending of Latin Christian frontiers as 'in *Hispania* [in the sense of Iberia], where a master also is in the council with the king'.[69] Stibor drew his knowledge first-hand, since his older brother John (Pol. Jan Bażyński) had been a delegate for the order at the court of the Portuguese king John I between 1419 and 1422. In these years, John must have witnessed the strong interdependence between monarchy and

---

in der Geschichte Preußens und Polens', in *Bürgertum, Handelskapital, Städtebünde*, ed. Konrad Fritze, Eckhard Müller-Mertens und Johannes Schildhauer (Weimar, 1975), pp. 210–29; Hartmut Boockmann, 'Zu den politischen Zielen des Deutschen Ordens in seiner Auseinandersetzung mit den preußischen Ständen', *Jahrbuch für Geschichte Mittel- und Ostdeutschlands* 15 (1966), 57–104.

67 Laurentius Blumenau, 'Historia de Ordine Theutonicorum Cruciferorum', ed. Max Töppen, in *SRP* 4: 35–70 (here 65). On this issue, see Marie-Luise Heckmann, 'Zwischen Anspruch und Wirklichkeit ...: Die Selbstsicht der Führungsgruppe des Deutschen Ordens beim Ausbruch des Dreizehnjährigen Krieges', in *Der Blick auf sich und die anderen: Selbst- und Fremdbild von Frauen und Männern in Mittelalter und früher Neuzeit. Festschrift für Klaus Arnold*, ed. Jürgen Sarnowsky, Lucie Kuhse und Sünje Prühlen (Göttingen, 2007), pp. 237–63.

68 *Geschichten von wegen eines Bundes*, ed. Max Töppen, in *SRP* 4: 71–211 (here 77, 86).

69 Paul Pole, 'Preussische Chronik', ed. Max Töppen, in *SRP* 5: 173–288 (here app. 3, p. 248). See Jürgen Sarnowsky, 'Die ständische Kritik am Deutschen Orden in der ersten Hälfte des 15. Jahrhunderts', in *Das Preußenland als Forschungsaufgabe: Eine europäische Region in ihren geschichtlichen Bezügen. Festschrift für Udo Arnold zum 60. Geburtstag, gewidmet von den Mitgliedern der Historischen Kommission für Ost- und Westpreußische Landesforschung*, ed. Bernhart Jähnig and Georg Michels (Lüneburg, 2000), pp. 403–22.

military orders on the Iberian Peninsula while taking part in the Luso-Moroccan frontier conflict over the North-African city of Ceuta (Berb. Sebta, Arab. Sabtah), which had been captured by the Christians in a campaign declared as a crusade in 1415.[70] The appeal to idealised conditions (from the Polish perspective) in the relationship between crown and military order in distant Iberia was to remain a popular argument used by Polish diplomats until the very end of the Teutonic Order's state in Prussia, as was shown for instance in the negotiations between both sides at the Poznań assembly in 1510.[71]

These rhetorical references in the political language of the Polish diplomacy are all the more remarkable when one considers that, especially after the conclusion of the *Reconquista* with the conquest of Granada in 1492 and the complete unification of the Iberian Peninsula under Latin Christian rule, the latter had been increasingly considered among the safe hinterland regions of Europe. The reverse was true for Poland which, in the early modern period, was finally given the generally accepted epithet of a permanent Latin Christian forewall or bulwark both in its own self-perceptions and in those from elsewhere. Together with 'Italy, France and other western realms', Hispania was now said to owe its integrity to the lands of the Polish king Sigismund, located 'on the enemy frontiers', as representatively emphasised on behalf of the Holy See by the papal legate and later bishop of Sebenico, Ivan Štafilić (Ital. Giovanni Stafileo), at the royal court in Cracow in 1512. The Jagiellonian dominions were being 'daily and incessantly devastated, their cities destroyed, their fortresses and fields burned' while their inhabitants 'were being partly slain by the sword, partly carried off as prisoners'.[72]

---

70 John of Baysen's participation in the Portuguese campaigns against the Moroccans is panegyrically summarised in John I's recommendation letter written to Grand Master Michael Küchmeister from (most probably) 24 January 1422. The letter was printed in Karl Scherler, *Hans v. Baisen der erste Gubernator in Preussen c. 1380–1459* (Danzig, 1911), pp. 24–26. See also Astrid Kaim-Bartels, 'Herausbildung und Rolle des Adels im mittelalterlichen Preußen', *Beiträge zur Geschichte Westpreußens* 17 (2000), 9–29 (here 21); Andrzej Feliks Grabski, 'O polskich rycerzach w Maroku w XV wieku parę uwag', *PrzH* 58 (1967), 515–17; Rudolf Grieser, 'Baysen, Hans von', *Neue Deutsche Biographie* 1 (1953), 680–81; Ulrich Wendland, 'Hans von Baysen', *Weichselland: Mitteilungen des Westpreußischen Geschichtsvereins* 37 (1938), 76–89 (here 76–77); Karol Górski, 'O Janie Bażyńskim w świetle dokumentów', *RH* 13 (1937), 304–17 (here 307–8); Rudolf Grieser, *Hans von Baysen: Ein Staatsmann aus der Zeit des Niederganges der Ordensherrschaft in Preußen* (Leipzig, 1936), pp. 12–13. On the Christian conquest of Ceuta, the subsequent Luso-Moroccan conflict over this region and the Latin Christian expansion in Africa as well as the crusading moments in it, see Adam Simmons, 'The African Adoption of the Portuguese Crusade during the Fifteenth and Sixteenth Centuries', *The Historical Journal* 65 (2022), 571–90; Vitor Luís Gaspar Rodrigues, 'The Portuguese Art of War in Northern Morocco during the 15th Century', *Athens Journal of History* 3 (2017), 321–36; A. R. Disney, *A History of Portugal and the Portuguese Empire: From Beginnings to 1807*, 2 vols (Cambridge, 2009–12), 2: 1–83; Luís Adão da Fonseca, Maria Cristina Pimenta and Paula Maria de Carvalho Pinto Costa, 'The Papacy and the Crusades in XVth Century Portugal', in *La Papauté et les croisades*, ed. Michel Balard (Ashgate, 2011), pp. 141–54; John L. Vogt, 'Crusading and Commercial Elements in the Portuguese Capture of Ceuta (1415)', *The Muslim World* 59 (1969), 287–99.
71 Pole, 'Preussische Chronik', app. 4, p. 287 (see also pp. 271 and 273–74).
72 *AT* 2, no. 19, p. 16.

The recategorisation of Iberia as a pacified and safe Christian region did not mean that the respective countries of the peninsula were no longer regarded as defenders of the faith. The opposite was the case, as becomes clear from the speech by Štafilić quoted above. In pursuit of one of the main aims of the Fifth Lateran Council (1512–17), the nuncio was sent to win the support of the Polish king for a pan-European crusade against the Muslims, the ultimate aim of which, of course, in the tradition of the late medieval crusade rhetoric, would be the liberation of the Holy Land. In Štafilić's portrayal, Sigismund together with his older brother Vladislas, king of Bohemia and of Hungary, was supposed to campaign against the Ottomans and Tatars. Štafilić styled King Ferdinand II of Aragon and the Two Sicilies as the western counterpart to the Jagiellons, since he had successfully 'been opposing the adversaries of the Apostolic See and our holiest Lord like an invincible wall both on land and at sea' for some years now and thus was also to take a leading role in the papal crusading plans against the Muslims.[73] Similar to the aforementioned speeches from the great fifteenth-century councils, an arc was rhetorically stretched from the Polish (and also Hungarian) to the Aragonese periphery by linking to the self-image of both areas and emphasising their faith-defending efforts and traditions — with the difference that, taking the geopolitical conditions into account, the Spanish *frontera* had now been relocated from Iberia to the southern Mediterranean and North Africa. In the years that followed, the appeal to the faith-defending self-images of Poland and Spain and the memorialisation of crusading traditions continued to play not unimportant roles in the diplomatic correspondence between both countries.[74]

For the Teutonic Order, increased recourses to the old crusade rhetoric can be recorded at the turn of the fifteenth to sixteenth centuries. Around 1500, Grand Master Frederick of Saxony attempted on several occasions to shake off Polish hegemony. Here the leadership of the order again exalted its position as a shield of Christianity and as a safe refuge for all those willing to take up the cross against the enemies of Latin Christianity. The ever-emerging conflict between the Livonian branch of the Teutonic Order and the grand duchy of Moscow in the late fifteenth and sixteenth centuries gave new fuel to the long-serving crusade argumentation and allowed the Teutonic Knights to uphold their faith-defending self-image — a view which was willingly adopted and propagated by contemporaries, such as Hartmann Schedel, for example, who praised Livonia as 'the last region and province of the Christians' in his well-known world chronicle from 1493.[75] The importance of Livonia for the order grew even further after the so-called Prussian Homage in 1525 (Pol. Hołd pruski), that is the formal investment of Albert of Brandenburg-Ansbach as duke of Prussia following the

---

73 *AT* 2, no. 19, p. 16.
74 As, for instance, in a letter of Sigismund I to Charles V from 1512, *AT* 6, no. 160, p. 160. See Srodecki, *Antemurale Christianitatis*, p. 268.
75 Hartmann Schedel, *Register Des buchs der Croniken vnd geschichten mit figuren vnd pildnussen wn anbeginn der welt bis auf dise vnnsere Zeit* (Nürnberg, 1493), fol. 278v.

dissolution and transformation of the Teutonic Order state in Prussia into a secular hereditary duchy under Polish suzerainty.[76] Against the background of the growing 'Muscovite threat' and in particular the Livonian War from 1558 to 1583, the land at the eastern shores of the Baltic Sea appeared in numerous Western (mostly German-language) depictions as 'the bulwark of the Catholic Church' and 'the wall of the Holy [Roman] Empire and other realms and provinces of [Latin] Christianity'.[77] However, unlike in the aforementioned cases from the fifteenth and early sixteenth centuries, explicit references to a pan-European crusading movement can hardly be found in these and similar depictions in these years and the period to follow.

Concluding Thoughts

The Teutonic Order was undoubtedly one of the pioneers in the adoption of the faith-defending rhetoric for self-referential descriptions and for legitimising its own existence. With their power-political striving for independent territorial rule (first in in the Bârsa Land, but above all later in Prussia and Livonia), the Teutonic Knights carefully developed the image of the order as a crusading 'shield', 'wall' or 'bulwark' of the Catholic faith, indispensable for the welfare of the Christian West. The order drew the foundations for the perception of itself and the outside world as an association of shared belief from the high medieval ideology of the crusade. Also used, albeit to a lesser extent, by the Templars and Hospitallers, it is no coincidence that the appeal to the New Testament *scutum fidei* formula of Paul the Apostle formed the core of the Teutonic Knights' self-perception. Nevertheless, whereas the use of these *topoi* was rather occasional in the thirteenth and fourteenth centuries, they experienced a noticeable increase around 1400, that is after the Christianisation of Lithuania and at a time of growing tension with the kingdom of Poland. As shown in this chapter, particularly in the run-up to and during the Great War (1409–11), as well as in the subsequent diplomatic disputes with Poland at the great councils of the first half of the fifteenth century, the order

---

76 Juhan Kreem, 'Crusading Traditions and Chivalric Ideals: The Mentality of the Teutonic Order in Livonia at the Beginning of the Sixteenth Century', *Crusades* 12 (2013), 233–50. See also Almut Bues, '"Die letst gegent und provintz der cristen", Or: Where is the Baltic?', in *Zones of Fracture in Modern Europe: The Baltic Countries, the Balkans and Northern Italy*, ed. Bues (Wiesbaden, 2005), pp. 27–43.

77 Olaus Magnus, *Carta marina et descriptio septemtrionalium terrarum ac mirabilium rerum in eis con tentarum diligentissime* (Veneciis, 1539) <https://w.wiki/7WN2> [accessed 29 September 2023]; *EFE* 8, nos 55–56, pp. 89–94. The latter quote is taken from the inner-dynastic correspondence between Holy Roman emperor Ferdinand and his nephew, Spanish king Philip II, from the late 1550s and early 1560s. The extent to which these euphemisms fell back on the rhetorical models of Andrés Dias de Escobar and others of his ilk or were brought in by the Habsburgs as a German aristocratic family, who, following the tradition of the Hohenstaufens and Luxemburgers, saw themselves as protectors of the Teutonic Order, is difficult to establish.

Fig. 26. *The Prussian Homage* (painting by Marcello Bacciarelli, 1796).

increasingly relied on its self-image as defenders of the faith. While the Polish ambassadors in Constance still sporadically defended their King Vladislas II Jogaila as Christ's champion in front of the council public, deputies of the order such as Peter of Wormditt, Ardicino della Porta or Andrés Dias de Escobar repeatedly referred to the order's crusading past and its supposedly still relevant and necessary crusading existence in the present. Furthermore, although the planned but not realised Holy Land crusades were still unquestionably given much greater priority (even though the indulgences granted were the same), the comparison of the southern and eastern Baltic Sea region to the various other theatres of religious warfare (foremost to the Outremer and Iberia), particularly at the church councils at the beginning of the fifteenth century, was intended to serve to upgrade the legitimacy of the Teutonic Order's Baltic crusades. These rhetorical comparisons, however, not only reflect the mentality of certain intellectual elites, who took the side of the Teutonic Knights in bilateral diplomatic correspondences or in the private parties of closed council meetings. They were also evident in the actual habitus of Latin Christian chivalry, who, with a unique self-understanding, raised their swords under the sign of the cross against the numerous enemies of the Catholic West on various fronts: one year in Spain, the next in Prussia, and then in the Balkans.[78]

On closer inspection, the order's increased recourse to shield or bulwark allegories reflects the changed political framework conditions in the fifteenth century. In contrast to the twelfth or thirteenth centuries, the order's self-portrayal was no longer about expanding Christianity's borders. This was hardly possible after the conversion of Lithuania, her union with Poland and the harsh defeat at Tannenberg in 1411. Rather, the order now drew solely on the image of a hard-pressed Christian bulwark — harassed by the only allegedly Christianised Lithuanians, the schismatic Rus, the evil Muslim Tatars from the vast Eurasian steppes and, last but not least, their allies: the 'false' Christians from Poland. Drawing parallels to the Holy Land and Iberia was intended to emphasise the special status and thus the unquestionability of the Teutonic Order. Just as in the Mediterranean, Latin Christianity, oppressed from all sides, would also be defended in the south-eastern and eastern Baltic Sea region.

Another change went hand in hand with this shift from expansive to defensive rhetoric: in the fifteenth century, explicit bulwark allegories borrowed from the terminology of fortification notably gained in popularity, at the expense of the previously more popular shield allegories and the not clearly-defined border area stylisations. This rhetoric, as used by various intellectuals such as Ardicino della Porta and others of his ilk in Constance, would cast its shadow on the further development of the idea of the crusades in the late Middle Ages: apart from the

---

[78] A representative overview of the European nobles' restless crusade voyages in the later Middle Ages is provided in the aforementioned reports of the Franco-Flemish knight Gilbert of Lannoy. For a general overview, see Paravicini, *Preussenreisen*; Timothy Guard, *Chivalry, Kingship and Crusade: The English Experience in the Fourteenth Century* (Woodbridge, 2013).

Iberian *Reconquista*, which was fast approaching its end in the fifteenth century, the crusaders now largely defended Latin Christianity on the walls of besieged cities in Prussia, Livonia, eastern Poland, (and later — after her Christianisation) Lithuania or the Balkans. Large scale crusading campaigns, such as those of Nicopolis or Varna, now became a rarity. This also reflects the changed emphasis within the Teutonic Order's and its supporters' crusade rhetoric and, after a process of adaptation, also within the Polish diplomatic language. In fact, the polemical disputes with the Teutonic Knights at the councils in Constance and Basle were to prove constitutive for the Polish bulwark *topoi* of later decades. While most of the Polish representatives at the councils were still primarily trying to refute the accusations made by the order against the neophyte Jogaila and to portray the Polish king primarily as a true defender of the faith, from the second half of the 1430s onwards there was a remarkable shift in the Polish self-perception. What was considered a novelty in the rhetoric of Polish elites at Arras, the juxtaposition of the Polish existence on the border with the Spanish *frontera*, had already, as early as 1500, become a self-evident *epitethon ornans* of Poland as *the* crusading 'bulwark of the Christian faith'.[79]

---

79 See, with further references, Paul Srodecki, '"Universe Christiane reipublice validissima propugnacula" — Jagiellonian Europe in Bulwark Descriptions around 1500', in *The Jagiellonians in Europe: Dynastic Diplomacy and Foreign Relations*, ed. Attila Bárány (Debrecen, 2016), pp. 57–74; Srodecki, *Antemurale Christianitatis*, pp. 217–65.

SERGEY POLEKHOV

Zwischen Kreuzzugsrhetorik und Bündnissen

Die Ostpolitik des Großfürsten Witold von Litauen (1392–1430)

Das Großfürstentum Litauen, einer der flächenmäßig größten Reichsverbände des östlichen Europa im ausgehenden Mittelalter, nimmt zurecht einen festen Platz in den Forschungen zur spätmittelalterlichen Kreuzzugsbewegung ein.[1] Die Rolle der Litauer als letzte Heiden Europas (bis 1387 für das eigentliche Litauen und 1417 für Samogitien) und Sieger in der Schlacht von Tannenberg (1410) wird zwar immer betont.[2] Das Interesse der Forschung galt aber lange Zeit Litauen als einem Ziel der baltischen Kreuzzüge, während die Frage nach dem Wechsel von einem Kreuzzugsobjekt zu einem Kreuzzugsakteur nach dem Übertritt Litauens zum Christentum von der Geschichtswissenschaft weitestgehend vernachlässigt worden ist. Und wenn die Aneignung der Kreuzzugsidee durch die Litauer thematisiert worden ist, dann zumeist (und größtenteils recht rudimentär) im Hinblick auf die Maßnahmen Witolds und Jogailas am Ende des 14. Jahrhunderts, als es den Vettern am Vorabend der Schlacht an der Worskla (12.

---

1 So beispielsweise bei Eric Christiansen, *The Northern Crusades: The Baltic and the Catholic Frontier, 1100–1525* (London, 1980); Norman Housley, *The Later Crusades, 1274–1580: From Lyons to Alcazar* (Oxford, 1992); *Crusading in the Fifteenth Century: Message and Impact*, hg. v. Housley (London, 2004); Housley, *Contesting the Crusades* (Oxford, 2006); *The Crusade in the Fifteenth Century: Converging and Competing Cultures*, hg. v. Housley (London, 2017); *Reconfiguring the Fifteenth-Century Crusade*, hg. v. Housley (London, 2017); *Holy War in Late Medieval and Early Modern East-Central Europe*, hg. v. Janusz Smołucha, John Jefferson und Andrzej Wadas (Kraków, 2017).

2 Darius Baronas und Stephen C. Rowell, *The Conversion of Lithuania: From Pagan Barbarians to Late Medieval Christians* (Vilnius, 2015). Siehe auch mit weiteren Literaturhinweisen Sławomir Jóźwiak et al., *Wojna Polski i Litwy z Zakonem Krzyżackim w latach 1409–11* (Malbork, 2010). Zu den Auswirkungen der Schlacht und des Krieges: Rimvydas Petrauskas, 'Iki ir po didžiojo mūšio: politiniai pokyčiai Rytų Pabaltijyje Žalgirio mūšio epochoje', in *Jogailos ir Vytauto laikai*, hg. v. Zigmantas Kiaupa et al. (Kaunas, 2011), S. 8–20. Zum Forschungsstand und den Forschungsperspektiven: Krzysztof Kwiatkowski, *Memoria continenter historiam denotat: Bitwa pod Grunwaldem/Tannenbergiem/Žalgirisem 1410 w najnowszych badaniach* (Toruń, 2015).

August 1399) gelang, durch ihre Diplomaten eine entsprechende Kreuzzugsbulle gegen die Goldene Horde bei Papst Bonifatius IX. zu erwirken.[3]

Die Dringlichkeit dieses bisher nur in geringem Maße bearbeiteten Forschungsfeldes wird aber umso deutlicher, wenn man die Bedeutung der litauischen Expansion nach Osten für den Fortbestand des Großfürstentums im ausgehenden Mittelalter betrachtet — die Eroberungszüge waren eine wichtige Quelle des materiellen Wohlstands der litauischen Fürsten und ihrer Umgebung, sei es nun hinsichtlich des territorialen Zuwachses, der gemachten Kriegsbeute oder der zahlreichen erkämpften Kontributionen und Tribute.[4] In der Regierungszeit des Großfürsten Witold (1392–1430, katholischer Taufname 1383: Wigand; orthodoxer [vermutlich 1384 und 1387] und erneut katholischer [1386 und zuletzt 1389/90] Taufname: Alexander[5]) erreichte die litauische Ostexpansion ihren Höhepunkt.

Tatsächlich stieg die Kreuzzugsidee schon recht bald nach der Christianisierung Litauens neben weiteren legitimistischen Vorzügen, die der Übertritt zum christlichen Glauben mit sich brachte, zu einem sehr effektiven Mittel in der Expansion gen Osten auf, als es darum ging, die weitläufigen Länder der zersplitterten orthodoxen Rus, die zum Teil noch unter dem Einfluss der an Macht schwindenden Goldenen Horde standen, nach und nach zu erobern oder der Macht des litauischen Herrschers zu unterwerfen.[6] Unter welchen Umständen benutzte Witold die Kreuzzugsidee und -rhetorik? Kann hier zurecht von der bloßen Ideenausnutzung und einer rhetorischen Vereinnahmung gesprochen werden oder wollte der Gediminide ernsthaft die östlichen Nachbarn zum Katholizismus bekehren? Welche Rolle spielte dabei das Königreich Polen, mit dem das Großfürstentum Litauen durch eine dynastische Union verbunden war? Um diese Fragen beantworten zu können, bedarf es einer genauen Analyse der Witoldschen Ostpolitik — ein Untersuchungsfeld, das bisher immer noch weitgehend

---

3 An dieser Stelle sind zwei Aufsätze von Stephen C. Rowell nennenswert: 'Lietuva — krikščionybės pylimas? Vienos XV amžiaus ideologijos pasisavinimas', in *Europos idėja Lietuvoje: istorija ir dabartis*, hg. v. Darius Staliūnas (Vilnius, 2002), S. 17–32, und 'Naujieji kryžiaus žygiuotojai: LDK ir Bizantijos santykiai XIV–XV a. sandūroje. Ar Vytautas Didysis buvo Lietuvos kryžiaus žygių prieš turkus bei totorius pradininkas?', in *Kryžiaus karų epocha Baltijos regiono tautų istorinėje sąmonėje*, hg. v. Rita Regina Trimonienė und Robertas Jurgaitis (Šiauliai, 2007), S. 181–205.

4 Henryk Łowmiański, 'Uwagi w sprawie podłoża społecznego i gospodarczego unii jagiellońskiej', in Łowmiański, *Studia nad dziejami Wielkiego Księstwa Litewskiego* (Poznań, 1983), S. 365–454.

5 Zu den Taufen und Taufnamen Witolds siehe Jan Tęgowski, *Pierwsze pokolenia Giedyminowiczów* (Poznań, 1999), S. 211.

6 Zu diesen Innovationen siehe Alvydas Nikžentaitis, 'Litauen unter den Grossfürsten Gedimin (1316–41) und Olgerd (1345–77)', in *Die „Blüte" der Staaten des östlichen Europa im 14. Jahrhundert*, hg. v. Marc Löwener (Wiesbaden, 2004), S. 65–75; Darius Baronas, 'Der Kontext der litauischen Kriegskunst des 13. Jahrhunderts und die militärischen Innovationen von der zweiten Hälfte des 14. Jahrhunderts bis zum Beginn des 15. Jahrhunderts', in *Tannenberg — Grunwald — Žalgiris 1410: Krieg und Frieden im späten Mittelalter*, hg. v. Werner Paravicini, Rimvydas Petrauskas und Grischa Vercamer (Wiesbaden, 2012), S. 159–73.

unerforscht ist und mehr Fragen aufwirft als Antworten bietet.[7] In diesem Aufsatz sollen Witolds Beziehungen zu seinen östlichen Nachbarn nur skizzenhaft nachgezeichnet werden, wobei das Augenmerk auf den Mitteln ihrer Durchsetzung liegen wird.

Als Witold sich 1392 mit seinem Vetter Jogaila, der als Wladislaus II. (poln. Władysław II Jagiełło) 1386 zum polnischen König gekrönt worden war, aussöhnte, war des ersteren territoriale Machtbasis noch vergleichbar gering: Der polnische König bestätigte Witold nur in seinem „Erbland", dem Fürstentum Trakai, während alle anderen litauischen Teilfürsten ihre Besitzungen beibehielten.[8] In den nächsten Jahren konnte Witold schrittweise die anderen litauischen Fürsten teils durch geschicktes Taktieren, teils mittels Gewalt aus ihren ruthenischen Fürstentümern (Nawahradak, Witebsk, Polazk, Wolhynien, Kiew und Podolien) entfernen und ernannte stattdessen selbst eigene Statthalter, um seine Stellung im Großfürstentum Litauen zu stärken.[9] Diese Handlungen bereiteten den Weg für die Durchsetzung der Ostpolitik, die nach den Kriegszügen des Algirdas (ca. 1296–1304–77, Großfürst ab 1345) eine Renaissance erlebte. Witolds neuaufgegriffenes Interesse am Osten des europäischen Kontinents war sowohl den Machtkämpfen nach dem Tod von Algirdas als auch den gestiegenen Aktivitäten des Deutschen Ordens gegen Litauen und des Großfürstentums Moskau in den russischen Ländern, die nicht unter der litauischen Oberhoheit standen, geschuldet. Witolds außenpolitische Interessen im Osten wurden dadurch erschwert, dass er auf Gebiete stieß, die vom eigentlichen Litauen (*Lithuania propria*), dem historischen und politischen Kern des Großfürstentums, weit entfernt waren und unter mehr oder weniger starkem Einfluss der Moskauer Herrscher standen oder mit ihm ein Bündnis gegen Witold schließen konnten — so etwa im Falle von Nowgorod, Pleskau, Nowossil-Odojew, Rjasan aber auch Smolensk und Twer. Auch

---

7 Antoni Prochaska, *Dzieje Witolda wielkiego księcia Litwy* (Kraków, 1914); Vytautas Didysis, hg. v. P. Šležas (Kaunas, 1930); Joseph Pfitzner, *Großfürst Witold von Litauen als Staatsmann* (Brünn, 1930); Jarosław Nikodem, *Witold, wielki książę litewski (1354 lub 1355–27 października 1430 roku)* (Kraków, 2013). Vgl. auch die wichtigsten Synthesen der Geschichte des Großfürstentums Litauen und seiner Union mit Polen (eine Auswahl): Mykhailo S. Hrushevs'kyj, Історія України-Руси. Т. 4. XIV–XVI віки — відносини політичні (Kyjiv, 1993); Oskar Halecki, *Dzieje unii Jagiellońskiej*, 2 Bde. (Kraków, 1919–20); Ludwik Kolankowski, *Dzieje Wielkiego Księstwa Litewskiego za Jagiellonów*, 1 vol (1377–1499) (Warszawa, 1930); Grzegorz Błaszczyk, *Dzieje stosunków polsko-litewskich od czasów najdawniejszych do współczesności*, 2 Bde. (Poznań, 1998–2007), 2: *Od Krewa do Lublina*.

8 Es wird zuweilen in der Wissenschaftsliteratur zu Unrecht behauptet, Witold sei von Jogaila 1392 mit der großfürstlichen Würde ausgestattet und als dessen Statthalter in Litauen eingesetzt worden. Zum Problem vom Machtumfang Witolds nach 1392 siehe zuletzt Jarosław Nikodem, 'Charakter rządów Skirgiełły i Witolda na Litwie w latach 1392–1394', *Lituano-Slavica Posnaniensia: Studia Historica* 11 (2005), 153–63; idem, *Jadwiga król Polski* (Wrocław, 2009), S. 306–18; idem, *Witold*, S. 157–66.

9 Die Auffassung, dass Witold diese Handlungen initiierte bzw. provozierte, während Jogaila sie nur sanktionierte, scheint mir überzeugend, weil sie gerade im Witolds Interesse lagen. Siehe hierzu Jarosław Nikodem, 'Charakter rządów Skirgiełły i Witolda na Litwie w latach 1392–1394', *Lituano-Slavica Posnaniensia: Studia historica* 11 (2005), 153–63; Nikodem, 'Kaributo maištas', *Lietuvos istorijos metraštis* 1 (2007), 5–20; Nikodem, *Jadwiga król Polski* (Wrocław, 2009), S. 306–18; Nikodem, *Witold*, S. 157–66.

wenn ihm insbesondere die Geschichtsforschung des 19. und 20. Jahrhunderts eine gut durchkalkuliertes außenpolitisches „Programm" zuzuschreiben suchte, muss seine Politik insgesamt als pragmatisch und als den jeweiligen tagespolitischen „Wetterlagen" angepasst beurteilt werden.[10]

Im Folgenden geht es darum, wie sich Witolds Ostpolitik unter diesen Umständen gestaltete (mit besonderer Rücksicht auf ihre Mittel und die Rolle der Kreuzzugsrhetorik).

Bereits zwischen 1393 und 1395 setzte Witold im vom Großfürstentum Litauen abhängigen Fürstentum Smolensk statt seines Bruders Jurij Svjatoslavič, der bereits 1386 Wladislaus II. Jogaila und seinem Bruder Skirgaila gehuldigt hatte, Gleb Svjatoslavič als Fürsten ein. Letzterer hatte Witold nach Preußen begleitet. Bald nach dem Tod seines Hauptrivalen Skirgaila eroberte Witold zum ersten Mal Smolensk und gliederte es in das Großfürstentum Litauen ein (1395).[11] Die nächsten Ziele in der Rus waren Nowgorod und wahrscheinlich auch Pleskau, wie dies die späteren Ereignisse besonders klar zeigen sollten. Gegen Groß-Nowgorod waren zunächst gemeinsame Handlungen Witolds und Wassilis I. gerichtet. Letzterer war durch seine Ehefrau Sophia seit 1391 Schwiegersohn des litauischen Großfürsten. Nach einem Treffen beider Herrscher in Kolomna im Herbst 1396 forderten sie gemeinsam die Nowgoroder dazu auf, den „Deutschen" — also dem livländischen Ordenszweig — den Frieden aufzukündigen.[12] Nachdem die Nowgoroder sich weigerten dies zu tun, interpretierte der Moskauer Großfürst das als einen feindlichen Akt und begann mit Kriegshandlungen gegen Nowgorod.[13] Noch Anfang 1398 bat er Witold um Hilfe gegen Nowgorod, doch bereits im Sommer desselben Jahres sowie insbesondere im Folgejahr reagierte der Moskauer Herrscher zurückhaltend auf die Versuche seines Schwiegervaters, sich für das litauische Eingreifen gegen Nowgorod im Gegenzug freie Hand im Herrschaftsbereich Moskaus zu sichern. Wassilis Zusage wäre einer Unterwerfung gleichgekommen. Der Moskauer Großfürst fühlte sich in seiner zunehmenden Zurückhaltung durch die sich zugunsten Witolds veränderten politischen Rahmenbedingungen bestätigt: So hatte der Gediminide am 12. Oktober 1398 den Vertrag von Salinwerder mit dem Deutschen Orden geschlossen. Beide Parteien verständigten sich hier auf gegenseitige Hilfe bei der Durchsetzung der eigenen Interessen in Pleskau und Nowgorod. Ein Affront gegenüber Wassili![14]

---

10 Ausführlicher dazu Sergej Polechov, 'Eine Litauische alternative für die ganze Rus'? Die Ostpolitik der litauischen Herrscher im ausgehenden Mittelalter: Ansprüche und Wirklichkeit', *Studia historica Brunensia* 2 (2019), S. 45–62.
11 *PSRL* 4.1: 378–79.
12 Es kann damit verbunden sein, dass Witolds Waffenstillstand mit dem Orden nach dem 29. September 1396 auslief. Danach schloss er den neuen Waffenstillstand erst ab Januar 1397. Siehe Sebastian Kubon, *Die Außenpolitik des Deutschen Ordens unter Hochmeister Konrad von Jungingen (1393–1407)* (Göttingen, 2016), S. 73, 77.
13 *PSRL* 25: S. 227.
14 *LUB* 4, Nr. 1469, Sp. 201–4 (zur Datierung des Briefes: Kubon, *Außenpolitik*, S. 93); *NPL*, S. 393–94; *PLP* 2: 30; *PSRL* 25: 228. Der Vertrag von Salinwerder abgedruckt bei *SVDOP* 1, Nr. 2, S. 9–12. Die

Neben dem politischen Movens der territorialen Expansion leitete Witold bei seiner Ostpolitik insbesondere der Wunsch, als konvertierter Katholik dem Abendland zu zeigen, dass er ein christlicher Fürst sei. Es war umso wichtiger, dass unter seiner Hoheit die Samogiten standen, die immer noch Heiden waren und deren Gebiete einen ständigen Zankapfel zwischen Litauen und dem Deutschen Orden bildeten.[15] Dazu kamen die weitläufigen ruthenischen Gebiete, die unter Gedimin und seinen Nachfolgern im 14. Jahrhundert dem Großfürstentum Litauen unterstellt worden waren. Unter diesen Umständen konnte der Orden behaupten, Witold sei kein wahrer Christ, sei er doch Herr „ungläubiger" beziehungsweise „schismatischer" Untertanen und trage so keinesfalls zur Ausbreitung des katholischen Glaubens bei. Witold versuchte diesem Vorwurf schon recht früh entgegenzuwirken und so schlug er bereits im Sommer 1395, als er diplomatische Kontakte mit dem Deutschen Orden nach dem Amtsantritt Konrads von Jungingen aufnahm, letzterem vor, über die Ausbreitung des christlichen Glaubens zu verhandeln. Dieser Vorschlag wurde jedoch während der Verhandlungen nicht weiter thematisiert, da der polnische König es seinem Vetter untersagte. Dieses Thema tauchte aber immer wieder in den Kontakten Witolds mit dem Deutschen Orden in den nächsten Jahren auf.[16] Unter anderem wurde die Problematik 1398 im ersten Artikel des Vertrages von Salinwerder angeregt als Witold feierlich versprach, den katholischen Glauben auszubreiten.[17] Dieses Versprechen sollte den Nährboden für einen künftigen Kriegszug gegen Groß-Nowgorod (und/oder Pleskau?) vorbereiten. Ein anderer Weg wurde aller Wahrscheinlichkeit nach schon früher, auf dem Treffen mit Wassili I. und dem Metropoliten Kiprian in Smolensk im Frühling 1396 besprochen, um danach Boten nach Konstantinopel zu schicken und die Verhandlungen über die Kirchenunion zu veranlassen.[18]

Es mag also kaum verwundern, dass Witold und Wladislaus II. Jogaila in dieser Zeit die Idee eines Kreuzzuges aufgriffen, um die Erweiterung ihres Machtbereichs zu legitimieren.[19] Schon in der Mitte der 1390er Jahre mischte sich Witold in die Kriege der tatarischen Khane ein. Er unterstützte Toktamisch (tat. Tuqtamış), der von seinem Rivalen Timur Qutlugh (tat. Timer Qotlığ) vertrieben worden war, 1397 nach Litauen floh und Witold die ruthenischen Länder offiziell mit einem Jarlyg (einer Anordnungsurkunde) verlieh.[20] Schon 1395 behauptete

---

ausführliche Analyse seines Aushandeln- und Schließungsverfahrens sowie der dahinterstehenden Interessen: Kubon, *Außenpolitik*, S. 58–123.
15 Vytenis Almonaitis, *Žemaitijos politinė padėtis 1380–1410 metais* (Kaunas, 1998).
16 Kubon, *Außenpolitik*, S. 69–73.
17 *SVDOP* 1, Nr. 2, S. 9–12; Kubon, *Außenpolitik*, S. 58–123.
18 Mikhail D. Prisyolkov, *Троицкая летопись: Реконструкция текста* (Leningrad, 1950), S. 447; Boris N. Floria, *Исследования по истории Церкви: Древнерусское и славянское Средневековье* (Moskva, 2007), S. 334–35.
19 Zum folgenden siehe Rowell, 'Naujieji kryžiaus žygiuotojai'.
20 Antoni Prochaska, 'Z Witołdowych dziejów: I. Układ Witołda z Tochtamyszem 1397 r.', *PH* 15 (1912), 259–64; Dariusz Kołodziejczyk, *The Crimean Khanate and Poland-Lithuania: International*

Witold, er ziehe gegen Timur Qutlugh, was ihm erlaubte, Smolensk zum ersten Mal zu erobern.[21] 1397 und 1398 unternahm Witold sodann mehrere Feldzüge nach Süden, wo er einige Burgen errichten ließ. In der Außendarstellung sollten sie das christliche Hinterland vor der Goldenen Horde schützen, nüchtern betrachtet galten sie aber allem voran der Sicherung der neu eroberten Gebiete.[22] Das letzte Beispiel zeigt, dass Witolds primäres Ziel nicht die Abwehr oder gar Christianisierung der Tataren war, sondern vielmehr die Erweiterung des großfürstlichen Territoriums sowie die Verschaffung einer günstigen Machtposition gegenüber der Goldenen Horde. Im Laufe dieser Kämpfe zeichnete sich eine direkte Konfrontation Witolds mit Timur Qutlugh ab. Der Deutsche Orden war seit 1398 mit Witold verbündet, der sich gerade im Vertrag von Salinwerder verpflichtet hatte, den christlichen (also genauer gesagt: römisch-katholischen) Glauben auszubreiten. Zum entscheidenden Feldzug gegen die Goldene Horde bot der Deutsche Orden sogar seine militärische Hilfe an und schickte ein größeres Kontingent von mehr als 300 Deutschrittern unter dem Komtur von Ragnit, Marquard von Salzbach, nach Litauen.[23]

In dieser Zeit, unmittelbar nach dem erfolglosen Nikopolis-Kreuzzug von 1396, war die Idee eines Kreuzzuges gegen die „Ungläubigen" wieder aufgeflammt. Diese Umstände sowie die Zusammenarbeit mit dem polnischen König führten dazu, dass Papst Bonifatius IX. den Krakauer Bischof Wojciech Jastrzębiec am 4. Mai 1399 aufrief, einen Kreuzzug „gegen die verfluchte Tollwut [...] der Tataren, Heiden, Türken und anderer barbarischen Völker" in Polen, Litauen, Ruthenien und den Donaufürstentümern zu predigen.[24] In diesem Schreiben ist die Rede zwar von Wladislaus II. Jogaila und seinen Ländern, aber seine Ausstellung lag offensichtlich im Interesse des litauischen Großfürsten mit seiner

---

Diplomacy on the European Periphery (15th–18th Century). A Study of Peace Treaties Followed by Annotated Documents (Leiden, 2011), S. 8–9. Den russischen Chroniken zufolge wollte Witold einen Jarlyg für die ganze Rus von Toktamisch erwirken (*PSRL* 4.1: 384–85). Das scheint aber vielmehr eine literarische Fiktion zu sein als eine realisierbare Forderung. Wenn Toktamisch trotz seines Machtverlusts einen Jarlyg für die ruthenischen Länder dem Großfürsten von Litauen ausstellte, hinderte ihn nichts, auf dieselbe Weise die ganze Rus seinem Verbündeten zu verleihen. Andererseits zeigt die angeführte Darstellung der Entwicklungen in der Rus, wie schwer es dem Großfürsten von Litauen fiel, diese Verleihung durchzusetzen. Siehe Jaroslaw Pelenski, *Russia and Kazan: Conquest and Imperial Ideology (1438–1560s)* (The Hague, 1974), S. 156–70.

21 *PSRL* 4.1: 378–79.

22 Johann von Posilge, 'Chronik des Landes Preussen', hg. v. Ernst Strehlke, in *SRP* 3: 79–388 (hier 216, 222). Einen weiteren Beleg liefert der Brief des Kaufmanns Johann Ryman aus Polazk nach Riga vom 25. Juli 1399: [...] *de Ploschowers sid ut der reise comen, dar ze myt Vitoweten weren* [...]. *Ok seghet men, wo Vitowe hefft in Taterie II slod upslagen II dach vard van Kaffe to dem mere werd an enen water het Bochowe Rekkee* [...]. (Latvijas valsts vēstures arhīvs, 673. f, 4. apr., 18. k., 80 l.).

23 Jürgen Sarnowsky, 'The Teutonic Order Confronts Mongols and Turks', in *The Military Orders: Fighting for the Faith and Caring for the Sick*, hg. v. Malcolm Barber (London, 1994), S. 253–62 (hier 258).

24 *VMPL* 1, Nr. 1041, S. 771: [...] *contra detestandam rabiem* [...] *Tartarorum, Paganorum, Turkorum et aliarum barbararum nationum* [...]. Vgl. Jan Drabina, *Papiestwo — Polska w latach 1384–1434* (Kraków, 2003), S. 36.

aktiven Ostpolitik. Witolds Feldzug endete mit der berühmten Schlacht an der Worskla am 12. August 1399, in der der Gediminide und seine Verbündeten eine vernichtende Niederlage erlitten.[25] Die Bulle konnte Polen und Litauen erst nach Witolds Aufbruch nach Süden erreichen und beeinflusste somit nicht die Kriegshandlungen.[26] Auch wenn es Pläne gab, einen Kreuzzug noch im nächsten kommenden Jahr zu organisieren und die Niederlage an der Worskla wettzumachen, entspannten sich die Beziehungen zur Goldenen Horde recht schnell mit dem Tod Timur Qutlughs, der nur kurze Zeit nach dem Sieg über das Kreuzfahrerheer in einem inneren Konflikt sein Leben verlor.[27] Bald darauf, nach der Erneuerung der Union mit Polen, wandte sich Witold westwärts, nach Samogitien, das wieder zu einem Zankapfel zwischen Litauen und dem Deutschen Orden wurde, was schließlich zum Krieg mit diesem in den Jahren 1401–4 führen sollte[28].

Schon während dieses Krieges aktivierte Witold seine Ostpolitik erneut, war doch das 1395 unterworfene Smolensker Land in der Zwischenzeit (1401) erneut vom Großfürstentum Litauen abgefallen. Infolge der Feldzüge der Jahre 1403–4 gelang es den Litauern, das Fürstentum Smolensk dem Großfürstentum wieder einzuverleiben[29]. Witolds nächstes Ziel war die Unterwerfung Pleskaus, wie die späteren Ereignisse erkennen lassen, obwohl dieses Land nach dem Vertrag von Salinwerder zum Interessenbereich des Deutschen Ordens gehörte. Anfang 1406 griff der Gediminide das Pleskauer Land an und übte gleichzeitig Druck auf Nowgorod aus, damit es ihm den geflohenen letzten Fürsten von Smolensk Jurij Svjatoslavič ausliefere. Wassili I von Moskau ergriff für Pleskau Partei und eröffnete die Kriegshandlungen gegen das Großfürstentum Litauen.[30] Diesmal war der Deutsche Orden wieder ein Verbündeter Witolds. Am Kriegszug Witolds gegen Moskau 1406 nahmen nicht nur Ordenstruppen teil, sondern auch Preu-

---

25 Stephen C. Rowell, 'Ne visai primintinos kautynės: Ką byloja šaltiniai apie 1399 m. mūšį ties Vorsklos upe?', *Istorijos šaltinių tyrimai* 1 (2008), 67–89.
26 Das betont Stephen C. Rowell, 'Naujieji kryžiaus žygiuotojai', wie auch den Umstand, dass der entscheidende Feldzug Witolds gegen Timur Qutlugh eine Antwort des Großfürsten auf die Forderungen des Khans darstellte.
27 VMPL 1, Nr. 1042–43, S. 771–73; CEV, Nr. 214, S. 64–65.
28 Almonaitis, *Žemaitijos*, S. 132–12; Błaszczyk, *Dzieje stosunków* 2: 283–95; Kubon, *Außenpolitik*, S. 132–74.
29 PSRL 4.1: 395–96.
30 Diesem Krieg ist folgender Aufsatz gewidmet: Roman A. Bespalov, 'Литовско-московские отношения 1392–1408 годов в связи со смоленской, черниговской и рязанской политикой Витовта и Василия I', *SR* 12 (2016), 129–82. Leider übersah der Verfasser fast völlig die Rolle der Stadtrepubliken der nordwestlichen Rus als eines Erisapfels in den Beziehungen zwischen Witold und Wassili I, indem er den ganzen Krieg mit Jurij Sviatoslavic und Švitrigaila verbindet. Auch die Briefe der Jahre 1406–8 aus dem Tridentiner Formelbuch blieben ihm unbekannt. Siehe hierzu Sergey V. Polekhov, 'Литовско-русские отношения в начале XV века в свете малоизвестных документов', *DRVM* 3 [69] (2017), 105–6; Polekhov, 'Псков во внешней политике великого князя литовского Витовта в первом десятилетии XV века', *DRVM* 4 [90] (2022), 39–60.

ßenreisende aus dem Westen, unter ihnen beispielsweise die Herolde der Herzöge von Straubing-Holland und Burgund.[31]

Einen Hinweis darauf, dass Witold versuchte, sich der alten Deutschordenstraditionen des Heidenkampfs zu bedienen, kann man in der Ankunft der *dutschir lande erbar geste* sehen, die über die Zwischenstation Preußen sich weiter auf den Weg nach Litauen zur Teilnahme an Witolds „Reise" in die Rus machten.[32] Ein direkter Hinweis wird durch die Chronik des pomesanischen Offizials Johann von Posilge sowie durch den Brief des Ordensprokurators in Rom, Peter von Wormditt, an den Hochmeister Konrad von Jungingen geliefert: In beiden Quellen wird berichtet, wie die Gesandten Jogailas und Witolds, nämlich ein Mönch und ein *polonisscher doctor, der vormols des konigs sachen im hofe hatte geforderd*, sich im Frühling 1407 um einen Ablass (*applas*) für die Teilnehmer des Kriegszuges gegen *die Russin und heydin* bemühten. Wegen des Widerstands des Ordensprokurators (trotz des Bündnisses des Ordens mit Witold!) bewilligte Papst Gregor XII. den Herrschern von Polen und Litauen einen solchen Kriegszug nicht.[33] Der als Beilage zu diesem Brief überlieferte kurze Text der Supplik beider Herrscher ist dadurch interessant, dass er nicht aus der päpstlichen Kanzlei, sondern von Polen ausging.[34] Neben Polen wird hierbei auch Litauen erstmals explizit als eine Schutzmacht der lateinischen Christenheit dargestellt.[35]

War der päpstliche Segen für den Feldzug gegen Pleskau oder gegen Moskau vorgesehen? Unterschieden die Herrscher Polens und Litauens überhaupt die beiden Ziele? Es scheint, dass die Stelle aus der preußischen Chronik sich eher auf Pleskau bezieht: Die Ordensgäste sollten *betwingen czu dem geloubin die Russin und heydin, dy den landen gelegin werin czu twingen*. Gerade Pleskau war dem Orden (*den landen*) im Vertrag von Salinwerder zugeschrieben worden. Offensichtlich ist, dass der polnische König auch in diesem Fall, wie acht Jahre zuvor, als „oberster Fürst von Litauen" auftrat und seine Gesandten mit der Erwirkung des päpstlichen Segens beauftragte, während der Feldzug vor allem im Interesse Witolds lag. Es ist wiederum zu betonen, dass die Idee der „Reisen" des Deutschen Ordens gegen die Heiden oder „unwahre Christen" noch sehr lebendig war — die letzten Litauenfahrten fanden 1402–3 statt. Auch diesmal war Witolds Ziel nicht die Bekehrung der „ungläubigen" Russen, sondern die Erweiterung

---

31 *Das Marienburger Tresslerbuch der Jahre 1399–1409*, hg. v. Erich Joachim (Königsberg, 1896), S. 407.
32 *CEV*, Nr. 358, S. 140. Vgl. auch Nr. 359, S. 141.
33 Posilge, 'Chronik', S. 288. Vgl. GStA PK, XX. HA, OBA 861 (Teildruck in *BGDO*, 2, Nr. 31; hier ist die Rede nur von den „Ungläubigen" und „Schismatikern", und nicht von den Ruthenen). Dieser Fall wurde in der Literatur bereits analysiert, jedoch ohne detaillierten Bezug auf die Ostpolitik Witolds, siehe Hartmut Boockmann, *Johannes Falkenberg, der Deutsche Orden und die polnische Politik: Untersuchungen zur politischen Theorie des späteren Mittelalters* (Göttingen, 1975), S. 80; Axel Ehlers, *Die Ablasspraxis des Deutschen Ordens im Mittelalter* (Marburg, 2007), S. 74.
34 GStA PK, XX. HA, OBA 861, fol. 2, abgedruckt als Quellenanhang dieses Beitrags.
35 Zur Entwicklung solcher Vorstellungen siehe Paul Srodecki, *Antemurale Christianitatis: Zur Genese der Bollwerksrhetorik im östlichen Mitteleuropa an der Schwelle vom Mittelalter zur Frühen Neuzeit* (Husum, 2015).

seines Machtbereichs. Noch im Herbst, nach der Schließung des Waffenstillstands mit Wassili I. und der darauffolgenden Rückkehr nach Litauen stellte Witold das Land seines damaligen Gegners in einem Brief an den neuen Hochmeister Ulrich von Jungingen als ein Gebiet der „Ungläubigen" dar.[36] Es war in Preußen jedoch sehr gut bekannt, dass Witold der Schwiegervater Wassilis I. war (seine Tochter wurde 1390 über Danzig und Nowgorod nach Moskau geschickt, als sich Witold in Preußen aufhielt).[37] Wie früher setzte der litauische Herrscher nicht nur die Rhetorik des Krieges gegen die „Ungläubigen" ein, sondern wirkte auch diesmal auf der kirchenpolitischen Ebene. Nachdem der Metropolit Kiprian im Sommer 1406 gestorben war, schickte Witold den Polazker Erzeparchen Theodosios als seinen Anwärter auf den Metropolitenstuhl nach Konstantinopel: Wenn er vom Patriarchen geweiht würde, könnte das auch zur Erweiterung des Einflusses Witolds beitragen.[38]

Bald musste Witold auch den Krieg gegen Moskau und Pleskau aufgeben, nicht zuletzt wegen des Aufstandes seines Vetters Švitrigaila, der im Sommer 1408 mit einer großen Gruppe der Anhänger aus den tschernihiwschen Landen zu Wassili I. abritt, von ihm umfangreiche Besitzungen bekam und an der Abwehr gegen Witold teilnahm. In den Jahren 1408–9 söhnte sich Witold mit dem Großfürsten Wassili I. von Moskau sowie mit Pleskau aus.[39] Der litauische Herrscher sicherte sich nicht nur die freundliche Neutralität der östlichen Nachbarn, sondern auch die Teilnahme der Tataren aus der Goldenen Horde am neuen Krieg mit dem Deutschen Orden, dessen Heer am 15. Juli 1410 bei Tannenberg die wohl größte Niederlage seiner Geschichte erlitt.[40]

Bald nach diesem Sieg, der durch den ersten Thorner Frieden 1411 besiegelt wurde, kehrte Witold zur aktiven Politik im Osten Europas zurück mit dem Versuch, seine Position in den Ländern der Rus zu stärken.[41] Auf den ersten Blick scheint das zweite Jahrzehnt des 15. Jahrhunderts in Witolds Ostpolitik „friedlich" zu sein und bleibt somit im Schatten der großen Kriegszüge, die er

---

36 *CEV*, Nr. 384, S. 162–63.
37 Posilge, 'Chronik', S. 167; *LUB* 3, Nr. 1269, Sp. 570–71; *PSRL* 4.1: 368; 15.1, Sp. 158–59. Der Hochmeister Konrad von Jungingen bezeichnet Wassili I. in einem Brief an den livländischen Meister Wennemar von Brüggenei vom 19. April 1398 als Witolds *swoger* (*LUB* 4, Nr. 1469, Sp. 202).
38 Акты, относящиеся к истории Западной России, 5 Bde. (Sankt-Peterburg 1846–53), 1: Nr. 25, S. 36. Siehe hierzu auch den Brief Witolds an den Großfürsten Iwan von Twer: Yuriy Yu. Afanasenko, 'Новогрудский собор 1415 г. в церковной политике великого князя Витовта', *Studia Historica Europae Orientalis* 8 (2015), 91–122 (hier 120).
39 Sergey V. Polekhov, *Наследники Витовта: Династическая война в Великом княжестве Литовском в 30-е годы XV века* (Moskva, 2015), S. 137–38; *PLP* 2: 35; Leonid Arbusow, 'Zwölf Urkunden zu O. Stavenhagen: "Livland und die Schlacht bei Tannenberg"', *Sitzungsberichte der Gesellschaft für Geschichte und Altertumskunde der Ostseeprovinzen Russlands aus dem Jahre 1911* (Riga, 1913), Nr. 1, S. 265–66.
40 Jóźwiak et al., *Wojna Polski i Litwy*, S. 33–44.
41 Weiterführend siehe Sergey V. Polekhov, 'Лугвень, Новгород и восточная политика Витовта (1411–14) в свете малоизвестных источников Кёнигсбергского архива', in *Мсціслаў і Мсціслаўскі край*, hg. v. A. A. Miatselski (Minsk, 2019), S. 58–78.

sowohl früher als auch später nach Süden und nach Osten führte. Es gab in dieser Periode wirklich keine Unternehmen dieser Art und dieses Ausmaßes, aber Witolds Versuche, in der Rus festen Fuß zu fassen, waren somit nicht weniger aktiv — und die Kreuzzugsrhetorik spielte dabei eine wichtige Rolle, was ich im Folgenden zeigen werde.

Im Sommer 1411 bereisten die Herrscher von Polen und Litauen ihre ruthenischen Gebiete. Dabei besuchten sie die Städte Polazk, Witebsk, Smolensk und Kiew sowie die südwestruthenischen Länder Podolien und Wolhynien und empfingen unterwegs die Boten aus Nowgorod und Pleskau sowie den Großfürsten von Rjasan, der ihnen sogar huldigte. In Kiew fand ein großes Zusammentreffen der weltlichen Herrscher und Kirchenfürsten statt mit der Teilnahme des Großfürsten von Moskau Wassili I., des tatarischen Khans, des russischen Metropoliten Photius und des Fürsten Lengvenis Simon, des Bruders des polnischen Königs, der zu jenem Zeitpunkt ein Dienstfürst in Nowgorod war. Nach einer Nachricht des Boten des römisch-deutschen Königs Sigismund an König Wenzel IV. von Böhmen schlossen sich diese Fürsten gegen den Deutschen Orden zusammen. Die Herrscher Polens und Litauens versuchten zu dieser Zeit, einen neuen Krieg gegen den Orden zu provozieren und Nowgorod darin zu verwickeln, was nicht nur ihre Stellung gegenüber dem Deutschen Orden, sondern auch ihren Einfluss in Nowgorod stärken sollte.[42] Nowgorod war zwar an einem Bündnis mit dem Großfürstentum Litauen interessiert, wollte es aber nutzen, um seine Handelsinteressen in Livland und gegenüber den Hansekaufleuten zu bewahren; mit dem Orden wollten die Nowgoroder allerdings Frieden halten. Nachdem sie sich Ende 1411 geweigert hatten, dem Orden den Frieden aufzusagen, beriefen Witold und Wladislaus II. Jogaila ihren Dienstfürsten aus Nowgorod ab und versuchten, auch dieser Stadt mit einem Angriff zu drohen, was aber nicht zum gewünschten Ergebnis führte. Bereits 1413–14 söhnte sich Witold mit Nowgorod aus. Dabei lehnten die Nowgoroder seinen Vorschlag ab, Lengvenis wieder als einen Dienstfürsten anzunehmen.[43]

Somit war Witolds Versuch, seine Position in Nowgorod zu stärken, gescheitert. Noch 1414–15 versuchte er, Druck auf Nowgorod auszuüben, indem er in Kontakten mit den Nowgorodern behauptete, es sei ihm gelungen, einen großen Teil Preußens im Krieg zu erobern.[44] Es ist wichtig anzumerken, dass der Großfürst von Moskau Wassili I. fast nichts (oder nur relativ wenig) gegen den gestiegenen Einfluss Witolds in der Rus unternahm. 1413 reiste Wassilis Ehefrau Sophia zweimal zu ihrem Vater nach Litauen, und 1414 schickte der Moskauer Großfürst gar ein Heer, um am Krieg Polens und Litauens gegen den Deutschen Orden teilzunehmen. Es ist anzunehmen, dass Wassili seine Stellung in der Rus

---

42 Das zeigte überzeugend kürzlich Adam Szweda, 'Zakon krzyżacki wobec Polski i Litwy w latach 1411–1414', *PR* 141 (2014), 531–53.
43 GStA PK, XX. HA, OBA 591. Ediert in *CEV*, Appendix, Nr. 29, S. 1058 (datiert vage „nach 1410"); Polekhov, 'Лугвень', S. 76–77 (hier auch mit Datierung).
44 LMAVB RS, F 15–73, S. 399–400.

aus Rücksicht auf die Tataren nach 1408, dem Jahr als der tatarische Emir Edigü (tat. İdegäy; Edigej der russischen Chroniken) Moskau angriff und plünderte, nicht oder nur sehr behutsam ausbauen wollte.

Gleichzeitig versuchte Witold, seine Position in der orthodoxen Kirche zu stärken. Seine Versuche, einen eigenen Kandidaten zum Metropoliten der ganzen Rus nach dem Tode Kiprians zu erheben, waren gescheitert, und letztendlich weihten am 15. November 1415 die in Nawahradak versammelten orthodoxen Bischöfe aus Polen und Litauen den Bulgaren Grigorij Zamblak zum Metropoliten der ruthenischen Bistümer.[45] Witold hatte vor, seine kirchliche Macht auch auf andere russische Länder außerhalb des Großfürstentums Litauen auszudehnen, also auf Nowgorod, Pleskau und Twer.[46] Schon früher, da im Februar 1415, hatte Gegenpapst Johannes (XXIII.) Wladislaus II. Jogaila zum Generalvikar über Nowgorod und Pleskau ernannt und ihm erlaubt, die Verhandlungen über die Bekehrung der Bewohner dieser Städte zu führen und die Gegner des Glaubens zu bekriegen.[47] Dennoch begab sich der von den Nowgorodern erwählte Erzbischof Anfang 1416 nicht nach Nawahradak oder Wilna, sondern nach Moskau zum Metropoliten Photius.[48] Zudem versuchten Witold und Jogaila, die Person des Metropoliten Grigorij Zamblak für die Verhandlungen über die Kirchenunion auf dem Konstanzer Konzil in Anspruch zu nehmen.[49] Kurz vor seiner Abreise, am 25. August 1417, stellten beide Herrscher einen Brief an das Konstanzer Konzil aus, in dem sie es zur Anerkennung der orthodoxen Taufe durch den Heiligen Stuhl aufforderten.[50] Die Unionsverhandlungen waren ein wichtiges Instrument im Streit mit dem Deutschen Orden auf dem Konstanzer Konzil ebenso wie die Behauptung, dass Witold und Jogaila die Tataren zum christlichen Glauben bekehren würden, und die Anwesenheit von tatarischen Gesandten auf dem Konzil.[51]

In Wirklichkeit waren Witolds Erfolge in der benachbarten Rus viel bescheidener. Nach einer Mitteilung der Ritterschaft von Harrien und Wirland an

---

45 Anatoliy A. Turilov, 'Григорий Цамблак', in *Православная энциклопедия* 12 (Moskva, 2006), 583–92.
46 *LUB* 5, Nr. 2047, Sp. 107–8; Anatoliy A. Turilov, 'Послание митрополита Григория Цамблака великому князю тверскому Ивану Михайловичу (1415 г.)', *DRVM* 4 (62) (2015), 104–6.
47 *CESDQ* 2, Nr. 58, S. 69–71.
48 *NPL*, S. 406; *PSRL* 4.1: 414–15.
49 Florya, *Исследования по истории Церкви*, S. 336–48.
50 *Copiale Prioratus Sancti Andree: The Letter-Book of James Haldenstone Prior of St. Andrews (1418–43)*, hg. v. J. H. Baxter (Oxford, 1930), Nr. 20, S. 38–41; Jerzy Kłoczowski, 'Jagiełło i Witold wobec prawosławnych: próba ich dowartościowania w 1417 roku', in *Balticum: Studia z dziejów polityki, gospodarki i kultury XII–XVII wieku ofiarowane Marianowi Biskupowi w siedemdziesiątą rocznicę urodzin*, hg. v. Zenon H. Nowak (Toruń, 1992), S. 175–79.
51 *LUB* 5, Nr. 2359, Sp. 525–26 (Volltext ohne Datierung) = *BGDO* 2, Nr. 130, S. 275–77 (Teildruck mit dem genauen Datum 25. Oktober 1415). Zur tatarischen Gesandtschaft siehe Boris N. Florya, 'Татарские послы на Констанцском соборе', *Русское Средневековье: Источники. 2000–01 гг.* (Moskva, 2002), S. 17–22; Vladislav P. Gulevich, 'Татары в кругу высокой европейской политики на церковном соборе в Констанце', *Studia Historica Europae Orientalis* 10 (2017), 60–75.

den livländischen Ordensmeister 1416, gelang es Witold zwar, einen litauischen Statthalter in Pleskau einzusetzen.[52] Als es jedoch tatsächlich dazu gekommen war, sollte dieser nur sehr kurz amtieren, denn schon in der ersten Hälfte des Jahres 1417 lehnten die Pleskauer Witolds Forderungen ab, dem livländischen Ordenszweig den Frieden aufzusagen.[53] Stattdessen wandten sich letztere an den Großfürsten von Moskau, dessen Gesandte an den Verhandlungen zwischen seinem „Erbland" Pleskau und dem Orden in Livland beteiligt gewesen waren.[54] Die Nowgoroder setzten ihre Politik des Lavierens zwischen Moskau und Wilna fort: Während des großen Handelskonflikts mit den hansischen (vor allem den livländischen) Kaufleuten sowie mit dem livländischen Ordenszweig 1416 wandten sie sich gleichzeitig an Wassili I. Dieser betonte in seinen Schreiben an Witold Moskaus Macht über Nowgorod und Pleskau.[55] Dabei wurde deutlich, dass der Moskauer Großfürst diese Kontakte trotz der Spaltung der russischen Kirche nicht unterbrach.[56] Denn auch die Nowgoroder schickten Gesandte nach Konstanz.[57]

Dass die Unterwerfung Nowgorods noch am Ende des zweiten Dezenniums des 15. Jahrhunderts zu den Zielen Witolds und Jogailas zählte, zeigt sehr gut eine Stelle in einem Brief des Vogts der Neumark, Sander Machwitz, an den Hochmeister Michael Küchmeister. In dem Schreiben berichtet Machwitz von den Verhandlungen zwischen den Räten des dänischen Königs Erich von Pommern und des polnischen Königs. Nachdem letzterer die Antwort Witolds bekommen hatte, äußerten sich seine Räte nur ungern im Gespräch mit den Gesandten Erichs zur Witoldschen Ostpolitik:

> [...] der sachen drie weren, do der Cristenheyt macht anlihet. Die eyne were, das sie den Orden zu Prussen welden uffnemen und welden in setzen by den koning von Cypern und by den meister von Roddys, wann sie das also bestelen welden, das her do der Cristenheit nutczer were wenn hy. Die andere were, das sie welden wynnen das Heilige Grab. Die dritte were, das sie welden wynnen Grossen Nowgarten.[58]

---

52 Davon ist die Rede in zwei Schreiben aus Livland an den Hochmeister im Juni 1416 (*LUB* 5, Nr. 2071, 2074, Sp. 133–34, 137–38).

53 *LUB* 5, Nr. 2119, 2142, Sp. 205–6, 232–34.

54 *LUB* 5, Nr. 2166, 2172, 2176, Sp. 267–70, 278–82, 285–88; Natalya A. Kazakova, *Русско-ливонские и русско-ганзейские отношения: Конец XI начало XVI в.* (Leningrad, 1975), S. 51–55.

55 *LUB* 5, Nr. 2113, Sp. 195–97; vgl. *CEV*, Nr. 763, S. 402–3. Es ist nicht ganz klar, ob die Nowgoroder sich auch an Witold wandten, wie die Datierung eines mit dem Jahresdatum nicht versehenen Schreibens durch seinen Bearbeiter vermuten lässt. Eine paläographische Analyse wäre in diesem Fall sehr wünschenswert. Siehe hierzu *Hansisches Urkundenbuch*, hg. v. Konstantin Höhlbaum, 11 Bde. (Halle, 1876–1916), 6: Nr. 104, S. 45–46. Vgl. auch Kazakova, *Русско-ливонские и русско-ганзейские отношения*, S. 95–99.

56 Davon zeugt auch die Heirat des Fürsten Alexander (genannt Olelko) von Kapyl und Sluzk, Witolds Neffen zweiten Grades, mit Anastasija, der Tochter Wassilis I. und Enkelin Witolds (*LUB* 5, Nr. 2158, Sp. 256–58; *CEV*, Nr. 740, S. 392–93; vgl. auch *LUB* 5, Nr. 2047, Sp. 107–8).

57 Florya, *Исследования по истории Церкви*, S. 343–44.

58 Zenon H. Nowak, *Współpraca polityczna państw unii polsko-litewskiej i unii kalmarskiej w latach 1411–25* (Toruń, 1996), App. 3, S. 99; *BGDO* 2, S. 576, Anm. 2.

Diese Fragen sollten auf einer baldigen Zusammenkunft von vielen „christlichen und heidnischen Fürsten" besprochen werden, auf dem nicht nur die Herrscher von Polen und Litauen, sondern auch die Räte des römisch-deutschen und ungarischen Königs Sigismund von Luxemburg, des Großfürsten von Moskau und des Khans der Goldenen Horde anwesend sein sollten. Davon berichtete der Vogt der Neumark an den Hochmeister in einem Schreiben vom 2. Oktober 1418, aber die Zusammenkunft der Räte beider Könige, wie aus dem Kontext seines Briefes hervorgeht, sollte viel früher stattfinden, und zwar zwischen dem 2. Februar und dem 24. Juni 1418, wahrscheinlich im Februar oder März.[59] Also bediente sich Witold nicht nur der Rhetorik der Bekehrung der Russen zum katholischen Glauben, um Nowgorod und Pleskau zu unterwerfen, wie die erneute Ernennung von ihm und Wladislaus II. Jogaila zu Generalvikaren in Nowgorod sowie Pleskau durch den neu gewählten Papst Martin V. zeigte.[60] Es handelte sich auch um die Anerkennung der Witoldschen Interessen seitens seiner mächtigsten östlichen Nachbarn, des Großfürsten von Moskau und des Khans der Goldenen Horde. Es sollte hierbei hervorgehoben werden, dass Nowgorod zum postulierten „Erbe" der Moskauer Großfürsten gehörte und dass die politischen Beziehungen in der Rus vom Khan der Goldenen Horde anerkannt werden mussten, der sie durch einen Jarlyg sanktionierte.[61]

Die Tatarenpolitik war in dieser Zeit ein weiteres Aktivitätsfeld Witolds, was ihn gleichzeitig an der Durchsetzung seiner Pläne in der Rus hinderte. Der Großfürst von Litauen versuchte, die innere Krise und den allmählichen Zerfall der Goldenen Horde für seine Zwecke auszunutzen. Die Deutschordensgebietiger berichteten mehrmals, dass sich ein „Tatarenkhan" in Litauen bei Witold aufgehalten habe.[62] Manchmal führten sie auch die Einzelheiten der Kämpfe verschiedener Gruppierungen innerhalb der Horde auf.[63] Da sich die Situation in der Goldenen Horde sehr rasch änderte, ist es für diesen Zeitraum besonders schwer, die namentlich nicht genannten Dynasten zu identifizieren und den Verlauf der Kämpfe genau zu rekonstruieren, selbst mithilfe des Vergleichs der Nachrichten der westlichen, orientalischen und russischen Quellen. Unbestritten bleibt, dass die Maßnahmen Witolds in dieser Hinsicht viele Ressourcen banden. Ungeachtet

---

59 Nowak, *Współpraca polityczna*, S. 35–36; Antoni Gąsiorowski, *Itinerarium króla Władysława Jagiełły, 1386–1434* (Warszawa, 2015), S. 87. Witold weilte im Februar im eigentlichen Litauen: Sergiej Polechow, 'Itinerarium Witolda, wielkiego księcia litewskiego: 4/5 VIII 1392–27 X 1430', *RL* 5 (2019), S. 9–120, hier S. 72. Danach veränderte sich die Situation wesentlich nach der Flucht Švitrigailas aus dem Gefängnis Ende März.
60 Martin V. stellte beide Bullen für Jogaila und Witold am 13. Mai 1418 aus, *Historica Russiae Monumenta, ex antiquis exterarum gentium archivis et bibliothecis deprompta*, hg. v. Aleksandr I. Turgenew et al., 2 Bde (Sankt-Peterburg, 1841), Bd. 1, Nr. 119–20, S. 117–19.
61 Dazu ausführlich Anton A. Gorskiy, *От земель к великим княжениям: «примыслы» русских князей второй половины XIII–XV в.* (Moskva, 2010).
62 *CEV*, Nr. 683, S. 352–53 = *LUB* 5, Nr. 2079, Sp. 143–45. Vgl. auch *LUB* 5, Nr. 2113, 2150, 2195, Sp. 195–97, 246–48, 312–14.
63 *CEV*, Nr. 754, S. 397–98 = *LUB* 5, Nr. 2182, Sp. 296.

der Witoldschen Erfolge, wie etwa der Teilnahme der Tataren am sogenannten „Hungerkrieg" gegen den Deutschen Orden 1414, war seine Politik nicht immer zielführend. Sein größter Misserfolg war die Plünderung Kiews durch den tatarischen Emir Edigü im Sommer 1416.[64]

In den Kontakten mit den westlichen Mächten verfolgte Witold die Idee der Bekehrung der Tataren. Mit dieser Absicht erschien eine tatarische Gesandtschaft auf dem Konstanzer Konzil. Es ist jedoch nicht ganz klar, ob die in Konstanz weilenden tatarischen „Kaiser" wirklich Macht ausübten oder sich einfach bei Witold aufhielten und welchen Teil der zersplitterten Tataren sie vertraten.[65] Das war umso wichtiger, da der Deutsche Orden Witolds Zusammenarbeit mit den „Heiden und Ungläubigen" zum Schaden der Christen betonte, wie in Paul Srodeckis Kapitel zum Disput zwischen dem Orden und den polnisch-litauischen Verbündeten in diesem Buch dargestellt.

Trotz der aktiven Ostpolitik Witolds, taucht die Kreuzzugsidee in dieser Zeitspanne nur ein paar Mal auf. Kurz nach der Wahl des Gegenpapstes Johannes (XXIII.) bemühte sich eine polnische Gesandtschaft an der Kurie um einen päpstlichen Segen für den Kreuzzug gegen die Tataren. Johannes (XXIII.) verweigerte ihn angesichts des Kreuzzuges gegen den König von Neapel.[66] Diese Bitte Jogailas gerade während einer Zeit guter Beziehungen mit der Goldenen Horde konnte der Unterstützung einer der tatarischen Gruppierungen durch Polen und Litauen dienen (ähnlich wie am Ende des 14. Jahrhunderts) sowie ein Gegenstück zu den Anschuldigungen durch den Orden darstellen.[67] In den nächsten Jahren versuchten sowohl der Deutsche Orden als auch Polen und Litauen, den päpstlichen Kreuzzugssegen zu erwirken. Ende Mai 1412 schrieb der Hochmeister Heinrich von Plauen an den Erzbischof Johann von Riga, der Ordensprokurator an der Kurie sei angewiesen, *das her mit den ambasiaten dornoch stee, das unser heiliger vater der pabest das cru[cze] obir herczog Wit[out] gebe.*[68] Schon im Juni berichtete Nikolaus von Buseck, Titularbischof von Sebastopolis und Weihbischof von Würzburg, dem Hochmeister, dass der Papst eine Bulle und einen *bichtbriff* signiert habe. In der Bulle sei erklärt worden:

> *wer by uch sye und helffte uch ubir dy heyden, der ist absolviret a pena et culpa, aber ich hett gern gesehen, daz dy bulle hette behalden, wer wider den Ordin mit den heiden tett und mit yn hilde, daz dy wern in excommunicacione; dez konde nicht gesin.*[69]

---

64 Posilge, 'Chronik', S. 364; Jan Długosz, *Annales seu cronicae incliti regni Poloniae*, hg. v. Jan Dąbrowski et al., [11 Bde.] (Warszawa, 1964–2005), [8]: Buch 11, S. 65; *PSRL* 6.1: 537; *LUB* 5, Nr. 2079, Sp. 143–45 = *CEV*, Nr. 683, S. 352–53; *LUB* 5, Nr. 2113, Sp. 195–97.
65 Florya, 'Татарские послы'; Gulevich, 'Татары'. Es sei hier angemerkt, dass jeder Dschingiside schon wegen seiner Herkunft als ein „Khan" auftreten durfte.
66 Długosz, *Annales* [8], Buch 11, S. 183–84; Drabina, *Papiestwo*, S. 48–49.
67 Gulevich, *От ордынского улуса*, S. 132–39.
68 *BGDO* 2, Nr. 70, S. 142–43 = *CEV*, Nr. 493, S. 231–32.
69 GStA PK, XX. HA, OBA 1949; ausführlicher Regest mit Teildruck in *BGDO* 2, Nr. 80, S. 169–70.

Diese Stelle zeigt, dass der Bischof darüber besorgt war, dass die Bulle offensichtlich gegen Jogaila und Witold gerichtet sei, die in dieser Zeit durch den Orden als Verbündete der Heiden und Ungläubigen dargestellt wurden. Vielleicht bemühten sich gleichzeitig die Herrscher Polens und Litauens auch um *cruczefartbriffe*, so eine Formulierung im Brief des Ordensprokurators Peter von Wormditt an den Hochmeister Heinrich von Plauen vom 18. Oktober 1413. Der Ordensvertreter betonte, dass der Papst ihnen eine solche Bulle nicht verweigern könne, wenn sie schon für den Deutschen Orden ausgestellt worden wäre. Der Prokurator war durch den Hochmeister angewiesen worden, das zu verhindern, auch wohl deshalb, da eine solche Bulle zur Stärkung Polens und Litauens gegenüber dem Orden geführt hätte.[70] Gerade in dieser Zeit versuchte Witold, wie schon oben erwähnt, gegen Groß-Nowgorod ins Feld zu ziehen. Allerdings ist es zu einem solchen Kriegszug nicht gekommen, da Witold versuchte, sich mit Nowgorod auf friedlichem Weg zu versöhnen und seinen Einfluss dort zu behaupten, wenn auch nicht ganz erfolgreich. Schon im Oktober 1416, bald nach der Plünderung von Kiew durch Edigü, bat der Erzbischof von Gnesen, Mikołaj Trąba, auf dem Konstanzer Konzil *vor allen nacionibus* im Namen des polnischen Königs, an alle Fürsten und Herren zu schreiben, damit sie dem polnischen König in seinem Krieg mit der Goldenen Horde helfen.[71] Hierin kann man noch einen Bezug auf die Kreuzzugsidee erkennen.

Schließlich scheinen die von den polnischen Räten 1418 genannten drei Sachen, *do der Cristenheyt macht anlihet* — der Kampf mit den Türken mittels des Deutschen Ordens, die Wiedereroberung des Heiligen Grabs und die Unterwerfung Groß-Nowgorods — für einen Kreuzzug sehr geeignet gewesen zu sein, obwohl in dem Schriftstück keine direkte Rede davon ist und auch nichts von weiteren Schritten in dieser Richtung bekannt ist. Diese Bemühungen trugen zum Bild Jogailas und Witolds als für einen Kreuzzug geeigneter Herrscher bei.[72] Das galt zumindest für die Außendarstellung, denn beide bedienten sich tatsächlich überwiegend friedlicher Instrumente in ihrer Ostpolitik, wie es sich in der oben geschilderten Kirchenpolitik oder den Verhandlungen mit den östlichen Nachbarn (neben den Kriegsdrohungen) widerspiegelte.

Obwohl Witold, wie erwähnt, auch während der Spaltung der russischen Metropolie Kontakte mit Wassili I. pflegte, spricht man zu Recht von einer Wende in seiner Ostpolitik am Ende der 1410er Jahre.[73] Sie wurde durch eine Reihe von

---

70 GStA PK, XX. HA, OBA 1998; Teildruck in *BGDO* 2, Nr. 84, S. 178–82.
71 *BGDO* 2, Nr. 182, S. 367.
72 So mahnte das Konstanzer Konzil neben dem König von Polen auch Witold samt der litauischen Großen wie auch den Deutschen Orden, dem König von Ungarn, Sigismund von Luxemburg, in seinem Krieg gegen die Türken zu helfen (*CESDQ* 2, Nr. 62, S. 75–76). Siehe hierzu Rowell, 'Lietuva — krikščionybės pylimas?', S. 21–22.
73 Die weiteren Ereignisse sind ziemlich gut erforscht, siehe hierzu vor allem Dmitrij I. Ivanov, 'Московско-литовские отношения в 20-е годы XV столетия', *SR* 2 (1999), S. 79–115. Hier stütze ich mich auf die Ergebnisse seiner Forschung und ergänze nur die wichtigsten Quellenaussagen sowie diejenigen, die er nicht berücksichtigte.

verschiedenen Faktoren verursacht. In den Jahren 1418–19 hatte der litauische Herrscher sich mit innenpolitischen Schwierigkeiten auseinanderzusetzen: Sein Rivale Švitrigaila floh aus dem Gefängnis in Wolhynien, weshalb Witold und Jogaila befürchteten, dass er in der südlichen Rus Fuß fassen und damit Witold bedrohen könnte.[74] Darüber hinaus brach in Samogitien ein Aufstand aus, den der Deutsche Orden für seine Interessen auszunutzen vermochte.[75] Wenn man auch die Misserfolge der Anhänger Witolds in den tatarischen Kämpfen berücksichtigt, wundert es nicht, dass Witold und Jogaila den geplanten Krieg mit dem Deutschen Orden aufschoben und den abgelaufenen Waffenstillstand verlängerten. Im Streit mit dem Orden um Samogitien stellte sich der römisch-deutsche König Sigismund von Luxemburg erneut auf die Seite des Ordens, was besonders in seinem Schiedsspruch in Breslau Anfang 1420 Ausdruck fand.[76] Deswegen entschied sich Witold zu kriegerischen Handlungen gegen die Deutschritter und begann mit der Söldnerwerbung.[77] Die Nowgoroder versöhnten sich gerade zu jener Zeit mit den Pleskauern. Schon Ende 1418 brach eine Gesandtschaft Witolds nach Moskau auf, die eine Reihe von Gesandtschaften eröffnete[78].

Zur Annäherung an Moskau trug zusätzlich der Tod des Kiewer Metropoliten Grigorij Zamblak Ende 1419 bei, nachdem die kirchliche Macht des in Moskau residierenden Metropoliten Photius auch über die ruthenischen Länder durch Witold und Jogaila anerkannt worden war.[79] Diese Annäherung war von Moskauer Seite offensichtlich auch dem Gesundheitszustand Wassilis I. geschuldet. Sein gleichnamiger Sohn und Erbe, Wassili II., war erst 1415 geboren worden. Es war kein Geheimnis in Moskau, dass der Bruder Wassilis I., Fürst Jurij von Zvenigorod, nach dem Tod des Großfürsten den Anspruch auf den Moskauer Thron anmelden würde, denn er war im letzten Testament von Dmitri Donskoi

---

74 Polekhov, Наследники Витовта, S. 139–40.
75 Robert Krumbholtz, *Samaiten und der Deutsche Orden bis zum Frieden am Melno-See* (Königsberg i. Pr., 1890), S. 193–98; Rimvydas Petrauskas, 'Žemaičių diduomenė ir politinė padėtis Žemaitijoje XIV a. pabaigoje — XV a. pradžioje', in *Žemaičių istorijos virsmas iš 750 metų perspektyvos*, hg. v. Antanas Ivinskis (Vilnius, 2004), S. 151–72, hier S. 159–60.
76 Siehe hierzu Paul Srodecki, 'Mediating Actors in the Conflict between the Teutonic Order and the Kingdom of Poland in the Early Fifteenth Century', in *Der Deutsche Orden auf dem Konstanzer Konzil: Pläne — Strategien — Erwartungen*, hg. v. Helmut Flachenecker (Ilmtal-Weinstraße, 2020), pp. 15–33.
77 GStA PK, XX. HA, OBA 3173–74, 3330, 3652.
78 *LUB* 5, Nr. 2291, Sp. 447–48. Ivanov, 'Московско-литовские отношения', S. 83, datiert diese Annäherung zu Unrecht auf Ende 1419 oder Anfang 1420.
79 Manchmal taucht erneut der alte Gedanke auf, Grigorij Zamblak sei Ende 1419 nicht verstorben, sondern habe sich nach Moldau begeben, so beispielsweise bei Melchisedec Ştefănescu, *Viaţa şi scrierile lui Grigorie Ţamblac* (Bukarest, 2010). Die Argumente, die hierfür eingebracht werden, scheinen mir jedoch nach wie vor nicht überzeugend zu sein (vgl. dazu auch in der rumänischen Geschichtsforschung Ştefan S. Gorovei, 'Addenda et corrigenda. 2. Iarăşi Grigore Ţamblac?!', *Studii şi Materiale de Istorie Medie* 32 (2014), 427–31). Wenn man sogar annimmt, dass der Kiewer Metropolit 1419 nicht verstarb, sondern von seinem Stuhl entfernt wurde, ist das ein weiteres Indiz für die Annäherung Litauens und Moskaus, die jedoch bereits viel früher anfing. Für die Literaturhinweise bedanke ich mich sehr herzlich bei Mihai-Dumitru Grigore und Mihail Ciobanu.

zum zweiten Erben nach Wassili I. ernannt worden. Deswegen benötigte Wassili I. Unterstützung seitens seines mächtigen litauischen Schwiegervaters. Dieser war auch daran interessiert, diese Situation für die Stärkung seiner Stellung in Osteuropa auszunutzen. Seit den frühen 1420er Jahren entwickelten sich auch die Machtverhältnisse innerhalb der Goldenen Horde zugunsten des Gediminiden, wo sein Verbündeter Ulug Mehmed (tat. Oluğ-Möxämmät) zum Khan erhoben worden war.

Bereits 1422 nahm das Moskauer Heer am Krieg Polens und Litauens mit dem Deutschen Orden teil. In den nächsten Jahren bestätigte Witold zweimal das Testament Wassilis I. Beide Urkunden sind erhalten; es wurde aber erst vor Kurzem festgestellt, dass sie mit dem Siegel Witolds versehen worden waren, was dessen Stellung hinsichtlich der Thronfolgeprobleme in Moskau betonen sollte.[80] Nach Wassilis I. Tod im Februar 1425 und der Thronbesteigung durch seinen Sohn Wassili II. gelang es Witold, von dieser Situation politisch zu profitieren. Während seiner großen Reise durch die ruthenischen Länder im Sommer 1427 huldigten ihm die Fürsten von Nowossil-Odojew und Rjasan, was auch durch den minderjährigen Großfürsten von Moskau anerkannt wurde (seine Mutter, Witolds Tochter Sophia, traf sich mit ihm im Sommer).[81]

Zu den kriegerischen Aktivitäten Witolds in dieser Zeit gehören seine Feldzüge gegen Pleskau 1426 und Nowgorod 1428. Beide waren im Voraus geplant und gehörten zu den schon früher bekannten Richtungen der Witoldschen Ostpolitik. Bereits 1421 und 1424 reisten Pleskauer Boten zu Witold nach Wolhynien und Podolien mit wertvollen Gaben, die er demonstrativ verschmähte.[82] Die langen Reisewege zeugen von der Bedeutung, die die Pleskauer den Beziehungen zu Witold beimaßen. In denselben Jahren äußerte Witold mehrmals seinen Wunsch, ins Feld gegen Pleskau zu ziehen. Dazu kam es aber erst im Sommer 1426.[83] Zuvor versuchte Witold, Pleskau auf der internationalen Bühne zu isolieren und sich die Hilfe verschiedener Länder und den Beistand Polens und des livländischen Ordenszweiges zu sichern.[84] Witolds Versuch, die Festungen des Pleskauer Landes noch im August zu erobern, scheiterte, und er beschränkte sich auf hohe Kontributionszahlungen. Danach richtete Witold seine Aufmerksamkeit auf Nowgorod, wie die Gesandtschaften der Nowgoroder an den litauischen Herrscher 1427

---

80 Sergey V. Polekhov, 'Последнее завещание Василия I и политическая ситуация в Восточной Европе', *DRVM* 3 (61) (2015), 97–98; Polekhov, 'Последние завещания Василия I и печати Витовта', *SR* 12 (2016), 183–200. Da die Testamente Wassilis I. kein Datum enthalten, wurden sie in der Vergangenheit durch die Forschung und in allen bisherigen Editionen fälschlich zugeordnet. Zum Problem ihrer Reihenfolge siehe überblickshaft Anton A. Gorskiy, 'Завещания Василия I Дмитриевича: проблемы последовательности и датировки', *DRVM* 1 (67) (2017), 20–34.
81 *CEV*, Nr. 1298, 1329, S. 778–80, 798–800; Ivanov, 'Московско-литовские отношения', S. 100–3.
82 *Oeuvres de Ghillebert de Lannoy, voyageur, diplomate et moraliste*, ed. Charles Potvin (Louvain, 1878), S. 56; *PLP* 2: 39–40.
83 Ivanov, 'Московско-литовские отношения', S. 91–92, 95–100.
84 LMAVB RS, F 15-73, S. 29; *LUB* 7, Nr. 490, 500, S. 337–38, 342–43; Długosz, *Annales* [8], Buch 11, S. 219–20.

und 1428 indirekt bezeugen. Schon im März 1428 schrieb er dem Hochmeister, er habe den Entschluss gefasst, im Sommer gegen Nowgorod zu ziehen.[85] Aber die Kriegshandlungen verliefen ähnlich wie gegen Pleskau zwei Jahre zuvor — die Belagerung von Porchow blieb erfolglos und Witold begnügte sich mit einer Kontributionszahlung.[86]

In diesem Kontext sind Witolds Versuche von Interesse, sich als katholischer Herrscher darzustellen und damit abendländische Hilfe zu erhalten. An beiden Feldzügen nahmen nicht nur „ungläubige" Untertanen und Verbündete Witolds teil, wie Ruthenen, Tataren und Moldawier, sondern auch Ritter aus Polen und Deutschland.[87] Witold bediente sich dabei der Rhetorik des gerechten Krieges gegen die ungläubigen Russen. Der Subdiakon der Dominikaner im sewerischen Nowgorod, Mikuła von Kopyłów, betonte im Kolophon eines liturgischen Buches, dass Witold „mit etlichen namhaften katholischen Fürsten, nämlich Švitrigaila, seinem leiblichen Bruder Sigismund, Herzog Kasimir von Masowien" und zahlreichen polnischen Würdenträgern und Rittern, gegen Nowgorod gezogen war — anders als der polnische Historiograph Jan Długosz, der die Teilnahme der Ruthenen an diesem Feldzug hervorhob.[88] Stephen C. Rowell zufolge sind Witolds Kriegshandlungen gegen die Rus höchstwahrscheinlich mittels einer

---

85 *CEV*, Nr. 1269, 1329, S. 757, 798–800; LMAVB RS, F 15–73, S. 231; Ivanov, 'Московско-литовские отношения', S. 104–5.
86 In der sogenannten „Bychowiec-Chronik" aus den 1520er Jahren wird berichtet, dass Witold seine Hauptleute nach Nowgorod und Pleskau geschickt haben soll (*PSRL* 17, Sp. 520–21). Diese Behauptung ist meines Erachtens sehr unwahrscheinlich, weil sie keine Bestätigung in den ziemlich „dicht" überlieferten zeitgenössischen Quellen findet.
87 Dazu Sobiesław Szybkowski, 'Rycerscy goście z Polski na dworze wielkiego księcia Witolda — próba portretu grupy', in *Litwa i jej sąsiedzi w relacjach wzajemnych (XIII–XVI w.)*, hg. v. Anna Kołodziejczyk, Rafał Kubicki und Marek Radoch (Olsztyn, 2014), S. 81–105. Vgl. auch eine etwas rätselhafte Stelle im späteren Brief des südwestdeutschen Ritters und Abenteurers Friedrich von Flersheim an den Papst Calixt III. Der deutsche Adelige behauptete, er sei *mit hertzog Widelt wieder die grossen Nauhartten, und mit dem könig von Mussgau wieder die von Blessgau* in den Krieg gezogen — so nachzulesen in: *Die Flersheimer Chronik: Zur Geschichte des XV. und XVI. Jahrhunderts*, hg. v. Otto Waltz (Leipzig, 1874), S. 30. Großfürst Wassili II. von Moskau führte jedoch zeit seines Lebens keine Kriege gegen Pleskau. Zudem befand sich der Flersheimer während Witolds Feldzugs gegen Nowgorod im Juli 1428 bei Golubac, wo er im Kampf gegen die Osmanen angeblich Sigismund von Luxemburg das Leben gerettet haben soll, und später in Wien (*Die Flersheimer Chronik*, S. 25–27). Es ist nicht auszuschließen, dass er 30 Jahre nach den eigentlichen Ereignissen, von denen er so blumig berichtet, die Liste seiner Heldentaten und Abenteuer um weitere „Feinde des Abendlandes" erweiterte. Zum Kontext vgl. Steffen Krieb, '"Unnd maihne, das das kheinem ritter nie wiederfahren sey, als mir." Die Briefe Friedrichs von Flersheim als Selbstzeugnisse', in *Kommunikation mit dem Ich. Signaturen der Selbstzeugnisforschung an europäischen Beispielen des 12. bis 16. Jahrhunderts*, hg. v. Heinz-Dieter Heimann und Pierre Monnet (Bochum 2004), S. 135–46, hier S. 143 mit Anm. 42, wo diese Stelle mit anderen Kriegen, aber sehr unpräzis, verbunden wird.
88 *Catalogus codicum manuscriptorum Bibliothecae Ossolinianae Leopoliensis*, hg. v. Wojciech Kętrzyński, 3 Bde. (Lwów, 1881–98), 2: Nr. 372, S. 433–34; Długosz, *Annales* [8], Buch 11, S. 243–46. Zur Teilnahme der ruthenischen Untertanen Witolds aus Wolhynien und Podolien an diesem Feldzug vgl. Volodymyr D. Sobchuk, *Від коріння до крони. Дослідження з історії князівських і шляхетських родів Волині XV — першої половини XVII ст.* (Kremenez, 2014), S. 387–406.

Bulle Martins V. abgesegnet worden.[89] Ein entsprechendes Schreiben ist bisher allerdings nicht gefunden worden. Bedenkt man die große Anzahl päpstlicher Bullen zur Hussitenfrage und überhaupt die Überlieferungsdichte zur Geschichte des Großfürstentums Litauen und seiner Nachbarn im 15. Jahrhundert, so erscheint es wahrscheinlicher, dass ein solches Schreiben nie existierte. Als Grund hierfür kann vermutet werden, dass der unmittelbare päpstliche Segen Witold gestört hätte, als er die Situation im und um das Großfürstentum Moskau für die Durchsetzung seiner Pläne ausnutzen wollte. Witold und Jogaila trafen sich in diesen Jahren mehrmals mit dem Großfürsten von Moskau, seiner Mutter, dem Metropoliten Photius und ihren Gesandten. Gerade im Sommer 1428, als Witold gegen Nowgorod zog, hielt sich Metropolit Photius in Polen auf und traf sich sogar mit Jogaila.[90] Viel nützlicher für Witold in seinen Kontakten mit dem Abendland war der grobe Hinweis auf die Notwendigkeit der Abwehr des Erzbischofs und Kapitels von Riga durch Witold „gegen die Angriffe der Ungläubigen und anderer Ruhestörer und Verwirrten", zu der Martin V. den Großfürsten von Litauen in seinem Schreiben vom 30. Dezember 1426 aufgefordert hatte.[91]

Jedenfalls wurde Witold in dieser Zeit von seinen abendländischen Zeitgenossen als ein von den „Heiden" und „Ungläubigen" bedrängter Fürst betrachtet, der diese nicht nur bekämpfen und zum katholischen Glauben bekehren, sondern auch das Heilige Land für die Christen zurückerobern könnte.[92] Diese Vorstellung fand Ausdruck in der Politik des römischen und ungarischen Königs Sigismund von Luxemburg, der mit Witold Pläne der Abwehr gegen die Osmanen auf der Tagfahrt zu Luzk — also am Rande der „christlichen Welt" — besprach.[93] In Wirklichkeit lagen jedoch Witolds Interessen, wie die oben angeführte Analyse zeigt, gar nicht im Heiligen Land, sondern vielmehr in der Rus, wo seine Erfolge viel bescheidener waren, als er sie darzustellen versuchte.

Zusammenfassend kann festgehalten werden: Die Idee eines Krieges gegen die „Ungläubigen" — seien es Tataren oder die orthodoxen „Schismatiker" der Rus — tauchte mehrmals in der Politik des Großfürsten Witolds von Litauen auf. Die Bemühungen um die päpstliche Absegnung eines Kreuzzuges dieser Art waren ein Feld der Zusammenarbeit Witolds mit Jogaila und der in ihren Diensten stehenden Gelehrten, Geistlichen und Diplomaten.[94] Sie blieben jedoch

---

89 Rowell, 'Lietuva — krikščionybės pylimas?', S. 22.
90 Długosz, *Annales* [8], Buch 11, S. 240; 'Podwody kazimierskie 1407–32', hg. v. Stanisław Krzyżanowski, *Archiwum Komisji Historycznej* 11 (1909–13), 392–465 (hier 435). Zu Unrecht wird dieses Treffen von Ivanov, 'Московско-литовские отношения', S. 100–1, umdatiert.
91 *LUB* 7, Nr. 554, S. 383–84. Vgl. Anti Selart, 'Political Rhetoric and the Edges of Christianity: Livonia and Its Evil Elements in the Fifteenth Century', in *The Edges of the Medieval World*, hg. v. Gerhard Jaritz und Juhan Kreem (Budapest 2009), S. 55–69.
92 *CESDQ* 2, Nr. 182, S. 246; *CEV*, Nr. 1394, S. 881.
93 Długosz, *Annales* [8], Buch 11, S. 249; *Scriptores rerum Silesiacarum*, hg. v. Gustav Adolf Stenzel et al. (Breslau, 1835–1902), 6, Nr. 113, S. 83–84.
94 Witolds Zusammenarbeit mit Jogailas Vertretern war eine gute Lösung für den meisten Teil seiner Regierung, erwies sich aber als die Schwäche seiner Diplomatie in seinen letzten Lebensjahren

größtenteils erfolglos. Die einzige im Interesse Witolds erwirkte Kreuzzugsbulle von 1399 hatte keinen unmittelbaren Einfluss auf den Verlauf seines Krieges mit den Tataren und konnte höchstens zur Formierung seines Bilds als eines Glaubensverfechters beitragen, was allerdings auch nicht bedeutungslos für seine Stellung war. Das Ziel Witolds war es, seine Position in Osteuropa zu stärken und seinen Machtbereich zu erweitern. Eine Bekehrung der Ruthenen und Tataren zum katholischen Christentum konnte dabei keine unmittelbare Aufgabe sein, besonders wenn man die Probleme der nichtkatholischen Bevölkerung im Großfürstentum Litauen berücksichtigt sowie andere Mittel zur Durchsetzung der Witoldschen Politik wie seine Tätigkeit auf dem Kirchenunionsfeld oder seine Bündnisse mit den Tataren und den Ländern der Rus, die er gleichzeitig im Westen als „Ungläubige" darstellte. Gerade die Nutzung dieser Bündnisse und überhaupt der günstigen internationalen Situation in Osteuropa in den 1420er Jahren erlaubte es Witold, in seinen letzten Lebensjahren den größten Einfluss in dieser Region zu erreichen. Durch die Instrumentalisierung der Kreuzzugsrhetorik konnte er zudem das Bild seiner Person als das eines katholischen Fürsten, ja, eines Glaubensverteidigers in weiten Teilen des Abendlandes verbreiten und verankern.

1429–30, als es der Streit mit Polen entstand über Witolds Recht, die ihm von Sigismund von Luxemburg angetragene Königskrone anzunehmen. Dem Gutachten der Krakauer Juristen konnte Witold damals nur ähnliche Schreiben der Gelehrten König Sigismunds entgegenstellen. Ausführlich dazu Grzegorz Błaszczyk, *Burza koronacyjna: Dramatyczny fragment stosunków polsko-litewskich w XV wieku* (Poznań, 1998); Žydrūnas Mačiukas, 'Teisinis Vytauto karūnacijos ginčas', in *Lietuvos valstybė XII–XVIII a.*, hg. v. Zigmantas Kiaupa, Artūras Mickevičius und Jolita Sarcevičienė (Vilnius, 1997), S. 271–83; Přemysl Bar, 'Der „Krönungssturm": König Sigismund von Luxemburg, Großfürst Witold von Litauen und das gescheiterte politische Bündnis zwischen beiden Herrschern', *RH* 83 (2017), 65–101; Sergey V. Polekhov, 'Как короновать великого князя? Из истории «коронационной бури» (1429–1430) и инсигний, предназначавшихся для Витовта', *Istorijos šaltinių tyrimai* 7 (2021), 9–74. Über die Gelehrten im Dienste Witolds siehe Sobiesław Szybkowski, 'Polish Staff as a Social Group in the Chancery of Grand Duke Witold', *QMAN* 3 (1998), 75–94.

Quellenanhang[95]

1407 [März] (vor April 9.). Eine Supplik des polnischen Königs Wladislaus II. Jogaila und des litauischen Großfürsten Alexander Witold von Litauen um den gleichen päpstlichen Ablass für diejenigen Kombattanten, die mit Ungläubigen und Schismatikern Krieg führen würden, wie für die Teilnehmer einer Kreuzfahrt ins Heilige Land.

B: GStAPK, XX. HA, OBA 861 (olim Ia 103), Fol. 2. Papier ohne Wasserzeichen, 22,2×15 cm. Gleichzeitige Abschrift. Am unteren Rand links mit Bleistift: „ad I. a. 103". Überliefert als eine Anlage zum Brief des Ordensprokurators Peter von Wormditt an den Hochmeister Konrad von Jungingen vom 14. Mai 1407 (ebd., Bl. 1).

Da die Supplik vor Papst Gregor XII. am 9. April 1407 gelesen wurde (GStAPK, XX. HA, OBA 861, Fol. 1 = BGDO 2, Nr. 31), war sie wahrscheinlich im März in der polnischen königlichen Kanzlei verfasst worden.

Beatissime pater. Quia Regnum Polonie ac partes Russie et Lytwanie, que sub dicione fidelis Sancte Romane Ecclesie et s[erenissimi] r[egis] Wladislai, regis Polonie, consistunt, et eciam terre devoti vestri Allexandri alias Voitholdi[a]*, fratris dicti regis, ducis Lytwanie, consueverunt cum terris Thartarorum necnon quorundam aliorum Sarracenorum et infidelium ac eciam scismaticorum [confinere]*[b]*, unde ipsis regi et duci pro fide catholica contra ipsos infideles inierunt frequencia bella et eis propter nimiam multitudinem eorum ipsi rex et dux indigent strennuis auxiliacionibus et bellatoribus ad resistendum viriliter perfidis nacionibus antedictis, quod si non fieret, de levi omnes terre Christianorum in illis partibus consisten[tes] destruerentur aut subicerentur perpetue servitutis iugo sub infidelibus ipsis. Quapropter supplicant E[ius] S[anctitati] predicti rex et dux, quatenus zelo fidei predictis ipsis et Christianis huiusmodi pie compacien[do] omnibus Christifidelibus, qui sequentur vexilla regis et ducis predictorum contra eosdem infideles aut scismaticos, confessis tamen et contritis, quos mori bellando aut in via illic eundo vel redeundo contigerit, plenam remissionem omnium suorum peccaminum, illam vero, quam qui Terram Sanctam visitare consueverunt, indulgeri dignemini. Item illis, qui per se ipsos ad hoc abiles non existunt, sed miserint iuxta facultates eorum alios bellatores pro eis seu alias pro armis et victualibus contribuerint, eciam remissionem similem concedere dignemini. Item et alias literas opportunas in premissis cum arduis et neccessariis fidei prefate negociis concedere dignemini iuxta informacionem eis dandam ex parte supradictorum non obstantibus quibuscumque.*

Sine alia lectione.

[a] So in B statt Witholdi. [b] Fehlt in B, ergänzt nach dem Sinn.

„Heiligster Vater! Da das Königreich Polen und die Länder der Rus und Litauens, die sich unter der treuen Gehorsamkeit der Heiligen Römischen Kirche und des allerdurchlauchtigsten Königs Wladislaus von Polen befinden, wie auch die Länder Eures Getreuen Alexander alias Witold, des genannten Königs Bruder [genauer: Vetter], des Fürsten von Litauen, gewohnt sind, an die Länder der Tataren sowie etlicher anderer Sarazenen und Ungläubigen und auch Schismatiker [zu grenzen], sollten deshalb der genannte König und der genannte Fürst um des katholischen Glaubens willen zahlreiche Kriege gegen

---

95 Für die Hilfe bei der Vorbereitung der Edition dieser Supplik bedanke ich mich sehr herzlich bei Darius Antanavičius (Wilna) und Alexandra Čirkova (St. Petersburg).

diese Ungläubigen führen, und wegen ihrer übergroßen Zahl brauchen derselbe König und derselbe Fürst tatkräftige Helfer und Krieger, um den genannten hinterlistigen Völkern zu widerstehen; andernfalls würden alle christlichen Völker dieser Länder vernichtet oder dem Joch ewiger Sklaverei dieser Ungläubigen unterworfen werden. Deswegen bitten der genannte König und der genannte Fürst Eure Heiligkeit, aus Glaubenseifer zu ihnen und Christen barmherzig, allen Christengläubigen, die den Heeresfahnen des vorgenannten Königs und Fürsten gegen diese Ungläubige oder Schismatiker folgen, gebeichtet und reuig, die im Krieg oder auf dem Wege hin oder zurück sterben, völligen Ablass aller ihrer Sünden zu erteilen, ähnlich wie denjenigen, die das Heilige Land besuchten. Auch möget Ihr denjenigen, die selber dazu nicht fähig sind, aber andere Krieger nach ihren Möglichkeiten schicken oder in anderer Weise zu Waffen und Viktualien beitragen, denselben Sündenablass gewähren. Auch möget Ihr weitere geeignete Schreiben in der genannten Angelegenheit mit den schwierigen und notwendigen Aufgaben erlassen, gemäß, den Informationen von Seiten der Genannten, wenn dem nichts entgegensteht.

Ohne andere Lesung."

PAVEL SOUKUP

Legitimising the Hussite Wars

Anti-Heretical Crusading in the Fifteenth Century[*]

From the point of view of canon law, the crusades against the Hussites were a continuation of the trial of Jan Hus and of the inquisition which was introduced against his followers. Hus's trial ended with the execution of the convict at the stake in July 1415. Since Jan Hus was sentenced as a heretic, holding, defending, and spreading his views was also heretical. In February 1418, Pope Martin V formally established an inquisition to proceed against the Wycliffite heretics in Central Europe. Among the faculties bestowed on bishops and inquisitors was the right to call upon the secular authorities if the heretics proved overly obstinate. While the inquisition did achieve some success outside Bohemia, it never truly began to function in the territory of the kingdom. The crusade proclaimed on 1 March 1420 can thus be seen as the ultimate measure in the long-term struggle against the Hussite heresy, with Sigismund of Luxemburg — king of the Romans, of Hungary, and Bohemia — fulfilling the role of the aforementioned secular authority.[1] On the military level, the first round of crusades, fought between 1420 and 1431, failed spectacularly. In the Second Hussite War, from 1467 to 1471, the crusaders' luck was not much better.[2] Despite these practical failures, the means employed by the curia and the princes represented a well-established instrument: crusading against heretics was endorsed by the legal and theological theories developed since the twelfth century. Was there any further need for

---

[*] This study was prepared at the Institute of Philosophy of the Czech Academy of Sciences and supported by a grant from the Czech Science Foundation (GA ČR), *From Performativity to Institutionalization: Handling Conflict in the Late Middle Ages (19–28415X)*. ORCID: 0000-0001-8864-9530.

[1] For the documents establishing the persecution of the Hussites, see *Conciliorum oecumenicorum generaliumque decreta*, ed. Giuseppe Alberigo et al., 4 vols (Turnhout, 2006–16), 2.1: 580–89; MVRGB 7: no. 218, pp. 98–108 (here 107); no. 565, pp. 247–49.

[2] For basic information, see Frederick G. Heymann, 'The Crusades against the Hussites', in *A History of the Crusades*, ed. Kenneth M. Setton, 6 vols (Madison, 1969–89), 3: 586–646; František Šmahel, *Die Hussitische Revolution*, 3 vols (Hannover, 2002); Pavel Soukup, 'Religion and Violence in the Hussite Wars', in *The European Wars of Religion: An Interdisciplinary Reassessment of Sources, Interpretations, and Myths*, ed. Wolfgang Palaver, Harriet Rudolph and Dietmar Regensburger (Farnham, 2016), pp. 19–44.

The Defence of the Faith, Outremer: Studies in the Crusades and the Latin East, 15 (Turnhout: Brepols, 2024), pp. 361–376
BREPOLS PUBLISHERS 10.1484/M.OUTREMER-EB.5.136544

legitimisation? In this article, I will identify some areas where this need arose, and outline briefly how the ideologues of the anti-Hussite crusade attempted to provide legitimacy.

A War against Christians

A striking symptom of the Hussite crisis was the rich theological output which accompanied the war on heresy. A certain need for legitimisation can be discerned in the very fact that Catholic theologians continued to argue that the ideas of the Hussites were erroneous. Strictly speaking, this was superfluous: the verdicts mentioned above should have established heresy beyond doubt. The authority of the judgement was unproblematic even in constitutional terms: the sentences passed at the Council of Constance were confirmed and built upon by the pope, so there was every reason for the condemnation to be accepted, regardless of the struggle over ecclesiastical primacy. None the less, theologians continued to produce new refutations of Hussitism. The number of anti-Hussite treatises, ranging from short and privately-circulated ones to extensive and widely-copied ones, can be estimated at around three hundred.[3] A polemical production as voluminous as the one which accompanied the anti-Hussite crusades is unheard of in other theatres of crusading.

One possible explanation could be Hussite apologetics: the enemy himself argued within the same framework of Christian scholarship. With their typical proselytising verve, the Hussites repeatedly proclaimed themselves to be the true followers of Jesus Christ. The learned polemics against them acknowledged implicitly that the victims of the crusade were Christians, albeit erring Christians. In Martin V's bull proclaiming the first crusade, the enemies were designated as 'Wycliffites and Hussites', terms developed according to the tradition of naming Christian sects. Alongside these terms, crusade-related documents from the papal chancery kept using the less-specific expressions 'Bohemian heretics' or 'heretics in Bohemia'.[4] However *pessima*, *prava*, and *perfidissima* this heresy was, it still had a Christian pedigree, i. e. it represented a distortion and perversion of the Christian faith.

The terminology used in narrative sources points to the reception and adaptation of this conceptual framework. The Catholic chronicler of the Hussite wars, Andrew of Ratisbon, usually referred to the two sides as 'Catholics' and 'heretics'.[5]

---

[3] *Repertorium operum antihussiticorum*, online database, ed. Pavel Soukup <www.antihus.eu> [accessed 31 October 2018].

[4] Pavel Soukup, 'The Waning of the "Wycliffites": Giving Names to Hussite Heresy', in *Europe after Wyclif*, ed. J. Patrick Hornbeck II and Michael Van Dussen (New York, 2017), pp. 196–226 (here 202).

[5] E. g. Andreas von Regensburg, *Sämtliche Werke*, ed. Georg Leidinger, Quellen und Erörterungen zur bayerischen und deutschen Geschichte, NF 1 (München, 1903), pp. 368, 376, 422, 425, 429–30, 448, 451.

In a few cases, however, he identified the Catholics generally as the 'faithful of Christ' (*Christi fideles*).[6] Attributing the Christian status only to the Catholics meant pushing the heretics outside of Christianity. The Lübeck chronicler, Hermann Korner, also considered the Hussites to be the 'enemies of Christ', while he referred to the crusaders simply as the 'Christian army'.[7] Preachers of the Cross — such as Oswald Reinlein in 1426 — sometimes went to the extreme of applying the term 'infidels' to the Hussites, a term usually reserved for non-Christian enemies such as Muslims and pagans.[8] Reinlein's colleague Thomas Harder mixed all the above concepts in 1467, saying that the Catholic Church and 'we Christians' were attacked by the 'infidels and heretics', the enemies of Christ, the Hussites.[9]

Naturally, the extent to which the opponent could have been considered Christian had profound consequences for the lawfulness of war. In the context of the anti-Hussite crusades, did anyone have any scruples about killing people who had been baptised? For the papacy, this seems not to have been a problem. Martin V not only saw extermination as the right way of dealing with the Hussite problem, but he even assured crusaders, and especially those of clerical status, that they were not guilty of murder. In February 1422, the pope addressed the issue of killing in a *motu proprio*. He said that some clerics were afraid they would incur excommunication and irregularity as they had taken part in the anti-Hussite expedition in which many people were killed, the villages and towns of heretics were sacked, and churches — including their clerical leadership — were burnt. The pope declared that the clerics involved did not deserve any ecclesiastical penalties; on the contrary, he authorised clergy to partake in the extirpation of heretics and to fight with actual weapons (*armata manu*). He substantiated this rather exceptional provision with the fear that even greater dangers would arise if the heretics continued spreading 'like venomous reptiles' and attacking the souls of the people.[10]

The papal brief was quite widely received (the edition lists six copies in Bohemian manuscripts). Several decades later, it was briefly discussed by the Erfurt Carthusian Johannes Hagen. In one of his notebooks, Hagen summarised the decree and remarked that it seemingly contradicted canon law, which stated that any cleric who killed a heretic or pagan became irregular. Then, however,

---

6 Andreas von Regensburg, *Sämtliche Werke*, p. 423.
7 Constantin Hruschka, *Kriegsführung und Geschichtsschreibung im Spätmittelalter: Eine Untersuchung zur Chronistik der Konzilszeit* (Köln, 2001), pp. 385–86.
8 MS Nürnberg, Stadtbibliothek, Cent. I 78, fol. 71rb. Reinlein said the pope *congregat fideles suos ad militandum contra infideles et eorum fautores*. '[...] summons those loyal to him to fight against the infidels and their supporters'.
9 MS Klosterneuburg, Stiftsbibliothek, CCl 993, fol. 122r: *Ecclesia katholica et nos christiani, eiusdem ecclesie filii et filie, inpungnamur et inquietamur per infideles et hereticos, fidei katholice persecutores et Christi inimicos, quales sunt perfidi Hussite Bohemi*. 'The Catholic Church and we Christians, sons and daughters of the same Church, are attacked and harrassed by the infidels and heretics, persecutors of the Catholic faith and enemies of Christ, which are the faithless Bohemian Hussites'.
10 *MVRGB* 7, no. 900, pp. 369–71.

Hagen referred to a number of authors who agreed that irregularity was part of the positive law and, as such, was subject to the pope's jurisdiction. Thus, Martin V's lifting of the penalty for homicide was superior to previous general regulations.[11] Hagen's discussion concerned only the special case of clerical killers; the killing of heretics by the secular arm was less problematic. In one of his crusading sermons, the Klosterneuburg Canon Regular, Thomas Harder, asked whether it was just to fight against heretics and kill them. In answering, he provided two unequivocal authorities: Thomas and Bernard. According to Aquinas, heretics deserved not only to be separated from the Church through excommunication, but also to be excluded from the world by death. Falsifying the faith was more serious than forging money, for which princes imposed capital punishment. Bernard of Clairvaux declared in *De laude novae militiae* that the knights of Christ kill safely, i. e. with no guilt, because he who kills a malefactor is not a murderer but a *malicida*—killer of evil.[12]

Another crusading preacher, the Viennese Augustinian Oswald Reinlein, judged the Hussite heretics unworthy to receive sacraments or any human grace because they had not repented for so many years.[13] While perhaps anticipated

---

11 MS Erfurt, Bistumsarchiv, Bestand Domarchiv, Hs. Hist. 1, fol. 43v: *Hcc nota bene, quia de iure occidens hereticum aut paganum est irregularis, L. distinccione 'Si quis viduam' cum similibus. Sed dicit Iohannes Calderinus, Panormitanus, Iohannes Andree et communiter omnes doctores, quod sine metu irregularitatis potest hoc papa concedere, quia de iure positivo introducta est irregularitas homicide, ideo papa tollere potest. Concordat Thomas, Scotus et alii theologi.* 'Note this well, for according to law, one who kills a heretic or pagan is irregular, as stated in distinction 50 "Si quis viduam" and similar. But Giovanni Calderini, Niccolò 'Panormitanus' Tedeschi, John of Andrea and all the doctors say in common that the pope can permit this with no fear of irregularity, because irregularity due to homicide was introduced by positive law, and so the pope can lift it. Thomas [Aquinas], [John Duns] Scotus and other theologians agree'. For the canon (D. 50, 8), see *Corpus iuris Canonici*, ed. Emil Friedberg, 2 vols (Leipzig, 1879), 1: 179–80.
12 MS Klosterneuburg, Stiftsbibliothek, CCl 993, fol. 131v: *Quod autem iustum sit pungnare contra hereticos et eos interficere, hoc ostendit sanctus Thomas 2ᵃ 2ᵉ, quescione 11, articulo 3° dicens: 'Heretici propter ipsorum peccatum meruerunt nedum ab ecclesia per excommunicacionem separari, sed eciam per mortem a mundo excludi'. [...] Dicit enim beatus Bernhardus in quodam tractatu De milicia [...]: 'Sane cum occidit malefactorem, non homicida est, sed, ut dixerim, malicida. Christus enim vindex est in hiis, qui male agunt, et defensor christianorum reputatur'.* 'Saint Thomas shows in Secunda secundae, question 11, article 3, that it is just to fight against heretics and to kill them, saying: "Because of their sin, heretics have deserved not only to be separated from the Church through excommunication, but also excluded from the world through death". [...] Indeed, saint Bernard says in a certain tract "On knighthood": "Certainly he who kills an evildoer is not a murderer but, so to say, a killer of evil. For Christ is an avenger against those who do evil and is held to be a defender of Christians"'. See Thomas Aquinas, 2ᵃ 2ᵃᵉ, q. 11, a. 3, in *Sancti Thomae Aquinatis Doctoris angelici Opera omnia iussu impensaque Leonis XIII P. M. edita*, 13 vols (Roma, 1882–1918), 8: 100; Bernhardus Claraevallensis, 'De laude novae militiae' 3, in *Sancti Bernardi Opera*, ed. Jean Leclercq et al., 9 vols (Roma, 1957–98), 3: 217.
13 MS Nürnberg, Stadtbibliothek, Cent. I 78, fol. 69ra: *O quomodo ergo nos illam hereticam gentem Hussitarum non iudicamus indignam eciam omni gracia humana et sacramentis ecclesie, cum per tot annos exspectati sunt ad penitenciam, quam agere nolunt?* 'Oh, how should we not judge those heretical Hussite people to be unworthy of all human grace and the sacraments of the Church, when they were expected for so many years to do penance, and refuse to do so?'

in a crusading sermon, such a view cannot be taken for granted. The Heidelberg theologian Nicholas Magni of Jauer resolved the question of killing heretics in a dedicated *quaestio* in 1425. This did not appear in an immediate crusade context, but rather in connection with Nicholas's involvement as one of the judges in the inquisition process against the German Hussite John of Drändorf in 1425. The author asked whether heretics renouncing their error should be received by the Church as many times as they repent, and he answered in the affirmative. He insisted that such heretics who pose a threat to other people, especially to the simple folk, must be sentenced to death. Heretics who do not infect others need not be killed if there are people firm in faith who could interact with them. Nicholas did not want to contradict Thomas Aquinas, and thus admitted that even those heretics who do not corrupt the faithful may be killed, but he clearly preferred not to. In any case, he insisted that heretics who repent must not be refused or repelled, even though repentance does not excuse them from temporal sentence. After all, heretics were still human, and thus charity dictated one love them.[14]

These considerations show that the physical destruction of heretics was not always a straightforward consideration. In the view of some thinkers, legitimacy needed to be substantiated with a nuanced classification of crime and punishment. If the Hussites were considered obstinate and dangerous heretics, a crusade against them was in order. When they were classified otherwise, questions may have arisen. The agreement between the Hussites and the Council of Basle, negotiated in 1433–36, ended the first wave of crusades and removed the stain of heresy from the Bohemians. Johannes Cotbus of Sommerfeld, a Celestine from Oybin in Upper Lusatia, wrote his *Tractatus de cruce signatis* during the Second Hussite War in 1468. Among other questions, he considered the legitimacy of the crusades against schismatics and other Christian rebels. Proclaiming the Cross against Saracens and heretics was beyond doubt, because these were precisely the groups which Hostiensis mentioned as the targets of crusades. Cotbus spent some time considering disobedient Christians before accepting them amongst the targets of a legitimate crusade. In the end, their Christian status counted against the Hussites. As Cotbus said, Christians who split themselves from the Church sinned more than Saracens, because they rejected the faith that they had previously accepted. While Muslims or Jews cannot be coerced into accepting

---

14 Adolph Franz, *Der Magister Nikolaus Magni de Jawor: Ein Beitrag zur Literatur- und Gelehrtengeschichte des 14. und 15. Jahrhunderts* (Freiburg i. Bg., 1898), pp. 221–23 (for context, see 114–19); *Drei Inquisitions-Verfahren aus dem Jahre 1425: Akten der Prozesse gegen die deutschen Hussiten Johannes Drändorf und Peter Turnau sowie gegen Drändorfs Diener Martin Borchard*, ed. Hermann Heimpel (Göttingen, 1969), p. 148. For Nicholas's later views on dealing with heretics, see Jiří Petrášek, *"Meide die Häretiker": Die antihussitische Reaktion des Heidelberger Professors Nikolaus von Jauer (1355–1435) auf das taboritische Manifest aus dem Jahr 1430* (Münster, 2018), pp. 231–33.

Christianity, schismatics must be compelled. Cotbus deemed the extirpation of the Bohemian schism and heresy as the greatest good.[15]

Comparing the imminent danger posed by the Hussites to previous crises which the Church resolved by means of crusade was among the easiest and most widespread strategies of legitimisation. Transferring the traditional privileges reserved for the crusaders to the Holy Land to the anti-Hussite struggle seemed to be advantageous, yet there were also voices calling for caution. The Heidelberg lawyer Job Vener penned an expert opinion in 1421 in which he advocated a limitation of traditional crusading privileges as set by the Lateran IV decree *Ad liberandam* and exploited by the organisers of the current anti-Hussite crusade. He was afraid that an overly liberal policy of granting grace for financial contributions would jeopardise the credibility of the crusade.[16]

Vener's reformist considerations sought to keep an eye on the papacy and their use of the crusade, but not to question the anti-Hussite crusade as such. The admissibility of the war against the Bohemian heretics was grounded in the classical theory of just war. The three basic conditions as summarised by Aquinas entered even the preaching of the Cross against the Hussites.[17] Just cause, right intention, and legitimate authority were all related to the crucial assumption that Christian warfare may only be defensive. In the particular case of the war

---

15 MS Praha, Národní knihovna České republiky, IV E 15, fol. 84r: *Si enim crux pro recuperacione Terre sancte merito predicatur, multo forcius pro unitate ecclesie servanda crux contra scismaticos erit predicanda, XXIIII. q. 1 'Loquitur' et canone sequenti. Maius enim periculum imminet in hoc quam in illo, quia anima est preciosior rebus. Preterea si personarum offensas attendamus, magis peccant christiani inobedientes et scismatici, qui ad fidem semel susceptam cogi precise debent, quam Sarraceni, qui fidem recipere non coguntur inviti, XXIII. q. V 'Ad fidem', XLV^ta di. 'De Iudeis'. Preterea nullum est scisma, quod sibi non consurgat ad aliquam heresim, XXIII. q. 1 'Scisma siquidem'. Patet ergo: et contra tales et quosvis alios secundum determinacionem pape et ecclesie crux rite predicatur.* 'If indeed the Cross is rightly preached for the recuperation of the Holy Land, still more boldly should the Cross be preached against schismatics for the preservation of ecclesiastical unity (Causa 24, question 1 "Loquitur" and the following canon). Indeed, in the latter there is a greater threat than in the former, for the soul is more precious than things. Besides, if we attend to offences caused by persons, disobedient Christians and schismatics sin more and should immediately be compelled to the faith they once had accepted, while the Saracens should not be compelled to accept the faith against their will (Causa 23, question 5 "Ad fidem"; Distinction 45 "De Iudeis"). Moreover, there is no schism which does not aspire to some heresy (Causa 23, question 1 "Scisma quidem"). Therefore, it is clear that against such people as well as any others the Cross is duly preached following the determination of the pope and the Church'. The quoted legal norms are C. 24, 1, 18–19; C. 23, 5, 33; D. 45, 5; and C. 24, 1, 34, in *Corpus iuris Canonici* 1: 971–73, 939, 161–62 and 979–80. See MS IV E 15, fol. 81v: *Igitur econtrario maximum bonum et opus valde virtuosum erit laborare pro extirpacione heresis atque scismatis Bohemorum, qui ecclesiam Dei scindunt, maculant et opprimunt.* 'Therefore, on the contrary, it would be the foremost good and a very virtuous business to work for the extirpation of the heresy and schism of the Bohemians, who tear, pollute and oppress the Church'.

16 Hermann Heimpel, *Die Vener von Gmünd und Strassburg 1162–1447: Studien und Texte zur Geschichte einer Familie sowie des gelehrten Beamtentums in der Zeit der abendländischen Kirchenspaltung und der Konzilien von Pisa, Konstanz und Basel*, 3 vols (Göttingen, 1982), 2: 898–912.

17 See the discussion of Thomas Harder in MS Klosterneuburg, Stiftsbibliothek, CCl 993, fols 131v–132r.

against the Hussites, however, it was more than obvious that it was the crusaders' troops who first invaded Bohemia. Quite naturally, then, the Hussites claimed for themselves the status of defenders under attack. To assure legitimacy, the crusaders portrayed their fight as a defence of the faith and the Church, regardless of who struck first.[18]

The frequent defeats of the crusaders, however, challenged their status as warriors for the true faith. Why would God permit his defenders to succumb? The eternal question of all defeated holy warriors arose in the Hussite wars as well. The answer of theoreticians was a classic one: it was not because the enterprise was unjust and the cause wrong, but because of the sins of individual participants. Johannes Cotbus of Sommerfeld insisted on such an interpretation for the military failures of the Breslau (mod. Wrocław, Poland) troops in the 1460s. He gave examples from the Old Testament of instances when God denied his warriors victory because of their demerits, and he reused a long passage from Bernard of Clairvaux's *De consideratione* concerning the failure of the Second Crusade.[19] In 1430, the chronicler Andrew of Ratisbon composed an entire *Dialogus* to explain the recurrent defeats of the Catholic troops. He also named a number of examples from biblical and post-biblical history to illustrate his point that prolonged suffering was necessary before God would eventually grant victory.[20]

If defeats were necessary and suffering meritorious, why would Christians even want to prevail? In this logic, the enemy was seen as a scourge of God, fulfilling His judgement. Was it licit, then, to oppose? A short anonymous text attests that such a doubt arose contemporaneously with the Hussite wars in the context of the Turkish crusade. The work with the incipit *Diceret aliquis: Videtur, quod cristianis non licet occidere Turcos* has been preserved in a manuscript now in New York's Morgan Library.[21] The codex contains writings by Walter Burley, Giles of Rome, Jean Gerson, Bartolus de Saxoferrato, and others. The two dated items were copied in 1437 and 1457, the earlier of them in Basle; the manuscript also features a treatise addressed to the Council of Basle by Jean Mauroux. The *dubium* about killing the Turks appears as the antepenultimate item in the codex. It is followed by a short note on how to sign people with the cross, and a one-page query about why sins are forgiven through a pilgrimage to the Holy Land, answered with an excerpt from Alexander of Hales. All these three texts are written in the same hand on three leaves now glued to the last quire of the codex.

---

18 King Sigismund, for instance, was called *pugil et defensor fidei christiane* in a papal letter of 1422: MVRGB 7, no. 937, p. 384. For claims concerning the defensive character of warfare, see Soukup, 'Religion and Violence', pp. 24–26.
19 MS Praha, Národní knihovna České republiky, IV E 15, fols 78bisv–79v; Bernardus Claraevallensis, 'De consideratione' 2, 1–3, in *Sancti Bernardi Opera*, 3: 410–12.
20 Andreas von Regensburg, *Sämtliche Werke*, pp. 657–91; see Norman Housley, 'Explaining Defeat: Andrew of Regensburg and the Hussite Crusades', in *Dei gesta per Francos: Etudes sur les croisades dédiées à Jean Richard*, ed. Michel Balard, Benjamin Z. Kedar and Jonathan Riley-Smith (Aldershot, 2001), pp. 87–95.
21 MS New York, Morgan Library and Museum, B.23, fols 255r–256v.

The two short appendices confirm that the text on killing the Turks belongs to a crusading context.

Doubts arose due to the following consideration: those who are incited by God to do something do not sin; in the Old Testament, many infidel peoples were incited to punish Jews and did not sin while killing them. In the 'present case', God aroused the Turks to punish the sins of the Christians, and so the latter are not allowed to resist unless they want to resist God. This observation, as well as parts of the following solution (but not all of it), are borrowed from Alexander of Hales' *Summa theologica*.[22] Alexander distinguished between those who punish sins without knowing it, and those who do so intentionally. In the first case, God incites only the action, in the second, the intention of the 'scourges' as well. The author of the *dubium* says that, in the Turkish war, it is the Christians who are in the second category.[23] Even if God wanted to punish the faithful through the Turks, he also wants Christians to resist the infidels. When resisting the Turks, Christians do act against what God wants (*volitum*), but not against the divine will (*voluntas*).[24] This subtle distinction is illustrated by the following example: If God wants my father to die and I do not want it, I resist the *volitum*, but not the will of God, who wants me not to want my father to die. While the dialectics of opposing and not opposing the divine will are demonstrated by way of proof, the fact that the Turks are tormenting Christians unjustly is stated on a purely rhetorical level with no further argumentation.[25] In this way, by pointing at the

---

22 Alexander de Halis, 'Summa theologica' 3, 125–26 and 357, in *Doctoris irrefragabilis Alexandri de Hales Ordinis Minorum Summa theologica*, ed. Collegium S. Bonaventurae, 4 vols (Quaracchi, 1924–48), 4: 176–78 and 530–31.

23 MS New York, Morgan Library and Museum, B.23, fol. 255v: *Isto 2° modo excitantur in casu currenti contra infideles Turcos divino honori contrarios, ecclesie sancte molestos, fidei et crucis Christi hostes perfidos iuxta illud Luce 19: Inimicos meos illos, qui noluerunt me regnare super se, adducite huc et interficite ante me.* [Luke 19:27]. 'In this second way, people are incited in the present case against the faithless Turks, who oppose themselves to the honour of God, trouble the Holy Church, and are treacherous enemies of Christ's Cross according the Gospel of Luke 19: "As for those my enemies, who would not have me reign over them, bring them hither, and kill them before me"'.

24 MS New York, Morgan Library and Museum, B.23, fol. 255v: *Nec Cristi fideles sic agentes volunt contra voluntatem divinam, ymo volunt secundum voluntatem divinam ei se conformantes in modo volendi, licet velint contrarium voliti, quia Deus vult fideles sic velle et agere, scilicet resietere Turcis et eosdem pro viribus delere.* 'Nor do the Christians who act in this way desire anything against the divine will; on the contrary, they desire according to the divine will, conforming themselves to it in the manner of their desiring, even though they desire that which is contrary to what God wants, for God wants the faithful to desire and act in this way, i.e. to resist the Turks and destroy them with all force'.

25 MS New York, Morgan Library and Museum, B.23, fol. 255v: *Licet ergo multorum demeritis exigentibus fidelium saltem numero, si non merito, res et persone digne paccantur ab infidelibus, non tamen infideles iuste puniunt, quia Turci infestant membra ecclesie non pro vindicta iniurie Deo illate, sed ut inimici Verbi incarnati et crucis Cristi ad subiciendum sibi fideles et trahendi in errorem detestandi Machameti. Hinc est, quod cristianorum est arma movere ad huiusmodi maleficos occidendum et delendum.* 'Even though the belongings and persons of many of the faithful are righteously seized by the infidels, because at least the quantity, if not the quality of their demerits requires it, nevertheless the infidels do not punish us justly, for the Turks vex the members of the Church not in order to avenge the injustice caused

danger and suffering of the Church, any doubts about killing the human enemy in a crusade — be they infidels or heretics, Turks or Hussites — could have been, and indeed were, relatively easily suppressed.

Competing Interests

The anti-heretical discourse of the period seems to imply that there was no alternative to exterminating the venomous dogma and the perfidious people who held it. This is, however, not true. Nicholas Magni's suggestion that experienced, orthodox people may talk to heretics rather than destroying them indicated that persuasion was a possible way of dealing with heresy. This was perhaps possible in the case of individual heretics, yet much more difficult on a larger scale. Prospective negotiations between the Roman Church and the Hussites as a group was an eminently political question that deserved complex deliberation. From the very beginning of the Hussite crusade in 1420, King Sigismund considered the option of achieving a peaceful solution through talks. For the king, the question was a pragmatic one: he would prefer whatever solution would secure him the Bohemian crown, be it war or negotiation. Pope Martin V and the legates he commissioned with organising the anti-Hussite campaigns preferred military confrontation, calling upon the king and the princes of the empire to take part in crusades. In the understanding of the curia, only the pope could authorise peaceful contact with heretics. Even if such talks materialised, the only admissible way forward was via *informatio*, i. e. the heretics' unconditioned acceptance of the instruction given by the Church hierarchy.[26] A disputation between the Hussites and the Roman Church on equal terms was not realised until the Council of Basle in 1433. Even then many insisted on the doctrinal submission of the Hussites, and some prominent Basle representatives never entirely abandoned the idea of military intervention.

Let us cite some examples of the argumentation of those who preferred crusade to other means of returning the Hussites back into the Church. The Polish king Vladislas II Jogaila played the Hussite card to exert pressure on Sigismund who, as king of the Romans, acted as arbiter in the long-term conflict between Poland and the Teutonic Order. Although Vladislas never granted the Hussites a full theological disputation about doctrinal issues, he maintained various diplomatic contacts with them. Some of the Hussites offered Vladislas the Bohemian throne, and his nephew Sigismund Korybut spent several years as a governor in

---

to God, but rather as enemies of the incarnate Word and Christ's Cross, to subjugate the faithful and draw them into the error of the detested Muhammad. Hence Christians should raise arms to kill and destroy such evildoers'.

26 The best survey of the attempts during the 1420s to organise a disputation between the Hussites and the Roman Church is Dušan Coufal, *Polemika o kalich mezi teologií a politikou 1414–31: Předpoklady basilejské disputace o prvním z pražských artikulů* (Praha, 2012), pp. 159–280.

Bohemia.[27] To face the threat of the emerging Polono-Hussite alliance, Sigismund of Luxemburg sent his ambassador Martín Talayero to Poland. On 22 April 1422, the Parisian master of theology and diplomat in Sigismund's service gave a speech before Vladislas II Jogaila. He summarised the errors and atrocities of the Bohemians and strove to discourage the king from any contact with them. He stressed that the Hussites had been isolated from the Church *de iure*, i. e. through excommunication, as well as *de facto*, i.e. through proclamation of a crusade. Thus, no faithful Catholic was allowed to communicate with them in any way and, in allowing a debate, Vladislas would spurn the decrees of the general councils. In his argumentation in favour of a crusade, Talayero also exploited some concepts of social theory, insisting that the duty of kings and secular lords was 'to protect and defend the traditions of the fathers with iron and weapons'. Disputing with heretics would disqualify the king for any future war.[28]

Similar arguments came from the Roman curia. On behalf of the legate Branda da Castiglione, Giuliano Cesarini presented a diplomatic message to Vladislas II Jogaila in early 1424. Here, too, the basis of the argumentation was provided by an enumeration of Hussite felonies: not only do the heretics infect other people with their theological errors, but they also aim to destroy the social order by rebelling against their king, refusing to pay levies, and challenging private property in general. Cesarini also used a variety of specifically crusading tropes: he applied the topos of *tempus acceptabile* to Vladislas's conversion to Christianity, although it happened almost four decades earlier. Nevertheless, according to the ambassador, the time had come when all peoples would praise the day of Vladislas's baptism if he would stand up for the Christian faith. The rhetorical figure *quantum magis* followed: if the king used to wage war for temporal, earthly things, how much more should he now fight for his Creator and for eternal life? By doing so he would fulfil his role in the world's order: 'Although every faithful Christian is obliged to persecute heresies, kings and princes are obliged in the first place, having been given a sword from God to praise the good but take vengeance on the wicked'. Practical aspects also speak for Vladislas's participation in the crusade, since he is not only a faithful Christian and mighty king, but also a neighbour of Bohemia and someone with experience and good luck in warfare.[29]

The Polish king was not the only one to earn admonition and crusading exhortation. Whenever King Sigismund pondered the possibility of a disputation with the Hussites, he would be admonished by the curia in the same way. For example, in June 1426, the new papal legate Giordano Orsini reminded Sigismund about his unconditioned acceptance of the anti-Hussite rulings at Constance. Since the falsity of the Hussite faith was proven beyond doubt by the authoritative

---

27 Jarosław Nikodem, *Polska i Litwa wobec husyckich Czech w latach 1420–33: Studium o polityce dynastycznej Władysława Jagiełły i Witolda Kiejstutowicza* (Poznań, 2004).
28 Jaroslav Kadlec, 'Magister Martin Talayero aus Tortosa im Kampf gegen die Hussiten', *AHC* 12 (1980), 269–314 (here 302).
29 *CEV*, no. 1122, p. 615.

decision of the general council, any negotiation on theological topics was ruled out. The legate spurred Sigismund, who had always been the 'defender of the faith and one who drove out the schism', not to desist from the fight against heresy. Again, the extermination of the Hussites was legitimised by their heresy and proven by the authority of the Church.[30]

The political flexibility of anti-heretical argumentation is shown in a proclamation of the University of Paris from 14 December 1428. The structure of the argument is similar to the previous examples. The memorandum starts by pointing out the errors of the Bohemians and the dangers they pose to Christendom. The negligence of 'Christians' allowed the spread of Hussitism; given the Muslim advance in the east, it is now time to take action if Christianity is to be saved. 'Oh, faithful of Christ', the university exclaims, 'gird on, fight manfully against the old snake and his infidel servants!' The roles assigned to social groups corresponded to the structure of the Lateran IV model of crusading: the clergy contributes through prayers, the princes take arms, and everyone else offers resources and subsidies. A precondition is peace, unity, and moral improvement in Latin Christendom. At this point, the Parisian masters reveal their real agenda: they call for an accelerated convention of the Council of Basle, the appropriate forum to meet these requirements. In the Paris proclamation, the crusading argumentation does not stand in service of the papacy but rather of the general council — the actor who eventually opened negotiations with the Hussites.[31]

The way out of the first phase of the anti-Hussite crusades demonstrates how much the struggle against the Hussite heresy was affected by political divides within the Catholic camp. The internal politics of both the Holy Roman Empire and the Roman Church were marked by opposition and competition. With their invitation of the Hussites to negotiate on the faith, the Basle fathers earned the ire of Pope Eugene IV. In his bull of dissolution from 18 December 1431, the pope used the proposed disputation with heretics as an argument against the Council of Basle. He insisted that the invitation violated both the determination of the Councils of Constance and Siena and apostolic authority itself.[32] In the subsequent exchange of opinions, the Council and the curia defended their respective approaches to the reduction of the Bohemians, to Church reform, and to other ardent matters. Not even the conciliarists rejected crusade as such, but rather considered negotiation a more promising alternative at the time; they did not turn their back to military proposals coming from the German nobility or princes which might prove useful if the talks would fail.[33] Thus, the crusade

---

30 *RTA ÄR* 8, no. 406, p. 491.
31 Dušan Coufal, 'Pařížská univerzita a husité v letech 1428–1429', *Mediaevalia Historica Bohemica* 18 (2015), 205–35 (here 225–33).
32 *MCG* 2: 74. For a discussion of the two versions of the dissolution bull, see Loy Bilderback, 'Eugene IV and the First Dissolution of the Council of Basle', *Church History* 36 (1967), 243–53.
33 The proposal of Duke William of Bavaria-Munich to summon military forces to Basle was accepted in October 1432. For references, see Ladislav Hofman, 'Husité a koncilium Basilejské v letech 1431 a 1432', *Český časopis historický* 7 (1901), 1–13, 142–62, 293–309, 408–15 (here 306–7).

against the heretics was not called into question as such, but was rather endorsed or dismissed based on the particular political orientation prevailing in the papalist–conciliarist controversy at the moment.

The papacy held the legalist position as outlined in Eugene's bull of dissolution, i. e. no talks with condemned heretics were permitted. Few further arguments in favour of the crusade were made. The pope insisted on the 'extirpation' rather than the 'reduction' of the heretics. In his reply to Sigismund's embassy, given on 25 April 1432, he imparted his conviction that it was the duty of the king of the Romans as the *advocatus ecclesie* to destroy the Hussite heresy. He wondered why the resources of all of Hungary and Germany had not sufficed to fulfil this task.[34] A memorandum sent at the same time from the curia to various European courts pointed to the papacy's expertise in crusading. Even though the council fathers were approached by knights' eager to renew the struggle with the Hussites, the pope doubted that the Council would be able to organise such an expedition. The assembly was too small and insignificant to levy a tax in all Christian kingdoms, and it would not collect the necessary subsidies even in thirty years. The pope said sarcastically that he would be happy to send the money to Basle if the conciliarists would really wage the war, but he was sure that somebody other than the German princes must be found to lead such an expedition. 'This matter requires something other than words', he remarked, and he cited the crusading experience of his predecessor, Martin V.[35]

On 22 August, Eugene IV's ambassador, Andrew of Petra, the archbishop of Colossus (Rhodes), gave a long speech at Basle in which he explored yet another way of legitimising the anti-Hussite crusade rather than negotiation. According to Andrew, there was no profit in negotiating with the Bohemians because they had nothing to offer. While the union with the Greeks could provide incontestable cultural as well as geographical gains, the Hussites were nothing but a virus, worse than any other heresy in Christian history. Were these savage wolves able to turn into sheep, the pope would make every effort to help them, but as they are not, their extirpation is the only option available to save the rest of the faithful.[36]

Even in cases where there was a consensus about the desirability of extirpation, some aspects of the war were subject to debate. In the politics of the empire, the legitimate leadership in a crusade was at stake. Unsuccessful though it was on the practical level, the battle against the Hussites was still seen as a source of prestige. The traditional concept of the emperor as defender of the Church was challenged by the princes, who claimed a share in the decision-making. At the meeting in Bingen in January 1424, the electors agreed that, in periods of the king's absence from the empire, his powers should pass to them. The struggle against the Bohemian heretics was mentioned as their primary task: 'the almighty

---

34 *MCG* 2: 169.
35 *MCG* 2: 158.
36 *Sacrorum conciliorum nova et amplissima collectio*, ed. Giovanni Domenico Mansi, 53 vols (Venezia, 1759–1927), 29: 475–77.

God has honoured us and assigned us the task of standing properly against any crime that might arise in the Holy Church and Christendom and the Holy Roman Empire, and especially a crime against the holy Christian faith...'[37] Yet even the prerogative of the princes could be contested. After the failure of the 1431 crusade, the representatives of several south-German knightly societies met in Windsheim and agreed that a new crusade should be launched without the princes. This proposal reached the president of the Council of Basle, Giuliano Cesarini, who supported it and shared it with the pope when resisting the dissolution of the Council.[38] Like the Electors, the lower nobles were also anxious about 'the Holy Church, Holy Roman Empire, all of Christendom, and especially the nobility in the German regions'.[39]

Responding to the Electors' announcement from Bingen, Sigismund reminded them that it was he, the king, who had invested great effort and resources into the war with the various enemies of the faith: 'Although we have to wage a daily yet significant war against the Turks, against the Bosnian heretics called the Patarines, and against many other infidels, and to pay great costs, we still do not want to desist from [fighting] the Bohemian heretics'.[40] The concurrence of the crusading enterprises was another problem that generated the need for a legitimisation of the chosen battlefront. The optimistic vision Sigismund expressed in his letter to the Electors was a delusion: no one could fight the Hussites and the Turks at the same time, and the king knew this best. Already on 17 January 1422, his diplomat Martín Talayero excused Sigismund before Pope Martin V from the accusation of insufficient involvement in the war against Hussites. Talayero pointed out instances when Sigismund had to leave the Hussite battlefront due to the Ottoman threat to Hungary. On other occasions, the king did not seize the opportunity of an intervention in Turkey and gave priority to suppressing the Hussite heresy.[41] In late 1431, the Hungarian bishops referenced the dual burden of the defence against the Hussites and the Turks to excuse themselves from personal presence at the Council of Basle.[42]

In practice, the conundrum of simultaneous wars against heretics and infidels was hardly resolvable. On the ideological level, it seems that the defence against the external enemies of Christendom was considered a greater priority than the anti-heretical war. The anti-Ottoman crusade remained the ultimate goal.

---

37 *RTA ÄR* 8: 347. See Sabine Wefers, *Das politische System Kaiser Sigmunds* (Stuttgart, 1989), pp. 111–26.
38 *MCG* 2: 96.
39 *RTA ÄR* 9, no. 463, p. 625; Joachim Schneider, 'Überregionale Integrationstendenzen im deutschen Niederadel: Zwei Briefzeitungen von 1427 und die Auseinandersetzungen der Hussitenzeit', in *Strukturen der Gesellschaft im Mittelalter: Interdisziplinäre Mediävistik in Würzburg*, ed. Dieter Rödel and Joachim Schneider (Wiesbaden, 1996), pp. 115–39 (here 132–39).
40 *RTA ÄR* 8, no. 312, p. 379.
41 Johannes Hollnsteiner, 'Ein neues Dokument zur Hussitengeschichte', in *Festschrift zu Ehren Emil von Ottenthals*, ed. Raimund von Klebelsberg (Innsbruck, 1925), pp. 66–78 (here 74 and 76).
42 *Sacrorum conciliorum nova et amplissima collectio* 30: 72–76.

Participation in the Hussite crusade rather than fighting the Turks might need justification. Upon entering the war against Bohemia, the Hungarian king Matthias Corvinus proclaimed on 8 April 1468: 'We think that this war is not less pious than that one we have been waging for such a long time against the Turks, the fiercest enemies of all faithful'.[43] The motif of multiple threats to Christendom was exploited for various political agendas. It could be used as an argument to invite princes to join the common battle, as when Talayero praised Vladislas II Jogaila for his fight against the pagan 'barbarians' and exhorted him to join the war against the Hussites because a concerted military effort would be more efficient.[44] The necessity of ending the Hussite crisis in order to face the Turks was beyond doubt. For some, this would legitimise the Hussite crusade which, consequently, needed to be as quick as possible. Others, as expressed by Cesarini in his welcome speech upon the arrival of the Hussite delegates to Basle on 10 January 1433, understood the simultaneous conflicts as mutual obstacles, and suggested a concord with the Hussites for the sake of those Christian brothers suffering from 'the Turks, Saracens, Tatars, and barbarians'.[45] Once again, concluding peace appeared to be a tactical move in preparing the ultimate war.

***

The need to legitimise the anti-Hussite crusade arose in two major areas. One was religious and moral, regarding whether it was admissible to fight physically against erring Christians; the other was diplomatic, regarding the justification of the crusade as the most appropriate option for dealing with heresy. Doubts about killing humans were relatively easy to overcome by reference to the danger posed by the Hussites to Christian society. Most justifications of the crusade were produced in response to politically-motivated disinterest. The stable set of arguments included the binding condemnations of Hussitism, the necessary prophylaxis against its spread, and the urgent need to protect the Church and society from the attacks of the heretics. Given the age, weight, and almost general acceptance of these arguments, it was negotiation rather than crusade which needed legitimacy. Indeed, more innovative reasoning, rooted in an alternative ecclesiological model, was presented by the partisans of settlement with the Hussites.[46]

In political manoeuvring, the traditional, somewhat rigid crusader argumentation had a flexible application: since the war for the faith provided legitimacy, it was claimed by various political players as their own exclusive duty and vocation.

---

43 *Scriptores rerum Silesiacarum*, ed. Gustav Adolf Stenzel et al., 17 vols (Breslau, 1835–1902), 9: no. 390, pp. 262–63.
44 Kadlec, 'Magister Martin Talayero', pp. 303–4.
45 *MCG* 2: 315. See Norman Housley, 'Ending and starting crusades at the council of Basel', *Crusades* 16 (2017), 115–45 (here 119–20).
46 One of the most important contributions to justify talks with the Hussites has been analysed by Olivier Marin, 'Pourquoi débattre avec les hussites: le tournant stratégique bâlois à la lumière du Tractatus de iustificatione vocationis Bohemorum (1432)', in *La coexistence confessionnelle en France et en Europe germanique et orientale*, ed. Catherine Maurer and Catherine Vincent (Lyon, 2015), pp. 107–29.

This duty became overwhelming when more theatres of holy war opened, and the choice of battlefield required justification. The question regarding the admissibility of war on Christians reappeared in a new context — rather than debating the war as such, its drain on the fight against the infidels was emphasised. Finding alternative means of dealing with the Bohemian heresy or schism could release resources for the fight against the Turks. In connection with both the Hussites and the Greeks, the issues of *unio* and *reductio*, rather than *exterminatio*, became cardinal. Too often, the anti-Hussite crusade proved weak in practice and sterile in theory. Venerable tradition turned out to be a burden when it came to innovating the rhetoric of legitimacy.

Index

Due to limited space and easier readability, instead of listing the various subordinate polities belonging to a crown we have decided to list only the dominant kingdom within a *corona regni*, thus 'king of Hungary' instead of 'king of Hungary and Croatia-Dalmatia', 'king of Aragon' instead of 'king of Aragon, Valencia, Sicily, Naples, Sardinia etc.', 'king of Castile' instead of 'king of Castile, Leon etc.' and so on. Note also that country names and demonyms are not separately indexed. Affiliations to religious orders are given as follows: OCarm = Carmelites; OCart = Carthusians; OCist = Cistercians; OFM = Franciscan Order; OFS = Secular Franciscan Order; OP = Dominican Order; OSA = Augustinian Order; OSB = Benedictine Order; OSBCel = Celestines; OT = Teutonic Order

Acontius of Viterbo (*fl.* early 13th cent.), papal legate, 240–41
Acre, Israel, 83
    Christian siege and conquest (1189–91), 315
    Mamluk siege and conquest (1291), 40, 51, 83
Adalia (mod. Antalya, Turkey)
    crusade (1361), 39, 177, 218
Adolf IV (1220–59), count of Berg, 143
Adriatic Sea, 179
Aegean Sea, 37
Ahmed (*c.* 1465–1513), Ottoman prince, 115–16
Akkerman, *see* Cetatea Albă
Aksakovo, Bulgaria, 234
al-Andalus, Andalusians, 96, 100–1, 109, 329
al-Kāmil Muḥammad al-Malik (*c.* 1176/77–1238), sultan of Egypt, 143
al-Nasir (1158–1225), Abbasid caliph, 318
al-Nāsir Muḥammad (1285–1341), Mamluk sultan, 82
Albania, Albanians, 78, 227, 229–31, 250

Albert (d. after 1317), mayor of Cracow, 283
Albert II the Magnanimous (1397–1439), Romano-German king, duke of Austria (as Albert V), king of Bohemia and of Hungary (as Albert I), 220
Albert III (1349–95), duke of Austria, 138
Albert of Brandenburg-Ansbach (1490–1568), OT, grand master, duke of Prussia, 44, 279, 334
Albert of Sarteano (1385–1450), OFM, 86–90
Alcácer Quibir (Mor. Ksar el-Kebir), Morocco
    crusade and battle (1578), 34, 51
Alcalá de Henares, Spain
    treaty (1308), 102
Aldona Anne of Lithuania (*c.* 1311/13–39), queen consort of Poland, 286
Alexander III the Great (356 BCE–323 BCE), king of Macedonia, 131
Alexander IV (*c.* 1199–1261), pope, 318

Alexander VI (1431–1503), pope, 71, 120, 262–63, 275
Alexander Karijotaitis (c. 1330–c. 1380), duke of Volodymyr-Volynskyi, of Lutsk and of Podolia, 159, 255, 304
Alexander of Hales (c. 1185–1245), theologian, 367
Summa theologica, 368
Alexander the Jagiellonian (1461–1506), grand duke of Lithuania, king of Poland, 168–69, 261–63
Alexander (aka Olelko) Vladimirovich (d. 1454), duke of Kapyl and Slutsk, 350
Alexandria, Egypt, 218
Alfonso III the Liberal (1265–91), king of Aragon, 97–98
Alfonso IV the Benign (1299–1336), king of Aragon, 103
Alfonso V the Magnanimous (1396–1458), king of Aragon, 106, 108, 222
Alfonso X the Wise (1221–84), king of Castile, of Leon and of Galicia, Romano-German anti-king, 34, 97, 100, 111
Alfonso XI the Avenger (1311–50), king of Castile, 102–3
Algeciras, Spain
crusade, Castilian siege and conquest (1342–44), 104
Algirdas (c. 1296/1304–1377), grand duke of Lithuania, 267–68, 289–90, 341
Almohads, dynasty, 318
Alonso de Cárdenas (c. 1423–93), grand master of the Order of Santiago, 105
Alps, mountain range, 77
Alsace, Alsatians, 134
Amadeus VI (aka 'the Green Count', 1334–83), count of Savoy, 177, 218
Amposta, Spain, 106, 108–9
Anatolia, Anatolians, 60, 107, 117, 174–75, 177–78, 181, 184, 196, 224, 230

Andrew II (c. 1176–1235), king of Hungary, 240, 242–43
Andrew of Castagno (1421–57), painter, 61
Adrew of Grumbach (d. 1500), OT, German land master, 276
Andrew of Petra (d. 1440), archbishop of Rhodes, theologian, 372
Andrew of Ratisbon (c. 1380–c. 1442/44), chronicler, 362
Dialogus, 367
Angevins (Capetian branch), dynasty, 34, 60, 82, 178, 199, 201, 255, 287, 303
Angyal, Dávid (1857–1943), historian, 41
Anna of Moscow (1393–1417), Byzantine empress consort, 165
Annals of Vienne, 182
Anselm of Meissen (c. 1210–78), bishop of Warmia, 129
Antequera, Spain
Castilian siege and conquest (1410), 104
Anthony of Fluvià (d. 1437), grand master of the Knights Hospitaller, 107
Antioch (mod. Antakya, Turkey), 83
Apollo, Graeco-Roman deity, 193
Apulia, Apulians, 189
Aquinas, Thomas (1225–74), OP, theologian, 364–65
Arabia, Arabs, 119, 153, 193–94, 332
Arad, Romania, 207
Aragon, Aragonese, 55–56, 82, 89, 95–111, 222, 258, 327, 334
Archer, Thomas Andrew (1853–1905), historian, 40, 48
Arnheim, The Netherlands, 143
Arnold, Udo (b. 1940), historian, 43
Arnold of Vilanova (c. 1238–1311), physician and religious reformer, 91
Arras, France
congress (1435), 329–30, 338

Artois, Artoisians, 329
Ascanians, dynasty, 284
Ascoli Satriano, Italy, 222
Aşıkpaşazade (aka Devish Ahmet Âşıkî, c. 1400–c. 1484), historiographer, 224
Asilah, Morocco
  crusade, siege, battle and Portuguese conquest (1471), 34
Atiya, Aziz Suryal (1898–1988), historian and Coptologist, 47–48
Atlantic Ocean, 34
Attila (*fl. c.* 406–53), king and chieftain of the Huns, 195
Austria, Austrians, 41, 70, 130, 138, 181, 220, 231
Avignon, France, 78, 284, 289, 295, 299, 302, 304, 306
Ayala Martínez, Carlos de (b. 1957), historian, 100, 103–4
Aydin, Turkey, 175

Babinger, Franz (1891–1967), historian and orientalist, 42
Bad Windsheim, Germany, 373
Bak, János M. (1929–2020), historian, 42
Bakócz, Tamás (1442–1521), archbishop of Esztergom, cardinal, 119
Baldassare da Santa Maria (*fl.* 15th cent.), OFM, custodian of the Holy Land, 89
Baldwin I (1060s–1118), count of Edessa, king of Jerusalem, 326
Balkan Mountains, mountain range, 234
Baltic Sea, 34, 43–44, 48, 99, 127, 129, 131, 134, 138, 145, 150, 177, 268, 289, 316, 318, 322, 325–27, 331, 335, 337
Banat, geographical and historical region, *see* Temesköz
Bárány, Attila (b. 1971), historian, 42, 60, 153, 174
Barbary pirates
  crusade (1390), *see* Mahdia Crusade

Baronas, Darius (b. 1973), historian, 59
Bârsa Land, geographical and historical region, 204, 208, 267, 316, 335
Bartholomew of Alverna, OFM, vicar of Bosnia (in off. 1367–1406), 312
Bartholomew of Camerino (*fl.* 1480s), papal legate, 167–68
Bartolus de Saxoferrato (1313–57), jurist, 367
Basil Karijotaitis, duke of Novgorodok and Podolia, 159
Basle, Switzerland
  council (1431–37), 55, 68–69, 77–80, 220, 222, 320, 328–29, 338, 365, 367, 369, 371–74
Battle of the Strait (1274–1350), 95, 100, 102–3
Bavaria, Bavarians, 133, 181, 190, 196, 372
Bayezid I the Thunderbolt (c. 1360–1403), Ottoman sultan, 181, 183, 189–90, 192–97, 199–201, 208
Bayezid II (1447–1512), Ottoman sultan, 114–16, 274
Baza, Spain
  Castilian siege and conquest (1489), 105
Bażyński, Jan, *see* John of Baysen
Bażyński, Mikołaj, *see* Nicholas of Baysen
Bażyński, Ścibor, *see* Stibor of Baysen
Beauvoir, Yonne, France, 331
Beheim, Michael (1416–c. 1474/78), poet and singer, 226, 231–32, 234
Beirut, Lebanon, 51
Béla IV (1206–70), king of Hungary, 180, 243–45
Belardi Arrigoni, Giacomo (d. 1435), OP, bishop of Lodi, of Trieste and of Urbino, theologian, 324
Belastena, Serbia, 206
Bełch, Stanisław F. (1904–89), historian, Catholic priest, 320

380 INDEX

Belgrade, Serbia, 200, 207, 212–13, 224, 259
  Ottoman siege (1440), 203
  Ottoman siege (1456), 70, 249
  Ottoman siege and conquest (1521), 122
Benedict XII (1285–1342), pope, 103, 286–87, 295, 298
Beneš of Cvilín (d. 1265), Bohemian nobleman, 130
Berbers, 318
Berka of Dubá, Hynek (c. 1297–1348), Bohemian nobleman, 135
Berlin, Germany, 43
Bernard (c. 1291–1326), duke of Świdnica, 132–33
Bernard of Cimburk (d. after 1351), Bohemian nobleman, 133–34
Bernard of Clairvaux (1090–1153), St, OCist, theologian
  De consideratione, 367
  De laude novae militia, 364
Bernard of Breydenbach (c. 1440–97), jurist, traveller
  Perenigratio in Terram Sanctam, 93
Bernardino Amico (*fl.* late sixteenth and early seventeenth centuries), OFM, theologian, 93
Belisarius (c. 500–65), military commander, 210
Bessarion (1403–72), cardinal, theologian and humanist, 79
  Epistolae et Orationes contra Turcos, 68
Bethlehem, Palestine, 83, 85–87
Beumann, Helmut (1912–95), historian, 43
Bihać, Bosnia and Herzegovina, 208
Bihar, geographical and historical region, 213
Bilhorod-Dnistrovskyi, *see* Cetatea Albă
Bingen, Germany, 372–73
Birago, Lampugnino (d. 1472), humanist, 72

Biskup, Marian (1922–2012), historian, 45
Black Sea, 162, 166, 168, 179, 231, 257 270, 313
Blumenau, Laurentius (c. 1415–84), jurist, historiographer, 332
Bobovac, Bosnia and Herzegovina, 208
Bobrzycki, Leszek (d. 1444), Polish knight, 234
Bočac, Bosnia and Herzegovina, 203, 208
Boček of Jaroslovice and Zbraslav (d. 1255), castellan of Znaim, 130
Bogislas V the Great (c. 1317/18–74), duke of Pomerania-Stolp, 289
Bogomilism, Bogomils, 44, 64
Bohemia, Bohemians, 58–59, 115, 121–22, 127–39, 151, 165, 170, 181, 208, 220–21, 275, 283–84, 287, 289, 295, 299, 301, 303, 306, 328, 334, 361–75
Bonet Donato, Mariá (b. 1964), historian, 55–56
Bonfini, Antonio (1427–1502), humanist, historiographer and poet, 225–26, 228, 230
Boniface IX (c. 1350–1404), pope, 162, 200, 246, 257, 263–64, 340, 344
Boockmann, Hartmut (1934–98), historian, 43, 74
Borbás, Benjámin (b. 1992), historian, 58–59
Boris Karijotaitis (d. 1386/1388), duke of Podolia, 159
Boreš of Rýzmburk (1210/15–77), Bohemian nobleman, 130
Bosna, river, 208
Bosnia, Bosnians, 61, 70, 122, 179, 182, 187, 201–3, 208–9, 211–13, 215–17, 224–25, 227, 229, 231, 237–52, 291, 373
Bracciolini, Gian Francesco Poggio (1380–1459), humanist, historian and translator
  Historiae de varietate fortunae, 187

Vita di messer Filippo Scolari, 207
Bran, Romania, *see* Törcsvár
Branda da Castiglione (1350–1443), cardinal, diplomat and humanist, 370
Brandenburg, Brandenburgians, 43–44, 275, 284, 334
Brandenburg (Frisches Haff) (mod. Ushakovo, Russia), 157, 272–73
Brandon, Jean (d. 1428), OCist, chronicler, 194
Bratislava, Slovakia, *see* Pressburg
Brauner, Alois, historian, 41
Brčko, Bosnia and Herzegovina, 202
Breslau, *see* Wrocław, Poland
Brieg, *see* Brzeg, Poland
Brodnica, Poland, *see* Strasburg (Drewenz), 150
Brown, Walter (*fl.* 1370s), salesman, 152
Bruno of Schauenburg (*c.* 1205–81), bishop of Olomouc, 128–30
Brzeg (Ger. Brieg), Poland, 258
Bucharest, Romania, 116
Buda (western part of mod. Budapest, Hungary), 72, 178–79, 181–82, 185, 223, 225
Bulgaria, Bulgarians, 113, 173, 177, 179, 181–83, 203, 210, 219–20, 225–36
Buonaccorsi, Filippo 'Callimachus' (1437–96), humanist, diplomat and writer, 276
   Historia de rege Vladislao, 225–27, 232–34
Buondelmonti, Cristoforo (*c.* 1385–*c.* 1430), traveller, cartograph, 165
Burgundy, Burgundians, 85–87, 89, 91, 149, 151, 180–83, 190–91, 193, 195, 222, 230, 249, 258, 260, 329–30, 346
Burley, Walter (*c.* 1275–1344/45), philosopher, 367
Bychowiec Chronicle (aka *Lithuanian Chronicle*), 261, 356
Byzantine Empire, Byzantines, 37, 39, 41, 113, 130, 134–36, 141, 166, 170, 176, 180, 182, 219–20, 222, 229–30, 234, 242

Caffa (mod. Feodosia, Ukraine [de jure] / Russia [de facto]), 270
Calais, France
   siege (1346/47), 151
Calderini, Giovanni (*c.* 1300–65), lawyer and canonist, 364
Callixtus III (1378–1458), pope, 88–89, 167, 249–50, 356
Calvet, Gerárd, OFM, custodian of the Holy Land, 86, 167, 249–50
Campisio, Giovanni (*fl.* 1444), humanist, 228
Çandarlı Halil Pasha, the younger (d. 1453), Ottoman grand vizier, 226–27
Capgrave, John (1393–1464), OSA, historiographer and scholastic theologian, 323
Capuchins, 84
Carninaus, archbishop of Kalocsa (in off. 1421–22), 207
Carpathians, mountain range, 287, 313
Carvajal, Juan (*c.* 1400–69), cardinal, papal legate, 78, 249
Casimir II (1401/3–1442), duke of Płock, Rawa, Sochaczew, Gostynin, Płońsk, Wizna and Belz, 356
Casimir III the Great (1310–70), king of Poland, 136, 268, 286–90, 292–93, 295, 297–312, 319
Casimir IV Andrew the Jagiellonian (1427–92), king of Poland, grand duke of Lithuania (as Casimir I Andrew), 167–68, 260–61, 265, 270, 273, 275, 279, 332
Casimir the Jagiellonian (1458–84), St, Polono-Lithuanian prince, 168
Castile, Castilians, 34, 55–56, 89, 95–111, 168, 262, 329–30
Catalonia, Catalans, 101, 105–8, 110
Catharism, Cathars, 64, 239

Cătlăbuga, lake
  battle (1485), 274
Caucasus, mountain range, 185
Čepek, Jan (*fl.* 1440s), Hussite
  mercenary leader, 224
Cesarini, Giuliano, the elder (1398–
  1444), cardinal, 72, 77–78, 220–21,
  223–25, 227, 229–30, 233, 235–36,
  370, 373–74
Cetatea Albă (mod. Bilhorod-
  Dnistrovskyi, Ukraine; Turk
  Akkerman), 168, 262, 270, 274
Ceuta (Berb. Sebta, Arab. Sabtah), Spain,
  101, 333
  crusade, siege, battle and Portuguese
  conquest (1415), 34, 333
Chalkokondyles, Laonikos (*c.* 1430–70),
  historiographer, 170
Charles I Robert (1288–1342), king of
  Hungary, 34, 60, 246
Charles IV (1316–78), Holy Roman
  emperor, king of Bohemia, 133, 135–
  36, 138, 268, 289, 291–92, 304
Charles V (1500–58), Holy Roman
  emperor, king of Spain (as Charles I),
  108–9, 334
Charles VI the Beloved (aka 'the Mad',
  1368–1422), king of France, 86, 149,
  188–89, 191
Charles VII the Victorious (1403–61),
  king of France, 331
Chełm, Poland, *see* Kholm
Chełmno, Poland, 167
Chełmno Land, 129
Chernihiv, Ukraine, 164
Chilia (mod. Kiliya, Ukraine; Turk.
  Kilya), 119, 168, 262, 270, 274
Christburg (mod. Dzierzgoń, Poland),
  130
Chronicle of Fredegar, 187
Chronicon Dubnicense, 288
Chronique des quatre premiers Valois, 193–
  94

Cimburks, Bohemian noble family, 133–
  34, 137
Ciołek, Erazm (1474–1522), bishop of
  Płock, diplomat, royal secretary, 262
Ciudad Rodrigo, Spain, 324–25
Clamecy, Nièvre, France, 86
Clarey, Pierre (*fl.* 15th cent.), OFM, 87
Clausewitz, Carl von (1780–1831),
  general and military theorist, 64
Clement IV (*c.* 1190–1268), pope, 131,
  254
Clement V (*c.* 1264–1314), pope, 99, 101
Clement VI (1291–1352), pope, 84, 175,
  287, 298, 303
Clement VII (1478–1534), pope, 107
Clermont (mod. Clermont-Ferrand,
  France)
  council (1095), 40, 121
Cluny, France, 324
Cold War (1947–91), 39
Coloman (1208–41), prince (king from
  1215/16) of Galicia, duke of
  Slavonia, 243–44
Colombe, Jean (*c.* 1430–93), painter and
  manuscript illuminator, 186
Condulmer, Francesco (*c.* 1390–1453),
  cardinal, 229
Conrad I (1187/88–1247), duke of
  Masovia and of Cracow, 129
Conrad III the Red (1448–1503), duke
  of Czersk and of Warsaw, 276
Conrad of Erlichshausen (*c.* 1390/95–
  1449), OT, grand master, 222
Conrad of Jungingen (*c.* 1355/60–1407),
  OT, grand master, 145, 256, 343,
  346–47, 359
Constance, Germany
  council (1414–18), 44, 55, 68, 73–
  78, 80, 150, 164–65, 167, 268,
  320–25, 327–30, 337–38, 362,
  370–71
Constantine II (*c.* 1447–1505), king of
  Georgia, king of Kartli, 168, 261

Constantine Karijotaitis (1335–89), duke of Podolia, 159
Constantinople (mod. Istanbul, Turkey), 78, 114, 116–19, 121–23, 165–67, 170, 176, 187, 219, 222, 230–31, 269, 306, 343, 347
  Ottoman siege (1422), 166
  Ottoman siege and conquest (1453), 78, 123, 187, 269
Cotbus of Sommerfeld, Johannes (*fl.* 15th cent.), OSBCel, theologian
  Tractatus de cruce signatis, 365–67
Covaci, Valentina, historian, 92
Cracow, Poland, 73, 75, 136, 167, 222, 279, 283, 285–87, 306, 321, 323, 333, 344, 358
  assembly (1364), 292, 304
Craiovești, dynasty, 116
Crimean Khanate, Crimean Tatars, 41, 116, 169, 270
Croatia, Croats, 36, 69–70, 182, 213, 222, 236, 246
crusades
  against schismatics, 43
  against the Hussites, 34, 44, 55, 63–64, 74, 77, 151, 153, 224, 231, 247, 259, 327–29, 357, 361–75
  against the Iberian Muslims, 95–111
  against the Mongols and Tatars, 36, 41, 52, 54, 61, 63, 75, 115, 147, 159, 161–62, 164–69, 180, 193, 256–57, 259–65, 268, 270, 275, 277, 279, 285–90, 292, 295, 299–304, 306–7, 318–21, 329–31, 334, 337, 343–44, 347–49, 351–52, 354, 356–59, 374
  against the Ottomans, 36–37, 42, 45, 51, 59–60, 113–23, 168, 173–97, 199–236, 247–52, 338, 344
  against the Wends, 43
  German Crusade (1197), 315
  into Lithuania, 43, 99, 127–39, 141–70, 253–56, 285–93, 319
  into Livonia, 43, 156–58
  into Pomerania, 43, 319
  into Prussia, 76, 99, 127–39, 319
  into the Aegean Sea, 37, 39
  into Bosnia, 237–46
  into the Eastern Mediterranean and North Africa, 81–93
  First Crusade (1096–99), 40
  Second Crusade (1147–49), 367
  Third Crusade (1189–92), 315
  Fifth Crusade (1217–21), 141–43
  Eighth Crusade (1270), 51
  Lord Edward's Crusade (1271–72), 51
Csák, Ugrin (*c.* 1190–1241), archbishop of Kalocsa, 242, 244
Csanád, geographical and historical region, 207, 213
Csongrád, Hungary, 207
Cuyavia, Cuyavians, 283, 292
Cyprian (*c.* 1330–1406), St, metropolitan of Kiev and all Rus, 343, 347, 349
Cyprus, Cypriots, 37, 83, 86, 175, 177, 218, 292, 304, 322, 330, 350
Cyriacus of Ancona (1391–1452), humanist and antiquarian, 222
Czechia, Czechs, 51, 58, 127–39, 220, 222, 224, 236, 328, 361–75
Czelej, Mścigniew (*c.* 1298–1341), voivode of Cracow, 286

Da Lezze, Donado (1459–1526), humanist historiographer, 195
Dąbrowski, Jan (1890–1965), historian, 41, 219
Đakovo, Croatia, 245
Dalmatia, Dalmatians, 201, 213, 240, 250
Damietta, Egypt
  crusade (1218–21), 143
Dan I (*c.* 1354–86), voivode of Wallachia, 204
Dan II the Brave (d. 1432), voivode of Wallachia, 204

Daniel of Kunheim (c. 1430–1507), Lotharingo-Prussian nobleman, Teutonic land judge, 272–73
Danube, river, 61, 69, 113, 117, 119, 177, 179, 181–84, 194, 199, 203, 207, 210, 212, 214, 216, 223, 225–26, 229, 232, 235, 270–71
Danutė Anna (c. 1358–1424), duchess consort of Warsaw, 157
Daugava, see Western Dvina
Dávid, Géza (b. 1949), historian, 42
Debrc, Serbia, 206
Delfino, Giacomo (fl. 15th cent.), OFM, custodian of the Holy Land, 86
Della Porta, Ardicino, the elder (1370/80–1434), cardinal, jurist, 326–27, 337
Deltuva, Lithuania, 168
Denmark, Danes, 45, 322, 350
Deutschbrod (mod. Havlíčkův Brod, Czechia), 328
Dias de Escobar (aka Díaz, Didaci etc.), André, bishop of Ciudad Rodrigo (c. 1366/67–c. 1448), OSB, bishop of Ciudad Rodrigo, of Ajaccio and of Megara, theologian, 73, 324–26, 335, 337
Dederick of Legendorf (c. 1360–c. 1425), mayor of Elbing, 154
Diceret aliquis: Videtur, quod cristianis non licet occidere Turcos, 367
Dieren, The Netherlands, 143
Dijon, France, 88–89
Długosz, Jan (1415–80), historiographer
  Annales seu cronicae incliti regni Poloniae, 221–22, 228, 232–33, 356
Dmitry Donskoy (1350–89), prince of Moscow, grand prince of Vladimir, 354–55
Dmytro Dedko (d. c. 1349), voivode of Peremyshl, *de facto* ruler of Galicia, 298, 300–2

Dnieper, river, 162
Dobrogost of Nowy Dwór (1355–1401/2), bishop of Poznań, archbishop of Gniezno, 291
Dombó (mod. Dubovac, Serbia), 207
Dragoman, Bulgaria, 227
Drankó (mod. Drencova, Romania), 207
Drina, river, 209
Dubica, Bosnia and Herzegovina, and Croatia, 201
Dubočac, Bosnia and Herzegovina, 202, 208
Dubrovnik, Croatia, see Ragusa
Dubysa, river, 160
Duklja, Dukljanians, 238
Dünaburg (mod. Daugavpils, Latvia), 257
Đurađ Branković (1377–1456), despot of Serbia, 200, 221, 223, 225–26, 229, 231–32, 236
Dzierzgoń, Poland, see Christburg

Edigu (1352–1419), White Horde emir, 349, 352–53
Edirne, Turkey, 182, 224, 229, 231, 234
Edward I Longshanks (1239–1307), king of England, duke of Aquitaine, 51, 144
Edward III (1312–77), king of England, 145
Edward IV (1442–83), king of England, 145
Egerberk, Czechia, 133–34
Egypt, Egyptians, 47, 88, 90, 118–19, 143, 177
Ekdahl, Sven (b. 1935), historian, 43
Elbing (mod. Elbląg, Poland), 130
Elizabeth of Luxemburg (1409–42), Romano-German queen consort, queen consort of Hungary and of Bohemia, 221–22

INDEX 385

Elizabeth of Bosnia (c. 1339–87), queen consort of Hungary and of Poland, regent of Hungary, 291
Elizabeth of Poland (c. 1326–61), duchess consort of Pomerania-Stolp, 289
Emeric (1174–1204), king of Hungary, 239
England, English, 41, 45, 47, 49–51, 58–59, 90, 121–22, 135, 141–54, 176, 178, 180–81, 193, 222, 236, 319, 326, 329
Erfurt, Germany, 364
Eric of Pomerania (c. 1382–1459), king of Denmark (as Eric VII), of Norway (as Eric III) and of Sweden (as Eric XIII), duke of Pomerania (as Eric I), 256, 350
Eric (aka Henry) of Winsen (d. 1391), bishop of Przemyśl, 312
Erpingham, Thomas (c. 1357–1428), English soldier, 142
Estonia, Estonians, 45, 48
Esturmy, William (d. 1427), English nobleman, knight of the shire, 142
Esztergom, Hungary, 119, 206–7, 213, 240, 245
Ethiopia, Ethiopians, 88
Euboea, island, see Negroponte
Eugene IV (1383–1447), pope, 69, 77–78, 86–90, 177, 219–23, 231, 329, 371–72
Evangelisti, Paolo, historian, 84–85
Evesham, UK
  battle (1265), 144
Exeter, UK, 143

Falkenberg, Johannes (c. 1364–c. 1429), OP, 74–76, 267, 320, 322–25
Liber de doctrina, 320
Satira, 76, 320
Farine, Charles, see René de Mont-Louis
Favreau-Lilie, Marie-Luise, historian, 43

Ferdinand I (aka Ferrante, 1424–94), king of Naples, 108
Ferdinand I (1503–64), Holy Roman emperor, king of Bohemia and of Hungary, archduke of Austria, 335
Ferdinand I of Antequera (aka 'the Just', 1380–1416), king of Aragon, 104, 258–59
Ferdinand II the Catholic (1452–1516), king of Aragon and of Castile (*jure uxoris* as Ferdinand V), 89, 95, 105–9, 334
Ferdinand IV (1285–1312), king of Castile, 99
Ferenc, Salamon (1825–92), historian, 42
Fernández de Heredia, Juan (c. 1310–96), grand master of the Knights Hospitaller, 98–99, 107
Crónica de los conqueridores, 99
Ferrante of Naples, see Ferdinand I, king of Naples
Ferrara, Italy
  council (1438–45), 77, 219, 320
Fichet, Guillaume (1433–c. 1480), theologian and humanist, 68
Fidentius of Padua (d. after 1291), OFM, 55, 81, 93
Filipović, Emir O. (b. 1984), historian, 61, 70
Filippo Maria Visconti (1392–1447), duke of Milan, 233
Flanders, Flemings, 165, 181, 321, 337
Florence, Italy, 60–61, 70, 207, 210
  council (1445–49), 77, 219–20, 320
Florentin, Bulgaria, 232
Fodor, Pál (b. 1955), historian, 42
Forstreuter, Kurt (1897–1979), historian, 43
France, French, 39, 41, 45, 47, 51, 76, 86, 97, 109, 121–22, 135–36, 148–51, 165, 174, 176–78, 180–83, 185, 188–91, 193–94, 196–97, 222–23, 236,

318–19, 321, 324, 326, 329, 331, 333, 337
Francesco I Sforza (1401–66), duke of Milan, 89
Francesco de Comitibus Aquae Vivae (*fl.* early 15th cent.), 170, 259
Frankfurt (Main), Germany, 68–69, 331
Reichstag (1454), 68
Frederick II (1194–1250), Holy Roman emperor, king of Sicily (as Frederick I), 143
Frederick III (1415–93), Holy Roman emperor, archduke of Austria (as Frederick V), 72, 221
Frederick V the Elder (1460–1536), margrave of Brandenburg-Ansbach and of Brandenburg-Kulmbach, 275
Frederick of Flersheim, the elder (*c.* 1396–1473), German knight and adventurer, 258, 356
Frederick of Saxony (1473–1510), OT, grand master, 279, 334
Frederick the Fair (*c.* 1289–1330), Romano-German anti-king (1325–30 co-king), duke of Austria and of Styria, 133
Frick of Chyš and Egerberk (*fl.* 1317–27), Bohemian nobleman, 134
Froissart, Jean (*c.* 1337–*c.* 1405), historiographer, poet
Chroniques, 188–89, 192, 194, 196
Fruzhin (*c.* 1380–*c.* 1460), Bulgarian prince, 235

Galicia, Galicians (Eastern Europe), 63, 159, 286–87, 289, 291, 296, 300, 304–5, 311
Galilee, Galileans, 67
Gallipoli, peninsula, 122
crusade (1366), 39, 177
Galvano da Levanto (*fl. c.* 1300), OFM, 55, 93
Gandolfo of Sicily, OFM, custodian of the Holy Land, 86, 88

Gaposchkin, M. Cecilia (b. 1970), 92
Garai, László (*c.* 1410–59), palatine of Hungary, ban of Mačva, 222
Garai, Miklós (*c.* 1367–1433), palatine of Hungary, ban of Mačva, 150
Gascony, Gascons, 144
Gay, Jules (1867–1935), historian, 47
Gediminas (*c.* 1275 – 1341), grand duke of Lithuania, 286, 290
Gediminids, dynasty, 59, 255, 286, 290, 340, 342, 345, 355
royal branch, *see* Jagiellons
Genghisids, dynasty, 353
Genoa, Genoese, 37, 39, 175–76, 222, 230–31, 234
George II Boleslas (d. 1340), prince of Galicia-Volhynia, 299–300, 304
George Karijotaitis (after 1330–1374/75), duke of Podolia, 159
George of Lydda (d. 303), St, 102, 136–37
George the Bearded (1471–1539), duke of Saxony, 279
Germany, Germans, 41, 43–45, 48, 68–70, 72, 75, 79–80, 121–22, 131–33, 136, 142, 151, 157, 163, 166, 170, 174, 181, 183, 185, 190, 193–95, 220–21, 224, 231, 238, 243, 253–60, 265, 271, 275–76, 279, 283–85, 289, 300, 315, 318–21, 323–25, 335, 341–49, 351–56, 363, 365, 371–73
Gerson, Jean (1363–1329), theologian and poet, 68, 367
Gerward of Ostrów (d. 1323), bishop of Włocławek, 284
Gibbons, Herbert Adams (1880–1934), journalist and historian, 195
Gibraltar, UK, 95, 100, 102–4, 109–10
Gilbert of Alneto (*fl.* 1444), Burgundian knight, 151
Gilbert of Lannoy (1386–1462), traveller and diplomat, 165, 321, 337

Gilbert of Tournai (c. 1200–84), OFM, 55, 93
Giles of Rome (c. 1243–1316), OSA, archbishop of Bourges, philosopher and theologian, 367
Giovio, Paolo (1483–1552), physician and historiographer, 195
Giurgiu, Romania, 203, 236
Glarentza, Greece, 83
Gleb Svyatoslavich (c. 1355–99), grand prince of Smolensk, 342
Gniezno, Poland, 167, 271, 285, 301
Godfrey of Bouillon (1060–1100), duke of Lower Lotharingia, advocate of the Holy Sepulchre, 88, 326
Golden Horde, 41, 159, 161, 164–67, 257, 286–91, 296, 300, 304–5, 321–22, 330, 340, 343–45, 347, 351–53, 355
Goll, Jaroslav (1846–1929), historian, 127
Golub War (1422), 328
Golubac, Serbia, 199–200
siege (1428), 199, 211, 214, 356
Gospel of Luke, 368
Goštautas, Albertas (c. 1480–1539), voivode of Vilnius, grand chancellor of Lithuania, 264
Goštautas, Martynas (c. 1430–83), grand marshal of Lithuania, voivode of Novgorodok, voivode of Kiev, voivode of Trakai, 260
Gotland, island, 152
Granada, Spain, 95, 97–105
crusade (aka Fourth Granada War, 1482–92), Castilian siege and conquest (1491–92), 34, 51, 105, 109–10, 333
Great Schism (aka East-West Schism of 1054), 39
Great War (1409–11), 44, 141–42, 146–49, 153, 164, 258, 313, 321, 335, 337, 339, 347

Great Western Schism (1378–1417), 178, 188, 324, 327
Great Yarmouth, UK, 152
Greater Poland, Greater Poles, 284, 313
Greece, Greeks, 55, 77–79, 83, 113, 118, 159, 165–66, 187, 233, 306, 372, 375
Gregory IX (c. 1167/70–1241), pope, 243, 291
Gregory X (c. 1210–1276), pope, 99
Gregory XI (1330–78), pope, 159, 178, 255
Gregory XII (c. 1327–1417), pope, 154, 209, 264, 346, 359
Grigore, Mihai D. (b. 1975), historian, 56, 354
Grunwald, Poland
battle (1410), *see* Tannenberg
Guillaume de Machaut (c. 1300–77), composer and poet
Le confort d'ami, 135
Gunter of Hohenstein, OT, commander of Brandenburg (mod. Uskakovo, Russia), 157
Guy II of Châtillon (d. 1397), count of Blois and of Soissons, 189
Győr, Hungary, 221

Habart of Žerotín-Adlar (*fl.* early 14th cent.), Bohemian nobleman, 133
Habsburgs, dynasty, 72, 133, 220–21, 335
Hagen, Johannes (1415–76), OCart, theologian, 363–64
Hainaut, Hainautiens, 136
Halecki, Oskar (1891–1973), historian, 42, 219, 310
Halmás (mod. Almaș, Romania), 213
Halych, Ukraine, 291, 306–7, 311
Hamidids, dynasty, 177
Hammer-Purgstall, Joseph von (1774–1856), historian and orientalist, 41–42
Hanseatic League, 59, 145–46, 148–50, 152, 348

Haram (mod. Nova Palanka, Serbia), 206
Harder, Thomas, preacher, 363–64, 366
Hartleb of Deblín and Dubno (d. 1294), Moravian nobleman, 130
Hátszeg (mod. Haţeg, Romania), 204
Havlíčkův Brod, Czechia, *see* Deutschbrod
Házmburks, Bohemian noble family, 137
Hedwig of Anjou (1373/74–99), queen of Poland, 309–12
Heidelberg, Germany, 365–66
Heidenkampf, Heidenmission, 43, 193, 253–57, 259, 261, 263, 265, 316, 339, 343–44, 346, 352–53, 357
Helmrath, Johannes (b. 1953), historian, 80
Henrique de Coimbra (c. 1465–1532), OFM, bishop of Ceuta, 91
Henry I of Hradec (d. 1237), Bohemian nobleman, 130
Henry I of Lipa (c. 1275–1329), supreme marshal of Bohemia, 134
Henry II (1133–89), king of England, 144
Henry II of Lichtenburk (d. after 1356), Bohemian nobleman, 133, 135
Henry II the Iron of Lipa (c. 1297–1336), supreme marshal of Bohemia, 135
Henry III (1207–72), king of England, 141–44
Henry IV (c. 1367–1413), king of England, earl of Derby, 138, 145–49
Henry IV the Impotent (1425–74), king of Castile
crusade (1455), 105
Henry V (1386–1422), king of England, 149, 151
Henry VI (1165–97), Holy Roman emperor, king of Sicily, 315
Henry VI (1421–71), king of England, 151
Henry VIII (1491–1547), king of England, 153

Henry Beaufort (c. 1375–1447), bishop of Lincoln and of Winchester, cardinal, 151
Henry 'Hostiensis' of Segusio (c. 1200–71), canonist, 73, 365
Henry of Plauen, the elder (1370–1429), OT, grand master, 147–48, 164, 322, 352–53
Henry Reuss of Plauen (1400–70), OT, grand master, 146
Herman (*fl.* 1338), OT, commander of Jindřichův Hradec, 138
Herman of Miličín, Bohemian nobleman, 134
Herman of Salza (c. 1162–1239), OT, grand master, 141, 143
Herman of Wartberge (c. 1330–80), OT, chronicler
Chronicon Livoniae, 267–68
Hertzberg, Gustav Friedrich (1826–1907), historian, 41–42
Hobbins, Daniel (b. 1966), historian, 68
Hohenstaufens, dynasty, 289, 315, 335
Holland, Hollanders, 136, 258, 346
Holy Land, 33, 41, 51–52, 55, 81–93, 97–99, 101, 105–6, 109, 131, 134, 163, 182, 189, 243, 267, 292, 295, 303, 314–16, 319, 325–27, 330, 334, 337, 357, 359, 366–67
Holy Roman Empire, 41, 69, 121, 135, 138, 143, 221, 231, 236, 256, 263, 269, 289, 315, 321, 323–24, 335, 371, 373
Holy See, *see individual popes*
Homer (c. 8th cent. BCE), poet, 187
Honorius III (c. 1150–1227), pope, 240, 242
Horváth, Malm, diplomat, 118
Horváth, Mihály (1809–78), historian and theologian, 42
Hospitallers, 48, 78, 95–98, 101–10, 122, 144, 168, 175–76, 315, 326, 335

Housley, Norman (b. 1952), historian, 50, 54–55, 156
Hrvoje Vukčić Hrvatinić (c. 1350–1416), grand voivode of Bosnia, 201–2, 208–9
Hull, UK, *see* Kingston upon Hull
Humbert II de la Tour-du-Pin (1312–55), dauphin of Vienne, 176
Hundred Years' War (1337–1453), 150–51, 153, 188, 222, 330
Hungary, Hungarians, 34, 36, 41–43, 56, 60–62, 69–70, 72, 74, 78–79, 88, 114–19, 121–23, 136, 147, 150–51, 153, 159, 165, 178–83, 189, 199–226, 233, 235–36, 238–47, 250–51, 255, 259–60, 262–64, 268–69, 272, 275, 287–88, 291, 295–96, 299, 301–3, 309, 311, 320, 334, 351, 353, 357, 361, 372–74
Hunger War (1414), 352
Hus, Jan (c. 1370–1415), theologian, 361
Hussitism, Hussites, 34, 44, 55, 63–64, 74, 77, 151, 153, 224, 231, 247, 259, 327–29, 357, 361–75

Ibrahim II (d. 1464), bey of Karaman, 223–24, 229
Idík of Švábenice (before 1232–68), Moravian nobleman, 130
Ilyéd (mod. Ilidia, Romania), 213
Imber, Colin (b. 1945), historian, 220
India, Indians, 88
Innocent III (1161–1216), pope, 238
Innocent IV (c. 1195–1254), pope, 129, 245, 254, 288, 316
Innocent VI (1282–1362), pope, 176, 298, 303
Innocent VIII (1432–92), pope, 120, 271
Insterburg (mod. Chernyakhovsk, Russia), 136
Iorga, Nicolae (1871–1940), 47
 Notes et extraits pour server à l'histoire des croisades au XVe siècle, 46

Isaac II Angelos (1156–1204), Byzantine emperor, 242
Isabella I the Catholic (1451–1504), queen of Castile, queen consort of Aragon, 89–90, 95, 105, 108, 168, 262
Isabella of England (1214–41), Holy Roman empress consort, queen consort of Sicily, 143
Islam, Muslims, 33, 36, 60, 84, 95–103, 106, 109–10, 123, 164, 176–77, 182, 184–85, 193–96, 224, 227, 234, 292, 295, 316, 318, 320, 325, 327, 329–30, 333–34, 337, 363, 365, 371
Isvalies, Pietro (d. 1511), archbishop of Reggio Calabria, cardinal and papal legate, 71–72
Italy, Italians, 34, 48, 69–70, 78, 80, 83, 121–22, 128, 165, 187–88, 194, 225, 250, 274, 288, 319, 326–27, 333
Ivan III the Great (1440–1505), grand prince of Moscow, 168–69
Ivan Mikhaylovich (1357–1425), prince of Mikulin and Tver, grand prince of Tver, 347
Ivan Shishman (c. 1350–95), tsar of Bulgaria-Tarnovo, 232, 235
Ivan Sratsimir (1324–97), tsar of Bulgaria-Vidin, 183, 232
Ivan Štafilić (Ital. Giovanni Stafileo, 1472–1528), bishop of Šibenik, 333
Izyaslav, Ukraine, 168

Jacques de Helly (*fl.* 1390s), French nobleman, 197
Jaffa (southern part of mod. Tel Aviv, Israel), 83
Jagiellons, dynasty (royal branch of the Gediminids), 60, 62, 115–19, 121, 147, 159, 161, 163–68, 169, 211, 220–26, 228–31, 234–36, 260–61, 263, 265, 268, 270, 273, 275, 309–10,

313, 319–21, 323, 329–30, 333–34, 337, 369–70, 374
Jähnig, Bernhart (b. 1941), historian, 43
Jajce, Bosnia and Herzegovina, 203
Jakub Świnka (d. 1314), archbishop of Gniezno, 285
Jalal al-Din (1380–1412), Golden Horde khan, 321
James I (1208–76), king of Aragon, 97
James II (1267–1327), king of Aragon, 99, 101, 105, 108, 111
Jan Jiskra of Brandýs (c. 1400–69/70), mercenary leader, 222
Jan Lutkowic z Brzezia (c. 1405–71), bishop of Cuyavia-Pomerelia, bishop of Cracow, deputy crown chancellor of Poland, 167
Jan Muskata (c. 1250–1320), bishop of Cracow, 285
Jan of Klingenberg (c. 1290–1345), Czech nobleman, 135
Jan of Lipá (fl. first half of the 14th cent.), Boehmian nobleman, 135
Jan Pakosławic of Strożyska (d. c. 1374), diplomat, 288, 290, 304–5
Jan Volek (d. 1351), bishop of Olomouc, 135
Janiš, Dalibor (b. 1973), historian, 56–57
Janusz I the Old (c. 1346–1429), duke of Warsaw, 157
Jaros, Sven (b. 1986), historian, 63
Jaroš of Schlieben, Lusatian nobleman, 130
Jaroslav of Žerotín-Adlar (fl. early 14th cent.), Bohemian nobleman, 133
Jastrzębiec, Wojciech (c. 1362–1436), bishop of Poznań, bishop of Cracow, archbishop of Gniezno, primate and grand crown chancellor of Poland, 344
Jauer (mod. Jawor, Poland), 365
Jean II Le Maingre (aka Boucicaut, 1366–1421), marshal of France, 174, 191

Jean de Lastic (1371–1454), grand master of the Knights Hospitaller, 106
Jean de Vincelles (d. 1439), OCist, abbot of Cluny, 324
Jefferson, John, historian, 220
Jenec of Deblín (d. 1287), Moravian nobleman, 130
Jerusalem, Israel and Palestine, 33–34, 40, 55, 60, 81–92, 95, 101, 114, 120, 123, 170, 218, 259, 326
Ješek of Boskovice (d. 1362), supreme land chamberlain of Moravia, 135
Ješek II of Michalovice (d. 1354), Bohemian nobleman, 135
Jesus of Nazareth (c. 6/4 BCE–30/33 CE), prophet, preacher, religious leader, 33, 188, 242, 250, 362, 364
Jiménez de Cisneros, Francisco (1436–1517), OFM, cardinal, archbishop of Toledo, primate of Spain, regent-governor of Castile, 90–91
Jindřichův Hradec (Germ. Neuhaus), Czechia, 130, 137–38
Bohemian noble family, 130, 137–38
Joachimitism, Joachimites, 91
Jobst (1351–1411), margrave of Moravia, 185
Jogaila (Pol. Jagiełło), see Vladislas II Jogaila
John (fl. 1st cent. CE), St, apostle, 162
John I (1357–1433), king of Portugal, 332–33
John I Albert (1459–1513), king of Poland, 169, 275–79
John II of Châtillon (c. 1342–81), count of Blois, 138
John II (1405–54), king of Castile, 329
John II the Lame (1270/75–1340), count of Sponheim-Kreuznach, 134
John V Palaiologos (1332–91), Byzantine emperor, 176, 178

INDEX 391

John VIII Palaiologos (1392–1448), Byzantine emperor, 165, 219–20, 222
John XXII (1244–1334), pope, 97, 101, 284
John XXIII (c. 1370–1419), antipope, 324, 349, 352–53
John Angelos (c. 1193–1253), Byzantine prince, governor of Syrmia, 242
John Duns Scotus (c. 1265/66–1308), OFM, philosopher, 364
John Lackland (1166–1216), king of England, duke of Normandy and of Acquitaine, lord of Ireland, 144
John of Andrea (c. 1270–1348), jurist and canonist, 364
John of Baysen (d. 1459), governor of Royal Prussia, 332–33
John of Capestrano (1386–1456), St, OFM, 78–79, 81, 86, 88–90, 248
John of Casamari (fl. early 13th cent.), OCist, papal envoy, 238–39
John of Drändorf (c. 1390–1425), preacher, 365
John of Frankfurt, OT, commander of Beauvoir, 331
John of Gubbio (fl. 1390s), papal legate, 180
John of Hunyad (1407–56), regent-governor of Hungary, voivode of Transylvania, 36, 62, 88, 123, 203, 211, 213, 220–21, 223, 225–26, 228–29, 231, 235–36
John of Luxemburg (1310–46), king of Bohemia, 58–59, 127–28, 133–38, 284, 287
John of Posilge (c. 1340–1405), OT, chronicler, 148, 316, 346
John of Sommerfeld, see Cotbus of Sommerfeld, Johannes
John of Thurocz (c. 1435–c. 1488/89), chronicler, 204, 223, 225, 230
John of Tiefen (1440–97), OT, grand master, 275–79

John of Wallenrode (c. 1370–1419), archbishop of Riga, bishop of Liège (as John VII), 150
John of Wildeshausen, OP, bishop of Bosnia, 243
John the Fearless (1371–1419), count of Nevers, of Artois, of Flanders and of Charolais, duke of Burgundy, 86, 181, 190–91, 196

Kadold II Orphan (d. 1260), Bohemo-Austrian nobleman, 130
Kahl, Hans-Dietrich (1920–2016), historian, 43
Kaliakra, Bulgaria, 234
Kaliningrad, Russia, see Königsberg
Kalocsa, Hungary, 207, 213, 242, 245
Kanizsai, János (1350s–1418), archbishop of Gran, primate and chancellor of Hungary, 180, 206
Karaca Bey (d. 1444), Ottoman military commander, 235
Karaman, Turkey, 78, 116, 223, 229, 231
Karijotids, dynasty (cadet branch of the Gediminids), 159, 255, 304
Kasejovice, Czechia Bohemian noble family, 137
Kasim Pasha (fl. 1442–43), beylerbey of Rumelia, 226
Kastrioti, Gjergj 'Skanderbeg' (1405–68), Albanian prince and military commander, 78, 227, 236, 250
Kaunas, Lithuania, 168
Kavarna, Bulgaria, 234
Kenna Joan Algirdaitė (c. 1351–68), duchess consort of Pomerania-Stolp, 289
Kęsgailai, Jonas (aka Kęsgailaitis, d. 1485), captain of Samogitia, 168, 253
Kęstutis (c. 1297–82), duke of of Trakai, grand duke of Lithuania, 157–58, 255, 268, 288

Keve (mod. Kovin, Serbia), 206–7, 212–13
Kholm (mod. Chełm, Poland), 291
Kiev, Ukraine, 25, 162, 166, 260, 262, 270, 341, 348, 352–54
Kiliya, *see* Chilia
King's Lynn, UK, 149
Kingston upon Hull, UK, 149
Kiška, Stanislovas (d. 1513/14), grand hetman of Lithuania, grand marshal of Lithuania, voivode of Smolensk, 169, 262
Kladovo, Serbia, 232
Kličevac, Serbia, 209
Kling, Gustav, historian, 41
Klingenbergs, Bohemian noble family, 137
Klosterneuburg, Austria, 364
Koblenz, Germany, 146
Koeppen, Hans (1913–77), historian, 43
Kolarov, Hristo (1877–1950), historian, 220
Kolomna, Russia, 342
Kolomyia, Ukraine, 274
Kölpény (mod. Kulpin, Serbia), 206
Komotin, Bosnia and Herzegovina, 203
Königsberg (mod. Kaliningrad, Russia), 134, 152, 275–76, 331
Konya, Turkey, 224
Korkut (1467/69–1513), Ottoman prince, 116
Korner, Hermann (*c.* 1365–1438), OP, chronicler, 363
Korosno (mod. Krosno, Poland), 307
Kosovo Field
battle (1389), 114, 179, 189
crusade and battle (1448), 114, 187
Krassó, geographical and historical region, 179, 207, 213
Kreva (Pol. Krewo, Lith. Krėva), Belarus
union (1385), 267, 286, 293, 311, 313
Kristó, Gyula (1939–2004), historian, 42

Kromer, Marcin (1512–89), bishop of Warmia, historiographer, 228
Kronstadt (mod. Brașov, Romania; Hung. Brassó), 122, 200, 203–4, 208, 228
Krosno, Poland, *see* Korosno
Krupski, Jerzy (1472–1534), diplomat, 118
Krushevats, Serbia, 226
Ksar es-Seghir, Morocco
crusade, siege, battle and Portuguese conquest (1458), 34
Küchmeister, Michael (1360/70–1423), OT, grand master, 151, 333, 350
Kulin (d. *c.* 1204), ban of Bosnia, 238–39
Kulmerland, *see* Chełmno Land
Kuna of Zbraslav and Kunštát (1220/25–95), Moravian nobleman, 130
Kunovitsa, Serbia
battle (1444), 226, 229
Kutná Hora (Ger. Kuttenberg), Czechia, 328

La Mota, Spain
Labuda, Gerard (1916–2010), historian, 45
Ladislas the Magnanimous (1377–1414), king of Naples, 201
Ladislas the Posthumous (1440–57), king of Hungary and of Bohemia, 221
Lampsakos (mod. Lapseki, Turkey)
crusade (1359), 39, 176
Lancasters, dynasty, 142
Landštejns, Bohemian noble family, 135, 137
Lasocki, Mikołaj (*c.* 1380–1450), royal secretary, diplomat, 329–30
Lašva, river, 202, 209
Lateran Councils (1123–1517)
fourth (1215), 366, 371
fifth (1512–17), 120, 334
Latvia, Latvians, 45, 48

Lazarists, 144
Le Livre des fais du bon messire Jehan le Maingre, 174
Legnica (Ger. Liegnitz), Poland, 258
Leighton, Gregory, historian, 49
Lengvenis Simon (c. 1360–after 1431), prince of Novgorod, prince of Mstislav, 348
Leo X (1475–1521), pope, 113–23
Leopold III the Just (1351–86), duke of Austria, 138
Lepanto (mod. Nafpaktos, Greece) battle (1571), 51
Lépes, Loránd, deputy voivode of Transylvania (in off. 1415–38), 212
Lesser Poland, Lesser Poles, 283–84, 286, 303, 307, 309, 311
Leutschau, *see* Levoča, Slovakia
Levantine crusades, *see* crusades
Levoča (Hung. Lőcse; Ger. Leutschau), Slovakia
congress (1494), 275, 277
Librazsd (mod. Liborajdea, Romania), 207
Lichtenburks, Bohemian noble family, 130, 133, 135
Liegnitz, *see* Legnica, Poland
Litauerfahrten (aka *Litauerreisen*), *see* crusades into Lithuania
Lithuania, Lithuanians, 40, 43–45, 48, 58–61, 63–64, 73–74, 99, 115, 119, 121, 132, 135–36, 138, 141–70, 177–78, 194, 214, 253–65, 267–68, 270, 285–93, 296, 299, 301–8, 310–13, 316, 320–23, 328–29, 331–32, 335, 337–39, 341
Litice, Czechia
Bohemian noble family, 137
Liubartas (d. c. 1383), prince of Lutsk and Liubar, prince of Volhynia, 290
Livonia, Livonians, Livs, 43, 45, 149, 156–58, 256, 258, 267, 272, 276–78, 290, 292, 313, 316, 328, 332, 334–35, 338, 342, 347–48, 350, 355
Llull, Ramon (c. 1232–1316), OFM, philosopher and theologian, 55, 93, 101
Liber de fine, 101
Lőcse, *see* Levoča, Slovakia
Lombardy, Lombards, 181, 194
London, UK, 149
López de Carvajal, Bernardino (1456–1523), cardinal, 263
Los Angeles, CA, USA, 48
Lotharingia, Lotharingians, 257
Louis I the Great (1326–82), king of Hungary and of Poland, 34, 60, 136, 178–79, 287–89, 291–92, 302–3, 309, 312
Louis I (1372–1407), duke of Orléans, 86
Louis II (1384–1436), duke of Brzeg and Legnica, 258
Louis II the Jagiellonian (1506–26), king of Hungary and of Bohemia (as Louis I), 122
Louis IV the Bavarian (1282–1347), Holy Roman emperor, duke of Bavaria, 133
Louis IX (1214–70), king of France, 51, 326
Louis of Erlichshausen (c. 1410/15–67), OT, grand master, 270
Lübeck, Germany, 151, 363
Lublin, Poland, 163, 287, 303
union (1569), 313
Ludolf König of Wattzau (1280s–1348), OT, grand master, 136
Lugubre et multum inauditum, 73–74
Luigi da Bologna (c. 1430s–after 1479), OFS, diplomat, 86
Lusatia, Lusatians, 365
Lusignans, dynasty, 177, 218, 292, 304
Luther, Martin (1483–1546), OSA, theologian, 122

Lutsk, Ukraine
  congress (1429), 258, 357
  war (1431), 328
Luttrell, Anthony T. (b. 1932), historian
  A History of the Crusades, 48
  The Papacy and the Levant (1204–1571), 48
Luxembourg City, Luxembourg, 133
Luxemburgs, dynasty, 36, 58–60, 74, 127–28, 133–38, 147, 149–50, 159, 164–65, 170, 178–82, 188–89, 199–206, 208–9, 212–15, 218, 220, 246–47, 258–60, 268–69, 275, 284, 287, 289, 291–92, 304, 320–21, 323–24, 328, 330, 348, 351, 353–54, 356–58, 361, 367, 369–73
Lviv (Pol. Lwów), Ukraine, 278, 307, 311
Lynn, UK, *see* King's Lynn
Lyon, France
  councils
    second (1274), 33

Maccabees, 315
Macsó, geographical and historical region, 179, 207–8
Macedonia, Macedonians, 187, 231
Machwitz, Sander (d. after 1420), OT, land advocate of the New March, 350
Madara, Bulgaria, 233
Madrid, Spain, 102–3
Magdeburg, Germany
  city law/rights, 309
Maglaj, Bosnia and Herzegovina, 209
Mahdia, Tunisia
  crusade (1390), 39
Mahmud Bey (*fl.* 1443/44), Ottoman military commander, 226
Malta, Maltese, 109–10
Mályusz, Elemér (1898–1989), historian, 42
Mamluk Sultanate, Mamluks, 81–82, 84–85, 90, 117–19, 177
Manichaeism, Manicheans, 246–47, 249, 251

Mantua, Italy, 69, 79–80
Manuel I (1469–1521), king of Portugal, 90–91
Manuel Angelos Philantropenos (before 1373–after 1420), lord of Thessaly, diplomat, 165–66
Mariano of Siena (1401–67), OFM, preacher, 250
Marienburg (mod. Malbork, Poland), 75, 145, 258, 272
Markvard of Dunajovice (*fl.* 1250s), supreme land chamberlain of Bohemia, 130
Marmara Sea, 181
Maróti, László, ban of Mačva (in off. 1441–43), 235
Marquard of Salzbach (d. 1410), OT, commander of Ragnit, commander of Brandenburg (Frisches Haff), 256, 344
Marquet (de Valombreuse), Jean, OFM, 89, 91
Martin V (1369–1431), pope, 86, 104, 165, 170, 323, 325, 327–28, 351, 357, 361–64, 369, 372–73
Martin Truchsess of Wetzhausen (*c.* 1435–89), OT, grand master 271, 273–75, 279
Mary of Anjou (1371–95), queen of Hungary, 309
Mary the Virgin (*fl.* end of the 1st cent. BCE / beginning of the 2nd cent. CE), St, 145, 166
Marzec, Andrzej (b. 1971), historian, 63, 177, 268, 297, 304, 319
Maschke, Erich (1900–82), historian, 43
Masovia, Masovians, 129, 157, 276, 290–91, 293, 303–4, 309, 356
Matejko, Jan (1838–93), painter, 44, 307–8, 314
Matijević, Jeronim, diplomat, 118

Matthias I Corvinus (1443–90), king of Hungary, king of Bohemia, 36, 70–72, 75, 79, 374
Maugest, Hans (fl. 1440s), German mercenary, 231
Mauro Hispano (fl. late 15th / early 16th cent.), OFM, custodian of the Holy Land, 90–91
Mauroux, Jean (1365–1437), theologian, 367
Maximilian I (1459–1519), Holy Roman emperor, archduke of Austria, duke of Burgundy (jure uxoris), 263, 275–78
Mediterranean Sea, 33–34, 45, 55, 69, 78, 83, 95, 97–99, 101–2, 105–10, 118, 128, 153, 177, 179, 329, 334, 337
Mehmed (1486–1504), Ottoman prince, 115
Mehmed I (c. 1386–1421), Ottoman sultan, 203
Mehmed II the Conqueror (1432–81), Ottoman sultan, 42, 70–71, 78, 195, 250
Mellini, Domenico (c. 1531–1620)
 Vita di Filippo Scolari, 210
Melno, lake
 peace treaty (1422), 328
Michalovice (part of Mladá Boleslav), Czechia
 Bohemian noble family, 135, 137
Michaud, Joseph-François (1767–1839)
 Histoire des croisades, 46–47
Michelozzo di Bartolomeo Michelozzi (1396–1472), architect and sculptor, 69
Mieszko I (c. 922/45–92), duke of Poland, 292
Miethke, Jürgen (b. 1938), historian, 80
Mihailoglu Mehmed, Ottoman bey, 116
Miháld (mod. Mehadia, Romania), 213
Mihnea the Evil (c. 1462–1510), voivode of Wallachia, 115

Mikuła of Kopyłów (fl. 1428), OP, subdiacon of Novhorod-Siverskyi, 356
Milan, Italy, 70, 89, 93, 222, 233, 249, 328
Miličín, Czechia
 Bohemian noble family, 134, 137
Militzer, Klaus (1940–2022), historian, 43
Mills, Charles (1788–1826), historian, 40, 47
Mindaugas (c. 1203–63), grand duke and (since 1253) king of Lithuania, 254
Mircea I the Old (c. 1355–1418), voivode of Wallachia, 123, 181, 200, 203–4
Mityev, Neven, historian, 60–61
Mohács, Hungary
 battle (1526), 122
Moldavia, Moldavians, 113, 117–19, 121–23, 168–70, 179, 182, 212, 261–62, 271–72, 274, 277–79, 321, 354
Mongolian Empire, Mongols, 36, 41, 52, 54, 63, 69, 147, 159, 161, 164, 176, 180, 244, 285, 292, 300, 318–19, 321, 329–30
Mont-Louis, René de (aka Charles Farine, 1818–83), historian, 40, 48
Moors, 99, 193, 318, 325–26
Moravia, Moravians, 58, 127–39, 185
Morocco, Moroccans, 73–74, 97, 100, 332–33
Moscow, Russia, 25, 28, 40, 52, 59, 61, 161, 163–66, 168, 262–64, 272, 276–77, 279, 334–35, 341–42, 345–51, 354–57
Mudéjars, 102
Mühldorf (Inn), Germany
 battle (1322), 133
Mülich, Hektor (c. 1420–89/90), salesman, chronicler, 182
Murad I (1326–89), Ottoman sultan, 193, 195, 197

Murad II (1404–51), Ottoman sultan, 166, 203, 206, 224, 226–27, 229, 231–32, 234
Mureşan, Dan Ioan (b. 1974), historian, 68
Murray, Alan V., historian, 49, 156
Muscovy, Muscovites, *see* Moscow, Russia

Nagyszeben (mod. Sibiu, Romania), 204
Naker, Liborius (1440–1502/3), OT, secretary and writer, 278
Naples, Italy, 70, 82, 108–9, 201, 249
Narbonne, France, 150
Nasrids, dynasty, 104
Navarre, Navarrese, 107
Neagoe Basarab (c. 1482–1521), voivode of Wallachia, 56, 58, 114, 116–19, 121–22
Negroponte (Gr. Euboea), 79, 83
Neidenburg (mod. Nidzica, Poland), 274
Neman, Russia, *see* Ragnit
Nepričava, Serbia, 206
Neşri, Mehmed (c. 1450–c. 1520), historiographer, 224
Netherlands, Netherlandish, Dutch, 143, 154
New March, New Marchians, 350–51
New York, NY, USA, 367
Nicholas Magni of Jauer (c. 1355–1435), theologian, 365, 369
Nicholas of Buseck, auxiliary bishop of Würzburg (in off. 1403–23), 352
Nicholas of Cusa, bishop of Brixen, cardinal, philosopher and theologian, 72
Nicholas IV (1227–92), pope, 99
Nicholas V (1397–1455), pope, 72, 78–79, 106, 247–48
Nicholas of Baysen (d. 1503), governor of Royal Prussia, voivode of Marienburg, 272

Nicholas of Jeroschin (d. after 1344), OT, chronicler, 316
Nicholas of Redwitz (d. 1437), OT, advocate of Stuhm, 151
Nicholas of Tüngen (d. 1489), bishop of Warmia, 271
Nicholson, Helen J. (b. 1960), historian, 141
Nicopolis (mod. Nikopol, Bulgaria), 116
crusade, siege and battle (1396), 36–37, 42, 45, 51, 59–60, 114, 173–97, 199–201, 208, 229, 232–33, 338, 344
Nicosia, Cyprus, 83
Nish, Serbia, 224, 226
battle (1443), 227, 229
Norbury, John (d. 1414), lord high treasurer of England, 142
Norwich, UK, 152
Novara, Italy, 165, 326
Novgorod, Russia, 166, 258, 264, 272, 341–43, 345, 347–51, 353–57
Novgorodok (mod. Navahrudak, Belarus), 166, 341, 349
Novo Brdo, Kosovo, 209
Novosil, Russia, 341, 355
Novotný, Václav (1869–1932), historian, 127
Nowak, Zenon Hubert (1934–99), historian, 45
Nowy Dwór Mazowiecki, Poland, 291
Nuremberg, Germany
Reichstag (1460), 79

Occitania, Occitans, 150
Odoyev, Russia, 341, 355
Oka, river, 164, 166
Oldrado da Ponte (d. before 1348), jurist, theologian, 326–27
Oldřich II of Hradec (d. before 1312), Bohemian nobleman, 137
Oldřich III of Hradec (d. c. 1348), Bohemian nobleman, 137–38

Oldřich Pluh of Rabštejn, Bohemian nobleman, 135
Oleśnicki, Zbigniew, the elder (1389–1455), bishop of Cracow, cardinal, 167, 222, 229
Oleśnicki, Zbigniew, the younger (1430–93), archbishop of Gniezno, primate of Poland, 271–73
Olomouc, Czechia, 128, 130–31, 135
Ondřej of Všechromy (d. 1277), lord of Říčan, 130
Opatowiec, Poland, 302
Opava, Czechia, 128
Opole, Poland, 291, 309, 312
Oradea, Romania, see Várad
Orléans, France, 86, 331
  English siege (1428/29), 151
Orsha, Belarus
  battle (1514), 169
Orsini, Giordano (1360/70–1438), cardinal, papal legate, 370
Orshova, Romania, 199, 207, 213, 232–33
Orthodox Church, 39–40, 43–45, 56, 63–64, 71, 73–74, 77, 117, 119, 123, 129, 159, 161–64, 167, 169, 177, 183, 185, 188, 200, 227, 229, 233, 237, 239, 246, 251, 264, 268, 272, 276, 278–79, 283, 285–86, 290, 299, 302, 304–5, 306, 312–13, 319–21, 324–26, 329, 337, 340, 343, 346, 349, 357, 359–60, 365
Oruç Bey (aka Oruç bin Âdil, fl. late 15th and early 16th cs.), historiographer, 231
Oryahovo, Bulgaria, 183, 191, 232
Ostrožac, Bosnia and Herzegovina, 208
Otranto, Italy
  Ottoman siege and conquest (1480), 80
  Christian siege and recapture (1481), 168

Otto of Bergow (fl. first half of the 14th cent.), Germano-Bohemian nobleman, 135
Ottokar I Premislas (d. 1230), king of Bohemia, 128
Ottokar II Premislas (c. 1230–78), king of Bohemia, duke of Austria, of Styria and of Carinthia, 58–59, 127–34, 137–38, 254
Ottoman Empire, Ottoman Turks, 36–37, 39, 41–43, 45, 48–49, 52, 54–56, 59–62, 69–72, 74–75, 78–79, 81, 87–89, 91, 106, 109, 113–23, 161, 164–68, 170, 173–97, 199–213, 215–16, 218–38, 246–53, 257–63, 259, 261–62, 268–72, 274–79, 292, 317, 322, 324, 327, 329–30, 334, 344, 353, 356–57, 373–74
  civil war (1509–13), 114–15
Ovech, Bulgaria, 233
Oybin, Germany, 365

Paikalas, Antonios (fl. early 16th cent.), diplomat, 118–19
Pajorin, Klára (b. 1942), historian, 70
Palacio, Andrea (fl. 1440s), writer, 233
Palatinate, Palatines, 256
Palestine, Palestinians, 76, 182, 316
Pálosfalvi, Tamás (b. 1968), historian, 42
Pamplona, Spain, 107
Panormitanus, see Tedeschi, Niccolò
papacy, popes, see individual popes
Paravicini, Werner (b. 1942), historian, 43
Paris, France, 185, 191, 321, 370–71
Paris, Matthew (c. 1200–59), OSB, chronicler, 143–44
Pasłęk, Poland, see Preußisch Holland
Paul (c. 5–c. 64/65), St, apostle, 335
Paul II (1417–71), pope, 70
Paul of Rusdorf (c. 1385–1441), OT, grand master, 154

Paul Walter of Guglingen (fl. 15th cent.), OFM, 85, 93
Paulus Vladimir, see Włodkowic, Paweł
Paviot, Jacques (b. 1955), historian, 87
Pavlov, Plamen (b. 1958), historian, 232
Pecorara, Giacomo (c. 1170–1244), papal legate, 243
Pécs, Hungary, 213
Pentek, Zdzisław (b. 1964), historian, 236
Peremyshl (mod. Przemyśl, Poland), 291, 299, 307, 312
Persia, Persians, 116, 119, 194
Peter I (1311–56), duke of Bourbon, 136
Peter I of Lusignan (1328–69), king of Cyprus, 177, 218, 292, 304
Peter I the Cruel (1334–69), king of Castile, 100
Peter II the Catholic (1178–1213), king of Aragon, 102
Peter III (1240–85), king of Aragon, 97
Peter IV the Ceremonious (1319–87), king of Aragon, 98, 104
Peter of Dusburg (d. after 1326/30), OT, chronicler, 130, 132–35, 316, 318
  Chronica terrae Prussiae, 130
Peter of Kremenets, Volhynian nobleman, 167
Peter of Rožmberk (d. 1347), supreme land chamberlain of Bohemia, 134
Peter of Wormditt (c. 1360–1419), OT, jurist, 73, 320, 322, 324–25, 337, 346, 353, 359
Peter of Žitava (c. 1275–1339), OCist, chronicler, 285
Peter Thomas (1305–66), St, OCarm, papal legate, 176–77
Petrauskas, Rimvydas (b. 1972), historian, 61
Petrich, Bulgaria, 234
Philip (c. 1285–1338), count of Sponheim-Bolanden, 134

Philip II (1527–98), king of Spain and of Portugal (as Philip I), 335
Philip II the Bold (1342–1404), duke of Burgundy, count (*jure uxoris*) of Flanders and of Artois, 88, 181
Philip III the Good (1396–1467), duke of Burgundy, 87–89, 93, 195, 330
Philip IV (1605–65), king of Spain and of Portugal (as Philip III), 93
Philippe de Mézières (c. 1327–1405), author, 169–70, 176, 180, 187
  Epistre lamentable et consolatoire, 189, 195
  Le songe du vieil pelerin, 169, 187, 189
Photius (d. 1431), metropolitan of Kiev and all Rus, 166, 348–49, 354, 357
Piasts, dynasty, 63, 129, 135, 258, 268, 277, 283–86, 288, 291–93, 297, 299–300, 304, 309, 312, 319
Picardy, Picards, 197
Piccolomini, Enea Silvio (1405–64), 68–72, 78–79, 194–95, 221, 228, 233
  Asia, 187
  Constantinopolitana clades, 68, 70, 75
Pintoin, Michel (c. 1350–c. 1421), OSB, chronicler
  Chronica Karoli Sexti, 185, 188, 190–91, 193–95, 321
Piotrków, Poland
  Sejm (1488), 274–75
Pipo of Ozora, see Scolari, Filippo
Pirot, Serbia, 224
Pius II, pope, see Piccolomini, Enea Silvio
Plichta III of Žerotín-Adlar (1291–1322), Bohemian nobleman, 132–33
Plovdiv, Bulgaria, 224
Podolia, Podolians, 159, 255, 269, 275–77, 287, 305, 309, 341, 348, 355–56
Poland, Poles, 34, 36, 40, 44–45, 48, 56, 60–61, 63, 73–76, 78, 110, 113–15, 117–19, 121–22, 123, 128, 130, 135–36, 138–39, 145, 147–52, 159, 161, 163–70, 181, 214, 219–20, 222–24,

228–29, 236, 255, 257–58, 260–65, 267–79, 283–93, 295–338, 340–41, 343–46, 348–49, 350–53, 355–59, 365, 367, 369–70
Polekhov, Sergey (b. 1986), historian, 64
Polatsk, Belarus, 341, 344, 347–48
Pomerania, Pomeranians, 43, 63, 133, 289, 319–20
Pomerelia, Pomerelians, 133, 284
Poppo of Osterna (c. 1200–67), OT, grand master, 129
Porkhov, Russia, 166, 356
Portugal, Portuguese, 34, 73, 90, 95, 102, 104, 109, 121–22, 324, 332–33
Porziuncola, Italy, 83
Pósa (d. 1270/72), OP, bishop of Bosnia, 244–45
Poznań, Poland, 333
Pozsezsin (mod. Pojejena, Romania), 207
Prague, Czechia, 77, 128, 132
Premislas (1257–96), duke of Greater Poland (as Premislas II), of Cracow and of Pomerelia (the latter both as Premislas I), king of Poland (as Premislas I), 285
Přemyslids, dynasty, 56, 58–59, 127–34, 137–38, 254, 283
Pressburg (mod. Bratislava, Slovakia), 88, 247
Preußenfahrten (also *Preußenreisen*), *see* crusades into Prussia
Preußisch Holland (mod. Pasłęk, Poland), 278
Prizren, Kosovo, 209
Proctor, George (1795/96–1842), historian, 40, 48
Provadiya, Bulgaria, 233
Protestantism, Protestants, 122
Prussia, Prussians
    duchy (1525–1701), 44
        Homage (Pol. *Hołd pruski*, 1525), 44, 63, 279, 334, 336

kingdom (1701–1918), 41, 43
Old Prussians (Baltic people), 43, 58, 63, 128–39, 170, 254, 316–17, 319
Royal (1466–1569), 44, 271–75, 277, 331–32
Teutonic, *see* Teutonic Order, Teutonic Knights
uprising (1242–49), 129
uprising (1260–83), 131
Przemyśl, Poland, *see* Peremyshl
Pskov, Russia, 165–66, 258, 276, 341–43, 345–51, 354–56

Qansuh al-Ghuri (c. 1441/46–1516), Mamluk sultan, 90
Qizilbash, 116
Quaresmio, Francesco (1583–1650), OFM, writer and orientalist, 93
    Terrae Sanctae Elucidatio, 93

Radu II the Bald (d. 1431), voivode of Wallachia, 204
Radu IV the Great (1467–1508), voivode of Wallachia, 114, 116
Radvila, Mikalojus II 'Amor Poloniae' (1470–1521), land marshal of Trakai, voivode of Trakai, voivode of Vilnius, grand chancellor of Lithuania, 263
Radvilas, Lithuano-Polish noble family, 263
Ragnit (mod. Neman, Russia), 344
Ragusa (mod. Dubrovnik, Croatia), 69, 117–18, 222, 230, 240, 243
Rama, river, 244
Rashka, geographical and historical region, 223
Ratisbon, Germany, 362, 367
    Reichstag (1454), 167
    Reichstag (1471), 68–69
Reconquista, 34, 55–56, 81, 95–111, 325, 330, 333, 337

Reichartinger, Leonhard (d. 1396), Bavarian nobleman, 190
Reinlein, Oswald (d. 1466), OSA, preacher, 363–64
religious and religious military orders
  Alcántara, 96–97, 103–4, 107
  Augustinians, 323, 364
  Aviz, 104
  Benedictines, 322, 324
  Calatrava, 96–97, 100–1, 103–4, 107
  Carmelites, 176
  Carthusians, 243, 363–64
  Celestines, 365
  Cistercians, 194, 238
  Dominicans, 76, 82–83, 243–45, 249, 320, 322, 324, 365
  Franciscans, 55, 70, 76, 78, 81–93, 107, 167, 248–50, 312, 326
  Jesuits, 84
  Hospitallers, *see the respective entry above*
  Military Order of Christ, 102, 104
  Montesa, 96, 101–3, 105, 110–11
  Santiago, 96–97, 99–100, 103–5, 107
  Saint Mary of Spain (aka Order of the Star), 100, 110–11
  Sword Brethren, 45
  Templars, *see the respective entry below*
  Teutonic Knights, *see* Teutonic Order
Reynolds, Burnam W. (b. 1948), historian, 49
Rhine, river, 132, 187, 256
Rhineland, Rhinelanders, 132–34
Rhode, Gotthold (1916–90), historian, 301
Rhodes, island, 48, 78, 88, 95, 98, 101, 103, 105–8, 110, 122, 167–68, 322, 372
Richard II (1367–1400), king of England, 145–46
Rider's War (1519–21), 153
Riga, Latvia, 150, 158, 272, 352, 357
Riley-Smith, Jonathan (1938–2016), historian, 156

Rimša, Edmundas Antanas (b. 1948), historian, 158
Ritsema van Eck, Marianne, historian, 55
Robert of Anjou (1278–1343), king of Naples, 82
Roger of Wendover (d. 1236), chronicler, 143–44
Rome, Italy, 69, 77–80, 86, 90, 107, 114, 118, 120, 165, 179, 188–89, 239, 242, 247, 249, 258, 269, 276–77, 279, 319, 361, 367, 372
Roman Empire, Romans, 170, 187
Roman Catholic Church, 34, 39, 44–45, 56, 68, 71, 73–75–78, 80–93, 95, 102, 105, 107–11, 120, 131, 151, 153, 155–56, 159–61, 165, 167–69, 173, 175–76, 188, 191, 207, 220, 236–37, 239–48, 251–52, 256, 264, 276, 285–86, 288–91, 293, 295, 297, 302, 305, 307–8, 311–12, 316, 319–21, 323–25, 327–28, 330–32, 335, 337, 359, 362–74
Romania, Romanians, 47, 58, 113, 115, 122, 179, 199–200, 203–4, 206–7, 213–14, 228, 233
Ronovs, Bohemian noble family, 137
Roques (also Roque or de Rocha), Jean, OFM, vicar general, 326
Rosetti, Radu (1853–1926), historian and politician, 41
Rossi, Ettore (1894–1955), historian and orientalist, 48
Rowell, Stephen C. (b. 1964), historian, 257, 356–57
Rus (Ruthenia), Ruthenians, 34, 43, 63, 159, 164, 166, 168, 236, 256, 268, 272, 276–79, 285–92, 295–312, 319–21, 329
Ruse, Bulgaria, 236
Russia, Russians, 44–45, 48, 134, 136, 170, 270, 272, 275, 299, 312
Ryashiv (mod. Rzeszów, Poland), 307
Ryazan, Russia, 164, 166, 341, 348, 355

Rýzmberks, Bohemian noble family, 137
Rzeszów, Poland, *see* Ryashiv

Sabtah, *see* Ceuta, Spain
Sacosta, Pere Ramon (d. 1467), grand master of the Knights Hospitaller, 107
Safavids, dynasty, 117
Sagundino, Niccolò 'Secundinus' (1402–64), humanist writer, diplomat, 195
Saint-Denis, Parisian commune, 185, 321
Saint-Oyend-de-Joux (mod. Saint-Claude, France), 324
Saladin, *see* Salah ad-Din Yusuf ibn Ayyub
Salado, river
  battle (1340), 102–4
Salah ad-Din Yusuf ibn Ayyub (aka Saladin, c. 1137–93), sultan of Egypt and Syria, 197
Salutati, Coluccio (1332–1406), humanist, chancellor of Florence, 185–88
Salynas (Ger. Salinwerder), River Neman islet
  treaty (1398), 162, 256, 342–46
Sambia, Sambians, 129, 131–32
Samogitia, Samogitians, 73–76, 135, 165, 168, 253, 257–58, 332, 339, 343, 345, 354
Sancha of Majorca (c.1285–1345), queen consort and regent of Naples, 82
Sanok, Poland, *see* Syanik
Sanudo, Marino, the elder (c. 1270–1343), geographer, 93
Saracens, 157, 193, 260, 318, 359
Sarnowsky, Jürgen (b. 1955), historian, 43
Sárói, László (*fl.* late 14th cent.), count of Temes, 178
Sava, river, 208
Saxony, Saxons, 130, 279
Schedel, Hartmann (1440–1514), humanist and historiographer, 334

Schiltberger, Johannes (c. 1380–1427), traveller and writer
  Reisebuch, 37, 174, 190, 195–96
Schlick, Kaspar (c. 1396–1449), jurist, chancellor of the Holy Roman Empire, 72
Scolari, Andrea (d. 1426), bishop of Zagreb, bishop of Várad, 207
Scolari, Filippo (aka Pippo Spano or Pipo of Ozora, 1369–1426), military leader, 60–61, 204, 207, 209–13
Sculteti, Michael (d. 1500), bishop of Curland, Teutonic procurator, 278
Scythia, Scythians, 119, 187
Sebes (mod. Turnu Ruieni, Romania), 213
Sebta, *see* Ceuta, Spain
Second Baron's War (1264–67), 144
Şehinşah (1474–1511), Ottoman prince, 114–17, 119, 122
Seleucid Empire, Seleucids, 315
Selim I the Grim (1470–1520), Ottoman sultan, 115
Seljuk Sultanate, Seljuk Turks, 174–75, 193
Serbia, Serbs, 113, 179, 181–82, 184–85, 199–200, 203, 206–12, 221, 223, 225–26, 229, 231–32, 236, 250
Setton, Kenneth (1914–95), historian, 48
  A History of the Crusades, 155
Sforzas, dynasty, 89, 222
Shiism, Shiites, 116–17
Shkorpil, Hermengild (1858–1923), archaeologist and museologist, 220
Shkorpil, Karel (1859–1944), archaeologist and museologist, 220
Shumen, Bulgaria, 233–34
Sibiu, Romania, *see* Nagyszeben
Sicily, Sicilians, 86, 88, 108, 144, 334
Sidon, Lebanon, 83
Siegfried IV Orphan (d. after 1265), Bohemo-Austrian nobleman, 130

Siemowit III (*c.* 1320–81), duke of Masovia, 291
Siena, Italy, 89, 203, 209, 215–17, 250, 371
Sienkiewicz, Henryk (1846–1916), writer
Krzyżacy, 45
Sigeher (*fl.* second half of the 13th cent.), poet, 131
Sigismund I the Old (1467–1548), king of Poland, grand duke of Lithuania (as Sigismund II), 115–16, 119, 121, 275, 333–34
Sigismund Kęstutaitis (*c.* 1365–1440), grand duke of Lithuania, 160, 167
Sigismund Korybut (*c.* 1395–1435), Gediminid prince, Hussite military leader, 369–70
Sigismund of Luxemburg (1368–1437), king of Hungary and of Bohemia, Holy Roman emperor, 36, 60, 74, 147, 149–50, 159, 164–65, 170, 178–82, 188–89, 199–206, 208–9, 212–15, 218, 220, 246–47, 258–60, 269, 320–21, 323–24, 328, 330, 348, 351, 353–54, 356–58, 361, 367, 369–73
Silesia, Silesians, 132, 134–36, 301, 306, 309
Silistra, Bulgaria, 235
Simon of Drahe (*fl.* late 15th / early 16th cent.), OT, commander of Holland (mod. Pasłęk, Poland), 278
Simon of Montfort (*c.* 1208–65), earl of Leicester, 144
Simon of Verdeau (*fl.* 15th cent.), OFM, 87
Šišić, Ferdo (1869–1940), historian, 41
Sixtus IV (1414–84), pope, 167–68, 260–61
Skanderbeg, *see* Kastrioti, Gjergj
Skirgaila (*c.* 1353/54–97), regent of the grand duchy of Lithuania, duke of Trakai, prince of Kiev, 160, 342

Slankamen, Serbia, 225, 228
Slavonia, Slavonians, 201–2, 213, 243, 245
Smederevo, Serbia, 221
Smil of Bílkov (d. 1278), castellan of Bítov, 130
Smil of Lichtenburk (*c.* 1220–69), supreme burgrave of Bohemia, 130, 133
Smil of Zbraslav and Střílky (*c.* 1222–73), castellan of Přerov, 130
Smolensk, Russia, 164, 169, 341–45, 348
Smyrna (mod. İzmir, Turkey), 107, 176
crusades (1343–51, 1472), 37, 45, 175–76
Sofia, Bulgaria, 224–26
Sokol, Croatia, 208
Soli, Solians, 242
Sophia of Lithuania (1371–1453), grand princess consort of Moscow, 161, 342, 348, 355
Soukup, Pavel (b. 1976), historian, 64
Spain, Spaniards, 34, 55–56, 90–91, 93, 95–111, 122, 259, 261–62, 326, 334, 337
Spano, Pippo, *see* Scolari, Filippo
Spěváček, Jiří (1923–96), historian, 127
Srebrenica, Bosnia and Herzegovina, 209
Srebrenik, Bosnia and Herzegovina, 202–3, 208
Srodecki, Paul (b. 1980), historian, 59–60, 63–64, 69–70, 73, 96, 110–11, 268, 297, 352
St Albans, UK, 143
Štafilić, Ivan (Ital. Giovanni Stafileo, 1472–1528), bishop of Sebenico, papal legate, 333–34
Stange, Heinrich (d. 1252), OT, commander of Christburg, 130
Stanges, German noble family, 130
Stebbing, Henry (1799–1883), historian, 40, 48

Stefan Lazarević (*c.* 1377–1427), prince and despot of Serbia, 184, 200, 209
Stephen III the Great (1438/39–1504), voivode of Moldavia, 113, 123, 168–69, 261, 270–71, 274, 278
Stephen IV the Young (1506–27), voivode of Moldavia, 118, 121–22
Stephen Thomas (*c.* 1411–61), king of Bosnia, 247–50
Stephen Tomašević (d. 1463), king of Bosnia, despot of Serbia, 250
Stephen Tvrtko I (*c.* 1338–91), king of Bosnia, 187, 247
Stephen Tvrtko II (before 1382–1443), king of Bosnia, 201, 203, 247
Stephen II Kotromanić (before 1295–1353), ban of Bosnia, 246
Šternberks, Bohemian noble family, 137
Stibor of Baysen (d. 1480), governor of Royal Prussia, 332
Strakonice, Czechia Bohemian noble family, 137
Strasburg (Drewenz), 150
Straubing, Germany, 346
Strożyska, Poland, 290
Stuhm (mod. Sztum, Poland), 151
Suceava, Romania, 169
Sudimantaitis, Alekna (d. 1490/91), voivode of Vilnius, grand chancellor of Lithuania, 260
Sudivojaitis, Stankus (d. 1481), lord lieutenant of Kaunas, 168, 263
Suleiman I the Magnificent (1494–1566), Ottoman sultan, 122
Sulejów, Poland congress (1318), 284
Šusta, Josef (1874–1945), historian, 127
Švitrigaila (*c.* 1370–1452), grand duke of Lithuania, prince of Volhynia, 160, 167, 260, 328, 345, 347, 351, 354, 356
Swabia, Swabians, 181
Sweden, Swedes, 40, 43

Swerd, John (*fl.* early 1370s), bowyer from York, 152
Syanik (Mod. Sanok, Poland), 307
Syria, Syrians, 83, 118–19, 194
Syrmia, Syrmians, 179
Szeged, Hungary, 212, 229
Székely, Székelys, 204, 206, 213
Szekfű, Gyula (1883–1955), historian, 42
Szilágy, Mihály (*c.* 1400–60), count of Beszterce, regent of Hungary, 235
Szinice (mod. Siviniţa, Romania), 207
Szolnok, Hungary, 213
Szörény (mod. Turnu Severin, Romania), 203, 206–7, 211, 213
Szweda, Adam (b. 1968), historian, 61–62, 96, 110

Tafur, Pero (*c.* 1405/9–80), traveller, historiographer and writer, 259
Talayero, Martín (*fl.* late 14th–early 15th cent.), diplomat, 370, 373–74
Talmács (mod. Talmaci, Romania), 206
Talovac, Croatian noble family
  Franko (d. 1448), ban of Slavonia, ban of Dalmatia and Croatia, 213
  Ivan (d. 1445), Hospitaller prior of Vrana, 203, 213
  Matko (d. *c.* 1445), ban of Slavonia, ban of Dalmatia and Croatia, 203, 213
  Petar (d. 1453), ban of Dalmatia and Croatia, 213
Tangier, Morocco
  crusade, siege and battle (1437), 34
Tannenberg (mod. Stębark, Poland)
  battle (1410), 44, 141–42, 146, 153, 164, 258, 313, 321, 337, 339, 347
Târgoviște, Romania, 118
Tarifa, Spain, 104
  Castilian siege and conquest (1292), 103
Tarnovo (since 1965 Veliko Tarnovo), Bulgaria, 179

Tarnowski, Jan Amor Maior, the elder (d. 1444), Polish nobleman and crusader, 234
Tarnowski, Jan Gratus Tarnowski (d. 1444), Polish nobleman and crusader, 234
Tatars, 41, 52, 61, 75, 115, 147, 159, 161–62, 164–69, 193–94, 256–57, 259–65, 268, 270, 275, 277, 278, 285–90, 292, 295, 299–304, 306–7, 318–21, 329–31, 334, 337, 343–44, 347–49, 351–52, 354, 356–59, 374
Tedeschi, Niccolò 'Panormitanus' (1386–1445), OSB, archbishop of Palermo, jurist, 364
Temesköz, geographical and historical region, 178–79, 199, 203–4, 206–7, 212–13, 217
Temesvár (mod. Timişoara, Romania), 212
  diet (1397), 214
Templars, 95, 97–98, 101–2, 143–44, 315, 322, 326, 335
Teutonic Order, Teutonic Knights, 39, 43–46, 48, 58–59, 61, 63, 69, 73–75, 96, 99, 110–11, 128–31, 133–35, 137–39, 141–55, 157–65, 168, 177, 193, 222, 253–60, 263–65, 267–79, 284–90, 292, 296, 303–5, 313–38, 341–55, 357, 359, 369
Thebes, Greece, 83
Theodore Karijotaitis (d. 1414), duke of Novgorodok and of Podolia, 159
Theodosios the Greek, archeparch of Polatsk (in off. 1391–1415), 347
Thessaly, Thessalians, 182
Thibault d'Aussigny (d. 1471), bishop of Orléans, 331
Thimo of Colditz, the elder (fl. 1314–40), lord of Krupka (Germ. Graupen), 135
Thirteen Years' War (1454–66), 44, 63, 146, 153, 269, 331–32

Thomas of Spalato (c. 1200–68), chronicler, 241
Thomas of Woodstock (1355–97), duke of Gloucester, 142
Thorn (mod. Toruń, Poland), 151, 271, 273, 300, 317
  peace treaty (1411), 74, 148, 268, 347
  peace treaty (1466), 269–70, 273–74, 277, 279, 332
Thrace, Thracians, 115–16, 182, 230–31, 235
Timish, river, 225
Timur Lenk (aka Tamerlane, 1336–1405), Timurid emir, 176, 196, 200
Timur Qutlugh (c. 1370–99), Golden Horde khan, 343–45
Toeppen, Max (1822–93), historian, 43
Tokhtamysh, Golden Horde khan, 343–44
Tommasini, Thomas (d. 1463), bishop of Lesina (Croat. Hvar), papal legate, 247
Törcsvár (mod. Bran, Romania), 206
Toričan, Bosnia and Herzegovina, 202
Totila (aka Baduila, d. 552), king of the Ostrogoths, 195
Toulouse, France, 51
Trąba, Mikołaj (c. 1358–1422), archbishop of Gniezno, primate and deputy crown chancellor of Poland, 353
Trakai, Lithuania, 157–58, 260, 265, 288, 341
Transylvania, Transylvanians, 116, 123, 199, 203–4, 208, 212–13, 216, 220–21, 226, 235, 267, 316
Trebizond (mod. Trabzon, Turkey), 115
Treitschke, Heinrich von (1834–96), historian, 43
Tripoli, Tunesia, 83
Troy (mod. Hisarlik, Turkey), 185, 187

Tsamblak, Grigoriy (c. 1364–c. 1420), metropolitan of Kiev, 349, 354
Tsvetkova, Bistra (1926–82), historian, 220, 225, 231, 235
Tudela, Spain, 107
Tunisia, Tunisians, 39, 51
Turahan Bey (d. 1456), military commander, governor of Thessaly, 226
Turkey, Turkish, 175–77, 218, 373
  for the Ottoman Empire and the Ottoman Turks see the respective entry above
Turnbull, Stephen Richard (b. 1948), historian, 49
Turnu Severin, Romania, *see* Szörény
Tutrakan, Bulgaria, 235
Tver, Russia, 341, 347, 349
Tyerman, Christopher (b. 1953), historian, 318
Tyre, Lebanon, 83
Tyutyundzhiev, Ivan (b. 1956), historian, 232

Ulrich of Etzenbach (c. 1250–1300), poet
  Alexandreis, 131–32
Ulrich of Jungingen (c. 1360–1410), OT, grand master, 154, 347
Ulugh Muhammad (1405–45), Golden Horde khan, 355
Una, river, 208
Urbach, Johannes (d. after 1422)
  Licet insignis, 73
Urban II (c. 1035–99), pope, 40, 121
Urban V (1310–70), pope, 290, 298, 304
Urban VI (c. 1318–89), pope, 257
Urban, William L. (b. 1939), historian, 48–49
Usora, Usorians, 202, 242
Ústí, Czechia
  Bohemian noble family, 137

Valdeks, Bohemian noble family, 137

Valencia, Spain, 96–97, 101, 104
Valentin, François (1796–1849), historian, 40, 48
Valois-Burgundy (ducal branch [Capetians]), dynasty, 87–89, 93, 181, 190–91, 195–96, 330
Vaněk of Vartenberk (1300–64/65), Bohemian nobleman, 135
Várad (mod. Oradea, Romania), 207, 213
Varna, Bulgaria
  crusade and battle (1444), 36–37, 42, 51, 59, 114, 168, 187, 220, 229–36, 338
Vartenberks, Bohemian noble family, 135, 137
Vasily I Dmitriyevich (1371–1425), grand prince of Vladimir and Moscow, 161, 164, 342–43, 345, 347–48, 350, 353–55
Vasily II Vasilyevich (1415–62), grand prince of Moscow, 355–56
Vatican City, 239
Velhartice, Czechia
  Bohemian noble family, 137
Venchan, Bulgaria, 233
Vener, Job (c. 1370–1447), jurist, 366
Venice, Venetians, 37, 56, 70–72, 78–79, 90, 109, 114, 118, 122, 128, 175–76, 179, 181, 222, 229–31, 234, 249–50
Vesconte, Pietro (fl. 1310–30), cartographer and geographer, 93
Vesela Straža, Bosnia and Herzegovina, 202, 208
Vidin, Bulgaria, 179, 183, 210, 232–33
Vienna, Austria, 72, 122, 325, 356
  battle (1683), 51
  Reichstag (1460), 79
Vilém of Chyš and Egerberk (fl. 1317–27), Bohemian nobleman, 134
Vilém of Hustopeče (c. 1240–after 1271), Bohemian nobleman, 134

Vilém of Landštejn (d. 1356), hetman of Moravia, supreme burgrave of Bohemia, 135

Villani, Matteo (c. 1290–1363), historiographer, 288

Vilnius, Lithuania, 158, 163–64, 167–68, 260–62, 264, 349–50, 359

Vinnytsya, Ukraine, 168

Visconti, dynasty, 233

Visegrád, Hungary
congress (1335), 301–2

Vistula, river, 272, 332

Vitebsk, Belarus, 341, 348

Vítek I of Hradec (d. c. 1259), castellan of Olomouc, 130, 137

Viterbo, Italy, 240

Vlad II Dracul (c. 1392/94–1447), voivode of Wallachia, 114, 123, 223, 233, 235

Vlad III the Impaler (c. 1431–76/77), voivode of Wallachia, 113–14

Vlad V the Young (1488–1512), voivode of Wallachia, 115–16

Vladislas I the Elbow-High (1260/61–1333), duke of Cuyavia, of Greater Poland and of Cracow, king of Poland, 135, 268, 283–86, 292–93, 319

Vladislas II (1326/30–1401), duke of Opole, palatine of Hungary, voivode of Ruthenia, 291, 309, 312

Vladislas II Jogaila (before 1362–1434), grand duke of Lithuania, king of Poland, 59–60, 62, 74, 76, 147–48, 159–61, 163–67, 169, 255–57, 259, 264, 267, 291, 297, 309–12, 319–23, 328–30, 337–39, 341–44, 346, 348–54, 357–60, 369–70, 374

Vladislas II the Jagiellonian (1456–1516), king of Bohemia and of Hungary, 115, 117–18, 121, 262, 264, 275, 334

Vladislas III Henry (c. 1160–1222), duke of Bohemia, margrave of Moravia (as Vladislas I Henry), 128

Vladislas III the Jagiellonian (1424–44), king of Poland and of Hungary (as Vladislas I), 168, 211, 220–26, 228–31, 234–36, 268

Vladislas the White (1327/33–88), duke of Gniewkowo, 292

Vok of Rožmberk (d. 1262), supreme marshal of Bohemia, 130–31

Volhynia, Volhynians, 63, 159, 167–68, 177, 287, 290, 296–97, 299–300, 304–5, 307, 311, 341, 348, 354–56

Volodomyr, Ukrainie, 290–91

Vorskla, river
crusade and battle (1399), 162, 256, 289, 305, 339–40, 345

Vranduk, Bosnia and Herzegovina, 202

Vrbas, river, 208

Vrbas, Serbia, 201, 209

Vukan Nemanjić (c. 1165–1208), lord of Duklja, grand prince of Serbia, 238

Vytautas Alexander the Great (c. 1350–1430), grand duke of Lithuania, 59–60, 64, 74–75, 147, 160–67, 169–70, 214, 256–60, 262, 264, 289, 305, 311, 321, 323, 328, 330, 339–60

Waleran of Wavrin (c. 1418–80), Burgundian knight, 235–36

Wales, Welsh, 144

Wallachia, Wallachians, Vlachs, 56, 58, 113–23, 179, 181–82, 200, 203–6, 208, 212–16, 223–24, 233, 235–236

Walsingham, Thomas (d. c. 1422), OSB, chronicler
Ypodigma Neustriæ, 322

Walters, Ludwig (1875–1968), historian, 324

Wanckel, Nikolaus (*fl.* early 16th cent.), OFM, 85, 92

Wapowski, Bernard (1475–1535), historian and cartographer, 228, 232
Warmia, Warmians, 129, 271, 275–77
Waterton, Hugh (*c*. 1340–1409), Lancaster servant, 142
Watzenrode, Lucas (1447–1512), bishop of Warmia, 275–77
Weber, Benjamin, 78
Weise, Erich (1895–1972), historian, 43
Wenceslas II (1271–1305), king of Bohemia and of Poland (as Wenceslas I), 128, 283
Wenceslas III (1289–1306), king of Bohemia, of Hungary (as Ladislas V) and of Poland (as Wenceslas II), 283
Wenceslas IV the Idle (1361–1419), king of Bohemia, Romano-German king, 138, 328, 348
Wends, 43
Werner of Orseln (*c*. 1280–1330), OT, grand master, 133, 135
Western Dvina, river, 166
Westphalia, Westphalians, 130, 243
Wigand of Marburg (*fl*. end of the 14th cent.), OT, chronicler, 136
Wilken, Friedrich (1777–1840), historian and orientalist, 40, 47
William III (1375–1435), duke of Bavaria-Munich, 372
William of Isenburg-Grenzau (*fl*. 1460s–1532), OT, writer and theologian, 278–79
William the Good (*c*. 1286–1337), count of Holland, of Zeeland and of Hainaut, 136
Windeck, Eberhard (*c*. 1380–1440/41), chronicler, 260
Winrich of Kniprode (*c*. 1310–82), OT, grand master, 145

Wittek, Paul (1894–1978), historian and orientalist, 42
Winchester, UK, 143
Wittelsbachs, dynasty, 133, 284
Włocławek, Poland, 284
Włodkowic, Paweł (*c*. 1370/73–1435), lawyer, theologian, 44, 73–74, 76, 326–27
  Articuli contra cruciferos, 73
  Conclusiones, 73, 76, 326
Wojciech of Opatowiec (d. 1360), diplomat, 302
World War II (1939–45), 320
Wrocław, Poland, 130, 134–36, 290, 301, 354, 367
Wycliffism, Wycliffites, 74, 361–62

Yarmouth, UK, *see* Great Yarmouth
Yotvingia, Yotvingians, 319
Yury Dmitrievich (1374–1434), prince of Zvenigorod and Galich, grand prince of Moscow, 354
Yury Svyatoslavich (d. 1407), grand prince of Smolensk, 342, 345

Zagreb, Croatia, 207, 213
Žalgiris, battle (1410), *see* Tannenberg
Zamora, Spain, 325
Zaránd (mod. Zărand, Romania), 207, 235
Ždrelo (mod. Serbia), 208
Žemaitija, *see* Samogitia
Zlatitsa, Bulgaria battle (1443), 226
Zöllner of Rotenstein, Conrad (*c*. 1325–90), OT, grand master, 145, 160